Media Literacy

Ninth Edition

Sara Miller McCune founded SAGE Publishing in 1965 to support the dissemination of usable knowledge and educate a global community. SAGE publishes more than 1000 journals and over 800 new books each year, spanning a wide range of subject areas. Our growing selection of library products includes archives, data, case studies and video. SAGE remains majority owned by our founder and after her lifetime will become owned by a charitable trust that secures the company's continued independence.

Los Angeles | London | New Delhi | Singapore | Washington DC | Melbourne

Media Literacy

Ninth Edition

W. James Potter

University of California, Santa Barbara

Los Angeles | London | New Delhi
Singapore | Washington DC | Melbourne

FOR INFORMATION:

SAGE Publications, Inc.
2455 Teller Road
Thousand Oaks, California 91320
E-mail: order@sagepub.com

SAGE Publications Ltd.
1 Oliver's Yard
55 City Road
London EC1Y 1SP
United Kingdom

SAGE Publications India Pvt. Ltd.
B 1/I 1 Mohan Cooperative Industrial Area
Mathura Road, New Delhi 110 044
India

SAGE Publications Asia-Pacific Pte. Ltd.
18 Cross Street #10-10/11/12
China Square Central
Singapore 048423

Acquisitions Editor: Lily Norton
Editorial Assistant: Sarah Wilson
Production Editor: Bennie Clark Allen
Copy Editor: Christina West
Typesetter: C&M Digitals (P) Ltd.
Proofreader: Sally Jaskold
Indexer: Jean Casalegno
Cover Designer: Candice Harman
Marketing Manager: Staci Wittek

Printed in the United States of America

Library of Congress Cataloging-in-Publication Data

Names: Potter, W. James, author.

Title: Media literacy / W. James Potter.

Description: Ninth edition. | Los Angeles : SAGE, [2020] | Includes bibliographical references and index.

Identifiers: LCCN 2018040336 | ISBN 9781506366289 (paperback : alk. paper)

Subjects: LCSH: Media literacy.

Classification: LCC P96.M4 P68 2020 | DDC 302.23072/1—dc23
LC record available at https://lccn.loc.gov/2018040336

This book is printed on acid-free paper.

SUSTAINABLE FORESTRY INITIATIVE
Certified Chain of Custody
Promoting Sustainable Forestry
www.sfiprogram.org
SFI-01268
SFI label applies to text stock

19 20 21 22 23 10 9 8 7 6 5 4 3 2

BRIEF CONTENTS

DETAILED CONTENTS

PREFACE

Most of us think we are fairly media literate. We know how to access all kinds of media to find the music, games, information, and entertainment we want. We recognize the faces of many celebrities and know many facts about their lives. We recognize a range of musical styles and have developed strong preferences for what we like. We can easily create messages through photos, videos, and text then upload them to various sites on the Internet. Clearly, we know how to expose ourselves to the media, we know how to absorb information from them, we know how to be entertained by them, and we know how to use them to create our own messages and share them with others.

Are we media literate? Yes, of course. We have acquired a great deal of information and developed remarkable skills. The abilities to speak a language, read, understand photographs, and follow narratives are significant achievements, although we often take them for granted.

While we should not overlook what we have accomplished, it is also important to acknowledge that we all can be *much more* media literate. In many ways, your overall level of media literacy now is probably about the same as it was when you first became a teenager. Since that time, your information base has grown enormously about some types of media messages, such as popular songs, Internet sites, and video clips. However, your information base may not have grown much in other areas—about the economics of the mass media industry, who controls that industry, how decisions are made about the production of content, and how that constant flow of content affects you and society in all sorts of hidden ways. Thus, your current level of media literacy allows you to do many things with the media, but you could be exercising *much more control* and getting *more* out of your media exposures—if you grew your knowledge in additional areas.

The more you are aware of how the mass media operate and how they affect you, the more you gain control over those effects and the more you will separate yourself from typical media users who have turned over a great deal of their lives to the mass media without realizing it. By "turning over a great deal of their lives to the mass media," I mean more than time and money, although both of those are considerable. I also mean that most people *have allowed the mass media to program them* in ways they are unaware of. And because they are unaware of these ways, they cannot shape or control that programming.

The purpose of this book is to show you how the media have been shaping your beliefs and behavioral patterns. Until you become aware of how much your beliefs have been formed by media influence and how the media have accomplished all this shaping, you will continue to float along in a flood of media messages—oblivious to their constant, subtle influence. However, once you begin to see things from a media literacy perspective, you can see how this process of influence works, and this understanding will help you to gain control over this shaping process.

HOW TO GET THE MOST OUT OF THIS BOOK

As you read through this book, think frameworks and be strategic. If you keep these two ideas in the front of your mind, you will be able to read faster and at the same time get more out of your reading.

Frameworks are maps. When you have a map to guide your reading journey, you know where you are and where you have to go next. To help you perceive the most important frameworks, each chapter begins with a key idea followed by an outline of topics covered. Strategies keep you focused on what is most important. When you read through each chapter, be guided by several important questions, then be strategic in your reading; that is, actively look for the answers to those questions. By *actively*, I mean don't just scan the words and sentences; instead, start with an agenda of questions, then as you read through each section, look specifically for answers to your questions. After you have finished a chapter, close the book and see how much you can recall. Can you remember only a random mass of facts, or can you envision an organized set of knowledge structured by your questions?

This book is composed of 15 instructional chapters followed by six issues chapters. The purpose of the 15 instructional chapters is to provide you with the framework of ideas to help you organize your knowledge structures in four areas: knowledge about the media industries, knowledge about media audiences, knowledge about media content, and knowledge about media effects. These chapters also present you with some facts and figures to hang on those frameworks. To help you acquire more information to elaborate these frameworks on your own, the chapters include a list of books, articles, and websites for further reading; I have selected these as particularly interesting extensions of what I have presented in the chapter. Also, because things change so fast these days with the media, I have also provided several sources of information (typically websites) where you can access the most current information available on each topic. The first time you read through these 15 core instructional chapters, stay focused on the most important ideas as you build your own knowledge structures. Then once you have these structures, go back and reread the chapters to add the detail you need to elaborate your understanding.

You will get more out of each of the core instructional chapters if you try to incorporate the information you are learning into your own experience. The exercises at the end of each chapter help you do this. But do not think of the exercises as something that will only help you prepare for an exam. Instead think about the exercises as things you can continually do in your everyday life as you encounter the media. The more you practice the tasks that are laid out in the exercises, the more you will be internalizing the information and thus making it more a natural part of the way you think.

After you have finished with the core instructional chapters and building your initial set of knowledge structures, you will be ready to dig deep into the controversies within media studies. The six issues chapters give you a chance to use your knowledge structures and increase the strength of your skills as you take apart these controversies, appreciate the beauty of their complexity, and put together your own informed opinion on each. The first issue unpacks the controversy about whether or not the ownership of the mass media has become too concentrated; some critics argue that there are now too few owners of too many media businesses. The topic of sports is treated in Issue 2 by examining possible answers to the question: Is there too much money being spent on sports? Issue 3 examines "fake news." Issue 4 analyzes how we criticize advertising and whether those criticisms are valid. Issue 5 tackles the persistent controversy over whether there is too much violence in the media and whether the prevalence of violence in media content is harming individuals and society. This section concludes with Issue 6, which examines the growing concern about privacy and how the new media environment is making it much more difficult for you to protect your privacy.

If you engage these issues on a superficial level, then you will likely be frustrated by what seem like unsolvable problems. But if you dig deeper and apply your developing skills of media literacy, you will begin to see how the complexities of these issues may be causing problems in your own life. And when you recognize these problems, you will be able to use your greater level of media literacy to develop strategies to reduce their influence. Thus you will be taking more control over issues that you previously thought were too big, too complicated, and the fault of other people.

DIGITAL RESOURCES

The **password-protected instructor resources site** at **http://study.sagepub.com/ potter9e** includes:

- **Test banks** that provide a diverse range of prewritten options as well as the opportunity to edit any question and/or insert your own personalized questions to effectively assess students' progress and understanding.

- **Lecture notes** that summarize key concepts on a chapter-by-chapter basis to help with preparation for lectures and class discussions.

- Chapter-specific **PowerPoint® slides** that offer assistance with lecture and review preparation by highlighting essential content, features, and artwork from the book.

- **Tables and figures** in an easily downloadable format for use in papers, handouts, and presentations.

- **Sample course syllabi** for semester and quarter courses provide suggested models for structuring your courses.

- **Discussion questions** that help launch classroom interaction by prompting students to engage with the material and by reinforcing important content.

- **Chapter activities** for individual or group projects provide lively and stimulating ideas for use in and out of class that reinforce active learning.

- **A course cartridge** provides easy LMS integration.

The **open access student study site** at **study.sagepub.com/potter9e** includes:

- Mobile-friendly practice **quizzes** that allow for independent assessment by students of their mastery of course material.

- Mobile-friendly **eFlashcards** that strengthen understanding of key terms and concepts.

- Carefully selected chapter-by-chapter **video and multimedia content** that enhances classroom-based explorations of key topics.

- Exclusive access to influential **SAGE journal and reference content** that ties important research to chapter concepts to strengthen learning.

- Access to **online-only appendices.**

TO CONCLUDE

It is my hope that this book will stimulate you to think more deeply about your media habits and become motivated to increase your control over the process of influence from the media. The information presented in these chapters will get you started in this direction. Will the book provide you with *all* the information you need to complete this task fully? No. That would require too much information to fit into one book. You will need to continue reading. At the end of most chapters, I suggest several books for further reading on the topic of that chapter. Although some of those books are fairly technical, most of them are easy to read and very interesting.

This book is an introduction. It is designed to show you the big picture so you can get started efficiently on increasing your own media literacy. It is important to get started now. The world is rapidly changing because of newer information technologies that allow you to create and share your own messages in addition to accessing all kinds of information on just about any conceivable topic.

I hope you will have fun reading this book. And I hope it will expose you to new perspectives from which you can perceive much more about the media. If it does, you will be gaining new insights about your old habits and interpretations. If this happens, I hope you will share your new insights and "war stories" with me. Much of this book has been written to reflect some of the problems and insights my students have had in the media literacy courses I have taught. I have learned much from them. I'd like to learn even more from you. So let me know what you think and send me a message at wjpotter@comm.ucsb.edu.

See you on the journey!

ACKNOWLEDGMENTS

This book project has traveled a very long distance from its initial conceptualization in the mid-1990s. Since then I have had the privilege of using various versions of the book with more than a thousand students at Florida State University, UCLA, Stanford University, and the University of California at Santa Barbara. These students helped me form the idea into a useful book for a broad range of undergraduates and refine the material through eight subsequent editions. I thank them for every question, every puzzled look, and every smile of satisfaction from an insight gained. Over the years, *Media Literacy* has been translated from English into seven other languages, which makes it accessible to readers in many parts of the world. Some of those readers have provided me with their reactions, and I thank them.

I thank the many reviewers whom SAGE called on to critique the text in each edition. Some contacted me directly; others chose to remain anonymous. In all cases their comments were valuable. SAGE and I gratefully acknowledge the following reviewers for their kind assistance:

MaryAlice Adams, *Miami University*

Richard T. Craig, *George Mason University*

Donna L. Halper, *Lesley University*

Elizabeth R. Ortiz, *Cedar Crest College*

Phil Rutledge, *University of North Carolina–Charlotte*

I am grateful for the support of SAGE with its many highly skilled staff members over the years. First, I need to thank Margaret Seawell, who initially signed this project then shepherded it through three editions, then Todd Armstrong who took over for Margaret on the fourth and fifth editions, then Matt Byrnie who took over for Todd and gave me considerable help with the sixth, seventh, and eighth editions before turning it over to Terri Accomazzo for this ninth edition. In the production department, Astrid Virding skillfully took the first edition from manuscript to bound book, as did Claudia Hoffman on the second edition, Tracy Alpern on the third, and Astrid Virding again on the fourth, fifth, and sixth editions, Olivia Weber-Stenis on the seventh edition, Laura Barrett on the eighth edition, and Bennie Clark Allen on this edition. They made it look easy, though there must have been days when it was anything but. I also want to thank Carmel Withers in Marketing and SAGE salespeople for their enthusiastic support of the new edition. Finally, I must thank the many fine copy editors SAGE has assigned to this project over the years, especially Christina West, who demonstrated that she is the best of the best with her great job editing my work on this ninth edition.

If you like this book, then I share the credit of success with all the people I mentioned above. If you find a mistake, a shortcoming, or a misinterpretation, it is my fault for not fully assimilating all the high-quality help I have been privileged to experience.

ABOUT THE AUTHOR

W. James Potter, professor at the University of California at Santa Barbara, holds one PhD in Communication Studies and another in Instructional Technology. He has been teaching media courses for more than two decades in the areas of effects on individuals and society, content narratives, structure and economics of media industries, advertising, journalism, programming, and production. He has served as editor of the *Journal of Broadcasting & Electronic Media* and is the author of many journal articles and books, including the following: *Media Effects, The 11 Myths of Media Violence, Becoming a Strategic Thinker: Developing Skills for Success, On Media Violence, Theory of Media Literacy: A Cognitive Approach,* and *How to Publish Your Communication Research* (with Alison Alexander).

INTRODUCTION

PART I

iStock/Xavier Arnau

WHY INCREASE
MEDIA LITERACY?

Key Idea: To survive in our information-saturated culture, we put our minds on "automatic pilot" in order to protect ourselves from the flood of media messages we constantly encounter. The danger with this automatic processing of messages is that it allows the mass media to condition our thought processes.

Media literacy increases your ability to exercise control over the vast array of messages you encounter through daily media exposure.

The first challenge we all face when confronting a new body of information is motivation. We ask ourselves: Why should I expend all the effort to learn this? How will learning this help me enough to make all that effort worthwhile?

With media literacy, our initial answers to the above questions are likely to make us feel that learning about media literacy is not worth the effort because we feel that we already know a lot about the media. We are familiar with a large number of websites, apps, recording artists, and celebrities. We are already able to access a wide range of entertainment and information, so why would we need to learn a lot more about the media? This book will show you the answer to that question by presenting you with some key insights about the media. This information will expand your perspective into new areas and increase your power to exercise control over your media exposures so that you can get more value from those messages. Let's get started!

In this chapter, I will show you the big picture of our media environment so that you can see how enormous the information problem is. The way you deal with this problem typically works well on a day-to-day basis, but its effectiveness is questionable over the long run. That is, the disadvantages in the long term greatly outweigh the advantages in the short term.

THE INFORMATION PROBLEM

Our culture is saturated with media messages— far more than you may realize. Hollywood releases more than 700 hours of feature films each year, which adds to its base of more than 100,000 hours of films it has already released in previous years. In addition, a video platform such as YouTube has more than 1 billion videos available for viewing and users are uploading more than 300 new hours of video *every minute of every day* (YouTube, 2018). Commercial television stations generate about 48 million hours of video messages every year worldwide, and radio stations send out 65.5 million hours of original programming

NurPhoto/Getty Images

Apple produces new technology in every iteration of its phones, watches, and other products.

Social media continues to be the fastest growing area for media exposure, being consumed mostly on smartphones and other mobile devices.

each year. We now have more than 140 million book titles in existence, and another 1,500 new book titles are published throughout the world each day. Then there is the World Wide Web, which has been estimated to have almost 2 billion websites (Internet Live Stats, 2018a) but is so huge that no one knows how big it really is.

Growth Is Accelerating

Not only are we already saturated with media messages, the rate of that saturation is growing at an accelerating pace. More information has been generated since you were born than the sum total of all information throughout all recorded history up until the time of your birth. And the rate continues to accelerate! In 2012, Silver estimated that the amount of information was doubling every year and by now the rate of growth is even higher.

Why is so much information being produced? One reason is that there are now more people producing information than ever before. Half of all the scientists who have ever lived are alive today and producing information. Also, the number of people in the United States who identify themselves as musicians has more than doubled in the last 4 decades, the number of artists has tripled, and the number of authors has increased fivefold (U.S. Census Bureau, 2017).

Another reason is that the technology now exists to provide easy-to-use platforms to share information. Thus everyone can generate and share information with large numbers of people every day. You no longer need to be a musician to create songs; you can use GarageBand or other computer synthesizers. You don't need to be signed to a recording contract by a record company to distribute your songs. You can also be a journalist, a fiction writer, a photographer, a filmmaker, or even a video game designer as a hobby and make your messages easily available to millions of people, just like professional artists. Or you can generate and share smaller forms of information such as e-mails and tweets. There are now 3.2 billion Internet users worldwide, and they send and receive 300 billion e-mail messages each day; Twitter users generate more than 500 million tweets per day; and Facebook reports that 100 million photos are uploaded each and every day (Pingdom, 2017).

Each of us is adding to this information clutter like never before. Tucker (2014) explains:

> Between checking your phone, using GPS, sending e-mail, tweets, and Facebook posts, and especially streaming movies and music, you create 1.8 million megabytes a year. It's enough to fill nine CD-ROMs every day. The device-ification of modern life in the developed world is the reason why more than 90 percent of all the data that exists was created in just the last three years. (p. xv)

Tucker continues, "And it's growing exponentially, with 44 times as much digital information in 2020 as there was in 2009" (p. xvi).

High Degree of Exposure

The media are highly attractive, so we increase the time we spend with media messages each year. Over the last 3 decades, every new survey of media use has shown that people on average have been increasing their exposure time every year. For example, in 2010, people spent an average of 10 hours and 46 minutes with all forms of the media each day, and this increased to 12 hours and 14 minutes by 2014 (eMarketer, 2014). By 2017, people were spending more time with the media than with anything else, with the average person spending 12 hours and 1 minute per day on media (eMarketer, 2017b).

Multitasking, like using your smartphone while watching online videos, has increased the average young person's daily quantity of media exposure.

iStockphoto.com/damircudic

It is clear that the media are an extremely important part of our everyday lives. In our information-saturated culture, we are constantly connected to our friends, our society, and the entire world through the media.

Keeping Up

How do we keep up with all this information? One thing we try to do is multitask. For example, a person can listen to recorded music, text friends, and watch video on a pop-up window all at the same time—thus experiencing 3 hours of media exposure for each hour of clock time.

Multitasking, however, is not a good enough strategy for helping us keep up with the flood of information. If you wanted to view all the videos uploaded to YouTube in just 1 day, it would take you an entire year of viewing and you would have to multitask by watching 20 screens with no breaks! While multitasking helps increase our exposure, it is not enough to help us keep up with even a tiny fraction of media messages in the everyday flood of information.

DEALING WITH THE INFORMATION PROBLEM

Although we are all saturated with information, and each year the media are more aggressive in seeking our attention, we are able to deal with it. How is this possible? The answer lies in the way the human brain is wired and programmed—its hardware and software.

Our Mental Hardware

The most remarkable piece of hardware on Earth is the human brain. Although the human brain is relatively small (weighing less than 4 pounds), it has a remarkable capacity to take in information from the five senses (sight, hearing, touch, taste, and smell), process all that information by storing it or filtering it, and then make decisions that result in action. The human brain is composed of 100 billion neuron cells, which is the

iStock/andresr

The human brain is capable of taking in and processing large amounts of information about our surroundings.

number of stars in the Milky Way (Storr, 2014). Each cell is linked by synapses to as many as 100,000 others. That means your brain has created over 500 trillion string-like fibers called axons and dendrites that connect with other neurons at junctions called synapses. "These synapses constantly form and dissolve, weakening, and strengthening in response to new experiences" (Haven, 2007, p. 22).

As the human brain is constantly monitoring the environment, thousands of neurons are receiving stimulation from thousands of other neurons and must decide whether to ignore the input or respond in some way by sending a signal to another specific neuron. "Somehow, through this freeway maze of links, loops, and electric traffic jams, we each manage to think, perceive, consider, imagine, remember, react, and respond" (Haven, 2007, p. 22).

Our Mental Software

How does this complex piece of hardware know what to do? The answer to this question is that the brain has been programmed to fulfill certain functions. This programming or software, which is sometimes referred to collectively as *the mind*, tells the brain how to function, much like the software programs on your computers tell them what functions to perform and how to perform those functions.

Some of this software has been hardwired into the brain before birth. For example, the brain automatically oversees the body's internal states by constantly monitoring the performance of the organs (heart, lungs, kidneys, etc.) to keep them functioning properly. The brain also has been programmed to monitor a person's environment for threats. For example, an orienting reflex directs the brain to pay attention to the environment for sudden changes like loud noises or flashes of light; when a potential threat is identified, the brain creates an attentional state that forces the person to examine the thing that triggered the attention to determine whether it is an actual threat or not. Also, the brain has been hardwired with a **fight-or-flight** reflex so that when a potential threat is encountered, the body is automatically made ready (increased heart rate and blood pressure) to either fight off the threat or run away to safety.

In addition to the hardwiring of the brain to maintain *physical* well-being, the brain has also been hardwired to enhance its *social* well-being. For example, the ability for language has been hardwired into human brains so people can easily communicate. Throughout history, every culture has developed a language. While the basic ability to learn a language is hardwired, the learning of any particular language must occur after birth so that individuals can use their language facility to transmit meaning to others and receive meanings from their culture.

As we accumulate experiences in life, our minds accumulate additional programming that tells our brains how to perform additional functions, such as solving math problems, reasoning logically, working through moral problems, controlling one's emotions, and expanding and growing one's skills that would lead to rewarding careers and relationships. This additional programming initially comes from one's parents and siblings. It also comes from one's contact with cultural institutions, such as education, religion, politics, and government. It comes from one's friends, acquaintances, and even enemies. And it comes from the mass media. All of this additional programming shapes how we make decisions in our everyday world about what to wear, what to eat, what is important, how to act, and how to spend our resources of time and money. This programming is constantly running in our unconscious minds in the form of automatic routines.

The human brain not only oversees autonomic functions like breathing, but also manages our reactions to the environment and social well-being.

Automatic Routines

The human mind can be wondrously efficient. It can perform many everyday tasks quickly by using **automatic routines**, which are sequences of behaviors or thoughts that we learn from experience then apply again and again with little effort. Once you have learned a sequence—such as tying your shoes, brushing your teeth, driving to school, or playing a song on the guitar—you can perform it over and over again with very little effort compared to the effort it took you to learn it in the first place. As we learn to do something, we are writing the instructions like a computer code in our minds. That code then runs automatically in our unconscious minds and serves to guide us through the task with very little thought or effort. To illustrate, recall your experience in first learning to type. You had to think of the individual letters in each word, think about which key controlled which letter, and then command a finger to press the correct key. It took you a long time to type out each word. But now after much practice, your thumbs (or fingers) move over the keyboard quickly as you type out messages in seconds. Now when you message someone, you think only about the message while not having to think at all about the task of typing.

Psychologists refer to this automatic processing of information as **automaticity**. Automaticity is a mental state where our minds operate without any conscious effort from us. We encounter almost all media messages in a state of automaticity; that is, we put our minds on "automatic pilot" where our minds automatically filter out almost all message options. I realize that this might sound strange, but think about it: We cannot possibly consider every possible message and consciously decide whether to pay attention to it or not. There are too many messages to consider. Over time, we have developed automatic routines that guide this filtering process very quickly and efficiently so we don't have to spend much, if any, mental effort.

To illustrate this automatic processing, consider what you do when you go to the supermarket to buy food. Let's say you walk into the store with a list of 25 items you need to buy, and 15 minutes later you walk out of the store with your 25 items. In this scenario, how many decisions have you made? The easy answer is to say 25 decisions, because you made a separate decision to buy each of your 25 items as you put each item into your cart. But what about all the items you *decided not to buy*? The average supermarket today has about 40,000 items on its shelves. So you actually made 40,000 decisions in the relatively short time you were in the supermarket—25 decisions to buy the 25 products and all those other decisions not to buy the remaining 39,975 products. How did you accomplish such an extensive task in such a short period of time? You relied on automatic routines. See how these automatic routines govern your buying habits?

Our culture is a grand supermarket of media messages. Those messages are everywhere whether we realize it or not, except that there are far more media messages in our culture than there are products in any supermarket. In our everyday lives—like when we enter a supermarket—a program is loaded into our mind that tells it what to look for and automatically filters out the rest. This automatic processing guides most, but certainly not all, of our media exposures. With automatic processing, we experience a great deal of media messages without paying any attention to them. Every once in a while something in the message or in our environment triggers our conscious attention to a media message. To illustrate this, imagine yourself driving in your car and you have music from your iPod playing through your car's sound system, but your attention is on the conversation you are having with your friend who is seated next to you. Then your favorite song starts playing, and your attention shifts from the conversation to the music. Or perhaps your conversation is interrupted when your friend notices that the radio is playing her favorite song, and she starts signing along with the music. In both scenarios, you are being exposed to a stream of media messages from your car sound system without paying conscious attention to them, but then something happens to trigger your conscious attention to the music.

Advantages and Disadvantages

The huge advantage of automatic processing is efficiency. When the filtering software is running automatically it is making thousands of decisions for us without requiring us to expend any effort.

There are, however, some significant disadvantages. When we rely exclusively on our automatic routines, we get into a rut and miss out on paying attention to many messages that may be highly useful to us; we never know what we are missing. When our minds are on automatic pilot, we may be missing a lot of messages that might be helpful or enjoyable to us. We might not have programmed all the triggers we need to help us get out of automatic processing when a potentially useful message comes our way. Returning to the supermarket example from above, let's say you are very health conscious. Had you been less concerned with efficiency when you went into the supermarket, you would have considered a wider range of products and read their labels for ingredients. Not all low-fat products have the same fat content; not all products with vitamins added have the same vitamins or the same proportions. Or perhaps you are very price conscious. Had you been less concerned with efficiency, you would have considered a wider variety of competing products and looked more carefully at the unit pricing so you could get more value for your money. When we are *too* concerned with efficiency, we lose opportunities to expand our experience and to put ourselves in a position to make better decisions that can make us healthier, wealthier, and happier.

Another disadvantage is that over the long run we start to experience message fatigue. When we feel overwhelmed with too many media messages, we try to protect ourselves even more by narrowing down our focus and thus filtering out even more messages. Eventually we end up exposing ourselves to the same type of message over and over, and the value of each message keeps decreasing and we lose the ability to concentrate. In 1971, Nobel Prize–winning economist Herbert Simon observed that "a wealth of information crates a poverty of attention" (Angwin, 2009, p. 239). This is illustrated by a study where experimenters set up a jam tasting table in a food store. Half the time, they offered 6 jams, and the other half the time, they offered 24 jams. While the table with more jams attracted 50% more visitors and tasters, the table with fewer jams stimulated more sales. Among the visitors to the table with the larger number of jams, only 3% bought some jam, while among the visitors to the table with the smaller number of jams, 30% bought some jam (Anderson, 2006). The lesson here is that while choice is attractive, too much choice can paralyze us into inaction. When we feel overwhelmed, we rely more and more on automatic routines and this leads us into a deeper and deeper rut of doing the same things over and over.

iStock/mediaphotos

How is shopping in a supermarket similar to consuming media content?

THE BIG QUESTION

Given that we live in a culture highly saturated with information and given that we protect ourselves from this flood of information with automatic routines programmed into our minds, the big question becomes: Who benefits the most from the way that those codes have been programmed?

There is no simple answer to this question because many forces have been active in influencing how your code has been programmed over the course of your life so far. Some of this influence has come from parents, siblings, and friends who typically have had your best interests in mind, so their influence is likely to have been positive. Some of this influence has come from institutions and society, which are typically prosocial influences, but they have also been concerned with pushing you to conform to their ideas of what you should believe and how you should behave. Then there are the media programmers and advertisers who are most concerned about influencing you in order to satisfy their own goals, while convincing you that their products are satisfying your needs.

The task of sorting through all these influences requires some considerable analyses. This book will guide you through the media part of that analysis. Each of the 15 chapters in the instructional core of this book will show you how to ask the crucial questions about what you think about the world, what you believe to be true, and your habits of spending your resources of time and money. Through these analyses, you will gradually increase your awareness about the degree to which the media have programmed your automatic codes. This increased awareness will make it clear to you which parts of your code are not acting in your best interest and are likely training you to waste your personal resources, which leads you into frustration, anxiety, and unhappiness. This will put you in a position to reprogram those faulty bits of code. Those revisions to your code change the way it runs so that you will be much more likely to achieve your own personal goals and experience more happiness.

People who do not periodically examine their automatic routines are defaulting to influences outside their control. When we are not consciously paying attention and carefully evaluating our media exposures, the mass media continually reinforce certain behavioral patterns of exposure until they become automatic habits. We mindlessly follow these habits that are delivering less and less valuable information and experiences. We allow advertisers to increase their influence as they continually program an uneasy self-consciousness into our minds so that we are on the lookout for products that will make us look, feel, and smell better. Advertisers have programmed many of us into a shopping habit. People in America spend more time shopping than people in any other country. Americans go to shopping centers about once a week, more often than they go to houses of worship, and Americans now have more shopping centers than high schools. A few years ago, 93% of teenage girls surveyed said that shopping was their favorite activity (Schwartz, 2004). Advertising has programmed our automatic routines so that we shop even when it would be in our best interest to do other things. When you allow others to dominate the programming of your mind, then when your mind runs on automatic pilot you end up behaving in ways that achieve the goals of those programmers rather than in ways that would make you happier.

If you are bothered that the media have been programming your automatic routines in order to satisfy their objectives rather than your personal objectives, then you will likely have the motivation to learn how to take more control over this programming process. You will want to learn how to examine the code that has been programmed into your mind and sort through those programs that really do help you while eliminating those programs that are making you unhappy. Taking control is what media literacy is all about.

SUMMARY

We cannot physically avoid the glut of information that aggressively seeks our attention in our culture. Instead, we protect ourselves by psychologically avoiding almost all of the messages in the flood of information. We do this by keeping our minds on automatic pilot most of the time. This automaticity allows us to avoid almost all messages and to do so efficiently.

Automaticity, however, comes with a price. While we are in the automatic state, we allow the media to condition us to form all kinds of habits that consume our time and money. While some of these habits may be beneficial to us, others are not. Learning to tell the difference between the two requires a stronger media literacy perspective.

Further Reading

Gleick, J. (2011). *The information: A history, a theory, a flood*. New York, NY: Pantheon Books. (526 pages, including index)

This is a rather long book that gets very technical in places with mathematical and engineering-type descriptions. But it is a worthwhile if you really want to understand the nature of information and how it has changed forms over the years.

Schwartz, B. (2004). *The paradox of choice: Why more is less*. New York, NY: HarperCollins. (265 pages, including end notes and index)

Schwartz writes about how much choice the average person is now confronted with every day. He argues that increasing choice up to a point is a good thing but that beyond that point, increasing choice overwhelms people and they cease to make good decisions.

Silver, N. (2012). *The signal and the noise: Why so many predictions fail—but some don't*. New York, NY: Penguin Press. (534 pages with index)

The author documents the dramatic increase in information over the last several decades and argues that most of this information is noise, which makes it more difficult—rather than easier—to make good predictions and forecasts.

Wright, A. (2007). *Glut: Mastering information through the ages*. Washington, DC: Joseph Henry Press. (252 pages with index)

Wright, who characterizes himself as an information architect, takes a historical approach to showing how humans have evolved in the way they generate, organize, and use information. He argues that all information systems are either nondemocratic and top-down (a hierarchy) or peer-to-peer and open (a network). Tracing the development of human information, he uses perspectives from mythology, library science, biology, neurology, and culture. He uses this historical background to critique the nature of information on the Internet.

Keeping Up to Date

For some chapters, the material I talk about is very fluid and quickly changes. Therefore, some of the facts and figures I present may be out of date by the time you read a particular chapter. To help you find more up-to-date figures, I have included some sources of information that you can check out to get the most recent figures available.

Infoniac.com (http://www.infoniac.com/hi-tech/)

This site presents information about the growth of information in the world and more generally it provides information about new developments in technologies.

Pingdom (http://royal.pingdom.com)

This is a blog written by members of the Pingdom team on a wide variety of topics concerning the Internet and web tech issues. Begun in 2007, Pingdom is a company that provides Internet services to companies around the world.

Statistical Abstracts of the United States (https://www.census.gov/library/publications/time-series/statistical_abstracts.html)

Up until 2011, the Department of Commerce U.S. Census Bureau released a new statistical abstract from the data it gathered every year. Since then, this website presents links for reports based on data gathered by other organizations.

Getty/David Malan

MEDIA LITERACY APPROACH

Key Idea: Media literacy is a set of perspectives that we actively use to expose ourselves to the media and interpret the meaning of the messages we encounter. It is multidimensional and a continuum.

Media literacy is the ability to access and process information from any kind of transmission.

As you learned in the first chapter, we are constantly flooded with a huge number of messages from the mass media. We must screen out all but a tiny percentage. To help us do this screening with the least amount of mental effort, we default to automaticity, where our minds quickly screen out messages without any conscious awareness of this process. This automatic filtering process is governed by a set of procedures—much like a computer program—that runs unconsciously until something in a media message triggers our attention. While this filtering process is largely automatic, it is possible for us to gain greater control over it if we increase our media literacy.

WHAT IS MEDIA LITERACY?

The most standard use of the term *literacy* applies to a person's ability to read the written word. However, with the advent of technologies to convey messages in addition to print, the idea of literacy was expanded to also include things like visual literacy (the ability to process flat two-dimensional pictures of our three-dimensional world), story literacy (the ability to follow plots in books, television, and film), and computer literacy (the ability to creates one's own digital messages, to send them to others electronically, to search for messages, and to process meaning from electronic screens). In this book we do not focus on any one particular type of literacy but instead take a broad approach that considers all media.

Another characteristic within the writings about media literacy is a focus on the mass media as being harmful; that is, mass media messages expose people to risks of harmful effects. While acknowledging that media messages have the potential to increase the risk of harmful effects, this book attempts to show you that media messages also offer a great potential for positive effects—if we are open minded. To illustrate this point, let's consider the belief that newer forms of technology have harmed people's ability to write well. An illustration of this belief is John Sutherland, an English professor at the University College of London, who has argued that texting has reduced language into a "bleak, bald, sad shorthand," that Facebook reinforces narcissistic drivel, and that PowerPoint presentations have taken the place of well-reasoned essays (quoted in Thompson, 2009). He says that today's technologies of communication that encourage or even require shorter messages, like Twitter, have shortened people's attention spans and therefore have limited their ability to think in longer arcs, which is required for constructing well-reasoned essays.

In contrast, other people regard these newer formats for communication more positively. For example, Andrea Lunsford, a professor of writing and rhetoric at Stanford University, argues that the newer information technologies have actually increased literacy. She says, "I think we're in the midst of a literacy revolution the likes of which we haven't seen since Greek civilization" (quoted in Thompson, 2009). In addition, she argues that these new technologies of communication are not killing

Media literacy stimulates us to adapt to changing communication technologies and open our minds to new media messages.

our ability to write well but instead are pushing it in new directions of being more personal, creative, and concise. She reached this conclusion after systematically analyzing more than 14,000 student writing samples over a 5-year period. She explains that young people today are adept at understanding the needs of their audiences and writing messages especially crafted to appeal to them. For today's youth, writing is about discovering themselves, organizing their thoughts concisely, managing impressions, and persuading their readers.

When we open our minds, we see that there are both positive as well as negative effects of these newer forms of communication. The newer technologies of communication offer fewer opportunities to develop certain skills but at the same time increase the opportunities to develop other kinds of skills. Thus it is careless to regard the media's influence on our skill set as being either all good or all bad.

In addition to encouraging us to open our minds, media literacy also stimulates us to *adapt* to our changing world rather than to *ignore* those changes or to *deny* that those changes are happening. We adapt by opening ourselves up to a wider variety of messages, then by analyzing those messages for new elements and evaluating those elements so we can appreciate their value.

THE THREE BUILDING BLOCKS OF MEDIA LITERACY

The three building blocks of media literacy are **skills**, **knowledge structures**, and **personal locus**. The combination of all three is necessary to build your wider set of perspectives on the media. Your skills are the tools you use to build knowledge structures. Your knowledge structures are the organizations of what you have learned. Your personal locus provides mental energy and direction.

Skills

Many people who write about media literacy primarily consider it a skill, and the term they use to refer to this skill is *critical thinking*. While the term *critical thinking* sounds good, its use creates confusion, because everyone seems to have a different meaning for it.

Some people regard critical thinking as a willingness to criticize the media; other people define it as the need to examine issues in more depth; still others suggest a meaning of being more systematic and logical when interacting with the media; others imply that it means the ability to focus on the most important issues and ignore the rest; and the list goes on. In order to avoid this conglomeration of meanings, I will not use this term; instead, I will try to be clearer by showing you how media literacy relies on seven specific skills. These are the skills of analysis, evaluation, grouping, induction, deduction, synthesis, and abstracting (see Table 2.1).

These skills are not exclusive to media literacy tasks; instead, we use these skills in all sorts of ways in our everyday lives. We all have some ability with each of these skills, so the media literacy challenge is *not to acquire* these skills; rather our challenge is *to get better* at using each of these skills in our encounters with media messages. In the remainder of this section, I will define each of these skills and show how they are applied in a media literacy context. (For a more detailed treatment of each of these skills, please see Potter, 2018.)

Analysis is the breaking down of a message into meaningful elements. As we encounter media messages, we can simply accept these messages on the surface or we can dig deeper into the message itself by breaking it down into its components and examining the composition of the elements that make up the message. For example, with a news story, we can accept what a journalist tells us or we can analyze the story for completeness. That is, we can break the story down into its who, what, when, where, why, and how to determine if the story is complete or not.

Evaluation is making a judgment about the value of an element. This judgment is made by comparing a message element to some standard. When we encounter opinions expressed by experts in media messages, we could simply memorize those opinions and make them our own. Or we could take the information elements in the message and compare them to our standards. If those elements meet or exceed our standards, we

TABLE 2.1 ■ The Seven Skills of Media Literacy	
Skill	**Definition**
Analysis	Breaking down a message into meaningful elements
Evaluation	Judging the value of an element; the judgment is made by comparing a message element to some standard
Grouping	Determining which elements are alike in some way; determining how a group of elements are different from other groups of elements
Induction	Inferring a pattern across a small set of elements, then generalizing the pattern to all elements in the set
Deduction	Using general principles to explain particulars
Synthesis	Assembling elements into a new structure
Abstracting	Creating a brief, clear, and accurate description capturing the essence of a message in a smaller number of words than the message itself

conclude that the message—and the opinion expressed there—is good; but if the elements fall short of our standard, then we judge the message to be unacceptable.

There is a lot of evidence that people simply accept the opinions they hear in media messages without making their own evaluations. One example of this is the now widespread opinion that in the United States, the educational system is not very good and a big reason for this is that children now spend too much time with the media, especially TV. To illustrate, the National Center for Education Statistics is an agency of the U.S. federal government that uses standardized testing to assess the level of learning of America's youth in reading, science, and mathematics each year, then compares their levels of learning with youth in 65 other countries. The *2012 Program for International Student Assessment* report says that adolescents in the United States are ranked 24th in reading, 28th in science, and 36th in mathematics (National Center for Education Statistics, 2012). Critics of the U.S. educational system use information like this to argue that adolescents spend too much time with the media and this makes their minds lazy, reduces their creativity, and turns them into lethargic entertainment junkies. If this happens, children will not value achievement and will not do well in school.

iStock/media photos

Analysis, one of the seven skills of media literacy, breaks down a message into meaningful components.

This criticism is faulty for several reasons. One reason for its faulty nature is that it blames the media exclusively and fails to acknowledge that academic performance is influenced by a complex of favors, especially parents' values for education and student motivations. Another reason is that it focuses only on negative effects and recognizes no potential for positive effects that continually accrue from media exposures of all kinds. When we analyze this criticism in even a little depth, we can see that it is misleading.

To illustrate, let's examine the often-heard criticism that television viewing is negatively related to academic achievement. What makes this faulty is that this relationship is explained better by something else—IQ. School achievement is overwhelmingly related to IQ. Also, children with lower IQs watch more television. So it is IQ that accounts for lower achievement and higher television viewing. Research analyses that take a child's IQ into account find that there is no overall negative relationship; instead, there is a much more interesting pattern (see Potter, 1987a). The negative relationship does not show up until the child's viewing has passed the threshold of 30 hours per week. Beyond that 30-hour point, the more television children watch, the lower their academic achievement, and that effect gets stronger with the more hours they watch beyond that threshold. This means that academic achievement goes down only after television viewing starts to cut into study time and sleep. But there is no negative effect for less than 30 hours of viewing per week. In fact, at the lowest levels of television viewing, there is actually a positive effect; that is, a child who watches none or only a few hours a week is likely to do less well academically than a child who watches a moderate amount (around 12 to 15 hours per week). Thus, the pattern is as follows: Children who are deprived of the source of information that television provides do less well in school than children who watch a moderate amount of television; however, when a child gets to the point where the amount of television viewing cuts into needed study time, academic performance goes down. Television—as well as the Internet and all other forms of the media—has potentially positive as well as negative effects. Television exposure can displace constructive behaviors such as studying, but television can expand our experience, teach us valuable social lessons, and stimulate our imaginations. Preventing children from using television can prevent a potentially negative effect but it also prevents positive effects as well.

When we pose the question, "What effect does viewing television have on a child's academic performance?" we could give the simple, popular answer: There is a negative effect. But now you can see that this answer is too simple—it is simpleminded. It is also misleading because it reinforces the limited belief that media effects are negative and that the media are to blame.

The reason faulty beliefs are such a dangerous trap is because they are self-reinforcing. By this, I mean that as people are continually exposed to faulty information, they feel even more secure that their faulty beliefs are accurate. They feel less and less motivated to challenge them. When someone points out that the information on which their beliefs are based is faulty, they do not accept this criticism because they are so sure that they are correct. Thus, over time, they are not only less likely to examine their beliefs but are also less tolerant of the possibility that beliefs other than their own are correct.

Grouping is the determining of which elements are alike in some way, then determining how a group of elements are different from other groups of elements. This skill is so important that each of this book's core instructional chapters, from this chapter on, includes a Compare & Contrast illustration of key terms so that you can develop a greater appreciation for how pairs of terms share similarities as well as illustrate differences that are key to making them distinct from one another.

The key to applying the grouping skill well relies on employing the most useful classification rules. The media tell us what classification rules are, so if we accept their classification rules, we will end up with the groups they want us to use. But if we make the effort to determine which classification rules are the best ways for us to organize our perceptions of the world, we will end up with groupings that have more meaning and more value for us.

iStock/Wavebreakmedia

Media exposure can have both positive and negative effects on children's academic performance.

Induction is inferring a pattern across a small number of elements, then generalizing the pattern to all elements in the larger set. We see examples of induction all the time, some good examples and some not so good. One example is a public opinion poll. Surveyors ask a few hundred people a question then generalize the results to the entire population. If the surveyors use a sample of people that represent the entire population, then this use of induction is good. However, if surveyors sample only one particular kind of person, then it is misleading to generalize their findings to the entire population, which is composed of all kinds of people.

We use induction in our everyday lives when we make a few observations then generalize. For example, we might get sick and go to the emergency room for treatment and have to wait several hours before being seen by a doctor. We get angry and claim that the entire health care system is overburdened and that everyone has to wait too long to get medical care.

Deduction is using general principles to explain particulars, typically with the use of syllogistic reasoning. A well-known syllogism is as follows: (1) All men are mortal (general principle). (2) Socrates is a man (particular observation). (3) Therefore, Socrates is mortal (conclusion reached through logical reasoning).

The starting place for deductive reasoning is our general principles. If our general principles are accurate, then we are likely to reach good conclusions. But when we have faulty general principles, we will explain particular occurrences in a faulty manner. One general principle that most people hold to be true is that the media, especially television, have a very strong negative effect on other people. They have an unrealistic opinion that the media cause other people to behave violently. Some people believe that if you allow PSAs (public service announcements) on TV about using condoms, children will learn that it is permissible and even a good thing to have sex. This is clearly an overestimation. At the same time, people *under*estimate the influence the media have on them. When they are asked if they think the media have any effect on them personally, 88% say no. These people argue that the media are primarily channels of entertainment and diversion, so they have no negative effect on them. The people who believe this say that they have watched thousands of hours of crime shows and have never shot anyone or robbed a bank. Although this may be true, this argument does not fully support the claim that the media have no effect on them; this argument is based on the false premise that the media only trigger high-profile, negative, behavioral effects that are easy to recognize. But there are many more types of effects, such as giving people the false impression that crime is a more serious problem than it really is or that most crime is violent.

Synthesis is the assembling of elements into a new structure. This is an essential skill we use when building and updating our knowledge structures. As we take in new information, it often does not fit into an existing knowledge structure, so we must adapt that knowledge structure to accommodate the new information. Thus the process of synthesis is using our new media messages to keep reformulating, refining, and updating our existing knowledge structures.

Abstracting is creating a brief, clear, and accurate description capturing the essence of a message in a significantly smaller number of words than the message itself. Thus when we are describing a media message to someone else or reviewing the message in our own minds, we use the skill of abstracting. The key to using this skill well is to be able to capture the "big picture" or central idea of the media message in as few words as possible.

These seven skills are the tools we use to create, alter, and update our knowledge structures. We use these tools to mine through the flood of information to find those key bits we need for some purpose, then transform those bits in some way (judge their worth, look for a pattern, or draw a conclusion) so we can fit them into a meaningful knowledge structure. Skills are like muscles; the more you exercise them, the stronger they get. Without practice, skills become weaker.

Knowledge Structures

Knowledge structures are sets of organized information in your memory. If they were simply unorganized piles of random facts, then they would not be very useful. Instead, the information needs to be carefully organized into a structure that helps us see patterns that organize our worlds. We use these patterns as maps to tell us where to get more information and also where to go to retrieve information we have previously encoded into our knowledge structures. To help visualize this, think about your bedroom. Are your books, papers, clothes, food wrappers, and everything else randomly scattered all over your bed, desk, closet, and drawers? If so, is it difficult for you to find things?

Information is the essential ingredient in knowledge structures. But not all information is equally useful in the building of a knowledge structure. Some information is rather superficial. If all a person has is the recognition of surface information, such as lyrics to television show theme songs, names of characters and actors, settings for shows, and the like, he or she is operating at a low level of media literacy, because this type of information addresses only the question of "What?" The more useful information comes in the form of the answers to the questions of "How?" and "Why?" But remember that you first need to know something about the what before you can delve deeper into the questions of how and why.

In everyday language, the terms *information* and *knowledge* are often used as synonyms, but in this book they have meanings very different from one another. Information is piecemeal and transitory, whereas knowledge is structured, organized, and of more enduring significance. Information resides in the messages, whereas knowledge resides in a person's mind. Information gives something to the person to interpret, whereas knowledge reflects that which has already been interpreted by the person.

istock/scyther5

Knowledge structures help to organize the different kinds of social and factual information we are exposed to every day.

Information is composed of facts. Facts by themselves are not knowledge any more than a pile of lumber is a house. Knowledge requires structure to provide context and thereby exhibit meaning. Think of messages as the raw materials and think of skills as the tools you use to build your knowledge structures.

While I'm on the topic of distinguishing information from knowledge, I also need to define a few terms related to the idea of information: **message**, **factual information**, and **social information.** Messages are those instruments that deliver information to us. Information is the content of those messages. Messages can be delivered in many different media—computers, smartphones, television, radio, CDs, video games, books, newspapers, magazines, websites, conversations, lectures, concerts, signs along the streets, labels on the products we buy, and so on. They can be large (an entire Hollywood movie) or small (one utterance by one character in a movie).

Messages are composed of two kinds of information: factual and social. Facts are discrete bits of information, such as names (of people, places, characters, etc.), dates, titles, definitions of terms, formulas, lists, and the like. For example, when you watch the news and hear messages, those messages are composed of facts, such as the following: *Donald Trump was elected to the office of President of the United States in the fall of 2016.* This statement contains facts.

Social information is composed of accepted beliefs that cannot be verified by authorities in the same way factual information can be. This is not to say that social information is less valuable or less real to people. Social information is composed of lessons that people infer from observing social interactions. These lessons are inferred from the patterns of actions and consequences we observe.

COMPARE & CONTRAST
FACTUAL INFORMATION AND SOCIAL INFORMATION

Compare: Factual information and social information are *the same* in the following ways:

- Both are things we learn from exposure to media messages.
- Both are stored in our memories and recalled when we have a need to use them.

Contrast: Factual information and social information are *different* in the following ways:

- Factual information is raw, unprocessed, and context free; facts are discrete bits

of information, such as names (of people, places, characters, etc.), dates, titles, definitions of terms, formulas, lists, and the like.

- Social information is composed of lessons that we infer from observing social interactions both in real life as well as in media messages; these are guidelines we learn about how to dress, talk, and act in order for other people in society to consider us attractive, smart, athletic, hip, and so forth.

With media literacy, we need strong knowledge structures in five areas: media effects, media content, media industries, the real world, and the self. With good knowledge in these five areas, you will be able to make better decisions about seeking out information, working with that information, and constructing meaning from it that will be more useful in serving your own goals. People who have had a wider range of experiences in the real world have a broader base from which to appreciate and analyze media messages. For example, those who have helped someone run for political office can understand and analyze press coverage of political campaigns to a greater depth than those who have not had any real-world experience with political campaigns. People who have played sports will be able to appreciate the athletic accomplishments they see on television to a greater depth compared to those people who have not physically tested themselves with those challenges. People who have had a wide range of relationships and family experiences will have a higher degree of understanding and more in-depth emotional reactions to those portrayals in the media.

Knowledge structures provide the context we use when trying to make sense of each new media message. The more knowledge structures we have, the more confident we can be in making sense of a wide range of messages. For example, you may have a very large, well-developed knowledge structure about a particular television series. You may know the names of all the characters in that TV show. You may know everything that has happened to those characters in all the episodes. You may even know the names and histories of the actors who play the characters. If you have all of this information well organized so that you can recall any of it at a moment's notice, you have a well-developed knowledge structure about that television series. Are you media literate? Within the small corner of the media world where that one TV show resides, you are. But if this were the only knowledge structure you had developed, you would have little understanding of the content produced by the other media. You would have difficulty understanding trends about who owns and controls the media, about how the media have developed over time, about why certain kinds of content are never seen while other types are continually repeated, and about what effects that content may be having on you. With many highly developed knowledge structures, you could understand the entire span of media issues and therefore be able to see the "big picture" about why the media are the way they are.

Your level of media literacy is determined in large part by how well you have developed knowledge structures in four areas: media industries, media audiences, media content, and media effects. This book presents structures and information to help you with these. To make a simple assessment of how well developed your knowledge structures are in these four areas of the media, do Exercise 2.1. Do the best you can in answering the questions in that exercise, but don't be too shocked if you cannot come up with many answers. Think of this exercise as a diagnostic to tell you where you need to add more information, then keep those needs in mind as you actively read through the following chapters of this book. Also, at this point, don't worry about checking your answers for accuracy; you can do that later as you read the book. For now, let this diagnostic exercise simply help you assess where you think you have information.

Personal Locus

In order to develop and use the set of seven skills of media literacy to build useful knowledge structures, you need one more element: a strong personal locus. Your personal locus is composed of goals and drives. The goals shape the information processing tasks by determining what gets filtered in and what gets ignored. The more you are aware of your goals, the more you can direct the process of information seeking. And the stronger your drives for information are, the more effort you will expend to attain your goals. However, when your locus is weak (i.e., you are not aware of particular goals and your drive energy is low), you will default to media control where you allow the media to exercise a high degree of control over exposures and information processing.

The more you know about your personal locus and the more you make conscious decisions to shape it, the more you can control the process of media influence on you. The more you engage your locus, the more you will be increasing your media literacy.

Being media literate, however, does not require that your personal locus be fully engaged every minute of every day. That would be an unreasonable requirement, because no one can maintain a high a degree of concentration all the time. Instead, the process of increasing media literacy requires you to activate your personal locus in bursts. During these periods of high concentration, you can analyze your mental programs to make sure that they are set up to achieve your own personal goals rather than the goals of the media programmers or advertisers. These periods of analyses will generate new insights about what is working well and where the glitches are. Then you can use those new insights to reprogram your mental code and fix the glitches by correcting faulty information, repairing uninformed opinions, and changing habits that are making you unhappy. Then once these alterations are made to your **mental codes**, you can return to automatic processing where your newly programmed codes will better help you achieve your goals for information and entertainment.

THE DEFINITION OF MEDIA LITERACY

Now that I have laid the foundation for media literacy by setting out its three major building blocks, it is time to present its formal definition. *Media literacy is a set of perspectives that we actively use to expose ourselves to the mass media to process and interpret the meaning of the messages we encounter.* We build our perspectives from knowledge structures. To build our knowledge structures, we need tools, raw material, and willingness. The tools are our skills. The raw material is information from the media and from the real world. The willingness comes from our personal locus.

Notice that the definition begins with "a set of perspectives." What is a perspective? I'll illustrate this with an analogy. Let's say you wanted to learn about the Earth. You could build a 100-foot-tall tower, climb up to the top, and use that as your perspective to study the Earth. This tower would give you a good perspective that would not be blocked by trees so that you could see for perhaps several miles in any direction. If your tower were in a forest, you would conclude that Earth is covered with trees. But if your tower were in a suburban neighborhood, you would conclude that Earth is covered with houses, roads, and shopping centers. If your tower were inside a large professional football stadium, you would conclude something quite different. Each of these perspectives would give you a very different idea about Earth. We could get into all kinds of arguments about which perspective delivers the most accurate or best set of ideas about Earth, but such arguments miss the point. None of these perspectives is better than any other. The key to understanding Earth is to build lots of these towers so you have many different perspectives to enlarge your understanding about what the Earth is. And not all of these towers need to be 100 feet tall. Some should be very short so that you can better see what is happening between the blades of grass in a lawn. And others should be hundreds of miles away from the surface so that you can tell that Earth is a sphere and that there are large weather formations constantly churning around the globe. The more perspectives you have, the more you will be able to understand this planet. This principle also holds with media literacy; that is, the more perspectives you have on the media, the better you will be able to understand the phenomenon.

To illuminate this idea of media literacy further, I need to describe two of its most important characteristics. First, media literacy is a multidimensional concept with many interesting facets. Second, media literacy is a continuum, not a category.

Media literacy is multidimensional. When we build our set of perspectives, we need to ensure that we construct different *types* of perspectives to maximize the value delivered

Media literacy is a set of perspectives that we actively use to expose, process, and interpret the meaning of the messages we encounter.

by a variety of perspectives. Thus it is useful to think of our perspectives along four very different dimensions: cognitive, emotional, aesthetic, and moral. Each of these four dimensions focuses on a different domain of understanding. The cognitive dimension focuses our attention on factual information—dates, names, definitions, and the like. Think of cognitive information as that which resides in the brain. This is the most basic dimension for media literacy perspectives.

The emotional dimension focuses our attention on how we perceive the feelings of people in media messages and how we read our own feelings that are triggered by those media exposures. Think of emotional information as that which lives in the heart—feelings of happy times, moments of fear, and instances of embarrassment. Some people have little ability to experience an emotion during exposure to the media, whereas others are very sensitive to cues that generate all sorts of feelings in them. For example, we all have the ability to perceive rage, fear, lust, hate, and other strong emotions. Producers use easy-to-recognize symbols to trigger these emotions, so they do not require a high degree of literacy from audience members in order to perceive and understand those messages. But some of us are much better than others at perceiving the more subtle emotions such as ambivalence, confusion, wariness, and so on. Crafting media messages about these emotions requires more production skill from writers, directors, and actors. Perceiving these subtle emotions accurately requires a higher degree of literacy from the audience.

The aesthetic dimension focuses our attention on the art and craft exhibited in the production of media messages. When we look for aesthetic information in messages, we orient toward making judgments about who are great writers, photographers, actors, dancers, choreographers, singers, musicians, composers, directors, and other kinds of artists. It also helps us make judgments about other products of creative craftsmanship, such as editing, lighting, set designing, costuming, sound recording, graphic layout, and so forth. The ability to appreciate the aesthetic qualities in media messages is very important to some scholars (Messaris, 1994; Silverblatt, Smith, Miller, Smith, & Brown, 2014; Wulff, 1997). For example, Messaris (1994) argues that viewers who are visually literate should have an awareness of artistry and visual manipulation. By this, he means an awareness about the processes by which meaning is created through the visual media. What is expected of sophisticated viewers is some degree of self-consciousness about their role as interpreters. This includes the ability to detect artifice (in staged behavior and editing) and to spot authorial presence (style of the producer/director).

Think of aesthetic information as that which resides in our eyes and ears. Some of us have a good ear for dialogue or musical composition. Some of us have a good eye for lighting, photographic composition, or movement. The more perspectives we have constructed from this aesthetic dimension, the finer discriminations we can make between a great actress and a good one, between a great song that will endure and a currently popular "flash in the pan," between a film director's best and very best work, or between art and artificiality.

The moral dimension focuses our attention on values. Think of moral information as that which resides in your conscience or your soul. This type of information provides us with the basis for making judgments about right and wrong. When we see characters make decisions in a story, we judge them on a moral dimension—that is, the characters' goodness or evilness. The more detailed and refined our moral perspectives are, the more deeply we can perceive the values underlying messages in the media and the more sophisticated and reasoned are our judgments about those values. It takes a highly media-literate person to perceive moral themes well. You must be able to think past individual characters to focus your meaning making at the overall narrative level. You need to be able to separate characters from their actions—you might not like a particular character, but you could still appreciate his or her actions in terms of fitting in with (or reinforcing) your values.

When your set of media literacy perspectives is constructed across all four of these dimensions, the more you can understand and appreciate the media. But if your perspectives are limited to only one or two of these dimensions, then you will have a much lower ceiling for media literacy. For example, you may be able to be highly analytical when you watch a movie and quote lots of facts about the history of the genre, the director's point of view, and the underlying theme. But if you cannot evoke an emotional reaction, you are simply going through a dry, academic exercise.

Media literacy is a continuum, not a category. The final characteristic of media literacy I need to emphasize is that media literacy is not a category, like a box, where you are either in the category or you are not. For example, you are either a high school graduate or you are not; you are either an American citizen or you are not. In contrast, media literacy is best regarded as a continuum, like a thermometer, where there are degrees.

We all occupy some position on the media literacy continuum. There is no point below which we could say that someone has no literacy, and there is no point at the high end of the continuum where we can say that someone is fully literate; there is always room for improvement. People are positioned along that continuum based on the strength of their set of perspectives on the media. The strength of a person's set of perspectives is reflected by the number and quality of knowledge structures. And the quality of knowledge structures is based on the level of a person's skills and experiences. Because people vary substantially on skills and experiences, they will vary on the number and quality of their knowledge structures. Hence, there will be a great variation of media literacy across people.

People operating at lower levels of media literacy have fewer perspectives on the media, and those perspectives are supported by knowledge structures that contain little information and are less organized. Thus people at lower levels of media literacy have less ability to understand the media, to appreciate their wonderful advantages, and to protect themselves from dangerous risks. These people are also habitually reluctant or unwilling to use their skills, which remain underdeveloped and therefore more difficult to employ successfully.

THE DEVELOPMENT OF MEDIA LITERACY

Media literacy is a broad continuum, as you have seen from the previous section. It involves personal locus, knowledge structures, and skills along the four dimensions of cognitive, emotional, aesthetic, and moral. In order to make sense of all this detail in a way to illustrate how people can develop their media literacy, it is useful to think of various levels or stages. Table 2.2 displays a scheme with eight developmental stages. The first stage is Acquiring Fundamentals, which occurs during the first year of life. Language Acquisition occurs during years 2 and 3, then Narrative Acquisition happens during years 3 to 5. These are stages that are typically left behind by children as they age into adolescence and adulthood.

The Developing Skepticism stage occurs from about ages 5 to 9, and the Intensive Development stage is shortly after. Many people stay in this stage the rest of their lives because this stage is fully functional; that is, people in this stage feel they are getting exposure to the messages they want and getting the meaning out of those messages they want. They feel they are fully media literate and that there is nothing more they need to learn.

The next three stages can be regarded as advanced, because they require the continual use of higher-level skills and the active development of elaborate knowledge structures. People in the Experiential Exploring stage feel that their media exposure has been very narrow, and they seek exposure to a much wider range of messages. For example, people who have watched only prime-time action/adventure and situation comedy programs will begin to watch news, PBS documentaries, travelogues, MTV, science fiction, offbeat sports, and so on. They will pick up niche magazines and books about unusual topics. The thrill for these people is to see something they have never seen before. This makes them think about the variety of human experience.

People in the Critical Appreciation stage see themselves as connoisseurs of the media. They seek out better messages that offer greater appeal along the four dimensions—cognitively, emotionally, aesthetically, and morally. People in this stage exhibit strongly held opinions about who are the best writers, the best producers, the best news reporters, and so forth, and they have lots of evidence to support their well-reasoned opinions. They can talk fluently and at length about what makes a good writer and how these elements are exhibited in a particular writer's body of work.

Social Responsibility is characterized by people having critical appreciation of all kinds of media messages, but instead of having a primarily internal perspective (as with the previous stage), the perspective here is external. The person at this stage not only asks "What is best from my point of view and why?" but also is concerned with questions such as "What types of messages are best for others and for society?"

Now think of these eight stages as neighborhoods. You have a home neighborhood where you live, depending on your age, your personal locus, how well you have developed your skills, and how elaborate your key knowledge structures are. You can move around to other neighborhoods depending on your needs. We are usually able to move up a stage or two from our home neighborhood. But moving up a stage requires a conscious effort where we must expend more energy to apply higher-level skills. So we don't move up unless we are strongly motivated to do so. For example, when you are reading a book that is considered a classic novel for a college course, you may be able to move up to the Critical Appreciation level. But when you flick on the television and watch MTV's *Pimp My Ride* or *The Hills* to relax, you might sink down to the Intensive Development level. There is nothing wrong with this dropping down a level or two, because there are times when we just want to "veg out" and don't want to spend the effort to stay at the highest

TABLE 2.2 ■ Development of Media Literacy	
Stage	**Characteristics**
Acquiring fundamentals	• Learn that there are human beings and other physical things apart from oneself; these things look different and serve different functions • Learn the meaning of facial expressions and natural sounds • Recognize shapes, form, size, color, movement, and spatial relations • Rudimentary concept of time—regular patterns
Language acquisition	• Recognize speech sounds and attach meaning to them • Be able to reproduce speech sounds • Orient to visual and audio media • Have emotional and behavioral responses to music and sounds • Recognize certain characters in visual media and follow their movement
Narrative acquisition	• Develop understanding of differences: fiction vs. nonfiction ads vs. entertainment real vs. make-believe • Understand how to connect plot elements: by time sequencing by motive-action-consequence
Developing skepticism	• Discount claims made in ads • Sharpen differences between likes and dislikes for shows, characters, and actions • Make fun of certain characters even though those characters are not presented as foils in their shows
Intensive development	• Have strong motivation to seek out information on certain topics • Develop a detailed set of information on particular topics (sports, politics, etc.) • Develop high awareness of utility of information and quick facility in processing information judged to be useful
Experiential exploring	• Seek out different forms of content and narratives • Focus on searching for surprises and new emotional, moral, and aesthetic reactions
Critical appreciation	• Accept messages on their own terms then evaluate them within that sphere • Develop very broad and detailed understanding of the historical, economic, political, and artistic contexts of message systems • Have the ability to make subtle comparisons and contrasts among many different message elements simultaneously • Have the ability to construct a summary judgment about the overall strengths and weaknesses of a message
Social responsibility	• Take a moral stand that certain messages are more constructive for society than others; this is a multidimensional perspective based on a thorough analysis of the media landscape • Recognize that one's own individual decisions impact society, no matter how minutely • Recognize that there are some actions an individual can take to make a constructive impact on society

stages. However, remember there is a difference between people who stay at the lower stages because they are unable or unwilling to operate at higher stages and people who are able to operate at all stages but who choose to take it easier at lower stages occasionally.

ADVANTAGES OF DEVELOPING A HIGHER DEGREE OF MEDIA LITERACY

There are primarily three advantages to developing a higher degree of media literacy. First, with increases in media literacy, your appetite for a wider variety of media messages will grow. Second, with increases in media literacy, you learn more about how to program your own mental codes. Third, with increases in media literacy, you are able to exercise more control over the media.

Appetite for a Wider Variety of Media Messages

The media offer an incredible array of choices. The Internet contains websites on every topic that humans can conceive. Books are published each year on an extremely wide range of topics. Magazines, with their 7,200 titles published each year (Statista, 2018l), offer a much wider range than any one person can consume. Cable television is a bit narrower still, but with several hundred channels from most cable TV providers, the choice is much wider than any one person can keep up with. However, the mass media continually try to direct our choices to a smaller set. For example, about 10,000 magazines are published in this country. When you go into a magazine store, like in an airport, you will see only about 100 magazines on the shelves. You likely do not scan through all 100 before making your choice about which one to buy and take on the plane. Instead, you rely on your automatic filtering to narrow your choice down to about three or four magazines that you have found interesting in the past— that is, the media have conditioned you to like these magazines. Do you have a choice? Yes, of course. But see how the media—first through the bookstore, then through media conditioning—have narrowed your choice down considerably; in other words, the decision you made was determined 99.99% by factors other than you. The media have programmed you to think that you have choices when in fact the degree of choice is greatly limited. It is rather like parents laying out two pairs of dress pants, one black and the other dark blue, for their 4-year-old son and giving him the total power to choose what he will wear today. Whether you regard this as a real choice depends on how much you know about the real range of options. If the boy's perspective on pants is limited to dark dress pants, then he will view his parents' offering of two pairs as a real choice. However, if his perspective is broader to include knowledge about jeans, cargo pants, skater shorts, bathing trunks, and football pants, then he will think the two pairs of dress pants is not much of a choice.

The mass media continually try to constrain your choices so they can condition you into habitual exposure to a few types of media **vehicles**. This makes you more predictable from a marketing point of view.

The media literacy perspective encourages you to be more adventurous and explore a wider range of messages, so that you can be more involved in your choices. When you do so, you will likely find many of those messages are not interesting or useful to you;

however, you will also likely find a few types of messages that are highly useful, and these surprises will allow you to expand your exposure repertoire in a way that better fulfills your needs.

More Self-Programming of Mental Codes

The purpose of media literacy is to empower individuals to make more of their own decisions about which messages to expose themselves to and to construct meanings from those messages to serve their own goals. When you operate at higher levels of media literacy, you have more power in programming your mental codes. This means that you reduce the power of the media in programming those codes that limit your media exposures to the habits they have built for you. You can reprogram your mental codes to open yourself up to new experiences. Also, you examine your standards and beliefs to find those that are faulty and replace them with standards and beliefs that are more of your own making. Then when you apply those more personal standards, you are making evaluations that are more in line with your own goals.

More Control Over Media

Increasing your level of media literacy gives you more power to control media exposures and their eventual effect on you. At lower levels of media literacy, you default to media control; that is, the media will use you to achieve their own goals. The mass media are composed of businesses that are very sophisticated in knowing how to attract your attention and condition you for repeat exposures.

There are times when the media's business goals and your personal goals are the same, thus creating a win-win situation for both the media and you. But there are also many times when your personal goals are different from the media's goals; when this occurs, you need to make a decision about whether to go along with the media-conditioned habits or break away from those conditioned habits to pursue your own goals. Oftentimes, we do not realize there is a decision to make because we are so firmly entrenched in those media-conditioned habits. The media literacy perspective will help you recognize when you have choices, especially in situations where the media's goals are different from your own goals.

SUMMARY

The chapter presents a definition of media literacy as a perspective from which we expose ourselves to the media and interpret the meaning of the messages we encounter. Media literacy is not a category; instead, there are degrees of media literacy. Media literacy is also multidimensional, with development taking place cognitively, emotionally, aesthetically, and morally.

Media literacy is composed of three building blocks: skills, knowledge structures, and personal locus. The skills are the tools that we use to work on information in the media messages to build strong knowledge structures. The direction and drive to do this work lies in one's personal locus.

People who are highly media literate are able to see much more in a given message. They are more aware of the levels of meaning. This enhances understanding. They are more in charge of programming their own mental codes. This enhances control. They are much more likely to get what they want from the messages. This enhances appreciation. Thus, people operating at higher levels of media literacy fulfill the goals of higher understanding, control, and appreciation.

Further Reading

Jenkins, H., Purushotma, R., Weigel, M., Clinton, K., & Robison, A. J. (2009). *Confronting the challenges of participatory culture: Media education for the 21st century.* Cambridge, MA: MIT Press. (128 pages)

Funded by the John D. and Catherine T. MacArthur Foundation, this book focuses on the skills that are most important for dealing with the new media culture, which is characterized by interactive media making it possible for people to participate in society in ways not available before.

Mackey, M. (2007). *Literacies across media: Playing the text* (2nd ed.). Abingdon, UK: Routledge. (224 pages)

This book describes an 18-month-long project that was designed to study how a group of boys and girls, aged from 10 to 14, made sense of narratives in a variety of formats, including print, electronic book, video, DVD, computer game, and CD-ROM. The author's analyses reveal how those children developed strategies for interpreting narratives through encounters with a diverse range of texts and media.

Potter, W. J. (2018). *The skills of media literacy* (2nd ed.). Santa Barbara, CA: Knowledge Assets. (224 pages, including references and glossary)

This book presents a detailed description of the seven essential skills of media literacy along with exercises to help readers develop those skills.

Silverblatt, A., Smith, A., Miller, D., Smith, J., & Brown, N. (2014). *Media literacy: Keys to interpreting media messages* (4th ed.). Westport, CT: Praeger. (340 pages, including index)

This is a mass media book that presents some chapters with information about what is needed as far as knowledge about the media. It has the feel of a textbook for an introductory-level course with its use of photographs and exercises for students to undertake.

Tyner, K. (Ed.) (2010). *Media literacy: New agendas in communication.* New York, NY: Routledge. (243 pages with index)

The 10 chapters in this edited volume deal with how media literacy initiatives have taken place in the past and what they should emphasize going forward. These initiatives are organized into four contexts: community-based settings, K–12 classrooms, higher education, and virtual environments.

EXERCISE 2.1
ASSESSMENT OF KNOWLEDGE STRUCTURES ABOUT MASS MEDIA

Media Industries

1. Can you list the different mass media according to how old they are? Start with the oldest and continue to the newest one.

2. What does "convergence" mean within the media industries?

3. What are the stages that structure the development of each mass medium as an industry?

4. What are the key characteristics of the media economic game?

5. How can you use your knowledge about the development of the mass media industries and how they play the economic game to increase your level of media literacy?

Media Audiences

1. What are the key three information processing tasks we perform when we encounter media messages?

2. What is the difference between exposure and attention?

3. In what four exposure states do we experience media messages?

4. Why have media programmers shifted their view from a mass audience to niche audiences?

5. How do media programmers identify niche audiences?

6. What are the key strategies media programmers use to attract and condition audiences?

7. How have children been treated as a special audience?

8. How should young adults also be treated as a special audience?

9. How can you use the knowledge about information processing tasks, exposure states, attention, niche audiences, and media programmers' strategies to increase your level of media literacy?

Media Content

1. What is the next-step reality principle?

2. In what ways are "reality" TV programs real?

3. How has the idea of "news" changed?

4. How should we go about the task of determining who should be regarded as a journalist?

5. What are the ways people use to judge the quality of news and which of these are faulty?

(Continued)

(Continued)

6. What is the general formula for media entertainment?

7. Can you articulate patterns of how the following topics are portrayed in the media: character demographics, sexual activity, violence, and health?

8. Can you explain in detail the strategies used by advertisers in designing overall campaigns as well as copy platforms?

9. What strategies do electronic gamers use to develop and market their games?

10. How does the design of cooperative experiences differ from competitive experiences on interactive electronic platforms?

11. How can you use the knowledge about the principle of next-step reality, definition of news, standards for judging quality of media messages, and strategies used by media programmers to increase your level of media literacy?

Media Effects

1. Explain how the four-dimensional perspective broadens the view of media effects.

2. What are the differences between baseline and fluctuation effects in the process of influence?

3. What are the differences between process and manifest effects?

4. How can you use knowledge about the four-dimensional perspective and the process of influence to increase your level of media literacy?

INTRODUCTION TO THE CORE KNOWLEDGE STRUCTURE CHAPTERS

The core of this book is composed of 12 knowledge structure chapters. Now that you have read through the two introductory chapters, you know how saturated our culture is with a constant flow of media messages and you know the main features of the media literacy approach. Now you are ready to start building more elaborate knowledge structures in four areas.

The first of these four areas focuses on the audience. Chapter 3 focuses on the audience from the individual's perspective, while Chapter 4 focuses on the audience from the mass media industries' perspective. Chapter 5 poses the question: Should children be treated as a special audience? This chapter shows you that yes, children are a special audience in some ways, but so too are adolescents, young adults, and the elderly.

The second knowledge structure area focuses on the media industries. Chapter 6 helps you see the media industries from a historical perspective so that you can appreciate the challenges they have overcome to arrive at their current status. Using a life cycle structure, it shows what is behind the innovation and development of the media industries. An economic perspective is used in Chapter 7 to show the business foundations of the industries.

The third knowledge structure area focuses on media content and contains five chapters. Chapter 8 introduces the idea of content and presents the major characteristic of all media content—what I call "one-step remove" reality. Then, Chapter 9 focuses on news content, Chapter 10 on entertainment content, Chapter 11 on advertising content, and Chapter 12 on interactive content such as video games and social networking media.

The fourth knowledge structure area focuses on media effects. When we take a broader perspective on effects, we can more accurately assess the influence of the media in our lives. This also puts us in a much better position to manage the effects of the media. Chapter 13 will help you expand your vision about what constitutes a media effect. Effects are both long term as well as immediate. Although they can influence our behavior, they also have profound influences on us cognitively, affectively, emotionally, and physiologically. And they have positive as well as negative effects. Then the question of how the effects processes work on us is explored in Chapter 14. Those processes are hardly ever simple or direct. More often, the media work in concert with many other factors that each serve to increase the probability that an effect may occur.

When you read through each of these chapters, look first at the key idea; this is the most important thing you need to learn from a chapter. Then look at the outline that shows the structure of the chapter. These outlines should also guide you in elaborating your own knowledge structures on the topic. Use the key idea and the outline to stimulate your own questions for the topic then let those questions guide your reading through the chapter. If some of these questions become more important and interesting to you as you read through a chapter, then continue your reading starting with the Further Reading suggestions I provide. Also, the more you engage with the material and work with it, the better you will learn and the more useful this learning will be in your everyday life.

The exercises will help with this. This book has a self-help tone as it presents guidance and practical exercises to help you achieve higher levels of media literacy. Do not get caught in the trap of thinking that it is sufficient to memorize the facts in each chapter and then stop thinking about the material. Simply memorizing facts will not help you increase your media literacy much. Instead, you need to *internalize* the information by drawing it into your own experiences. Continually ask yourself, "How does this new information fit in with what I already know?" "Can I find an example of this in my own life?" and "How can I *apply* this when I deal with the media?" The exercises at the end of each chapter will help you get started with this. The more you think through the exercises and the more you develop new exercises for yourself, the more you will be internalizing the information and thus making it more a natural part of the way you think.

AUDIENCES

PART II

getty/David Hill

AUDIENCE: INDIVIDUAL PERSPECTIVE

Key Idea: In our information-saturated culture, individuals are constantly processing media messages as they make decisions either consciously or automatically about filtering, meaning matching, and meaning construction. They continually are making these decisions in one of four exposure states: automatic, attentional, transported, and self-reflexive.

The human brain has enormous capacity for information but can only pay attention to a relatively small number of stimuli at a given time.

Harry and Ann are discussing their relationship over lunch on campus.

"Harry, you never pay attention to what I say!"

"How can you say that? We spend almost all day together every day and you are constantly talking," Harry replies. "I hear what you say."

"Maybe, but you don't understand what I say."

"Yes, I do. I know a lot about you. I know the names of all your brothers and sisters, and where you went to high school, and your favorite color and —"

Ann interrupts, "Those are facts about me. They are not me! You don't seem to know me."

"I know the meaning of every word you say. I don't need a dictionary!"

"There is more to meaning than the definitions of the words I use!"

In interpersonal conversations, we often get ourselves into trouble if we are not careful to make a distinction between literal meaning—the dictionary-type meanings we all share for common words and phrases—and the deeper meaning that resides in how we say things, which engages a more complex process. To help make sense of all this complexity, this chapter will show you that there are three generic information-processing tasks—filtering, meaning matching, and meaning construction—as we continuously encounter media messages in our everyday environments. Once you understand these three information-processing tasks, we will move on to the distinction between exposure and attention. Finally, the chapter will show you how you can use this knowledge to increase your media literacy and thereby control these processes to a higher degree.

INFORMATION-PROCESSING TASKS

We are constantly engaged in a series of three **information-processing tasks** every day. These tasks are **filtering**, **meaning matching**, and **meaning construction** (see Table 3.1). First, we encounter a message and are faced with the task of deciding whether to filter the message out (ignore it) or filter it in (process it). If we decide to filter it in, then we must make sense of it—that is, recognize the symbols and match our learned definitions to the symbols. Next, we need to construct the meaning of the message.

Filtering

As you saw in Chapter 1, there has been a huge increase in the amount of information generated, which has led to media companies competing much more aggressively for our limited attention. While the human brain has enormous capacity for processing information, the way it functions (or at least the way we currently understand how it functions) limits our ability to pay attention to a relatively small number of stimuli at any given moment. While the human mind can take in 11 million pieces of information in an instant, our awareness is limited to only about 40 of these pieces of information at any given moment (Wilson, 2002). This means that the brain has the capacity to track a

TABLE 3.1 ■ Three Tasks of Information Processing			
	Filtering Messages	**Meaning Matching**	**Meaning Construction**
Task	To make decisions about which messages to filter out (ignore) and which to filter in (pay attention to)	To use basic competencies to recognize referents and locate previously learned definitions for each	To use skills in order to move beyond meaning matching and to construct meaning for oneself in order to personalize and get more out of a message
Goal	To attend to only those messages that have some kind of usefulness for the person and ignore all other messages	To access previously learned meanings efficiently	To interpret messages from more than one perspective as a means of identifying the range of meaning options, then choose one or synthesize across several
Focus	Messages in the environment	Referents in messages	One's own knowledge structures

huge amount of stimuli in our environments but provides us with a very limited ability to be aware of all that activity. While our brains are constantly processing an enormous amount of stimuli from our environments, only a tiny percentage of all that stimuli makes it into our conscious awareness; the rest of the stimuli are being processed unconsciously with the use of automatic routines.

The automatic routines that run in our minds are like the automatic routines that run on our computers, where this programming guides your computer through thousands of complicated tasks without continually pausing to ask you dozens of bothersome questions about how you want that program to run. To illustrate this point, think about your e-mail account. Your e-mail provider uses **spam filters** to screen out all those e-mails that they determine are coming from spammers. Research has shown that 45% of the 14.5 billion e-mails sent each day are spam (Bauer, 2018). Because the average response rate is one reply to every 12.5 million spam e-mails sent, spammers regularly send out tens of millions of e-mails each day to find those few people who will buy things like pseudo-wonder drugs, pet rocks, and other products that 99.99% of us would never buy. Spam filters are automatic routines that do a considerable amount of filtering for you without asking you whether you want to receive e-mails from various addresses. However, because you don't see the tens of thousands of addresses that the automatic filter is using as spammers' addresses, you don't know whether the spam filter is blocking out some messages you might want to read. For the sake of efficiency, we don't make the considerable effort to check the long spam address list; instead, we let our spam filters run automatically.

Our minds also have programmed filters that guide the processing of messages. This raises the question of who programmed those filters; that is, who decided which messages to filter out? If it was you who fully programmed this code, then the filter is automatically following only your commands. But what if some of the filtering code was programmed by someone else? If this is the case, then you have let that someone else determine what you see and what you do not get to see.

Some media services do a significant amount of filtering for us. For example, when we shop for a book on Amazon, the keywords we use might generate a list of several thousand possible books, but Amazon shows us a screen of perhaps a dozen books. When we do a search for information on Google, the search might result in several million hits, but Google displays a screen with its top choices to save us from spending all day going through thousands of screens. For example, if you Google "information overload," you may get 4.28 million results in .4 seconds. While this is helpful in going from the 30 trillion webpages that Google says it searches down to 4.28 million pages, it still leaves you with far too many choices to process in a reasonable amount of time.

iStock/Prykhodov

Media search engines like Google use personal preferences to guide our searches.

These services proclaim they are providing us with efficiency, which is true. But they are also exercising considerable control over the filtering process. And they are continually seeking ways to increase their control over those filtering processes by claiming to "personalize" our searching and shopping experiences. Google CEO Eric Schmidt said that Google's goal was to guess what you are interested in. In December 2009, Google changed its algorithm to personalize searches. This means that your Google searches are not guided exclusively by the keywords you use; those searches are also guided by information Google has gathered about your personal preferences (to test this, do Exercise 3.1). In 2010, Google rolled out Google Instant, which guesses what you are searching for as you type in the keyword. Former Google Vice President Marissa Mayer said that the company hoped to make the search box obsolete; Google wants to guess at what you want to search for so that you won't even need to type a keyword (Pariser, 2011).

Where do these companies get their information about you in order to direct your choices? They collect some of the information themselves by recording your interactions with them; they also can buy a tremendous amount information about you—all your financial transactions and your media usage, including how often you use social media, e-mail, and text as well as what you talk about. For example, Acxiom is a large marketing research firm that has a database of half a billion people worldwide including 96% of all Americans. The information that database has about you includes about 1,500 items including the names of your family members, your current and past addresses, how often you pay your credit card bills, whether you own a dog or cat and its breed, whether you are right-handed or left-handed, and what kinds of medication you use based on your pharmacy records (Pariser, 2011). These large marketing data firms collect even more information on individuals than the government. Remember the terrorist attack on the World Trade Towers on 9/11? The major U.S. intelligence agencies (FBI, CIA, DEA, etc.) worked around the clock to identify the terrorists and 3 days later announced that they had identified 11 of the 19 terrorists involved—names, past addresses, current and past associates. Those intelligence agencies received most of their information from Acxiom (Pariser, 2011).

Internet companies employ sophisticated algorithms to churn through all the information they have about you in order to infer conclusions about what you like, then use those inferred conclusions to direct you to particular products while walling you off from other products in the name of efficient filtering. Because these powerful algorithms direct your attention to a narrow range of products and media messages, they serve to limit your experiences. And they do this without your awareness.

The media create much of our filtering code for us. They do this primarily by conditioning us for repeat exposures of the messages we like. This conditioning creates and reinforces exposure habits. When we follow our exposure habits, we leave no time to explore other media or other types of messages.

Meaning Matching

Meaning matching is the process of recognizing elements (referents) in the message and accessing our memory to find the meanings we have memorized for those elements. This is a relatively automatic task. It may require a good deal of effort to learn to recognize symbols in media messages and to memorize their standard meanings, but once

BOX 3.1
IMPLICATIONS OF FILTERING ALGORITHMS

Imagine the following scenario. Let's say a marketing company assembles a huge database about college students by pulling together information from Facebook pages, credit history, health history, parents' income level, and so on. Then someone in that marketing company develops an algorithm that churns through all that data and rank orders all the college students on potential for success and economic wealth.

Now, imagine that the marketing company's algorithm ranks you at the bottom as a loser but ranks your roommates at the top as potential winners. The marketing company sells its rankings to advertisers who then send your roommates all kinds of great offers for low-interest credit cards, coupons for exciting trips, opportunities to network with successful professionals, and so on. Meanwhile, you are ignored by these advertisers because you are regarded as an undesirable target audience.

Your roommates go on to live very successful and happy lives because of all the opportunities offered by advertisers who bought data that told them that your roommates were highly desirable targets. Your roommates get higher-paying jobs at graduation than you because employers looked at the rankings. Your roommates get bigger raises and promotions, have better health care plans, travel more and meet more interesting people, and so on. Marketers can set people off in different life paths by the opportunities they offer certain people and not others.

Questions

Do you think this is fair?

Should advertisers offer the same opportunities to everyone?

In a society where people's needs are so varied and fragmented, does it make sense to expect all advertisers to spend the money necessary to send their messages to everyone when they know that many of those people will never buy their products?

learned this process becomes routine. To illustrate, think back to when you first learned to read. You had to learn how to recognize words printed on a page. Then you had to memorize the meaning of each word. The first time you saw the sentence "Dick threw the ball to Jane," it required a good deal of work to divide the sentence into words, to recall the meaning of each word, and to put it all together. With practice, you were able to perform this process more quickly and more easily. Learning to read in elementary school is essentially the process of being able to recognize a longer list of referents and to memorize their **denoted meanings**. Some referents in media messages were words, some were numbers, some were pictures, and some were sounds.

iStock/yngerman

The relatively automatic task of meaning matching allows you to connect elements to meaning—for instance, recognizing the particular sound your cell phone makes when you've received a text message.

This type of learning develops **competencies.** By competency, I mean that either you are able to do something correctly or you are not. For example, when you see the phrase "2 + 2," you either recognize the "2" referents as particular quantities or you do not. You either recognize the "+" referent as addition or you do not. You can either perform this mathematical operation and arrive at 4 or you cannot. Working with these referents does not require, or allow for, individual interpretation and creative meaning construction. Competencies are our abilities to recognize standard referents and recall the memorized denoted meanings for those referents. If we did not have a common set of referents and shared meanings for each of these referents, communication would not be possible. Education at the elementary level is the training of the next generation to develop the basic competencies of recognizing these referents and memorizing the designated meaning for each one.

When your cell phone makes a particular sound, you know that means you have received a text. You look at the screen and see a name and know which friend has sent you that text. You tap the screen at a specific icon and your text message is revealed. That message has words and emoticons that convey meaning to you. In this example, the sound, name, icon, words, and emoticons are each symbols that have a specific meaning that you have learned in the past and are now able to match with a learned meaning with almost no effort. This task is accomplished automatically because you have acquired those competencies.

Meaning Construction

In contrast to meaning matching, meaning construction is a much more challenging task. It is not an automatic process but instead it requires us to think about moving beyond the standard denoted meaning and to create meaning for ourselves by using the skills of induction, deduction, grouping, and synthesis. We engage in a meaning construction process either when we have no denoted meaning for a particular message in our memory banks or when the denoted meaning does not satisfy us and we want to arrive at a different meaning.

Let's say you get a text from your friend Christopher, who has just broken up with his girlfriend Christine, and the text message says, "Chris is not happy with your help. Thanks a bunch." This message is too ambiguous for meaning matching. For example, does the Chris in the message refer to the sender or his ex-girlfriend? Is the sender being sarcastic when he says, "Thanks a bunch" because he resents your interference? Or is he sincere because you helped him break up when he couldn't do it himself? To answer these questions, you need context about your friendship with Christopher, about his relationship with Christine, his intention to break up with her or not, and so on. So you need skills rather than competencies to analyze the situation, evaluate his intention, and see how this message fits into the pattern of your relationship, so synthesis is an appropriate response.

Many meanings can be constructed from any media message; furthermore, there are many ways to go about constructing that meaning. Thus, we cannot learn a complete set of rules to accomplish this task; instead, we need to be guided by our own goals, and we need to use skills (rather than competencies) to creatively construct a path to reach our goals. For these reasons, meaning construction rarely takes place in an automatic fashion. Instead, we need to make conscious decisions when we are constructing meaning for ourselves. Also, every meaning construction task is different, so we cannot program our minds to follow the same one procedure automatically when we are confronted with a range of meaning construction tasks.

Much of our processing of media messages utilizes meaning construction. There is a large body of research that clearly shows that each of us brings a considerable number of factors with us to any media message exposure and that these factors constitute a **frame** that we use to interpret the message. For example, Kepplinger, Geiss, and Siebert (2012) conducted a study to see how people constructed meaning in news stories. They wanted to see if the way the media presented the story influenced how viewers interpreted the events and people in those stories. The researchers found that the way the media told the story did indeed influence the respondents' interpretation of meaning but that the meaning was also strongly influenced by the personal frames of the individual respondents.

While meaning matching relies on competencies, meaning construction relies on skills. This is one of the fundamental differences between the two tasks of meaning matching and meaning construction. Competencies are categorical; that is, either you have a competency or you do not. However, skill ability is not categorical; on any given skill there is a wide range of ability. That is, some people have little ability, whereas other people have enormous ability. Also, skills are like muscles. Without practice, skills become weaker. With practice and exercise, they grow stronger. When the personal locus has strong drive states for using skills, those skills have a much greater chance of developing to higher levels.

The two processes of meaning matching and meaning construction do not take place independently from one another; they are intertwined. To construct meaning, we first have to recognize referents and understand the sense in which those referents are being used in the message. Thus, the meaning matching process is more fundamental, because the product of the meaning matching process then is imported into the meaning construction process.

It's important to avoid getting the two mixed up. Consider the example of a physics exam where the professor asks students how they could use a barometer to measure the height of a building. If the professor is treating this as a meaning matching task, then there is one sanctioned answer: Take a reading of barometric pressure at the foot of the building and again at the roof then, using a particular formula, translate the differences in readings into feet, thus computing the height of the building. But what if a student is creative and can think of other ways to use the barometer to measure the height of the building, such as what Niels Bohr did in a physics exam at the University of Copenhagen in 1905? Bohr

Richard Levine/Alamy Stock Photo

Research shows that how a media message such as a news story is framed, or presented, will influence how an audience interprets the message.

answered the question by saying that he would go up onto the roof of the building, tie a string to the barometer, lower the barometer to the ground, then measure how long the string was. The professor gave him an F. When Bohr went to talk to his professor and explain his reasoning, the professor did not change the grade. Bohr then explained that there were many ways to answer the exam question. For example, he could throw the barometer off the roof, count the number of seconds it took to hit the ground, and then calculate the distance; or he could measure the length of the shadow of the barometer and the building, and then calculate the ratio. While all of these alternative methods could yield an accurate measure of the height of the building, the professor did not care, because he was looking for one particular answer that required matching the problem to the one solution he taught in his physics class. Bohr took the F that day but continued to use his creative mind to become a very successful physicist, winning the Nobel Prize in physics in 1922 for his contributions to atomic structure and quantum mechanics.

BOX 3.2
METAPHORS FOR HOW THE HUMAN MIND WORKS

Philosophers have been speculating for millennia how the human mind works, and scientists have been conducting research tests of the human mind for perhaps a century. However, we are still in the early stages of understanding this wonderfully complex phenomenon. Thus it helps to think about the human mind metaphorically. Two popular metaphors have been clocks and clouds (Brooks, 2011).

Clocks are self-contained, orderly systems that can be examined in a reductive manner; you can take apart a clock into component pieces and see how they all fit together in one and only one way. This metaphor captures what neurologists do; they focus on the parts of the human brain and how they function.

Clouds, in contrast to clocks, are irregular, dynamic, and idiosyncratic. They change minute to minute and can be formed in many different ways. The essence of clouds cannot be captured in numbers or fixed structures. The cloud metaphor reflects how humanists regard the human mind.

There are scholars who continue to debate which conception of the human mind is more accurate. But as you can see, both are useful ways to think about what the human mind does.

When we take a broad perspective on media literacy, we can see there are times when the human mind seems to act like a clock and there are other times when it appears more as a cloud. With meaning matching tasks, the human mind acts more like a clock as it automatically clicks through the routine of recognizing symbols and accessing their meanings that are connected to the symbols in memory. With meaning construction tasks, the human mind acts more like a cloud as it makes associations in a more amorphous and constantly changing manner

Questions

Can you think of examples in your life where your mind acted more like a clock?

Can you think of examples in your life where your mind acted more like a cloud?

Which metaphor describes the way your mind works better?

ANALYZING THE IDEA OF EXPOSURE TO MEDIA MESSAGES

In everyday language, the terms **exposure** and **attention** are often used synonymously. However, now that you have seen that we are exposed to a great number of media messages without paying attention to them, it is important to highlight the difference in meaning across these two terms.

Exposure and Attention

As we clarify the difference between exposure and attention, it is helpful to analyze the idea of exposure and see that there are several kinds. Let's look at a sequence of three types of exposure: **physical exposure**, **perceptual exposure**, and **psychological exposure** to media messages.

Physical Exposure

The most foundational criterion for exposure is physical presence. A person must experience some proximity to a message in order for exposure to take place. Physical exposure means that the message and the person occupy the same physical space for some period of time. Thus space and time are regarded as barriers to exposure. If a magazine is lying face up on a table in a room and Harry walks through that room, Harry is physically exposed to message on the cover of the magazine but not to any of the messages inside the magazine unless he picks it up and flips through the pages. Also, if Harry does not walk through that room when the magazine is on the table, there is no physical exposure to the message on the cover of the magazine.

Likewise, if a TV is turned on in the lunch room during the noon hour then is turned off at 1 p.m., anyone who walks through that room after 1 p.m. is not physically exposed to TV messages.

Physical proximity is a necessary condition for media exposure, but it is not a sufficient condition. A second necessary condition is perceptual exposure.

Perceptual Exposure

The perceptual consideration refers to a human's ability to receive appropriate sensory input through the visual and auditory senses.

iStock/PeopleImages

Three types of exposure— physical, perceptual, and psychological—are needed before we pay attention to a media message.

We are constantly immersed in a wide range of stimulus elements, but we perceive only a small fraction of these elements because of the limits on our sense organs and processing ability. We live in a world where information is encoding on each of billions of different frequencies along the electromagnetic spectrum. One of these frequencies is called light and our eyes are sensitive to perceive some of that information on that frequency. At other frequencies (e.g., television signals, radio signals, cell phone signals,, etc.) we cannot hear that encoded information, but we have invented devices to translate that information into a form where it occurs within our ability to perceive it (e.g., radio receivers translate that information into sound waves within our range of hearing).

COMPARE & CONTRAST
MEANING MATCHING AND MEANING CONSTRUCTION

Compare: Meaning matching and meaning construction are *the same* in the following ways:

- Both are essential tasks in the process of information processing.

- Both are mental tasks triggered when people notice an element in a media message.

Contrast: Meaning matching and meaning construction are *different* in the following ways:

- Meaning matching is largely an automatic process relying on competencies where media symbols are efficiently matched with previously learned meanings.

- Meaning construction is a process requiring a person's attention and engagement of cognitive processes involving skills where people move beyond simply accepting the previously learned meaning of symbols and infer (or create) fresh meanings that fit better with the context of the present situation and/or the person's own needs for meaning.

The perceptual criterion, however, has a feature beyond simple sensory reception; we must also consider the sensory input–brain connection. Frequently, when the sensory input gets to the brain, it must be transformed into something that we can understand. For example, when we watch a movie in a theater, we are exposed to individual static images projected at about 24 images per second. But humans cannot process 24 individual images per given second in a conscious manner; instead, those individual images run together and appear as continuous motion. Also with film projection, there is a brief time between each of those 24 individual images every second when the screen is blank, but the eye-brain connection is not quick enough to process the blanks, so we do not see those blanks as blanks; instead we only see smooth motion. If the projection rate of images were to slow down to under 10 images per second, we would begin to see a flutter; that is, our brains would begin to see the blanks, because the replacement of still images is slow enough for the eye-brain connection to begin processing them.

Stimuli that are outside the boundaries of human perception are called subliminal. Subliminal messages can leave no psychological trace because they cannot be physically perceived; that is, humans lack the sensory organs to take in stimuli and/or the hardwiring in the brain to be sensitive to them.

There is a widespread misconception that the media put people at risk for "subliminal communication." This belief indicates confusion between the terms *subliminal* and *subconscious*. There is an important distinction that needs to be made between subliminal and subconscious, because they are two very different things and they have two very different implications for exposure. Subliminal refers to being outside a human's ability to sense or perceive; thus it is always regarded as non-exposure. However, once media stimuli cross over the subliminal line and are able to be perceived by humans, this is regarded as exposure. However, this does not mean that all exposure is conscious, and this brings us to the third criterion in our definition: psychological.

BOX 3.3
LIMITS OF HUMAN PERCEPTUAL ABILITY

Seeing: With the human eye, we have three kinds of cones in the retinas at the back of our eyes. One code recognizes red, one blue, and one green. Thus, the human eye perceives three primary colors, and every color we see is a combination of these three.

Some animals, such as skate fish, have no cones, so they experience the world only in white and black (presence of light and absence of light).

Some birds and insects have up to six types of color receptors (Storr, 2014), so they can perceive much more of a range of color than we can.

Hearing: Human sensitivity to sound frequency extends from around 16 Hz and 20,000 Hz, but sounds are heard best when they are between 1,000 Hz and 4,000 Hz (Metallinos, 1996; Plack, 2005).

A dog whistle is pitched at a frequency higher than 20,000 Hz, so humans cannot perceive that sound; that is, it is outside their range of human sensitivity to sounds.

Bats have very poor sight compared to humans, but their hearing is much more developed, so they live in a world of sounds.

Smelling: Many animals have a much more sensitive perceptual ability to experience a wider range of smells. For example, dogs have a much better sense of smell than do humans, so they live in a world of smells much more than do humans.

Questions

Can you think of other ways in which your human senses are better than other animals?

Can you think of other ways in which your human senses are more limited than other animals?

Psychological Exposure

In order for psychological exposure to occur, there must be some trace element created in a person's mind. This element can be an image, a sound, an emotion, a pattern, and so on. It can last for a brief time (several seconds in short-term memory then cleared out) or a lifetime (when cataloged into long-term memory). It can enter the mind consciously (often called the central route), where people are fully aware of the elements in the exposure, or it can enter the mind unconsciously (often called the peripheral route), where people are unaware that elements are being entered into their minds (see Petty & Cacioppo, 1986). Thus there is a great variety of elements that potentially can meet this criterion for psychological exposure. The challenge then becomes organizing all these elements into meaningful sets and explaining how different kinds of elements are experienced by the individual and how they are processed as information.

Attention

In order for attention to occur, a person must first clear all three of the exposure hurdles described above—physical, perceptual, and psychological exposure. However, these three things alone do not guarantee attention; something else must also occur. That something else is conscious awareness of the media message. As you can now see, there are a lot of things that have to happen in order for us to "pay attention" to a media message. For this reason, it is rare for a media message to achieve attention. Harold Pashler, who wrote *The Psychology of Attention* (1998), explains that at any given moment, awareness encompasses only a tiny proportion of the stimuli impinging on a person's sensory systems. Furthermore, while we are paying attention to one thing, our attention can be distracted away to another thing. Pashler says there are times when "attention is directed or grabbed without any voluntary choice having taken place, even against strong wishes to the contrary" (p. 3). For example, when you are paying attention to a conversation with your roommate, your attention can be grabbed by a sound or an image that pops up on your computer screen and you shift your attention away from your roommate to the screen.

Exposure States

Thus far I have made a distinction between automatic processing and paying attention to particular media messages. This suggests two **exposure states**, but to understand better the experience of media exposure, we need to consider two additional exposure states. Thus, the four media literacy exposure states are **automatic**, **attentional**, **transported**, and **self-reflexive**. Each of these states is a qualitatively different experience for the audience member. By this I mean that these four are not arrayed along a single continuum where they are distinguished simply by the degree of attention. Instead, crossing the line from one state to another results in a qualitatively different experience with the message.

Automatic State

In the automatic state of exposure, people are in environments where they are exposed to media messages but they are not aware of those messages; that is, their mind is on automatic pilot as it filters out all the messages in the environment. This screening out continues automatically with no effort until some element in a message breaks through people's default screen and captures their attention.

In the automatic processing state, message elements are physically perceived but processed automatically in an unconscious manner. This exposure state resides above the threshold of human sense perception but below the threshold of conscious awareness.

The person is in a perceptual flow that continues until an interruption stops the exposure or "bumps" the person's perceptual processing into a different state of exposure or until the media message moves outside of a person's physical or perceptual ability to be exposed to it.

In the automatic state, people can look active to outside observers, but those people are not thinking about what they are doing. A person in the automatic state can be clicking through a series of websites without paying attention to the messages on those sites. While it may appear to an observer that the person is actively searching the web, the person may be just randomly clicking through webpages while thinking about something else. Even when there is evidence of exposure behavior, this does not necessarily mean that people's minds are engaged and that they are "making" decisions. Rather the decisions are happening to them automatically.

Exposure to much of the media is in the automatic state. People have no conscious awareness of the exposure when it is taking place, nor do they have a recollection of many of the details in the experience if they are asked about it later. This is especially the case when people are multitasking. Someone might be listening to music, surfing the web, and talking to a friend on the phone; while the person may be paying attention to the phone conversation, he is in an automatic exposure state with regard to the music and the webpages. If his attention suddenly shifts to an image on a webpage, then he slips into the automatic state with the phone conversation and no longer pays attention to what his friend is saying. Multitasking severely reduces a person's cognitive advantages (i.e., ability to concentrate on a particular message) but enhances emotional gratifications (i.e., receiving pleasure from more than one thing at a time) (Wang & Tchernev, 2012).

Attentional State

Attentional exposure refers to people being aware of the messages and actively interacting with the elements in the messages. This does not mean they must have a high level of concentration, although that is possible. The key is conscious awareness of the messages during exposures.

Within the attentional state there is a range of attention depending on how much of a person's mental resources one devotes to the exposure. At minimum, the person must be aware of the message and consciously track it, but there is a fair degree of elasticity in the degree of concentration, which can range from partial to quite extensive processing depending on the number of elements handled and the depth of analysis employed.

iStock/by_nicholas

In the transported state, people are pulled into the message so strongly that they lose their sense of separateness from the message.

Transported State

When people are in the attentional state but then are pulled into the message so strongly that they lose awareness of being apart from the message, they cross over into the transported state. In the transported state, audience members lose their sense of separateness from the message; that is, they are swept away with the message, enter the world of the message, and lose track of their own social world surroundings. For example, when we watch a movie in a theater, we often get so caught up in the action that we feel we are involved with that action. We experience the same intense emotions as the characters do. We lose the sense that we are in a theater. Our concentration level is so high that we lose touch with our real-world environment. We lose track of real time. Instead we experience narrative time; that is, we feel time pass like the characters feel time pass. This transported state typically occurs when people are playing video and computer games.

The transported state is not simply the high end of the attentional state. Instead, the transported state is qualitatively different than the attentional state. While attention is very high in the transported state, the attention is also very narrow; that is, people have tunnel vision and focus on the media message in a way that eliminates the barrier between them and the message. People are swept away and "enter" the message. In this sense, it is the opposite of the automatic state, where people stay grounded in their social world and are unaware of the media messages in their perceptual environment; in the transported exposure state, people enter the media message and lose track of their social world.

Self-Reflexive State

In the self-reflexive state, people are hyperaware of the message *and of their processing of the message.* It is as if they are sitting on their shoulder and monitoring their own reactions as they experience the message. This represents the fullest degree of awareness; that is, people are aware of the media message, their own social world, and their position in the social world while they process the media message. In the self-reflexive exposure state, the viewer exercises the greatest control over perceptions by reflecting on questions such as these: Why am I exposing myself to this message? What am I getting out of this exposure and why? Why am I making these interpretations of meaning? Not only is there analysis, but there is meta-analysis. This means that the person is not only analyzing the media message, but she is also analyzing her analysis of the media message.

While the self-reflexive and transported states might appear similar because both are characterized by high involvement by audience members, the two exposure states are very different. In the transported state, people are highly involved emotionally and they lose themselves in the action. In contrast, the self-reflexive state is characterized by people being highly involved cognitively and very much aware of themselves as they analytically process the exposure messages.

THE MEDIA LITERACY APPROACH

The ideas presented in this chapter will help you understand how you can increase your media literacy. That is, you can get better at making decisions about filtering, meaning matching, and meaning construction. This does not mean that you must encounter all media messages in a state of attention or self-reflexivity in order to make better decisions;

instead, you can alter your decision algorithms so that when they run in an automatic state or transported state they will deliver better choices.

As for the filtering task, you can periodically examine your media exposure habits and ask yourself why you are spending time with particular media and particular messages while ignoring others. If you have good reasons for your habits, then it is likely that those filtering habits are helping you achieve your own goals. But if you are puzzled by some of your habits, it is time to think about changing those habits to see if your needs can be met better through exposure to different media and different kinds of messages.

As for meaning matching, you can periodically check some of the meanings you have memorized. Perhaps you have acquired some of those meanings by simply memorizing the opinions of so-called experts, such as newscasters, pundits, cultural critics, and so on. Perhaps the experts were later found to be wrong, yet you still hold onto a memorized opinion that is now faulty. Or perhaps you should not have memorized an expert's opinion but instead constructed your own opinion that fits better with your own personal beliefs and experiences. It is likely that your large set of memorized meanings contains elements that are out of date, are causing friction with what you now believe, or are faulty in some way. If you don't identify them and clear them out of your "mental dictionary," you will automatically continue to use those meanings, and this can take you further away from your goals.

As for meaning construction, you can identify areas where decisions are most important in your life. As you use the media messages to gather more information, ask yourself if you are simply accepting that information as is or are transforming it to fit into your needs and goals. The more you work on transforming the raw material of information into knowledge that helps achieve your own goals, the more your meaning construction process will operate under your control.

The meaning of media messages is not always the way it might seem on the surface. There are often many layers of meanings. The more you are aware of the layers of meaning in messages, the more you can appreciate all the options for meaning construction that are available. And when you recognize multiple options for meaning construction, you can exercise more control over selecting the meanings that are most useful to you.

Some people perform these information-processing tasks better than others and are therefore more media literate than other people. Increasing one's level of media literacy requires a strong personal locus. We need to be aware of our personal goals and needs, then exert the drive energy to take control of our meanings.

We also need tools to execute our plans. Those tools are competencies and skills. Competencies are the tools people have acquired to help them interact with the media and to access information in the messages. Competencies are learned early in life, then applied automatically. Competencies are categorical; that is, either people are able to do something or they are not able. For example, either people know how to recognize a word and match its meaning to a memorized meaning or they do not. However, having competencies does not make one media literate, but lacking these competencies prevents one from being media literate because this deficiency prevents a person from accessing particular kinds of information. For example, people who do not have a basic reading competency cannot access printed material. This will greatly limit what they can build into their knowledge structures. This will also suppress the drive states in the personal locus; people who cannot read will have very low motivation to expose themselves to printed information.

In addition to competencies, people need a set of media literacy skills, especially with the task of meaning construction. Skill development is what can make a large difference in a person moving from lower to higher levels of media literacy. People who have weak skills will not be able to do much with the information they encounter. For example, if their skill of analysis is weak, they will not be able to dig out the good information from media messages. If their skill of evaluation is weak, they will not be able to judge the quality or usefulness of information well, so they cannot tell which information is good and which is faulty. If their skills of grouping induction are weak, they will not be able to see patterns across different messages. If their skills of abstraction are weak, they will struggle to see the "big picture" in a message. And if their skills of deduction and synthesis are weak, they will have great difficulty incorporating new information into their knowledge structures. They will organize information poorly, thus creating weak and faulty knowledge structures. In the worst case, people with weak skills will try to avoid thinking about information altogether and become passive; as a consequence, the active information providers (such as advertisers, entertainers, and news workers) will increase their power as the constructors of people's knowledge structures and will take control over of how people see the world by altering their beliefs and by giving people faulty standards that they then use to create their attitudes.

Skills and competencies work together in a continual cyclical process. With certain information-processing tasks, some skills or competencies may be more important than others. For example, with the task of filtering, the skills of analysis and evaluation are most important. With the task of meaning matching, the competencies are most important. And with the task of meaning construction, the skills of grouping, induction, deduction, synthesis, and abstracting are most important. However, the value of the individual skills and competencies varies by particular challenges presented by different types of messages.

SUMMARY

As we encounter the flood of media messages each day, our brains engage in three interlocking information-processing tasks of filtering, meaning matching, and meaning construction. The task of filtering is performed automatically where almost all messages are processed unconsciously and only a very few break through into consciousness. The meaning matching task is also performed unconsciously like a machine, where message stimuli (such as words, sounds, and images) are matched with recalled meanings. In contrast, the meaning construction task requires a conscious process using skills to create novel meanings for the messages we encounter.

Because so much of the information processing takes place automatically, we need to periodically examine the mental codes that govern that processing to determine if they are operating in our best interests. It is important to analyze our media habits periodically so that we can identify which habits are working to achieve our goals and which are diverting our time and attention away into wasteful or harmful practices. Once we can make this distinction clearly, we can reprogram our automatic codes so that when we return to the state of automaticity and our minds make thousands of decisions while on automatic pilot, those decisions will make us smarter, happier, and more productive.

Further Reading

Brooks, D. (2011). *The social animal: The hidden sources of love, character, and achievement.* New York, NY: Random House. (424 pages, including index and endnotes)

This is an easy-to-read book about the human brain. It presents a lot of interesting information about what is known, and what scientists think they now know, about this complex organ.

Konnikova, M. (2013). *Mastermind: How to think like Sherlock Holmes.* New York, NY: Penguin Books. (273 pages, including index)

This book is a blend of psychological text, literary analysis, and self-help. Konnikova, who is a fan of the Sherlock Holmes stories and has a Ph.D. in psychology, examines how Holmes thinks and how he solves his mysteries. She shows readers how the well-known fictional detective uses psychological principles and thinking skills to solve crimes. This easy-to-read book shows readers how they can apply the same skills to solve problems in their everyday lives. Konnikova focuses on the skills of induction and deduction, which are two of the key skills of media literacy. Its eight chapters are organized in four sections: (1) Understanding Yourself, (2) From Observation to Imagination, (3) The Art of Deduction, and (4) The Science and Art of Self-Knowledge.

Pariser, E. (2011). *The filter bubble: How the new personalized web is changing what we read and how we think.* New York, NY: Penguin Books. (294 pages with index and endnotes)

In this fascinating book, Pariser provides many examples of how the mass media are making filtering decisions for you.

Potter, W. J. (2018). *The skills of media literacy.* Santa Barbara, CA: Knowledge Assets. (224 pages, including references and glossary)

In this book, I show you a step-by-step approach to improving each of the seven skills of media literacy. This book presents lots of examples and exercises for each skill.

Storr, W. (2014). *The unpersuadables: Adventures with the enemies of science.* New York, NY: The Overlook Press. (355 pages, including index and endnotes)

Storr is a journalist who has interviewed people who hold beliefs at odds with scientific evidence (creationists, Holocaust deniers, etc.) to find out why they hold their beliefs. He concludes that all of human reasoning and knowledge is based on stories that we tell ourselves and that it is too psychologically troubling to change our stories, so we deny all those versions of the truth that do not conform to what we believe.

EXERCISE 3.1
CONDUCT A GOOGLE SEARCH TO OBSERVE THE RESULT OF PERSONALIZED SEARCHES

1. Get together with some friends in a group.

   While this exercise can be performed with as few as two people, it works better with a larger number. Also, this exercise works better when the group is composed of people with a wider divergence of interests.

2. Brainstorm a list of searches.

   The list of searches should be specific; that is, the searches should refer to specific interests and hobbies of the different people in the group.

3. Develop a list of keywords for the searches.

   Try to use words that have more than one meaning. For example, the word *fish* could refer to the action of trying to catch food from a boat, searching for information, the victim in a con game, and so on. The word *green* could refer to a color, a person who is new at something, a person's last name, and so on.

4. Conduct the searches simultaneously on Google.

   Each person should be connected to the Internet on his or her own device (laptop, notebook, smartphone, etc.), be on the Google search page, and enter the exact same keyword at the same time.

5. Analyze the results of each search.

   Notice differences in the time of search, number of hits, and sites ranked highest.

   Can you explain the differences in search results by the personal characteristics of the different people who conducted the searches?

6. Repeat the process above with relatively general terms, such as *news*, *clothing*, *advertising*, *reality*, and *effect*.

   Analyze the results of each search on a general term. Are there as many differences across people when you use a general term compared to when you use a specific term?

4

AUDIENCE: INDUSTRY PERSPECTIVE

Key Idea: The mass media segment the general population into marketing niches then construct niche audiences by creating special content to attract certain kinds of people to each niche so that access to those audiences can be sold to advertisers.

Some members of the cast of HBO's *Game of Thrones* at the 2017 San Diego Comic Con, one example of a niche media audience.

Alan and Jean were having coffee when Alan started to complain, "I'm starting to feel old these days."

"Oh, Alan, don't be ridiculous. You're not old. You still have all your hair and it hasn't even started to turn gray. You don't even need to wear glasses yet."

"I know that, but I still am feeling old."

"Are you starting to have mysterious aches and pains?"

"No. I feel fine."

"Is it hard for you to wake up in the morning and have enough energy to get through the day?"

"No. I still have lots of energy."

Jean was frustrated. "I don't get it. Why are you feeling old?"

"Well, it's my favorite shows on television."

"Are they being canceled?"

"No, it's not that. It's the ads in my shows. All the ads are for old people products like Geritol, denture cream, electric wheel chairs, retirement cruises, stuff like that!"

"Is that all that's bothering you?" Jean replied, feeling relieved. "That's no big deal. You can easily fix that. I had that same feeling last year and all I needed to do was watch other TV shows."

"What shows?"

"There are lots of shows with ads for cheap trucks, beer, and fast food."

"Watching those shows helped you feel young again?"

"Yes, it did. I no longer think about whether I have enough health insurance when I'm retired and whether I should strap on a diaper when I go to bed."

"Like, that is so awesome, dude." Alan was already feeling younger.

"Of course, there is one problem with this," said Jean. *"The TV shows you have to watch seem so juvenile and silly."*

The mass media construct audiences so they can sell advertisers access to those audiences. In constructing those audiences, the media focus on particular niches where they can provide content that serves a need not already being met. They attract particular kinds of people into those audiences then condition them for repeat exposures. In this chapter, we will examine the strategies that media businesses use to attract and condition audiences for repeat exposures. But first, we need to examine the more fundamental issue about how mass media businesses have shifted their perspective on the audience as being a mass to being a wide variety of smaller niche audiences.

SHIFT FROM MASS TO NICHE PERSPECTIVE ON AUDIENCE

Media programmers no longer think of the audience as a large general mass of all people. Now they think of audiences as many niches of smaller specialized sets of people as defined by their particular interests.

What Is a Mass Audience?

Until fairly recently, many media programmers and researchers believed there was something called a "**mass**" **audience** for the media. The term **mass communication** came into use about a century ago, when social philosophers were arguing that newspapers, magazines, and books communicated their ideas to all audience members in roughly the same way. It was assumed that every person in the entire population was pretty much the same as far as his or her needs for information and entertainment. It then followed that if a particular media message worked well with one person, it would work well with all people. Thus, the term *mass* was used in a qualitative way instead of a quantitative way, meaning it referred to a certain *type* of audience instead of the size of the audience. This shift away from a quantitative indicator solved the problem of determining how large an audience needed to be in order to be considered a "mass" audience; no one had been able to determine that magic threshold below which audiences were too small to be considered a mass.

At first, this shift to a qualitative perspective on the audience seemed to be an improvement over trying to figure out a quantitative threshold. The basis for this shift in thinking arose out of scholars noticing profound changes in societies that were experiencing the industrial revolution, which began in the mid-1800s in the United States and Western European countries. Because these countries were heavily industrialized, it was believed that this technological progress had shaped the lives of people in ways that were not evident in less industrialized countries. Sociologists observed that in less industrialized societies, people were tightly integrated into social networks in which they interacted continually with others on a daily basis. In industrialized societies, most people worked in factories doing jobs that rendered them extensions of machines because of the repetitive specialized tasks they performed. Sociologists believed that the industrial revolution had created a mass society; that is, while factories were producing standardized products, they also were standardizing society. They believed that the industrialization of work, where most people labored in factories at 9-to-5 jobs, had served to turn people into parts of a machine in a mass society that had four characteristics (Blumer, 1946). First, although society is heterogeneous (i.e., composed of everyone regardless of gender, ethnic background, or any other characteristic), everyone had been transformed into having one lifestyle. Second, the individuals in a mass society were anonymous to media businesses and advertisers. The message designers didn't know the names of anyone in the audience—nor did they care to—because the designers regarded everyone to be the same and interchangeable. Third, there was no interaction among the members in the audience. People didn't talk to each other about the media messages, so the meanings of messages did not get discussed and modified in conversations. Instead, those messages had a direct effect on each person in a uniform manner. And fourth, the mass audience had no social organization, no body of custom and tradition, no established set of rules or rituals, no organized group of sentiments, and no structure or status roles.

Because it was believed that communication did take place in a mass-like fashion, it was assumed that each media message reached everyone in the same way and was processed by everyone in the same manner. It was also believed that the processing itself was very simple; that is, people were vulnerable and had few psychological defenses against messages because they did not discuss messages with other people.

As evidence for this position, social critics pointed to the way that Adolf Hitler used the mass medium of radio in the 1930s to mobilize the German population to support him. Kate Smith's radio telethons for war bonds, in which she raised millions of dollars, were also offered as evidence that people were highly susceptible to media messages. Another often-cited example of the public's seeming lack of defense against media messages is provided by the widespread reaction to Orson Welles's 1939 Mercury Theater presentation of *War of the Worlds*, which was a fictional radio play presented as if it were a real newscast. Initial reports of listener reactions to the radio play indicated that everyone was panicked by the belief that Martians were landing in New Jersey. These examples led sociologists to became vocal in their warnings about the dangers of mass communication throughout the 1930s and 1940s.

As time went by, scholars moved beyond their fear of the power of mass media on a defenseless mass society and began to look more rationally at the changes in society. A more careful analysis of the three examples mentioned revealed that most people were *not* affected by those messages (Cantril, 1947). Furthermore, it was later shown that the people who were affected were not all affected in the same manner, nor did they all react in the same way. Thus, the idea of mass audience and its supporting belief that all audience members reacted to the messages in the same way started breaking down.

Rejection of the Idea of Mass Audience

By the 1950s, it became apparent to many scholars that the assumption of the audience as a "mass" was incorrect. Friedson (1953) was the first to criticize this view of the audience. He argued that people attended movies, listened to the radio, and watched television within an interpersonal context. Discussions of media material frequently took place before, during, and after exposure. He acknowledged that there was a well-developed web of organized social relationships that existed among audience members. This social environment continually influenced what audience members exposed themselves to and how messages affected them. Media behavior was merely a part of their more general social behavior. Friedson warned that "the concept of mass is not accurately applicable to the audience" (p. 316). Since Friedson made this point, many other researchers have supported this position (Bauer & Bauer, 1960).

Today, the term *mass communication* is still used, but there is no evidence to support the belief in a mass audience. Instead, there are many audiences, some with structures and leadership and others without these characteristics. While people may be isolated from one another across niches, they use the media to communicate a lot with people within their niches or networks. Also, it is very rare for a media event to attract everyone. Even with events such as the Super Bowl, less than half of all Americans watch. And more important, the people who do watch the Super Bowl do not all experience the same thing. Some viewers are elated as their team is winning, others are depressed as their team is losing, some are happy that there is a reason to party, and others have no idea which teams are playing the game. There is little common experience. Also, during the viewing, people talk to each other and help each other interpret events.

iStock/Maxiphoto

PhotoAlto/Belen Majdalani/Alto Agency RF Collections/Getty Images

Media programmers have shifted attention away from the large anonymous mass audience (left) toward more targeted and individualized niche audiences (right).

The Idea of Niche Audience

Mass media programmers and product marketers long ago abandoned the idea of mass audience. They know that it is foolhardy to attempt to sell a particular product, service, or media message to everyone. Instead, media programmers construct special kinds of messages to appeal to particular kinds of people: **niche audiences**. Once a media business has identified a potential niche audience, they create messages specially designed to attract that kind of person. If they are successful in attracting enough people in that niche audience, they sell access to that audience to advertisers, who want to get their persuasive messages in front of those targets in order to condition them to buy their products and services. Thus, media programmers are in the business of constructing niche audiences. For example, if a website designer wants to attract an upscale, highly educated, professional audience, the designer must identify an interest these people would have, such as an interest in golf. The web designer would then need to create content that would satisfy a need that these people have that is not already being met by other websites, cable TV networks, magazines, and books. The web designer must then find out where this potential audience is spending its time with the media and put ads in those media messages to attract those people to the newly designed website on golf. Once the website starts attracting these people, a sales staff will sell access to this audience to certain advertisers, such as luxury car dealers, jewelers, travel agencies, and stores that sell golf equipment.

Each person is a member of many different niche audiences. You are a member of a local community that the local newspaper, radio stations, and cable TV franchise targets. You are a member of virtual communities when you get on the Internet—communities that quickly form and may last for only one evening. You are a member of certain hobby groups that are targeted by certain websites and magazines, although other members of your audience are spread out all over the world and will never meet you in person.

COMPARE & CONTRAST
MASS AUDIENCE AND NICHE AUDIENCE

Compare: Mass audience and niche audience are *the same* in the following ways:

- Both are conceptions of the audience for mass media messages.

- Both are used by marketers to build their strategies for attracting audiences, holding their attention, and conditioning them for repeated exposures.

Contrast: Mass audience and niche audience are *different* in the following ways:

- Mass audience is based on an industrial-type conceptualization where the mass media are viewed as a factory producing standardized products for a mass of people who are heterogeneous (includes everyone), anonymous, isolated from one another, and without social organization.

- The niche audience is conceptualized as a relatively small number of people who all share some interest (hobby, lifestyle choice, particular need); marketers view the people within a niche audience as homogenous (all share the same interest), personal, and members of a social network where they continually interact with one another as they recommend media messages and products to one another.

IDENTIFYING NICHES

A major challenge for mass media programmers is to identify useful niches. In order to meet this challenge, they begin by trying to divide the total population into meaningful segments. Then they select the segments—niches—of interest to them and develop messages to try to attract people in those niches.

Over the years, audience segmentation schemes have become more complex in an effort to generate more precise groupings. This is illustrated by showing the development of thinking over five types of segmentation methods: **geographic**, **demographic**, **social class**, **geodemographic**, and **psychographic**.

Geographic Segmentation

This type of segmentation scheme is most important to newspapers as well as broadcast radio and local television where there are geographical boundaries to their coverage areas. But it has also been useful to other media in thinking about getting their messages out to certain regions of the country.

This is the oldest form of segmentation. A company would begin a business in a certain locale and produce products that the people in that locale wanted. Because of limits on distribution, that company would only do business in that one area. If that company wanted to expand, it would move out from its home locale to other places in the region where the product met a need. If there was a nationwide need, then the company could

iStock/EXTREME-PHOTOGRAPHER

iStock/AHMCPHERSON

Geodemographic consumer segmentation explains why neighborhoods tend to be homogeneous, and that people will navigate to the neighborhoods that most align with their own characteristics.

expand into national distribution, which many companies did, and thus geographic segmentation has become less useful.

Demographic Segmentation

Demographics focus on the relatively enduring characteristics about each person, such as gender, ethnic background, age, income, and education. These are fairly stable characteristics and have been quite useful in classifying us into meaningful audience segments. Although people can change their status on some of these (such as education and income), such change requires a great deal of effort and takes a significant amount of time to evolve.

Like with geographic segmentation, the usefulness of demographics as an audience segmentation device has been diminishing. Decades ago, when adult women typically stayed home and raised children, it made sense to focus the marketing of household and child care products on women only. But now that there are so many single-parent households and the number of women in the workforce is about the same as men, gender has lost its value as a way of identifying a target market for most marketing campaigns.

Ethnicity also used to be a stronger demographic segmenter than it is today, as the range of income, education, political views, and cultural needs is much greater within any ethnic group than it is across ethnic groups. With the tremendous growth of credit, household income has not been as useful a segmenter. Educational level is also less useful. Seventy years ago, having a college degree put you in an elite category—the top 5% of the population. But now, about two-thirds of people who graduate high school go on to college and about 32% of American adults (over 25 years old) have at least one college degree (Statista, 2018a). While demographics are still valuable as a segmenter for some products and some media messages, other segmentation schemes are required for most products and media messages.

Social Class Segmentation

We could think of social class solely in terms of household income level, but then social class would mean the same thing as the demographic of income. Why would we need both types of segmentation schemes if they put the same people into the same groups? The reason is that social class relies on a mix of characteristics that includes income but also considers people's view on the world. To illustrate this point, being in the lower class, of course, means a low income. But you as a college student have a fairly low income. Do you consider yourself lower class? No, obviously there is more to the definition of social class. Being in the lower class means being governed by the psychological perspective that what happens in life is not under your control. Lower-class people feel that they were born into a situation with not much opportunity to better their lives, and thus they must struggle to maintain their existence. Because fate has put them in this situation, all they can do is to try to make the best of it when they can. Therefore, when they get a windfall of money, they want to have as much fun as they can before someone takes it away from them. There is no point in saving for a tomorrow that will never come.

Being middle class means holding the value that it is valuable to put off immediate pleasures for more important longer-term goals; that is, you are willing to make sacrifices today in order to make investments in your future. The fact that you are in college is a good indication that you hold a middle-class perspective. You believe that it is a good idea to make economic and lifestyle sacrifices for 4 years now so that later your college degree will allow you to receive much larger rewards. You believe that your current actions influence your future. You believe that you control your fate, not the other way around.

Being upper class does not mean simply having more money; it means being able to control more resources—yours and those of others. It means the ability to raise large sums and wield a high degree of power.

Geodemographic Segmentation

A relatively recent innovation in consumer segmentation is geodemographic, which is a blend of geographic and demographic segmentation. It is based on the assumption that the same types of people tend to cluster together in neighborhoods. So neighborhoods tend to be homogeneous on important characteristics, and these characteristics are very different across neighborhoods.

One example of geodemographic segmentation is the PRIZM scheme, which was developed by the Claritas Corporation in 1974. PRIZM is based on a complex analysis of the U.S. census data. It began with the 35,000 ZIP code neighborhoods and concluded that there were 40 different kinds of neighborhoods in the United States. It gave the clusters memorable (and trademarked) nicknames such as "sun belt singles" (which are southern suburban areas populated by young professionals), "Norma Rae-ville" (named after the movie about a working-class woman who unionized factory employees), "Marlboro country" (evoking a western rural area with rugged men on horses), "furs and station wagons" (typified by new money living in expensive new neighborhoods), and "hardscrabble" (which represents areas in the Ozark mountains, Dakota badlands, and south Texas border).

Psychographic Segmentation

Psychographics is the current cutting edge of segmentation schemes. It is not limited to one or two characteristics of people but uses a wide variety of variables to create its segments. Typically, a psychographic segmentation scheme will use demographics, lifestyle, and product usage variables in segmenting consumers. There are many examples of psychographic segmentation. Two stand out as being very influential.

Twelve American Lifestyles

William Wells, director of advertising research at Needham, Harper & Steers in Chicago, developed the 12 American lifestyles that include Joe the factory worker and his wife Judy, Phyllis the career woman and her liberated husband Dale, Thelma the contented homemaker, and Harry the cigar-chomping middle-aged salesman. Each of these creations represents a different lifestyle. For example, Joe is a lower-middle-class male in his 30s who makes an hourly wage doing semiskilled work. He watches a lot of television, especially sports and action/adventure programs; he rarely reads. He drives a pickup truck and knows a lot about automotive parts and accessories. In contrast, Phyllis is a career woman in her 30s with a graduate degree. She reads a lot, and when she watches television, it is usually news or a good movie. She likes fine food, dining out, and travel.

Psychographic segmentation looks at multiple characteristics of a person's lifestyle to develop the segmentations.

VALS Typology

VALS was developed at SRI (Stanford Research Institute) by Arnold Mitchell. After monitoring social, economic, and political trends during the 1960s and 1970s, Mitchell constructed an 85-page measurement instrument that asked questions ranging from people's sexual habits to what brands of margarine they ate. He had 1,635 people fill out the questionnaire, and the answers became the database for his book *Nine American Lifestyles*, published in 1980. In the book, Mitchell argued that people's values strongly influence their spending patterns and media behaviors. So if we know which value group a person identifies with, we can predict a great deal about the products and services he or she will want. For example, one of the groups is called Experientials. The people in this value grouping like to try new and different things to see what they are like. They like to travel. They are early users of new types of products. And they are constantly looking for something different.

The VALS typology has made SRI very successful, with income of more than $200 million per year. By the mid-1980s, SRI had 130 VALS clients, including the major TV networks, major ad agencies, major publishers such as *Time*, and major corporations such as AT&T, Avon, Coke, General Motors, P&G, RJ Reynolds, and Tupperware. For example, Timex, a giant corporation best known for its watches, wanted to move into the home health care market with a selection of new products, including digital thermometers and blood pressure monitors. It decided to focus on two VALS segments: Societally Conscious and the Achievers. Everything about the packaging and the advertisements was chosen with these two groups in mind. Models were upscale and mature in comfortable surroundings with plants and books. The tagline was "Technology where it does the most good." Within months, all of Timex's products were the leaders in this new and fast-growing industry.

Over the years, as the American culture has changed, VALS has changed its segments to keep up. Today, the VALS typology of segments looks very different than it did in the early 1980s. By keeping up with changes in people's lifestyles over the years, VALS has remained a valuable tool for mass media programmers and marketers.

ATTRACTING AUDIENCES

Attracting audience attention is critical for the thousands of advertisers who spend hundreds of billions of dollars each year to expose their target audiences to their carefully designed messages. But as more and more advertisers as well as media outlets compete for the attention of the public, attention has grown to become the most valuable resource within the information economy. In their fascinating book *The Attention Economy: Understanding the New Currency of Business*, Davenport and Beck (2001) argue, "In postindustrialized societies, attention has become a more valuable currency than the kind you store in bank accounts. . . . Understanding and managing attention is now the single most important determinant of business success" (p. 3).

After a media organization has selected a niche audience to target, it must develop content to attract people into that audience. The mass media employ two tactics to do this. First, they try to appeal to your existing needs and interests. Second, they use cross-media and cross-vehicle promotion to attract your attention.

Appeal to Existing Needs and Interests

The mass media do not develop vehicles and messages and then go looking for an audience; instead they conduct research to try to identify the message needs of potential audiences, then they develop that content. Not everyone has the same needs and interests, so the media can identify a range of different types of people as defined by those different needs. For example, some people are very interested in sports, but other people are more interested in news and public affairs. These are two important niches for the media. Each of these has sub-niches. Some sports fanatics might like baseball, whereas others cannot stand baseball but love football.

How do media companies know what the existing needs are? The easiest way to answer this question is to look at what messages are already being consumed. The messages that already are attracting the most attention within a niche audience demonstrate that there is a particular existing need. The new competitors then try to create their own messages to attract that same audience by appealing to that same need. This is why many new films, TV shows, and popular songs typically look and sound like last year's most popular films, TV shows, and songs. For example, in March of 2006, the cable TV channel Bravo premiered *The Real Housewives of Orange County*. Its success resulted in spin-off series located in New York and Atlanta (2008); New Jersey (2009); Washington, D.C., and Beverly Hills (2010); and Miami (2011). Other cable TV producers formulated their own shows featuring housewives (*Mob Wives*), and they even developed international versions such as *The Real French Housewives of Hollywood* (2013) and *The Real Housewives* series set in Athens, Greece, and Israel (2011); Vancouver, Canada (2012); Melbourne, Australia (2014); and Cheshire, England (2015).

Programmers know that we have a relatively narrow exposure repertoire—that is, a set of message types we attend to—so if the new competitors can make their messages very similar to what we are already attending to, we will likely pay attention to those new messages also. Messages that are too different from what we are already exposing ourselves to will not break through the state of automaticity to capture our attention. We typically stay in this state of automaticity until something triggers our attention, and then we pay attention to it. Therefore, media programmers look for what has triggered our attention in the past, and they construct their messages in a similar manner so their messages will also trigger our attention.

Although we have a wide variety of media and messages available to us, we usually select a small subset of them that tend to serve our needs best. This fact about a small set of message preferences—or media repertoire—was clearly established several decades ago when there were far fewer media choices than we have today. In 1992, Ferguson found that even in cable TV households with more than 100 choices of channels, TV viewers typically watched only 5 to 8 channels and ignored the rest. Also, having a remote control device to change TV channels or a device to record shows was not found to increase the size of a person's channel repertoire. Thus when the media expand the number of messages offered, individuals do not increase the range of their exposures; instead, the expanded number of messages increases the number of niche audiences. With a larger range of messages available, individuals can find particular messages that better serve their needs. Today, when we have an almost infinite number of choices for media messages, each of us still has a relatively narrow focus on the types of media and messages we like best.

Cross-Media and Cross-Vehicle Promotion

Media programmers must find potential members of their audience in other audiences so the programmers can promote their new messages and thus attract people to the audience they are trying to construct. Programmers therefore will engage in a great deal of **cross-media promotion** and **cross-vehicle promotion**.

Decades ago, media programmers became very focused on branding their particular vehicles and trying to build loyalty for those vehicles. For example, local television stations wanted you to watch only them. A newspaper wanted you to be loyal to that newspaper and get your news only there—not from magazines, television, or the radio. But with the rise of media consolidation, media programmers have shifted their focus to the message and away from the vehicle. So, for example, a political commentator on the radio might also be asked to post a column on a website and appear on a TV show where the company that owns the radio station also owns the website and the television station. That company might also own a magazine and book publishing firm, in which case the commentator would be encouraged to write a column for the magazine and publish a book. When this media conglomerate company brands its message (i.e., the commentator), the company then tries to market that message through as many media outlets and vehicles it owns as possible to increase the number of revenue streams without adding much to existing expenses. Therefore, media companies think of audiences more in terms of messages that would attract them rather than as groups of people limited to one medium or one vehicle.

Jerry Markland/Getty Images Sport/Getty Images

NASCAR cars that display several corporate logos are an example of cross-vehicle promotion.

Differences across media are also blurring over time. Newspapers have become more like magazines in their editorial outlook, featuring more soft news and human interest pieces that are not time sensitive and that appeal more as entertainment than as information. Trade books are becoming shorter and less literary. And computers, with their games, encyclopedias, and webpages, are becoming more like films, books, magazines, and newspapers. Given the focus on messages and the convergence of channels, the content is becoming much more of a focus than is the delivery system.

Several decades ago, some futurists argued that we are moving toward convergence, where all the media will be one: "a single, high capacity, digital network of networks that will bridge what we now know as the separate domains of computing, telephony, broadcasting, motion pictures, and publishing" (Neuman, 1991, p. x). This convergence has been happening and continues to happen (Jenkins, Ford, & Green, 2013). The differences between channels of disseminating information have become much less important; in contrast, the differences in consumer needs across niche audiences have become much more important.

CONDITIONING AUDIENCES

Once a mass media organization has attracted you to a message, it immediately tries to condition you for repeated exposures. This drive toward **audience conditioning** is an essential strategy for all mass media. The costs of attracting members of an audience to their first exposure to a message are so high that media organizations must rely on repeated exposures in order to recoup their initial investment and eventually make a profit.

Media exposures are inertial. This means that when we are paying attention to a particular message, we tend to keep paying attention to that message, and when we are in an automatic state, we tend to stay in that state and filter out all the messages around us. For example, let's say you go to YouTube and watch one of your favorite videos. YouTube will suggest additional videos you might want to view next. These suggestions are formulated based on your history of watching other videos. YouTube wants to hold onto you as a continuing audience member, so it keeps suggesting content you might like. Then as you watch each suggested video and are entertained, you are being conditioned to want to return to YouTube tomorrow and the day after and the day after that. Successful websites, whether they deal with information, entertainment, music, video, or the printed word, all try to do the same thing. They offer you apps that you can download and use for free on your mobile devices. They want to condition you to continually use their services so it becomes a habit that you cannot live without.

How much have the media conditioned you? And what is the pattern of that conditioning? To answer these questions, estimate how much time you spend with the various media during an average week. Because many media habits are governed by automatic routines, you may not be aware of the extent of your exposure, but that is okay at this point. Just estimate the best you can in Exercise 4.1.

When you have finished with your estimates in Exercise 4.1, look at the pattern across the different media. Which ones consume the most time? Which ones do you ignore? Think about why you apportion your time with the media like you do. Why do you ignore certain media altogether?

Now check to see how well your estimates of exposures to various media match your actual patterns of exposure by recording your actual exposures over the course of a week (see Exercise 4.2). I must warn you that this is an onerous task! Carrying around a diary (even if it is just a piece of paper) all week and remembering to record all exposures takes continual mental effort. But this exercise should demonstrate how much effort you save when you follow your habits automatically and don't have to think about them at all.

Compare what you think are your exposure habits (from Exercise 4.1) and your actual exposure habits (from Exercise 4.2). Do you see differences? Is your estimate of total weekly hours spent with the media the same as your actual hours? If your estimate is lower, then you can see that your habit is stronger than you previously thought; think about how the mass media have programmed you to expose yourself to a higher degree than you were aware. If your estimate is higher than your actual exposure, why do you think you overestimated your media habits? Now look for differences between the estimates and actual figures across different media. Where did you underestimate your exposures and why? Where did you overestimate your exposures and why?

The degree to which your estimates are accurate reflections of your actual exposure patterns is an indicator of how aware you are of your media habits. If you are highly aware, it is also likely that you are in control of those exposure patterns; that is, you have programmed your own exposure mental codes so that when those codes run automatically, they are serving your goals. If, however, you have found large differences between your estimates and your actual exposure patterns, this is evidence that your codes have been programmed largely by others without your awareness. It is possible that you have been so thoroughly conditioned by past exposures to particular media or particular types of messages that you are now addicted. This concern is especially serious with Internet sites that can microfocus on your particular needs, give you the content and experiences you want continuously, and provide a long series of immediate reinforcements. Internet addiction is a growing negative effect of media, especially with content such as pornography, gaming, and shopping (Alter, 2017). For more on this negative effect, see Chapters 13 and 14.

SUMMARY

This is an exciting time to be a part of our culture. The media are constantly working hard to identify our changing needs for information and entertainment. Once the media have identified a new need, they quickly design the kinds of messages that will attract people with that need; in this way, they construct audiences. Then once a media company has attracted an audience, it works hard to condition that audience for repeat exposures, even to the point of addiction.

When we are well aware of our needs, we can use the mass media as an essential resource to satisfy the entire range of those needs. But if we are not self-aware, the most aggressive of the mass media will herd us into audiences that they continue to use repeatedly to generate income from advertisers. You can gain more control over this process by becoming more media literate so you can use the mass media as a tool in achieving your needs, rather than allowing the mass media to use you as a tool to achieve their needs. After reading this chapter, you should be more sensitized to and more aware of your media exposures.

Further Reading

Alter, A. (2017). *Irresistible: The rise of addictive technology and the business of keeping us hooked.* New York, NY: Penguin Press. (354 pages, including endnotes and index)

Alter, a New York University business school professor, shows how behavioral addiction follows the same patterns and has the same causes as chemical addiction. He focuses his arguments on behavioral addiction to the Internet, especially shopping, social contacts, porn, and gambling. The first part of the book deals with the biology of addiction and how we have increased our understanding of behavioral addictions over the past few decades. Part 2 deals with how Internet designers engineer addiction. In Part 3, the author provides some suggestions for helping people avoid addiction and reducing it once it starts.

Davenport, T. H., & Beck, J. C. (2001). *The attention economy: Understanding the new currency of business.* Boston, MA: Harvard Business School Press. (253 pages with index)

This is a very readable book written by two business school professors who explain why attention deficit is such a serious problem in our economy. But they are not social critics who are interested in pointing out a problem then exploring recommendations for ameliorating the problem. Instead, they write more as marketing consultants who provide suggestions to businesses about how to attract the public's attention.

Napoli, P. M. (2011). *Audience evolution: New technologies and the transformation of media audiences.* New York, NY: Columbia University Press. (272 pages)

Written by a professor at Fordham University, this book shows how the conceptualization of audiences has changed over time, particularly with the development of the newer media technologies that serve to fragment society. The scholarly analysis of this phenomenon focuses on political, economic, and social perspectives.

Neuman, W. R. (1991). *The future of the mass audience.* New York, NY: Cambridge University Press. (218 pages)

Neuman begins with a good, balanced discussion of the difficult idea of postindustrialism and with the conflict between fragmentation and homogenization. He argues that education contributes to fragmentation, with people able to peruse their specialized interests. Family demographics changed as women entered the workforce in large numbers. Neuman also shows that media use has fragmented. He argues that this is not a new issue but is a continuing and central problem of political communications. The key issue is that of balance: balance between the center and the periphery, between different interest factions, between competing elites, and between an efficient and effective central authority and the conflicting demands of the broader electorate (p. 167). This is the conflict between community and pluralism.

Rowles, D. (2014). *Mobile marketing: How mobile technology is revolutionizing marketing, communications, and advertising.* Philadelphia, PA: Kogan Page. (266 pages)

This book begins with a good overview of recent changes in marketing and advertising then presents a good deal of practical information to help readers design their own campaigns to reach target markets.

EXERCISE 4.1
ESTIMATE YOUR MEDIA EXPOSURE

Try to estimate how many minutes and hours you spend with each of the following media during a typical week.

_____ Watching video (cable, broadcast, DVDs, streaming, etc.)

_____ Watching films at a theater

_____ Listening to radio (at home, in your car, etc.)

_____ Listening to recordings of music

_____ Reading newspapers

_____ Reading magazines of all kinds

_____ Reading books (texts for class, novels for pleasure, etc.)

_____ Surfing the Internet looking for information and entertainment

_____ Interacting with friends on social networking platforms, texting, etc.

_____ Playing games on a computer, TV screen, handheld device, etc.

_____ Creating media content to upload (photos to Facebook, videos to YouTube, etc.)

_____ TOTAL

EXERCISE 4.2
TRACK YOUR MEDIA EXPOSURES

Keep a Media Exposure Diary for 1 week. Get a small notebook—one you can carry with you wherever you go for 7 days. Every time you are exposed to a message from the media either directly or indirectly, make an entry of the time and what the message was.

Direct exposures are those where you come in contact with a medium and experience a message during that contact. For example, if you watch _The Simpsons_, then write, "Message: _The Simpsons_; Time: Monday 8–8:30." Listening to KXXX for 30 minutes in the car is also a direct exposure.

Indirect exposures are those where you see a reminder of a media message, such as seeing a title of a movie on the marquee or at a bus stop. You don't see the film itself (which would be a direct exposure), but you see something that reminds you of it. Also, listen to conversations. If people talk about something they heard from the media, then you have been exposed to that media message indirectly. For example, if you heard your friends talk about _The Simpsons_, then write, "Message: Talked with friends about _The Simpsons_; Time: Tuesday morning 10–11:30." If you happened to hear your roommate humming a popular song that is played often on the radio, then write, "Message: Roommate hummed X song; Time: Wednesday all day!"

At the end of the week, analyze the entries in your diary to answer the following questions:

1. How much total time were you exposed to media messages?

2. How much total time did you spend creating media content (photos, videos, etc.)?

3. How much total time did you use the media for social interactions?

4. How much time did you spend in competitions—that is, using media for games of all kinds?

5. What proportion of the exposures was direct and what proportion was indirect?

6. What proportion of media exposures was initiated by you (active) and what proportion just happened (passive)?

7. What kinds of experiences dominate your time with the media?

8. How do your diary data compare to your estimates from Exercise 4.1?

9. Now that you've conducted a careful inventory of your media usage, did you discover anything that surprised you?

EXERCISE 4.3
WHAT SEGMENTS ARE YOU IN?

1. Pick three of your favorite television shows. Write the name of each on the column heading line below. Then watch each of these shows and list the products being advertised in each commercial on the lines in the column for that show.

Show 1: _____

_____
_____
_____
_____
_____
_____
_____
_____

Show 2: _____

_____
_____
_____
_____
_____
_____
_____
_____

Show 3: _____

_____
_____
_____
_____
_____
_____
_____
_____

(Continued)

(Continued)

2. Now look at the lists of products and try to imagine who the advertisers had in mind as a target audience when they decided to advertise in these shows.

    - Are those products oriented more toward males or females, or doesn't it matter?

    - What age group are the products aimed at?

    - What economic level are the products aimed at?

    - What educational level are the products aimed at?

    - What geographical location are the products aimed at, or doesn't it matter?

    - What values do the advertisers think you have?

3. Did you notice any ads for other TV shows? If so, what other shows were those ads trying to get you to watch? Do you watch those other shows? Why or why not?

4. Now try the same exercise using three websites that you like.

5. Monitor the e-mails you receive from companies trying to sell you something. Think about how these companies got your e-mail address.

iStock/Goldmund Lukic

CHILDREN AS A SPECIAL AUDIENCE

Key Idea: Children are treated as a special audience because of their lack of maturation and experience; however, maturation and experience alone do not make someone media literate.

The public and policymakers regard children as a special audience that needs protection from potentially negative effects of mass media exposure.

Kyle sent his report on the Battle of Gettysburg to the color printer attached to his family's computer. He had done his research on Wikipedia, then pasted some pictures of the battlefield he had taken with his digital camera during his family's vacation the previous summer. He looked proudly at the report and thought that Mrs. Hawthorne, his fourth-grade teacher, would surely give him another A. To reward himself, he clicked on his favorite social networking website and began texting his growing list of friends when his brother Bobby interrupted him.

"Hey, Kyle. Let's play some online games. How about some poker?"

"Yeah, right. If Mom catches us playing poker again, she's gonna ban me from the computer for a month."

"Come on, she's not going to find out."

"No way."

"Then show me how to get on the poker site. I want to play."

"I already showed you a million times." Kyle tried changing the subject. "Did you do your homework, Bobby?"

"Boring. Besides I forgot how to get on that math site."

"I'll show you—again." Kyle was getting irritated with his big brother. Kyle felt that Bobby, who was in the sixth grade, should be teaching things to him, not the other way around.

Researchers, policymakers, and the public in general have treated children as a special audience because they believe that children are especially vulnerable to negative effects from the mass media. For example, reviews of the literature of effects of various content on children show that children are affected, positively as well as negatively, by playing video games (Prot, Anderson, Gentile, Brown, & Swing, 2014), browsing the Internet (Livingstone, 2014), as well as exposure to all kinds of media content such as food advertising (Harris, 2014), portrayals of drugs (Strasburger, 2014), and sex (Brown, El-Toukhy, & Ortiz, 2014).

Exposure to these same types of media content, however, has been shown to affect adolescents and adults of all ages. This leads us to ask: Why are children treated as a special audience?

WHY TREAT CHILDREN AS A SPECIAL AUDIENCE?

There are two beliefs about children that are used as reasons why they should be regarded as a special group when it comes to the mass media. One of these beliefs is that children have not lived long enough to have sufficient real-world experience to protect them from media messages. The second belief is that children have not matured enough to be able to process enough elements in particular kinds of media messages in order to protect themselves from potentially harmful effects. Let's examine each of these two beliefs about children in more detail.

Lack of Experience

It is obvious that children have less worldly experience than older people. So it follows that people with lower levels of real-world experience would have greater difficulty processing media messages, such as making good evaluations of the degree of fantasy in portrayals or the degree of credibility of information. Thus children can more easily be misled into believing that the media world is an accurate reflection of the real world. And if children are misled in this way, they are at risk for negative effects when they try to behave in the real world in ways they have learned from the media world. For example, Dorr (1986) uses this reasoning as the basis for her argument that "children may accept program content as accurate 'information' when other more knowledgeable viewers know it to be otherwise" (p. 13).

This belief has a good deal of face validity. Children have not had as much time as adolescents or adults to develop knowledge structures on most things. This is why a good elementary education is so important, so that children can acquire the basic ideas about science, history, civics, geography, and other topics. Until children have developed many knowledge structures, they don't have many perspectives from which to view the world. Children also need to develop knowledge structures about the media. For example, Piotrowski (2014) has shown that children who have more advanced story schema are able to comprehend stories and educational content better than children with less well-developed schema. Because schema must be developed by individuals through exposure to media messages, children who increase their exposure to the media—and do so mindfully—will be better able to develop the schema and knowledge structures necessary to understand and appreciate the media more. But this reveals an irony.

People who argue that children are at higher risk of negative effects from the media because children have lower levels of experience with the media will typically try to restrict children's exposure to media messages in an effort to protect those children from the potential of negative effects; however, this restriction serves to limit their media exposure and thereby keeps children in a condition of vulnerability.

Lack of Maturation

As we age from infancy through adolescence, many of our abilities mature, thus enabling us to do more things. This **maturation** is most obvious in the physical realm, where our bodies grow larger and stronger from infancy through adolescence, thus enabling us to lift heavier objects, move quicker, and cover longer distances. Childhood is a time when we mature in other ways beyond the physical. From a media literacy perspective, it is important that we consider other forms of maturation, especially **cognitive development**, **emotional development**, and **moral development**.

Think of maturation as a series of gates along the path to higher media literacy. When we encounter one of these gates, we must wait behind it until we mature to a certain level, then the gate opens and we can proceed. There are a series cognitive gates, emotional gates, and moral gates. These gates occur every few years throughout childhood and hold us back in the early stages of media literacy. For example, most humans are not capable of acquiring the skill of reading until they are beyond the age of 4 or 5 years because their minds have not matured to a point where such learning is possible. Trying to teach reading to 2-year-olds is very frustrating. No matter how hard you work as a teacher or how hard the children work to learn, they will not get much out of this effort because their minds have not matured enough to handle this task. But once a child's mind matures to the point where he or she can use those skills, the practice of reading begins to pay off.

Cognitive Development

When we are very young, our minds are not developed enough to allow for an understanding of abstract thoughts, such as what is required by mathematical reasoning. A task of reasoning (such as multiplying four times five) is very difficult for us when we are 4 years old but very easy for us a few short years later.

The most influential thinker on the topic of cognitive maturation during childhood has been the Swiss psychologist Jean Piaget. From years of research, Piaget found that a child's mind matures from birth to about 12 years of age, during which time it goes through several identifiable stages (Piaget, 2012). Until age 2, children are in the sensorimotor stage and then advance to the pre-operational stage from 2 to 7 years of age. Then they progress to the concrete operational stage, and by age 12, they move into the formal operational stage, where they are regarded as having matured cognitively into adulthood. In each of these stages, children's minds mature to a point where they can accomplish a new set of cognitive tasks. For example, in the concrete operational stage (ages 7–12), children are able to organize objects into series. If you try to teach this skill to a child at age 3, you will fail, no matter how organized and clear your lessons are. Another skill that is developed throughout childhood is conservation, which is the ability to realize that certain attributes of an object are constant, even though that object is transformed in appearance (Pulaski, 1980). For example, ask children to make two balls of clay exactly the same size. Then roll one of them out into a long, thin shape like a snake, and ask them which of the two shapes has a bigger amount of clay. Younger children will say the snake has more clay than the ball because the snake is longer; they do not yet have the ability to understand that the amount of clay is still the same even when it changes shapes; that is, the amount has been conserved even though the shape has changed. By the time children reach the age of 7, their minds have matured enough to understand the idea of conservation.

Cognitive maturation also influences how children watch television. Although children begin paying attention to the TV screen as early as 6 months of age (Hollenbeck & Slaby, 1979), and by age 3 many children have developed regular patterns of viewing of about an hour or two per day (Huston et al., 1983), their viewing is primarily exploratory. This means that they are looking for individual events that stand out because of certain motions, color, music, sound effects, or unusual voices. They look for action, not dialogue. They have difficulty in understanding how individual events are ordered into plots, how characters' motives influence the action, and why characters change as a result of what happens in the plot (Wartella, 1981). The reason for this is that young children have not developed a very sophisticated understanding of narratives. Until they learn more of the principles of narrative progression, they will have difficulty making sense out of stories longer than a minute or two (Meadowcroft & Reeves, 1989).

iStock/Vesna Andjic

By about age 4, children are spending less time in the exploratory mode and more time in a search mode. This means that children begin developing an agenda of what to look for; their attention does not simply bounce haphazardly around from one high-profile action to another. By kindergarten, a continuous story line holds their attention. They focus their attention on formal features in making their decisions about what is important in the shows. For example, they interpret that a laugh track signals that a program is a comedy.

Also by age 4, children begin trying to distinguish between ads and programs. At first this is difficult, until they develop the skills of perceptual discrimination. During this trial-and-error learning, children either express confusion about the difference or use superficial perceptual or affective cues as the basis for the distinction. With practice, they become more skilled at separating ads from program content.

Children must also acquire the knowledge that ads are paid messages that are designed to get them to buy something—or make them ask their parents to buy something. Only 10% of children 5 to 7 years of age have a clear understanding of the profit-seeking

Cognitive development influences how children watch television. At each new stage of maturation, children are capable of understanding more about what they see on screen.

motives of commercials, and about half of all children are totally unaware of the nature of ads and believe commercials are purely for entertainment. For example, Wilson and Weiss (1992) found that compared to older children (ages 7–11), younger children (ages 4–6) were less able to recognize an ad for a particular toy and comprehend its intent when it was shown in a cartoon program, even when the product spokesperson was a character from a different cartoon program.

Disclaimers placed before ads to alert children to the fact that the program is being interrupted and that an ad is about to be shown do not generally work well with children younger than age 7 because they do not fully understand what an ad is. However, when disclaimers are in both the audio and video tracks, children are better able to perceive them. Also, when disclaimers are reworded into the language of children, their comprehension dramatically increases. By the second or third grade, most children have overcome their difficulty distinguishing between programs and commercials. With the combination of cognitive maturation, experience, and active application of critical skills, children no longer have any trouble understanding the purpose of ads and distinguishing ads from the program content.

As children develop an understanding of the purpose of advertising, they also develop an ability for critically evaluating ads. By the fourth grade, children have developed a critical and skeptical attitude toward advertising. They are also cynical about the credibility of commercials and begin feeling that they have been lied to in an effort by the advertiser to get them to buy products that are not as desirable as the commercials' portrayal. However, this skepticism is usually limited to their experience with products. For example, the skepticism is high with ads for familiar toys. Presumably, they have had real-world experiences with these toys and have learned that the ads contain exaggerated claims. However, children are much less skeptical of ads for medical or nutritional products; understandably, they have much less technical knowledge about these products and have less of a basis for skepticism.

By ages 8 to 10, most children have developed a good understanding of fictional plots. They understand how motives of characters influence plot points and how characters change as a result of what happens to them. Children of this age are not limited to understanding characters on only their physical traits but can also infer personality characteristics.

By ages 10 to 12, children have a rudimentary idea of the economic nature of TV. They recognize that there are different businesses that produce media messages and that these businesses have a profit-making motive.

Emotional Development

Emotions are hardwired into our brains (Goleman, 1995). Regardless of the culture in which we are raised, we all can recognize in ourselves and others the basic emotions of anger, sadness, fear, enjoyment, love, surprise, disgust, and shame. Although we do not need to learn emotions in the sense that we must learn to recognize words in order to read, there are still developmental steps in dealing with emotions that indicate that there is a range of emotional maturity.

We develop higher levels of emotional literacy by gaining experience with emotions and by paying close attention to our feelings when we interact with the media. As we gain greater experience with emotions, we are able to make finer discriminations. For example, we are all familiar with anger because that is one of the basic emotions. But it takes experience with this emotion to be able to tell the difference between hatred, outrage, fury, wrath, animosity, hostility, resentment, indignation, acrimony, annoyance, irritability, and exasperation.

A lack of cognitive development can be a barrier to appropriate emotional reactions to media messages. For example, very young children cannot follow the interconnected elements in a continuing plot; instead, they focus on individual elements. Therefore, they do not fully understand suspense and, without such an understanding, their emotional connection with the plot is limited as the suspense builds. Thus, a child's ability to have an emotional reaction to the media messages is limited not because of a lack of ability to feel emotions but because of a lack of ability to understand why certain things are happening at particular parts of a story.

By adolescence, children have reached cognitive maturity, and all the gates are open to a full understanding of all kinds of narratives. But some adolescents and adults still do not have much of an emotional reaction to media stories. Some people can be very highly developed cognitively but very undeveloped emotionally. Goleman (1995) argues that a person's emotional intelligence interacts with IQ:

> We have two brains, two minds—and two different kinds of intelligence: rational and emotional. How we do in life is determined by both—it is not just IQ, but emotional intelligence that matters. Indeed, intellect cannot work at its best without emotional intelligence. (p. 28)

Therefore, emotional development is tied to cognitive development. Children who cannot read or follow visual narratives will have their emotional reactions limited to reactions of micro-elements in messages. As people mature emotionally, they are better able to "read" emotions in themselves and others by having a higher degree of empathy and a greater self-awareness. In contrast, people at lower levels of emotional development are less able to experience emotions vicariously through characters or they experience the wrong emotions.

This connection between emotional development and cognitive development is especially important when it comes to helping children understand advertising. It is widely assumed that helping children understand the nature of advertising makes them less susceptible to advertising effects. However, empirical research does not provide convincing evidence for this view (Rozendaal, Lapierre, van Reijmersdal, & Buijzen, 2011). Because so much of advertising is focused on manipulating emotions, the more we understand about the emotional development of people, the better we can help them cope with this type of message.

Moral Development

We also develop along a moral dimension. We are not born with a moral code or a sensitivity to what is right and wrong. We must learn these as young children, and children learn these things in stages. Like Piaget, Lawrence Kohlberg has studied the development of children. While Piaget was concerned with cognitive development, Kohlberg focused on moral development. He suggested that there are three levels of moral development:

pre-conventional, conventional, and post-conventional. The centerpiece is *conventional*, which stands for fair, honest, concerned, and well regarded—characteristics of the typically good person (Kohlberg, 1966, 1981).

The pre-conventional stage begins at about age 2 and runs to about age 7 or 8. This is when children depend on an authority to tell them what is right and wrong. Thus the child's conscience is external. Children try out all kinds of behaviors and wait to be told by others if the behavior was good or bad.

During the conventional stage, children develop a conscience for themselves as they internalize what is right and wrong. They distinguish between truth and lies. However, the threat of punishment is still a strong motivator.

The post-conventional stage can begin as early as middle adolescence. In this stage, adolescents try to move beyond the conventional norms about what is right and wrong as they encounter moral dilemmas where none of the alternative courses of action are all right or all wrong. Adolescents in this stage search for fundamental principles that underlie the conventional norms, and this requires the ability to think abstractly. They move beyond the *what* and think more deeply about the *why*. Thus, the stages in this level are characterized by a sense that being socially conscious is more important than adhering to rigid legal principles.

Kohlberg's stages are not fixed steps that everyone follows in the same sequence. People can move around among the steps, given particular problems and moods. However, each stage is very different, and those stages are hierarchically ordered such that the more evolved person is likely to operate most often at higher levels.

There appears to be a gender difference in moral development. Men more typically base their moral judgments on rights and rules, whereas women tend to think in terms of care and cooperation. So in a conflict situation, women are likely to try to preserve relationships. In contrast, men are likely to search for a moral rule and try to apply it even if it hurts their relationship (Gilligan, 1993).

Let's examine these stages with a media example. Joey is a young child in a family that allows him to spend a lot of time playing highly competitive and aggressive video games and watch a great deal of television unsupervised. There is no parent or authority figure to help him process the messages or to show him alternatives to what is portrayed in the media world. Therefore, his moral development during the pre-conventional stages is shaped by the themes in the television messages, mainly cartoons, action/adventure shows, and situation comedies. From his steady exposure to these types of shows and values, Joey is likely to learn the following moral lessons: Aggression (both physical and verbal) is an acceptable and successful way to solve problems; with a little hard work, everyone can be successful, that is, be wealthy, powerful, and famous; family relationships are full of conflict and deceit, but everyone still loves each other; and romantic relationships are exciting but superficial and temporary.

As Joey moves into the conventional stages, much of his behavior will be governed by these moral lessons. He feels that the best way to get approval from others is to be funny, live dangerously, and have lots of peer relationships filled with conflict—the active, interesting life.

Finally, as Joey reaches late adolescence and confronts the post-conventional stages, he should begin asking questions such as the following: How can I resolve moral dilemmas so that I don't decide on a purely selfish basis? How can I live my life so as to benefit society in general? Given Joey's moral development and the lessons learned, it is unlikely that he will be interested in these post-conventional questions. It is probable that he will stay at the conventional stage and continue to make moral decisions based on the principles he learned while watching TV as a preschooler. This example illustrates that as people age, they become more capable of engaging in more sophisticated moral thinking, but if they are not motivated to progress, they will stay at a lower level of development.

BSIP/Newscom

Exposure to aggressive video games at the pre-conventional stage of development (ages 2 to 7 or 8) can affect moral development by conveying the idea that aggression is an acceptable way to solve problems.

SPECIAL TREATMENT FROM REGULATORS

Advocates of protecting children from negative media influence have focused their attention primarily on television because this medium has been so pervasive for more than a half-century. These advocates have been most concerned about the influence of the violence that seems to permeate the entire television landscape, and they continue to pressure governmental agencies to do something to protect children. In response to this pressure, Congress has been periodically holding hearings on television violence and its possible effects on children ever since the 1950s. As a result of all these hearings, Congress has not passed legislation regulating content but has over time exerted pressure on television networks to adopt some changes. In 1975, the TV industry tried a self-regulatory policy called the "family hour," where programmers pushed violent content and other material regarded as harmful to children later into the evening, leaving the first hour of **prime time** solely for content appropriate for so-called family viewing. However, several stations filed suit citing infringement of free speech and won their suit in court. Then the omnibus Telecommunications Act of 1996 included an amendment mandating that all TV receivers sold in the United States after 1999 should have a V-chip, which is a screening device that allows TV owners to program their sets to avoid programs with certain ratings for violence, sex, and language.

The Federal Communications Commission (FCC) has been more aggressive in regulating indecent material, such as sexual depictions as well as specific words deemed offensive. In one instance during the 1970s, the FCC took steps to fine a radio station that aired a George Carlin skit entitled "Filthy Words," where he repeatedly said the seven words explicitly prohibited on the airwaves. The station appealed, but the FCC ruling was upheld by the Supreme Court, which reasoned that it was in the public's interest to protect radio listeners from hearing those words during parts of the day when children were likely to be in the audience. In the late 1990s and early 2000s, shock jock Howard Stern was fined multiple times for making explicit sexual references on air, as was the company that controlled the radio stations that broadcasted his show.

Critics of television's influence on children have also been concerned about how advertisers can exploit youngsters. Kunkel and Wilcox (2001) point out that there have been two types of regulations designed to protect children from unfair practices in television advertising. One type of regulation has been to limit the amount of time devoted to advertising in programs aimed at children. The limits are 12 minutes per hour on weekdays and 10.5 minutes per hour on weekends. While compliance is relatively good, there are exceptions. For example, Viacom was cited for 600 violations in 1 year and fined $1 million. Viacom blamed the problem on human error (Shiver, 2004).

A second type of regulation aimed at protecting children has been the requirement to keep a clear separation between program content and commercial content on television programs aimed at children. Young children are fuzzy about the difference between entertainment and advertising content. Thus the FCC requires bumpers, which are 5-second segments before and after commercial breaks to alert young children about the switch in content. These bumpers typically take the form of "And now a word from our sponsor." The FCC also prohibits host selling, which uses a character from a TV show as the product spokesperson for products depicted in ads inserted into that program. This too has relatively high compliance, but again there are exceptions. For example, Disney aired 31 half-hour episodes in which commercials for products associated with the children's program were also aired. Disney was fined $500,000 and blamed the problem on human error (Shiver, 2004).

SPECIAL TREATMENT FROM PARENTS

Think back to when you were a child and how your parents controlled your media exposure, especially your television viewing. If you were like most children, your parents used one of four kinds of treatments: imposing restrictions, co-viewing, active mediation, or using program ratings.

Perhaps you were raised in a household where your media exposure was limited by rules about how much, when, and which types of television you were allowed to watch. Media exposure was used as a reward for good behavior, and your media use was restricted when you were bad. Researchers, however, have found that only about half of American households have any rules for media use (Rideout, Foehr, Roberts, & Brodie, 1999) and that parents are more likely to say they have media exposure rules compared to their children (Jordan, 2001).

Co-viewing involves parents and children watching TV together. No conversation is required. The assumption here is that when parents are in the room while children are viewing, children will avoid watching harmful content. There is a discrepancy in the research about how often co-viewing occurs. Some surveys have found co-viewing to be very common (Sang, Schmitz, & Tasche, 1992; Valkenburg, Krcmar, Peeters, & Marseille, 1999), with as many as 93% of parents saying they watch TV with their children at least once in a while (Jordan, 2001). Other surveys have found co-viewing to be rare (Dorr, Kovaric, & Doubleday, 1989; Lawrence & Wozniak, 1989), with as many as 95% of children 7 years of age and older saying that they never watch TV with their parents and 81% of children ages 2 to 7 saying they never watch with their parents (Rideout et al., 1999).

In a recent national probability sample of 2,326 parents of children aged 8 and under, Connell, Lauricella, and Wartella (2015) looked at parent–child co-using of media across six types: books, TV, computers, video games, tablets, and smartphones. Results indicate that parents are more likely to co-use traditional media such as books and television, whereas they are least likely to co-use video games.

Active mediation consists of conversations that parents or other adults have with children about television. An analysis of the literature on active mediation studies over the years has revealed four types of mediation approaches that parents use when viewing with the children (Austin, Bolls, Fujioka, & Engelbertson, 1999). These are non-mediators (parents who talk about television with their children infrequently), optimists (those whose discussion primarily reinforces television content), cynics (those whose discussion primarily counters television content), and selectives (those who use both positive and negative discussion techniques, depending on the situation). Thus the key difference in mediation style is **positive mediation**, which is pointing out the good things in television messages as well as encouraging children to emulate those good things, and **negative mediation**, which is pointing out the bad behaviors of characters and being critical of what is portrayed. Active mediation has been found to be rare over many decades of research (Austin, 1993; Himmelweit, Oppenheim, & Vince, 1958; Mohr, 1979; Nathanson, Eveland, Park, & Paul, 2002).

Program ratings have been available for decades but few parents use them. The Motion Picture Association of America (MPAA) has been rating Hollywood movies released to theaters since 1984. However, in repeated studies, about one third of parents or fewer use the MPAA age-based ratings system (Abelman, 1999; Bash, 1997; Mifflin, 1997). Since 1999, all televisions sold in the United States have a V-chip where users can program their sets to screen out certain types of programs based on the industry ratings of those shows for violence, language, and sexual situations. However, only a minority of parents use these ratings to protect their children from TV content. Over the years, parental usage has ranged from about one third (Foehr, Rideout, & Miller, 2000; Greenberg, Rampoldi-Hnilo, & Hofschire, 2000; Jordan, 2001; Kaiser Family Foundation, 1999; Rampoldi-Hnilo & Greenberg, 2000) down to less than 20% (CBSNews.com, 2009). Also, studies find that the ratings given to shows typically fail to warn viewers accurately about the levels of violence, sexual portrayals, and language. The authors of one recent study concluded that "TV Parental Guidelines ratings were ineffective in discriminating shows for 3 out of 4 behaviors studies. Even in shows rated for children as young as 7 years, violence was prevalent, prominent, and salient" (Gabrielli, Traore, Stoolmiller, Bergamini, & Sargent, 2016). These findings are not surprising given that the shows are rated by the producers rather than an impartial group.

iStock/Lise Gange

Co-viewing and the type of active mediation adults have with children can influence children's media exposure and experience.

The research on how parents help their children to be more media literate leads us to three conclusions. First, it appears that most parents do little to screen viewing choices for their children. Of course parents say they are concerned, and of course they care about the well-being of their children. But parents do not behave in a way that follows through on that concern. Parents think they are doing much more than they are, if children's perceptions of their parents' guidance can be believed. If parents are co-viewing with children, laying down rules, and actively mediating their television exposures, this is not making an impression on many of those children.

Second, almost all of the research on parents attempting to help children with the media is limited to TV viewing. Thus far, we know little about how parents help children with Internet exposures, especially with social networking sites and games. And the little research that is available on this topic so far is not promising. For example, Byrne and Lee (2011) conducted a national survey of 456 parents of children 10 to 16 years of age and found that there was considerable disagreement between children and their parents over what treatments were being used and what was working.

Third, it appears that many parents do not know what to say to their children to help them become more media literate, nor do they have an educated rationale for viewing rules. Unless parents themselves are media literate, their help is likely to lead to negative effects rather than truly help their children.

RE-EXAMINING THE CASE FOR SPECIAL TREATMENT OF CHILDREN

Clearly young children are at a disadvantage compared to adolescents and adults; young children have lower levels of maturation and experience. Therefore, it is understandable why children are treated as a special group that needs protection from risks of negative media effects. However, we must also realize that many adolescents and even adults are subject to significant deficiencies in maturation and experience. Let's examine these deficiencies in more detail and look at the implications of these deficiencies for media literacy.

Maturation

It is tempting to think that once we have completed childhood, we have matured to the point cognitively, emotionally, and morally that we can take care of ourselves during media exposure and that we do not need help. Evidence for such a belief comes from Piaget and his stage theory of cognitive development. Most people think that because Piaget's stages end at age 12 that we all become adults cognitively at age 13. However, this is a misinterpretation of Piaget's stage theory. While it is true that Piaget's theory does stop its explanation at adolescence, there is no evidence in his writing that he believed cognitive development ends at age 12. He simply confined his investigation and explanations to children. However, over time, Piaget's lack of attention to older age levels has been used as an argument that humans plateau at age 12 and stay at this level of cognitive development; that is, their capacity stays the same. People at other age levels share the same stage cognitive ability, and their differences in learning are then attributable to other things such as IQ, experience, and persistence. For example, Eron, Huesmann, Lefkowitz, and Walder (1972) argue that once children reach adolescence, their behavioral dispositions and inhibitory controls have become crystallized. But this appears to be a faulty belief, because there is a growing literature that documents how adults continue to experience cognitive changes throughout their lives. For example, Patricia King (1986) conducted a review of the published literature that tested the formal reasoning abilities of adults and concluded that "a rather large proportion of adults do not evidence formal thinking, even among those who have been enrolled in college" (p. 6). This conclusion holds up over the 25 studies she analyzed, including a variety of tests of formal reasoning ability and a variety of samples of adults 18 to 79 years old. In one third of the samples, less than 30% of respondents exhibited reasoning at the fully formal level; in almost all samples, no more than 70% of the adults were found to be fully functioning at the formal level. Therefore, the claim in Piaget's stage theory of cognitive development that humans mature into the stage of formal development at 12 years of age is faulty. Perhaps humans are *ready* to exhibit the skills of formal development beginning at age 12; however, most do not follow through on this readiness.

The ability to reason morally is not always shown to be more advanced with age. For example, van der Voort (1986) found no evidence that children judge violent behavior more critically in a moral sense as they age. He found no reduction in the approval of the good guys' behavior. And as children aged, they were even more likely to approve of the violent actions of the bad guys. So although children acquire additional cognitive abilities with age, they do not necessarily acquire additional moral insights. There is a range of moral development among people of any given age. Also, older children are not automatically more highly developed morally than are younger children.

In summary, there is ample evidence that people develop cognitively, emotionally, and morally over the course of childhood and that this development does not stop at adolescence but continues throughout one's entire life. Furthermore, it is important to note that not everyone at a given age is at the same level of development; there are significant differences across people at any particular age. It is likely that there are many adults who are not as highly developed cognitively, emotionally, or morally as many children.

Experience

While it is true that young children have spent less time on Earth than have adults, it does not necessarily follow that experience is the same as age. There are many adolescents and adults who have been having the same experiences over and over so that as they age, their experiences stay the same. Their lives are so routinized that they do pretty much the same thing every day. In contrast, there are children who are trying very different things every day. This is especially true with new technologies; children are the eager users of all kinds of innovations, while many adults lag behind in their willingness to try many of the newer technologies. Also, younger people are much more willing to try different kinds of messages; for example, they are more likely to view newly released movies, try video games, keep up with changes in popular music, and try a wider range of Internet sites.

iStock/STEEX

Regardless of your age, the more eager you are to embrace new experiences and new perspectives, the more media literate you will become.

Every age group has different challenges along the path of increasing media literacy. With children, the special challenges are their lower levels of development—cognitively, emotionally, and morally—as well as their lower amounts of experience with the real world. Adults also have special challenges. For example, older adults are likely to have very well-established media habits that can be very difficult to alter. Also, older adults have experienced many decades of media conditioning to form their beliefs, which then form standards for evaluating all kinds of people and experiences. The challenge for older adults is to examine their existing knowledge structures to weed out faulty or out-of-date information and to systematically incorporate new information to keep up with our rapidly changing world. Younger adults also have special challenges as you will see in the next section.

YOUNG ADULTS AS A SPECIAL AUDIENCE

Recall from the definition of media literacy that the more perspectives people have, the more media literate they are. These perspectives are abstract constructs, so they are not possible to examine directly, but you can infer what your perspectives are by assessing how broad, or narrow, your life experience has been so far by doing Exercise 5.1.

After you have completed this exercise, think about how eager you have been to try new experiences, new media, and new kinds of messages. Your eagerness as well as your follow-through on engaging in new experiences and making sense of them can be explained by a set of cognitive and emotional abilities. The stronger these abilities are, the easier it is to embrace new experiences and make the most of them.

Cognitive Abilities

There are four natural abilities that are most related to media literacy. These are **field independency**, **crystalline intelligence**, **fluid intelligence**, and **conceptual differentiation**.

Field Independency

Perhaps the most important ability related to media literacy is field independency. Think of field independency as your natural ability to distinguish between the noise and the signal in any message. The noise is the chaos of symbols and images. The signal is the information that emerges from the chaos. People who are highly field independent are able to sort quickly through the field of chaos to identify the elements of importance and ignore the distracting elements. In contrast, people who are more field dependent get stuck in the field of chaos—seeing all the details but missing the patterns and the "big picture," which is the signal (Witkin & Goodenough, 1977). For example, when field-in-dependent people are reading a news story on a website, they will be able to identify the key information of the who, what, when, where, and why of the story. They will quickly sort through what is said, the graphics, and the visuals to focus on the essence of the event being covered. People who are field dependent will perceive the same key elements in the story but will also pay an equal amount of attention to the background elements of pop-up pictures, ads, borders, and so on. To the field-dependent person, all of these elements are of fairly equal importance, so they are as likely to remember the trivial as they are to remember the main points of the story. This is not to say that field-dependent people retain more information because they pay attention to more; on the contrary, field-dependent people retain less information because the information is not organized well and is likely to contain as much noise (peripheral and tangential elements) as signal (elements about the main idea).

Let's try one more example of this concept. Have you ever had to read a long novel and gotten so lost about 100 pages into it that you had to quit in frustration? You may have felt that just when the author was getting the story going with one set of characters, he or she would switch to a different setting at a different time with a totally new set of characters. This may have been happening every few pages! There were too many characters talking about too many different things. You were overwhelmed by all the detail and could not make sense of the overall story. This indicates that the novelist was making demands on you to be much more field independent than you were able to be when you tried to read the novel. If you had been more field independent, you would have been able to sort through all the details and recognize a thematic pattern and then use that thematic pattern as a tool to sort through all the details about characters, settings, time, dialogue, and action to direct your attention efficiently to those elements that were most important.

The value of being field independent increases as our culture, and your everyday life, grows more and more cluttered with media messages. Think about all the text messages, e-mails, and phone calls you receive and send or make each day. Think of all the words, pictures, images, and videos you see on all your screens every day. Are they all of equal importance or are you able to navigate through all the noisy clutter to award your attention to the best stuff exclusively? If you can do this efficiently and accurately, you are likely field independent. But if you get distracted easily, go off on long tangents, and burn through many hours following trivia, then you are likely more field dependent; that is, you allow the field to take you in all kinds of directions rather than controlling your journey yourself. The sheer bulk of all the information makes it more difficult to sort the important from the trivial, so many of us do not bother to sort. Instead, we default to a passive state as we float along in this stream of messages. The advantage of this automatic processing is that it screens out the noise, but the disadvantage is that it screens out much of the signal too. When we are more field independent, we can better program our attention triggers to maximize the filtering *in* of signal and at the same time maximize the filtering *out* of noise.

iStock/DOUGBERRY

Crystalline Intelligence

It is helpful to make a distinction between two types of intelligence: crystalline and fluid. Both types of intelligence are important for media literacy. Crystalline intelligence is the ability to memorize facts. It is best measured by tests requiring knowledge of the cultural milieu in which one lives, such as vocabulary and general information.

Crystalline intelligence, one of the four natural cognitive abilities, is the ability to memorize facts such as vocabulary.

Highly developed crystalline intelligence gives us the facility to absorb the images, definitions, opinions, and agendas of others. With most adults, crystallized intelligence seems to increase throughout the life span, although at a decreasing rate in later years (Sternberg & Berg, 1987). This means that as adults get older, they do better on tests requiring factual knowledge of their world, such as vocabulary and general information. In general, older people can more easily add new information to existing knowledge structures and more easily retrieve that information from those knowledge structures they use most often. When you have a well-developed knowledge structure on a topic, it is easy to sort through new information as you are exposed to it, compare the new information to what you already have in your knowledge structure, and make a determination whether the new information is useful to remember. If the new information is worthwhile to remember, it is easy to catalog it in a way that it is easy to recall later. However, if you are exposed to a message on a brand-new topic (one for which you do not have a knowledge structure), it is difficult to process that new information. To test this, pick a topic that is of equal interest to you and your parents (your neighborhood, your family, politics, sports, etc.) and then see how much detail your parents remember compared to you.

People strong in crystalline intelligence are good at what is called **vertical thinking**. Vertical thinking is systematic, logical thinking that proceeds step by step in an orderly progression. This is the type of thinking we need in order to learn the introductory information on any topic. We need to be systematic when we are trying to learn basic arithmetic, spelling, and dates in history. People high in crystalline intelligence are likely to have a more extensive list of competencies because they have memorized a much larger set of symbols and their denoted meanings.

Fluid Intelligence

In contrast to crystalline intelligence is fluid intelligence, which is the ability to be creative, make leaps of insight, as well as perceive things in a fresh and novel manner. People strong in fluid intelligence are good at what is called **lateral thinking**. Lateral thinking, in contrast to vertical thinking, does not proceed step by step in a straight line. Instead, when confronted with a problem, the lateral thinker jumps to a new and quite arbitrary position, then works backward and tries to construct a logical path between this new position and the starting point. Lateral thinkers tend to arrive at a solution to a problem that other thinkers, who are locked into a vertical form of thinking, would never arrive at. Lateral thinkers are more intuitive and creative. They reject the standard beginning points to solving problems and instead begin with an intuitive guess, a brainstorming of ideas, or a proposed solution "out of the blue."

Few people have a natural aptitude for lateral thinking. However, those people who do have an aptitude for lateral thinking typically use it a lot. For example, many inventors are lateral thinkers because they approach old problems in fresh ways. For example, Thomas Edison invented so many things that by the end of his life, he had more than 1,300 patents in the areas of the telegraph, telephone, phonograph, movie camera, and projectors. This suggests that there is a capacity for generating new ideas that is better developed in some people than in others. This capacity does not seem to be related to sheer intelligence but more to a particular way of thinking. There are smart and not-so-smart lateral thinkers, just like there are smart and not-so-smart vertical thinkers.

There are advantages and disadvantages to both forms of thinking. Vertical thinkers tend to do best at solving traditional problems for which the solutions can be learned. However, when their traditional methods of solving problems break down and they reach a dead end, they are stuck and have nowhere to go because their systematic step-by-step method of proceeding has led them down a path to a dead end. When others are stuck at a dead end of thinking, it is the lateral thinkers who break through the barriers. However, lateral thinkers can often be flighty and may come up with many new ideas that might not be a feasible way of solving a problem. People who are good at both and who know when to try each approach are, of course, the most successful problem solvers.

Being strong on both these abilities helps with increasing one's level of media literacy. Highly developed crystalline intelligence gives us the facility to absorb the images, definitions, opinions, and agendas of others. This helps us a great deal in the meaning-matching task because we are likely to have acquired a large set of accurate matches of symbols and meanings. Highly developed fluid intelligence gives us the facility to challenge what we see on the surface, to look deeper and broader, and to recognize new patterns. This helps us a great deal in the meaning construction task because we are able to move beyond the surface meaning and construct meanings that are more useful for our own purposes.

COMPARE & CONTRAST
CRYSTALLINE INTELLIGENCE AND FLUID INTELLIGENCE

Compare: Crystalline intelligence and fluid intelligence are *the same* in the following ways:

- Both are natural cognitive abilities where individuals vary along a continuum from low natural ability to high natural ability.

- Both can be developed to higher levels with training and practice.

- Both are related to a person's level of media literacy, where higher abilities reflect a higher level of media literacy.

Contrast: Crystalline intelligence and fluid intelligence are *different* in the following ways:

- Crystalline intelligence refers to a person's natural ability to memorize facts and absorb information as presented. It is reflected in vertical thinking, which follows a systematic, logical progression and is most valuable in learning spelling of words, dates in history, and steps in solving arithmetic problems.

- Fluid intelligence refers to a person's natural ability to be creative, make leaps of insight, as well as perceive things in a fresh and novel manner. It is reflected in lateral thinking, which is solving problems not by taking logical steps but by thinking "outside the box."

Conceptual Differentiation

Conceptual differentiation refers to how people group and classify things. People who classify objects into a large number of mutually exclusive categories exhibit a high degree of conceptual differentiation (Gardner, 1968). In contrast, people who use a small number of categories have a low degree of conceptual differentiation.

Related to the number of categories is category width (Bruner, Goodnow, & Austin, 1956). People who have few categories to classify something usually have broad categories so as to contain all types of messages. For example, if a person only has three categories for all media messages (news, ads, and entertainment), then each of these categories must contain a wide variety of things. In contrast, someone who has a great many categories would be dividing media messages into thinner slices (breaking news, feature news, documentary, commercial ads, public service announcements, action/adventure shows, sitcoms, game shows, talk shows, cartoons, and reality shows).

When we encounter a new message, we must categorize it by using either a leveling or a sharpening strategy. With the leveling strategy, we look for similarities between the new message and previous messages we have stored away as examples in our categories. We look for the best fit between the new message and one of remembered messages. We will never find a perfect fit; that is, the new message always has slightly different characteristics than our category calls for, but we tend to ignore those differences. In contrast, the sharpening strategy focuses on differences and tries to maintain a high degree of separation between the new message and older messages (Pritchard, 1975). To illustrate this, let's say two people are comparing this year's Super Bowl with last year's Super Bowl. A leveler would argue that the two games were similar and point out all the things the two had in common. The sharpener would disagree and point out all the differences between the two Super Bowls. Levelers tend to have fewer categories so that many things can fit into the same category, whereas sharpeners have many, many categories. In our example, the first person would likely have only one category for Super Bowls, feeling that all the Super Bowls are pretty much the same. A sharpener might have a different category for every Super Bowl, treating each one as unique. Increasing one's level of media literacy requires one to do more sharpening of categories for media messages, media companies, and media effects.

Emotional Abilities

In addition to the four cognitive abilities outlined above, there are three natural emotional abilities that can help you considerably in meeting the challenge of increasing your media literacy. These three emotional abilities are **emotional intelligence**, **tolerance for ambiguity**, and **nonimpulsiveness**.

Emotional Intelligence

Our ability to understand and control our emotions is called emotional intelligence. Emotional intelligence is thought to be composed of several related abilities, such as the ability to read the emotions of other people (empathy), the ability to be aware of one's own emotions, the ability to harness and manage one's own emotions productively, and the ability to handle the emotional demands of relationships.

Those of us with stronger emotional intelligence have a well-developed sense of empathy; we are able to see the world from another person's perspective. The more perspectives we can access, the more emotional intelligence we have. When we are highly developed emotionally, we are more aware of our own emotions. We also better understand the factors that cause those emotions, so we are able to seek the kinds of messages to get us the emotional reactions we want. In addition, we are less impulsive and are able to exercise more self-control. We can concentrate on the task at hand rather than become distracted by peripheral emotions.

Tolerance for Ambiguity

Every day, we encounter people and situations that are unfamiliar to us. To prepare ourselves for such situations, we have developed sets of expectations. What do we do when our expectations are not met and we are surprised? That depends on our tolerance level for ambiguity. If we have a low tolerance for ambiguity, we will likely choose to ignore those messages that do not meet our expectations; we feel too confused or frustrated to work out the discrepancies.

In contrast, if we are willing to follow situations into unfamiliar territory that go beyond our preconceptions, then we have a high tolerance for ambiguity. Initial confusion does not stop us. Instead, this confusion motivates us to search harder for clarity. We do not feel an emotional barrier that prevents us from examining messages more closely. We are willing to break any message down into components and make comparisons and evaluations in a quest to understand the nature of the message and to examine why our initial expectations were wrong.

During media exposures, people with a low tolerance encounter messages on the surface. If the surface meaning fits their preconceptions, then it is filed away and becomes a confirmation (or reinforcement) of those preconceptions. If the surface meaning does not meet a person's preconceptions, the message is ignored. In short, there is no analysis.

People with a high tolerance for ambiguity do not have a barrier to analysis. They are willing to break any message down into components and make comparisons and evaluations in a quest to understand the nature of the message and why their own expectations were wrong. People who consistently attempt to verify their observations and judgments are called scanners because they are perpetually looking for more information (Gardner, 1968).

Nonimpulsiveness

Nonimpulsiveness refers to how quickly people make decisions about messages (Kagan, Rosman, Day, Albert, & Phillips, 1964). People who rush to a decision are impulsive. In contrast, people who take a long time and consider things from many perspectives are reflective or nonimpulsive.

Typically, there is a trade-off between speed and accuracy. Impulsive people are most concerned with speed; they feel overwhelmed by decisions, so they want to have things resolved as quickly as possible. For them, it is worth the risk to make a bad decision as long as they can quickly end the worry that comes with being faced with a decision-making task. Reflective people are most concerned with accuracy; they dread being wrong, so they think about all the options of a decision, even if it takes a long time.

How much time we take to make decisions is governed by our emotions. If we feel comfortable encountering new information and like to work through problems carefully, we are likely to act reflectively and take our time. However, if we feel a negative emotion (such as frustration), we tend to make decisions as quickly as possible to eliminate the negative emotional state.

SUMMARY

The public and policymakers regard children as a special audience that needs protection from potentially negative effects of mass media exposure. There has been a good deal of research to show that children are indeed vulnerable to certain types of messages. However, adolescents and adults have also been found to be vulnerable to certain types of messages. Therefore, every audience should be regarded as special because each audience has different vulnerabilities and challenges when it comes to media literacy.

The argument for protecting children is based on the idea that children are at lower levels of development—cognitive, emotional, and moral—as well as lower levels of experience. These deficiencies make them especially vulnerable to negative effects. However, the research shows that many adolescents and adults are also vulnerable.

Media literacy can help children, adolescents, and adults reduce negative effects and increase positive effects of exposure to media messages. Media literacy can be developed. That development is easier among people who keep improving on their natural abilities, who keep searching for a wide range of experiences in both the media as well as the real world, and who keep applying their skills actively to build more elaborate and useful knowledge structures.

Further Reading

Goleman, D. (1995). *Emotional intelligence.* New York, NY: Bantam. (352 pages with index)

In this very readable best-seller, Goleman argues that there is an emotional IQ, not just an intellectual one. He challenges the long-held belief that a person's intelligence, as measured by a narrow IQ test, is an inadequate predictor of success or ability. First, he broadens the conception of intelligence, and then he shows how a person's emotional development interacts with a broad range of cognitive abilities. He cites physiological data to show that emotions are part of the brain and are triggered by the capacity of the body.

Jordan, A. B., & Romer, D. (Eds.). (2014). *Media and the well-being of children and adolescents.* New York, NY: Oxford University Press. (288 pages, including index)

This edited book presents 16 chapters written by various experts on children and media. Each chapter focuses on a different type of media content or effect where children are shown to be vulnerable.

Kohlberg, L. (1981). *The philosophy of moral development: Moral stages and the idea of justice.* New York, NY: Harper & Row. (428 pages, including references and index)

Kohlberg lays out his moral development scheme of three stages, each with two substages. There are many examples relating this structure to how people come to understand the concept of justice.

Lemish, D. (2015). *Children and media.* Malden, MA: Wiley & Sons. (278 pages, including references and index)

Lemish, a professor and founding editor of the *Journal of Children and Media*, focuses on the topics of childhood development, health, literacy, and children's perceptions of self. She also describes efforts at media literacy education and policies that have been designed to help children deal with the media.

Pulaski, M. A. S. (1980). *Understanding Piaget: An introduction to children's cognitive development* (Rev. and exp. ed.). New York, NY: Harper & Row. (248 pages with index)

This book is a very clear, well-organized description of most of Piaget's thinking and research. Many drawings illustrate key concepts.

Singer, D. G., & Singer, J. L. (Eds.) (2001). *Handbook of children and the media*. Thousand Oaks, CA: SAGE. (765 pages, including index)

This is a definitive handbook on the topic of children and the media. It consists of 39 chapters, each written by an expert in the field. The chapters are clustered to address the following topics: children's uses of the media and the gratifications they obtain from them; cognitive functions and school-readiness skills; hazards of TV viewing; personality, social attitudes, and health; the media industry and its technology; and policy issues and advocacy.

Keeping Up to Date

Journal of Children and Media (https://www.tandfonline.com/loi/rchm20)

This scholarly journal is published quarterly and presents research articles in the areas of children as consumers of media, how children are portrayed in media messages, and how media organizations produce content for children.

MediaSmarts (http://mediasmarts.ca)

This website is a good source of information about how children are affected by media exposures and how parents and others can help increase their coping with these influences.

EXERCISE 5.1

THINKING ABOUT THE BREADTH OF YOUR LIFE EXPERIENCES

1. Friends
   - Do you have lots of friends or just a few?
   - Are your friends all pretty much the same as far as background, values, political attitudes, personality, and so on? Or is each friend very different from the rest?

2. Daily routines
   - Do you march through life structured by the same routines, or do you try to make each day different?
   - Do you wake up each day at the same time and go to bed at the same time?

(Continued)

(Continued)

- Do you eat your meals at the same time each day?
- Do you commute to school or work the same way every day or are you curious to find new routes?

3. Shopping

- Do you shop at the same stores or are you always looking for new shopping experiences?
- When you enter a store, do you walk around the merchandise the same way each time?
- When shopping for groceries, do you buy the same foods and same brands each week?
- When shopping for clothes, do you always look for the same styles and same brands?

4. Education

- Think about the range of courses you have taken in college or high school. To what extent is the range of courses due to mandatory requirements for your degree and to what extent is the range due to your curiosity for exploring new areas of knowledge?
- How much of your education has been motivated by a desire to get a degree and how much has been motivated by your curiosity?

5. Media use

- Do you routinely access certain media (such as the Internet) and routinely avoid others (such as print newspapers)?
- When you listen to recorded music, is it typically the same artists and same genre?
- When you watch movies or TV programs, is it typically the same types of shows?
- To what extent do you have media habits; that is, how structured are your days by media exposure routines?

INDUSTRY

PART III

6

DEVELOPMENT OF THE MASS MEDIA INDUSTRIES

Key Idea: Historically the mass media industries have followed a life cycle pattern of development (innovation, growth, peak, decline, and adaptation stages) but now the most powerful force shaping its current nature is convergence.

In 2017, Amazon acquired the grocery store chain Whole Foods for $13.7 billion.

Heather was determined to do well and earn a high grade in a course entitled Development of the Mass Media. She had bought the textbook, which included a dozen chapters, each one on a different type of mass medium. She had read each chapter carefully and high-lighted the important facts in green. Now as she prepared to study for a major test, she noticed that almost every word on every page was green. She felt frustrated and thought, "How am I ever going to learn all this material!?! It's too much. There are a million tiny facts. There is no way I can memorize all these facts."

It is likely that many of you have felt like Heather when you were confronted with a subject that is composed of a great number of facts. The mass media industries is a topic composed of a great amount of detail—dates, names of inventors, historical occurrences, business practices, names of businesses, complicated charts of who owns what, and tons of financial data. When I first started writing about this topic, I too was overwhelmed. As a writer, I could have made it easy on myself and simply presented one fact after another in a long and boring historical sequence. But that way of presenting facts would not have made it easy on you—the learner. Learning proceeds much more efficiently when you start with a simple, clear map that organizes the material you plan to study. With such a map, you can see all the topics and how they fit together, so you can avoid getting lost as you navigate through all the detail. Even more importantly, conceptual maps give you the context you need to understand each idea and catalog each effectively into your memory.

In this chapter, as well as the next, I present you with conceptual maps of the most important ideas about the mass media industries. These maps will show you the overall shape of the important knowledge structures and help you efficiently navigate through all the detail. Once you understand the structure of the most important ideas, then you can fill in the details. Many of those details about the media industries are provided for you in Appendix A, which you can access at http://study.sagepub.com/potter9e. If you want even more details, then you can continue acquiring facts by looking at the suggestions for Further Reading and Keeping Up to Date at the end of this chapter.

This chapter will focus your attention on three topics. First, we will examine the patterns in how the different mass media industries have developed over time. Second, we will look at those patterns across the mass media industries. Then third, we will take a close look at the factors that are shaping the mass media industries today.

PATTERNS OF DEVELOPMENT

Some of the mass media industries are relatively old and have been around for more than 2 centuries (e.g., books, newspapers, and magazines), while others are relatively young (e.g., cable TV and especially the Internet). While each industry has been shaped by different historical influences, technologies, regulations, and audience needs, all the mass media industries have exhibited a high degree of commonality in the way they have grown and developed over time. When we focus our attention on the changes that have been common to all the media industries, we can develop a better appreciation for the nature of all mass media.

The **life cycle pattern** provides a useful framework for examining the media industries because it focuses your attention on how the industries have gone through changes and why. The life cycle pattern contains five stages: **innovation** (or birth), **penetration** (or growth), **peak** (maturity), **decline**, and **adaptation**.

Innovation Stage

Each of the mass media industries began as an innovation. The innovation stage of a medium's development is characterized by a technological innovation that makes a channel of transmission possible. For example, there would be no film industry if someone had not invented the motion picture camera and projector. However, technology by itself is not enough to create a mass medium. A mass medium is more than an invention; there have been many technological innovations for the dissemination of information that have failed. So the innovation stage is also characterized by **marketing innovations** in addition to **technological innovations**. This means that someone had to create a business that would use the technology to deliver messages and thus build audiences.

A successful marketing innovation begins with an entrepreneur recognizing a need in the population, then using a new technology to satisfy that need in a way that people begin recognizing the value of the new medium and how it can help them. To do this, the entrepreneur must have a mass-like orientation; that is, he or she must exploit a technological channel's potential to attract particular audiences then continue to use that channel to condition those audiences for repeat exposures. For example, in the early 1900s, after the motion picture camera and projector were invented, some entrepreneurs

iStock/mbortolino

Launching a new mass medium successfully requires more than just technological innovations; it also needs marketing innovations.

turned their living rooms into theaters and began charging people to watch the movies they showed in their homes. These entrepreneurs found that there was a market for this kind of entertainment, so they took steps to grow a business by renting out storefronts to accommodate larger audiences; then they rented concert theaters, and then built their own theaters that were primarily for the showing of films. This growing number of large theaters not only met the demand for movies but also served to increase the demand. This increasing demand stimulated other entrepreneurs to create film production companies to make and distribute films to the growing number of theaters. Without all these marketing entrepreneurs who recognized a public need and marketed their services to grow that need into a habit, the technology of the motion picture camera and projector would never have developed beyond a curious invention.

COMPARE & CONTRAST
TECHNOLOGICAL INNOVATIONS AND MARKETING INNOVATIONS

Compare: Technological innovations and marketing innovations are *the same* in the following ways:

- Both involve the creation of new ways of crafting messages and disseminating them to target populations.

- Both are required characteristics of the innovation stage in the development of the mass media industries.

Contrast: Technological innovations and marketing innovations are *different* in the following ways:

- Technological innovations are engineering-type inventions that have created new ways to capture, store, and transmit information in print, graphic, photographic, audio, and video formats.

- Marketing innovations are strategic-type inventions that have created new ways to identify audiences and their needs, attract their attention, and present messages in a way that holds their attention and conditions those audiences for repeated exposures.

Penetration Stage

Once an innovation has created a new mass media channel, that channel needs to appeal to a very large, heterogeneous population if it is to be effective as a mass medium. This stage is called "penetration," because it highlights the growing acceptance of a medium from being used by only a few innovators then expanding to being used by early adopters, then the majority of a population, and finally everyone. The rate of penetration is determined by how fast the public regards the new medium as being able to satisfy their existing needs better than any alternative.

Sometimes, the public has a need that is already being satisfied by existing media, but a new medium comes along that can satisfy those needs better in some way. For example, in the 1940s, people were satisfying their need for entertainment with radio and with films.

But then broadcast television came along and was better than radio because it offered pictures in addition to sound. Thus, television provided more to audiences in return for the same attention. Television was better at satisfying many people's need for entertainment compared to film because television brought many hours of entertainment into a person's home each and every day, so there was no need to leave the house, get a babysitter, find a parking place, or buy a ticket. Television was much more convenient. Television is also credited with increasing the American public's appetite for entertainment. The amount of time spent viewing television steadily increased since television was first introduced until the early 2000s, when Internet use started to grow dramatically because the Internet could provide all the entertainment and news that TV could plus it could satisfy an even broader range of needs. In 2007, people spent an average of 4:21 hours per day viewing live TV (broadcast and cable) and an average of 2:18 additional minutes per day with the internet. By 2017, TV viewing had declined slightly to 4:04 hours per day while internet usage had increased dramatically to 5:50 hours per day (Dunn, 2017). This pattern illustrates two ideas. First, the internet has started taking some time away from TV, which indicates that the internet is satisfying better the needs that TV viewing used to do. Second, the rise of the internet illustrates that it is growing the needs of the population because the time spent with both of these media combined has grown from 6:39 hours per day in 2007 to 9:54 hours per day in 2017.

As each medium grows, it is influenced by factors that shape its growth. These factors include the public's need and desire for the medium, additional innovations that change the appeal of other competing media, political and regulatory constraints, and the economic demands of the private enterprises that own and operate the mass media.

Peak Stage

The peak stage is reached when the medium commands the most attention from the public and generates the most revenue compared to other media. This usually happens when the medium has achieved maximum penetration; that is, a very high percentage of households have accepted a medium, and the medium cannot grow in penetration any more. Of course, it can continue to absorb a greater proportion of an audience member's time and money. For example, broadcast television reached a peak in the 1960s after taking audiences away from radio and film. Broadcast television also had taken national advertisers away from magazines and radio. Until the 1990s, broadcast television remained at a peak as the most dominant mass medium because people were spending more time with broadcast television everyday compared to any other medium. Also, most people regarded broadcast television as their primary (and often only) source of entertainment and news.

Decline Stage

Eventually, a peak medium will be challenged by a newer medium and go into a decline. In the decline stage, the medium is characterized by a loss of audience acceptance and therefore by a loss in revenues. A decline in audience size results not from a decline in need for a particular kind of message but by those message needs being satisfied better by a competing medium that is growing in penetration and moving toward its own peak. For example, broadcast television experienced a decline in audiences and advertisers throughout the 1990s with the increase in cable channels. People were reducing the amount of time they were watching television shows designed to appeal to everyone and increasing the amount of time they were watching particular kinds of content that they wanted, such as news (CNN and Fox News), sports (ESPN), movies (TCM), comedy (Comedy Central), and music (MTV and VH1). Because cable television offered a wide range of content choices to people in just about every niche of interest, cable grew to a peak by taking audiences and advertisers away from broadcast television. Now in the new millennium, cable has been experiencing declining audiences as people shift to Internet services to provide them with entertainment and information.

Internet music provider Spotify appeals to the needs of niche audiences by offering personalized stations based on individual preferences.

Jaap Arriens/Sipa USA/Newscom

Adaptation Stage

A medium enters the adaptation stage of development when it begins to redefine its position in the media marketplace. Repositioning is achieved by identifying a new set of needs that the medium can meet, because the old needs it used to fulfill are now met better by another medium. For example, after radio lost its audience to television, radio adapted by doing three things. First, radio stopped competing directly with television by eliminating its general entertainment programs such as soap operas, situation comedies, and mystery dramas. Instead, radio shifted to music formats where disc jockeys would play popular songs one after another. Second, radio abandoned its strategy of trying to appeal to a general audience and instead segmented the market according to musical tastes, and each station aimed its programming at the people in one of those niches. So now in each radio market, there is likely to be a top 40 station, a rhythm and blues station, a jazz station, an album-oriented rock station, a golden oldies station, a country and western station, a classical music station, and so forth—each appealing to a different set of listeners. Third, radio realized that with the invention of the transistor radio in the 1950s, it could be portable whereas television could not. So radio developed playlists that formed a kind of background mood-shaping experience as people drove in their cars, laid out on beaches, and talked on the phone.

For the past several decades, broadcast television has been in decline as it fights off challenges by cable TV and computers. Broadcast television is trying to adapt much like radio did in the 1950s by trying to be more mobile and programming to niche audiences.

COMPARISONS ACROSS MASS MEDIA

Now let's look at the big picture *across* the media industries. We'll compare the development of the different mass media industries to get a sense of which are the newest and when each was the strongest.

Life Cycle Pattern

Take a minute to look at the life cycle patterns displayed in Figure 6.1. Notice that the print media of books, newspapers, and magazines are the oldest, with each of them moving out of their innovation stage more than a century ago. Computers are the newest mass medium, with its innovation stage finishing about the time you were born. Notice also that all of the mass media, with the exception of cable TV and computers, are currently in the adaptation stage. This means they are all trying to figure out how to coexist with the other up-and-coming media as well as with each other.

Although the life cycle pattern is a good template for showing patterns, it is not perfect. For example, notice that several of the media (books, magazines, and recordings) never reached a peak. This does not mean that those media are not important or successful; it only means that those media never achieved dominance as the most important mass medium at a given time.

Indicators of Peak

We are at an interesting time in the development of the media industries. Broadcast television has left the peak stage, which lasted for about 40 years, during which time it accounted for almost all of the television audience. But cable channels have been eroding broadcast television's hold on the audience; broadcast television has slipped below 50% of the television-viewing audience, and its revenues are now lagging behind that of cable television. Cable has been at the peak for more than a decade but is threatened by the medium of computers (which includes receiving media messages on desktops, laptops, notebooks, mobile phones, and the like). The computer medium is showing that it can be the delivery system for books, newspapers, magazines, recordings, film, and video; it can deliver those messages anywhere through a wire or wirelessly; and it provides the additional feature of being interactive so that users can easily make copies of messages, transform them, and pass them along to others. For all of these reasons, the medium of computers is well on its way to a peak.

When a medium is at its peak, it is usually the dominant medium; that is, it is the most important medium to the greatest number of people. This can be seen in terms of how much money the industry generates and how much time people spend with that medium. Given these criteria, it appears that cable television (along with its satellite delivery services) is still the most dominant medium. Cable and satellite TV now has revenues greater than any other medium. Radio is in second place with the amount of time that people spend with it per year. Does this mean that radio should be considered the second most dominant medium? The answer is no—for several reasons. First, although people spend a lot of time with their radios on, they are using the medium for background noise; that is, they are not really paying much attention to those messages. When radio was at its peak in the 1920s and 1930s, its programming commanded listeners' full attention. That programming included a wide range of genres that are now seen on television. People would listen to soap operas, detective shows, game shows, and comedies. But now, most of radio listening is background music. While listening to this music, people are typically exposing themselves to other media (such as reading books, magazines, and newspapers), or they are doing something else (such as talking on the phone, jogging, or working) that requires more attention. Even though the radio is on for so many hours in the lives of so many people, it does not hold people's full attention for very long.

FIGURE 6.1 ■ Life Cycle Patterns

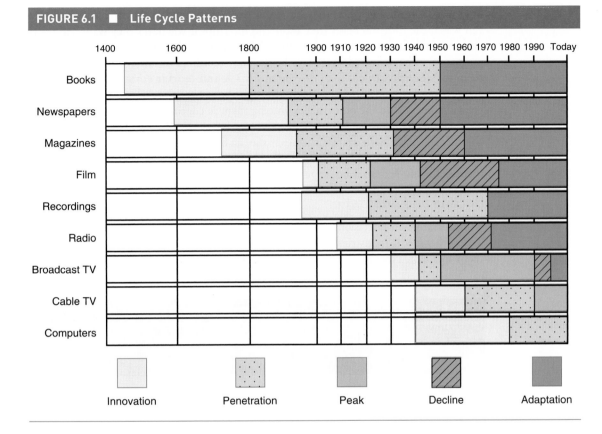

Second, radio does not generate as much revenue as other media. Does this mean people do not spend money on types of media such as radio and broadcast TV? Of course not. It means that these media do not get any income *directly* from the consumer. People must buy receivers, but that money goes to Best Buy, Walmart, or wherever people buy their sets. Broadcast radio and television get almost all of their revenue from advertising, which comes from consumers but only indirectly.

We are currently in a very dynamic and interesting time with the development of the mass media. The newer technologies that can be grouped under the title of computer are changing the way audiences access media messages by giving them much more control and variety. Take film for example. By 2010, Americans were spending almost twice the money on home viewing of movies (on-demand videos, digital downloads, and DVDs) than going to theaters ("Unkind Unwind," 2011). By 2014, Americans spent more on movie streaming and downloads (Netflix, Amazon Prime Video, etc.) than they did buying tickets at movie theaters (Rigby, 2014). When people are limited to theaters to view films, they have only about a dozen choices at any given time and they must be at the theater when the film starts and sit there for the entire running of the film unless they want to miss some of it. However, when people watch a film through their cable provider or especially from a website, they have a virtually unlimited range of choices and they can watch the film whenever they want and interrupt it whenever they want. Access to news is much faster and up to date on websites than waiting for printed newspapers or magazines to be delivered. Access to books and recordings is faster when downloading them to handheld devices than driving to a **brick-and-mortar store**. The newer media are growing fast and moving quickly through the penetration stage. They are putting growing pressure on the older media, forcing them to continue adapting.

It appears that computer/Internet is now entering the peak stage. The time spent with this medium has grown dramatically over the last decade (see Table 6.1). Notice that time spent with TV, radio, and print has declined a bit, while time spent with the Internet has increased by more than 3 hours per day!

Decline and Adaptation

Notice that when television penetrated the culture in the 1950s and quickly rose to a peak, other media industries—especially radio and film—went into a decline that forced them to adapt. Newspapers adapted by presenting longer stories of in-depth reporting

TABLE 6.1 ■ Time Spent With Various Mass Media		
	Hours: Minutes Spent per Day	
Mass Medium	**2007**	**2017**
Internet	2:18	5:50
Mobile devices	—	3:14
Desktop/laptop	—	2:08
Other devices	—	0:28
Television	4:21	4:04
Cable and satellite TV	2:51	—
Broadcast TV	1:50	—
Radio	2:05	1:26
Print	1:03	0:25
Newspapers	0:26	—
Magazines	0:19	—
Books	0:18	—
Other	—	0:22
Total	**9:47**	**12:07**

Time figures are hours and minutes per person per day on average.

Sources: U.S. Census Bureau (2009) and eMarketer (2017a).

that the short format of radio and television news could not provide. Newspapers survived for a time with this adaptation but now with the rise of the computer/Internet, newspapers are experiencing a steep decline in terms of readership and revenues, which has led to many newspapers going out of business.

As the Internet is growing into a peak, all the traditional media are in decline (see Table 6.1). In the decade from 2007 to 2017, time spent with traditional media of television, radio, and print has declined from 7:29 to 5:51 hours, while time spent with digital media increased from 2:18 to 5:50 hours. In 2007, 76% of our exposure time was with traditional media and that eroded to 50% a decade later, even though our overall time spent with the media increased 19% during that period from 9:49 hours per day to 11:41 hours. This is a significant shift that can be explained by the newer medium of Internet and mobile devices that allow us to satisfy all the needs that traditional media have been doing plus more and to satisfy these needs quickly and anywhere with our mobile devices. The typical smartphone now has more computing power than Apollo 11 had when it landed a man on the moon (Gibbs, 2012). It allows users to make phone calls, send texts, play music, read books, take pictures, and record video. With the use of apps, smartphones can access the Internet, play games, present coupons and pay for purchases at brick-and-mortar stores, track people on GPS, trade stocks, and follow traffic patterns in real time. In the United States, 77% of all adults own a smartphone (Statista, 2018f), 46% of all smartphone users say that it is something they could not live without (Rainie & Perrin, 2017), and one quarter of all users say they use their phone to stay online almost constantly (Perrin & Jiang, 2018).

At this point, let's see if you can use the information you have learned thus far in this chapter about the patterns of development of the mass media industries. Exercise 6.1 gives you a chance to apply your knowledge about how the mass media industries spring into being through technological and marketing innovations then grow larger and more powerful to a peak stage. Think about what that peak stage really means to a media industry and how the industry at a peak affects all the other media industries. This exercise has no right or wrong answers because it asks you to speculate what will happen in the computer/Internet industry 5 and 20 years into the future. So think outside the box of the present time and have some fun predicting the future!

CURRENT PICTURE

Now that you have seen the big picture about how the various mass media industries have developed over time, it is time to shift our focus to what is happening now. First we examine the most powerful force shaping the media industries today—convergence. Then we will profile the industries in terms of their workforces.

Convergence

The key to understanding the nature of the mass media industries today is to realize how the influence of **convergence** has been so powerful over the past decade and will continue to be well into the future. In the most general sense, convergence simply means the moving together over time of things that were previously separated. With

The movement from analog to digital—from audio cassettes to MP3s and music streaming, for example—has been key to technological convergence.

the media, convergence means the blending together of previously separate channels of communication such that the characteristics that have divided those channels into distinctly different media have been eroding. In this section, we'll examine how three types of convergence—technological, marketing, and psychological—have been changing the nature of the mass media.

Technological convergence refers to how innovations about storing and transmitting information have brought about changes to the mass media industries. The key technological innovation that has been driving convergence is not the computer per se but the software code that runs computers. This software code is digital; that is, it is written, stored, and read as discrete, individual numbers that are arranged in sequences to communicate patterns. While computers and digital code have been around for more than half a century, it was not until about 2 decades ago that the media largely replaced **analog coding** with **digital coding**.

Analog coding is the recording, storage, and retrieval of information that relies on the physical properties of a medium. Print information is stored as ink marks on paper. Sound recording information was stored as fluctuations within the grooves in vinyl disks. As a vinyl disk revolved on a turntable, a needle was dragged through the groove and picked up the tiny fluctuations pressed into the walls of that groove. Those fluctuations were translated into electrical impulses that were sent to an amplifier and then to a speaker where those impulses were translated into movements in the speaker, which sent out waves of compressed air to human ears. In the 1970s, recording companies began shifting from vinyl disks to magnetic tapes but the analog system of coding was still used.

Digital coding refers to using a sequence of symbols or bytes (usually numbers) that are not dependent on the physical characteristics of any one medium. Digital recording of information offers several major advantages over analog recording. Perhaps the biggest advantage is that digital code is standard and can be read by any medium, while the analog code is different for each medium. This standard digital code allows for ease of making copies of a message and accessing those copies on many different kinds of platforms (your MP3 player, computer, smartphone, car radio, home television, etc.). Another big advantage is that the digital code can be compressed so that all the music on an album can be put on a CD, which is much smaller than the old vinyl disks. Advances in compression technologies have now made it possible to store thousands of albums on a device the size of your thumb. Because of these advantages, all of the mass media have been switching over from analog to digital means of recording, storing, transmitting, and retrieving their messages.

While digitization of messages has been the major technological development leading to convergence, there have also been several other important technological developments that have helped this trend. One of these is the switching from copper wire to fiber optics in the sending of signals to televisions and computers. With the combination of compression of digitized information and fiber optics, both the amount of information and its speed have been increased thousands of times over the past few decades. Now with the availability of Wi-Fi and Bluetooth technologies, even greater amounts of information can move around at faster speeds. This has led to the availability of two-way communication. Now computer users can both upload and download enormous files—like huge software programs and videos—in a matter of seconds. People can engage in texting, instant messaging, and video conferences without wired connections.

Marketing convergence is a powerful influence that has changed the way media programmers regard audiences and how they develop their messages. In the past, media companies used to define themselves by channels; that is, newspapers saw themselves as a print medium only. However, technological changes have forced media businesses to move away from distinctions by channels of distribution and focus much more on the messages and the audiences. In the past, movie studios produced only films for theaters, magazine companies produced only print magazines, and recording companies produced only records. The channel limited their distribution and kept them in a box where they competed only with other like companies in the same box. But now media companies think outside the box (previously limited by their channel of transmission) and have broadened their marketing by thinking about all the ways they can distribute their messages across as many channels as possible.

With technological convergence, channels are much less important than are audience

Karwai Tang/Wireimage/Getty

Director Sam Taylor-Johnson (far left) and author E. L. James (far right) accompany actors Jamie Dornan and Dakota Johnson, who helped bring the popular book series *Fifty Shades of Grey* to life on the big screen.

needs and messages. Now mass media companies think first about the needs of different niche audiences, then develop messages to satisfy those audience needs. They translate that message into as many forms as possible to attract and hold that niche audience (film, TV, websites accessed through computers, notebooks, cell phones, etc.). This procedure has two major advantages. One advantage is that a single message can generate many streams of revenue, so once the media company pays to have the message produced, it can collect revenues several times. The second advantage is that when the message appears in one channel, it stimulates audience members to expose themselves to the message in other channels. For example, people who read the *Harry Potter* books are stimulated to see

Harry Potter movies. They want to read about the actors in those movies on fan websites and in magazines and newspapers.

This trend toward convergence also has changed the way media companies view audiences. In the past, the big media companies would try to attract the largest audiences possible. In order to do this, they would design their messages so they appealed to everyone without offending anyone with language or with certain themes that a part of the general audience might find distasteful. Thus they adopted the programming principle of the **lowest common denominator** (LCD). Programming has now shifted to what is called **long tail marketing**. To understand what a long tail is, think of the bell curve, which is referred to as a normal distribution by statisticians and college professors who "grade on the curve." On any characteristic (height, weight, IQ, scores on tests, etc.), people are arranged in a distribution that ranges from lowest to highest, and most people cluster in the middle of the distribution. Let's take height, for instance. Adult males can range from under 4 feet tall to over 7 feet tall, which is a range of about 40 inches. Within this overall range, about two thirds of adult males are clustered in the middle 5 inches (between 5 foot 7 inches and 6 feet), which forms the fat part of the curve. On either side of this fat part are fewer people who are either shorter or taller than the majority; these small areas on either side of the fat part are the tails. The tails are rather short on both sides of the fat part of the height distribution—there are almost no adult males who are taller than 7 feet or shorter than 4 feet. However, when it comes to personal interests like preferences for music or entertainment, the fat part of the distribution is not so fat; that is, there are fewer people who share the same preferences. For example, the highest rated television series draws less than 3% of the U.S. population. Does this mean that people are watching less TV? No, to the contrary, people are spending more time watching TV but they are spread out over hundreds of viewing options, each with a small audience. That is, we are spread out over a very long tail of different preferences satisfied by many different viewing options. Long tail marketing refers to finding out what the special needs are for each of the many small niche audiences that form the long tail, then developing the kind of content to attract that niche audience.

Long tail marketing is now a viable marketing strategy given the trends discussed above. Huge media conglomerates have deep pockets and can afford to pay for the research necessary to discover these new niche interests then accept the risk of developing new messages. The Internet allows for more experimentation and creativity. To illustrate, old-time brick-and-mortar book stores had limited shelf space, so they had to be selective in choosing which books to stock. But Amazon is web based, so it can market all books and thus has something to offer to every niche market—no matter how tiny—throughout the entire long tail of interests. This means that Amazon does not need to focus only on best-selling books (books ranked in the top 10 of sales). Now Amazon sells over 300,000 book titles a year, and the average book sells only 250 copies a year or less than 3,000 over the course of its lifetime (Ranson, 2017). Therefore, it is more typical for Amazon to generate sales of 1 million copies by selling 250 copies each of 4,000 different books than by trying to sell 1 million copies of a single book. That is long tail marketing.

Convergence is not just a technological or marketing force; it also has profoundly changed the psychology of the audience (Jenkins, 2006). **Psychological convergence** refers to changes in people's perceptions about barriers that previously existed that are now breaking down or totally eliminated due to recent changes in the media. These changes have served to help people see things in a different way and have provided them with tools to act on those changes in perception. One of these changes in perception concerns geography; that is, geographical barriers are no longer important. With e-mail, instant messaging, social networking websites, and mobile phones, people can stay in close contact psychologically with friends and colleagues even when those people are not physically present. There has also been the breaking down of sociological barriers. With newer media platforms, a person can cross all those barriers to make contact with anyone, regardless of social class, occupation, ethnicity, or age. With the removal of these geographical and sociological barriers, people have redefined their social spheres.

iStock/Fakhri-sa

Marketing convergence gives media businesses the opportunity to send their messages through many different channels.

Convergence has changed the way people think about the media and use them. That is, digitization has allowed people to access messages from various platforms and merge those into their own messages. The interactive features of many platforms have allowed users to bring together all kinds of previously unacquainted people into a single network of friends or professional colleagues. Thus there is a convergence of people's individual needs with the available ways to satisfy those needs. People are more active now and do not have to wait for media companies to recognize their needs; instead they can assemble their own messages as their needs arise. People do not think of themselves only as consumers of the media but also as essential contributors.

Special Case of the Computer Industry

Now the computer medium is moving into dominance. This industry is very dynamic as it grows and changes each year. The media businesses in this industry can be organized into three categories. One category includes those businesses that have been primarily the developers of hardware and software that they have sold to relatively large audiences. A second group includes conglomerates that have acquired many media companies over the years and now market messages across many different channels. This segment includes huge media conglomerates like The Walt Disney Company and WarnerMedia. These are examined in more detail in Issue 1 ("Ownership of Mass Media Businesses") later in this book. The third group includes companies that provide Internet-based services, such as Facebook (see Timeline 6.1) and YouTube (see Timeline 6.2).

Profile of Mass Media Workforce

While the number of media businesses has remained relatively stable over the past decade, there have been significant changes across sectors within the overall media

TIMELINE 6.1
Profile of Facebook

2000

2004: Facebook was launched by Mark Zuckerberg and his roommate Eduardo Saverin while they were undergraduates at Harvard University. The website's membership was initially limited to Harvard students but was expanded to other colleges in the Boston area, the Ivy League, and Stanford University. It later expanded further to include any university student.

2005: Facebook was a much smaller website than MySpace, with just 10 million monthly visitors compared with 24 million for MySpace. But Facebook grew quickly as it opened up membership to high school students.

2005: Facebook continued to grow by adding several new features such as the News Feed, which provided members with updates about their friends' activities.

2005

2006: Facebook opened it membership to anyone at least 13 years old with a valid e-mail address.

2007: Facebook released a guidebook that enabled software developers to write programs called widgets (small slide shows) that could run on Facebook's website. This allowed widget developers to use Facebook as a platform to make money through selling advertising on their own Facebook pages. MySpace prohibited third parties from advertising, thus controlling all the advertising themselves. By July, developers had built more than 2,000 widgets for Facebook.

2007: Microsoft bought a 1.6% stake in Facebook for $240 million.

2009: Facebook surpassed 250 million active users worldwide, making it bigger than MySpace. It employed 700 people and generated over $300 million a year.

2010: Facebook invited users to become beta testers for new features.

2010

2011: Facebook became the largest online photo host with its photo aggregator Pixable. Facebook was adding 20 million new users a month and had signed up 700 million users worldwide, including 150 million users in the United States. Also, 50% of those Facebook users were found to log in every day. One third of Facebook users (350 million) were regularly accessing the platform using mobile phones.

2011: Facebook settled charges brought by the U.S. Federal Trade Commission that Facebook was engaging in deceptive practices concerning users' privacy.

2012: Yahoo sued Facebook for infringing on 10 of its patents covering advertising, privacy controls, and social networking.

2012: Facebook went public; that is, it began selling shares on the NASDAQ with a valuation of $104 billion. At the same time, it created an App Center, a store that sold applications that operate on the Facebook site, and offered 500 apps that were mostly games.

2015

2014: After 10 years of operation, Facebook had over 1.2 billion active users worldwide, with 1 billion using mobile devices to access their accounts.

2015: Facebook added a "dislike" button, then several months later also added buttons for "love," "ha-ha," "wow," "sad," and "angry."

2015: Facebook announced it would no longer allow fake news publishers to use its ad-selling services.

2017: Facebook rolled out a Related Articles feature providing links to fact-checking sites such as Snopes and PolitiFact. Facebook had 2.13 billion monthly active users around the world and employed over 25,000 people.

2018: Zuckerberg testifies in Congressional hearings about how Facebook protects (or fails to protect) users' privacy.

2020

2018: More than two thirds of U.S. adults are regular users of Facebook, with three quarters of users accessing the site at least once each day. Also, 45% say they get their news from Facebook, which makes it by far the most used news source.

Sources: Angwin (2009), CNN Library (2018), Facebook (n.d.), Gramlich (2018b), Olivarez-Giles (2011), and "The New Tech Bubble" (2011).

TIMELINE 6.2
Profile of YouTube

2005

2005: Three former PayPal employees created YouTube as a video-sharing website on which users can upload and share videos. Unregistered users can watch the videos, while registered users are permitted to upload an unlimited number of videos. The first YouTube video uploaded was entitled "Me at the Zoo," which showed one of the founders, Jawed Karim, at San Diego Zoo.

2005: The site was opened to the public. It used Adobe Flash Video technology to display a wide variety of user-generated video content, including movie clips, TV clips, and music videos, as well as amateur content such as video blogging and short original videos.

2006: More than 65,000 new videos were being uploaded every day, and the site was receiving 100 million video views per day.

2006: YouTube was bought by Google Inc. for $1.65 billion.

2007: YouTube was consuming as much bandwidth as the entire Internet did in 2000.

2008: YouTube's bandwidth costs were estimated at approximately $1 million a day.

2008: Annual revenue had increased to $200 million due to advertising sales.

2008: YouTube reached an agreement with MGM, Lions Gate Entertainment, and CBS, which allowed the companies to post full-length films and television shows on the site, accompanied by advertisements.

2010

2009: YouTube was the dominant provider of online video in the United States, with a market share of around 43% as 2 billion videos were being viewed on YouTube per day. About 20 hours of new videos were being uploaded to the site every minute, and three quarters of the material was coming from outside the United States.

2011: YouTube had 500 million monthly viewers with more than 3 billion videos being viewed each day. Users were uploading 48 hours of videos every minute; more video was being uploaded to YouTube in a 60-day period than the three major U.S. networks had created in 60 years.

2015

2015: YouTube was now in 61 countries, with 80% of its traffic coming from outside the United States. It had over 1 billion unique viewers, with more than 6 billion videos being viewed each day. Users were uploading more than 100 hours of video every minute.

2017: The youngest YouTube star was 6-year-old Ryan ToysReview, who made $11 million from his YouTube site.

2018: YouTube has local versions in more than 88 countries and can be navigated in 76 different languages. The site has 1.3 billion regular users with almost 5 billion videos being watched every day; 200 hours of video are being uploaded every minute.

Sources:
Chmielewski (2011), Danny (2018), and YouTube (2018).

2020

industry. Table 6.2 shows that the print sector has lost almost one quarter of its businesses and that the broadcasting sector has also lost a large percentage of its businesses. During that same period of time, the number of businesses in the Internet sector has more than doubled. This shift in businesses across media sectors illustrates the strong influence of the rise of the digital media over the last decade.

When we move beyond counting the number of businesses in the media sectors and try to count the number of people by media occupations, the counting gets challenging because the traditional job titles have been losing their value as a way to identify what people do in occupations. For example, Table 6.3 shows that in 2011, there were 275,200 people categorized as working at advertising jobs, which has typically referred to people who were working full-time in either an advertising agency or an advertising department within a company (e.g., Proctor & Gamble, General Motors) doing traditional tasks of message design and placement in traditional media. While these types of jobs still exist, there are many other jobs that could be considered advertising but maybe not. For example, let's say you own a local restaurant and hire several people to engage in text messaging with customers who have posted ratings of your restaurant on Yelp and other sites where customers can rate businesses. While these employees spend their time designing and sending messages to your target audience in order to influence them to develop a more positive attitude about your restaurant and to eat there more, should these employees be considered as working in the advertising sector? Or should they be considered as being an author/writer or actor (if they are posing as fellow customers of your restaurant)? As another illustration of this problem with job classification, let's say you start your own blog and each day upload words you wrote, pictures you shot, and video you edited of you singing songs. Are you a producer, an editor, a sound engineer, an author, a photographer, or a singer? Although you work at all of these jobs, should you be counted as being employed in each of these job categories? If so, should we also count all the millions of people who upload videos to YouTube as

TABLE 6.2 ■ Changes in Number of Establishments Across Media Industries			
Mass Medium	**Number of Establishments**		
	2007	**2018**	**% Change**
Print (newspapers, periodicals, books)	22,683	17,256	−23.9%
Motion picture and video	20,164	21,936	+8.3%
Broadcasting	10,188	8,311	−18.4%
Software publishers	8,275	10,230	+23.6%
Internet	3,446	8,065	+134.0%
Sound recording	3,727	3,561	−4.5%
Totals	**68,483**	**69,259**	**+1.1%**

Source: Statista (2018b).

TABLE 6.3 ■ Media-Related Occupations, Growth Rates, and Median Salaries			
Occupation	Number of People	Growth Rate	Median Salary
Computer app development	514,800	21%	$85,430
Producers and directors	98,600	11%	$64,430
Advertising	275,200	24%	$51,280
Editors (film and video)	25,500	11%	$50,560
Editors (print)	129,600	12%	$49,990
Camera operators	26,300	11%	$41,670
Sound engineers	114,600	8%	$38,050
Authors and writers	151,700	8%	$35,010
Journalists	138,600	–6%	$34,850
Photographers	152,000	12%	$29,440
Musicians and singers	186,400	8%	$21.24/hour
Actors	56,500	11%	$16.59/hour

Source: Bureau of Labor Statistics (2015).

videographers, the tens of millions of people who post pictures on the web as photographers, and the hundreds of millions of people who e-mail everyday as writers? If we do count all these people as media workers, then most people would get counted multiple times, which would inflate the employment totals way beyond the total work force, and this would render the categorization of people into occupations meaningless.

The most important thing to understand about employment in the media industries is that there are about 2 million people working full-time in some traditional job of designing and distributing media messages (news, entertainment, and advertising) for an established media company. But almost everyone else in the total population is also continually designing and distributing their own messages through the media using the same skills (albeit at a much wider range of performance) as the full-time professionals. So while these occupational numbers are useful in giving you some sense of the relative sizes of workforces, they need to be regarded with skepticism.

iStock/andresr

Today, more than half of U.S. journalists are younger than 35.

When looking at the total labor force in this country, we can see a trend toward more and more women becoming employed outside the home. A report by the *Boston Globe* found that among the 151,436,000 people 16 years of age and older working in the United States, 46.9% were women (Rocheleau, 2017). When this total figure is broken down into occupational sectors, we can see a wide range of percentages of women across those sectors (see Table 6.4)

TABLE 6.4 ■ Media-Related Occupations by Gender		
Occupation Category	Percentage of Women	Total Number of People Employed
Writers and authors	62.8%	229,000
Public relations specialists	58.9%	121,000
Advertising and promotions managers	56.5%	67,000
Technical writers	55.7%	61,000
Market research analysts and marketing specialists	55.0%	302,000
Editors	52.4%	167,000
Photographers	47.7%	205,000
Advertising sales agents	45.5%	222,000
Musicians and singers	40.4%	192,000
Web developers	33.6%	205,000
Computer and information systems managers	25.5%	597,000
Computer hardware engineers	24.7%	69,000
Computer programmers	22.6%	466,000
Information security analysts	21.8%	89,000
Television, video, and motion picture camera operators and editors	21.4%	54,000
Announcers	20.9%	59,000
Software developers, applications and systems software	20.0%	1,483,000
Network and computer systems administrators	17.1%	218,000
Broadcast and sound engineering technicians and radio operators	15.2%	111,000
Computer network architects	9.7%	115,000

Source: Adapted from Rocheleau (2017).

A popular profession within the media industries is journalism. In this journalistic community, there are about 67,000 reporters and correspondents, 23,000 writers and editors, and 67,000 radio and television announcers and newscasters. Most are male. The Women's Media Center continually monitors the visibility of women in the media. Their 2017 report showed that only about one quarter of all broadcast news was being reported by women; 38.1% of print news and 64.1% of online news were being reported by women (Women's Media Center, 2017).

The data presented in this section are general figures to give you a broad idea about the media workforce. These patterns might not hold in any one particular media industry or business. Check this out for yourself by doing Exercise 6.2.

SUMMARY

The development of the media industries generally moves from the innovation stage to growth, peak, decline, and then adaptation. Remembering this pattern will help you understand how the media industries start, how they grow, and where they are today.

Historically, the mass media industries have been defined by their channels of distributing messages—book, newspaper, magazine, film, recording, radio, broadcast television, cable television, and computer. But over the past few decades, the mass media industries have undergone profound changes due to the forces of convergence—technological, marketing, and psychological. These forces of convergence have eroded the old channel distinctions and have shifted the focus away from the characteristics of distribution and onto the needs for media messages in distinct niches of audiences.

Further Reading

Drapes, M. (2009). *Vault guide to the top media & entertainment employers*. New York, NY: Vault Inc. (137 pages, including appendices)

This guidebook gives practical advice about getting hired in the media industries, particularly film, magazines, and book publishing. There is also a section that describes in detail what industry people do in their day-to-day jobs, whether on the business or creative side of the industries.

Drapes, M. R., & Lichtenberg, N. R. (2008). *Vault guide to the top media & entertainment employers*. New York, NY: Vault.com, Inc. (326 pages)

This book provides profiles of 41 large companies covering all facets of the mass media. While there is practical information about how to go about getting a job in these companies, the profiles provide much more detail about the companies themselves—how they are organized and how they developed over time.

Fellow, A. R. (2012). *American media history* (3rd ed.). Boston, MA: Wadsworth/Cengage. (438 pages with endnotes and index)

If you are interested in learning more about how the mass media developed in America, this book

(Continued)

(Continued)

is a good source. Each of its 14 chapters focuses on the development of the various media from the colonial years to the present. The book presents brief biographies of important media figures as it tells the story of the men and women whose inventions, ideas, and struggles helped shape the nation and its media system.

Neuman, W. R. (Ed.). (2010). *Media, technology, and society: Theories of media evolution.* Ann Arbor: University of Michigan Press. (231 pages with index)

This edited volume consists of 10 chapters written by various scholars. Seven chapters trace the development of a different mass medium—newspapers, telephone, film, radio, television, cable, and the Internet. The remaining three chapters focus on theories of media evolution, privacy and security policy, and the future of ownership.

Seguin, J., & Culver, S. H. (2012). *Media career guide: Preparing for jobs in the 21st century* (6th ed.). Boston, MA: Bedford/St. Martin's. (122 pages with index)

This is a practical guide to help college students prepare for a career in any facet of the mass media industries. Its seven chapters offer a lot of practical advice about how to develop a job search strategy; how to get an internship and maximize that experience; and how to write cover letters, resumes, and thank-you notes.

Keeping Up to Date

Bureau of Labor Statistics (https://www.bls.gov/ooh/management/advertising-promotions-and-marketing-managers.htm)

This federal government agency reports information on all kinds of occupations in the United States, including salaries, duties, and required educational training. This link directs you to the *Occupational Outlook Handbook* page for advertising, promotions, and marketing managers.

Statistical Abstract of the United States (https://www.census.gov/library/publications/time-series/statistical_abstracts.html)

The Department of Commerce previously released a new statistical abstract every year, ending with the 2012 edition. For updates on this material in this chapter, go to the section on Information and Communication.

Vault.com (http://www.vault.com)

This website provides useful information about various industries; particularly relevant to media literacy are the industries of publishing, newspapers, Internet and new media, music, broadcast and cable television, advertising, and public relations.

Zap2It (http://www.zap2it.com/)

This website provides ratings of television shows and data on the popularity of various Hollywood movies.

EXERCISE 6.1
SPECULATE ABOUT THE FUTURE OF THE COMPUTER/INTERNET INDUSTRY

This exercise gives you a chance to use what you have learned so far about how the media industries develop over time and what the current state is.

5-Year Vision

Can you imagine the media world 5 years from now? What will the computer/Internet industry be like? Let your speculation be guided by the following questions:

1. How long do you think it will take for the computer/Internet industry to reach its peak?

2. When the computer/Internet industry reaches its peak, how will the remaining media industries adapt in order to survive and stay successful?

3. Do you think any of the other media industries will collapse and all those companies go out of business? Which ones and why?

20-Year Vision

Try to imagine what the computer/Internet industry will be like 20 years from now. Let your speculation be guided by the following questions:

1. Will the computer/Internet industry still be at its peak?

2. Which of the other media industries will still be around by then?

3. Can you imagine what the next new media industry will be? If so, in what stage will that new industry be 20 years from now?

EXERCISE 6.2
EXAMINING INDIVIDUAL MEDIA BUSINESSES FOR WORKFORCE PATTERNS

I. Select a media company to analyze.

If you are thinking about pursuing a career in the media, select a company that you might like to work for and go to that company's website. Search the website to find answers to the following questions.

1. How many people work at this company?

2. How are the employees organized?

    By different levels (management, mid-level, low-level clerks)

    By departments (for different functions: production, sales, etc.)

3. How many employees are women and how many are men?

(Continued)

(Continued)

4. Are there gender differences across levels or departments?

5. Can you find any recruiting information?

   Profiles of the kinds of employees who work there

   Listings for actual jobs for which they are soliciting applications

II. Select a second media company to analyze.

   Find a second company in the same industry and same location if possible. If you selected a radio station in Part I, then try to find a second radio station in the same market to analyze in this part.

   Answer the same five questions as above.

III. Select a third media company to analyze.

   Find a third company in a different industry. If you selected radio stations in Parts I and II, then try to find a TV station, newspaper, magazine, recording studio, or computer/Internet company to analyze in this part.

   Answer the same five questions as above.

IV. Look for patterns.

   1. Compare and contrast the two companies you analyzed in Parts I and II.

      A. How were the two companies the same as far as workforce patterns?

      B. How were the two companies different as far as workforce patterns?

      C. Did the patterns you found match the general patterns presented in the text?

      D. Based on your analysis, which company would you prefer to work for and why?

   2. Compare and contrast the companies across the two industries you analyzed.

      A. How were the two industries the same as far as workforce patterns?

      B. How were the two industries different as far as workforce patterns?

      C. Did the patterns you found match the general patterns presented in the text?

      D. Based on your analysis, which industry would you prefer to work for and why?

A company's website might not present all the information you need to answer the complete set of questions in this exercise. Be creative in looking for other sources of information. Do a search of business periodicals (such as the *Wall Street Journal*, *Money Magazine*, *Fortune*, etc.). Look for blogs. Search for books; most large media companies have at least one book written about them.

MARVEL

7

ECONOMIC PERSPECTIVE

Key Idea: The businesses in the media industries are in strong competition with each other to acquire limited resources, play the high-risk game of appealing to audiences, and achieve a maximum profit.

Actors Chris Evans and Jeremy Renner ring the NYSE opening bell in celebration of Marvel's *Captain America: Civil War* at the New York Stock Exchange on May 3, 2016.

The other day I was talking to my neighbor Blaine, who had just graduated from college with a degree in economics. He was telling me how important it was to maximize resources in one's personal life. "When it comes to the mass media, I try to keep my costs down. That's why I go to the library and borrow books rather than buy them," he told me. "I also read newspapers and magazines there for free."

"What if you want a book that someone else has checked out or what if someone else is reading the newspaper when you want to read it?"

"Then I wait." He switched the subject, "I check out movies and documentaries then take them home and copy them for free."

"But don't you have to buy blank DVDs and flash drives to store your copies?"

"Okay, it's not completely free, but it's a lot less expensive than buying all that stuff. I also make copies of music for my MP3 player for free. I now have 10,000 songs in my music library."

"Doesn't that take a lot of time to make all those copies and keep organizing your library?"

"Yes, it takes some time but it's a hobby."

"How much time do you spend watching all these videos?"

"That's the beauty of having a large film library. I have so many choices that if one doesn't grab my interest right away, I just start watching another one until I find one I like. There are so many bad movies these days that you need a large library to find one that's any good."

"And your music? How much time do you spend listening to all that music?"

"Not as much as I would like. There's just not enough time in the day!" He thought for a minute then added, "Also, after a while all the new songs sound so derivative of other songs; they all begin to sound alike."

"Blaine, it sounds to me that you are very careful about not spending much money on the media but you do spend an awful lot of time. And it also seems that you don't get much in return for this investment of time."

"How can you say that? I have amassed a huge library of movies and songs."

"But what's the point of having acquired all those messages if you don't enjoy them much? The real payoff is personal enjoyment. It doesn't seem to me that your huge investment of time has much payoff."

The economic perspective focuses on resources. When we think of our personal resources we usually focus on money. Before you read on, take a few minutes to complete Exercise 7.1 to estimate how much money you typically spend on the media.

As a consumer of media messages, it is also important to think of time, which can be an even more valuable resource than money. How much time do you spend with the media? To see if your perception of time with the media is accurate, do Exercise 7.2.

The mass media are very successful each year at getting us to give them large amounts of our money and time in exchange for our exposures to a wide range of media messages. Now that you have a better idea of how much of your resources you are spending on the media, the material in this chapter might make more sense to you. As you read through the following sections, keep asking yourself: How well am I playing the economic game?

THE MEDIA GAME OF ECONOMICS

We play a game of economics each and every day; we cannot avoid playing. At the end of each day, we have spent our full 24 hours. What have you received back from this expenditure of time? Do you feel you are better off having traded away all that time? Or do you feel that your time has been wasted and that you have received little in exchange for those 24 hours?

iStock/STILLFX

How much time and money do you spend on media each year? Turn to the exercises at the end of the chapter to find out.

The Players

Because we spend so much time with the media, it is important to examine this part of the overall economic game. Within the media part of the game, there are four types of players: (a) you the consumer, (b) the advertisers, (c) the media companies, and (d) the employees of media companies. Each type of player brings a different set of resources to the game.

We are the consumers, and our resources include not only our money but, even more importantly, our time and our attention. We seek to exchange our money and time for entertainment and information. We as consumers are the largest group, with almost 330 million people in this country and over 7 billion people worldwide. We have the greatest amount of resources. If we pulled out of the game entirely, the game would collapse. However, our resources are dispersed over so many people that no one individual feels he or she has that much power in playing the game. This feeling is a mistake. While no one individual has a significant amount of power to change the overall game, each of us has the power to alter the game significantly for ourselves. If we play the game well, we continually increase the value of the entertainment and information we get in return for our time and money. But playing the game well requires that we keep track of our resources as well as our changing needs and that we negotiate better exchanges of resources. If we don't play the game well, we will make poor economic exchanges and continually get short changed on our expenditures of time and money.

The advertisers are a second group of players. Advertisers bring money to the game. They negotiate an exchange of their money for time and space in the media in order to expose their ads to their target audiences. Advertisers are very sophisticated in their economic exchanges, because they want to get access to their target audiences for the lowest cost possible. For example, sellers of tennis rackets want to get their ad messages in front of as many people who play tennis as possible, but they do not want to pay a lot of money to get access to a large audience that might also include toddlers, invalids, and people who hate tennis. So they look for media vehicles (such as particular sports TV shows, Internet sites, and magazines) that have constructed an audience of only tennis players and negotiate a good ad price to get access to that smaller, niche audience.

The media companies are the third group of players. These businesses bring money, messages, and audiences to the game as they compete in three different markets simultaneously. First, each media business competes in the talent market to try to get the best writers, journalists, actors, directors, musicians, website designers, and so on under contract to them. They try to keep these personnel costs low, but because the top talent is in short supply, their expenses escalate each year. Second, media businesses compete in the audience market; that is, they present the messages produced by their talented employees in such a way to attract the greatest number of people within certain types of audiences. In the media industries of magazines, newspapers, cable, and Internet, those companies sell subscriptions, so they want to maximize their revenue by attracting as many subscribers as possible. Media companies also sell messages in the form of books, recordings (music and movies), and theater tickets. Third, media companies compete in the advertising market. When media companies have constructed quality niche audiences, they have something valuable to offer advertisers who want to get their messages in front of particular types of consumers.

The media employees comprise the fourth group of players. Employees bring their time, skills, and **talent** to the game. Their goal is to increase the pay and benefits they receive for each hour worked. In the media, we make a distinction between **below-the-line employees** and **above-the-line employees**. Below-the-line employees are typically the crafts and clerical people who apply fairly common skills in the performance of their jobs. These skills can be learned by many people and can be improved with practice. That is, with the proper training and motivation, most people could perform well in most

below-the line jobs, such as a lighting techni-
cian, sound boom operator, copy editor, ticket
taker, cable installer, secretary, or receptionist.
There is a very large number of people who
potentially could do these jobs, so the supply
(people wanting these jobs) is much larger than
the demand (number of these jobs available).
Therefore, the payments to the people who
perform these jobs is relatively low.

The above-the-line employees are the creative types, and this requires talent much more
than training or effort, although training and
effort are also important. These above-the-line
people are the writers, producers, directors,
photographers, actors, singers, web designers, choreographers, and so on. We typically
regard talent as being artistic ability, but for the mass media industries, talent is regarded
more as the ability to attract large audiences then make them want to return for repeated
exposures. Sometimes, the two conceptualizations of talent are the same, but more often
the two are very different. For example, the singing ability of Lady Gaga, Miley Cyrus,
and Justin Bieber, although good, cannot alone account for their huge popularity; that
is, these recording artists have some inexplicable ability to attract large audiences that
cannot be explained solely by the artistic quality of their singing ability. Also, there are
many television stars who are not particularly good actors, yet they are in high demand
by television producers because these actors can attract large audiences.

Kevin Mazur/WireImage/Getty Images

Taylor Swift
accepts an
award at the
2018 Billboard
Music Awards in
Las Vegas. Her
contribution as
an above-the-line
talent is due not
only to her singing
talent but also to
her ability to draw
large audiences.

COMPARE & CONTRAST
BELOW-THE-LINE COSTS AND ABOVE-THE-LINE COSTS

Compare: Below-the-line costs and above-the-
line costs are *the same* in the following ways:

- Both are expenses that media companies
  pay to people as a necessary cost of doing
  business in a mass medium industry.

- Both are payments made to individuals to
  compensate them for their skills and efforts.

Contrast: Below-the-line costs and above-the-
line costs are *different* in the following ways:

- Below-the-line costs are payments to
  people whose skills are widespread in

the general population, so there are
many people who could do their jobs with
a relatively small amount of training.
Because there is a large supply of these
people, payments are relatively low.

- Above-the-line costs are payments to
  people whose skills are rare; these skills
  are largely based on talent and while
  training can improve upon that talent,
  training alone cannot create that special
  talent. Because there is a very small
  supply of these people, payments are
  relatively high.

Above-the-line people are paid a lot more than below-the-line people (at least twice as much on average), and the difference in wages is growing. Why are above-the-line people paid so much more? The reason is because this kind of talent is in short supply. For example, many people can sing and play musical instruments well, but very few musicians can attract enough fans who will pay to download their recordings in large numbers. The celebrities who can attract the most attention are paid the most (see Table 7.1).

TABLE 7.1 ■ Annual Income in 2017 of Highly Paid Media Celebrities		
2017 Income in Millions ($)	Person	Profession
130	Sean Combs	Musician
105	Beyoncé Knowles	Musician
95	J.K. Rowling	Novelist
94	Drake	Musician
90	Howard Stern	Radio personality
88	Coldplay	Musicians
87	James Patterson	Novelist
84	Guns N' Roses	Musicians
67	Rush Limbaugh	Radio personality
84	Justin Bieber	Musician
79	Dr. Phil McGraw	Personality
77	Ellen DeGeneres	TV personality
75	Bruce Springsteen	Musician
69	Adele	Musician
69	Jerry Seinfeld	Comedian
68	Mark Wahlberg	Actor
67	Metallica	Musicians
65	Dwayne Johnson	Actor
60	Garth Brooks	Musician
60	Elton John	Musician
60	Gordon Ramsay	TV personality
58	Ryan Seacrest	Radio and TV personality
57	Chris Rock	Comedian
54	Paul McCartney	Musician
52	Louis C.K.	Comedian

Source: Forbes (2018a).

Another elite strata of people in the media industries are the top executives who run the largest media companies (see Table 7.2). It tasks an enormous degree of managerial talent to run such large companies in such a risky industry. Notice the figures in the column labeled "Ratio," which indicate how many times more these executives are compensated compared to the median pay of their employees. For example, Leslie Moonves is the top executive at CBS, where the median pay for an employee is $116,470. This means that the Board of Directors at CBS in 2017 thought that Moonves was 595 times as valuable to the company compared to the average employee.

The Goal

For all four types of players, the general goal is to maximize the value of the exchange for themselves. Those who play the game well become **net winners**; that is, they have negotiated resource exchanges so well that their payoffs are of greater value than their costs. Because the resource exchange game is zero sum, the other players who give up resources more valuable than they receive in return are the **net losers**.

Determining value is computed in very different ways for different players. For the media businesses and advertisers, value can be computed quantitatively in numbers of dollars. These businesses compare the dollars they have to spend to create messages and

TABLE 7.2 ■	2017 Compensation of Top Executives of the Largest Media Companies		
Name	Pay ($, in Millions)	Ratio	Company, Job
Leslie Moonves	69.3	595	CBS, president and CEO
Jeff Bewkes	49.0	651	Time Warner, chairman and CEO
David Zaslav	42.2	522	Discovery Communications, president and CEO
Bob Iger	36.3	NA	The Walt Disney Company, chairman and CEO
Jon Feltheimer	35.3	NA	Lionsgate, CEO
Brian Roberts	32.5	458	Comcast Corporation, chairman and CEO
Rupert Murdoch	29.3	NA	21st Century Fox, executive chairman
Reed Hastings	24.4	133	Netflix, chairman and CEO
Bob Bakish	20.3	NA	Viacom, CEO

Pay figures include total compensation including base salary and bonuses paid in 2017. Ratio is the comparison of the executive's salary to the median pay of employees in that company. NA indicates data not available.

Source: Lang and Lieberman (2018).

attract audiences (expenses) to the dollars that those exposures generate (revenue). When they keep expenses lower than revenues, they generate a profit. The larger the profit they generate each year, the more of a net winner they are.

For consumers, our media costs are relatively easy to track because they are quantitative. Our financial costs are tracked in dollars and our other huge cost of time can be tracked in hours, which then can be translated into dollar amounts. But our payoffs (what we get in return for paying the costs) are very difficult to track quantitatively. Typically we assess these payoffs intuitively; that is, as long as we are feeling some satisfaction with a media exposure, we typically allow ourselves to continue in that exposure instead of asking the harder question about whether the exposure is delivering *enough* satisfaction to warrant the continuing expenditures of our resources. This process results in us getting by with less satisfaction than we would have achieved had we consciously and continuously asked for more in return.

The Rules

The most central rule of this economic game is that to play, you must have resources and a willingness to exchange them for other resources. If you lack either the resources or the willingness to engage in exchanges, you are irrelevant to the game.

All the other rules are made up by players as they negotiate. These rules are made up in order to maintain a sense of fairness in the exchange. Players who begin to perceive the game as unfair will cease to trust the other players and will stop playing; this diminishes the game. For the game to remain viable, it must attract huge numbers of players who willingly exchange their resources every day.

Although there are few rules, many characteristics guide the play of the game. These characteristics are illuminated in the next section.

CHARACTERISTICS OF THE GAME

To understand more about how the economic game is played with the mass media, you need to understand four characteristics of that game. These characteristics are as follows: the importance of valuing resources well, the complex interdependency among players, digital convergence, and the nature of competition. An understanding of this set of principles will help you comprehend how the negotiation for resources takes place.

Importance of Valuing Resources Well

The key to being successful in negotiations is to value resources accurately. If one player can do this and the second player cannot, the second player is at a real disadvantage. There are two considerations that go into resource valuation, and both of these require considerable skill to do well. One factor in valuing one's resources is to consider supply and demand. This factor favors the consumer because media companies supply a great many messages of all kinds constantly and media companies are always trying to increase demand. Because there is no scarcity of media messages on any conceivable topic, consumers have no motivation to pay more of their resources as a premium for access to scarce messages. A second factor that is important in valuing resources is making an assessment about how well the resource will achieve a particular goal. This factor favors the media businesses when we either have no goal or when we avoid evaluating how well our exposures are meeting our goals. Oftentimes we have no goals for our media exposures; that is, we are just going through exposures to kill time, which means we are trying to give away our time resource for free. And when we do have a goal for exposures (i.e., wanting to be entertained), we are typically willing to accept whatever is easily available.

The more skill people apply in valuing their resources, the more successful they will be in negotiating. For example, let's say you find something in your parents' attic that you think may be valuable. You take it to an antique dealer to sell it. The dealer offers you $60 for it. Should you accept the $60 and sell it to the dealer? If you have no knowledge of antiques and no idea about how rare the piece is, you are operating in the dark. You might think you are savvy and ask for $100, then settle for $80, feeling good that you "got the dealer to raise her price" $20. But maybe the piece is worth $1,000. If you don't have a good operating knowledge about what your resources are worth, you will continually fall into one of two traps. One trap is to *over*-value your resources, and other people will avoid making exchanges with you. The other trap is to *under*-value your resources, in which case you make lots of exchanges, but you continually are shortchanged. When you have little knowledge of the value of your resources, you can only play the game to lose.

Complex Interdependency Among Players

Some exchanges are relatively simple, such as when two people make an exchange and no one else is affected or concerned with that individual exchange. For example, let's say you are an employee of a video game company, and you want a raise in pay and benefits. If you are a receptionist or secretary, most of the negotiating power lies with the company and not with you, because there is a very large supply of people with these skills relative to the demand. The company is likely to offer you compensation not much above the minimum wage. Either you take this offer or you look for work elsewhere.

There are, however, many times when the negotiations are more involved, and this illustrates the **complex interdependence** among the different players in the media economic game. For example, let's say a radio station wants to attract more advertisers, so it cuts the price of its ads by 20% in its highest rated show. Advertisers want to buy those ad times (called avails), so demand for the avails at this station increases. The station, which used to air 15 minutes of ads during an hour, decides to air 20 minutes of ads, thus increasing its supply of avails to meet the increasing demand. The station likes this because even though it has cut its income per ad by 20%, it is now selling 33% more avails, and thus the station has increased its total revenue. But the audience notices this change and becomes upset that there are so many ads and not nearly as much music. Most of the audience switches channels during the ads and never comes back. The station's ratings drop dramatically. Then advertisers become unhappy because it is no bargain to get a 20% discount on ads if the audience they expected to reach is almost gone. Advertisers begin feeling they are wasting their money, so they stop buying those ads.

Three other characteristics make this interrelationship even more complex. First, the situation is highly dynamic and interrelated. When a person at one media company makes a decision, it can often have an impact on other companies in the same industry and perhaps other media industries. Returning to the radio station example above, when advertisers flocked to the station to get the discounted price for the avail, other radio stations (as well as television stations, newspapers, and local magazines) most likely lost advertising revenue. So when the revenues of one vehicle dramatically increase in the short term, the revenues of other competing vehicles are affected and usually go down. The same ripple effect can be seen with expenses of the media companies. For example, if several media companies started paying writers more money, then the better writers would be attracted to those better paying companies, and the other companies would either have to pay more or else make do with lesser talented writers, which would lower the quality of their shows and result in losing audience size and hence lower revenue. When something changes in an industry where all the components are tightly linked, that change ripples outward and affects other players.

A second characteristic that contributes to the complexity is that sometimes decision makers are conflicted because they are experiencing cross-purposes. An example of this is when a decision maker might be a member of more than one group—each with a different economic goal. Let's say you work at a small newspaper and also own half of the newspaper company. As an employee, you might want a raise in salary, but this would increase overall personnel expenses and therefore reduce profits, making your investment less valuable. On a different scale, let's say you work for a large newspaper and own stock in the company that owns the newspaper. A raise in your wages will benefit you a great deal more than a non-raise would benefit shareholders. So your needs as an employee greatly outweigh your needs as an owner.

Third, media vehicles compete in different markets. A market is a segment of the audience to which you offer your product or service. Markets differ in size, with the largest market in the United States being the national one. Only a few vehicles (such as television network prime-time broadcast programs, *USA Today* newspaper, and major Hollywood movies) see themselves competing in a national market. More typically, vehicles carve out a special niche. One way of identifying a niche is by geography, such as the case with newspapers, radio stations, and broadcast television stations. Media vehicles in these industries have their own geographical locale, such as a city or a limited region. Another way of identifying a niche is by audience interest, which is common with magazines, books, and websites. For example, *Surfer* magazine appeals to a very different audience niche than does *Ladies' Home Journal*. College texts are marketed very differently than religious books. A website about repairing motorcycles appeals to a very different audience than a fan website about Taylor Swift.

Clearly, the economics of the mass media industries are complex. The complexity can be traced to the fact that there are many different components, each with its own needs that are most often in conflict with the needs of other components. This requires a constant negotiation process, and as decisions are made, effects ripple out and influence the decisions of others. All parties are strongly interlinked.

Digital Convergence

Recall from Chapter 6 that digital convergence has eroded the characteristics that previously made the various traditional media so different from one another. Now, when a media company creates any kind of a message, that message is stored in digital form that makes it available to distribute in any media channel. This has created many more opportunities to market content simultaneously across all media channels.

The digitization of content has also lowered the barriers to entry for entrepreneurs. All of this recently available technology has made it relatively easy for anyone to create content and disseminate it instantly to people all over the world. Now anyone can create a newspaper or magazine by setting up a blog. Anyone can set up a book publishing company by using a very low-cost platform such as Amazon. Anyone can create their own music through easy-to-use programs like GarageBand and distribute as much music as they want on YouTube or their own blogs. Now the distribution problem has shifted away from getting access to media channels and much more toward identifying niche audiences that would spend their time in exposures to the message.

Nature of Competition

Economists make a distinction between monopolistic industries and competitive industries. In monopolistic industries, one company controls the market; consumers must buy their products from that one company by paying high prices or go without the product. In contrast, competitive industries have many companies producing the same (or very similar) products; in order to be successful in generating sales, these companies continually improve the quality of their products while keeping their prices low enough to be competitive. Thus, competitive markets are regarded as much more favorable to consumers.

Within the media industries, there are few examples of purely monopolistic or purely competitive markets. Instead there is a co-existing of the two, which has been referred to as **monopolistic competition**—*monopolistic* because each firm is large relative to the size of the market for its products and *competition* because firms in an industry compete aggressively for resources. In a monopolistic competitive market, the barriers to entry are relatively low, so many companies can enter the market and compete for audiences; however, only a few companies are enormously skilled at continuously making the right economic exchanges so that they are able to attract the majority of audiences and advertising revenue. While new companies enter the media market all the time, almost all struggle to stay in business. Those new companies that are able to identify a niche audience with an unmet need develop the right kinds of messages to attract those audience members, and then condition those audiences for repeat exposures that will grow stronger. If these newer companies can continue to satisfy the message needs of their niche audience better than the competitors, they grow more powerful even to the point of becoming an extremely powerful company themselves (e.g., Apple, Amazon, Google). But if the smaller companies cannot keep up with the competition, they soon go out of business. "Monopolistic competition occurs when many firms compete by selling 'differentiated' products, meaning products that are similar but not identical to one another" (Taylor, 2012, p. 62). For example, the film industry is dominated by a small number of Hollywood studios. While the action/adventure films that they produce have different titles, actors, settings, and dialogue, they are very similar in many other ways (plot structure, emotions they trigger in the audience, etc.). Likewise, video games all look different from one another on the surface, but the structure of the games themselves as well as the experience of playing them are largely similar across those games.

MEDIA INDUSTRY PERSPECTIVE

Now that you have seen the basic ideas of the economic game with the mass media, let's look at this game in more detail first from the industry's perspective. In this section, I will show you how successful the mass media industries have been in playing this game. Then I will show you the strategies they have developed in order to be so successful.

Overview of Success

Until recently, financial information about the mass media businesses was organized by traditional channels that included television (broadcast and cable), radio, film, recordings, and print (newspapers, magazines, and books). But with the rise of digital technologies, this categorization scheme has lost its ability to organize companies by the types of media messages they market. Almost all of the media messages that are produced and disseminated today could be included in at least two of these traditional categories. For example, the major motion picture studios that defined the film industry have over time become conglomerates that produce and distribute not only films but also television shows, recordings, newspapers, magazines, and books. Now it is common to see the industry referred to as the Media and Entertainment (M&E) industry because of its use of all kinds of media channels to market messages with an emphasis on entertainment, even with news and advertising. The M&E industry comprises businesses that produce and distribute motion pictures, television programs, and commercials, along with streaming content, music and audio recordings, broadcast, radio, book publishing, and video games as well as ancillary services and products.

The M&E industry in the United States now generates over $700 billion a year in revenue, which is expected to reach $804 billion by 2021 (SelectUSA, 2018). This industry is organized into four segments: film, music, books, and video games.

Film Segment

The film segment of the M&E market generates its revenue from audiences buying, renting, or exposing themselves to any kind of motion picture messages regardless of platform (movie theater, TV set, mobile device, etc.). So it includes revenue from box office ticket sales and TV subscriptions to all kinds of video services (cable, video on demand, streaming, downloading, etc.). Annual box office receipts for this segment now exceed $11 billion and home video has reached $108 billion (Nead, 2018).

Music Segment

The U.S. recorded music industry (including concerts and touring) now generates over $18 billion annually. Digital music sales (downloading and streaming) surpassed physical sales (CDs) for the first time in 2014. Streaming music is expected to increase almost 20% to $7.4 billion by 2021, as more consumers switch to buying subscriptions to music services rather than buying one song at a time. The businesses in this segment are also developing a wider array of revenue streams, including marketing their music to satellite radio, restaurants, and airlines for in-flight entertainment (Nead, 2018).

Digital technologies have revolutionized the music industry by creating high-quality, low-cost recording technologies and digital distribution, along with the proliferation of devices to download and listen to music. Future industry growth is likely to come from diversified services, such as packaging consumer experiences around touring and live music as well as bundling music services with other online content services. Also, it is expected that streaming services will continue to grow as they offer more personalized services for consumers (SelectUSA, 2018).

Book Segment

The U.S. book publishing segment, which includes both physical and digital books, is the largest in the world, with annual sales now at $37 billion. It includes three sectors: professional, educational, and consumer publishing. Consumer books cover the largest market share by far, followed by educational and then professional books.

Book publishing is moving strongly into digital formats. For example, online retailer Amazon has opened physical bookstores (for both physical and e-books). In addition to e-readers, which are designed to only display e-books, mobile devices of all kinds are being used to bring entire libraries to users' fingertips. By 2021, digital publishing will account for 45% of all publishing (SelectUSA, 2018).

Video Game Segment

The U.S. video gaming segment generates $23 billion in revenues annually. Today's consumers have access to multiple devices for gaming, including PCs, mobile phones, digital or physical consoles, and tablets. The video game segment is subdivided into three sectors: (1) physical, digital, and online games; (2) mobile apps; and (3) virtual and augmented reality (VR/AR) (SelectUSA, 2018).

The industry is constantly innovating and bringing new applications to market, such as VR and AR games. VR games place users inside the virtual world by using digital technology to replace reality with a complete and realistic, immersive simulation. In contrast, AR overlays virtual objects on the user's real world, augmenting it. Using VR/AR, U.S. developers and scientists are producing cutting-edge solutions in health care, education, online shopping, and entertainment (Nead, 2018).

Media products tend to compete within a realm of familiar features. The morning talk shows *The View* on ABC and *The Talk* on CBS, for instance, share many similarities.

Official White House Photo by Pete Souza. Wikimedia Commons, 28 July 2010.

CBS Photo Archive/CBS/Getty Images

Advertising

Advertising is the engine that drives the growth of the media industries. The cost of doing business in the United States has greatly increased as advertising continually becomes a stronger economic force. In 1900, about $500 million was spent on all forms of advertising. By 1940, it was $2 billion, so it took 40 years to multiply four times. In 1980, it was $60 billion, or a growth of 30 times in those 40 years. Now it is $207 billion (Statista, 2018g). It is important to note that while the overall amount of money spent on advertising each year continues to increase, some segments of the media industry are generating less revenue. Massive growth in the digital segment is driving the overall increase (see Table 7.3).

Why is advertising so important to our economy? Advertising has been the engine for growing the economy. Advertising makes it possible for new goods to enter markets and lets us know immediately that they are available. With more product successes, more and more companies are willing to introduce an even wider range of new products. These companies fuel advertising agencies with money, which is passed through to the media. As the media grow, they offer more information and entertainment to us. More of us spend more time with the media, which creates a greater demand for messages. We are exposed to more ads and are more likely to buy advertised products. Money cycles from us to the advertised products, to the manufacturers of those products, to those companies' advertising agencies, to the media. Advertising drives this cycle faster and faster each year. If we stopped buying advertised products, the cycle would slow down and eventually stop.

Media Strategies

The media industries have developed some general economic strategies over the years that make them successful at playing the economic game and achieving their goals. Three major strategies are illuminated in this section: maximizing profits, constructing audiences, and reducing risk.

TABLE 7.3 ■ Breakdown of Advertising Spending in the United States by Media Segment From 2010 to 2020		
Media Segment	**2010 (%)**	**2020 (%)**
Digital	17.1	44.9
Television	38.4	32.9
Radio	9.9	6.1
Magazines	9.9	5.6
Newspapers	14.8	5.5
Other	9.8	5.0

Source: Statista (2018g).

Maximizing Profits

Almost all mass media are profit-oriented enterprises. As businesses, they are run to make as large a **profit** as possible. Remember that profit is the payoff or reward for doing business. Profits increase when companies increase revenue while driving down expenses.

Increasing Revenue. A major strategy employed by media businesses to maximize their overall revenue is to increase the number of **revenue streams**. Given the way audiences have been fragmenting into smaller and smaller slivers, the level of revenue that can be generated by any one audience has been decreasing. So to work around this problem of fragmenting audiences, media businesses have had to develop multiple revenue streams. One way to do this is to try to appeal to more than one audience. Another way to do this is to try to develop several ways to generate money from the same audience. For example, a film studio will develop an action/adventure movie to attract a certain kind of audience to buy tickets at a theater when the movie is first released. Although movie studios typically spend $50 million advertising a film, they know that many films will not earn this much at the box office. So the studios sell the movie on DVDs and through downloads from Internet sites. They also lease the movie to foreign distributors, and this adds another revenue stream. They lease the film to the airlines for showing during flights. They also sell downloads of the music from the film. Often, they try to produce toys, clothing, or other artifacts from the film and sell those to the public. They sometimes hire writers to turn the movie into a book. Or they could hire someone to translate the movie into a comic book format. And they also sell product placements in the films. All these revenue streams increase the total revenue and thus give the film more of a chance to be profitable. This strategy is not limited to film but applies to all the media industries.

As media companies merge and acquire other media companies, they increase their access to more channels and vehicles. Thus larger media companies can be more successful with the strategy of increasing the number of revenue streams. As a media company grows, it can more easily market a single message across many channels and thus quickly create multiple revenue streams for that one message. Thus their revenues increase while their costs remain the same, and this translates directly to larger profits.

Beyond traditional outlets, media companies look for additional streams of revenue like licensing their films and television programs for viewing on airplanes.

istock/robertbupuis

Minimizing Expenses. One of the largest expenses across all the media industries is personnel. Recall from earlier in this chapter that I made a distinction between below-the-line and above-the-line employees. Because the talent of above-the-line employees is at a premium, media companies must pay huge sums to hire this talent. To compensate for this increasing cost of talent, companies are pressured to keep the blow-the-line costs down. Most of the positions in the media industries are fairly low-level jobs that entail routine assignments that can be done by many different people with little training. These are the secretaries, receptionists, ticket takers, and low-level craftspeople. A bit higher than this are the assistant producers, camera operators, disc jockeys, and the like. Some of these people have special talent and quickly move up to the top of their industry, but most of them do not.

The media pay the people with a lot of talent a lot of money because these people are required for a company to generate large revenues. To counterbalance the large payments to talent, companies reduce expenses by paying clerical people as little as possible. Because the supply of potential workers for entry-level positions is so much larger than the demand, media companies can pay near minimum wage and get good workers.

The media reduce expenses through **economies of scale** and **economies of scope**. Economies of scale exist when marginal costs are lower than average costs—that is, when producing an extra unit of a good decreases as the scale of output expands. Large production runs are good because they spread out the start-up expenses over many units; thus, with each additional unit manufactured, the per-unit cost continues to go down (Doyle, 2002). To illustrate, let's say you are a magazine publisher and your cost of operation (cost of paying all your reporters, editors, salespeople, office staff, building rent, equipment depreciation, supplies, phones, other utilities, etc.) is $60,000 per week. This is your fixed cost. If you print only one copy of the magazine each week, you will have to sell it for $60,000 just to cover your fixed costs. If you print two copies, you would have to sell each for $30,000 to cover all your costs; your average fixed cost per copy is cut in half. If you print 60,000 copies, your average fixed cost per copy is only $1. Thus, your average fixed costs keep going down as these costs are spread over more and more copies.

However, when you print more copies, the cost of paper, ink, and distribution increases; these are your variable costs because they vary according to how many copies you print. The more copies you print, the more paper and ink you will need, and the price you pay for a roll of paper or a gallon of ink will go down because you can buy these materials in bulk and get big discounts. Although your total cost for ink and paper will go up when you print more copies, your *average* variable cost for these items will go down. This is known as economies of scale. The bigger the scale of your business, the more likely your costs will go down either through the ability to demand greater discounts or because you are able to operate more efficiently beyond a certain point.

The media companies, like any business, want to keep their expenses down, so they will find the point at which the combination of both their average fixed costs and their average variable costs is lowest. Beyond this point, distributing more copies only serves to increase unit costs and thus reduce profit. So newspapers, magazines, books, and recordings each seek the point where their average total costs (the sum of average fixed costs and average variable costs) are lowest.

With economies of scale, broadcast television, radio, and websites are different from the other media. They have no variable costs, only fixed costs. For example, with broadcast television, there is no cost to the station of adding an additional viewer to the audience. Viewers pay for their own television receivers, and they pay for the electricity to run them. The station has no distribution costs other than the electricity of the broadcast signal, and the power used to broadcast a station's signal is the same whether 100 or 100,000 sets are tuned in. It is fixed. With no variable costs and with a very high first-copy fixed cost, broadcast television stations keep dropping their average total costs with each additional audience member added. For this reason, the broadcast media (both radio and television) are strongly motivated, more than any other media, to increase the size of their audiences. The same pattern holds with websites.

Economies of scope also serve to reduce a firm's expenses per unit. Economies of scope are achieved through multi-product production; that is, there are variations on the product produced. Recall the example above about a movie company generating many revenue streams for a single movie. As the revenues increase for each new revenue stream, the expenses remain relatively low; that is, once you have produced the movie, it is relatively inexpensive to record it on videocassettes and DVDs. By increasing the scope of distributing the same product, very little additional costs are incurred, and yet the potential for increased revenues is great.

Digitization has made economies of scope even more attractive, because it creates little cost to retransmit a message in many different channels. Also, digitization allows for compression of greater amounts of data or more layers of content to be packed into a product. Now you can buy a DVD with an entire movie, which may also include bonus material such as outtakes, alternative endings, a director's cut, or interviews with the writer, director, and stars.

Let's see if you can apply this general information about revenues and expenses to specific media companies by doing Exercise 7.3. To get this information, access a company's website and see if you can find its annual financial report.

Constructing Audiences

A second strategy that media businesses use to maximize profits is to construct desirable audiences then rent them out to advertisers. A media business builds an audience by recognizing where there is a need for entertainment or information, then providing those products and services to satisfy those needs. This can be done generally in one of two ways. A media business can use either (a) a **quantity audience strategy** (i.e., try to attract as *large* a general audience as possible) or (b) a **quality audience strategy** (i.e., try to attract a certain *kind* of niche audience).

The dominant mass media in the past have typically used a quantity audience strategy. They tried to present whatever content they felt would attract the greatest number of people without caring much about who they were; they simply sought after the greatest number of people they could attract. This is what the commercial television networks have done in the past, especially for their prime-time period (8 to 11 p.m. each night). During the peak of broadcast television, a prime-time show that generated a rating of 10 was regarded as a failure. Now with audience fragmentation, a prime-time show that generates a rating of 10 is regarded as a hit show.

Attracting People to Niche Audiences. The radio and magazine industries have been very successful for years in attracting a **niche audience**. Recall from the previous chapter that radio was displaced by television as the dominant medium in the middle of the last century. In order to pull itself out of a decline and adapt, radio switched from a quantitative to a qualitative audience strategy and each radio station developed a certain sound to appeal to one kind of listener. For example, one station will use rap music to attract urban youth, whereas another station will use golden oldies to attract the aging baby boomers. The audience for each of these stations was relatively small compared to the audience for broadcast television, which was at its peak and used a quantity strategy to try to appeal to everyone. Now television is no longer at a peak and it is trying to adapt by switching to a quality audience strategy.

Relatively small, highly targeted audiences have great value to many advertisers, because special groups of people have special needs. Businesses that are marketing products for a special audience will pay a premium to the media vehicles that attract that special audience. For example, joggers as a group have a special need for information on running practices, equipment, and training techniques. They support several magazines that publish nothing but this type of information. Manufacturers of jogging equipment pay a premium to place ads in these magazines, knowing that the buying of advertising space in these magazines is a very efficient purchase, because the ads placed there will be reaching their most likely customers.

This niche orientation is called long tail marketing, which was introduced in the previous chapter. The market for products of all kinds as well as media messages is now much less concentrated on a few hits and is much more spread out across thousands of alternatives, each of which generates a small amount of sales. Our economy has shifted away from a focus on relatively few hits (mainstream products) and is moving toward servicing the needs of thousands of tiny markets forming a long tail. To illustrate, the recording industry used to focus on signing only those musical groups that could produce hit records. The recording industry was interested only in best sellers with only those songs on the Billboard Top 100 list as having any value. But then with the introduction of MP3 players in 2001 and the widespread use of music sharing platforms on the Internet, the recording industry moved much more into long tail marketing, and by 2006 there were 8 million unique song tracks being sold and shared.

Long tail marketing relies on aggregators, which are platforms that bring together buyers and sellers of all kinds of products and services. Anderson (2006) explains that there are five kinds of aggregators: physical goods (Amazon, eBay), digital goods (iTunes), advertising services (Google, Craigslist), information (Google, Wikipedia), and communities/user-created content (Facebook). These aggregators rely on recommendations to direct users to the products and services they are most likely to buy. That is, the aggregators make filtering decisions so that users can have a more efficient buying experience and not have to slog through all the hundreds of thousands of choices.

What makes long tail marketing so successful is the widespread use of technologies that many people can use to create products and messages, the removal of limitations in bottlenecks of distribution, and limits on product lines in stores. Now everything is available (Anderson, 2006). Now it is easier than ever to create media messages in many forms (print, musical recordings, video) and make them widely available (blogs, Amazon, iTunes, YouTube, Facebook, etc.)

We are now in the middle of a major retailing shift away from brick-and-mortar stores to web-based stores. Brick-and-mortar stores have limited shelf space and can only offer a small percentage of products, but virtual stores on the Internet can offer a much more extensive selection of products.

Conditioning Audiences. Once a mass media business has constructed an audience, it needs to keep that audience so it can continue to rent it out to advertisers. The mass media businesses are not especially interested in providing a message for a single exposure, like a rock concert promoter might. The mass media want to stay in business over the long term, and this requires that they maintain their audiences. Therefore, they must condition their audience members so that they develop a habit of exposure.

Reducing Risk

While all businesses face risk, the degree of risk is especially high for media businesses. For example, 80% of all television series introduced in prime time do not attract an audience large enough for networks to ask for a second season of production (Goldberg, 2018). Also, very few Hollywood films earn enough at the box office to cover their initial production costs, and less than 2% of films released each year in the United States account for 80% of box office returns (Schumpeter, 2011). Look at the assortment of movies displayed in Table 7.4 to see how costly it is to make a Hollywood film. Some of these films make enormous amounts of money but many do not even cover their production costs.

TABLE 7.4 ■ Hollywood Movies: Big Reward or Big Failure			
Name of Movie	Production Budget ($)	Domestic Gross ($)	Worldwide Gross ($)
Avatar (2009)	425	761	2,780
Pirates of the Caribbean: On Stranger Tides (2011)	411	241	1,046
Avengers: Age of Ultron (2015)	331	459	1,408
Star Wars: The Force Awakens (2015)	306	937	2,059
Avengers: Infinity War (2018)	300	664	2,015
Pirates of the Caribbean: At World's End (2007)	300	309	963
Dark Knight Rises (2012)	275	448	1,084
Lone Ranger (2013)	275	89	260
Green Lantern (2011)	200	117	220
Evan Almighty (2007)	175	100	174
King Author: Legend of the Sword (2017)	175	39	140
Wolfman (2010)	150	62	143
Sahara (2005)	145	69	122

(Continued)

TABLE 7.4 ■ (Continued)			
Name of Movie	**Production Budget ($)**	**Domestic Gross ($)**	**Worldwide Gross ($)**
Harry Potter and the Sorcerer's Stone (2001)	125	318	975
Monster Trucks (2016)	125	33	62
Speed Racer (2008)	120	44	93
Star Wars: Episode I—The Phantom Menace (1999)	115	475	1,027
Around the World in 80 Days (2004)	110	24	72
The Lord of the Rings: The Fellowship of the Ring (2001)	109	315	887
Ice Age: Collision Course (2016)	105	64	404
Town and Country (2001)	105	7	10
The Wolf of Wall Street (2013)	100	117	390
Land of the Lost (2009)	100	49	70

Values are in millions of dollars.

Source: IMDbPro (2018).

How do media companies reduce the risk that their messages will fail to attract a large enough audience to recover their initial costs of production? Media businesses have shifted their thinking toward something called the **marketing concept**. Instead of beginning with messages then trying to find audiences for those messages, media businesses begin with audience needs then construct messages to meet those needs. With the marketing concept, managers conduct research to identify particular niche audiences, then find out what the unmet needs are for those audiences. Then the media develop messages to meet those previously unmet needs. Beginning with research first and product development second reduces risk of message failure once the messages are released into the market.

This procedure is used frequently by the media industries. Researchers look at what works, then develop shows that are sequels or spin-offs of successful shows. Also, in the magazine industry, a large conglomerate will do market testing for unmet needs for magazines; once a need is found, the company will develop a magazine to reach that niche audience, then rent those consumers to a particular set of advertisers who need to expose that particular audience to their ad messages. Hollywood is fond of sequels because they reduce risk. In 2016 alone, Hollywood released 20 movies that were sequels; and at the time, 17 of the top 20 grossing movies of all time were sequels (Cheang, 2016). Notice in Table 7.4 that there are many movie series (e.g., *Pirates of the Caribbean*, *Avengers*) that earn huge worldwide revenues that more than pay back their huge production costs. Moviegoers like paying for new stories about their favorite characters.

CONSUMERS' STRATEGIES

We as consumers follow strategies just like the media industries do. However, our strategies are quite different from the profit-maximizing strategies of the mass media. We have two options for strategies. We can follow a default strategy, or we can follow a media literacy strategy.

Default Strategy

The **default strategy** typically runs continuously in our unconscious minds. It guides us to follow our preprogrammed habits because this requires very little effort and delivers familiar satisfactions. If we get on Facebook every morning, we will continue to get on Facebook each morning. If we typically send 20 tweets per day, we will continue sending a similar number of tweets each day. If we like a half-dozen music groups, we follow their new releases and typically ignore the music of other groups and are completely unaware of the music in other genres. We follow these habits because it is easy to continue doing what we have in the past without thinking about it much. These habits were developed in the past when we tried something new and felt it was a pleasant experience, so we continue with it without thinking much. We rarely search out the experience for a very different type of message, either because we are not sure what other messages are out there or feel that searching out those messages will entail much more effort than it is worth; that is, we will not feel more rewarded by them. Although the messages we currently experience are not providing huge rewards, they have almost no costs to us because they are routine habits. Therefore value is determined more by the low cost of the exposures than by the high return.

Media Literacy Strategy

People who follow a media literacy strategy understand the economic game and how to be a better player. This means they have higher expectations for a return on the resources they expend. They want more than minimal satisfaction from exposures. They think much more about the value of their own resources, and they want to negotiate a better exchange for those resources.

In thinking about how much of your resources you give to the mass media, it is important to make a distinction between direct and indirect support. Think of your direct support as being those financial payments you make directly to a media company. For example, when you subscribe to a website, magazine, or cable TV service, you pay a subscription fee to a media company. When you buy a book, you pay a fee to a bookstore. When you download a movie or recording, you make a payment to a media store. When you buy hardware, such as TVs, DVD players, MP3 players, video games, and other media products, you pay money to a store. These are all direct payments because you are involved in an exchange with a media company who gives you access to a media message in exchange for your money.

Think of indirect support of the media as the time you invest when you expose yourself to media messages. Media companies then translate your time into money by selling your time to advertisers. Advertisers then add this expense to the selling price of their products. So when you buy a heavily advertised product, you are indirectly supporting the media. By paying more for products of all kinds (e.g., toothpaste, hamburgers, cereal, etc.), you subsidize the advertising industry, which sends a good deal of this money on to the mass media. Thus the mass media receive **direct support** from consumers in the form of payments to mass media organizations as well as **indirect support** from consumers who buy advertised products.

The media of books, films, and recordings are supported almost entirely by direct costs paid by consumers of those messages. There are a few examples of ads being stuck in books and recordings and displayed before films, but the revenue from these ads is minor compared to direct costs. With magazines, newspapers, cable TV, and now the Internet, the costs are split between direct (subscriptions) and indirect (advertising). With broadcast television and radio, there is often no direct cost for exposure to a program, but there is a high cost for purchasing the means to receive a program (radios and television sets), in addition to indirect costs in the form of advertising.

The balance between direct and indirect support is shifting from direct to indirect payment. The reason for this is that the costs of hardware (computers, mobile devices, TVs, etc.) are coming down each year, while the revenues generated through advertising of all kinds increase each year. This shift also makes consumers believe they are paying less each year for media messages; however, the reality is that consumers are paying more.

COMPARE & CONTRAST
DIRECT SUPPORT AND INDIRECT SUPPORT

Compare: Direct support and indirect support of the media are *the same* in the following ways:

- Both are ways the general population participates in the economic game to make the mass media industries viable.

- Both are the continual exchanges people make of resources, where they give up their money and time in exchange for exposures to media messages.

Contrast: Direct support and indirect support of the media are *different* in the following ways:

- Direct support refers to monetary payments made by people directly to various media companies in order to purchase hardware to receive media messages (television sets, computers, mobile devices, etc.), purchase individual copies of messages (newspaper, magazines, books, etc.), or make regular payments for subscriptions to access media messages (cable TV, Internet access, etc.)

- Indirect support refers to expenditures of time with the media (such as viewing TV programs that programmers translate into money by selling audience attention to advertisers) as well as monetary expenditures (of advertised products).

Why do some people follow the default strategy exclusively, while others also employ the media literacy strategy? The answer lies in the strength of one's personal locus. People with a weak personal locus will settle for little in the exchanges because it requires too much effort to become a better player in the economic game. In contrast, people with a strong personal locus are driven to become more of a winner at this game. They find that expending the greater effort required to improve their skills and build more elaborate knowledge structures (see Table 7.5) is fun because it pays them back with much more interesting experiences.

TABLE 7.5 ■ Types of Skills and Knowledge Structures Needed to Understand the Economic Nature of the Mass Media		
	Skills	**Knowledge**
Cognitive	Ability to analyze reports on media industries and companies to determine revenue, expenses, and profits	Knowledge of revenue, expenses, and profits of media industries and specific companies
	Ability to compare/contrast across industries and companies on economic indicators	
	Ability to evaluate the economic health of media industries and companies	
	Ability to generalize from particular companies to industry trends	
	Ability to synthesize a prediction for future trends in the media industries and companies	
	Ability to analyze media industries and companies to recognize the operation of the five economic characteristics	
Emotional	Ability to analyze your feelings in reaction to the economic practices of media	Knowledge of your experiences in buying and using media products
Moral	Ability to analyze the moral implications of economic decisions	Knowledge of values in the media
	Ability to compare/contrast the moral implications across different companies	Knowledge of your ethical system
	Ability to evaluate the ethical responsibilities of the mass media to society	

SUMMARY

When you add the economic information from this chapter to your knowledge structure about the media, you develop a deeper understanding about how decisions are made. Remember that the media industries are composed of businesses that are run to make as large a profit as they can. Each of the media industries does this well, and each earns a profit much higher than the average of almost all other industries in the United States.

The media businesses play the economic game very well because they follow three strategies. First, they maximize profits by increasing revenue and decreasing expenses. Second, they construct niche audiences, then condition audience members into habits of continual exposures. Third, they reduce their risks by using the marketing concept.

We as consumers have two strategies available to us. One strategy is the default strategy, where we follow habits conditioned by the media. By following this strategy, we exchange our resources of time and money for a continual state of satisfaction with our habitual exposures; our focus is on keeping our costs low by limiting our exposures to content we have liked in the past and avoiding the risk of trying new content that would require more effort to find and understand. The alternative is to follow a media literacy strategy, where we expend more effort to develop our skills and knowledge structures *so that we profit by using the media better to fulfill our own needs for entertainment and information.*

Further Reading

Albarran, A. B. (2010). *The media economy.* New York, NY: Taylor & Francis. (202 pages with index)

The author covers a lot of ground in this relatively short book. He includes chapters on theories, technologies, regulatory issues, globalization, and labor issues.

Anderson, C. (2006). *The long tail: Why the future of business is selling less of more.* New York, NY: Hyperion. (238 pages, including index)

Anderson convincingly shows that marketers of media messages—as well as all products—have moved away from depending on hits for generating all their sales and instead are now mining sales from thousands of non-hits, each of which has low sales but added together generate huge revenue.

Doyle, G. (2013). *Understanding media economics* (2nd ed.). London, England: SAGE. (216 pages, including references and index)

This book was written for people who do not have a background in economics but want to learn about how the media industries operate along economic principles. Although the examples are primarily from Great Britain and Europe, they illustrate economic trends and principles that also operate in the United States.

Picard, R. G. (2011). *The economics and financing of media companies* (2nd ed.). New York, NY: Fordham University Press. (274 pages with glossary and index)

While taking a broad economic perspective on the mass media, Picard also focuses on how these companies are capitalized and how they use the principles of financial management to make decisions about how to acquire and exchange resources.

Sowell, T. (2008). *Economic facts and fallacies.* New York, NY: Basic Books. (262 pages, including endnotes and index)

The author provides a refreshing analysis about many beliefs that the general public and academics hold to be true about the economy, both within the United States as well as globally. While Sowell focuses neither on the media nor literacy, he shows how faulty beliefs can mislead people as well as governments to make bad economic decisions, which is a dominant theme within media literacy thinking.

Vogel, H. L. (2014). *Entertainment industry economics: A guide for financial analysis* (9th ed.). New York, NY: Cambridge University Press. (655 pages, including appendices, glossary, and index)

This textbook presents a wealth of details about the economics of each of the media industries in 15 chapters. It presents a lot of facts and figures (rather than anecdotes and insider stories) about the economic history and current nature of the entertainment industries primarily in the United States.

Keeping Up to Date

Advertising Age (http://adage.com/datacenter/article?article_id=106352)

This website provides lots of information about the leading media companies.

Forbes (http://www.forbes.com/lists/2008/54/400list08_The-400-Richest-Americans_Rank.html)

This website provides stories on economics and rank-ordered lists of wealthy people.

EXERCISE 7.1
ESTIMATING YOUR PERSONAL EXPENDITURES OF MONEY ON THE MEDIA

1. Before you go any further, stop and make a general estimate about how much money you spent on all forms of the media over the past year. Write your estimate here: $_____.

2. Now, let's itemize those expenditures. Think back 1 year from today and try to remember how much money you spent on each of the following over the past 12 months. If you want to do this accurately, get out your checkbook register and credit card receipts.

   $_____ Cable subscription (take your monthly bill and multiply by 12)

   $_____ Magazine subscriptions

   $_____ Buying individual issues of magazines

   $_____ Newspaper subscriptions

   $_____ Buying individual newspapers

   $_____ Buying textbooks

   $_____ Other books (pleasure reading, gifts, reference books, etc.)

   $_____ Movie theater admissions

   $_____ Rental and downloading costs of movies

   $_____ Buying radios, televisions, DVD players, MP3 players, etc.

   $_____ Repairs on media equipment

   $_____ Buying computer hardware and peripherals (printer, game controllers, etc.)

   $_____ Buying computer software and/or manuals

   $_____ Subscription to computer services (Internet service provider, website access, etc.)

   $_____ Buying musical recordings

   $_____ Buying video or computer games

   $_____ Playing video games at arcades

   $_____ TOTAL (sum of all the figures down the column)

3. How close are your figures in questions 1 and 2?

4. Does the amount of money you spent surprise you? Why?

EXERCISE 7.2
ESTIMATING YOUR PERSONAL EXPENDITURES OF TIME ON THE MEDIA

1. Begin with a wild guess about how much time you spend with the media each year. Write your estimate here: _____ hours.

2. Now, let's itemize those expenditures of time. To make this task manageable, think about an average week. In the spaces below, estimate how many hours and minutes you spend with each of the following activities. Remember that you can be doing more than one of these at the same time.

    _____ Reading magazines (print and online)

    _____ Reading newspapers (print and online)

    _____ Reading textbooks and other materials for classes

    _____ Reading books (print and electronic) for pleasure

    _____ Listening to the radio (in your car, portable players, at home, etc.)

    _____ Listening to recorded music (non-radio; MP3 player, stereo system at home, etc.)

    _____ Watching films at theaters

    _____ Watching videos on screens of all kinds (televisions, computers, mobile devices, etc.)

    _____ Working on a computer (word processing, doing research, etc.)

    _____ Communicating on computers and mobiles (e-mailing, texting, **social networking**, etc.)

    _____ Playing on computers and mobiles (games, visiting websites for entertainment, etc.)

    _____ TOTAL (sum of all the figures down the column)

3. How close are your figures in questions 1 and 2?

4. Does the amount of time you spent surprise you? Why?

EXERCISE 7.3
FINANCIAL ANALYSIS

1. Go to the library and get a list of media companies. Try the *Hoover's Guide to Media Companies* or get your reference librarian to help you. Find two media companies that look interesting to you.

2. For each company, do a brief financial analysis by answering the following questions:

    a. How much revenue did the company have last year?

b. What were the major sources of that income?

c. Given the sources of income, would you say that the company is primarily concerned with media businesses, or are media businesses really a sideline to other more important businesses?

d. What were the company's expenses for the year?

e. What was the company's profit margin? (Can you get both a return on revenues [ROR] and a return on assets [ROA]?)

f. What did the company do with its profits? Did it disperse all or part to the shareholders who invested in the company? Or did the company keep all or most of the profits for investing in additional media properties or other businesses?

3. Given your two analyses of the companies, in which would you rather invest your money? Why?

CONTENT

PART IV

8

MEDIA CONTENT
AND REALITY

*Key Idea: The media spin reality to make it appear more
exciting and thus attract people away from their real lives.*

Host Chris Harrison (right) stands with *The Bachelor* season 19 star Chris Soules as he addresses a room full of contestants.
The popular television show blends reality and fantasy media messages.

"This is a great idea for a show I call Act Real," said Cosmo as he started his pitch for a reality television show to Sylvia, who was a television network vice president of reality programming. *"So Sylv, my idea is to get about 8 to 10 aspiring young actors and stick them in a house in downtown New York City. Every few days they audition for a part in a major Broadway show or TV show. After each round of auditions, only one gets hired and that person moves out of the house. The rest of them stay in the house and we hear them complain and get all depressed. Each week the number of actors in the house goes down and we are left with the actors who feel more and more like losers."*

"Well, then where's the payoff?" asked Sylvia.

"Get this, Sylv, the payoff is that the last guy ends up getting the best acting job of all of them. But he doesn't know that until the last episode when he is the most depressed and the most pissed off because all the other actors who he thinks are not as good as him are all given jobs. It's beautiful!"

"What kind of support do you need from the network?"

"First, I want you to put out a casting call for actors for a new show on your network. We should get thousands of applications. We choose the most unstable actors, the real drama queens. Then we need to hire some writers to give the actors cool nicknames and backstories. Also the writers should write some lines here and there for the actors so we get some feuds going. We need your best editors to cut down all our footage because we will have cameras in every room in that house and end up with about 3,000 hours of footage."

"Sounds like a lot of production. What makes this a 'reality' show?"

"We don't pay the actors!"

"I don't know about that. The actors' union will not allow that."

"Yes they will, Sylv. These guys are actors in real life but on our show they are just ordinary people who want to be hired as actors. We don't have to pay ordinary people to be on a reality show. It's beautiful!"

A popular way to group media messages has been to put them into two categories: reality and fantasy. These two categories appear to be very different from one another, so it should be an easy task to group media messages. However, the task of grouping becomes very difficult when we start analyzing media messages and find a blend of reality and fantasy in almost all those messages. And this distinction between reality and fantasy seems to break down totally when we analyze the content from the newest television genre of "reality programming."

In this chapter, we will examine the role of reality in media content formulas where scholars have been trying to figure out how audiences make judgments about what is real in media messages. Then we will analyze patterns across television shows within the emerging genre of reality programming.

ROLE OF REALITY IN MEDIA CONTENT FORMULAS

Reality is one of the most difficult concepts to define in any context. Philosophers have been trying to define it for millennia, and ever since the field of psychology was founded more than a dozen decades ago, psychologists have been focused on the fundamental problem of how the human mind encounters the world and seeks to make sense of what is real. The more that scholars study this idea, the more it becomes clear that determining what is reality requires a complex judgment that involves many criteria and differs across individuals.

Complex Judgment

With media studies, it would seem as if the task of delineating reality would be easier by simply drawing the line of reality between the media world and the real world. The real world is real, and the media world is fantasy. But this is far too easy a distinction, and drawing the line in this way would be highly inaccurate and misleading. Still, we do have to make a distinction because developing a sophisticated understanding of the nature of reality is very important when trying to gain control over media effects. Let's begin by examining how scholars have analyzed how people make this distinction.

Magic Window

For years, media scholars assumed a clear distinction between reality and fantasy in media messages. Early thinking was that the media, especially television, simply held a window up to the actual world when it covered real events and real people. Thus news and informational shows were considered reality and everything else, which was fiction, was considered fantasy. They used this simple distinction to argue that children initially believed that all of television was a **magic window** that showed literal reality and that until children learned how to tell the difference between reality and fantasy, they were vulnerable to many negative effects. The results of early research on this topic claimed that very young children (younger than 3 years of age) regarded television as a magic window, but as children's minds mature cognitively (as you saw in Chapter 5), they developed a skepticism—called the adult discount—about the literal reality of media messages, and they were better able to distinguish reality from fantasy (Taylor & Howell, 1973). As they accumulate more experience with the media, children increase their skepticism and fully embrace the adult discount by about age 12 (Hawkins, 1977).

Subsequent research, however, began to show that not all people apply an adult discount consistently by the time they reach age 12. For example, van der Voort (1986) found that although children's perceptions of reality decreased from ages 9 to 12 for fantasy programs, there was no change in their perceptions

Very young children may view television as a "magic window" on the world, but they can distinguish fictional programming from news by age 5.

of the reality of so-called reality programs. It appears that children base their perceptions of reality not on the *accuracy* of portrayals or information but on the *probability* that something could occur in their lives. This suggested that people were making judgments about the reality of media messages not simply using a magic window distinction, but that they used multiple criteria for judging the reality of media messages.

Multiple Dimensions of Reality

Researchers have found that while the beginning point of judging reality is usually with an assessment of whether a portrayal actually happened, people frequently use more criteria, such as factuality, perceptual persuasiveness, social utility, identity, emotional involvement, plausibility, typicality, and narrative consistency (Cho, Shen, & Wilson, 2014; Dorr, 1981; Hall, 2003; Hawkins, 1977; Potter, 1986) (see Table 8.1).

Furthermore, it appears that people make judgments on these various criteria in an independent manner; that is, if a message is perceived as highly realistic on one criterion, the person may or may not perceive the message as being realistic on the other criteria. For example, *Star Trek* is likely to be regarded as fantasy when using the factuality criterion, but it could be regarded as highly realistic by many on the other criteria.

While space ships and aliens may be more fanciful than college students, in what ways are the science fiction *Star Wars* films more realistic than the telenovela-style TV drama *Jane the Virgin*?

TABLE 8.1 ■ Criteria for Determining Reality of Media Messages	
Criterion	**Questions**
Factuality	Does the message show what actually happened? This is the idea of the magic window that asks: Is the media message an accurate, undistorted view of actual events and people from the real world?
Perceptual persuasiveness	Does the media message present characters and settings that convince us to perceive them as real?
Social utility	Does the media message portray social lessons that can be used by people in their everyday lives?
Identity	Does the way characters are portrayed in media messages lead people to believe that those characters are very much like people in their everyday lives, so that they develop attachments to those characters like the attachments they have with real people?
Emotional involvement	Does the media message engage people's feelings so they are pulled into the action and feel that the action portrayed is really happening?
Plausibility	Does the media message portray something that *could* happen?
Typicality	Does the media message portray something that *usually* happens?
Narrative consistency	Does the plot of the story make people believe that the sequence of actions is believable?

Differences Across Individuals

As you have seen with the arguments laid out above, reality is a complex idea. There are many dimensions. There are also considerable differences across individuals in how they make their judgments of reality of media portrayals. These judgments of reality can vary widely even among people of the same age and experience. Not every child of the same age is making the same judgments about reality. For example, van der Voort (1986) reported that perceptions of reality and the degree of identification with characters vary substantially at any given age. He found that some children became absorbed in watching violent videos and judged the violence to be realistic, which led to a stronger emotional reaction, which led to a belief that the violence was terrible, which did *not* lead to aggressive behavior in real life. In contrast, other children who were also absorbed in viewing violence and believed it to be realistic had an uncritical attitude toward program violence, which led to them being more jaded and less emotionally involved, which led to more aggressive behavior in real life.

To further illustrate the idea of a range of perceptions of reality, consider the situation as described in Box 8.1 regarding the television show *Gilligan's Island*. The people who wrote to the Coast Guard, begging them to rescue Gilligan and his friends from the island, appear silly. You might be thinking that such a problem with reality is rare, and you would probably be right because this is such an extreme situation. But consider how much variation across people there is on perceptions of reality on shows like *Undercover Boss*, *World Wrestling Federation*, *Jersey Shore*, *The Hills*, *Amish Mafia*, and *COPS*. Which of these shows do you think are more real than others? Do you think everyone else would agree with your judgments, or would there be many differences across people?

BOX 8.1
GILLIGAN'S ISLAND

In 1964, Sherwood Schwartz produced a show called *Gilligan's Island.* This was a farcical comedy where seven characters who had been on a pleasure cruise encountered a storm that left them shipwrecked on an island somewhere in the Pacific Ocean. After about six episodes had aired, Schwartz was contacted by the Coast Guard and told that it had received several dozen telegrams from people who were complaining that the military should send a ship to rescue these seven people. Those telegrams were serious. Schwartz was dumfounded, calling this the "most extreme case of suspension of belief I ever heard of." He wondered, "Who did these viewers think was filming the castaways on that island? There was even a laugh track on the show. Who was laughing at the survivors of the wreck of the *S. S. Minnow*? It boggled the mind" (Schwartz, 1984, p. 2).

The cast of *Gilligan's Island.*

© Ronald Grant Archive / Alamy

Up to this point in the chapter, I have shown you how complex the idea of reality can be. We must consider multiple criteria that are independent from one another. We must also consider that children are less capable than adults in making certain kinds of judgments about reality but become more sophisticated in applying different criteria as they age. Furthermore, we must consider that there is a wide range of sophistication in making reality judgments across adults.

How can we simplify this complex array of ideas so that we can focus attention on why all this should matter to media literacy? What do people really need to know about the nature of the reality of media messages to be literate and protect themselves from harmful effects?

Organizing Principle: Next-Step Reality

Much of the complexity in the research about perceptions of reality can be explained simply by what I call "**next-step reality**." When we think about what audiences really want from media messages, we can see that many of their exposure decisions are guided by a desire for next-step reality. Also, when we look at decisions from a programmer's perspective, we can again see the emergence of next-step reality. This idea is embedded in how media messages get produced and why certain messages attract large audiences whereas other messages do not. In this section, I bring this idea to the surface and show you how it serves as a useful organizing principle for thinking about all kinds of media content.

Audience's Perspective

Why do people expose themselves to media messages? At the most fundamental level, they expose themselves to the media to find messages that they cannot get in real life. If people were getting all the messages they needed in real life, they would have no motivation to go to the expense (money and time) to search through the media for these messages. There are two reasons why people are motivated to get certain messages but go to the media rather than get those messages in real life. One reason is that it is impossible for them to get those messages in real life. For example, for most people, it is impossible to know what the Earth looks like from outer space or what the surfaces of other planets look like. It is impossible to know what it was like to live on a farm during the American Civil War, to be a knight of the Round Table in medieval England, or to watch Jesus Christ preach. To get access to these images, sounds, and emotions, people must access messages from the media.

A second reason that motivates people to get messages from the media instead of real life is because the costs of getting those messages in the media are far lower than the costs required in real life. For example, it is easier to watch a 1-hour travelogue on France than to pay the money to travel there for a week. It is far easier to watch a presidential news conference on television than it is to go to journalism school, get a job at a major newspaper or television service, get credentialed as a White House reporter, and attend the press conference in person. And it is less costly emotionally to watch characters in a movie try to meet each other, establish relationships, break up, and learn from their mistakes than it is to go through all of that in real life to learn the same social lessons.

Audiences therefore have a strong, continuing motivation to seek out messages in the media. They search for messages that have two general characteristics. First, those messages must appear real. They must have many elements that signal to viewers that they are real; that is, they are close enough to resonate strongly with a viewer's experience of everyday life, and thus those messages are accurate representations or at least plausible and probable. If they do not appear real, then audiences will not trust that the information is useful enough to bring it back into their everyday lives. Second, those messages must present something more than everyday reality. Without this something extra, there is no reason to search out the media message because the person is already getting those experiences in his or her real life. This is what I mean by next-step reality—the message is presented as reality to resonate with the audience's experience and make it have the potential to be useful in everyday situations, but the message is also "sweetened" by an extra added ingredient that takes it one step outside of the audience's everyday existence.

Therefore, people want media messages that are not so real that they are identical to the experiences in their everyday lives. But neither do they want media messages that are so far removed from their experiences that the messages have no immediate relevance. So people want messages that are one step removed from real life; they want messages that show what is easily possible and make it seem probable and even actual.

Programmers' Perspective

Programmers intuitively know that to attract an audience, they must take their audience's sense of reality and tweak it a bit to make it seem more interesting. Thus, the producers of media messages typically keep the elements of their messages anchored in the real world as much as possible so those depictions can resonate with the audience's experiences in real life. But producers of media messages also know they cannot simply reproduce those messages; there would be no point to this because it would be easier for people to stay with their own real-world experiences.

Producers of fiction know that the essence of their challenge is to tell stories that are "bigger" than life in some way. Producers typically start with an ordinary setting and a standard plot (boy meets girl) then sweeten the story by making it more dramatic. They make their characters a little more attractive or a little more interesting than people in real life. They make plots unfold at a faster pace than real-life events, and they put their characters in situations where their decisions are tougher and the consequences of those decisions are more serious. Skilled producers can take the audience on a journey by removing the audience from actual reality one step at a time until they have taken them willingly to an absurd place. This is the formula with farce. The story begins with what looks like an ordinary everyday situation; then, step by step, the producer takes the audience far away from that reality but does it in a way that the audience is not lost but willingly awaits each new step. Thus, producers depend on viewers' willing suspension of disbelief. To make people willing, producers must take it one step at a time.

The next-step reality is also easy to understand with persuasive messages. For example, the typical problem–solution advertising message shows ordinary people with an ordinary problem, such as bad breath, a headache, dirty laundry, hunger for a good lunch, and so on. The advertiser invites the audience to take the step of faith into a solution, that is, to buy and use the advertised product on the promise that it will solve the problem better than any other solution—more quickly, more completely, more cheaply, or more satisfying emotionally.

The next-step reality is a bit more difficult to understand with information-type messages. For example, if the purpose of news organizations is to report the events of the day, how can the next-step reality apply to journalists? The answer is that when journalists select what gets reported, they are not as interested in the typical events as they are in the anomalous events. Recall the old saying that if a dog bites a man, it is not news, but if a man bites a dog, that is news. The twist in the event makes it news. Crimes are news because they are aberrant behaviors. Violent crimes are more newsworthy than are property crimes because they are more aberrant and more rare—in the real world.

All kinds of messages—entertainment, persuasion, and information—are crafted to retain the appearance of a high degree of reality, but all are really one step removed from reality. The more skillfully this one-step remove transforms the reality, the more interesting the message will be and the more likely it will attract and hold people's attention.

Because we spend so much time with the media world in addition to the real world, and because the boundary between the two is often obscured, we can often get confused. This is especially the case after thousands of hours of automatic processing of both the mundane real-world messages and the massive flow of media-world messages. In all of that continuous flow, there is a constant intermingling of perceptions about what is real and what is fantasy.

REALITY PROGRAMMING AS A GENRE

While television has had examples of reality programming throughout its history (with game shows, *Candid Camera*, etc.), it did not become a recognizable genre until about 2000, when three of the most popular TV shows were unscripted series using real people instead of professional performers (*Survivor*, *American Idol*, and *Big Brother*). This type of show was popular with audiences because it appealed to the public's voyeuristic interest in following real people as they struggle then succeed in competitions.

While the reality series is a relatively new genre, there are now several hundred different reality programs where ordinary people (not professional actors) find love, friendship, treasure, a job, a new family, or financial backing for inventions; where ordinary people get their houses rebuilt, their wardrobes upgraded, their vehicles tricked out, and their bodily appearance reshaped; and where ordinary people compete with others to attain the honor of being the best singer, dancer, entertainer, chef, or human punching bag.

One of the most popular of the reality series has been *Survivor*, which typically takes 16 real people and puts them in a wilderness setting where the individuals depend on each other for survival (food, shelter, fire). Even before the first episode aired, CBS received 6,000 applicants who wanted to be marooned on a small island in the South China Sea and compete for $1 million (Bauder, 2000). When we apply the eight reality criteria (Table 8.1) to *Survivor*, we can see that the show is realistic in some ways but not in others. Furthermore, it might appear to be realistic on the surface in some ways, but when we analyze the show's characteristics, we can see that these judgments might change. For example, the players are real people, not actors hired to deliver scripted lines. However, those players were not selected from thousands of applicants because they were ordinary people; instead they were selected on the basis of their potential attractiveness to audiences and their ability to generate conflict. The situation is artificial in the sense that none of these people live their typical life in the wilderness, nor (with the exception of the all-star seasons) have they played this game before—or any game for $1 million. Although the setting looks like a deserted wilderness, the players are not really alone. There are dozens of production people (including camera crews, sound engineers, and crews to design and build sets for the challenges and tribal councils) and the host, Jeff Probst. Where do these production people live? How do they get to the survivors' camps to record their actions? Are there helicopter and boat crews? How do all these production people eat? Are there cooks? How does their food get to the wilderness location? The show is not scripted in the sense that dialogue has been written by a member of the Writers Guild of America. However, each contestant carefully writes his or her own lines in the sense that the contestant's interactions are highly calculated to put that individual in the best position to win the game. Also, the show is carefully edited to present to the viewing public the most dramatic version of what takes place. Multiple cameras are constantly recording what happens over the 40 days of the game, and these thousands of hours of footage are edited down to about 20 hours that are shown to the public. Thus the audience is shown much less than 1% of what actually happened during those 40 days. The editors and producers of "reality" media messages never tell the audience the full story; they edit out what they think is boring then assemble the pieces they think will be the most dramatic into interesting story lines.

The popularity of *Survivor* quickly generated a slew of other entries into this genre of reality programming. What these shows have in common is that each takes a handful of real people and puts them in a competitive situation. As the participants compete and reveal their personalities, audience members begin to identify with (or at least root for) certain players. For example, on *The Bachelor*, a young man who is looking for a wife is introduced to 25 beautiful women. Each week, he eliminates some of the women until he gets it down to one woman (the winner) and proposes marriage to her (the prize). Another example is *American Idol*, where thousands of people go to auditions all over the country and about a dozen are chosen as contestants. The contestants compete as one is let go each week until only one winner remains and is awarded a recording contract.

The popular reality television show, *Dancing With the Stars*, places real well-known people in a competitive situation.

Andy Martin Jr/Alamy Stock Photo

Within a decade, the number of reality shows on television had grown from 4 in 2000 to 320 in 2010. By 2018, that number had climbed to over 750 different reality shows; an analysis of the top 400 shows on broadcast and cable television in 2017 found that 188 of them were reality shows (Dehnart, 2018).

Much of this growth came from **knock-offs** and **spin-offs**. An example of a knock-off series is *Hardcore Pawn*, which is a television series about a pawn shop in Detroit airing on truTV. This series is a knock-off of *Pawn Stars*, which was a successful series on the History Channel about a pawn shop in Las Vegas (Passy, 2014). An example of a spin-off is the *Real Housewives* franchise (as described in Chapter 4), which began with Bravo's *The Real Housewives of Orange County* in 2006 and has since expanded to other U.S. and international locations. Other TV cable producers formulated their own shows featuring housewives (*Mob Wives*).

COMPARE & CONTRAST
SPIN-OFF SERIES AND KNOCK-OFF SERIES

Compare: The spin-off series and knock-off series are *the same* in the following ways:

- Both are television shows in a series, which is a progression of episodes using the same settings and characters (or real people) and where some plot lines are resolved within a single episode and other plot lines are played out over multiple episodes in the series.

- Both are new television series that substantially copy the formulas used by a previously successful television series.

Contrast: The spin-off series and knock-off series are *different* in the following ways:

- The spin-off series is produced by the same people who produced the previously successful television series on which the spin-off is based.

- The knock-off series is produced by different people who are copying the formula used by other people who produced the successful television series on which the knock-off is based.

The genre of reality TV has grown so large that it requires eight sub-genres and many sub-sub-genre categories to capture all its variety (see Table 8.2). Now that there are so many reality shows, the audience is so split that the ratings for even the most popular shows have dropped. For example, *American Idol* was the most watched TV show for eight seasons in the early 2000s then dropped to 22nd place by 2014 (Passy, 2014).

TABLE 8.2 ■ The Sub-Genres of the Reality TV Genre		
Sub-Genre	**Description**	**Shows**
Documentary style	Cameras record what happens in everyday life	Real people (*Big Brother, Jersey Shore, The Real Housewives of Beverly Hills*)
		Workers (*Undercover Boss, Dog Whisperer, American Chopper*)
		Celebrities (*The Osbornes, The Anna Nicole Show*)
		Fringe groups (*Sister Wives, Amish Mafia*)
Reality-legal	People's behavior is recorded as they deal with legal problems	Court shows (*The People's Court, Divorce Court*)
		Law enforcement documentaries (*COPS*)
Reality competition/ game show	People compete for some prize as one or more contestants are eliminated each episode	Performance (*American Idol, America's Got Talent, Dancing With the Stars*)
		Dating competitions (*The Bachelor, For Love or Money*)
		Job search competitions (*Top Chef, America's Next Top Model, Last Comic Standing*)
Self-improvement/ makeover	Viewers are amazed as a real-world person or object is drastically improved	Personal makeovers (*The Biggest Loser, Extreme Makeover*)
		Home makeovers (*Extreme Makeover: Home Edition*)
		Vehicle makeovers (*Pimp My Ride*)
Social experiment	People are put in unusual situations and a camera records their reactions	*Wife Swap, Secret Millionaire*
Hidden camera	People's actions are recorded without their awareness	*What Would You Do?, Cheaters*
Supernatural/ paranormal	People are put in frightening situations that purportedly involve paranormal forces	*Scariest Places on Earth, Ghost Hunters*
Hoax	People are fooled to believe something false and their reactions are recorded	*Catfish, My Big Fat Obnoxious Boss, Hell Date, Punk'd*

TV programmers also like reality shows because they are less expensive to produce. According to Passy (2014), "Even on a show like 'American Idol,' contestants who make it to the top 12 earn just a few thousand dollars in performance fees" and unlike "writers for scripted television, reality-TV writers often work without union contracts, which means they're paid less than union members. Consequently, a reality series can cost less than $500,000 an episode—less that what a high-profile sitcom actor gets paid in a single week" (p. F3).

THE IMPORTANCE OF MEDIA LITERACY

We all live in two worlds: the real world and the media world. Attaining higher levels of media literacy does not mean avoiding the media world. Instead it means being able to tell the two worlds apart as the two merge together under pressures from newer message formats and newer technologies that seem to make the boundary lines between the two worlds very fuzzy.

Most of us feel that the real world is too limited; that is, we cannot get all the experiences and information we want in the real world. To get those experiences and information, we journey into the media world. For example, you might feel that your life is too boring and you want to experience some exciting romance. You could read a novel, go to a movie, or watch a television program to get this kind of experience. Or you might be curious about what happened in your city today, so you watch the evening news, where reporters take you to all the places of the day's actions—crime scenes, fire locations, courthouses, sporting arenas. Although these are all real-world locations, you are not visiting them in the real world. Instead, you enter the media world to visit them.

We are continually entering the media world to get experiences and information we cannot get very well in our real lives. We enter the media world to expand our real-world experience and to help us understand the real world better. But those experiences we have in the media world are different than if we had experienced them directly in the real world. We often forget this as we bring media-world experiences back into our real world. As we constantly cross the border between the real world and the media world, the border sometimes gets blurred, and over time we tend to forget which memories are from experiences in the real world and which were originally experienced in the media world.

This blurring of the line and the interlacing of memories makes it important that we spend some mental energy considering the nature of reality and how the reality of the two worlds is different. Increasingly, the border between our real world and the media world is becoming harder to discern. More and more often, the media do not wait for us to cross over into their world; they bring their messages into our world. Because much of our exposure to media messages is not planned by us, we don't realize how much we are exposed to the media. Consider the exposure you have to media messages every day in your real world without you being aware of them. For example, there are radio messages coming out of other people's cars as you walk down the street in your real world; you pass messages on kiosks, billboards, newspapers lying on tables, and people talking about the media messages they have experienced. As the media pump messages into our world at an ever increasing rate, the borderline becomes blurred. We take almost all of this for granted.

There are many places where the border between the real world and the media world is not so clear. Think about what makes the following programs real, as the media claim: *Big Brother, Extreme Makeover, Ink Master, American Idol, Pimp My Ride,* and *Hardcore Pawn.* To what extent do these shows fit into your real world and resonate with your real experiences?

As genres change and the line between reality and fantasy programming becomes even more blurred, we must avoid falling into the trap of debating which shows are real and which are fantasy. This is why the next-step reality is so fundamental to media literacy because it shifts the question and hence the focus of our attention. The question should *not* be: How real are media messages? The next-step reality organizing principle shows us that every media message is a mix of reality and fantasy. Instead, the question should be: Which elements in this message reflect reality and which elements are removed from reality in some way? When you are guided by the organizing principle of next-step reality, you need to analyze media messages to answer these more appropriate questions. This analysis will help you develop a sensitivity to how big of a step you usually tolerate in the one-step remove messages. Some people will tolerate only a very small step and limit themselves to messages that very closely match their own experiences and knowledge. On the other end of that spectrum are people who insist on radical departures from what their everyday lives provide them.

The key to becoming media literate is not in how close we move to the reality end of the spectrum; that would only limit our range of information and emotional reactions. Instead, the key to media literacy is to be flexible and aware. Being flexible means being willing to traverse the entire spectrum of messages and being willing to enjoy the full range of messages. Being aware means realizing where you are in the spectrum as you experience each type of message and knowing the different standards of appreciation to apply to different places on the spectrum of reality. By being both flexible and aware, you can much better enjoy the enormous variety of messages in the media and, at the same time, control the effects of those messages so that you avoid the negative ones that usually come from automatic exposure and instead more intensely enjoy the positive effects that can result from any media message.

All of us must continually decide how closely media messages reflect real life and what the implications of those differences are on our beliefs about reality. Sometimes, these decisions about what is real are relatively easy; it is simple for most of us to understand that there is nothing like *Gilligan's Island* in real life. But some of the decisions are harder to make accurately—especially when they are subtly shaped over a long period of time by the accumulation of thousands of journeys into the media world. Over time, we have come to accept much of the media world as the real world. For example, who is the current president of the United States? Are you sure? Have you ever met him? If you have not met him, how do you know he really exists? If you have met him, how do you know he is who he says he is? I am not trying to make you paranoid. I am only asking you to consider the degree to which you trust the information and experiences you bring back from the media world into your real world. When encountering some of that information, you should have a high degree of skepticism, but other information should be accepted by you with a feeling of trust. Are you sure you know which is which?

This is why being media literate is so important. Media messages are not always the way they seem. For example, with reality programming, we need to be careful to discern what is the reality and what is the fantasy in those programs. Passy (2014) writes,

> Producers and networks acknowledge that reality TV involves a fair amount of fakery. Show producers shape situations to beef up story lines—in the case of competition-style shows sometimes by simply prompting contestants to do something unusual to boost their chances with the judges. Producers argue that truly spontaneous and unplanned situations often take too long to unfold or lack dramatic impact—and that the public understands "reality TV" isn't meant to mirror reality. (p. F3)

There are often many layers of meanings. Some of those layers are highly unrealistic (never happened in actuality, never will happen, and never could happen), but they are interlaced among layers of realistic elements that could transform the overall message in your perception from "fantasy" to "it might happen" to "it is likely to happen" to "I need to try this." The more you are aware of the layers of meaning in messages, the more you can control the selection of which meanings you want. Being more analytical is the first step toward controlling how the media affect you. If you are unaware of the meanings, then the media stay in control of how you perceive the world.

When you understand this organizing principle of next-step reality, you can better appreciate media content. You can focus your analysis on how different media, different vehicles, and different artists achieve the resonance of reality and then take that one step to remove their message from that reality. This is where the artistic talent comes into play. So a good understanding of this concept can help you develop a keener aesthetic sense as you experience individual messages. Also important, this concept should motivate you to ask questions about patterns in the one-step remove. There are patterns of life in the real world, and there are patterns of stories in the media world. The two patterns are not the same. The more you recognize the story patterns and how they are different from real-world life patterns, the less trouble you will have in recognizing the border between reality and fantasy. To get started on this path, try Exercise 8.1. As you analyze television programs for their reality and fantasy elements, try to push yourself beyond the easy-to-spot elements. Dig deeper to identify the less obvious elements.

SUMMARY

Clearly, the issue of reality entails more than making a simple decision about whether something actually happened. People are able to think in terms of degrees of reality, and when they are assessing the degree of reality, they consider more than one dimension. It is also important to understand that there is not a huge gap between children's ability to perceive reality accurately and adults' ability. This is a trap into which adults frequently fall. Being in this trap gives those adults a false sense of security that they do not need to think carefully about the reality of media messages because they are no longer children and therefore are protected by the adult discount. Because the degree of belief in reality is associated with higher negative effects, adults are vulnerable, as are children (Potter, 1986; Rubin, Perse, & Taylor, 1988).

The most useful way to think about reality is with the "next-step reality" organizing principle. This focuses your attention on the degree to which media messages are both real and fantasy. This then sets up more important questions: Which elements in the message do I regard as real, and how did I arrive at that perception? Which elements in the message do I regard as fantasy? To what extent am I attracted to the fantasy and willing to try to make it my reality? Keep these questions in mind as you read through the next four chapters on different types of media content.

Further Reading

DeVolld, T. (2016). *Reality TV: An insider's guide to TV's hottest market* (2nd ed.). Studio City, CA: Michael Wiese Productions. (172 pages, including appendices)

The author begins with an overview of the history of reality TV and some schemes to organize all the different types of shows. However, most of the 12 chapters in this book are organized by topics that help readers understand the process of planning, producing, editing, and marketing reality TV programs.

Dill, K. E. (2009). *How fantasy becomes reality: Seeing through media influence.* New York, NY: Oxford University Press. (306 pages with endnotes and index)

This is a very readable book by a media psychology scholar. In her nine chapters, Dill explores the various ways the media's use of fantasy leads to real effects among individuals. Topics include violence, beauty, race, gender, advertising, and political coverage.

Essany, M. (2008). *Reality check: The business and art of producing reality TV.* Burlington, MA: Focal Press. (260 pages with index and glossary of TV production terms)

This is an easy-to-read book with a self-help tone. The author is an industry insider who produced and starred in his own reality television series telecast on E! The book presents a lot of practical information about what goes on during the planning and production of a reality series for American television.

Ouellette, L., & Murray, S. (Eds.). (2009). *Reality TV: Remaking television culture.* New York, NY: New York University Press. (377 pages with index)

This edited volume consists of 17 chapters written by critical and cultural scholars. The chapters are organized into four groups: genre, industry, culture/power, and interactivity.

Pozner, J. L. (2010). *Reality bites back: The troubling truth about guilty pleasure TV.* New York, NY: Seal Press.

The author is a journalist, social critic, and founder of Women In Media & News (WIMN), a media justice group that amplifies women's presence and power in the public debate through media analysis, education, and advocacy. This book presents an extended criticism of so-called reality television programs.

Keeping Up to Date

JobMonkey.com   (http://www.jobmonkey.com/realitytv/reality-tv-statistics.html)

This general website posts information about lots of different kinds of job opportunities.

The link above presents a lot of information about productions and casting opportunities for a wide range of reality programs.

EXERCISE 8.1
DELINEATING THE ELUSIVE LINE BETWEEN REALITY AND FANTASY

1. *Analyze Television Programs:* For each of the genres of programs listed below, pick one particular program and analyze it.

   • Situation comedy
   • Drama (police drama or family drama)
   • "Reality" program (such as *Survivor, The Bachelor, Extreme Makeover, Big Brother, Undercover Boss,* etc.)
   • News program

   For each program, take a sheet of paper and write the name of the program at the top. Then draw a vertical line down the middle of the page. Label the left column as "Reality Indicators" and list in the column all the things about the program that you think would lead someone to believe that the program content is real (that is, depicts reality). Then label the right column "Non-Real World" and list in that column all the things about the program that you think would lead someone to believe that the program was not real.

2. *Tabulate Lists:* Count all the items you have listed in the Reality Indicators column and write that number at the bottom of that column. Then count all the items you have listed in the Non-Real World column and write that number at the bottom of that column. Do the same for all sheets, so that you have two totals at the bottom of the page for each program you have analyzed for reality. Turn totals into percentages. For example, if on one sheet you listed five things in the left column (reality items) and five things in the right column (non-reality items), then this would compute to 50% reality and 50% non-reality. If instead you had one item in the reality column and four items in the unreality column, this would compute to 20% and 80%.

3. *Check for Patterns:* If you are a perceptive television viewer, you are likely to have at least a handful of items in each column. No program is purely reality—there are all kinds of production decisions (about characters, plot, settings, customs, makeup, dialogue, camera placement, editing, etc.) that take messages out of the pure reality realm. Also, no program is purely fantasy—there are character types,

(Continued)

(Continued)

situations, language, settings, and so forth that are very much like the real world.

Look at the pairs of percentages at the bottom of each page. Are the splits in percentages favoring the first types of shows, which are the more fantasy types of shows? Or are they favoring the more reality types of shows, which are the second two genres? Or is there no difference? Now try this exercise again with the following media types:

- Movies
- Stories in magazines
- Newspaper stories
- Internet sites
- Video games

Do reality proportions vary across the medium?

9

NEWS

Key Idea: News is not a reflection of actual events; it is a construction by news workers who are subjected to many influences and constraints.

Eight months after the 2016 presidential elections, tabloids still advertise headlines about Hillary Clinton. The news media played an important role in shaping this story.

Kristen was shopping at the mall when a person came up to her holding a clipboard and said, "I'm taking a survey. Could you answer a few questions for me?"

"Okay, what are they about?"

"This is a survey about news. My first question is: What newspapers do you read?"

"I don't read any newspapers," said Kristen.

The interviewer made a mark on her form then asked, "What news magazines do you read?"

"None."

"Do you listen to newscasts on the radio?"

"No."

"How about the evening news on television?"

"No."

The interviewer glanced over her form then looked up at Kristen. "So you avoid all news?"

"No. I love news and watch about 2 hours of it every night on TV. I always watch the Daily Show With Jon Stewart. Then I watch the Late Show With David Letterman."

"But those aren't news shows. They're comedy shows."

"They present lots of news. I always learn a lot more about what is going on in the world by watching those shows than when I used to watch the evening news programs. And they're fun to watch."

"Those shows make stuff up to be funny!"

"Yes, they do. But I can always tell when they are making something up. With the so-called real news shows, I am never sure what they are making up."

Concern about recent changes in the news industry has been growing among the public. In his classic book *The Sociology of News*, Schudson (2003) argued that the audience for news has been fragmenting and that journalists have been trivializing the news in order to satisfy what the news industry perceives as what the public now wants. Schudson brought his criticism to a climax by asking, "Can journalism continue to be publicly important?" McCaffrey (2010) wrote, "The news industry is in the midst of a period of profound transition. The advent of the Internet Age has rendered obsolete long-standing models of how to gather and communicate the news." Given the "breakneck pace at which change has occurred over the past two decades, it's likely that we are in for an era of perpetual transformation, one with few certainties and no fixed outcome" (p. 3). Critics ranging from current U.S. President Donald Trump to members of the public have labeled media news reports they do not like or agree with as "fake news" (for more on this, see Issue 3).

These recent alarms and criticisms, however, are nothing new. Critics have been complaining about the nature of news for centuries. For example, when Thomas Jefferson was president of the United States, he delivered one of the most strident criticisms of the press in 1807 when he said, "The man who never looks into a newspaper is better informed than he who reads them." Jefferson took the position that "he who knows nothing is nearer to truth than he whose mind is filled with falsehoods and errors" (quoted in Jensen, 1997, p. 11). Thus, Jefferson was arguing that nothing printed in a newspaper could be believed. His harsh criticism of news after he became president is in direct contrast to his more often cited support of the press in 1787 before he was president, when he said, "Were it left to me to decide whether we should have a government without newspapers or newspapers without a government, I should not hesitate a moment to prefer the latter" (quoted in Jensen, 1997, p. 11). This pair of quotes from Jefferson illustrates that Americans have had a love-hate relationship with news for as long as there have been Americans. We seem to revere the institution of the press as essential to creating an informed citizenry, but then we use this idealism to hold the press to standards so high that they are impossible to achieve.

In this chapter, I will first provide you with some history about the development of the press so that you can see that it has gone through several major changes since the founding of this country. Then we will analyze the standards that people use to evaluate the quality of news. Finally, the chapter builds to some recommendations for dealing with the news in a more media literate manner. This topic is then explored in more detail in Issue 3 on fake news.

DYNAMIC NATURE OF NEWS

Changes in the conception of news are not new; journalists, social critics, and the public have all been experiencing transformations in the way they think about news for centuries. So in order to understand the meaning of the current transformations, we need to draw some context from history.

The desire for news goes back to preliterate culture; humans have always expressed an interest in the events surrounding them (Harrison, 2006). News was personal and local; that is, people were most concerned about events that impacted their daily lives (e.g., threats from invaders, impact of weather on their crops, changes in local regulations) as

Newspapers have played an important role in American life from the very beginning. The first newspaper to print the Declaration of Independence was the *Pennsylvania Evening Post* on July 6, 1776.

well as the lives of their families and friends. News was transmitted almost exclusively through interpersonal conversations, so it was composed largely of gossip and rumors.

Newspapers did not begin until the 16th century, when a group of men in Italy collected information and sold it to their clients in news pamphlets. By the 17th century, these news pamphlets evolved into daily newspapers first in Germany then throughout Europe. These early newspapers presented a simple listing of facts, which made them hard to read because the facts were not presented as a story with any context or flow. The audience for these early newspapers were elites—that is, people who could read and who could afford to pay for information. "Merchants, in particular, had a keen awareness of the value of information, and the dangers of acting on false rumour" (Pettegree, 2014, p. 3). Therefore, these early journalists were most concerned with accuracy of their information, so they worked to corroborate their facts to give them greater credibility.

The early settlers in America clustered into colonies, each with its own local problems and challenges. People in each colony wanted to be kept up to date about shipping schedules, changes in regulation from England, and their own local politics. Each colony had several newspapers, each with its own political point of view.

Rise and Fall of "Big News"

Following the American Civil War and the rise of the industrial revolution in the mid-19th century, the population was undergoing fundamental change as people moved from farms to cities. After the American Civil War, the population was developing a greater sense of nationhood and wanted information about political leaders and America's place in the world. And due to compulsory education, literacy rates had greatly increased. Some entrepreneurs (e.g., William Randolph Hearst and Joseph Pulitzer) saw this as a chance to develop newspapers with very large circulations in the growing population centers. But these entrepreneurs realized that in order to appeal to a large readership, they needed to move away from obvious political partisanship in their stories and make them appear as being "objective" so as not to offend any group of readers.

The growth of huge-circulation newspapers ushered in an era of "big news." Editors of these newspapers regarded the population as hungry for news but needed to be told what was most important. When radio became a mass medium in the 1920s, networks created national news broadcasts using this idea of big news where expert journalists decided what events should be covered. When radio became a mass medium in the 1950s, it followed the big news model.

This idea of big news reached a peak in the 1980s, then circulation began declining for newspapers, and audiences began eroding for radio and television news. This erosion was slow at first but then increased with the rise of the Internet and the news alternatives it offered in the form of news blogs and bulletin boards.

These declines were dramatic for newspapers. The number of daily newspapers decreased from 1,750 in 1970 to 1,350 in 2012 (Pew Research Center, 2014). The circulation for daily newspapers in the United States was 63.3 million in 1984 and declined to 30.9 million by 2017. Some of this loss of circulation was offset by these newspapers attracting visitors to their online sites. In 2006, there were 8.2 million unique visitors each month to a daily newspaper website, and this had increased to 11.5 million by 2017. However, during this time, the number of journalists shrank. Employment at daily newspapers peaked at 74,410 employees in newsrooms in 2006, down to only 39,210 by 2017 (Barthel, 2018).

As for TV news, 50% of Americans said in 2017 that they get news from television, while 43% said they get news from online sources (Shearer & Gottfried, 2017). Unlike newspapers, TV news exposure has not been showing a decline recently. The combined viewership of network-produced evening news (ABC, CBS, and NBC) was 22.8 million in 2008, and it increased slightly to 23.8 million by 2016 (Matsa, 2017a). However, exposure to local TV newscasts has been falling. Viewership of newscasts decreased from 12.3 million in 2007 to 10.8 million in 2016 for local morning news, from 25.7 million to 20.7 million for early evening news, and from 29.2 to 20.3 million for late-night news (Matsa, 2017b).

Shift to Online Sources of News

The dramatic erosion of audiences for "big news" should not be interpreted as Americans losing interest in being informed; instead, there has been a shift toward exposure to online news sources, which indicates that Americans are still interested in keeping up with the events of the day. This trend of news exposure away from traditional media to online media was initially driven by younger people. The Kaiser Family Foundation (2010) conducted a survey of young Americans ages 8 to 18 and found that from 2005 to 2010, time spent reading magazines and newspapers dropped (from 14 to 9 minutes for magazines and from 6 to 3 minutes for newspapers). The proportion of young people who read a newspaper in a typical day dropped from 42% in 1999 to 23% in 2009 (Pew Research Center, 2012). A few years later, the Pew Research Center (2014) reported that 48% of 18- to 29-year-olds watch online news videos, while only 27% of 50- to 64-year-olds and 11% of those 65 and older do the same. By 2017, 43% of all adults said they got their news from online sources and 67% of people 65 and older were getting their news on a mobile device; furthermore, 67% of Americans said they get at least some of their news on social media sites such as Twitter, YouTube, and Snapchat (Bialik & Matsa, 2017).

This shift from traditional news sources to online sources illustrates changes in the need for news. First, it indicates that Americans want more efficient access to news. They do not want to wait for a newspaper to be delivered or for a broadcast news site to report the news of the day; instead, they want continuous access at any time and anywhere. Online news sites offer this convenience, especially when people access those online sites with their mobile devices. By 2014, 36% of all adults were watching online news videos, 82% of Americans said they got news on a desktop or laptop, and 54% said they got news on a mobile device (Pew Research Center, 2014). By 2017, 85% of U.S. adults said they were getting their news on a mobile device (Bialik & Matsa, 2017).

iStock/GoodLifeStudio

Younger Americans increasingly get their news from web-based outlets.

Second, the shift from traditional sources to online sources also illustrates that people want a different kind of news. By moving away from traditional news sources that are staffed by professional journalists who use their expertise to select what they regard as the most important events of each day and use their professionalism to search out credible information to tell their stories in a balanced manner, people are indicating that they prefer news stories that are much more local, in the sense that those stories are about what their friends are doing or the things that users—not journalists—think are the most important (Lee, Choi, Kim, & Kim, 2014; Moon & Hadley, 2014; Revers, 2014; Xu & Feng, 2014). Evidence for this is seen in the rise of social networking sites being used to access news. Over the past decade, surveys show that 30% of the general population says it gets its news from Facebook, 10% gets its news from YouTube, and 8% gets its news from Twitter. Furthermore, 26% of the population gets its news from two social networking sites, and 9% get news from at least three (Holcomb, Gottfried, & Mitchell, 2013). Donsbach (2010) writes, "Younger people are increasingly using blogs, chatrooms or community networks such as Facebook and MySpace to receive what they think is 'news'" (p. 43). Facebook founder and CEO Mark Zuckerberg bragged that Facebook may be the biggest source of news in the entire world; in 2007, he said, "We're actually producing more news in a single day for our 19 million users than any other media outlet in its entire existence" (Pariser, 2011).

It appears that the shift in what is news has been away from what traditional news outlets have determined as important events and much more toward what individuals seek out as useful information. When Purcell and Rainie (2014) asked people if they feel that digital technologies have made them feel better informed than 5 years ago, they found that 81% of respondents said they were better informed about products and services to buy, 75% about national news, 72% about popular culture, 68% about hobbies and personal interests, 67% about their friends, 65% about their health and fitness, and 60% about their family. Notice how important "news" about products, friends, family, and personal health is.

As you can now see, the idea of what is news has always been in a state of dynamic change. Until the rise of news pamphlets and newspapers in Europe in the 16th and 17th centuries, people's idea of news was limited to the current events taking place in their immediate vicinity in their everyday lives. Then the idea of news shifted to pamphlets presenting daily listings of facts. Then there was a shift to newspapers presenting stories from a particular political point of view to audiences that wanted up-to-date information to support their political orientations. Then there was a shift to newspapers telling readers that they were presenting objective facts rather than editorializing particular political positions. Then there was a shift toward making news more entertaining rather than purely factual. Then there was a shift to offering a wide variety of platforms—many interactive—to offer every kind of niche audience a different kind of up-to-date information.

DIFFERENT PERSPECTIVES ON NEWS

There are many perspectives on what constitutes this thing we refer to as "news" (Table 9.1). Some of these perspectives are complementary and work together, while others are in conflict with one another. Let's examine five of these perspectives in some detail.

Political Philosophy Perspective

The political philosophy perspective specifies what news *should be*. Thus this is a normative perspective rather than a descriptive perspective. People who take this perspective on the news argue that news should focus on the most important events and people in a society in order to keep people up to date about what is most significant. News stories should be constructed from accurate facts rather than journalists' opinions so that people can become educated about what is really happening and make up their own minds about what positions to take on issues and which candidates to vote for in elections of their leaders. This position is espoused by philosophers and social critics who view the purpose of the press to educate the public every day about their world and thus create and maintain an informed public that would make the best decisions possible in electing their leaders and supporting issues in a democratic society.

This perspective builds from the first amendment to the U.S. Constitution, which protects the news media from governmental interference so that they can be free to report

TABLE 9.1 ■ Five Perspectives on News	
Perspective	**Description**
Political philosophy perspective	News is the daily reporting of the key, accurate facts about most significant events of the day in order to inform the public so that individuals have enough information to make rational, informed choices.
Traditional journalism perspective	News is that which is reported by journalists who are professional because of their knowledge, their membership in professional journalism organizations, and their autonomy from outside influences.
News-working perspective	News is the flow of stories produced by newsworkers who learn how to be successful (get their stories published and read) through a continuing process of socialization within news organizations.
Economic perspective	News is that which is presented by news businesses and as such is shaped by decisions regarding the allocation of scarce resources in a way to increase profits by maximizing revenue and minimizing expenses.
Consumer personal perspective	News is that which people seek out and expose themselves to in order to keep up to date about the events and issues they regard as being most important to them.

on public issues "so that crucial features of liberal society can be maintained, for example the protection of rights such as free speech, or the monitoring of abuses of power" (Ward, 2014, p. 3). People holding this perspective on the news believe that the press should not be an instrument used by powerful elites (such as the government or powerful businesses) to achieve their own goals. The press should be independent from political or economic pressures so that it can present the public with an objective representation of major events every day. Kaplan (2010) argues that the quest for objectivity is "American journalism's proudest, if most difficult to sustain, achievement. Considered a crucial tool for democracy, objectivity supposedly secures a space for neutral, factual information and public deliberation outside the corruption, rancor, and partisan spin that normally characterizes public discourse" (p. 25).

Traditional Journalistic Perspective

The traditional journalistic perspective is also a normative perspective because it encapsulates what journalists believe to be the purpose and nature of news and presents this encapsulation as a template for what news should be. Journalists essentially believe that their purpose is to inform the public, rather than persuade the public, which they refer to as editorializing and should be avoided. This perspective typically focuses on seven criteria to specify the characteristics an event must have in order to be considered newsworthy. These seven criteria are timeliness, significance, proximity, prominence, conflict, human interest, and deviance.

Timeliness is the most obvious criterion for newsworthiness. An event has to be current in order to be considered news. Significance refers to the magnitude of the consequences of an event. Thus a shooting resulting in the death of five people is more newsworthy than a shooting that results in only one death. Proximity refers to how close the event is to the news audience. Thus a shooting that takes place in a news outlet's home town is more newsworthy in that town compared to a shooting that takes place a thousand miles away. Prominence refers to how well known people and institutions are in the event being considered as newsworthy. Thus if the mayor of a town is arrested for drunk driving, that is more newsworthy than if one of the town's file clerks is arrested for drunk driving. Conflict refers to the degree to which the parties in an event disagree. Human interest refers to how strongly the event would appeal to human emotions.

Deviance refers to the degree to which an event is out of the ordinary. Thus if a dog bites a man, that is not newsworthy; but if a man bites a dog, that is newsworthy. The irony is that we depend on the news to tell us what the norm is. To be well informed, we need to know how things typically work, what is likely to happen tomorrow, and what the relative risks of harm are. But the news media focus our attention on the deviant. Because we see so many portrayals of the deviant, we come to believe that the deviant is the norm.

News-Working Perspective

Unlike the previous two perspectives, the news-working perspective is not a normative one; instead, it has been developed by scholars who study what journalists, editors, and other news workers actually do in the everyday performance of gathering news and presenting it. For example, Altheide (1976) found that while news workers are aware of normative news perspectives that tell them what they should do, they frequently cannot achieve the prescribed standards because of **unavoidable constraints**, such as deadlines, limited access to sources, and limited financial resources. Journalists learn how to work around these constraints to do the best they can but it always falls short of the ideal. Thus journalists are socialized into their work environment through trial and error as they learn what they must do in order to survive. Over time, they develop what has been called the "**news perspective**," which is not something that is consciously imposed by the owners of the media, but instead grows naturally out of their everyday practices. The news perspective is so pervasive and common among journalists that it is taken for granted. It is also generally shared by journalists in all kinds of vehicles and all media; as a result, there is a widespread commonality to all news in traditional news organizations. To illustrate this point, let's consider the topic of health and how it is covered in the news. First, let's examine what is covered. In a content analysis of 14,849 local television news stories from across the United States, Haberkorn (2009) kept track of how often the major causes of death (heart disease, lung cancer, and diabetes) were covered. She found that of all news stories, only 5.9% deal with a health issue of any kind. And among that small number of health stories, only 5.8% focused on the top three causes of death. She concluded that there is a poverty of information on local television news programs concerning serious health risks that affect most people. Another content analysis of news (local and national newspapers, television, and magazines) found that news coverage underrepresented the contribution of lung cancer; furthermore, the news media presented almost no information concerning the prevention and detection of cancers (Slater, Long, & Bettinghaus, 2008). However, while the news media underreported serious illnesses common throughout the population, they increased their coverage of elective plastic surgeries (Cho, 2007).

A key part of the news perspective are **story formulas**. These are the procedures that journalists learn as shortcuts to help them quickly select and write stories. As far as gathering information on a story, journalists follow the formula of asking six questions: Who? What? Where? When? Why? How? Journalists confronted with a new story begin by asking these questions, then structure their story to answer each of these questions.

One popular news-writing formula is the inverted pyramid. This formula tells the journalist to put the most important information at the beginning of the story, then add the next most important set of information. Journalists move down their list of information, ranked according to importance, until all the information is in the story. This formula was developed in the early days of the telegraph, when journalists in the field would send their stories to their newspapers over telegraph lines. They needed to send the most important information first in case the telegraph line went dead before they were done transmitting the entire story. We are way past the days of dependence on telegraph lines, but the formula still has value because editors will cut stories if they run too long. For example, a newspaper editor might want to use a reporter's 20-inch story but only has room for 16 inches, so the editor will typically cut off the last 4 inches.

Another popular formula is to use a narrative to tell a story in an entertainment format. Journalists who use this formula will begin the story with a heated conflict, a gruesome description, or an unusual quote—all designed to grab the reader's attention in an emotional manner. The journalist then presents each bit of information in a narrative much like a storyteller would.

Perhaps the most popular formula for telling stories in the news is what I call **simplified extended conflict** (SEC).When covering a story, journalists look for some angle of conflict that appears very simple. They believe that a story that has no conflict will not *grab* the audience's attention, but if the conflict is complex, the story will not *hold* the audience's attention. Furthermore, if the story can be played out over several days—or longer—so much the better. Political elections offer lots of good examples of the SEC. Campaigns always involve conflict between the candidates, and this can usually be reduced to two people. Also, the campaign, which goes on for weeks or months, can be portrayed as a race, with one candidate ahead and the other candidate running hard to catch up. If the conflict is focused on the finer points of complex issues, the story will not appeal to as large an audience. Therefore, journalists look for a simple form of conflict, and that is best seen in the "horse race" metaphor. Political coverage is much more about who is winning and whether the challenger can come from behind and close the gap than it is about issues. Other examples of SEC are the United States against Iraq, various crusaders against Congress, the little guy against city hall, and the forces of pro-life against the forces of pro-choice. The press can present the conflict in these situations in a very simple manner and keep the conflict going for a long time. It does this by polarizing the people or issues in the conflict, inviting the audience to identify with one side, then playing out the fight with lots of drama.

When the press has a big story that will consume news space for several weeks or months, it has an opportunity to more fully develop the nuances of the parties in the conflict. With political issues, the press could choose to tell the story of how competing interests have some common ground and how compromise is crafted. With criminal trials, the press could choose to tell the story of how humans can go astray and what justice means in each situation. Instead, the press rarely digs deep into a story—illuminating its complexity and educating the public about the underlying nature of the problem. The press typically focuses on the surface information—polishing it to a more glitzy finish to make it more attractive to passive viewers.

While these guidelines and story formulas instruct journalists, they are not definitive prescriptions; that is, journalists are free to deviate from them, and many times in the everyday world, journalists must think beyond the guidelines. This is especially the case in determining what gets covered. For example, let's say that a local official was arrested for a minor misdemeanor in your town 1 hour ago. This event is high on timeliness and proximity but low on significance. In contrast, let's say that yesterday an earthquake in a small country halfway around the world killed thousands of people. Which story is more newsworthy? This multi-characteristic definition forces us to compare apples and oranges; that is, when determining what is news, is the characteristic of proximity more important than the characteristic of significance? And what does significance really mean—significant to governments, significant to the people involved in the event, or significant to you?

This perspective has been criticized for distorting events. Altheide (1976) argues that "the organizational, practical, and other mundane features of news work promote a way of looking at events which fundamentally distorts them. . . . In order to make events news, news reporting decontextualizes and thereby changes them" (pp. 24–25).

Economic Perspective

The economic perspective on news focuses on how news organizations operate as businesses in the way they allocate their resources in order to achieve their primary business goal, which is to increase profits by maximizing revenue and minimizing expenses. From the early days of newspapers up until today, the organizations that gather and report news are businesses. Some are very small and some are huge conglomerates, but the one thing they all have in common is that they must generate revenue to pay for all their materials and employees. The two most salient characteristics of the economic perspective are commercialism and marketing.

Arguably, the strongest influence on the construction of news is its commercial nature (Altheide, 1976). News organizations are in the business of constructing large audiences so they can rent those audiences to advertisers. The larger the audience, the higher the rent and the more revenue the news organization generates. Therefore, the ultimate goal of news is a commercial one, and journalists are driven to construct stories that will attract large audiences. Therefore, news organizations must be careful not to run hard-hitting stories that would offend audiences. Also, news organizations must be careful not to offend their advertisers (Lee & Solomon, 1990). Furthermore, news organizations seek to find what kinds of stories audiences want most, then journalists are directed by marketing managers to present those kinds of stories in order to satisfy the existing needs in the market—just like manufacturing companies do when determining which products to produce.

Commercialization is not new. The commercialization of newspapers in the United States dates back to about the 1830s, when newspapers shifted away from financial dependence on political parties to dependence on circulation and advertising revenues (Hampton, Livio, & Sessions Goulet, 2010). Pettegree (2014) argued that news first became a commercial commodity, not with the invention of the newspaper, but much earlier in the 15th century with the invention of the printing press, which resulted in printers growing the public appetite for news and information.

The economic perspective has been criticized for several reasons. One reason is that when news decisions are made by marketers instead of journalists, the news coverage is confounded with advertising. For example, Kaniss (1996) criticized news shows in the Philadelphia area by pointing out that during the November 1996 sweeps month, the local CBS affiliate on its evening news show ran nine stories on the *Titanic*, a ship that sank 84 years prior to those "news" stories but was the subject of a CBS mini-series. The Philadelphia ABC affiliate was cited as frequently running "news" stories about Mickey Mouse because the ABC network is owned by Disney. Local affiliates in many TV markets are also found to frequently run news stories about stars on their network series, and they often run soft news stories on topics of made-for-TV movies appearing that night on the network.

Another criticism of the economic perspective is that it tends to change the content of news in a way that is somehow harmful to the public. For example, journalists operating under the marketing perspective are more likely to present stories that grab the attention of large audiences by highlighting the unusual so as to shock people. This marketing perspective has led news workers to believe that the public wants more soft news items than stories about the government, the economy, and political matters. In a content analysis of

13,000 items in 12 daily newspapers, it was found that newspapers with a strong market orientation publish fewer items about government and public affairs and more items about lifestyle and sports than do newspapers with a weak market orientation.

> Today, the newsrooms of hundreds of U.S. newspapers, magazines, and television stations have embraced, to greater or lesser extents, this approach to making news. Typically a market-driven organization selects target markets for its product, identifies the wants and needs of potential customers in its target markets, and seeks to satisfy those wants and needs as efficiently as possible. (Beam, 2003, p. 368)

And one of the widespread needs in any population is the need for information that confirms one's beliefs rather than challenges them (Knobloch-Westerwick & Meng, 2009). Therefore the more successful news organizations use the marketing perspective to identify their audience's beliefs then provide them with information that supports those beliefs.

Boczkowski and Mitchelstein (2013) argue that a foundational issue about the news is "whether journalists supply the news that citizens need and whether citizens want such information or prefer information on sports, crime, and entertainment—subjects that are interesting but don't contribute to the health of a democratic society" (p. 6). Perhaps there is a gap between the stories that professional journalists think are the most newsworthy (i.e., politics, economics, and international matters) and those that attract audiences most strongly. Gans (2003) observes that journalists expect as an integral part of their professional identities to provide stories that are most newsworthy rather than most attractive. Boczkowski and Mitchelstein (2013) conducted a major 2-year study in which they interviewed dozens of news editors and analyzed the content of 40,000 news stories as well as audience attractions to 20 news sites across seven countries. They found a large and growing gap between the supply of what they called public affairs stories (stories thought by journalists to be the most important and newsworthy) and public demand for non–public affairs (sports and entertainment). They said,

> There was a gap despite the presence of substantive differences in the media systems among the countries in which the sites are located and tin the sites' ideological orientations. Moreover, the lack of major geographic variation persists at the regional level. (p. 17)

Consumer Personal Perspective

When we look at the current exposure patterns to news content, we must conclude that many people are seeking a kind of information that does not conform to the old traditional journalistic perspective on news. One pattern we see is that people are seeking out information strategically that benefits them. That is, they are not sitting back waiting for "authorities" to tell them what the most important events and issues are; instead, they already have a good idea of their interests and they seek out information that satisfies their personal needs for information they can use. This shows up in two trends: hyper-localism and selective exposure.

Hyper-localism

As the audience for news fragments, news vehicles are getting more and more specialized, which is known as **hyper-localism**. The news watchdog group the Project for Excellence in Journalism says that the mass media are having a very hard time holding onto their audiences for news and the overall audience is shrinking for newspapers, TV news, and even Internet news. Also, the smaller and smaller number of people who care about exposing themselves to news messages have more and more options, beyond newspapers and network news programs

Today, people tend to seek out news that satisfies their own particular personal needs, in contrast to decades ago, when people let news organizations tell them what was important and should be considered news.

(Rainey, 2007). Cable news is pulling away a lot of viewers who like personality-driven news shows (such as Bill O'Reilly), comedy news shows (such as the *Daily Show* or the *Colbert Report*), sports-focused news shows (such as *SportsCenter*), or celebrity-focused news (such as *E!*). These news seekers are less interested in global or national issues than they are in more local or hobby-type things that interest them personally. News organizations realize this, so they are developing more and more specialized vehicles to appeal to these many niche audiences.

Selective Exposure

The idea that people selectively expose themselves to news content has been around for a long time, but it is even more important today with the fragmentation of audiences and the proliferation of choices. Selective exposure is a psychological concept that says people seek out information that conforms to their existing belief systems and avoid information that challenges those beliefs. In the past when there were few sources of news, people could either expose themselves to mainstream news—where they would likely see beliefs expressed counter to their own—or they could avoid news altogether. Now with so many types of news constantly available to a full range of niche audiences, people can easily find a source of news that constantly confirms their own personal belief system. This leads to the possibility of creating many different small groups of people, each strongly believing they are correct and everyone else is wrong about how the world works.

The consumer personal perspective appears to be gaining importance with the rise of Internet platforms of news, although this perspective is not new—it has always been around. The locus of this perspective is the individual who determines for himself or herself what is news rather than relying on an outside authority such as a journalist, news company, or philosopher. This perspective is a pragmatic one, where an individual's standard for what is news is purely personal and focuses on what is most important or interesting to the individual. Thus people with a particular hobby will define news as those events currently impacting their hobby—meetings of hobbyists, new regulations on their hobby, new inventions that help them with their hobby, and so on. People who are family oriented are most interested in what is happening to people with whom they are related—who is sick, who is traveling and where, who is dating or getting engaged, married, or divorced, and so on. Thus sources such as Facebook provide much more "newsworthy" information than *USA Today*, *Time Magazine*, and *CBS Evening News* put together. For many people, when the president of the United States delivers a State of the Union address and lays out economic plans, this is not newsworthy; instead, when their closest friends lay out their plans for how they plan to spend their time and money on vacations and shopping trips, this is highly newsworthy. Other journalistic criteria such as proximity or prominence are relatively unimportant. When a sibling or close friend announces her engagement, this is highly newsworthy regardless of whether she lives next door or far away. What your brother is doing for the holidays is newsworthy to you regardless of whether he is a college student or a congressman.

CONSUMER STANDARDS FOR EVALUATING THE QUALITY OF NEWS

As you have seen thus far in this chapter, there is a lot of criticism of the news. Criticism is stimulated when people are upset that something, like news, does not meet their standards. So in order to understand the nature of this criticism, we need to analyze what the standards are for making evaluations about news stories. In this section, we will look at the three most often mentioned standards in some detail—objectivity, accuracy, and neutrality.

Objectivity

The most often mentioned criterion of news quality is objectivity. There is a strong ethic of objectivity in journalism (Parenti, 1986), and Kaplan (2010) adds, "For over a century, the US press has embraced the ethic of objectivity as defining its core public mission" (p. 25).

The idea of objectivity, however, is a very general philosophical concept that means a separateness from the object being observed so that the object is perceived accurately and that the perception is not distorted by human limitations. This, of course, is an impossible standard for humans—even journalists—to achieve. When humans observe objects, their perceptions are always shaped by their expectations, their abilities, and their histories. Furthermore, journalists are limited by time constraints imposed by deadlines, by the size of the story they can write, by their network of sources, and by their ability to interview people and judge whether those people are telling the truth.

The use of objectivity as a standard for journalists is unrealistic. Journalists can never been purely objective. Even when they try to avoid being influenced by their biases, they cannot know all of their biases. And these unconscious biases serve to shape how they make their many daily decisions about what things to cover, what kinds of information to gather, how much information to gather, and how to assemble their research into a story.

Accuracy

Accuracy seems to be a good criterion for judging the quality of news. It is typically obvious when a story reports facts that are wrong. If a story reports one fact and that fact is easy to check, then accuracy becomes a very useful criterion. But almost no news stories present only one fact, and this raises the issue of completeness. What if a story presents

20 facts and 19 are accurate? Does this make the entire story faulty? This is a difficult question to answer in general because if the one inaccurate fact is trivial, we could conclude that the entire story is accurate. But if the one inaccurate fact is central to the story, then it is likely that we would conclude that it does not matter that 95% of the facts were accurate, the story itself is inaccurate. You can see that the judgment about accuracy can soon become complicated.

Completeness

Such an evaluation gets even more complicated when we start to think about facts that are not reported in a story; that is, what about a news story that reports lots of facts accurately but all of those facts are peripheral to the story, while the facts that are central to the story are left out? Presenting only a partial story is a type of distortion that is not usually regarded as bias because there does not seem to be an intention by the journalist to mislead the audience. Instead, the journalist has run out of time or does not have enough sources or ability to tell the entire story. Even though the journalist is not trying to mislead the audience, people exposed to a partial story are still shown a distorted picture of the occurrence, and therefore the story cannot be regarded as being objective.

One form of a partial story is when a major story stops getting covered, even though important events continue to occur. An example of this is the $21 billion settlement by the tobacco industry that was covered during negotiations. But then the press stopped covering the story as the tobacco companies began paying billions of dollars to state governments between 2000 and 2002.Why would it be important to cover how the money was used? The settlement specified that states should spend the money for health care and to educate people, especially children, about the health risks of smoking. But only 5% of this total payout went toward anti-smoking efforts as it was intended. Instead, the money was funneled to all sorts of pork barrel projects across the 50 states; in North Carolina, much of the money went to subsidize tobacco farmers. These subsidies did not go to help tobacco farmers transition to other crops; instead, much of the money went to modernize their tobacco farms (Mnookin, 2002). Also, the press did a poor job of educating the public about where the money for the payout was coming from. Most people know that it is from the major tobacco companies, but most people do not know where the tobacco companies get much of the revenue that they use to make their payments to states in the tobacco settlement. Each of the major tobacco companies now controls hundreds of brands of all kinds of food products in supermarkets. So the payout was likely financed by a rise in prices of crackers, cereals, peanut butter, dog food, soups, and so on.

Another type of partial story is when a journalist tells a story from a single point of view. American journalists typically tell their stories from the point of view that America is always justified in its military actions, and those we aggress against are not justified. For example, Fishman and Marvin (2003) analyzed 21 years of photographs appearing on the front pages of the *New York Times*. They focused on violence and found that non-U.S. agents were represented as more explicitly violent than U.S. agents and that the latter are associated with disguised modes of violence more often than the former. The recurring image of non-U.S. violence is that of order brutally ruptured or enforced. By contrast, images of U.S. violence are less alarming and suggest order without cruelty. Thus, violence is associated more with out-group status than with in-group status.

Context

Context is what helps audiences understand the meaning of the event in the news stories. Without context, the story has ambiguous meaning. For example, a story could report that Mr. Jones was arrested for murder this morning. That fact can convey very different meanings if we vary the context. Let's say that the journalist put in some historical context that Mr. Jones had murdered several people a decade ago, was caught and convicted, served time in prison, but was recently let go because of a ruling of an inexperienced and liberal judge. In contrast, let's say that Mr. Jones, one of the candidates running for mayor, was arrested despite the fact that police had in custody another man who possessed the probable murder weapon and who had confessed. The fact of the arrest takes on a very different meaning within different contexts.

This raises an important question: Can a news story be accurate if the journalist provides no context? Most scholars would answer, no. For example, Bagdikian (1992) argues that the most significant form of bias in journalism appears when a story is reported with a lack of context. The fear is that context is only the journalist's opinion, and opinion must be avoided in "objective reporting." Bagdikian continues, "But there is a difference between partisanship and placing facts in a reasonably informed context of history and social circumstance. American journalism has not made a workable distinction between them" (p. 214). He says that "there are powerful commercial pressures to remove social significance from standard American news. Informed social-economic context has unavoidable political implications which may disturb some in the audience whose world view differs" (p. 214). So the media report undisputed facts about things but ignore the meaning behind the facts and, in so doing, severely limit our ability to see that underlying meaning.

Although contextual material is very important, many stories present very little context (Parenti, 1986). For example, the many stories about crimes that we see reported every day are each limited to the facts of that one crime. Rarely is there any context about crime rates or how the particular crime reported in the story matches some kind of a pattern—historical, social, economic, and so forth. Crime stories are like popcorn for the mind. Each story is small, simple, and relatively the same. These stories give our mind the sense that it is consuming information, but they have little nutritional value. After years of munching on this information, we have come to believe that most crime is violent street crime and that it is increasing all around us. But the real-world figures indicate that most crime is white collar (embezzlement, fraud, forgery, identity theft, etc.) and property crimes (larceny, shoplifting, etc.) rather than violent crime (murder, rape, armed robbery, etc.). Yet it is the more rare violent crime that gets reported because it is more deviant and thus more likely to capture the attention of the news audience.

iStock/glegorly

A lack of context is the most significant form of bias in journalism.

Asking journalists to build more context into their stories presents two problems. First, journalists vary widely in talent, and it takes a very talented and experienced journalist to be able to dig out a great deal of relevant contextual information on deadline. Second, when journalists have the responsibility of constructing the context, they may be manifesting a lot of power to define the meaning of the event for the readers. Journalists can substantially change the meaning if they leave out (whether intentionally or through an oversight) an important contextual element.

Let's examine an example of a story reporting facts that are accurate but that leads readers to a wrong conclusion because the reporter does not provide an adequate context for those facts. In 2004, *Los Angeles Times* reporter Larry Stewart wrote a story from a report by a group calling itself the Institute for Diversity and Ethics in Sport. In his newspaper story, Stewart (2004) reported that the report said that it found six of the schools in the 2004 National Collegiate Athletic Association (NCAA) Sweet 16 basketball tournament had graduation rates no higher than 50%. This leaves the reader with the impression that universities (at least six) were exploiting their athletes. But what the reporter did not put in the story is that, nationwide, only about 50% of students who enter a 4-year program as a freshman end up graduating with a bachelor's degree. Therefore, the problem is not with basketball teams having unusually low graduation rates, which is what the story implied. The real issue is the relatively large dropout rate of all college students. Also, the reporter said that the report complained that only 3 of the 16 teams had an African American head coach. Why is this number bad? What should the number be? If the number should be proportional to the number of African Americans in the United States, then we should expect 12% of coaches to be African American, and that would make it two coaches. Or instead, should the number of African American coaches be proportional to the number of African American players on NCAA basketball teams? This would be a much larger percentage, but then this raises the issue that perhaps African Americans are overrepresented on these basketball teams and that the problem is that there needs to be better representation from non–African Americans on NCAA basketball teams—why are there not many more Hispanic or Asian American players? The determination of adequate representation is a complex issue. If news organizations see themselves as having the function of informing their audiences so those people can make good decisions, then journalists must provide more detailed contexts. If, instead, a journalist writes a superficial story that features only a controversy, then this serves to stir up negative emotions instead of educating audiences.

COMPARE & CONTRAST
NEWS OBJECTIVITY AND NEWS QUALITY

Compare: News objectivity and news quality are *the same* in the following ways:

- Both are criteria people apply to make assessments of the news.

- Both are abstract standards that are difficult to articulate.

Contrast: News objectivity and news quality are *different* in the following ways:

- News objectivity is an impossible criterion to achieve because it requires journalists to perceive news events without bias or limitations (such as time deadlines, access to sources, etc.).

- News quality refers to criteria such as truthfulness, neutrality, and accuracy, which are possible but still difficult criteria for journalists to meet.

Who would you consider to be a more qualified journalist: Katie Couric (pictured), or John Oliver of HBO?

In summary, you can see that accuracy is a complex concept with many layers of meaning. This makes it complicated to use as a standard for judging the quality of a news story.

Neutrality

As a criterion for the quality of news, neutrality means that the story is free from journalistic bias or editorializing. This means that the journalist does not slant the story to convince the audience to think a certain way; that is, the journalist focuses on informing and not on persuading. Neutrality is observed in lack of bias and balance.

Lack of Bias

Bias—like fabrication—is a willful distortion on the part of a journalist, but it is difficult for audiences to recognize when this is occurring. This highlights the distinction between actual bias (where a journalist willfully distorts a news story) and perceived bias (when audiences think that the story is slanted). Examples of actual bias in traditional news organizations are rare but this does not mean that the stories themselves are free of bias. Jensen (1997) points out that there is little evidence of a conscious conspiracy among journalists to censor the news.

> News is too diverse, fast-breaking, and unpredictable to be controlled by some sinister conservative eastern establishment media cabal. However, there is a congruence of attitudes and interests on the part of the owners and managers of mass media organizations. That non-conspiracy conspiracy, when combined with a variety of other factors, leads to the systematic failure of the news media to inform the public. While it is not an overt form of censorship, such as the kind we observe in some other societies, it is nonetheless real and often equally as dangerous to the public's well-being. (pp. 14–15)

In his book *Censored: The News That Didn't Make the News—And Why*, Jensen (1995) describes many seemingly important stories that did not receive much, if any, coverage by the news media. For example, in 1985, the National Institute for Occupational Safety and Health (NIOSH) found that more than 240,000 people were in danger in 258 work sites around the United States. The purpose of NIOSH is to monitor safety in the workplace and to inform workers when they are in serious danger of contracting life-threatening diseases from exposure to chemicals and other hazardous materials in the workplace. By 1995, NIOSH had informed less than 30% of the people who it had found to be in daily danger a decade earlier. Thus, NIOSH knew that 170,000 people were working in highly risky environments every day and let 10 years go by without telling them. The news media ignored this governmental negligence for more than a decade.

Those who follow the media closely often complain about a liberal or a conservative news bias, or they say that there is too much negativism. In an analysis of Gallup public opinion data, it was found that more than half of Americans felt that the media were influenced by advertisers, business corporations, Democrats, the federal government, liberals, the military, and Republicans (Becker, Kosicki, & Jones, 1992). The newspaper industry itself has found the same thing in its own surveys. For example, a survey by the American Society of Newspaper Editors found that most people believe the media have political leanings (Jeffres, 1994).

Perception of news bias has been explained by in-group/out-group differences. Citizens' political leanings influence how much variation they perceive; politically dissimilar media are seen as having a more uniform partisan bias and politically similar media are seen as having more diverse partisan biases (Stroud, Muddiman, & Lee, 2014).

What is interesting is that conservatives feel that the media have a generally liberal leaning, whereas liberals feel that the media are conservative. Conservatives complain that most news reporters are liberal in their own views, and these liberal journalists show their bias when they present their stories. In contrast, liberals feel that conservative commentators have too much power and have redefined the American agenda to stigmatize liberals.

In the early days of the United States, most newspapers were founded by people who had a clear political viewpoint that they wanted to promote. Towns had multiple newspapers, each one appealing to a different niche of political thinking. Newspapers were biased politically, and the bias was clearly labeled. But by the late 1800s, newspapers had shifted from a political focus to a business focus, with the goal of building the largest circulation. To do this, newspapers lost their political edge so as to avoid offending any potential readers. This business focus still underlies the mass media. Decisions are made to build audiences, not to espouse a political point of view. Sometimes, arguing for a particular political point of view can be used as a tool to build an audience, but these instances are usually found within those media with a niche orientation. Instead, the large national news organizations such as the television networks and the large newspapers try to present both sides of any political issue so as to appear objective and balanced because they want to appeal to all kinds of people across the political spectrum. This conclusion has been supported by D'Alessio and Allen (2000), who conducted a meta-analysis of 59 quantitative studies of news bias in presidential campaigns since 1948. They found no evidence of bias with newspapers or magazines and only an "insubstantial" bias in network television news.

Bernard Goldberg, an Emmy award–winning reporter who worked for CBS news for 30 years, published a book entitled *Bias: A CBS Insider Exposes How the Media Distort the News* in 2003. Goldberg argued that the news is slanted with a liberal bias rather than providing objective, disinterested reporting. Written in a personal style, Goldberg tells insider stories about how the news is gathered and reported that show how almost everyone working in television news fosters a liberal bias in their reporting.

It is important to be sensitive to whether particular news vehicles present either a liberal or conservative bias. But it is far more important to be sensitive to the broader bias underlying all news vehicles—that is, the bias of commercialism, entertainment, and superficiality. If all we do is debate the liberal-conservative issue when it comes to news bias, we are in danger of missing the larger picture that the news media are providing us with a worldview that determines not only what we think about (as in agenda setting) but also what we think, how we think, and who we are.

Lack of bias means truthfulness. Pettegree (2014) points out that the earliest concern about quality of news concerned truthfulness: "Merchants, in particular, had a keen awareness of the value of information, and the dangers of acting on false rumour" (p. 3). This led to the importance of corroboration of facts across several sources so that lies and falsehoods could be weeded out.

Truthfulness also requires that journalists not make up facts to fill in the gaps of their stories or to "sweeten" their stories to make them more attractive or compelling to audiences. Jamieson and Waldman (2003) point out that sometimes journalists are tempted to tell a good story and ignore facts that get in the way of telling that story.

Fortunately, there are not many examples of fabrication, but the few major instances that have been revealed have really damaged journalism's credibility. In an article published in the *American Journalism Review*, Lori Robertson (2001) highlighted almost two dozen high-profile acts of ethical violations that resulted in the firing of journalists. The problem seems to be in all kinds of print vehicles, including well-known magazines (*Time, New Republic, Business Week*), large newspapers (*Wall Street Journal, New York Times, Boston Globe*), and small newspapers (*Myrtle Beach Sun News* in South Carolina, *Bloomsburg Press Enterprise* in Pennsylvania, and *Owensboro Messenger-Inquirer* in Kentucky), and cuts across all kinds of reporters, including sports, business, general news, columnists, and arts critics.

Perhaps the most publicized ethical problems were perpetrated by Jayson Blair, a 27-year-old reporter on the fast track at the *New York Times*. In order to enhance his career, he tried to write stories that would be so interesting that they would be selected for publication in the most prominent places in the newspaper. However, in order to write such stories, he liberally embellished the facts, even going so far as to make up whole stories. When *Times* editors finally began checking his stories, they found many fabrications and quickly fired Blair. But the damage to the credibility of the *Times* was done, and the editors felt compelled to publish a 14,000-word apologia on its front page (Wolf, 2003).

Sometimes newsmakers will fabricate facts and present them to journalists who must then decide whether to publish the fabricated facts or to expose them as being false. This is especially the case in political campaigns where the public relations staffs of candidates often manufacture "facts" to strengthen the position of their candidate. The 2012 presidential campaign was a good one for fact checkers like PolitiFact and FactCheck.org, which uncovered many instances of bending the truth as well as outright lies and brought these to the attention of the public. However, this exposure seemed to have had little effect on either voters or the campaigns. For example, the Romney campaign claimed that Barack Obama was ditching welfare work requirements. This was found to be false and reported as false by the fact checkers. However, when this campaign lie was exposed, it did not harm Romney's campaign. Either the electorate did not hear that it was a lie or did not care, because polling numbers were found to increase support for Romney as a result of the claim. When Romney pollster Neil Newhouse was confronted with the lie, he replied, "We're not going to let our campaign be dictated by fact checkers" (Poniewozik, 2012).

Balance

The criterion of balance means that journalists present all sides of an issue in an equal manner. Again, this is a simple concept that becomes complicated as we analyze it. If an issue is simple, it has only two sides, each of which has an equal number of potential arguments to support it. If we believe that issues meet these conditions, then we can design a relatively simple test for balance. For example, Fico and Soffin (1995) looked at balance in newspaper coverage of controversial issues such as abortion, condoms in schools, and various governmental bills. Balance was assessed by examining whether both sides of an issue were illuminated in terms of sources interviewed for both sides and whether assertions for both sides were in the headline, first paragraph, and graphics. They found that 48% of stories analyzed were one-sided; that is, a second side was not covered at all. They counted the number of story elements that illuminated the different sides of each issue and found that, on average, one side received three more elements compared to the other side—therefore, the average story was imbalanced. Only 7% of stories were completely balanced. The authors concluded that professional capability or ethical self-consciousness are lacking in many journalists.

Most issues, however, have more than two sides. For example, let's take abortion, which is almost always presented as having two and only two sides. But when we start asking questions about when life begins—conception, zygote, when a child is able to function on his or her own if induced, birth—then we can see there are multiple positions that can be taken on this issue and the criterion of balance would require that all positions be acknowledged in a news story.

Another problem with achieving balance arises when we realize that not all positions on an issue have an equal amount of potentially supporting information. For example, let's say journalists must cover a story where a person argues that the Earth is flat. Must those journalists work extra hard to find enough facts to support the flat Earth claim in order to write a good news story? Do those journalists have an obligation to make both sides of the "controversy" appeal equally credible? Clearly, in this example, if journalists give credence to the flat Earth claim equal to the spherical Earth claim, they will be misleading their audiences. The problem then shifts to determining which issues are equally balanced controversies and which are not and who should be trusted to determine which is which.

In summary, while it is important that we continually make good evaluations of news stories, all of the criteria we could use to engage in such evaluations require us to think through the complexity that each presents.

HOW CAN WE BECOME MORE MEDIA LITERATE WITH NEWS?

The information we acquire every day from what we consider news providers molds our view of the world. The gradual accumulation of information about what we think is important shapes our beliefs about how things work and about how things *should* work. These beliefs become the standards we use when evaluating people, events, and places. Thus over the long run, our exposure patterns to news are about more than acquiring information about current occurrences; it is more fundamentally an unavoidable process of constructing knowledge structures, beliefs, and attitudes. Therefore the more we think about our exposure patterns and the implications of those patterns, the more we can gain control over the process and make it work in our favor. Becoming more media literate involves the periodic assessment of exposure and quality.

Exposure Matters

The traditional news media cover the same events and present their stories in a very similar way. Thus if you wanted to be informed about national or international events every day, it doesn't matter whether you watch the ABC, CBS, or NBC evening news or read a daily newspaper—you would be exposed to the same stories. This pattern led scholars to observe that the traditional media set the agenda each day by deciding what to cover and what to ignore. Agenda-setting theory explains that the media are selective in what they present as news and what they emphasize as being the most important news. This selection and emphasis set the agenda; that is, the public accepts what the media highlight as most important (see McCombs & Reynolds, 2009; McCombs & Shaw, 1972). While the theory was created to explain how the news shapes public opinion for political campaigns and issues, it has moved into a broader realm beyond politics over the years. McCombs and Reynolds (2009) also say that beyond the "specifics of politics and election campaigns, the larger political culture is defined by a basic civic agenda of beliefs about politics and elections. Exploration of yet other cultural agendas is moving agenda-setting theory far beyond its traditional realm of public affairs" (p. 13).

In the past, we could control whether we exposed ourselves to traditional news media or not, but if we did, then the control shifted to the traditional news media which told us what was important. With the rise of nontraditional news media, we now have many alternative sources of news. Thus, the control of what we are exposed to shifts to us. Our exposure decisions are likely to be shaped by what we consider to be news. To think of this choice, consider the dimension of global to personal. At one pole of this dimension is global, which consists of patterns of events worldwide; this exposure takes you to countries, cultures, and historical periods of which you have little or no direct contact. The next "neighborhood" along this dimension is national, which consists of events taking place in your home country where you are likely to know the language, culture, and history and want to be kept up to date with current happenings. The next neighborhood is your region, which is likely the geographical area that you frequently visit on a regular basis. At the other end of this dimension is the personal pole. The news here is not limited by geography but by your sense of personal contacts; that is, you desire to know what is happening to people with whom you have a personal relationship. Where you focus your news exposure experiences along this dimension is determined in large part by your perspective on the news. If your perspective is outward directed, then you are likely to be highly curious about things that are foreign to you. In contrast, if your perspective is inward directed, then you are likely driven to search for exposures that involve personal contact with individuals. Media literacy is not associated with either pole of this dimension; instead, media literacy is reflected in the scope of your perspective. That is, the more neighborhoods that generate curiosity in you, the more broad will be your exposure. Thus media literacy warns against a narrow focus. If we limit ourselves to a narrow perspective that focuses only on our personal social networks, then we become blind to how governments work, the shape of the economy, and what is happening in other parts of the world.

Let's see where you are in your exposure patterns (see Exercise 9.1). First, rate how your news exposure is divided among the four neighborhoods. Then move on to the questions about your curiosity and knowledge to see how those differences are related to your exposure patterns.

The culture is becoming fragmented into smaller and smaller interest groups, and the people within each group seem to have a different need for news. Thus over time, the common experience is evaporating; that is, there is a diminishing knowledge base that we all share. Instead we each have a different set of facts about the world, which leads to a multiplicity of beliefs and attitudes. Thus when the public must make a choice about electing political leaders or supporting issues, there are many groups, each with a different approach, shouting at each other that they are right and all others are wrong. Thus the political discourse gets more diverse, more loud, more polarized, and less tolerant or understanding of other points of view.

It is more difficult to see commonalities. However, one likely commonality is the movement toward a culture of fear. This is because news outlets, regardless of niche audience, use the tool of triggering emotions to attract audiences and hold their attention. Fear is an easy emotion to trigger. News outlets focus on deviance and this triggers a fear in audiences that their well-being and lifestyle may be threatened by criminal activity, higher taxes and fewer services, a faltering economy leading to layoffs, selfish or incompetent leaders making bad decisions, and even bad weather. Rarely does any one of these individual messages paralyze us with fear, but over time the gradual reminder of risks and threats builds in each of us an uneasy fear that things are getting worse somehow.

Quality Matters

If we don't periodically evaluate the quality of our news sources, we run the risk of believing we are well informed when in reality we are not. Check out Table 9.2. Notice that most of the items in the table are concerned with accuracy and credibility. But quality also refers to scope. Because of selective exposure, we are likely to gravitate to stories that confirm our existing beliefs. It is comforting to continually be reminded that other people think the same way we do. And it is easier to avoid the dissonance that typically arises when we are presented with evidence that our beliefs are weak or wrong.

Interactivity with news has created a paradox. On the one hand, interactivity makes features available that draw people into news and make it more useful to them; these features include searchable archives, hyperlinks, discussion forums, and easy downloading of information. These things bring people closer to the news (Brown, 2001). On the other hand, the interactive features require considerable cognitive and emotional cost by demanding more patience, expertise, and cognitive resources that increase the likelihood of confusion and frustration (Bucy, 2004). Because we often get involved in interactive experiences with news, we think of the information we experience in these interactions as highly accurate, but this is not always the case.

Now, let's see how well you can apply the insights you learned in this chapter. Begin with Exercise 9.2 and think about the skills and knowledge structures that help you process meaning of news stories. Then move on to Exercise 9.3, which asks you to use those skills and knowledge structures to analyze and evaluate a news story. Then if you are ready for a more advanced experience of analyzing the news, do Exercises 9.4 and 9.5 to see how well you can see beyond the elements of a news story and picture the practices used by the journalists to work around constraints.

TABLE 9.2 ■ Types of Skills and Knowledge Needed to Deal With News and Information Messages in a Media-Literate Manner		
	Skills	**Knowledge**
Cognitive	Ability to analyze a news story to identify key points of information Ability to compare and contrast key points of information in the news story with facts in your knowledge structure Ability to evaluate the veracity of information in the story Ability to evaluate if the story presents a balanced presentation of the news event/issue	Knowledge of topic from many sources (media and real world)
Emotional	Ability to analyze the feelings of people in the news story Ability to put oneself into the position of different people in the story Ability to extend empathy to other people contiguous to the news story	Recall from personal experience how it would feel to be in the situation in the story
Aesthetic	Ability to analyze the craft and artistic elements in the story Ability to compare and contrast the artistry used to tell this story with that used to tell other stories	Knowledge of writing, graphics, photography, and so on Knowledge of good and bad stories and the elements that contributed to those qualities
Moral	Ability to analyze the moral elements in a story Ability to compare and contrast this story with other stories Ability to evaluate the ethical responsibilities of the journalists on this story	Knowledge of criticism of news and knowledge of the meaning of bias, objectivity, balance, and fairness Knowledge of other stories on this topic and how those journalists achieved balance and fairness Highly developed moral code for journalism

SUMMARY

The idea of what is news has undergone many changes over time and has influenced different perspectives, particularly the political philosophy, traditional journalism, news-working, economic, and personal perspectives. These changes also lead us to question what a journalist is and how we should judge the quality of news. These questions are especially important now that we are in the new media environment in which nontraditional news outlets are so prevalent, so niche oriented, and open to so much interactive participation among audiences, journalists, and newsmakers.

Further Reading

Henry, N. (2007). *American carnival: Journalism under siege in an age of new media*. Berkeley, CA: University of California Press. (326 pages with index)

This book is written by a journalist who is concerned about how traditional journalism can survive in the new media environment.

Jensen, C. (1995). *Censored: The news that didn't make the news—and why*. New York, NY: Four Walls Eight Windows. (332 pages with index)

Begun by the author in 1976, Project Censored invites journalists, scholars, librarians, and the general public to nominate stories that they feel were not reported adequately during that year. From the hundreds of submissions, the list is reduced to 25 based on "the amount of coverage the story received, the national or international importance of the issue, the reliability of the source, and the potential impact the story may have" (p. 15). A blue-ribbon panel of judges then selects the top 10 censored stories for the year.

Mindich, T. Z. (2005). *Tuned out: Why Americans under 40 don't follow the news*. New York, NY: Oxford University Press. (172 pages with index)

The author clearly documents that the last two generations of Americans have exhibited drastic declines in attention to news in the traditional media. Furthermore, only 11% of young people even attend to the news on the Internet. He develops some explanations for why news has become so irrelevant to the younger generations, then speculates about how this will impact the political system and society in general.

Paul, R. P., & Elder, L. (2006). *How to detect media bias & propaganda* (3rd ed.). Dillon Beach, CA: Foundation for Critical Thinking. (46 pages with glossary)

This short book focuses on critical thinking and the news. It presents a lot of practical advice on how to think about news stories critically and thereby protect oneself from bias, especially from novelty and sensationalism.

Roth, A. L., & Huff, M. (Eds.) (2017) *Censored 2018: The top censored stories and media analysis of 2016–2017*. New York, NY: Seven Stories Press.

This book presents 25 important news stories that were not covered at all or very little. It also includes seven other chapters that were written by social critics, such as Ralph Nader, that try to explain why the press favors certain types of stories while ignoring others that are potentially far more important to cover.

Schudson, M. (2003). *The sociology of news*. New York, NY: Norton. (261 pages, including end notes and index)

Schudson sharpens and clarifies many points in the argument that journalists "not only report reality but create it" (p. 2). He digs deep into the issue and offers explanations about how the news construction occurs and the effect those constructions have on the public. After providing a brief history of journalism, he identifies two criticisms as being especially salient today. The first is that news coverage of politics is critical and this promotes cynicism in the public. Second, news itself has gone soft; that is, it is a mix of information with entertainment rather than a legitimate effort to explain complex situations.

Keeping Up to Date

Journal of Broadcasting & Electronic Media (https://www.tandfonline.com/loi/hbem20)

Journalism & Mass Communication Quarterly (http://journals.sagepub.com/home/jmq)

These are scholarly journals that publish research that examines how news is presented in the content of the mass media, particularly newspapers and television

News Blogs

There are thousands of news blogs. Many are owned by major news organizations such as CNN (http://news.blogs.cnn.com) and the *New York Times* (http://www.nytimes.com/interactive/blogs/directory.html). Another popular news blog is the *Huffington Post* (http://www.huffingtonpost.com), which was started by Arianna Huffington independent of any news organization but was bought by AOL in 2011.

WikiLeaks (https://wikileaks.org)

Founded in 2007, WikiLeaks is a not-for-profit media organization that provides a secure and anonymous way for sources to leak information to the public. It relies on a network of volunteers from around the world. Leakers are typically whistle-blowers who work in private businesses and government agencies where they feel their organization is doing something harmful to the public so they steal the private information of that organization and make it available for the public to view.

EXERCISE 9.1
ASSESSING YOUR NEWS EXPOSURE

1. Think about the four neighborhoods along the global-personal dimension. What percentage of your time each day is spent searching out news on each of these neighborhoods?

   _____ % searching for news on international events

   _____ % searching for news on national events

   _____ % searching for news on regional events

   _____ % searching for news on personal events

   These percentages should sum to 100%.

2. Rate your curiosity about each of these four neighborhoods. That is, how interested are you typically every day to find out more detail about what is happening in each of these four neighborhoods? A rating of 10 means you are driven to find out everything; a rating of 0 means you have absolutely no interest in anything in that neighborhood.

   Degree of curiosity about news on international events: _____

   Degree of curiosity about news on national events: _____

Degree of curiosity about news on regional events: _____

Degree of curiosity about news on personal events: _____

3. Rate your existing knowledge base about each of these four neighborhoods. That is, how much information do you feel you have attained about the people and history of events in each of these four neighborhoods? A rating of 10 means you feel you are expert in your knowledge; a rating of 0 means you

know absolutely nothing about the people and events in that neighborhood.

Existing knowledge about news on international events: _____

Existing knowledge about news on national events: _____

Existing knowledge about news on regional events: _____

Existing knowledge about news on personal events: _____

EXERCISE 9.2
PREPARING TO ANALYZE A NEWS STORY

1. Take a blank sheet of paper and draw the structure of Table 9.2 on it. That is, create two columns: label one column "Skills" and the other column "Knowledge." Now create four rows and label them as "Cognitive," "Emotional," "Aesthetic," and "Moral." Your table should have eight blocks.

2. Think about an important issue that is triggering current events. For now, don't worry about seeking out any news stories on this issue or the events currently taking place. Instead, this is about the issue itself and what kinds of skills and knowledge you would need to get the most out of news coverage.

3. Write down the skills and knowledge you would need to achieve a basic minimal understanding of a story on this topic. Think in terms of your everyday viewing of news, where you just want to monitor the surface

facts to keep up with the day's major events.

4. Think about the skills and knowledge you would need to achieve a much more complete understanding about the meaning of the event in the news story. Think in terms of what it would take for you to be an expert on the event.

5. Look at what you have written in response to question 4. Does it differ much from what you have written in response to question 3? How much detail do you have in each of the eight blocks? With which blocks did you struggle the most? Why do you think you struggled there?

6. Compare the results of your tables with those of a friend. Did your friend have more details in certain blocks compared to yours? If so, did that additional detail extend your thinking? The more people's work you compare, the more you can see a range of differences.

EXERCISE 9.3
ANALYZING AND EVALUATING A NEWS STORY

After you have completed Exercise 9.2, find a news story on the topic you analyzed. It would be good to record the story so that you can look at it more than once.

1. How accurate are the individual facts in the story?

2. How complete is the set of facts?

   Are there obvious facts missing (who, what, when, where, why, and how)?

3. Are the facts presented in a meaningful context?

   Is there a historical context?

   Are events in this story compared/contrasted to other similar events?

4. Is the presentation of facts descriptive or persuasive?

   Does the journalist's voice come through in the story or does it appear that the facts speak for themselves?

Do you feel like you are being led to a particular conclusion rather than left alone to make up your own mind?

Do you feel that the journalist has an agenda?

5. Sources of information:

   Do you feel that the journalist used enough sources of information?

   Do you feel that the journalist used the best sources of information possible?

6. Do all the facts in the story confirm what you already knew or were you surprised by something?

   Does this story challenge you to think about things in a different way?

   Or does the story reinforce your existing beliefs and attitudes?

EXERCISE 9.4
INFERRING NEWS WORKERS' DECISIONS

Gather together three or four newspapers for the same day—the more the better.

1. Look at the composition of the first page across those newspapers, and think about the differences and similarities of the news perspectives.

a. What are the major stories in terms of placement and size?

b. What pictures and graphics are used? Are they used to present substance, or are they used merely to make the page more appealing to the eye?

c. How much of the front pages is composed of non-news matter?

2. Read the major news stories.

a. What criteria must have been used to select them?

b. What types of elements are emphasized in the stories? What are the facts that make this story news? What facts provide background context?

c. Is the story balanced, or are obvious viewpoints ignored?

3. Look at the sections of the newspapers.

a. Which sections are there (such as sports, women, business, etc.)?

b. Look at how the space is allocated. How much space is given to ads? How much to hard news? How much to soft, entertainment-type news?

4. What happened within the last 24 hours that did not get covered?

5. In summary, which of these newspapers do you think is the best and why?

6. Later today, listen to some news on the radio and watch some on television. How is the news different in these media compared to newspapers?

EXERCISE 9.5
EXERCISING YOUR SKILLS

Think of some current event of interest to you. Now pretend you are an editor of an online newspaper. What elements would you want to have in the story?

1. What sources would you want to access?

For people as sources, how will you go about getting access?

For non-people (such as the records of government agencies and businesses), are these sources considered private? If so, how can you get access to them?

2. What facts and figures would you want to gather?

List the questions you would ask.

Does the order of the questions matter?

3. What historical contextual factors would you want?

How far back should your coverage go?

During that time period, what are the key events that your readers should know in order to appreciate the event that is currently happening that makes this news?

4. Would you want to include visuals (such as graphics, photographs, or video) in your story?

If not, why?

If so, which visuals do you consider important?

If these visuals already exist, how will you get permission to use them?

If these visuals do not already exist, how will you go about producing them?

10

ENTERTAINMENT

Key Idea: Story formulas help designers of entertainment messages attract audience attention and condition audiences for repeat exposures.

Hulu's drama series *The Handmaid's Tale* has won multiple awards for its direction, acting, and writing.

Katherine, a freelance script writer, had waited 3 weeks to get an appointment with the vice president of Prestige Films and Entertainment Company so she could pitch her idea for a TV movie. If the vice president liked her idea, he would green-light the project, which would mean she would get paid to write the script. Prestige would then likely produce the 2-hour movie that could turn into a pilot for a television series.

Katherine was very nervous as she began her pitch. "This is a story about family values as seen through the eyes of a brother and sister who are suddenly orphaned. Chloe is 10 years old and Tony is her 14-year-old brother. The story opens with Chloe, Tony, and their parents on the run from some evil corporation thugs who are trying to track down the father for being a whistle-blower and exposing some illegal practices of the company where the father worked. The thugs find the family but the children narrowly escape as the thugs are killing the parents. Now orphans with no family or friends, the children have to keep moving around so that the thugs don't find them. Most of the movie is about how the brother and sister form a strong bond as they take care of each other. There is a series of scenes showing how they struggle to find transportation, shelter, and food as they evade the thugs chasing them. There are also some tender scenes where Chloe and Tony talk about their grief and fear. Finally, in the climax, the kids figure out a way to trick the thugs into an ambush where they are able to kill the thugs. They take the thugs' car and discover its trunk is full of cash. So the movie ends on a high note."

The vice president smiled broadly. "I love your idea. It's got so many great story elements. It's got tragedy. It's got action and suspense. It's got kids fighting to survive. It's got family values. It's got violence and retribution. I love it!"

"So you'll green-light the project?" Katherine couldn't believe that after 2 years of pitching various film projects, she finally had a winner.

"Yes. Definitely yes! But I'd like to see one change—one small, tiny change. If you agree to that, it's a go."

"What kind of change?"

"Could you make Tony a porpoise?"

"A porpoise—a fish?"

"Yes, let's make Tony a fish. TV viewers love animals!"

Humans have been telling stories for over 100,000 years. Haven (2007) points out that "every culture in the history of this planet has created stories: myths, fables, legends, folk tales" (p. 4). He says that not all cultures have created a written language, not all cultures have developed codified laws, and not all cultures have created logical argumentation, but all cultures have developed and used stories. What makes stories so useful for humans is that they are entertaining vehicles for communicating meaning. This communication of meaning depends on a sharing of story formulas.

This chapter begins with an examination of general storytelling formulas that producers of media messages use to create their entertainment stories. The formulas are the guides; that is, they tell storytellers what elements are available to put into their stories and how those elements should be assembled. These formulas tell producers how to begin their stories in a way that grabs the attention of the audience. These formulas tell producers how to keep the story going in a way to hold audience attention, and they also tell producers how to deliver a satisfying payoff to audiences so they will find the experience pleasurable and therefore want to experience more stories. Because we as the audience also understand these formulas (albeit unconsciously and intuitively), we can easily follow the progression of the action.

This chapter also examines challenges of storytelling in the media and the patterns that have been documented about elements frequently found in media stories. These patterns tell us things about what media storytellers have focused on most and what they have regarded as most important over time. Finally, the chapter concludes with a set of guidelines to help you increase your media literacy with entertainment messages.

STORY FORMULAS

On the surface, it appears that the media present a wide variety of entertainment messages. But when we analyze those messages, we can see that they follow standard designs. For example, all entertainment stories on commercial TV are designed to fit into standard time blocks (30 minutes, 1 hour, or 2 hours), all begin with teasers and story credits, and all have interruptions for commercial messages. Popular music follows standard musical formulas. None of those songs is a purely random sequence of notes. Musical formulas tell musicians which notes are played in sequence (melody progressions) and which notes are to be played together (chords). There are a small number of standard rhythms. All of the songs are creative variations on the standard formula. The same is true for any media message.

Story formulas are guides for both producers of media messages as well as for audiences. These formulas help producers navigate the process of making decisions as they select story elements and structure those selections in a meaningful sequence. They help audiences quickly process their ideas about characters and efficiently follow the unfolding action.

BOX 10.1
ANALOGY: CONSTRUCTING A HOUSE AND CONSTRUCTING A STORY

The processes of constructing a house and constructing a story are similar in many ways.

When architects construct a house, they know that all houses must have a foundation, an outer shell with windows and at least one door, and a roof. The foundation can be made of many different materials (poured concrete, cinder block, etc.) and sizes (footing, half basement, full basement), so architects have options, but they know they must have some kind of a foundation. The outer shell is required but again, architects have options of building materials (brick, stone, wood, aluminum, etc.).

Houses can be of different styles (such as ranch, two-story colonial, craftsman, Cape Cod, etc.). Each of these styles still must conform to the basic requirements for a house, but each comes with its own set of guidelines that build on the basic requirements for a house.

While all houses conform to architectural guidelines, there are so many options available

(down to lighting fixtures and color of paint on the walls) that no two houses are exactly the same.

When constructing an entertainment message, storytellers know that all stories must have a beginning hook to grab the attention of the audience, interesting characters, and a plot that audience members want to follow as characters struggle with conflict. The choice of characters offers many options (by age, ethnicity, personality characteristics, etc.). The conflict can be between two characters, a character and society, or a character and an idea.

Stories vary by genre (such as drama, comedy, romance, etc.). Each of these genres builds off the general story formula but still must conform to the basic requirements of that formula.

While all stories conform to storytelling formulas, there are so many options available to storytellers that no two stories are exactly the same.

There are many different storytelling formulas, depending on the constraints of different media and the conventions of different types—or **genres**—of stories. Think of the arrangement of these formulas in a tree structure. The trunk of the tree is composed of the most **general entertainment storytelling formulas**. These include guidelines about how to attract any audience, how to hold that audience's attention while the story unfolds and the audience is pulled into the action and forms virtual relationships with the story's characters, and how to resolve the action with a satisfying conclusion. Branching off this central trunk of guidelines are formulas about different kinds—or genres—of stories, such as mystery, action/adventure, romance, and comedy. Each of these major branches has its own sub-branches, and each of these has its own sub-sub-branches and twigs until we get out to the leaves, which are the different individual stories. Thus each individual story is a product of how a story producer has worked his or her way through all the design decisions from the general trunk outward.

General Story Formula

The most general of all storytelling formulas provides guidelines for what all stories must have. Such a formula says that all stories must begin with a problem for at least one character. The character struggles to overcome obstacles along the path of achieving what he or she wants and this involves the character coming into conflict with other characters, institutions, and ideas. This conflict is heightened throughout the story to a point of climax, where the conflict is resolved either by the character finally achieving the long-sought-after goal or by the character adapting to the conflict in some way.

Thus the general storytelling formula exhibits three essential guidelines. First, all stories must generate conflict. This pulls audiences into the action, and people continue to follow the story to see how the conflict will be resolved. Second, all stories are told through the point of view of a character; this is the protagonist. Audiences experience the action through the protagonists' point of view; that is, the values they use to justify their actions. Third, all stories need to trigger emotions in the audience; the more vivid the elements in the story, the more likely that strong emotions will be generated. The emotional journey is the payoff for audiences who want to be entertained.

This general formula is used not only by the creators of media messages; the formula is also used by us—the audience—to help us easily recognize the good and bad characters and to quickly find where we are in the story. Stories that follow the formulas the closest usually have the largest audiences, because they are the easiest to follow. The more experience we have with entertainment messages, the more we learn the story formula. We are conditioned to expect certain plot points, certain pacing, certain types of characters, and certain themes.

There is a very large scholarly literature that examines how media entertainment stories attract the attention of audiences, how audiences process those stories, and how those stories affect audiences. Story producers can find a lot of useful information in this research literature, even though the findings are more suggestive than definitive because many of those empirical studies present complex or equivocal results. For example, the research shows that violence is typically a story element that attracts and holds audience interest, but this does not hold for everyone, and it appears that it is not the violence per se but the arousing nature of violent portrayals that is the active element (Zillmann, 1991). Also, the research shows that humor is a desirable element to put into media stories. However, there are many different types of humor and because humor is personal, not all audience members "get" all types of humor (Boxman-Shabtai & Shifman, 2014). Suspense has been found to be a useful characteristic, but not all audience members enjoy suspense the same way (Shafer, 2014). Research has shown that in general, people enjoy stories more that have a higher degree of realism, but realism can be assessed along at least six different dimensions (Cho, Shen, & Wilson, 2014). Although disgust repels and offends us, it has functionally evolved over time to compel our attention to both core disgusts (i.e., blood, guts, body products) and socio-moral violations (i.e., injustices, brutality, racism), making it a quality of many entertainment messages that may keep audiences engrossed and engaged; however, not all people like to feel disgusted when being entertained (Rubenking & Lang, 2014).

Genres

The overall entertainment story formula is elaborated in different ways across different genres of entertainment. Let's examine the story formula in the genres of drama, comedy, and romance.

Drama. The drama genre has three basic sub-genres that illuminate three types of drama entertainment: tragedy, mystery, and action/horror (Sayre & King, 2003). Tragedy must have characters that are perceived by the audience as noble and good. However, bad things happen to these characters either because they have a fatal flaw they cannot get around (as is the case in Shakespearean tragedies) or because fate has conspired to do them in (such as what happens in the movie *Titanic*).What audiences enjoy about tragedies is the opportunity to compare themselves with the tragic characters and feel better off than those unfortunate characters.

With the mystery formula, an important element of the plot is missing. For example, in a "whodunit" mystery, the *who* is missing. A serious crime usually triggers the story, and a focal character must uncover information in order to figure out who committed the crime. Audiences are drawn into the story as they try to solve the mystery for themselves. In her book *Talking About Detective Fiction*, bestselling novelist P. D. James (2009) says that "the formula for a successful detective story is 50 percent good detection, 25 percent character and 25 percent what the writer knows best" (p. 115).

The action/horror formula is primarily plot driven as good and evil fight it out in ever-deepening conflict. Characters are stereotypes or comic book types. Within several seconds after being introduced to a character, we know whether that character is a hero or a villain. Characters are static and don't change. The plot relies on fast-paced action that maximizes arousal in the audience. The primary emotions evoked are fear, suspense, and vengeance. Violence is a staple in almost all of these stories. The formula of violence tells us that it is okay for criminals to behave violently throughout a program as long as they are caught at the end of the show. This restores a sense of peace—at least until the commercials are over and the next show begins. Also, we feel that it is permissible for police officers, private investigators, and good-guy vigilantes to break the law and use violence as long as it is used successfully against the bad guys.

Comedy. With the comedy formula, minor conflict situations flare up and set the action in motion. The conflict is heightened verbally, usually through deceit or insults. Characters are developed through their unusual foibles and quick wit. The action is neatly resolved at the end of the show, and all the main characters end up happy, because the tension created by their problems has been eliminated.

One sub-genre of comedy is the character comedy or comedy of manners. Here the humor arises out of character quirks that illuminate the craziness of everyday situations. Characters find themselves in difficult situations that we all encounter every day. As characters try to work their way through these situations, the absurdity of certain social conventions is illustrated, and this makes us laugh. Examples include *Seinfeld* and *Big Bang Theory*. Another sub-genre of comedy is the put-down comedy, where certain characters have power over other characters and exercise that power in humorous ways. Examples include *Two and a Half Men* and *The Office*.

AF Archive/Alamy Stock Photo

The Netflix series *Unbreakable Kimmy Schmidt* tells the story of a quirky young woman, played by Ellie Kemper, who is adjusting to life in NYC after she is rescued from a doomsday cult.

Romance. A romance story begins with a person experiencing either loneliness from a lack of a relationship or a relationship that is bad due to betrayal, jealousy, or fear. As audience members, we are led to identify with the main character and feel her pain. But she is full of hope for what seems like an unattainable goal. Through hard work and virtue, she gets closer and closer to her goal—even though she experiences frequent heart-rendering setbacks—until the story climaxes with the fulfillment of the goal, which transmits intense emotions to the audience.

Writers who have mastered this formula are very successful. For example, among all paperbacks sold in the United States, about half are in the genre of the romance novel. One romance novelist who really understood the formula is Barbara Cartland. She published 723 romance novels, all following the same basic romance formula. She was so successful that she sold almost 1 billion books. Did she produce a body of great literature that will be read for centuries? No, of course not. Did she recognize a market for a particular kind of story and manufacture many products to meet that need? There is no doubt of this.

After years of watching stories on television and in the movies, we have become adept at following the formulas about characters, plots, and themes. We know these formulas so well that many of us think we can write and produce our own shows. Perhaps some of us can, but producing a successful entertainment message for the mass media is very challenging. While the formulas are deceptively simple, making them work well is difficult.

COMPARE & CONTRAST
GENERAL STORY FORMULA AND GENRE STORY FORMULAS

Compare: The general story formula and genre story formulas are *the same* in the following ways:

- Both are guidelines that are used by creators of media entertainment messages when they are making decisions about how to tell their stories.

- Both are templates that audience members use to make sense of the media stories during their exposures; these formulas set their expectations about who the characters are and what they are likely to do.

Contrast: The general story formula and genre story formulas are *different* in the following ways:

- The general story formula presents the elements that all media stories should have to attract audience attention and hold that attention throughout the exposure.

- Genre story formulas build off the general story formula by adding elements that are characteristic of a particular genre.

CHALLENGES

Although these formulas are relatively simple for audiences to understand, they are exceedingly difficult for producers to follow well when creating entertainment messages. The challenges arise from using different media, changing public taste, and dealing with risk.

Different Media

Telling an entertaining story presents a different challenge as you move from one medium to another. If you plan to tell a story in print, you have only one perceptual channel (eyes), and you need to use words to trigger vivid images in the minds of the readers. If you plan to tell a story in song, you again need to trigger vivid images and strong emotions, but you must do this through the audience's ears, not their eyes. With a song, you need to use words that sound good, not just look good on a screen. That is, the words must have a certain cadence that goes along with the rhythm of the music. Often the song has a rhyming pattern, which also presents a special challenge to songwriters. With popular music, words must tell their full story in 2 or 3 minutes.

Commercial television is one of the most challenging media for telling stories. At first, it might seem the least challenging because it appears to have few perceptual constraints; that is, you can use audio as well as video elements. Also, you are not dependent on the reading abilities of audience members. But it is very difficult to attract an audience on commercial television because there are so many competing channels of broadcast, cable, and video on demand. Also, it is a huge challenge to hold onto an audience once it is initially attracted because commercial television interrupts stories frequently for commercials, and some of these breaks have a dozen or more ads and last for 4 or more minutes. Viewers can forget about the story or lose their motivation to stay tuned unless that story has really intrigued them. Therefore, storytellers on television must do things to catch the audience's interest right from the beginning; they must build the action to a high point before each commercial break so that the audience will want to stay tuned throughout the commercial pod and find out what happens when the show returns, and they must keep the action interesting every minute so that people who are flipping through channels will want to stop and watch the show.

With television programs, not only must producers use the well-known formulas, they must also be creative enough to break with the story formula to keep their stories fresh for viewers who have seen the same plot hundreds of times. These two tasks seem impossible to attain at the same time, and this is why the percentage of television series that have lasted more than several dozen episodes is small.

Netflix is one of the most popular streaming services that screens TV shows and movies on a variety of media devices.

Entertainment messages on the web (such as videos on YouTube and Hulu) do not have the constraints of timing (they can be any length and accessed at any time) that videos on traditional television channels have. However, web messages face a great deal more competition. More video is uploaded to YouTube in one month than the three major TV networks have created in 60 years (Bullas, n.d.). If you wanted to view the videos uploaded to YouTube last week, it would take you more than 40 years of viewing with no breaks. So if you want your uploaded video to attract a significant audience, you have a huge challenge of breaking through the clutter from all the competition.

Changing Public Taste

Storytelling formulas must evolve as public tastes change over time. People get bored with too much repetition and look for something slightly different. Producers of entertainment messages know that while they analyze messages that have been most successful in the past, they cannot simply copy those messages and expect to achieve equal success.

The public has certain expectations about what it will and will not tolerate in entertainment. We can see where this line of acceptability is when the public gets offended and complains—particularly in the areas of bad language, sexual portrayals, and violence. Television programmers are essentially conservative and fearful of offending viewers, so they present content that they believe reflects mainstream American values.

This line of acceptability, however, changes over time as people get over their shock at a new kind of portrayal, then eventually get used to it. For example, writing in the late 1980s, George Comstock (1989) pointed out that

> much of what is on television today would not have been considered acceptable by broadcasters or the public 20 or even 10 years ago. Public tastes and social standards have changed, and television has made some contribution to these changes by probing the borders of convention accompanying each season. . . . These conventions of popular entertainment provide television, as they do other media, with rules that minimize the possibility of public offense. (p. 182)

Since Comstock wrote that, television has continued to push the line of public acceptance, and what offended viewers in the 1980s hardly gets their attention today.

The same evolution of a formula has been occurring with popular music. The basic formula of popular songs is a story about love or sex. For example, Christianson and Roberts (1998) conducted a content analysis of 60 years of popular music. While they found that 70% of all songs have dealt with the topics of sex and love, the way those topics have been treated has changed. They noticed that in the early decades of their study, love was treated as an emotion, and the lyrics were symbolic; that is, the words suggested actions but left it up to the listeners to imagine the sex. In contrast, the later decades of their analysis found that love was treated as a physical act, and the lyrics were much more explicit in describing those acts.

Dealing With Risk

Producers of entertainment messages realize they are taking on a huge risk, because using the media to tell entertainment stories typically consumes a great deal of resources and the chance of earning back one's initial investment is very small. For example, videographers might spend several months shooting and editing a story, then put it on a video web platform where it attracts only several hundred visitors, which is too small of an audience to attract advertisers. If they choose stories that are too standard and formulaic, they risk boring viewers who will not return to view subsequent episodes in a series. On the other hand, if they break with the formulas too much, they risk confusing viewers or, worse, offending them.

When TV programmers guess right about breaking with entertainment formulas, they can attract fairly large audiences. The Fox television network rose to prominence in the 1990s by pushing the envelope of acceptability in TV storytelling with shows such as *When Good Pets Go Bad*, *World's Scariest Police Shootouts*, and *Who Wants to Marry a Multimillionaire?* While these shows drew a lot of criticism, they also attracted large audiences, and Fox grew to rival the big three dominant TV networks (ABC, CBS, NBC) at the time.

While disgust may be seen as a negative reaction, it may also keep an audience engaged with a story.

TV programmers are usually very conservative with risk and typically force others to share the risk with them. For example, the major television networks have developed compensation conventions by paying only about 80% of production costs for new shows, which forces producers to attract large audiences if they want to make money. To illustrate, let's say you have developed a new television show and the audience loved the pilot. The network contracts with you to produce a full season of 22 episodes. At this point you would be feeling extremely successful, because few producers are offered such an opportunity compared to the thousands of producers who are constantly pitching story ideas to network programmers. However, you are still facing a huge challenge. It will cost you about $40 million to produce those 22 episodes. Because the network pays a fee of only about 80%, you will lose about $8 million by the end of that season. If your show is cancelled after one season, you have a huge loss. So you feel a high degree of pressure to attract a large enough audience so that your contract will be renewed for a second season. If you are able to do this, you have the power to negotiate a much more favorable contract and you will start to make money. And the more times you get your show renewed for an additional season, the more you are demonstrating your ability to attract a large audience, and the more money you make.

Hollywood films are another very challenging medium because they cost so much to produce and the risk of failure is so great, with more than 90% of all Hollywood films failing to earn back their basic production costs at the box office. Producers continually analyze the most successful movies to try to find the magic formulas that made them so successful. For example, screenwriter Sue Clayton analyzed successful and unsuccessful Hollywood films to try to figure out which elements are most associated with success. From this analysis, she discovered a formula, which she calls the genetic blueprint for a successful movie. This blueprint calls for 30% action, 17% comedy, 13% good vs. evil, 12% love/sex/romance, 10% special effects, 10% plot, and 8% music. This formula shows that *Titanic* and *Toy Story 2* were perfect movies (C. Baker, 2003). While it is doubtful that we could ever reduce the formula for a successful movie or story to a precise mathematical formula, there are certain characteristics all stories must have in order to appeal to audiences.

PATTERNS

For almost a century, media scholars have been analyzing the content of media messages to identify patterns of elements used in these stories. These analyses have been conducted to generate answers to questions such as these: How much antisocial content (e.g., violence, irresponsible sexual behavior, bad language, or illicit drug use) is portrayed in the media? Are characters in entertainment stories portrayed in a realistic manner—in terms of gender, ethnicity, socioeconomic status (SES), professions, and so on? What are the underlying values portrayed in media entertainment stories?

Sometimes, scholars will attempt to answer these kinds of questions with a deep analysis of one novel, one movie, or one TV series. These scholars, who take a humanist approach to research, often reveal interesting patterns within one media message or the work of one producer. Other scholars, who are more interested in documenting broad patterns to reflect how stories are told across many entertainment messages, take a scientific approach by using a method called **content analysis**. Content analysis is a scientific technique of counting occurrences of various things (e.g., character's gender, age, ethnicity, occupations, etc.). The validity of the findings generated by content analysis relies on samples of shows that are analyzed as being representative of larger populations of shows. This method worked well until around the end of the 20th century. Throughout the 1900s, most people went to the same movies, listened to the same music, and watched the same TV shows, so it was relatively easy to identify the mainstream media messages and sample them in a representative way. For example, in the early days of TV broadcasting, content analysts knew that over 95% of all TV viewing was on shows offered by the three broadcast networks (ABC, CBS, and NBC). So if they sampled from the shows broadcast by those three networks, they could construct a sample that was representative of what almost all Americans were watching on TV. But over time the audience has been fragmenting so by the early 1990s, the content analysis conducted by the National Television Violence Study (NTVS) had to sample from 23 TV channels to capture even what 50% of the viewing audience was watching. Since then the audience has fragmented even more with Internet providers of video. Now in 2018, the top-drawing TV network (CBS) averages about 8 million viewers, which is a rating of about 2.4% of the total audience. Only four providers (CBS, NBC, HBO, and ABC) average as much as a 1% rating. Now if researchers wanted to conduct a content analysis that could document patterns across the entire TV landscape, they would have to include more than several hundred TV channels in their sample, which no one has yet attempted to do. Furthermore, with the fragmentation of the TV viewing audience and the proliferation of so many different sub-sub-sub-genres, it is unrealistic to expect any research study to be able to present patterns that represent the entire TV entertainment landscape. Instead, scientific studies now attempt to see if there are patterns only within tiny slivers of TV programming, such as body image themes in rap music videos (Zhang, Dixon, & Conrad, 2010), indirect aggression in animated Disney films (Coyne & Whitehead, 2008), or how characters on two TV series talk about gender (Van Damme, 2010).

It is still useful, however, for you to understand the dominant patterns that content analysts found in the past. This will sensitize you to issues about gender and ethnic equality or representation, about the prevalence of antisocial behaviors, and about the underlying values that may still be influencing media content.

Character Patterns

Content analyses of the television landscape in the 1970s to 1990s showed that producers of stories were featuring patterns of characters that were very different from patterns of people in the real world (see Table 10.1). The patterns of gender, ethnicity, age, marital status, SES, and occupations have been very different in the television world compared to the real world over the years. If we notice these demographic patterns in the television world and assume that they are the same in the real world, we will be creating faulty information for ourselves. For example, look at Table 10.2 to see the differences by occupation between the TV and real worlds.

TABLE 10.1 ■ Demographic Patterns in the Television World	
Demographic	**Patterns**
Gender	Males used to outnumber females three to one in the television world. Men were more likely to be shown as working and in a wider variety of jobs than were women, who were typically portrayed as stay-at-home moms or working at low status jobs.
Ethnicity	Eighty percent of all characters were White Americans. African Americans comprised only 2% of television characters until the late 1960s, when they jumped to about 10% of all characters. By the 1990s, African Americans had accounted for about 16% of the main and minor roles, which was larger than their percentage (12%) in the real-world population of the United States. Hispanics, however, have not fared as well. Although Hispanics made up about 9% of the U.S. population, only about 2% of all television characters were Hispanic.
Age	Three quarters of all television characters were between the ages of 20 and 50, but in the real world, only one third of the population is between these ages. Young children and the elderly are underrepresented on television. Fictional characters younger than age 19 make up only 10% of the total television population, even though they make up one third of the U.S. population. Also, characters older than age 50 accounted for about 15% of all television characters.
Marital status	Marital status was obvious with about 80% of the women and 45% of the men. Of those for whom you could tell their marital status, more than 50% of the women were married, whereas less than one third of the men were married.
Socioeconomic status	Almost half the characters on television were wealthy or ultra-wealthy, and very few (less than 10%) were lower class.

Sources: Comstock, Chaffee, Katzman, McCombs, and Roberts (1978); Davis (1990); Glascock (2001); Greenberg, Edison, Korzenny, Fernandez-Collado, and Atkin (1980); Mastro and Greenberg (2000); and Signorielli and Kahlenberg (2001).

TABLE 10.2 ■ Comparison of Occupation Prevalence in the TV World and the Real World		
Occupation	% in TV World	% in Real World
Medical workers	12.1	0.9
Police	11.4	0.9
Lawyers	08.3	0.7
Executives/managers	06.4	31.0
Media people	08.3	0.3
Space travelers	05.9	0.0001
Salespeople	02.6	11.8
Forensic specialists	04.5	0.01

Source: Medich (2002).

What could account for this dominance of males, Whites, and youthful adults? Perhaps it is due to the demographics of the people who are television writers. Turow (1992) pointed out that according to the Writers Guild of America, White males accounted for more than three quarters of the writers employed in film and TV. Minorities accounted for only 2% of all writers. In a survey of the age, gender, and ethnicity of writers working in Hollywood's television and film industries in 1985, it was reported that it was dominated by White males. In 2002, the same pattern was found as far as gender and ethnicity (Bielby & Bielby, 2002), and Glascock (2001) reported that males outnumber females 3.6 to 1 among creative personnel, which includes producers, directors, and writers.

Furthermore, the characters typically portrayed in television were two-dimensional stereotypes. Stereotypes are positive from the point of view that they are easy for viewers to recognize. But stereotypes can also have a negative effect because they are often inadequate as well as biased, they often serve as obstacles to rational assessment, and they are resistant to social change.

We use stereotypes in dealing with real-world information, not just media portrayals. For example, when we meet a new person, we try to "type" that person based on the characteristics we can immediately see, such as age, gender, appearance, how the person talks, and so on. Once we have typed someone, we have a set of expectations for that person. For example, if we see a 5-year-old girl in a fancy dress playing with a doll on the steps of a church, we would immediately call up a specific set of expectations. In contrast, if we see a middle-aged man with a beer belly straining through his dirty T-shirt, chewing tobacco, and cleaning a rifle, we would call up a very different set of expectations. Stereotypes provide us with a set of expectations that we can access quickly as we encounter people and events. They are a necessary mode of processing characters, especially when there are thousands of messages coming at us quickly every day and we need to create order out of "the great blooming, buzzing confusion of reality" (Lippmann, 1922, p. 96).

Characters in the television world are developed as stereotypes according to certain formulas, which make the characters easily and quickly recognizable to viewers. Look at the examples of stereotypes in Table 10.3. For each of these stereotypes, a clear image likely comes into your mind. You have seen each of these characters many times. When one of them appears in a story, it only takes a few seconds for you to recognize who that character is.

Stereotypes, however, can be harmful when they lead audiences to believe that all people of a given type share certain negative characteristics. This is why two groups—African Americans and women—are vocal in their complaints about how their demographic groups are stereotypically portrayed in television stories. Stereotypes in some other areas, such as occupations, families, the elderly, and body images, can also be harmful.

Controversial Content Elements

In the world of media entertainment, everything can be forgiven except dullness. When TV was being criticized for having so much violence, Howard Stringer, former president of CBS, was arguing against standards to clean up television by saying, "We don't want to turn the vast wasteland into a dull wasteland" (*USA Today*, July 1, 1993, p. 2A). And that is the key—TV and all the entertainment media must avoid being dull, so they titillate audiences by playing around with the line of acceptability on controversial topics such as sex, homosexuality, violence, and language.

Sex

A large number of people in the American culture are offended by sexual portrayals and nudity on television. The Federal Communications Commission (FCC) is sensitive to this and acts as a watchdog. For example, the FCC fined CBS $550,000 for a

TABLE 10.3 ■ Examples of Prevalent Stereotypes
The strong, self-reliant police detective who uses unconventional methods to deal with the scum on the street. He is irritated by his authoritarian bosses but always gets the job done using his own unorthodox methods.
The nurturing mother who has kooky kids and an idiot husband.
The sexy young female actress/model/nurse/secretary who becomes a romantic interest of a male hero.
The dumb blonde who is superficial, cares only about physical appearance and dress styles, and has no common sense.
The young street punk who commits petty and violent crimes, usually for drugs. He is tough and sassy until police intimidate him into making a plea bargain.
The nerdy male adolescent who displays hilariously dysfunctional social skills. Although he is very sensitive, he never learns from his social mistakes.

breast-baring incident at the 2004 Super Bowl in order to placate the large number of people who complained (Fabrikant, 2004). However, producers continually push the line to test the public's tolerance of sexual portrayals.

Sexual activity on television has been prevalent since the 1970s (Buerkel-Rothfuss, 1993; Cassata & Skill, 1983). If we limit our definition of sex to visual depictions of intercourse, the rate fluctuates around one (Greenberg et al., 1993) or two (Fernandez-Collado, Greenberg, Korzenny, & Atkin, 1978) acts per hour of prime time. In soap operas, the rate is even higher.

If we expand the definition to include all visual depictions of sexual activity, such as kissing, petting, homosexuality, prostitution, and rape, the hourly rates go up to about 3 acts on prime time and 3.7 acts per hour on soap operas (Greenberg et al., 1993). And when the definition is further expanded to include talk about sex as well as sexual imagery, the rate climbs to 16 instances per hour on prime time (Sapolsky & Tabarlet, 1990). Most of this talk about sex is on situation comedies in the early evening, when it is presented in a humorous context.

The most recent major set of studies was conducted from 1997 to 2002, which analyzed 2,817 programs across 10 channels and found that about two thirds of all shows (64%) contain some sexual content and 14% portray sexual intercourse. Among the 20 top-rated shows among teens, 83% contained sexual portrayals. The overall rate was about three scenes per hour. Two thirds (67%) of all network prime-time shows contain either talk about sex or sexual behavior, averaging more than five scenes per hour. And the rates of sexual portrayal continue to increase. Over that 5-year time span, the percentage of shows portraying sexual intercourse doubled from 7% to 14% (Kaiser Family Foundation, 2003; Kunkel, Eyal, & Donnerstein, 2007). However, when we take a longer time span, the opposite pattern is revealed. To illustrate, Hetsroni (2007) conducted a meta-analysis of the findings from content analysis about sexual portrayals on television. After examining the findings derived from 2,588 hours of broadcasts from 18 seasons, Hetsroni concluded that the frequency per hour of most of the sexual contents had decreased over the years. This is particularly notable for dialogues about sex and normative heterosexual conduct, but it is also true for illegal sexual interactions and messages about risks and responsibilities in sexual behavior.

Which conclusion should we believe? Are sexual portrayals increasing or decreasing on television? It appears the best way to answer these questions is to acknowledge that the rates of sexual portrayals change over time and that these changes go in cycles. Across some time periods, there appears to be an increase in portrayals as producers push the line of acceptability, while across other time periods, there appears to be a decrease in portrayals as producers cut back in response to public complaints. The bottom line here is that sexual portrayals will always be a part of media entertainment messages, because humans have always been—and will always be—interested in sex.

Most depictions of sexual behavior are not presented responsibly from a health point of view. Schrag (1990) reports that American children and teens view an average of more than 14,000 sexual references and innuendos on television each year. Of these, less than 150 refer to the use of birth control, so the rate of unprotected sex is very high, yet there is a very low incidence of sexually transmitted diseases (STDs) or pregnancies depicted in these stories. This situation may be changing. For example, by the 1997–1998 television season, about 9% of shows dealing with sex presented safe-sex messages, and this had increased to 15% of shows in the 2001–2002 television season (Kaiser Family Foundation, 2003). A few years later, the Kaiser Family Foundation (2010) released a follow-up study that found that the number of sexual scenes on television had nearly doubled since 1998. The report also said that while the inclusion of references to "safer-sex" issues—such as waiting to have sex, using protection, or possible consequences of unprotected sex—has also increased since 1998, that rate has leveled off in recent years. This finding was further amplified by Kunkel et al. (2007), who reported that topics related to sexual risks or responsibilities (e.g., condom use, abstinence) are increasingly included on television, but nonetheless remain infrequent overall. Such safe-sex messages occur most frequently in program environments where they are most relevant (i.e., when sexual intercourse is included in the story).

Try conducting your own content analysis of some media entertainment by doing Exercise 10.1. As you work through the challenges in setting up and conducting a content analysis, think about the implications of your decisions on the eventual patterns you will find.

Homosexuality

The U.S. television industry has a long history of ignoring, stereotyping, and marginalizing homosexuality (Harrington, 2003). Gay and lesbian issues or characters were virtually invisible on television in the 1950s and early 1960s. Then, in the 1970s, gay characters began to appear, but they were limited to two treatments. One treatment was the coming-out story, and the other was the "queer monster" story. Furthermore, although the 1970s ushered in prime-time shows about gay characters, they were typically played by straight actors and marketed to a straight audience.

In the 1980s, depictions of homosexuality declined dramatically due to the conservatism of the Reagan years and the growing concern about HIV/AIDS (and its association with gay male sexuality) (Gross, 2001). Gay characters began to appear in greater frequency throughout the 1990s, in part due to a growing stigma attached to anti-gay prejudice and a growing recognition of a gay consumer market (Gross, 2001). By the late 1990s, about 50 network series had lesbian, gay, or bisexual recurring characters, more than twice the total of all previous decades of television. In 1997, prime-time viewers witnessed comedienne Ellen DeGeneres, who played Ellen Morgan on ABC's *Ellen*, come out as the first lesbian lead actress/character on network television.

Matt Winkelmeyer/Getty Images Entertainment/Getty Images

Janet Mock, the transgender writer, TV host, and trans rights activist, exemplifies how the LGBTQ community is gaining increasing visibility in the media.

The following year, NBC featured the first network gay male lead in its hit show *Will & Grace*. During the fall 1999 television season, the big four television networks premiered 26 new series. There were 17 gay characters on the four major networks and about the same number of Black, Asian, and Latino characters combined. A big reason for this is that there are many gays in Hollywood and not many minorities (Brownfield, 1999).

In many respects, the 1990s seemed to transcend the longstanding "rules" for representing homosexuality on television: (a) Gay or lesbian characters must be restricted to one-time appearances in television series or one-shot television movies; (b) gay and lesbian characters can never be "incidentally" gay—instead, their sexuality must be the "problem" to be "solved"; (c) their problem should be explored in terms of its effects on heterosexuals; and (d) gay and lesbian erotic desire must be completely absent (Dow, 2001, pp. 129–130; see also Gross, 2001).

Although there are more representations of homosexuality than ever before, scholars caution against the presumption that these are necessarily more progressive representations. As throughout television history, gays and lesbians are still more likely to appear in comedies than dramas, where the line between "laughing with" and "laughing at" remains strategically ambiguous. Also, gay and lesbian characters are still often portrayed by straight (or not "out") actors and marketed to straight audiences (Battles & Hilton-Morrow, 2002; Dow, 2001; Gross, 2001).

The most recent analysis of sexual portrayals on television programs found portrayals of non-heterosexuals in about 15% of programs overall. Of 14 genres, only movies and variety/comedy shows had substantial percentages of programs that contained non-heterosexual content. Programs on commercial broadcast networks were less likely to have non-heterosexual content than those on cable networks, especially those on premium cable movie networks (Fisher, Hill, Grube, & Gruber, 2007). Also, in his meta-analysis of the findings from content analysis about sexual portrayals on television over 18 seasons, Hetsroni (2007) reports that the frequency of portrayals of homosexuality has increased considerably.

Violence

Violence was the most studied form of content in all of the mass media from the advent of television as a mass medium around 1950 to the turn of the century. Scholars continually monitored the amount of violence on television, producing at least 60 major content analyses (see Potter, 1999) but then interest waned.

Depending on the definition used, violence has been found in 57% to 80% of all entertainment programs (Columbia Broadcasting System, 1980; Greenberg et al., 1980; Lichter & Lichter, 1983; "NCTV Says," 1983; Potter & Ware, 1987; Schramm, Lyle, & Parker, 1961; Signorielli, 1990; Smythe, 1954; Williams, Zabrack, & Joy, 1982).

The most consistent examination of television violence has been conducted by Gerbner and his associates (e.g., see Gerbner, Gross, Morgan, & Signorielli, 1980). Since the late 1960s, they have documented the frequency of violent acts that fit the definition: the overt expression of physical force (with or without a weapon) against self or other, compelling action against one's will on pain of being hurt or killed, or actually hurting or killing. Signorielli (1990) reports that from 1967 to 1985, the hourly rate fluctuated from about four to seven violent acts, with peaks occurring about every 4 years.

The most comprehensive analysis of violence on television has been conducted with the NTVS (1996), which analyzed the content of a total of 3,185 programs across 23 television channels for all day parts from 6 a.m. until 11 p.m., 7 days a week, over the course of a television season. NTVS researchers report that 57% of all programs analyzed had some violence and that one third of programs presented nine or more violent interactions.

The numbers in the above paragraphs are limited to physical forms of violence, and they do not include verbal violence. Verbal violence is even more prevalent on television than is physical violence. For example, Williams et al. (1982) reported finding a rate of 9.5 acts of verbal violence as well as 9 acts of physical violence per hour on North American (United States and Canada) television. Potter and Ware (1987) found about 8 acts per hour of physical violence and an additional 12 acts of verbal violence on American television. Also, Greenberg and his colleagues (1980) reported that an average prime-time hour of television contains 22 acts of verbal aggression and 12 acts of physical aggression. In a comparison of rates of violence on television from the mid-1970s to the mid-1990s, Potter and Vaughan (1997) found that the rates of physical violence remained stable but that the rates of verbal violence had increased dramatically. They reasoned that programmers were wary of increasing physical violence because such an increase would trigger a public outcry, but the substantial increase in verbal violence was tolerated by the public, so the increase continued.

There have also been some scientific studies of the amount of violence in films. For example, the top-grossing 50 films of 1998 contained a total of 2,300 acts of violence, according to the Center for Media and Public Affairs, based in Washington, D.C. "Violence was not only a staple of popular entertainment, it was often portrayed as laudable, necessary or relatively harmless activity," said S. Robert Lichter, the center's president (Goldstein, 1999, p. B1). In another analysis of violent films, Sapolsky, Molitor, and Luque (2003) content analyzed popular slasher films in the 1990s and found more acts of violence in them than similar films from the 1980s. One change was that recent slasher films rarely mixed scenes of sex and violence. The researchers also posed the question about whether females were more victimized than males, and they concluded that in all slasher films, there were more male victims than there were female victims. But they did not stop with this conclusion; they also found that the ratio of female victims is higher in slasher films than in commercially successful action/adventure films of the 1990s. This means than when a female is shown in a slasher film, she has a greater chance of being victimized. Also, females are shown in fear longer than males.

Violence on television has been examined not only for its frequency but also for its context—that is, the way it is presented. For example, Potter and Ware (1987) found that with much of the violence, the perpetrator is rewarded and the victims are rarely shown with much pain and suffering. This was also the case in the NTVS studies, where violent acts were rarely punished, and rarely were victims shown as suffering any harmful consequences. Also, 37% of the perpetrators of violence were portrayed as being attractive, and 44% of the acts were shown as being justified. These patterns led the researchers to conclude that violence not only was prevalent throughout the entire television landscape but was also typically shown as sanitized and glamorized (see Potter & Smith, 2000).

This level of violence in the media is far higher than the real-world levels of violence and crime. This was demonstrated by Oliver (1994), who analyzed pseudo-reality-based police shows, such as *COPS*. She found that the Federal Bureau of Investigation (FBI) figures for murder, rape, robbery, and aggregated assault were 13.2% of all crimes, but in the television world, these four violent crimes accounted for 87% of all crimes. Also, the FBI reports that 18.0% of crimes are cleared, but on television, 61.5% are cleared—that is, the perpetrator is arrested, is killed, or commits suicide. Again, television focuses on the most arousing crimes rather than the dull ones. Also, there is a more satisfying resolution to crimes than there is in the real world.

Language

It appears as if "bad" language has broken the barrier on television and is here to stay. For example, Kaye and Sapolsky (2001) examined prime-time network programs to ascertain whether usage of offensive language increased throughout the 1990s when a content-based rating system was implemented. The per-hour rate of objectionable words increased between 1990 and 1994 but decreased in 1997 to a level slightly below that found in 1990. Although the FCC deemed the "seven dirty words" as too offensive for television, five of these words had made their way onto the prime-time airwaves.

People continue to complain about bad language on television, and the FCC monitors television programs to determine if they are obscene or not. In making their determination, the FCC takes context into consideration. For example, many people complained about indecency in the movie *Saving Private Ryan*, but the FCC ruled that it did not contain indecency although there was considerable profanity and violence. The FCC reasoned that the language was appropriate for soldiers fighting in a war ("FCC Finds No Indecency," 2005). Another study found that profanity on network TV, increased 69% from 2005 to 2010 and that the greatest increases were during the so-called family hour from 8 p.m. to 9 p.m. (Flint, 2010).

In addition to obscenity, bad language also includes racial and gender slurs. In the spring of 2007, radio shock jock Don Imus referred to the Rutgers University women's basketball team as "nappy headed hos" in an offhanded comment during one of his radio broadcasts. Many listeners were greatly offended and criticized his language. This triggered the attention of the media, which made it a prominent controversial story. African American and feminist leaders harshly criticized Imus's comments. Although Imus met with Rutgers officials and formally apologized and even though his apology was accepted by the members of the women's basketball team, Imus was fired from his job. Imus had found that after 3 decades as a popular shock jock where he insulted a wide range of politicians and public figures, his language in this instance had crossed a line where the consequences were severe and immediate.

Health

The television world is a generally healthy one when we look at patterns across all kinds of shows. While some parts of this pattern of health portrayals are very responsible in presenting healthy messages to viewers, other parts of this pattern are deceptive; that is, some portrayals present a very misleading message about health.

Deceptive Health Patterns

Although there are many indicators of deceptive health, I'll present only five in this section. First, although most characters are not shown having particularly healthy habits (eating responsibly, regularly exercising, and getting medical checkups to prevent illnesses), most characters appear healthy, fit, and thin. It has been estimated that 64.5% of the American population is overweight or obese (American Obesity Association, 2004), but on television, only 6% of the males and 2% of the females are. Furthermore, characters do not gain weight from their high-caloric diets, although eating and drinking are frequent activities on entertainment programs. About 75% of all shows display this activity. But eating is usually unhealthy. The traditional meals of breakfast, lunch, and dinner combined account for only about half of the eating; snacking accounts for the rest. Fruit is the snack in only 4% to 5% of the episodes.

Second, although there is a high degree of violence on many shows, few characters are portrayed as suffering any harm. In fact, most characters are portrayed as being healthy and active. Only 6% to 7% of major characters are portrayed as having had injuries or illnesses that require treatment. Pain, suffering, or medical help rarely follows violent activity. In children's programs, despite greater mayhem, only 3% of characters are shown receiving medical treatment. Prime-time characters are not only healthy but also relatively safe from accidents, even though they rarely wear seat belts when they drive. And they are rarely portrayed as suffering from impairments of any kind as a result of an accident.

A third indicator of deceptive health is that the everyday normal health maladies are rarely shown. Most health problems that are portrayed are serious and life-threatening. When help for medical problems is portrayed, it is not in a preventative or therapeutic manner but in a dramatic and social way. Hardly anyone dies a natural death on television.

Prime-time characters are not shown with any kind of physical impairments. Rarely does a character even wear glasses; even in old age, only one out of four characters wears them. Only 2% of characters on prime-time shows are physically handicapped. When they do appear, they tend to be older, less positively presented, and more likely to be victimized. Almost none appear on children's shows.

Fourth, mental health is portrayed in a dangerously stereotypical manner. In real life, mentally ill people are usually passive and withdrawn, frightened, and avoidant. But on television, mentally ill characters were found to be 10 times more likely to be a violent criminal than non–mentally ill television characters (Diefenbach & West, 2007). In television stories, mentally ill characters are typically shown to be active, confused, aggressive, dangerous, and unpredictable.

Fifth, doctors are greatly overrepresented on television compared to their numbers in real life. Health care professionals dominate the ranks of professionals, despite the paucity of sick characters on television. They are five times their numbers in real life proportionally. Only criminals or law enforcers are more numerous. Also, many of these doctors are shown making house calls and devoting far more time to individual patients than real-life doctors are able to.

Responsible Health Patterns

The use of alcohol, tobacco, and illegal drugs has dramatically declined over the years on television. Smoking was a frequent activity until the mid-1980s, until it almost completely disappeared except for reruns of old movies.

Alcohol use has also substantially declined. When alcohol is presented now, it is frequently shown with negative consequences. Until the mid-1980s, alcohol consumption was common on television. The drinking of alcohol was shown twice as often as the drinking of coffee and tea, 14 times that of soft drinks, and 15 times that of water. It was shown as sociable, happy, and problem free. Also, alcohol use was rarely portrayed with any negative consequences. When negative consequences were shown, they were usually very slight, such as a temporary hangover. Despite high rates of consumption across many characters, only 1% of television drinkers are portrayed as having a drinking problem.

Although television is showing more responsible portrayals of drug and alcohol use, the movies do not fare so well. An analysis of the 200 most popular movies of 1996 and

1997 reveals that characters frequently abuse drugs and alcohol. Moreover, these characters are not portrayed as worrying about the consequences (Hartman, 1999).

Body image. A content analysis of three magazines from 1967 to 1997 found that male bodies were portrayed as more lean, muscular, and V-shaped. This fits with the male body image ideal of thin and athletic. "Sociocultural standards of beauty for males emphasize strength and muscularity" (Law & Labre, 2002, p. 697).

Hollywood movies are also a target of critics of the media's obsession with a certain type of body image. Alexandra Kuczynski wrote *Beauty Junkies: Inside Our $15 Billion Obsession With Cosmetic Surgery*, in which she argued that Hollywood has created a standard of beauty that does not exist in nature. "This standard is pert, symmetrical features atop a skinny body with large breasts (also called 'tits on sticks')" (Kantrowitz, 2006). She says that Hollywood creates celebrities with perfect bodies then floods the media with these images making them the standard that everyone tries to meet. When people cannot meet this standard, they undergo surgeries or get depressed. Also, Himes and Thompson (2007) conducted a study to examine how overweight characters were presented in movies and television shows. They found that fat characters were typically stigmatized; that is, non-overweight characters used humor to put down overweight characters often directly to their face. They also found that male characters were three times more likely to engage in fat stigmatization commentary or fat humor than female characters.

Hollywood is often criticized for creating unrealistic and unattainable standards of beauty and body image.

Values

Examining the arts within a culture is a way to determine the values of that culture. For example, the ancient Greek and Roman cultures exhibited the values of perfection, harmony, and beauty in their art. During the European Middle Ages, the art reflected the dominance of the Catholic Church, with its focus on the life of Christ, especially his birth, miracles, crucifixion, and resurrection. Earthly existence was mundane and painful, whereas the afterlife was glorious. During the Renaissance, the art reflected the values of a scientific approach to understanding the world. During the European Romantic era, the focus shifted from the logical and intellectual concerns that were dominant during the Renaissance to the emotions of humans. During the Modern era, the arts were decoupled from the church and political institutions. Art glorified the individual and his or her unique way of looking at the world and constructing meaning (Metallinos, 1996).

Today, we can examine the broad span of messages from the mass media and ask: What do our stories tell us about our current culture? Some researchers and social critics have attempted to answer this question. Table 10.4 shows what two media scholars have

TABLE 10.4 ■ Values Underlying Entertainment Messages

Comstock's (1989) List

1. Material consumption is very satisfying.

2. The world is a mean and risky place. There is a great deal of crime and violence throughout the television world.

3. The TV world has turned the social pyramid upside down by showing most characters as wealthy and powerful and very few of them as working class.

4. Males are more powerful than females in terms of income, job status, and decision making. This is slowly changing, but we are still far from a balance of power.

5. Occupational status is highly valued. Professional occupations are depicted as worthwhile, whereas manual work is uninteresting. People attain the status of a worthwhile profession through upward mobility from the middle class. This upward mobility is accomplished through self-confidence and toughness; goodness of character alone is not enough. The movement upward is usually quick and painless.

6. There are a few privileged professions in which the people are almost always shown as doing good and helping others. However, most businesspeople are shady. Businesses are frequently portrayed as taking advantage of the gullible public and abusing their power.

7. Law enforcers are overrepresented as being successful, strong, and justified. Private investigators are almost always shown as better than the police.

8. There is a belief in the occult, life on other planets, life after death, and hidden, malevolent purposes behind the inexplicable.

9. A person's self-interest is very important. People are motivated to get what they want regardless of the feelings of others. Examples include extramarital affairs, crime, hard-driving businesspeople, and police who disregard the rights of others to achieve their goals.

10. There are often truly heroic acts portrayed where there are daring rescues, selflessness, loyalty to others, and the struggle against difficult odds to do the right thing.

Walsh's (1994) List

1. Happiness is found in having things.

2. Get all you can for yourself.

3. Get it all as quickly as you can.

4. Win at all costs.

5. Violence is entertaining.

6. Always seek pleasure and avoid boredom.

observed to be the themes in television entertainment. Notice that the first of Comstock's (1989) themes deals with material consumption. Comstock is not referring to the ads in the stories but to the values in the stories themselves. He says, "It is not solely that so many stories revolve around the rich, but that in so many instances dwellings and their furnishings are beyond the means of those portrayed as occupying them" (p. 172). For example, the popular situation comedy *Friends* features Monica, a part-time cook, and Rachel, a waitress in a coffeehouse, who are shown supporting themselves in a well-furnished two-bedroom apartment in downtown Manhattan.

Notice also how the lists of Comstock (1989) and Walsh (1994) overlap. For example, Walsh is also concerned with the value of materialism, which he argues is at odds with a healthy society. Walsh also argues that the values of the marketplace are as follows: happiness equals wealth, instant gratification, and "me first." In contrast, the values of a healthy society are the following: self-esteem comes from within, moderation, tolerance, understanding, and social responsibility.

In complaining about the direction of programming on TV aimed at young people, *U.S. News & World Report* columnist John Leo (1999) said,

> These shows are also carriers of heavy cultural messages, the most obvious being that parents are fools. In the teen soap operas, parents are absent, stupid, irrelevant, zanily adulterous, on the lam, or in jail. The unmistakable message is that kids are on their own, with no need to listen to parents, who know little or nothing anyway. This helps the TV industry certify teenagers as an autonomous culture with its own set of ethics and consumption patterns. (p. 15)

Young people are a very important target for many Hollywood films, and a particular kind of film is believed to be the best draw for them. For example, in a profile of a literary manager, Warren Zide, *Los Angeles Times* reporter Claudia Eller (1999) examines the values operating in Hollywood. She said,

> When it came to getting the script for *American Pie* in shape to be sold, Zide said he and his colleagues advised [the writer] "to write the raunchiest script possible without worrying about the rating." Apparently it was good advice. The R-rated comedy about four high-school buddies who make a pact to lose their virginity before graduation piqued the interest of several studios before it was sold to Universal Pictures for $650,000. (p. C5)

Eller also quotes Zide on his reaction to a script about teenagers on a spring break: "I hated when I was growing up and you go to see some R-rated movie and there's no nudity in it, and you're like, 'Oh, man, I was gypped.'" So, now as a literary agent, Zide asks, "Do we have enough T&A in it?" (p. C5).

BECOMING MEDIA LITERATE WITH ENTERTAINMENT MESSAGES

With formulas, we are all fairly media literate. We can all follow stories, even complicated ones with flashbacks, irony, and many characters. We know how to read stereotypical characters from their physical appearance and attribute all kinds of personality characteristics to them. We can easily keep increasing our media literacy with story formulas by simply exposing ourselves to more stories, especially stories in a wider variety of genres and sub-genres.

With patterns, however, the challenge for media literacy is considerably higher. Patterns are insidious because we typically process each portrayal individually then unconsciously infer patterns often based on only a few instances or on faulty samples (Tversky & Kahneman, 1973). Thus after watching a small number of movies or television shows, we infer patterns about the real world, such as how people dress and act. These inferences typically result in unrealistic beliefs about attractiveness, romance, success, health, family, and so on.

Media stories typically ignore things that are not dramatic (e.g., housework, running errands, and small talk with neighbors) or visually interesting (e.g., thinking by ourselves, reading, walking, and other quiet activities). If we develop our expectations for real life from the pattern of dramatic stories we see in the media, our expectations will be unrealistic; if we try to achieve those unrealistic objectives, we will continually fail and become depressed.

Producers, however, are under no obligation to present an accurate account of the mundane world. Their task is to build as large an audience as possible. To do this, they must rely on all their creative powers to achieve a dramatic effect, so they deliberately distort the world to surprise and startle us. Some creative people produce fantasy that, by definition, is totally unlike real life—they do this to allow us to escape our lives and to see imaginative occurrences. Other producers who try to capture real life must do so in an intriguing manner. That is, they avoid presenting the mundane mainstream of real life and instead highlight the occurrences at the margins where there are particularly interesting people or events. This is real life in the sense that it could happen or even did happen.

Producers of entertaining stories are not psychologists or sociologists; they are not usually trying to educate us about how the human mind works or about how society works. However, the drama in their stories does have the side effect of tempting us to use those plots as lessons about the real world. The danger to us as viewers of these stories is that we gradually absorb social lessons from these fictional stories. Over time, we start to confuse the "one-step remove" elements from the more realistic elements. Eventually, we come to believe that the patterns of fantasy that we continually see in media stories should be how we live our real lives.

The way to deal with the unrealistic picture presented by entertainment media is *not* to pressure producers to make their world of fiction more realistic. That would be silly. Instead, the best way to deal with this situation is to educate yourself about the content patterns in the media world and to become more sensitive, recognizing where those patterns diverge from real-world patterns. Learn to appreciate the divergences as fantasy and limit yourself to being entertained by their unreality. And avoid being guided by unrealistic expectations based on what media characters look like and how they act.

Now that you have more information about patterns of characters, plots, and values of entertainment stories in the media, you have a stronger knowledge structure about media content. When you use this knowledge structure to guide yourself through your exposures to media stories in the future, you will be able to see much more in those messages. Table 10.5 shows the cognitive, emotional, aesthetic, and moral skills you will need to do this in a conscious, active manner. But do not restrict yourself to the specifics in Table 10.5; instead, use the information presented there to stimulate your thinking about other skills and knowledge. Then, during your exposures to media entertainment, recall the knowledge you will need and consciously apply the skills in all four domains.

	Skills	Knowledge
TABLE 10.5 ■ Types of Skills and Knowledge Structures Needed to Deal With Entertainment Messages in a Media-Literate Manner		
Cognitive	Ability to analyze entertainment content to identify key plot points, types of characters, and themes Ability to see entertainment formulas Ability to compare/contrast plot points, characters, and themes across vehicles and media	Knowledge of elements in entertainment formula
Emotional	Ability to analyze the portrayed feelings of characters Ability to put oneself into the position of different characters in the story Ability to control emotions elicited by the plot and themes	Recall from personal experiences how it would feel to be in the situation depicted in the story
Aesthetic	Ability to analyze the craft and artistic elements in the story Ability to compare and contrast the artistry used to tell the story with that used to tell other stories	Knowledge of writing, directing, acting, editing, sound mixing, and so on Knowledge of good and bad stories and the elements that contributed to those qualities
Moral	Ability to analyze the moral elements as evidenced by decisions made by characters, implications of those decisions revealed by the plot, and underlying themes Ability to compare and contrast ethical decisions presented in this story with other stories Ability to evaluate the ethical responsibilities of the producers and programmers	Knowledge of what moral systems say about different decisions as well as knowledge of the moral implications of your decisions Knowledge of other stories that have portrayed this topic, both good and bad Knowledge of values of people in the media industries

During exposure to the media, remember that entertainment messages follow a formula. Viewers want formulaic characters and plots so that the entertainment messages are easy to follow. Look at how closely stories follow formulas by working on Exercise 10.2. As you progress through the exercise, keep the following questions in mind. How do stories follow standard patterns and how do they deviate from them? How much can a story deviate from standard formulas before audiences are likely to become confused and lose sense of what is happening?

Keep asking questions about these stories. Be skeptical. Take nothing for granted. If you stay active during your exposures, you will be increasing your media literacy and thus gain more control over setting expectations for life that are both realistic and special to you.

SUMMARY

When producers create entertainment messages, they are guided by a general story, which outlines what all entertainment stories must have; a genre formula, which builds on the general story formula by adding elements specific to a genre; and knowledge about which particular storytelling elements (such as elements for arousal, types of humor, degree and type of realism, suspense, and triggers for emotional reactions) work with particular types of audiences. Thus entertainment messages within a particular genre share a lot of commonalities that differentiate them from messages within other genres. The more that we, as audience members, understand these formulas, the more effectively and efficiently we can follow their action and process their meaning.

Further Reading

Cantor, M. G. (1980). *Prime-time television.* Beverly Hills, CA: SAGE. (143 pages, including index)

Written by a sociologist who spent 10 years interviewing actors, writers, and producers, this book explains how decisions about content are made in the television industry. She develops a model to show that many forces shape the development of any television program. The examples in the book are dated, but most of the principles still apply.

Haven, K. (2007). *Story proof: The science behind the startling power of story.* Westport, CT: Libraries Unlimited. (152 pages, including references and index)

With his background as a professional storyteller, Haven examines the scientific literature to analyze what stories are and how they affect humans in all sorts of ways. He reviews the research literature across scholarly fields as a basis for constructing his own definition of a story, then shows how stories have always been a powerful form of communication.

Medved, M. (1992). *Hollywood vs. America: Popular culture and the war on traditional values.* New York, NY: HarperCollins. (386 pages)

This film critic argues that Hollywood has a value system that is very different from that of mainstream America. Hollywood glorifies the perverse, ridicules all forms of mainstream religion, tears down the image of the family, and glorifies ugliness with violence, bad language, and America bashing. Then the industry is puzzled why attendance is dropping and criticism is increasing.

Postman, N. (1984). *Amusing ourselves to death: Public discourse in the age of show business.* New York, NY: Penguin. (184 pages with index)

This is a strong, well-written argument about how the media, especially television, have conditioned us to expect entertainment. Because our perceptions of ideas are shaped by the form of their expression, we are now image oriented. We respond to pleasure, not thought and reflection.

Keeping Up to Date

Scholarly Journals

Journal of Broadcasting & Electronic Media (https://www.tandfonline.com/loi/hbem20)

Journalism & Mass Communication Quarterly (http://journals.sagepub.com/home/jmq)

These are scholarly journals that publish research studies that examine entertainment type messages in the mass media, particularly television, primarily using scientific type methods such as content analysis. The reported findings typically focus attention on broad patterns.

Critical Studies in Media Communication (https://www.tandfonline.com/loi/rcsm20)

Discourse & Society (http://journals.sagepub.com/home/das)

Film Quarterly (https://filmquarterly.org)

Sight & Sound (https://www.bfi.org.uk/news-opinion/sight-sound-magazine)

These are journals that publish scholarship from a humanistic perspective and therefore provide analyses of media content, especially film and television, from a cultural or critical perspective.

Magazines for General Audiences

Entertainment Weekly (https://ew.com)

TV Guide (https://www.tvguide.com)

Rolling Stone (https://www.rollingstone.com)

Hollywood Reporter (https://www.hollywoodreporter.com)

Billboard (https://www.billboard.com)

EXERCISE 10.1
ANALYZING THE ENTERTAINMENT CONTENT

1. Write a definition for *sexual behavior*. This is not as easy as it might seem. You must consider issues such as the following:

   - What must the characters do?

   - What are their intentions? Is a kiss or a hug always sexual?

   - What do they talk about? If a character talks about what he or she wants to do, does that count?

2. *Sampling:* Select a handful of media messages that have a chance of representing a larger set of messages. For example, you might want to select two different situation comedies on prime-time network television to represent mainstream situation comedies.

3. Code the messages in the sample. Count how many acts occur that meet your definition. Note the gender, age, and ethnic background of the characters.

4. Discuss your results with others in class who did their own content analyses of sex.

   a. What is the range in the numbers of acts found? Can this range be attributed to differences in definitions or differences in shows?

   b. Profile the types of characters who were most often involved in sexual activity.

   c. Are there any noticeable differences in character profiles across types of situation comedies?

5. Now try using your definition to analyze the content on soap operas, music videos, and action/adventure dramas.

   a. Do you see any big differences in the number of sexual acts across different types of shows?

   b. Do you see any big differences in the profiles of characters involved in sexual activity across shows?

6. Now think about how sex is portrayed in the television world.

   a. What types of activity are the most prevalent?

   b. How responsibly is sex portrayed in the television world? That is, are the physical and emotional risks often discussed or considered? Is sex portrayed as a normal part of a loving, stable relationship, or is it portrayed more as a game of conquest or a source of silliness?

   c. Did you find anything in the patterns that surprised you?

7. What do you need to know about how sex is portrayed in the media and the role of sex in the real world for you to construct a strong knowledge structure on this subject?

EXERCISE 10.2

PRACTICING MEDIA LITERACY SKILLS ON ENTERTAINMENT PROGRAMMING

Watch a television program, then think about the following tasks.

1. *Analysis:* Break down the program by doing the following:

   a. List the main characters.

   b. List the main plot points.

   c. Were there violent elements? If so, list them.

   d. Were there sexual elements? Is so, list them.

   e. Were there health-related elements? If so, list them.

2. *Grouping:* Select the two main characters.

   a. How are they the same/different demographically?

   b. How are they the same/different by personality characteristics?

(Continued)

(Continued)

c.   How are they the same/different in the way they move the plot forward?

3. *Evaluation:* Think about all the characters and make the following judgments.

   a. In your judgment, which character was the most humorous? Why?

   b. In your judgment, which character was the most ethical in his or her behavior? Why?

   c. In your judgment, which actor or actress displayed the best acting skills? Why?

   d. In your judgment, which of the plot points were the strongest? Which were the weakest?

   e. In your judgment, what is the theme of this show?

4. *Abstracting:* Describe your show (characters and plot) in 50 words or less.

5. *Generalizing:* Start with particular characters and particular happenings in your show, then infer general patterns of people and events in general.

   a. Think about the demographics of the characters in your show. Do those demographics in your show match the patterns of demographics in the real world?

   b. Think about the plot elements (sex, violence, health) in your show. Do these elements in your show match the patterns of these elements in the real world?

6. *Appreciating:* Consider the following questions.

   a. Emotional: Was the show able to evoke emotions in you? If so, list those emotions and explain how the show triggered those particular emotions.

   b. Aesthetic: Is there something about the writing, directing, editing, lighting, set design, costuming, or music/sound effects that you found of particular high quality? If so, explain what led you to appreciate that element so much.

   c. Moral: Did the show raise ethical considerations (either explicitly or implicitly)? If so, did you appreciate how the show dealt with those ethical considerations?

Stephen Lovekin/FilmMagic for
YouTube/Getty Images

11

ADVERTISING

Key Idea: We live in a culture saturated with advertising messages that have been carefully planned to fulfill the goals of each of the thousands of advertisers who flood our culture with messages every day.

YouTube CEO Susan Wojcicki speaks at a Google-presented event about the launch of YouTube Brandcast, which gives brands insight into how to best reach desired audiences on the video sharing site.

"I hate ads. They are so annoying the way they interrupt TV shows and all those pop-ups and banner ads on websites. I refuse to pay attention to any of them. I don't contribute much to advertisers. They must hate me."

"Not necessarily. Do you buy advertised products?"

"Like what?"

"Like when you go to the grocery store, you probably buy cereals, snacks, tooth-paste. Do you buy well-known brands or the generic house brands?"

"I buy the well-known brands. And not because they are well known or because they are so heavily advertised."

"Then why do you buy them?"

"They have higher quality."

"How do you know that?"

"Everybody knows that."

"If you read the labels carefully, you would see that the ingredients in the house brands are identical to the advertised brands. Also, the same governmental regula-tions that apply to advertised brands also apply to house brands, so house brands do not have impurities or harmful ingredients. And the house brands are almost always made in the same manufacturing plants as make the advertised brands. Yet you pay a lot more for the advertised brands, because you are not just buying the product. You are also buying the advertising."

"I still think the well-known brands are better."

"Then I think that advertisers must love you!"

Let's begin with a question: What are the products of advertising? Some of you might interpret "products" to mean the things we buy—clothes, pizzas, mobile phones, and so on. Others might think that the products are the ads we see—after all, that is what the people in the industry create and show to us constantly. While both of these interpretations have some truth to them on the surface, both miss the point of the real nature of advertising. The most important product of advertising is *you*.

Advertisers have trained you and all members of the public to give them your time, your attention, and your money—even money you don't have when you buy advertised products on credit. Advertisers have spent hundreds of billions of dollars over your lifetime to craft special messages

Advertisers have conditioned us to give them our time and money by appealing to what we think we need.

iStock/huseyintuncer

that have put hundreds of thousands of images, jingles, ideas, and desires into your memory banks. They have done this with your permission and even your blessing. And they have even convinced you to pay them for conditioning you.

This chapter is organized to achieve three objectives. The first objective is to sensitize you to the amount and pervasiveness of advertising in the culture. The second objective is to help you understand how advertising messages are designed. And the third objective is to get you started being more systematic in analyzing ad messages and evaluating the degree to which their appeals match your real needs.

ADVERTISING IS PERVASIVE

The United States is saturated with advertising. With about 4.3% of the world's population, the United States absorbs almost half of the world's advertising expenditures.

We are submersed in a culture saturated with advertising messages (see Table 11.1) and the number of ads in our culture increases each year. In the 1970s, the average American was exposed to about 500 ads per day; by the early 2000s, that number had grown to 5,000 ads per day (Johnson, 2006a). A decade later, with the proliferation of advertising on computers and mobile devices that number had doubled to 10,000 ads per day (Saxon, 2018), which means that you are being exposed to more than 10 ads every minute of every hour that you are awake each and every day! Is this possible? To check the accuracy of this figure, try doing Exercise 11.1. This exercise may fatigue you after an hour or two (or perhaps even after several minutes). If fatigue happens quickly, then you will have absorbed the lesson of this exercise—you are constantly being exposed to many more ad messages than you were aware.

Research shows 80% of consumers opt for the more expensive, advertised brand over a store brand.

iStock/PeopleImages

TABLE 11.1 ■ Pervasiveness of Advertising in America	
Medium	**Advertising**
Newspapers	Sixty percent of the typical newspaper is advertising. Newspapers are now primarily vehicles for ads more so than for news.
Film	Movie theaters bombard viewers with ads. A series of ads is projected on their screens while the audience waits for the show to begin. When the film begins, there are usually ads for the theater's concession stand. The ticket a person buys usually has an ad on it.
	Films themselves are full of ads in the form of paid product placements. There are more than 30 companies operating in Hollywood to place products within movies and TV shows.
Radio	For years, the industry standard for maximum number of ad minutes per hour has been 18; however, this is not a legally imposed limit, but rather a guideline. Many radio stations exceed this guideline and present up to 40 minutes of ads per hour during particular times of the day.
Television	The percentage of programming on television given to commercial messages has been increasing over the years; by 2009, it had increased to over 40%.
	TV advertising is now in airports, in elevators in high-end hotels, and in doctors' waiting rooms—all beaming messages to captive audiences.
Books	Advertisers are paying for product placement in novels. Cover Girl cosmetics got writer Sean Stewart to mention a particular kind of make up in his novel about adolescent girls, and the publisher increased the book run from 30,000 to 100,000 copies based on the promotional strength of the deal (Smiley, 2006).
Computers	By 2012, the number of ads shown to U.S. users of the Internet was more than 5.3 trillion, with 445 different advertisers each delivering more than a billion ads on websites in 2012. The typical Internet user is served 1,707 banner ads per month (Morrissey, 2013).
Nonmedia	Ads are on the sides of buildings, on taxis and buses, on police cruisers, in public restrooms, at gas pumps, on the back of store receipts, in church bulletins, in public school classrooms, and even on the clothing of people walking the streets.
	There are now talking billboards that are fitted with a low-power radio transmitter that tells motorists where to tune for more information on the product advertised on the billboard.
	Commercial companies now sponsor events such as Russian space launches (Pizza Hut) and trips by the Pope (Frito-Lay and PepsiCo) in exchange for advertising rights.

Each year, the amount of money spent on advertising grows dramatically. In 1900, about $500 million was spent on all forms of advertising in the United States. By 1940, it was $2 billion, so it took 40 years to multiply four times. In 1980, it was $60 billion, or a growth of 30 times in those 40 years. By 2018, it had grown to $220 billion per year (Statista, 2018c). These numbers are so large that they are difficult to comprehend. Let's break down the expenditures by number of people in the population. In 1940, the industry spent $16 on each person in this country; by 1980, it was $260, and now it is about $675 per person per year.

An advertiser who wants to introduce a new product nationally and break through the existing clutter to get consumers to realize that there is a new product on the market must now spend a minimum of $50 million in advertising to launch the product. Of course, all this new advertising adds even more to the clutter, making it even more expensive for the next product introduction. This growth in advertising expenditures, the number of ads, and the number of places where ads appear has been accelerating for the past few decades and likely will continue with no end in sight.

Why can we expect continued growth? Because we—the public—do not mind all this advertising. There are times when we might criticize certain ads, and sometimes we get upset when we watch television and have our shows repeatedly interrupted by commercial breaks. However, few Americans have a negative attitude about advertising—only about 15% of us.

Our criticisms are minor compared to our unthinking support of advertising. By "unthinking" support, I mean that most of us do not realize how much advertising exposure we experience every day and how it has shaped our attitudes and behaviors. We accept the saturation, and we allow our behavior to be shaped by it. I'll present two examples of this point to help you understand how much you have been influenced by advertising.

The first example illustrates our preference for advertised products. In supermarkets and drugstores, each product category has an unadvertised alternative on the shelves among all the advertised brands. The differences in ingredients of the unadvertised alternatives compared to the advertised brands are minuscule—and often identical—because the products are all manufactured by the same companies in the same factories. Although the advertised brands all cost more—often a lot more—than the unadvertised alternative, about 80% of all purchases are for the advertised brands on average across all product categories (Jones, 2004). Why are we willing to spend more on an advertised brand when we can buy the same thing for less money? The answer is that advertising has conditioned us to believe that the advertised brands are better and worth the extra expense to us. That is, when we purchase an advertised brand, we are not just buying the product ingredients—we are also buying the package of beliefs about the product. This is one clear indication about how advertising is successful.

A second illustration of the influence of advertising can be seen in how much you yourself voluntarily participate as an advertiser for all kinds of products. Look at the clothing you have on now. How many clothing logos are you displaying on your shirt, pants, shoes, hat, book bag, mobile devices, and so on? You are advertising those products everywhere you go by proudly displaying those logos. How much are those companies paying you to advertise for them? They pay you nothing, right? In fact, you are paying them. Had you bought the same piece of clothing without the prized logo, it would have cost you less money. Therefore, you have chosen to pay more for the privilege of wearing a particular brand and displaying its logo. This is a good deal for those manufacturers who have convinced you to work for them for free *and to pay them for this privilege!*

PROCESS OF CONSTRUCTING ADVERTISING MESSAGES

Because the cost of advertising is so high and continues to increase, advertisers engage in a very systematic process of design to maximize the probability that their ads will be successful. This process begins with the development of an overall campaign strategy where advertisers determine who their target audiences are and how they want to present their product to those audiences. Then advertisers think about whether they will focus their campaign on outbound marketing, inbound marketing, or both. **Outbound marketing** is the traditional method advertisers use to engage their targeted consumers by designing ads to attract their attention then placing those ads in traditional media outlets (television, radio, newspapers, and magazines) where advertisers know there are high concentrations of their targeted consumers in the audience.

Inbound marketing, in contrast, is a much newer method that uses the Internet primarily. Advertisers design a website for their product then wait for people to declare their interest in the product by visiting their website. Once these "inbound" potential consumers get on their website, advertisers take them through a procedure step by step to get them to buy the product. This procedure is called the **buying funnel** (see Table 11.2).

Let's examine this overall procedure by first looking at how advertisers put together their campaign strategy. Then we will examine how they use this campaign strategy with both outbound marketing and inbound marketing.

TABLE 11.2 ■ Contrasting Outbound and Inbound Advertising Perspectives	
Outbound Advertising	**Inbound Advertising**
Purpose is to reach out to potential customers by placing ads in media and places where those people normally spend their time	Purpose is to guide potential customers through a buying funnel once those people have expressed an interest in the product by visiting a website
Heavy use of traditional mass media to disseminate ads widely to target audiences	Heavy use of social media—social networking sites, blogs, video and photo sharing, chat rooms, message boards, listservs, wikis, social bookmarking, and mobile applications
Ads must be compelling enough to attract people to pay attention to those ads	Message flow is interactive across networks of consumers; companies interject themselves into these networks to befriend consumers, listen to their needs, and influence them in conversations
Message flow is one-way: advertiser to consumer	Advertising focuses on communicating with potential customers in an ongoing dialogue Messages are personal and immediate; messages are delivered at the precise moment a target person needs it
Success of the ad campaign is measured after all the ads have been run and focuses on two criteria: reach (percentage of the target group that was exposed to at least one ad during the campaign) and frequency (the average number of times each person in the target group was exposed to ads in the campaign)	Success of this advertising procedure is measured continuously by monitoring how well it moves potential customers through the buying funnel. When problems are identified, they are corrected immediately

Source: Adapted from Scott (2013).

Campaign Strategy

The planning document that companies or advertising agencies develop to sell a product or service is the **campaign strategy**. When developing a campaign strategy, advertisers are guided by three principles. The first principle is that the role of advertising evolves. Decades ago consumers were viewed as people who had a lot more in common compared to their differences. Over time, the population has been fragmenting in all sorts of ways so that there are many more recognizable lifestyle groupings. Each of these many different lifestyles has a different set of needs and problems. Advertisers work hard to identify these constantly changing niche audiences and develop products to satisfy their more specialized needs. And advertisers must be more creative in designing messages to appeal to these many different audiences. Now with the proliferation of media platforms, advertisers have more powerful ways to search out niche audiences and test their messages on them.

Second, planners realize that advertising is a risky endeavor. The stakes are high, as is the risk. For example, the average supermarket now has 40,000 to 50,000 products on its shelves, which is a huge increase from the 1990s when the average supermarket had 7,000 products (Malito, 2017). While several hundred new products are introduced each month, 90% of those new products fail to last more than a year, even though most of these new products are supported with advertising budgets upward of $50 million each.

Third, advertisers recognize that advertising is both a science as well as an art. Many people think of advertising primarily as an art form where creative people brainstorm about how to produce all kinds of compelling messages to stimulate us to buy the hundreds of thousands of products displayed in malls and showrooms and on webpages and supermarket shelves. Yes, a lot of creative people work in advertising. However, advertising is much more of a business enterprise than an artistic pursuit. The design of advertising campaigns is undertaken with rigorous planning by professionals with a great deal of technical expertise. Advertising relies on good information to make important decisions about who to target their ad campaigns to, how to present their products to those target audiences, and how to get their messages to the right targets. This requires a good deal of science to generate this information and to interpret it in a useful way.

Guided by these three principles, advertisers try to come up with the best answers they can to the following five questions as they design their advertising campaigns (Table 11.3).

1. Who should be my primary target of the advertising campaign? Advertising campaigns begin with an analysis of who is currently using the product. The big-time advertisers have well-established brands and large numbers of brand-loyal consumers; these people are their primary target for advertising campaigns. Companies know they must continually advertise to their consumer base in order to keep reinforcing their brand-loyal habits.

Companies are also always looking for opportunities to grow their sales by identifying additional targets beyond their primary target. These are called secondary targets. These are people who are either using the competitor's brand and need to be converted or who have a need for the product and are unaware of it. Also, advertisers are continually monitoring the culture to identify new needs then develop new products to satisfy those needs.

TABLE 11.3 ■ Key Questions Advertisers Ask When Constructing Their Campaign Strategy
1. Who should be my primary target of the advertising campaign?
2. What is my primary advertising campaign objective?
Awareness
Conviction
Action
Reinforcement
3. How do my targets make their purchasing decision?
More thinking or feeling
Degree of involvement
4. What is the key benefit I want to sell?
Physical features
Functional features
Characterizational features
5. Should I use a product spokesperson in my campaign?

In identifying targets, advertisers have typically used geographic indicators such as where people live (urban, suburban, rural) as well as region of the country, which is related to climate and cultural needs. Demographic indicators have also been important, particularly gender, age, and educational level. Over the past few decades, advertisers have also been looking at psychological indicators (need to achieve, need to socialize, etc.) as well as lifestyle indicators (patterns of consumption). So target markets are described as "women 18 to 34," "men working blue collar jobs who are sports fans," or "recent college graduates who are starting a family."

2. **What is my primary advertising campaign objective?** Advertisers work to specify the goal of their ad campaigns, and this involves one of four types of objectives: awareness, conviction, action, and reinforcement. Awareness is the objective of campaigns when a product is new, so advertisers must design a campaign to make sure that their target audience learns about the product's name, its main features, and where it can be bought. Conviction refers to attitudes; advertisers must move beyond simply providing knowledge and create positive attitudes about their products. Action campaigns focus on getting consumers to buy the product or at least try it. Reinforcement campaigns are aimed at existing customers to make them feel good about their buying habits so they will continue to buy and consume or use the product. Most advertising campaigns focus on the reinforcement objective because most advertising campaigns are conducted by companies who already have an established product and a well-established consumer base. So they advertise a great deal to protect that consumer base.

FIGURE 11.1 ■ Purchasing Decision Matrix		
	Thinking	Feeling
High involvement	Car, house, furniture	Jewelry, cosmetics, apparel, motorcycles
Low involvement	Food, household items	Cigarettes, liquor, candy

3. **How do my targets make their purchasing decision?** The more advertisers know about how their customers go about making purchasing decisions, the better they will be able to design a campaign. A relatively simple way to think about consumer purchasing decisions is to make a distinction along two dimensions of involvement (high and low) and thinking versus feeling (see Figure 11.1). With thinking decisions, we tend to want facts about the product and we make logical comparisons among alternative products to choose the one that can best satisfy our rational needs. With feeling decisions, we rely on our emotions and choose products that make us feel the best, regardless of what our head is telling us.

The involvement dimension refers to how important the purchasing decision is to us. When decisions are relatively unimportant (i.e., the consequences of choosing the wrong product are minor), we can make decisions very quickly. In contrast, when decisions are relatively important (high cost with long-term consequences), then we become highly involved in the decision and either want to gather a great deal of information before making a thinking decision or we spend a lot of time worrying over the choices before making a feeling decision.

4. **What is the key benefit I want to sell?** Any given product can be advertised in many different ways. When advertisers design their campaigns, they think about what it is about their product that they want to emphasize. There are three choices: **physical features**, **functional features**, and **characterizational features**. Physical features refer to the actual components of the product itself. For example, a toothpaste might contain fluoride to prevent tooth decay or a chemical to give it a minty taste. Functional features refer to the way consumers can use the product. A toothpaste might come in a pump dispenser that makes it more convenient to use. Characterizational features refer to how consumers feel when using the product. A toothpaste can be advertised in a way to make users feel sexy because their breath is fresh and their teeth are so white that they attract romantic partners as they walk around in public.

5. **Should I use a product spokesperson in my campaign?** Advertisers often use a product spokesperson in their ad campaigns. For most products, the product spokesperson needs to be credible, trustworthy, and attractive. Credibility refers to expertise; that is, the person really knows what she is talking about. Trustworthiness refers to the belief that the person is telling the truth rather than lying to the audience to get them to buy the product. Attractiveness can refer to physical appeal (Victoria's Secret lingerie models, Abercrombie & Fitch bare-chested guys showing off six-pack abs, etc.), but it can also refer to other qualities that make audiences want to watch ads.

Typically advertisers would like to have all three characteristics in their product spokesperson but at times one characteristic becomes overridingly dominant. For example, a doctor spokesperson for a medical procedure is important for credibility; in this case, attractiveness is not so important.

Outbound Advertising Perspective

Advertisers who follow through with a traditional strategy will focus on an outbound perspective on advertising. This means they design ads then place those ads in media vehicles in order to expose their targets to their messages. Therefore the design of messages is very important in order to get those ads to fulfill the purpose of the overall campaign strategy. The plan for the ads is called a **copy platform**. The copy platform is a document that translates the elements in their overall campaign strategy into a plan that creatives use as they design and produce the ads themselves. This plan is structured by six questions (Table 11.4).

1. **What message strategy should be used?** There are basically seven options for a message strategy: generic, preemptive, USP, brand image, positioning, affective, and

TABLE 11.4   ■   Key Questions Advertisers Ask When Constructing Their Copy Platforms
1. What message strategy should be used?
Generic
Preemptive
USP (unique selling proposition)
Brand image
Positioning
Affective
Resonance
2. What should be the tone of the ad?
Hard sell/soft sell
Degree of seriousness
3. How much information should be put into the ad?
4. What type of story should be used?
Problem-solution plot
Spokesperson presents information
Montage
5. Who should be cast in the ad?
6. What should the setting be?

resonance. The generic-type ad is a simple description of a key characteristic of the product. For example, if you are selling hamburgers, you could simply say something like "Buy our burger because it costs 99 cents." The pre-emptive strategy is descriptive like the generic strategy but it also makes a claim for superiority. For example, you could say, "Buy our burger because it is the cheapest one in town."

The USP strategy focuses on the product's unique selling proposition (USP). To use this strategy, advertisers must identify something that their product has that all the competitors lack. For example, "Buy our burger because it

Serena Williams's partnership with Gatorade is an example of how advertisers use celebrity appearances to create positive associations between the audience and their product.

is the only one with our secret sauce." The brand image strategy focuses attention on the positive aspects of the brand. For example, "Buy our burger because it is a McDonald's burger."

Positioning is a psychological strategy that focuses attention more on the consumer's mind than the product itself. Positioning does not refer to geographical location of the product in stores; instead it refers to psychological neighborhoods in consumers' minds. Positioning focuses on how your product is "thought of" in relation to your competitors. With burgers, two psychological neighborhoods in most consumers' minds are price and quality. The low-price neighborhood is evoked by names like McDonald's and Burger King. Let's say the highest-quality burgers in a person's town are associated with a restaurant named Ritzy Beef. Your ad then might be something like, "Buy our burger because it is high quality like Ritzy Beef but inexpensive like McDonald's." This ad attempts to position the burger in a psychological neighborhood that is both high quality and inexpensive.

The affective message strategy focuses on triggering an emotion, such as joy or relief. These ads might use humor to make people laugh and/or feel good in some way. Or they might trigger fear of some problem then lead consumers to a feeling of relief that will be brought on by the use of their product. Similar to the affective strategy, the resonance strategy involves the use of emotion. With resonance, the advertiser is trying to evoke a pleasant memory in the minds of consumers. For example, a burger company could show kids eating their burgers as a reward after a little league game, or teenagers eating the burgers after the prom. These images would resonate with targets' memories of good times and make them want to recapture those experiences.

2. **What should be the tone of the ad?** Think of tone along two dimensions. One of these dimensions is hard sell versus soft sell. Hard-sell ads are characterized by pressure, such as when a product spokesperson is yelling into the camera that you better get down to his store today while the huge sale is going on because tomorrow will be too late! A second dimension is the degree of seriousness.

3. **How much information should be put into the ad?** Many ads focus on presenting only one simple idea. Designers know that the ad environment is cluttered, so they are happy if they can get people to remember one thing about their product. But

oftentimes, advertisers will feel a need to pack more information into an ad in order to achieve their purpose of informing their targets or trying to get them to switch brands. High-information ads work better in print, so that people can read over the detail at their own pace and go back over certain parts if they need to understand them better. High-information ads also work better when the targets are more educated, because people with higher levels of education are more able and willing to handle more information.

4. **What type of story should be used?** The most standard story structure is problem-solution. The advertiser shows people struggling with a problem when suddenly someone uses their product and the problem goes away. This is what Procter & Gamble typically uses to show the value of their household products.

Another story structure is to show the product spokesperson talking into the camera directly to the targets. The spokesperson simply explains the features of the product in a way that makes targets want to buy it. Spokespeople who are attractive will capture the audience's attention and hold it, while their credibility and trustworthiness are important to make what they say persuasive. The story montage is a series of images that show the product in an attractive manner. Car companies often use this story structure in television ads where they may present several dozen quick shots of a car riding down a winding country road to evoke the sense of adventure and freedom.

5. **Who should be cast in the ad?** If an ad campaign uses a product spokesperson, then the casting decision is easy. However, many ads do not use a product spokesperson, so planners must decide first whether to use actors or real people. The key to casting is to feature people in the ad who will attract the attention of the target audience. Furthermore, if the copy platform calls for a problem-solution story, then it is important to make sure the person with the problem in the ad is someone with whom the targets can identify with and see themselves having the same problem that is then solved by the product.

6. **What should the setting be?** The setting of the ad also requires a lot of thought. In simple problem-solution stories, advertisers want to show the action in places where targets are most likely to experience the problems, such as in their own homes or places of work.

Advertisers begin with these six questions about the ad campaign and the copy platform then systematically work through all the options to create a set of ads that all contribute to the goals of the overall ad campaign. But if advertisers answer all six of these questions in standard ways, then their ads will look like everyone else's ads and thereby prevent their ads from breaking through all the clutter so that audiences pay attention to them and are influenced by them. Instead ad designers need to demonstrate some creativity. However, creativity does not refer to thinking so far out of the box that all these questions and their options are ignored. Instead, creativity starts with an awareness and understanding of the options for these questions then using those options in new ways.

Inbound Advertising Perspective

When advertisers use an inbound perspective, they commit to constantly monitoring their base of consumers to find out what they are thinking as new needs emerge. They design messages in the form of interactive experiences (e.g., blogging, e-mailing, and friending on social media sites) and design websites to capture consumers' attention.

COMPARE & CONTRAST
CAMPAIGN STRATEGY AND COPY PLATFORM

Compare: The campaign strategy and copy platform are *the same* in the following ways:

- Both are planning tools used by advertisers.

- Both require business awareness (of the company's goals and economics), scholarly awareness (about research findings of what works in different ads and why), and artistic interpretation (to be able to use business sense and research knowledge in a creative way).

Contrast: The campaign strategy and copy platform are *different* in the following ways:

- The campaign strategy translates a company's business goals and its marketing objectives into a plan about how to go about getting its messages out to a target market in the most effective and efficient manner possible.

- The copy platform translates a company's campaign strategy into a set of guidelines that can be used for designing the individual advertising messages.

When people demonstrate the initiative to access the website, the advertisers interact with those people with the intention of getting them to progress step by step through the buying funnel. This procedure starts with giving visitors some information to make them aware of the advertised product, then generating interest in the product. Next advertisers give visitors more information about the product's features then stimulate them to go shopping and eventually buy the product. But the buying funnel procedure does not end with the product purchase. Advertisers continue to interact with buyers to help them avoid buyer's remorse so that they will buy the product again and again. Finally, advertisers try to condition their buyers to act as advocates for the product as they interact with their friends on social media sites and in real life.

Advertisers continually monitor how potential customers navigate the Internet to get information on their products and eventually make decisions about whether to buy those products or not. Advertisers use what they learn to position their product more effectively on the Internet. This procedure is called **SEO (search engine optimization)**, which includes designing a website to make it easy to navigate, providing links to your site from other sites, and using the right keywords to get potential customers to your site and through the buying funnel.

Advertisers use the buying funnel to design keywords for searches and ad copy for webpages. By monitoring how people conduct Internet searches for products in a particular category, advertisers can examine how people change their keywords as they develop an interest in a product. Advertisers watch what key words people use at the top of the funnel; that is, what keywords do consumers use when they are not aware of your product? These keywords are very general and refer to typical needs. Advertisers monitor how the keywords change as people move through the funnel so they can incorporate those keywords into their messages at various levels of the funnel to increase the chances that potential consumers will move further through the funnel from the top with the wide mouth all the way to the narrow bottom where the product purchases are made.

Thus the inbound perspective on advertising is much more oriented toward continual interactions and trying to get consumers not just to buy the product but to like the product so much they in essence work for the company for free by sending their own messages that transform the advertising procedure into a viral movement.

BECOMING MORE MEDIA LITERATE WITH ADVERTISING

In our everyday lives, we can do things to avoid news messages and even entertainment messages, but we cannot avoid advertising messages. Advertising is too pervasive, and advertisers are aggressive in using new ways to expose you to their messages. We encounter almost all advertising messages in a state of automaticity, where we are unaware of how much exposure we are experiencing. Also, when we are exposed to ads in the state of automaticity, we do not process their claims and therefore cannot discount their influence. This is especially the case when we are multitasking, because we are much less likely to analyze the ad claims and counter-argue (Jeong & Hwang, 2012).

During unconscious exposure, advertisers can plant their messages into our subconscious, where the information from those ads gradually shapes our definitions for attractiveness, sex appeal, relationships, cleanliness, health, success, hunger, body shape, problems, and happiness. For example, we might have the radio on in the car as we concentrate on driving, and when ads come on, we do not pay much attention. Then later, we find ourselves humming a jingle, or a word phrase occurs to us, or we pass by a store and "remember" that there is a sale going on there. These flashes of sounds, words, and ideas emerge from our subconscious, where they had been put by ads that we did not pay attention to. Over time, all those images, sounds, and ideas build patterns in our subconscious and profoundly shape the way we think about ourselves and the world.

To increase your media literacy about advertising, you need to construct a good knowledge structure about advertising (Table 11.5) then use that knowledge structure periodically to check that the advertising aimed at you helps you satisfy your own needs more than the goals of the advertisers. To guide you in this task, I will present three steps in this section. Each step comes with an exercise to help you apply this information.

Analyze Your Personal Needs

The more you are aware of your needs, the more you can use advertising to control your life. If you are not aware of your needs, the constant flood of advertising messages will create and shape your needs—often without you knowing it. Stop reading this chapter now and complete Exercise 11.3.

How did you do on Part I of Exercise 11.3? Were you able to come up with a long list of needs, or could you think only of one or two? Was it easy or hard to rank order your needs? Then in Part II, were you surprised by how many products you have brought into your home? Were you surprised about how many were well-advertised brands?

TABLE 11.5 ■ Types of Skills and Knowledge Structures Needed to Deal With Advertising Messages in a Media-Literate Manner

	Skills	Knowledge
Cognitive	Ability to analyze an advertisement to identify key elements of persuasion Ability to compare and contrast key elements of persuasion in the ad with facts in your real-world knowledge structure Ability to evaluate veracity of claims in the ad	Knowledge on topic from many sources (media and real world)
Emotional	Ability to analyze the feelings of people in the ad Ability to put oneself into the position of different people in the ad	Recall from personal experiences how it feels to have a need for the advertised product
Aesthetic	Ability to analyze the craft and artistic elements of the ad Ability to compare and contrast the artistry used to craft this ad with that used to craft other types of ads	Knowledge of writing, graphics, photography, and so on Knowledge of successful and unsuccessful ads and the elements that contributed to those qualities
Moral	Ability to analyze the moral elements of an ad Ability to evaluate the ethical responsibilities of advertisers	Knowledge of criticism of advertising and knowledge of how ads can manipulate our attitudes and behaviors Highly developed moral code

Now ask yourself: How aware am I of my needs? Make a comparison of your rank-ordered list from Part I with how you spend your money and time as indicated in the inventories in Part II. Is your primary need (from Part I) reflected in the inventories of your possessions and time (from Part II)? For example, let's say your number one–ranked need was health. Did the inventory of your closet reveal more clothes for health-producing activities than any other type of clothes? Did your inventory of your kitchen reveal an absence of highly advertised, high-caloric, high-fat, high-sugar, or high-salt snacks? Did your inventory of your bathroom reveal more products for sore muscles or more for beauty? Is your toothpaste a decay preventer or a tooth whitener? Did the inventory of your time reveal that you are very active or mostly passive?

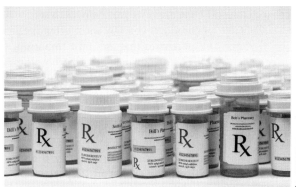

isotck/WendellandCarolyn

Prescription drug advertisements can manipulate people into believing they have additional needs.

If your self-reported needs (from Part I) closely matched your inventories (from Part II), then congratulations! You are aware of your needs and know how to spend your resources to satisfy them. But if there are discrepancies between your self-reported needs and where you spend your money and time, then you have a faulty sense of your needs. You might be telling yourself that your needs are A, B, and C, when your real needs are X, Y, and Z. You are satisfying your real needs even though you are not aware of what they really are. More typically, discrepancies exist because you are not able to satisfy your needs; that is, you are very aware of what your needs are. But when you go to the store, you end up buying lots of things that really do not address those needs but you hope they will because you want to believe the puffery in the ads. However, the will to believe is not enough. As time goes by, you become frustrated that you cannot fulfill your major needs, although it seems like you are doing what society (as channeled by advertisements) is telling you to do.

One of the biggest dangers concerning the manipulation of our natural needs is with prescription drugs. The number of ads for prescription drugs on television grows each year; until 2008, the average person was exposed to 16 hours of ads for prescription drugs each year, which is more time than they spent with their primary care doctors. These ads mislead the public by inflating their claims and by burying their risks in "a sea of unintelligible tiny print" (Foreman, 2009, p. E5). A content analysis of these ads found that while most ads (82%) made some factual claims and some rational arguments (86%) for product use, almost all of these ads (95%) used an emotional appeal. Many of the ads urged people to use their drug in order to achieve social approval (78%) and to regain control over some aspect of their lives (85%) (Frosch, Krueger, Hornik, Cronholm, & Barg, 2007). These ads lead people to diagnose themselves then pressure their physicians to prescribe the drugs they see advertised, so they can achieve the wonderful life the drugs depict.

Analyze Ads

The next step is to analyze some ads. Of course, there are too many ads in your environment to analyze them all. Make this step manageable by making a list of the advertised products you buy most often (i.e., your regular grocery store purchases) or the product purchases that are most important (cars, mobile devices, designer clothing, vacations). Then find some ads for those products and analyze them (Exercise 11.4). While you conduct your analyses, think most about how the advertiser constructed the campaign strategy and copy platform. Can you identify elements in those ads you are analyzing that would give you a good idea about what the copy platform was as a guide to these ads?

Are those ads simply giving you information to make you aware of the products or are they reinforcing existing beliefs and behaviors? Most people think that ads are designed to convince people to buy the product. Very little of the advertising we see has this intention. Many ads, especially those for new products, are intending only to establish our awareness that the product exists. Some ads are designed to create an emotion in us and link that emotion with the product. Some ads are designed to inoculate us against the claims of competitors so that when we see an ad for one of their competitors, we will not come under its influence. But the most prevalent intention of ads is reinforcement. Most ads are aimed at target groups of people who already use the product. Thus, the advertisement is designed to remind those customers that the product still exists and that it is a good one. People usually remember ads for products they already buy, so most of the effect of advertising is one of reinforcement of existing attitudes and behaviors. Thus, reinforcement is the powerful effect of advertising. Most ads are designed to make people feel good about the products they have already bought so that they will buy them again.

Evaluate Ads

The final step is to compare your personal needs to what the ads are telling you. This requires an evaluation of the ads; that is, you are making value judgments about how well the advertisers understand your real needs and how well they present their products as a best way of satisfying those needs (Exercise 11.5).

If you found a close match between your personal needs and the advertising appeals for the products you buy, then you can conclude that advertising is exerting a positive influence in your life. That is, advertisers have identified your actual needs and are helping you satisfy them. In contrast, if you find that advertisers are trying to make you believe you have needs that you really don't have, then you need to think about what you can do to prevent them from eventually convincing you that these false needs are real.

SUMMARY

We live in a culture that is saturated with advertising messages. In order to become more media literate and protect ourselves from the pervasive influence of this saturation, we need to understand more about the process advertisers use to design their ad campaigns and messages. When we have more knowledge about advertising campaign strategies and copy platforms, we will be more able to analyze and evaluate advertising messages.

Further Reading

Block, M. P., & Schultz, D. E. (2009). *Media generations: Media allocation in a consumer-controlled marketplace*. Worthington, OH; Prosper Press. (128 pages)

This book presents findings from SIMM (Simultaneous Media Usage), which is a marketing study of 170,000 responses over a 6-year period to media usage and consumer behavior. This is one illustration of how much data marketers are continually gathering and how those data form the basis for advertising campaigns that are effective.

Fennis, B. M., & Stroebe, W. (2010). *The psychology of advertising*. New York, NY: Psychology Press. (331 pages, including glossary and indexes).

Written by two European psychology professors, this book describes what the research in cognitive psychology and social psychology tells us so far about how humans process advertising messages and are affected by them, particularly their memory, attitudes, and behaviors. The authors give a very well-organized and detailed presentation of theories and research findings from within the field of psychology.

(Continued)

(Continued)

Geddes, B. (2014). *Advanced Google AdWorks* (3rd ed.). New York, NY: Wiley. (657 pages, including index)

The author is an Internet marketing consultant who has developed many procedures for Google to use in advertising. The book is composed of 17 chapters of practical information, sometimes very technical, which is useful for readers who want to apply the ideas in their own ad campaigns.

Lindstrom, M. (2016). *Small data: The tiny clues that uncover huge trends.* New York, NY: St. Martin's Press. (245 pages, including endnotes and index)

The author is a business consultant who uses close observation of people and details of cultures to uncover people's hidden beliefs, desires, and emotions. He sells these insights to large corporations that are looking to satisfy previously unknown consumer needs.

Scott, D. M. (2013). *The new rules of marketing & PR* (4th ed.). Hoboken, NJ: Wiley. (439 pages with index)

Written by a marketing consultant, this book offers a great deal of practical information about how the professions of advertising and public relations have been changing due to the opportunities offered by the Internet.

Keeping Up to Date

Advertising Industry Periodicals

    Advertising Age (http://adage.com)

    Adweek (https://www.adweek.com)

Professional Organizations

    American Association of Advertising Agencies (http://www.aaaa.org)

    Association of Magazine Media (http://www.magazine.org)

    Cable Television Advertising Bureau (http://www.thecab.tv)

    News Media Alliance (https://www.newsmediaalliance.org)

    Radio Advertising Bureau (http://www.rab.com)

    Television Bureau of Advertising (http://www.tvb.org)

    Video Advertising Bureau (http://www.vab.net)

Consumer and Educational Associations Concerned With Advertising

    Ad Council (http://www.adcouncil.org)

    American Advertising Federation (http://www.aaf.org)

    Better Business Bureau (http://www.bbb.org)

Scholarly Journals

    The following journals publish research examining the content and effects of advertising messages presented in the mass media, particularly newspapers, magazines, television, and websites.

Journal of Advertising (https://www.tandf online.com/loi/ujoa20)

Journal of Advertising Research (http://www .journalofadvertisingresearch.com)

Journal of Broadcasting & Electronic Media (https://www.tandfonline.com/loi/hbem20)

Journalism & Mass Communication Quarterly (http://journals.sagepub.com/loi/jmq)

EXERCISE 11.1
INCREASING YOUR AWARENESS OF THE AMOUNT OF ADVERTISING IN YOUR ENVIRONMENT

Purpose: This exercise is designed to test how much advertising you are exposed to on a daily basis. For 1 day, carry around a sheet of paper in your pocket and write down every time you are exposed to an advertising message.

1. Mobile devices and computers: Check screens for banner ads, pop-ups, and ads in the margins. For each app, look for logos or appeals to try new features on the app; those are advertising messages.

2. Television: Count how many times your program is interrupted. Each interruption is a commercial pod. Count the number of individual commercials in each pod. Don't forget to count ads for the show you are watching, for other upcoming shows, and for the channel.

   Look for ads in the form of product placement in the programs themselves. For example, if a family is eating breakfast, can you see product brand names for cereal, juice, and so on? If characters are on the highway, can you see brand logos of cars and names of products on billboards or signs on buildings and businesses?

3. Print: If you read magazines and newspapers on paper, count the number of individual ads as you are flipping through the pages. About 80% of the revenue of newspapers and magazines comes from advertising. So if your issue of a magazine cost $3, would you be willing to pay $15 to support a magazine without any advertising?

4. Pay attention to your unmediated world.

   Do you see people walking around with brand names on their clothing?

   Notice the brand name logos on products all around you.

   Count the ads on signs that announce upcoming events.

   Look for names on buildings and other structures that alert you to the presence of businesses that produce and sell you products and services.

   Listen for sounds that are designed to capture your attention and remind you of particular products.

   Listen to people talking about brands and products.

EXERCISE 11.2
INCREASING YOUR AWARENESS OF EFFECTS OF ADVERTISING

1. Test your recall of brands. Pick two product categories (e.g., breakfast cereals, shampoos, soft drinks, potato chips, etc.).

   On a piece of paper write all the brand names you can remember for one of your selected product categories. Then turn the paper over and list all the brand names you can remember for the second product category.

   Go to a supermarket or drugstore and look at how many brands there are on those shelves for each of the product categories you selected.

   Were you able to name them all? What percentage were you able to name?

   Of those you did not have on your list, can you recall anything about their advertising campaigns? If so, why do you think you could not remember them when you made your list?

2. Next time you go to the drugstore or the supermarket to shop, try buying nonadvertised products (the store brand or generic) in place of the advertised brands you usually buy.

   How much money did you save?

   Are the savings worth it, or do you feel that you have made a big mistake?

3. Run a taste test for your friends. Buy several brands of advertised cola and some obscure brands. Pour different brands into their own cups. Ask your friends to taste each and tell you which cola is in which cup.

   Could your friends guess the right brands?

   Were they sure of their choices, or were they making wild guesses?

EXERCISE 11.3
PERSONAL NEEDS INVENTORY

Part I

Take out a sheet of paper and write down your needs.

1. Begin by simply listing all your needs as they pop into your head.

2. Once you have a list, organize the elements into categories. Group all like needs together. For example, you might have several social needs (e.g., make more friends, become more popular), health needs (e.g., lose weight, exercise more, etc.), career needs, family needs, school needs, and so forth.

3. After you have your categories, rank order your groups. Which set of needs is most important to you? What set is second, and

so on? Now put this paper aside and go on to Part II.

Part II

1. Go through your clothes closet.

   How many changes of clothes (outfits) do you have? How many pairs of shoes? If you have one or two changes of clothes, you are operating at a functional level; that is, you are satisfied to protect your body from the elements and for the sake of being modest. If you have many sets of clothes, group them according to your needs; that is, which are your social clothes, your business clothes, your exercise clothes, and so on?

   Which set of clothes contains the greatest number of outfits? Why? Do you have the most clothes in an area that is the same as what you designated as your highest-ranked need area in Part I?

2. Go through your kitchen cabinets and pantry.

   How many prepared foods (in boxes, cans, and bags) do you have compared to natural foods (milk, fresh fruit, fresh vegetables, etc.)?

   What proportion of those products are advertised brands, and what proportion are unadvertised or generic?

3. Check your bathroom.

   How many "health and beauty" aids do you have?

   How many of those products are for basic health needs, and how many are image enhancers?

   What proportion of those products are advertised brands, and what proportion are unadvertised or generic?

4. Think about how you spend your time.

   How much time do you take getting washed, groomed, and dressed each day?

   How much time do you spend eating and snacking (how many times)?

   What do you do with your leisure time—are you active in satisfying your needs, or are you passively sitting in front of the TV or listening to music, where you are being told by others what your needs should be?

EXERCISE 11.4
ANALYZING ADVERTISING MESSAGES

Find ads for the products you buy the most (regular purchases in supermarkets). Look at several print ads from magazines and newspapers. Watch several ads on television. Use this set of ads in the following tasks.

1. What is the main product claim (reason for buying the product) of the ad?

2. Is the claim presented explicitly or implicitly (you have to infer it)?

(Continued)

(Continued)

3. What is the intention of the ad (awareness, positive emotion, change attitude, **inoculation**, reinforcement, buying product)?

4. Is the ad more emotional or rational?

If emotional, which emotion was evoked? Why this emotion?

If rational, how much information was presented? Were the right facts presented?

5. Did the ad use a product spokesperson? If so, why was this person chosen?

6. What was the message strategy of the ad?

7. What is the tone (humorous vs. serious; hard sell vs. soft sell) of the ad?

8. Look beyond the surface of the ad and the particular product; that is, think beyond how the ad is trying to get you to use a particular product. Can you see some underlying values that the ad is teaching?

What is the ad saying about the nature of problems and how advertised products can solve those problems?

What is the ad telling you about what it means to be healthy, attractive, and successful? Have those lessons become your internalized values?

EXERCISE 11.5
EVALUATING ADVERTISING MESSAGES

Find some ads for products that you typically use and evaluate those ads by asking yourself the following questions.

1. Which ads evoked the strongest emotions in you?

What were those emotions?

Explain how the ad triggered those particular emotions.

2. Which ads were the best from an aesthetic point of view? Is there something about the writing, directing, editing, lighting, set design, costuming, or music/sound effects that you found of particularly high quality?

If so, explain what led you to appreciate that element so much.

3. Which ads were most upsetting from a moral perspective?

What ethical considerations were raised?

4. Overall, which of the ads were most persuasive to you? Why?

5. Overall, which of the ads recognized your existing needs the best?

Did these ads present the best reasons for why the product would satisfy your needs?

6. Which ads were most exploitive—that is, tried to convince you of false needs?

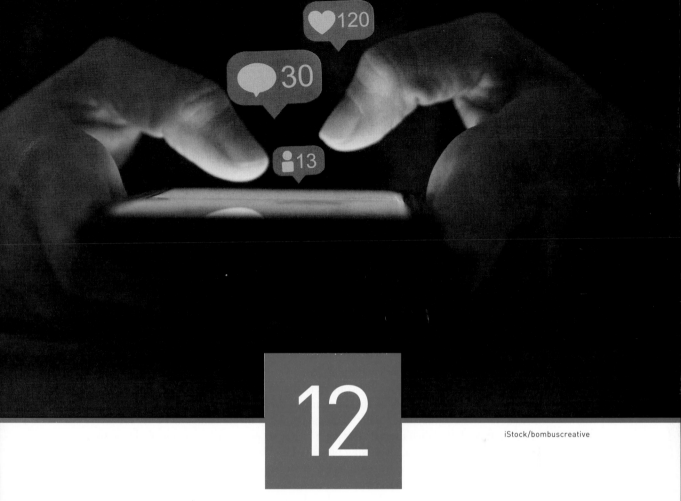

12

INTERACTIVE MEDIA

Key Idea: Interactive mass media are platforms that attract audiences who want to create their own media experiences for purposes of either competition or cooperation.

Interactive media platforms, such as Twitter, Facebook, and Instagram, allow people to create their own content based on personal interests.

The topic of **interactive media** is included in this section on content rather than in the industry section, because it is the content that is most characteristic of the interactive media. The content presented by noninteractive media is created by professional writers and producers who are highly skilled at applying message formulas that will attract particular kinds of audiences then condition them for repeat exposures. With interactive media, professional designers create platforms—rather than content—to attract audiences, then the audiences create the content as they interact with other users. These users are not paid for creating any of this content; to the contrary, users not only create the content for free but they often pay the interactive mass media companies a fee for access to the content. Even when users do not pay a fee for access to an interactive platform, they still agree to be exposed to advertising presented on these platforms.

There are essentially three types of interactive media platforms—those that offer users a competitive experience, those that offer users a cooperative experience, and those that offer users an acquisition experience. In this chapter, we will examine each of these three types in detail.

COMPETITIVE EXPERIENCES

Many interactive media platforms have been designed to attract users who want to compete against themselves, to compete against a computer, or to compete against one or many players. With the technology of computers, the Internet, and mobile devices, **electronic games** became part of the mass media.

What all of these games have in common are digital game codes that govern game appearance and play, visual and audio features that attract users into the game, and input devices that players use to communicate with the digital code in playing the game (Kerr, 2006). Also, electronic games are like all of the other forms of mass media, because the games are commercial products that have been created in a manner to be highly attractive to particular niche audiences and the games themselves are constructed so as to condition habitual use of them (Giddings & Kennedy, 2006). However, games are different than other types of media messages in the sense that they do not take players through a story in the conventional narrative sense (Friedman, 1995). Instead, games offer the potential for players to construct their own stories as they move through the game. These games force the player to pay a heightened level of attention to the message stimuli instead of simply absorbing the meanings as presented. Players must continually make decisions as responses to the game's stimuli. As the consequences of their decisions unfold, they are drawn more deeply into the experience of writing their own stories. This participation gives players a sense of power and a sense of wonder as they explore how far they can go on their personal quest.

Troy Harvey/Bloomberg via Getty Images

Attendees play *Super Smash Bros. Ultimate* during the E3 Entertainment Expo in Los Angeles. Video games offer the ideal platform for the competitive interactive experiences.

Attraction to Electronic Games

Why are people attracted to electronic games? The desire to compete is a fundamental part of being human, and the playing of competitive games is as old as civilization itself. For millennia, humans competed against themselves by trying to solve puzzles and mysteries. Humans invented card games and board games (such as checkers, chess, and Monopoly) to compete against one person or several other people. Then with the invention of computers, the competitive platform was greatly expanded. By playing a game on a computerized platform, we can start the game any time we want and pause the game for as long as we want, we can take as much time as we want to decide our next move, and we can receive immediate feedback on our performance. With the rise of the Internet, we can now play against opponents anywhere in the world, so geography is no longer a limitation. Also, we can compete with very large numbers of players, such as with **MMORPGs** (massively multiplayer online role-playing games). And with the proliferation of mobile devices, we can take our game-playing experiences everywhere we go.

Electronic games offer players a way to satisfy two kinds of needs—emotional as well as cognitive (Tamborini et al., 2011). As you saw in Chapter 10, people seek out entertainment messages in order to feel aroused and to experience strong emotions. Games arouse players and can trigger emotions both when they are losing (frustration, humiliation, anger) as well as winning (joy, elation). These emotions are often more intense than the emotions normally triggered in a person's real life. Playing electronic games also satisfies cognitive needs, especially the needs for competence and autonomy. We all want challenges to motivate us, and we also want the experience of meeting those challenges so that we can feel successful. Electronic games offer a sequence of gradually increasing challenges that begin with fairly easy tasks that we can finish quickly. The completion of these initial tasks serves to provide a feeling of satisfaction that is rewarding and this motivates us to continue toward more challenging tasks. As we complete these more challenging tasks, the feeling of reward intensifies and our confidence builds, which propels us toward even more challenging tasks.

Another reason we are attracted to electronic game playing is to give us an opportunity to exercise control. Many of us feel a lack of control over events in our real lives where we seem to continually work at things that fail to deliver adequate rewards. We feel that our lives are so routine that we never seem to make any progress, which Castronova (2005) refers to as the Sisyphus problem. Sisyphus was the character in Greek mythology who was doomed to push a heavy boulder up a hill; each time he neared the top, he would weaken from the exertion and the boulder would roll back down the hill. Sisyphus would have to start all over again, day after day. Castronova says that many people feel like some burdens of their everyday life are too onerous to push over the top of a hill, so they play electronic games where they can be successful—metaphorically, get that boulder all the way to the peak so it will roll down the other side. Thus game playing can make people feel more successful and more in control.

Another attraction of electronic games is the opportunity to socialize with others on a common task. Even though these games are highly competitive, enjoyment is increased when players band together into teams and develop strong attachments to their team members (Schmierbach, Xu, Oeldorf-Hirsch, & Dardis, 2012).

Psychology of Playing Electronic Games

Psychologists who study how people play electronic games have come up with two terms to describe key characteristics of the game-playing experience—**flow** and **telescoping**. *Flow* is a term coined by social psychologist Mihaly Csikszentmihalyi (1988). He observed people getting lost in tasks and called this experience flow. In order to achieve this state of flow, people must deeply immerse themselves in a task so that they lose all track of time and place. With digital games, players often get so involved in the playing of the game that it is as if they enter the world presented by the screen and lose the sense that they are in the real world. Players become so focused on the pleasure of the game that other needs (such as thirst, sleep, hunger, etc.) become secondary; that is, satisfying those secondary needs gets put off in the interest of satisfying the primary need of achieving the next objective in the game. The expectation of completing the next game objective is so pleasurable that everything else is forgotten while in the flow state.

Telescoping is a term used by another social psychologist, Steven Johnson (2006b). He used this term to refer to the way electronic game players focus on the steps within the process of moving through a game. At any given point in an electronic game, the player must focus on an immediate objective that follows from previous objectives that were successfully achieved and lead to upcoming objectives that take the player to the end of the game. This focusing on the immediate objective is viewed as the foreground, and all the other objectives are pushed into the background where they are used only as context for the foregrounded objective. Thus game players must keep the big picture in mind as context while they focus on the immediate objectives they face at a given point in the game. When they meet their immediate objective, they do not stop playing; instead, they feel immediately propelled onward to meeting their next objective. Johnson says "talented gamers have mastered the ability to keep all these varied objectives alive in their heads simultaneously" (p. 54). Telescoping is not the same as multitasking. Multitasking is handling a chaotic stream of unrelated objectives, such as talking on the phone, instant messaging friends, listing to music on an iPod, and googling topics. Telescoping focuses more on a sequence of ordered objectives in a hierarchy of priority then moving through them in the correct sequence.

Experiencing flow and telescoping can be very intense and rewarding. It can be like a narcotic that continually draws players back to gaming for a repeat of the experience. And once players feel the experience, they want it to continue uninterrupted. When it is interrupted, they want to get back to it as quickly as possible.

Designing Electronic Game Platforms

The process of designing of a new electronic game is a complicated task that requires teamwork in the blending of many different types of skills. Teams of about 12 to 20 people—each with different specialized skills—work on developing each game, which takes about 15 to 18 months to create and test. Some of these team members must have marketing skills to understand the electronic gaming industry and be able to identify a potential niche audience that is not currently having their gaming needs met. Other team members must understand human psychology well enough to design features to attract the right audience, pull them into the gaming experience, and condition them so they will want to play the game continually. Some team members must be artistic enough to develop a compelling look, feel, and sound of the game. And other team members must be skillful computer programmers in order to write the code to make all these ideas work on the screen.

This complicated process of electronic game design can be organized into nine steps (Castronova, 2001). First, an idea is conceived and sketched out in a demo. Second, a team of designers determines what a player will do while playing the game. Third, artists render the environments and characters. Fourth, programmers write the digital code to make the game work as envisioned by the game designers and artists. Fifth, when enough code is written, an alpha version of the game is tested to see how well it works. Sixth, corrections are made to fix bugs and to make the game run more smoothly. Seventh, a beta version is tested by making it available to more players. Ideally, this beta testing creates a community of avid game players by making the game available on downloads for free during a trial period. Eighth, when management is satisfied with the beta testing, the game "goes gold" and is released to the publisher. And ninth, the publisher designs the box, reproduces the game disks, and distributes them to wholesale and retail outlets.

Sykes (2006) elaborates on the game design process by pointing out that game developers must make three fundamental decisions about the game they want to design. These decisions concern category of play, formality of play, and the affective tone. As for category of play, Sykes says that there are six types as determined by the objective of the game. These six categories of play are agon (competition is the primary focus; enjoyment derives from competing), alea (games of chance), mimicry (play involving make believe; players take on a new identity), ilinx (players seek vertigo, which is the temporary destabilization of the perceptual system, such as fairground rides), exploration (fun experienced when exploring new places and discovering new things), and social play (contact with others by joining special clans with secret languages, nicknames, initiation rites, etc.). While there is a different niche audience for each of these six features, the popular games usually combine two or more of these features in a single game to appeal to a broader base of players.

As for formality of play, Sykes (2006) says there is a range in the number of rules that a game can have. At the informal end of this range are games with very few rules or rituals; players experience the spontaneous expression of the animalistic impulse to play. At the formal end of the range are games with many rules and rituals that require discipline to follow; players who learn the rules best and who are capable of using those rules to their advantage succeed the most.

Affective tone refers to the kinds of emotions designers want the game to trigger in players. Sykes again points out that there is a range open to game designers. One typically triggered feeling of these games is aggression; designers figure out ways to put players in conflict situations with other players and the computer so that players feel they must fight to survive. Game designers build in levels where a player must fight off increasingly stronger opponents to get their rewards. Another popular feeling that designers try to trigger is mystery or suspense, where players must figure out what is happening before something bad happens to them or others.

In addition to the design decisions outlined in the above paragraphs, designers also follow some generic-type rules to ensure that their games are able to attract players then condition them for repeat playing. There are six design rules that apply to all successful digital games. Game developers carefully follow these rules in order to reduce the risk that players will reject their games. First, there must be some reward to the player, and the rewards must only go to the good players. Bad players should be punished, but the punishment should never be for something that happened outside a player's control. Second, the game should be relatively easy to learn. Of course, some games are very complex, but the complexity is not revealed to a player in the beginning. Instead, the complexity is gradually revealed step by step as the player moves through the game. Third, the game should be predicable. The game should follow logical rules so that players can predict the outcome of their actions. Fourth, the game should be consistent. The outcome of a particular action must always be the same. Fifth, there should be a fair degree of familiarity. This means that designers should consider what players bring to the game and use it. And sixth, the game should be challenging. If it is too simple, players will quickly lose interest. Instead, designers must build in layers where players advance to greater and greater challenges to keep them playing.

Marketing Electronic Games

Who is the market for video games? You are probably thinking it is a nerdy teenage boy, but this perception would be wrong. The average electronic game player is 30 years old and has been playing for an average of 12 years; 68% of all electronic game players are 18 years and older. Also, 47% of all gamers are women, with women over 18 being the fastest growing market. In addition, game playing is widespread, with 67% of all U.S. households playing electronic games (Entertainment Software Association, 2017).

Marketers of electronic games have moved to psychographic descriptors to identify niches of game players, and they typically identify four types of audiences: explorers, socializers, achievers, and controllers. Each of these four niches is characterized by a different kind of player. Explorers are players who are curious and want to wander around inside the game world to discover all its territories and experiences. Socializers are players who like to interact with other players. They want the game to present challenges that require forming groups so that players have an opportunity to work together in accomplishing shared objectives. They want social interaction in the games, so they want opportunities to join clubs and engage in cultural activities with others, such as weddings, parties, and other social rituals. Achievers are players who are attracted to the games in order to build something, like a city, an empire, or great personal wealth. Finally, controllers are players who want to dominate others. They want games with a high degree of competition so they can figure out ways to defeat and dominate worthy opponents.

Game developers must promote their products to an increasingly wide variety of players.

While games are typically marketed to players, game developers also market their game code to other game developers. This is called the **middle-ware market**. There are would-be designers of games who lack a depth of programming skills required to design a game from scratch; these developers buy **game engines**, which is the basic programming needed to support a game. They use these game engines to construct the specifics of their games (characters, settings, decision points, etc.) from the basic code (Castronova, 2001).

The video game industry is very healthy, with revenue increasing each year, and it employs 220,000 people in the United States alone. In 2017 it generated a record high of $36 billion in revenue, which included sales of hardware, software, and peripherals (Entertainment Software Association, 2018). However, the video game industry is also very risky. Only about 3% of electronic games earn a profit because the costs of development are so high. For example, the cost of designing a prototype for a modest electronic game is typically about $1.5 million. The minimum cost of developing a console game is typically about $7.5 million and this figure escalates when game developers use characters and locations that require licensing permission (Havens & Lotz, 2012).

MMORPGs

A popular—and very addictive—electronic game is the massively multiplayer online role-playing game (MMORPG). Many of these games have been very successful at attracting large numbers of players and conditioning them for repeated play so well that they have convinced many of their players to believe that the cyberworld of the game is more important than the players' real worlds.

One of the most popular and elaborate MMORPGs is the *World of Warcraft* (WOW), which was released in 2004. Players of WOW "live" in a medieval type world called Azeroth. New players spend months building up their characters while avoiding being killed (called "ganked" in WOW) by more experienced players. After months of play, the good players get to level 60, where they join with other players in guilds and undertake intricately planned raids on dungeons to kill dragons and engage in massive rumbles against other guilds.

In order to play WOW, players must purchase the computer software for $19.99 then pay a monthly fee of $14.99 to play online. By 2009, WOW had 11.5 million players worldwide, making it the most successful online video game in the world (Fritz, 2009). But over time as other MMORPGs have grown in popularity, the intense competition for players has

MMORPG games like *World of Warcraft* create a flow and telescoping experience where players are deeply immersed in the tasks and experience of the game.

reduced the number of WOW's regular players significantly to about 5 million players in 2018 and this downward trend was forecast for at least the next 5 years (Statista, 2018d).

MMORPGs have been found to lead to addiction (Yee, 2002), even to the point of death. A Korean player was found dead of exhaustion after spending 80 continuous hours in *Lineage* without a break. An *EverQuest* user committed suicide triggered by a feeling of desperation conditioned by events within the game world (Castronova, 2005, p. 64). A less life-threatening, but more widespread, effect of playing MMORPGs is **displacement**. These games provide players with a cyberworld that is often much more attractive than their real worlds, so players shift their time and resources into these cyberworlds and thus displace their real worlds. For many players, the cyberworlds offer experiences they cannot get in their real world, so players move into the cyberworld and live their lives there, where they create economies, political systems, friendships, romantic attachments, and careers. In his book *Synthetic Worlds*, Edward Castronova (2005) argued that

> the synthetic worlds now emerging from the computer game industry . . . are becoming an important host of ordinary human affairs. There is much more than gaming going on there; conflict, governance, trade, love. The number of people who could be said to "live" out there in cyberspace is already numbering in the millions; it is growing and we are already beginning to see subtle and not-so-subtle effects of this behavior at the societal level in real Earth countries. (p. 2)

Furthermore, Castronova said that

> the fading of boundaries between our world and the synthetic worlds of cyberspace is what justifies serious inquiry, in my view. As the lines disappear, we move toward a state in which there is really no barrier to a complete translation of every interpersonal human phenomenon on Earth in the digital space. (p. 48)

Castronova conducted a study of users of these games and found that about 57% said they would quit their real-world job and work in the cyberworld if they could make enough money there to support themselves, and three quarters of players wish they could spend all of their time in the cyberworld of the game (p. 59).

The boundary between cyberworlds and the real world has also been breached in the realm of the economy. Each MMORPG cyberworld has its own internal economy where players are given opportunities to perform a range of work-like tasks and earn some type of "coin of the realm" for this work. Players can then enter into exchanges with other players. In this way, players can satisfy their game-playing needs and gradually amass wealth within the game. Then in the early 2000s, some players began trying to sell resources they earned within game worlds to people in the real world for real-world currency. For example, players of *EverQuest* would work at menial tasks in that particular cyberworld where they were paid around 300 platinum pieces an hour on average. Some of these players sold their platinum pieces on eBay to other *EverQuest* game players for U.S. dollars. The exchange rate at the time was about $3.50 USD for 300 *EverQuest* platinum pieces. Thus a person can go to work in *EverQuest* and make $3.50 per hour (Castronova, 2005). Of course, $3.50 an hour is far below the minimum wage in America, but in other countries it is a good income. So ambitious people in developing nations could enter the *EverQuest* cyberworld and perform a task like hammering metal into suits of armor by clicking a mouse all day, then sell these suits of armor to other *EverQuest* game players on eBay. As of 2004, eBay was hosting about $30 million of annual trade for goods that only exist in synthetic worlds. Much of this trade was for real currencies, meaning that eBay was in the foreign currency exchange market (Castronova, 2005, p. 149). eBay has since banned the sale of virtual goods on its site, but there are other sites (e.g., Craigslist) where virtual goods can be sold and many games have developed their own sites for the exchange of virtual goods. This has led game marketers to create their own cryptocurrencies, such as platinum pieces in *EverQuest* and Linder dollars in Second Life. Some entrepreneurs have also created cryptocurrencies outside of video game worlds. Bitcoin is one example of a cryptocurrency, as discussed later in this chapter. By the end of 2017, the exchange market for cryptocurrencies was averaging daily trading volumes of over $50 billion, which is more than the daily trading volume of the New York Stock Exchange (Williams-Grut, 2017).

How important are the competitive interactive platforms to you? Try working through Exercise 12.1 to take an inventory of your playing experiences. If you never play electronic games, then you cannot do Exercise 12.1, but do not ignore this issue. Instead, ask yourself why you have been avoiding them. Are all your needs currently being met by other ways you spend your time? Are there games that could help you develop skills you would find valuable? Are there games that could provide you with more emotional experiences?

COMPARE & CONTRAST
ELECTRONIC GAMES AND SOCIAL NETWORKING SITES

Compare: Electronic games and social networking sites are *the same* in the following ways:

- Both offer users a way to interact with other people without being in the same physical location.

- Both exist in cyberspace and can be accessed on one's computer, tablet, smartphone, or any other device that can connect to the Internet.

Contrast: Electronic games and social networking sites are *different* in the following ways:

- Electronic games feature competitive experiences primarily, although some offer opportunities to work with other people in teams but the purpose of team work is to compete against other teams.

- Social networking sites feature cooperative experiences primarily; that is, they are platforms for people to make friendships and share experiences that are mutually beneficial.

COOPERATIVE EXPERIENCES

Interactive media platforms that offer cooperative experiences have grown extremely popular. The most popular of these are what are called social networking sites (SNSs) such as Facebook (begun in 2004) and Twitter (begun in 2000). By 2008, 24% of the U.S. population were regular users of social media sites, and this percentage steadily increased to more than 81% in 2017 (Statista, 2018e).

Although SNSs are relatively new, there is already fascinating research that shows how certain kinds of people are using SNSs to fulfill their special needs and to overcome their particular challenges. These groups include juvenile delinquents (Lim, Vadrevu, Chan, & Basnyat, 2012), gays (Vivienne & Burgess, 2012), and people suffering with grief (Marwick & Ellison, 2012). However, research has also clearly demonstrated the risks of trying to maintain close personal relationships on SNSs that are rather public (Baym & Boyd, 2012; Bazarova, 2012; Van Der Heide, D'Angelo, & Schumaker, 2012). In an interesting ethnographic study, Ito and his colleagues (2009) hung out with American children and teenagers over a 3-year period to study why they spent so much time with the interactive media. The researchers made two major observations. First, they observed that interactive media offer two strong attractions for today's youth: friendship-driven participation and interest-driven participation. Second, the researchers observed that interactions with media vary by degree of involvement. The least engaging degree of involvement is "hanging out" with friends and extending social networks. As users get more involved with the interactive media, they are required to develop new skills or a different kind of media literacy. This new media literacy is characterized by "deliberately casual forms of online speech, nuanced social norms for how to engage in social network activities, and new genres of media representation, such as machinima, mashups, remix, video blogs, Web comics, and fansubs" (p. 25).

Social contact can take several forms. Some users want friendship, others want dating experiences, some want to live in a different world, and others want to share their opinions and values. It is likely the case that many of us want several of these or all four at times. Let's examine each of these in more detail below.

Friendship

The most prevalent platform for friendship is the SNS. These are web-based platforms that give individuals the opportunity to create a public profile, generate connections with visitors to their site, and share personal information. These sites provide tools to allow users to construct their sites easily with text, photos, and video. SNSs offer a sense of community that is much more psychological than geographic; in fact, geographic limitations are relaxed to the point where interactions can occur with anyone in the world.

The earliest SNS was Six Degrees, launched in 1997. Then Myspace started in the summer of 2003 by offering users a profile page with pictures and interests along with the ability to link to friends. Myspace also provided games, blogging (called journals early on), and even horoscopes. The early adopters were teenage girls who used it to keep in touch with their friends around the clock by posting photos and actively blogging. Myspace allowed them to customize their profiles, and this had strong appeal for the early users. They also downloaded songs and "mashed up" songs in remixes. Myspace also allowed "fakesters" by permitting users to be whoever they wanted to be—themselves, a celebrity, a pet animal, or a wholly made up person with a created identity. The major activity was "friending," which is getting people to add you to their friends list and agreeing to be on your friends list. Many users felt it was a competition to have the largest friends list (Angwin, 2009, pp. 59–62).

Until April 2004, only Myspace members could view the profiles of other Myspace members but because of the shifting focus to advertising support, Myspace was opened up to the outside world. By 2008, Myspace was by far the most used social networking site. However, Myspace went into a decline as its chief competitor, Facebook, provided people with superior technology and served their needs better, thus taking away most of Myspace's users and advertisers.

Sheryl Sandberg, Chief Operating Officer of Facebook, speaks at a Facebook event. Facebook provides many aspects of the cooperative experience such as friendship, opinion sharing, and entertainment.

Facebook, which was launched in 2004, quickly became a major competitor to Myspace. The website's membership was initially limited to Harvard students but was expanded to other colleges in the Boston area, the Ivy League, and Stanford University. During its first year, Facebook was much smaller than Myspace, with just 10 million monthly visitors compared with 24 million for Myspace, but it was growing quickly as it expanded to include any university student, then high school students, and, finally, anyone age 13 and over. Facebook also introduced several new features such as the News Feed, which provided members with updates about their friends' activities. By the summer of 2011, Facebook had 600 million users worldwide and virtually eliminated Myspace ("The New Tech Bubble," 2011). Now in 2018, Facebook has well over 2.2 billion active users worldwide, which is a 13% increase over the previous year. According to the digital marketing company Zephoria (Zephoria Digital Marketing, 2018), 76% of all females are regular users of Facebook and 66% of all males are regular users of Facebook.

Dating

While people frequently use a general friendship networking platform such as Facebook to move beyond friendships and into dating, there are SNSs specifically designed for partner seeking, such as Tinder, OkCupid, Coffee Meets Bagel, Hinge, Tastebuds, and Match.com, to name a few. These sites require you to set up an account where you fill out a questionnaire about yourself and the kind of potential dating partners you would like to meet. These sites differ in the ways they match people and what services they offer to subscribers. Some sites send users suggested matches, while others use GPS to help singles find dates in the vicinity then send them instant messages.

Dating sites are popular with people of partner-seeking age. Research has found that 49 million people in the United States have tried a dating site; 19% of adult singles are registered on at least one site, with the average person being on 2.4 dating sites (Dating Sites Reviews, 2018).

Living

For people who prefer to keep their contact with friends virtual and not interact in real life, there are virtual friendship sites. One of these is called Second Life, which is described as "A place to connect. A place to shop. A place to work. A place to love. A place to explore. A place to be different. A place to be yourself" (Second Life, n.d.). Second Life is an online virtual world developed by Linden Lab, which was launched in 2003. Anyone 13 years of age and older can join and create an avatar. These avatars, called residents, can explore the world (known as the grid), meet other residents, socialize, participate in individual and group activities, and create and trade virtual property and services with one another. By 2013, users had created 36 million accounts. It reached a peak of about a million regular users in 2007 and has since declined but still has about 600,000 active users (Jamison, 2018).

Opinion Sharing

The most popular type of interactive platform that allows people to share their opinions is the **blog**, which is a truncation of the words "web log." Blogs are websites where an individual posts personal opinions and invites responses from readers. Structurally, blogs consist of textual elements (diary notations, hobbies, quotes, lists of favorite sites, etc.), visual graphic elements (photographs, icons, weblinks), and interactive elements (online discussion, e-mails, etc.). Some blogs are focused on the authors themselves, while others are focused on issues or interests. Blogs offer the potential for an unlimited size audience, unlimited freedom to talk about anything, and unlimited size. Thus they can address issues outside the mainstream media. Blogs are dialogic; that is, they elicit responses, so bloggers post their thoughts with the expectation of receiving reactions.

The first blog went online in 1994; by 2012, there were more than 200 million blogs worldwide. Now it is impossible to tell accurately how many blogs there are but by 2018, there were over 440 million blogs on the three most popular platforms of Tumblr, Squarespace, and WordPress (Mediakix, 2017).

While most blogs feature the personal ramblings of opinionated individuals and receive only a few hundred visitors at most, there are other blogs that do qualify as examples of the mass media. These are highly organized sites usually focused on a particular topic with many postings designed to attract large numbers of a particular kind of audience; they are also supported by advertising messages. For example, the *Drudge Report* (with 1.6 million unique monthly visitors) and the *Huffington Post* (with 773,000 visitors) are political blogs but have postings on entertainment, business, media, lifestyle, and other topics. They rival major newspapers, both in the range and quality of their messages as well as their reach among readers.

Included in this blogosphere is Twitter, which began in 2006 by allowing users to post tweets of up to a limit of 140 characters. Tweets are typically impulse messages containing mundane information about users' everyday lives (such as what they ate for breakfast) and their opinions about whatever they care about.

By 2012, Twitter had increased to more than 555 million active registered users and they send an average of 58 million tweets each day (NumberOf.net, 2015). Since that time, the number of Twitter users has decreased but the number of tweets has grown enormously. By 2018, Twitter had 330 million active users who sent a total of 500 million tweets per day (Aslam, 2018a).

How important are the cooperative interactive platforms to you? Try working through Exercise 12.2 to take an inventory of your SNS experiences. If you never access a SNS, then you cannot do Exercise 12.2, but do not ignore this issue. Instead, ask yourself why you have been avoiding them. Are all your needs currently being met by other ways you spend your time? Are there SNSs that could help you develop skills you would find valuable? Are there SNSs that could provide you with more emotional experiences?

ACQUISITION EXPERIENCES

People use interactive media platforms to acquire things such as information and physical goods. Of course, people can acquire information and physical goods from brick-and-mortar places, but interactive media platforms are typically easier to use.

Information

There are many informational and educational websites available. Some of these websites simply present their own information. Some websites provide **search engines** that direct users to other websites where specific information exists, such as Google. When Google was launched in 1998, it began with about 10,000 search requests per day; 1 year later it was receiving 3.5 *million* per day. Now Google processes 3.5 *billion* queries per day. Each of these queries travels an average of 1,500 miles through 1,000 computers and back to the user in 0.2 seconds (Internet Live Stats, 2018b).

Some websites are truly interactive; that is, they allow users to contribute. The software technology that allows people to interact with these sites is called a wiki. A wiki is a website that allows any user to add material and to edit as well as delete what previous users have contributed. The term comes from the Hawaiian word *wikiwiki*, which means fast or speedy. In 1994, a computer programmer named Ward Cunningham developed an initial wiki server designed to be the simplest possible online database. He designed it to be democratic in the sense that users would be equal in their ability to easily access any information as well as make their own contributions to that information base.

The most well-known wiki so far is Wikipedia, which is a free web-based encyclopedia that does not hire experts to write the content but allows anyone access to add, delete, and edit content. Begun in 2001, Wikipedia's greatest initial challenge was generating interest among the general public to volunteer to create articles for the encyclopedia without being paid. It met this challenge and by 2018, users had generated over 27 billion words for 40 million articles in 293 languages (Wikipedia Statistics, 2018).

Wikipedia's greatest challenge has shifted away from attracting enough contributors to checking the contributions for accuracy. Also, there is a continuing challenge to ensure that people with certain political or religious orientations do not distort entries for their own purposes. For example, in 2006 Wikipedians noticed that unmet campaign promises of members of Congress were being deleted from articles on those representatives. It was discovered that these deletions were coming from web addresses of congressional aides for those members of Congress. Also, it was found that the justice department was removing references to certain groups they felt were involved in terrorist activities. Wikipedians also noticed that supporters of the Church of Scientology were entering a pro-Scientology viewpoint, while critics were editing that out in favor of a critical viewpoint. In all of these (and many more) instances, Wikipedia had to lock out those people from the editing function and prevent them from distorting the entries to serve their own purposes (Linthicum, 2009).

What makes Wikipedia successful is the large number of knowledgeable people who are willing to participate by making contributions, editing, and reading the entries. When errors show up in entries, they usually receive rapid correction because there are so many minds involved. This ensures a much more comprehensive resource than a small group of experts could produce. Also the great number of people involved contribute to the elaboration of each topic—thus more detail can be provided because it is coming from many different people. (For more on how the collective knowledge of groups is superior, see *Infotopia* by Cass Sunstein, 2006.)

Music

People have been acquiring music through sharing networks since software by the name of Napster became available in 1999. A computer hacker named Shawn Fanning created Napster as a file sharing software program while he was a student at Northeastern University in Boston. Napster was released in June 1999 and within a year, the software had been downloaded by 70 million people who used it primarily to share their owned music with other people. Napster used centralized file directories on the Internet to connect users to music files on thousands of individual computers, thus enabling any user to download virtually any recorded music in existence for free.

In December 1999, the Recording Industry Association of America (RIAA) sued Napster on the grounds that this music sharing service allowed **piracy** of copyrighted music. The RIAA eventually succeeded in shutting Napster down in July 2001, and the industry has worked on marketing music downloading for a fee.

While sharing of music for free on Internet sites has changed quite a bit since Napster was closed, there are still many sites available for this service. Some of these sites are Free Music Archive, NoiseTrade, Musopen, Jamendo, and SoundCloud.

Video

There are many sites where users can access and download videos. Some of these are interactive and allow users to upload videos. The most popular interactive video site is YouTube, which was created in February 2005. The first YouTube video was uploaded in April 2005, which was entitled "Me at the Zoo" and showed one of the founders, Jawed Karim, at San Diego Zoo. The site was opened to the public in November 2005, and it grew rapidly. By July 2006, the company announced that more than 65,000 new videos were being uploaded every day, and the site was receiving 100 million video views per day. By 2007, YouTube consumed as much bandwidth as the entire Internet consumed in 2000. And by 2018, YouTube was reporting over 1.6 billion unique visitors per month; users were viewing more than 5 billion videos every day, and users were uploading more than 100 hours of new video every minute (Aslam, 2018b).

Shopping

People have been shifting from buying products in brick-and-mortar stories to buying products online. Although this e-commerce is relatively new, it already accounted for $304 billion by the end of 2014, which was 6.4% of all retail sales in the United States that year. Online shopping continues to grow and is expected to reach almost $500 billion in sales by 2018 (Reingold & Wahba, 2014).

Two of the dominant platforms for e-commerce are Amazon and eBay. Amazon was created by Jeff Bezos in 1994 and went online the following year as a website for selling books. Over the years, Amazon diversified by also selling video, software, electronics, apparel, furniture, food, toys, and jewelry. The company further diversified by also producing a reader for electronic books, called the Kindle. Amazon is now the largest Internet-based retailer in the United States, with annual sales now over $178 billion (Market Mogul Team, 2018).

In September 1995, Pierre Omidyar started eBay as an online auction website where anyone who wanted to sell household items could post pictures and descriptions of their items online and allow viewers to bid on those items. When sellers accept a bid, they arrange for the sale of the item through eBay and then mail the item to the buyer.

Within 2 years, eBay had accounted for more than 1 million items sold. In 1998, the company went public, selling stock as a public corporation. By 2007, it had a quarter of a billion registered users worldwide with 100 million items on sale at any given time, ranging from items selling for a few dollars to a Gulfstream II business jet that sold for $4.9 million in 2001 ("The Basics of Selling on eBay," 2007). By 2013, eBay's annual revenue had increased to $16 billion but has since declined to about $9.5 billion in 2018 (MarketWatch.com, 2018).

Video sharing site YouTube has over 1 billion unique visitors a month and offers more than 100 hours of new video a minute. Luis Fonsi's "Despacito (Remix)" featuring Daddy Yankee and Justin Bieber, reached over 22 million views in 1 day and has won Fonsi multiple music awards.

AP Photo/Eric Jamison

MEDIA LITERACY WITH INTERACTIVE MESSAGES

What are the implications of interactive media platforms for media literacy? Some of these implications are personal and some are broader. The personal implications are things you need to consider as an individual so that you can avoid risks of negative effects and increase the probability of positive effects. The broader implications refer to the way the increasing use of the interactive platforms has been changing society and the economy.

Personal Implications

As you continue to rely on interactive media platforms, the most important thing you can do to increase your media literacy is to keep making a clear distinction between opportunity and addiction. Your control over using the media to satisfy your needs increases when you use SNSs and electronic games as opportunities to satisfy your personal needs more efficiently and more effectively. These interactive media platforms can really expand your experiences and give you many opportunities to move significantly beyond the limits imposed by your everyday life. These experiences can give you a much richer understanding of your strengths and much more ability to work on your weaknesses at your own pace and in your own way.

These same interactive platforms, however, can lead to addiction if you allow them to condition you so strongly that you cannot control your time with them. These interactive platforms can grow so addictive that they consume a great deal of your resources without delivering commensurate satisfaction. They can alter your mental programs to such a degree that you keep living your life through these platforms even though such an existence is making you unhappy and depressed. If you become addicted to one of these platforms, it takes over your personal goals and you slavishly work to achieve the platform's goals beyond the point where the game is bringing you any excitement or pleasure.

When you use these platforms, keep your own personal goals in mind. Prosocial goals are those that help you function better and more successfully with other people and in society. Thus users who spend time with electronic games that teach business princi- ples, leadership, interpersonal interaction, and the like are learning the value of prosocial behaviors and are developing their prosocial skills. However, almost all of these compet- itive games condition antisocial behaviors such as fighting, stealing, deceiving, and even killing. The players who spend time with these games will learn that antisocial behaviors are successful in resolving conflicts. Players become conditioned to use these antisocial behaviors in order to be successful in the game, and this learning may carry over into their real lives.

Broader Concerns

The growing popularity of interactive media platforms is changing economies and societ- ies. While there is little you can do as an individual to slow down these types of changes, you can position yourself to take advantage of these changes when you learn how to anticipate them.

As people shift their shopping behaviors away from brick-and-mortar stores and toward websites, they are forcing changes in the economy. Brick-and-mortar stores find it hard to compete with all their overhead and their limited selection of merchandise, so many of these stories are closing and the people who work there thus lose their jobs. But jobs open up in other places, like delivery companies or call-in centers for website merchants.

Another economic change is less visible now but is likely to have major implica- tions as we move into the future. When people spend their resources in virtual worlds, those resources get translated into currencies that are new and not well understood. For example, if people work in a virtual world like Second Life or a MMORPG and are paid for those efforts with goods and services there, it forces us to re-examine what it means to work and to get paid. This shift also transfers resources from the real world to virtual worlds and has the effect of reducing the vitality of the real- world economies. Thus the GDP (Gross Domestic Product) of real-world economies would shrink while the cyberworld GDP would grow. It appears that this is already happening.

This shift also has generated new forms of money. Cyberworkers typically are not paid in real-world currencies but instead are paid in currencies that exist only in par- ticular cyberworlds. This creates the need for new currency exchanges. For example,

Bitcoin is a cryptocurrency (form of money) that was invented in 2008 and already is used worldwide. Both Internet companies (such as Facebook, eBay, and Yahoo) and real-world companies (such as AT&T, Fidelity, and Western Union) accept Bitcoin, which is used in 100 countries; in the United States, over 200,000 companies accept it (Money Morning, 2013). Virtual currency is also attracting the attention of banks such as JPMorgan Chase, which filed a U.S. patent application in 2013 to develop a payment system utilizing "Virtual Cash."

The growth of e-commerce and new currencies has existing real-world governments struggling to adapt. In the United States, the Federal Reserve regulates the flow of U.S. dollars as a way of controlling the economy—slowing down inflation and preventing a depression. However, the Federal Reserve has no power to regulate the flow of Bitcoin or other virtual world currencies, so it loses power as these currencies increase in use.

When resources move back and forth from cyberworlds and real worlds, it raises questions about taxation. The Internal Revenue Service, which collects federal taxes on income earned in the United States, is struggling to figure out how to tax income that Americans earn in virtual worlds. If someone works in a cyberworld producing virtual products but then sells those virtual products in the real world, should that income be taxed? If so, what country should do the taxing? What if people work in a cyberworld and barter those virtual resources for real-world products? Should those be taxed as income? If so, how can we assess the value of those barter products in cyberworlds?

As people shift away from face-to-face interactions and toward more virtual interactions, the nature of society changes. Think about the nature of your friendships. Are your closest friendships with people who live thousands of miles away from you—people you will never interact with in person? With these friends, you cannot borrow tangible objects like a cup of sugar, a sweater, or their car. But you may be finding the opportunity to create deeper relationships based on a closer matching of interests than you could with the people you hang out with in your neighborhood. These changes in relationships are likely to have even more profound questions about romantic attachments: Can people develop truly meaningful romantic attachments by texting and Skyping? Is physical contact a necessary part of any romantic relationship?

SUMMARY

Interactive media platforms offer a wide variety of competitive as well as cooperative experiences for users. There is nothing inherently negative or positive in any of these experiences. Whether an experience is rendered negative or positive depends on how you engage with the platforms and how you use those platforms to achieve your own goals. When these platforms are used strategically as tools to provide you with experiences to satisfy your needs for arousal, emotion, skill building, and connecting with other people in meaningful and rewarding ways, they can be very valuable. However, when these platforms begin to dominate your life by consuming your resources while returning only frustration, false experiences, and isolation, they can be very harmful. The media literacy perspective offers you a way to make more conscious and more meaningful assessments about the degree to which various platforms are meeting your particular needs.

Further Reading

Angwin, J. (2009). *Stealing Myspace: The battle to control the most popular website in America*. New York, NY: Random House. (371 pages with index)

This is a detailed history of Myspace from its launch in the summer of 2003. It also includes some background on the website's founders (Chris DeWolfe and Tom Anderson) along with the companies that owned the website (eUniverse, Intermix, and News Corp.). It is written in a journalistic style by a reporter for the *Wall Street Journal*. The author also deals with some larger issues such as the development of advertising on the Internet and personal privacy.

Bollier, D. (2008). *Viral spiral: How the commoners built a digital republic of their own*. New York, NY: The New Press. (344 pages with index)

The thesis of this book is that the Internet was created as a **creative commons** where there is a great deal of sharing of resources for the common good. With free software in the 1980s and the rise of the World Wide Web in the 1990s, the Internet was created and is still maintained as an open source network that allows all people to interact freely in a wide variety of ways. By **viral spiral**, Bollier argues that this open networking structure feeds an upward spiral of innovation. The Internet's transformative power comes from allowing people free access to the ideas of other people so they can build on and alter those ideas. Therefore, change is not planned, ordered, or mechanical; rather change is messy and serendipitous. Threads of thinking radiate dynamically through countless nodes and influence all kinds of people in all kinds of ways to work collaboratively. Thus the Internet has been able to avoid the costly overhead that comes with centralized production and marketing and replaced it with a wide dispersion of vitality throughout the social commons.

Castronova, E. (2005). *Synthetic worlds*. Chicago, IL: University of Chicago Press. (332 pages, including index, appendix, and end notes)

Professor and economist Edward Castronova says that the computer industry is not only producing synthetic worlds in which their games are played, but it is stimulating the creation of other synthetic worlds by its players. People who use the games are not simply players; they often try to live the games and perform other human activities there, such as looking for friendships, love, employment, social connectedness, power, and prestige. There is much more than gaming going on there—conflict, governance, trade, love. The number of people who could be said to "live" out there in cyberspace is already numbering in the millions; it is growing and we are already beginning to see subtle and not-so-subtle effects of this behavior at the societal level in real Earth countries. He focuses primarily on massive multiplayer online role-playing games (MMORPGs), treating the phenomenon from an economic point of view by showing that there are economies within the game-playing worlds that extend out of cyberspace and into the real world.

Ito, M., Horst, H. A., Bittanti, M., Boyd, D., Stephenson, B. H., Lange, P. G., . . . Robinson, L. (2009). *Living and learning with new media: Summary of findings from the Digital Youth Project*. Cambridge, MA: The MIT Press. (98 pages; no index)

This book presents the results of a 3-year ethnographic study that examined how young people use the new media and how they learn from those exposures. The authors also wanted to find out how the newer digital media were changing "the dynamics of youth-adult negotiations over literacy, learning, and authoritative knowledge"

(p. xiv). They focus their attention on four ideas: new media ecology, networked publics, peer-based learning, and new media literacy.

Lih, A. (2009). *The Wikipedia revolution: How a bunch of nobodies created the world's greatest encyclopedia.* New York, NY: Hyperion. (246 pages with index)

This book tells the story about how the idea for Wikipedia was first conceived in 1995 then went online in 2001. Within 8 years, it had stimulated people to write 10 million articles across 200 languages for free. How was this made possible? Read the book!

Nayar, P. K. (2010). *An introduction to new media and cybercultures.* Malden, MA: Wiley-Blackwell. (216 pages, including glossary and index)

This book provides a descriptive overview of a lot of the terms, concepts, and issues arising from the new media and their creation of cybercultures.

Keeping Up to Date

Fileplanet (https://www.fileplanet.com/free-to-play/)

This website allows you to try demonstrations of many of the most popular video games.

Wikipedia (http://en.wikipedia.org/wiki/Main_Page)

This is the Wikipedia website's main page. Articles are constantly being added to this web-based encyclopedia. If you have not already done so, check out this amazing resource. Also, you can use this to get more up-to-date information on almost all concepts presented in this book.

EXERCISE 12.1
ASSESSING THE VALUE OF ELECTRONIC GAMES TO YOU

1. On a piece of paper list the electronic games you play on your computer and mobile devices (smartphone, iPad, etc.). Now estimate how much time you play each of those games in an average week.

2. Carry the piece of paper around with you for a week. Each time you play an electronic game, record how much time you spent playing that game.

3. At the end of the week, total up all the times recorded for actual game playing.

4. Compare your estimates at the beginning of the week with your totals for actual game playing at the end of the week.

5. Ask yourself the following questions:

   Was your actual playing time higher, lower, or the same as your initial estimate?

(Continued)

(Continued)

Did this surprise you?

In your initial estimate, were you able to list all the games you typically play?

What do these patterns tell you about how important electronic games are to you?

What percentage of your overall media use is devoted to playing electronic games?

What percentage of your waking hours is devoted to playing electronic games?

6. What do you get out of this game-playing activity?

What emotions are triggered as you play? Are these the emotions you want?

What skills are you developing as you play? Are these valuable skills to you?

Does game playing make you feel more confident or powerful? If so, are you able to transfer those feelings to your real life or are those feelings limited to the game?

7. How valuable is the playing of electronic games to you?

Compare your answers to question 6 with your answers to question 5 to see if you are getting enough payback for the time you are investing in game playing.

EXERCISE 12.2
ASSESSING THE VALUE OF SOCIAL NETWORKING SITES TO YOU

1. On a piece of paper list your favorite social networking sites (SNSs) where you build your network of friends/followers/contacts (e.g., Facebook, Twitter, LinkedIn, etc.). Now estimate how much time you spend on those sites in an average week.

2. Carry the piece of paper around with you for a week. As you use each SNS, record the time you spend there.

3. At the end of the week, total up all the times you recorded for actual use.

4. Compare your estimates at the beginning of the week with your totals for actual use at the end of the week.

5. Ask yourself the following questions:

Was your actual time on SNSs higher, lower, or the same as your initial estimate?

Did this surprise you?

In your initial estimate, were you able to list all the SNSs you typically use?

What do these patterns tell you about how important SNSs are to you?

What percentage of your overall media use is devoted to SNSs?

What percentage of your waking hours is devoted to SNSs?

6. What have you been getting out of the time you spend on SNSs?

How big is your network? Is that big enough? Too big to manage well?

What is the quality of your friends/followers/contacts?

What skills are you developing on these SNSs? Are these valuable skills to you?

What emotions are generated when you are on these SNSs?

Are you able to transfer these things to the real world?

Do you use the interpersonal skills you develop on SNSs in your real life?

Are the friendships you develop on SNSs limited to the SNS world?

7. How valuable has been your investment of time in SNSs?

Compare your answers to question 6 with your answers to question 5 to see if you are getting enough payback for the time you are investing in SNSs.

EFFECTS

PART V

BROADENING OUR PERSPECTIVE ON MEDIA EFFECTS

Key Idea: When we take a four-dimensional perspective—timing, valence, intentionality, and type—on media effects, we can better appreciate the broad range of effects the media are constantly exerting on us.

An awareness of the many effects media have on us is key to understanding media literacy, and helps us gain control over the messages we experience every day.

Suzanne is babysitting her two younger brothers, ages 7 and 10. She is reading a magazine while they are watching Spider-Man on television. She sees an ad for a new shampoo and tears out the coupon in the magazine ad, making a mental note to buy some of this brand when she is out shopping later today.

Her brothers are starting to shout at the television screen. Suzanne yells at her brothers to be quiet, then turns on her iPod to listen to some new music she has downloaded. As a new song starts playing, she starts to pay more attention to the lyrics and puts down her magazine. She begins to really like the song and wonders, "Who is singing this? I've never heard it before."

She begins to daydream about her date tonight. "I hope Tim takes me, like, to another, like, horror flick. It's, like, so much fun to, like, scream my lungs out and to attack him, like, during the bad parts."

When the song on the iPod finishes, she is in a happy mood, which is then shattered as her brothers begin yelling at each other and then wrestling around on the floor. Suzanne runs into the TV room and breaks up the fight. "You guys better behave yourselves or I won't let you watch your video of Spider-Man anymore! Get back in your own chairs now."

Peace restored, Suzanne picks up a newspaper and notices a story about a drive-by shooting where a gang of youths imitated some action in a recent movie. She thinks, "The media have such a bad effect on young kids. My brothers are going to end up in jail if they keep watching those shows. Thank goodness the media don't have any effect on me!"

Many of us have a narrow view of media effects. We look for high-profile tragedies as evidence of a media effect and use those isolated incidents to conclude that there are media effects. Although these high-profile tragedies are indications of media effects, they are rare in number, and this leads many people to think that media effects do not happen often and that when effects do occur, they happen to *other* people. This is faulty thinking. Media effects are happening all around us every day. And those effects are not just happening to other people; they are happening to *all* people, including Suzanne and us. For example, in the scenario above, Suzanne was persuaded to buy a new shampoo; she changed her mood by listening to the downloaded music to try to calm herself; she had fantasies triggered when she looked forward to a movie later that day; and she learned about a crime by reading the newspaper, then generalized from that one story to an unreasonable fear about her brothers ending up as convicts.

When you have a narrow perspective on what media effects are, you will not be able to perceive the many effects that are constantly occurring all around you. A sampling of some of those many effects is presented in Appendix A (https://study.sagepub.com/potter9e). When you increase your awareness of this variety of media effects, you will begin to see evidence for them constantly occurring in your life as well as with the people around you. And this awareness will help you decide which effects you want to continue experiencing and which you want to avoid, thus strengthening your personal locus with a better sense of direction about how you want to use the media to achieve your goals. Then as you use your improved sense of direction, you increase your control over media effects and put yourself in a position to enjoy the positive effects much more while reducing your risk of experiencing negative effects.

The purpose of this chapter is to help you become more aware of the great variety of media effects by expanding your perspective on what a media effect is. To guide your expansion of understanding, I present a four-dimensional analytical scheme. Those four dimensions are **timing**, **valence**, **intentionality**, and **type**. This chapter will show you how to use each of these four dimensions to understand much more about media effects.

TIMING OF EFFECTS

Media effects can be either immediate or long term. The timing of effects distinction focuses your attention on *when* evidence of the effect starts to show up more so than on *how long* the effect lasts.

An immediate effect is one that occurs during your exposure to a media message. The evidence of an immediate effect is observable during the exposure or very soon after. An immediate effect might last only for a short period of time (such as becoming afraid during a movie) or it might last forever (such as learning the outcome of a presidential election), but it is still an immediate effect because it changed something in you during the exposure. For example, when you visit your friends' Facebook pages, you learn what's new in their lives. When you read a website on sports, you might immediately feel happy when you learn that your favorite sports team won an important game. And when you watch an action/adventure film, you might begin jumping around in your seat and acting aggressively with the people around you. These are all immediate effects, because something happened to you during the exposure.

Long-term effects show up only after many exposures. No single exposure or single message is responsible for the effect. Instead, it is the *pattern* of repeated exposures that sets up the conditions for a long-term effect. For example, after years of being exposed to ads for all kinds of products, we become more materialistic; that is, we are more likely to believe that the way to solve our problems or live a happier life is keyed to greater consumption of advertised products (Opree, Buijzen, van Reijmersdal, & Valkenburg, 2014). No single exposure or event "caused" this belief; the belief is slowly and gradually constructed over years of exposures.

Immediate effects are much easier to notice than are long-term effects. There are two reasons for this. First, because immediate effects occur during an exposure to a particular message, it is easy to link the effect to the media message as a cause and conclude there was a media effect. By the time people notice a long-term effect, it is well after many media exposures and many other things are happening in their lives, so it is more difficult to link the effect to particular media exposures.

A second reason immediate effects are easier to notice is because they are usually sudden changes. For example, let's say you are visiting a friend's Facebook page and you see a posting that insults you; immediately you feel angry. Or your friend sends you a YouTube clip that makes you laugh. These sudden changes in your emotions are easy to notice.

VALENCE OF EFFECTS

The effect can be positive, neutral, or negative. Notice that these terms are value laden. Who is to decide what is positive and negative? The answer can be approached in two ways—from the perspective of the individual person and from the perspective of society in general.

From the individual perspective, a positive effect is one that helps you achieve a personal goal or satisfy a personal need. In this situation, you are usually aware of your goals and you use the media strategically to achieve those goals. For example, if your goal is to get some information to satisfy your curiosity, then finding facts in a book, in a newspaper, or on the Internet is a positive effect. This can move you toward a goal of having more information and achieving a higher level of knowledge. However, the media are constantly trying to use you and your resources to achieve their own goals; when their goals are in conflict with yours, this can lead to negative effects for you. For example, advertisers want you to spend more and more of your money on their products. If you buy products that actually do help you overcome problems you have, then this is a positive effect for both you and the advertiser. But if you allow advertisers to convince you that you are suffering from problems you do not actually have and you repeatedly buy their products, then this is a negative effect on you while being a positive effect for the advertiser.

We can also look at the valence of effects from a broad societal point of view by applying the values of society. The values of society are things like peacefulness, cooperation, freedom from threats, respect for one another, and the like. Media messages that reinforce these prosocial values can be regarded as positive effects. However, when media messages teach people how to commit crimes then trigger that criminal behavior, the media can be regarded from a social point of view as exerting a negative influence.

INTENTIONALITY OF EFFECTS

Oftentimes, we intend for an effect to happen, so we consciously seek out particular messages in the media to achieve that effect. For example, we may be bored and want to feel some excitement. To satisfy this conscious need, we go to a movie that presents a great deal of action and/or horror. During the movie, our blood pressure and heart rate go way up, and we are moved to the edge of our seat with fear. We have satisfied our need. Also, when we seek out factual knowledge in the media, we are consciously trying to achieve a particular effect. For example, you visit a sports website to learn about which teams won their games yesterday, you watch a cooking show to get ideas for new menus, or you access an app on your smartphone that tells you which groups will be appearing in concerts around your area. The information does not need to be extremely important, and it need not be remembered for more than a few minutes for an intentional effect to have occurred. Every day, there are dozens of examples where you intentionally use the media to learn to take advantage of some opportunity.

Many times, we expose ourselves to the media for one reason, but other effects that we were not seeking also occur. To illustrate, you get on a social networking site to connect with friends and find out what is new in their lives. We want to laugh at their funny pictures, and we want to celebrate their successes. During these exposures, we will usually have our intended effects occur; that is, we will laugh and get some information about our friends. But other effects are also occurring—effects we did not seek out and perhaps are not even aware of until someone later points them out. For example, our behavior is being conditioned for repeated exposures so that we spend more and more time each day on these platforms, and this can lead to unintended effects like **Internet addiction**.

Unintentional effects can be both long term and immediate. For example, after years of watching exciting movies, you develop a belief that the real world should be much more exciting. Also, your emotional and physiological reactions may have become desensitized; that is, it takes more excitement to make you happy. You did not intend for this to happen, but it happened anyway.

Even when you are experiencing an intentional effect, you may be subjected to unintended effects at the same time. For example, you watch a violent movie solely for the excitement, and the movie does deliver the excitement you wanted. However, the movie may also be delivering other effects, such as leading you to accept a belief that the world is a mean and dangerous place, which may make you irrationally fearful of traveling or meeting new people.

Unintentional effects frequently occur when you are in the state of automaticity because your defenses are not engaged. You are not aware that any learning is taking place, and hence you are not actively evaluating and processing the information. However, even when you are trying to be an active viewer, unintended effects can occur. For example, let's say you watch a news program or read a current affairs blog. You understand that the pundits are spinning the story in a way to reach their own particular goals. They are not there to inform you about the complexity of the situation; they do not want to reach a compromise or a synthesis of a higher realization on the issue. Instead, they dumb down the issue and present their polarized positions in a way to get viewers to agree with them. If you actively process this information, you can protect yourself from their influence by evaluating the credibility of their information then discounting their arguments. This is much better than simply accepting one of their polarized positions. By analyzing and evaluating the messages actively, you gain control over your opinion formation, which then leads to the formulation of a much more informed opinion.

TYPE OF EFFECTS

Most of the concern about the media focuses on the *behavior* of individuals. For example, there is a belief that watching violence will lead people to behave aggressively, that watching portrayals of sexual activity will make people promiscuous, and that watching crime will make people go out and commit the crimes they witness in media messages. However, we need to expand our focus beyond behavioral effects and also consider cognitive, belief, attitudinal, emotional, and physiological effects. Also, we need to think beyond effects on individuals and also consider effects on more macro things, such as society and institutions. Let's examine each of these in some detail.

Cognitive-Type Effect

Perhaps the most pervasive yet overlooked media-influenced effect is the **cognitive-type effect**. Media can affect what we know by planting ideas and information into our minds. This happens all the time and may be the most prevalent media effect. We are constantly acquiring information during every exposure to the media. But rarely do people credit the media with this type of effect when they are thinking about media effects. Think about all the information you now possess that got into your mind from your exposures to textbooks, magazines, and newspapers.

This cognitive learning is not limited to factual information; we also learn a great deal of social information from the media. As children, we learn a great deal about our world by observing role models—parents, older siblings, friends, and so on. Observation of social models accounts for almost all of the information communicated to children up until the time they begin school. The mass media provide an enormous number of models and actions from which children might learn. Given the large amount of time children spend with the media, pictorially mediated models (especially television and movies) exert a strong influence on children's learning about social situations.

Even as adults, we continue to pay careful attention to social models. When we do not have the social models we need in our real lives, we can usually find them in the media. Some of us want to learn most from social models who are powerful, extremely witty, physically attractive, or very successful in a particular career or sport. We develop a vicarious relationship with a professional athlete, famous actor, powerful politician, or wealthy role model. By observing these role models in the media, we gather lots of social information about what it takes to be successful and happy. Think of all the information you have in

Famous media personalities, such as Oprah Winfrey, can act as powerful social role models.

your memory about characters in television shows and movies you have seen; think about all those names, faces, behaviors, witty lines, and emotions they portrayed.

Belief-Type Effect

A **belief** is faith that something is real or true. For example, most humans have beliefs about the meaning of life, how we should treat one another, what happens when we die, and the existence of a supreme deity.

The media continually exert a **belief-type effect** by showing us the values used by people in the news and characters in fictional stories. Some of these beliefs are expressed by characters, so it is easy for us to tell what they are; in this case, we simply decide whether to accept or reject them. However, many of our beliefs have evolved over time as we watch what people and characters do in a variety of situations. For example, we might watch a lot of videos about people who have relationship problems with friends so that we can learn how they handle those problems; over time we develop beliefs about what friendships are and how we can develop the types of friendships we most want. Thus gradually over time media messages can shape our beliefs about important things like attractiveness, success, and human relationships.

Attitudinal-Type Effect

Attitudes are evaluative judgments about things. We compare the thing (like a person, a song, a political position, etc.) to our standard. If the thing meets our standard, we judge it to be okay; if it exceeds our standard, we judge it to be good, very good, excellent, outstanding, or super cool; and if it fails to meet our standard, we judge it to be bad, very bad, terrible, or uncool. The media can influence our judgments about all sorts of things. This is the **attitudinal-type effect**. We can listen to a political pundit, religious leader, or attractive character express an evaluative judgment and simply accept that attitude as our own. Or we can make up our own minds using a standard that has been shaped by media influence. For example, we might hear a new song on our friend's mobile device and immediately decide that it is one of the best songs we have ever heard; that is, we create a very positive attitude about the song. Or we could read the discussion of the performance of an elected official and judge her to be a good leader. In these examples, you might be thinking that these are not illustrations of media influence. But remember that the media can influence our standards so that when we make our own judgments, we end up using their standards. So think about what your standards are for "popular music" or "a good leader" and ask yourself the extent to which the media shaped those standards for you.

Attitudes rely on beliefs because beliefs are often the standards we use when making our evaluative judgments. For example, after years of observing glamorous men and women in Hollywood movies, fashion magazines, and Internet sites, we come to believe that we need to be tall and thin with six-pack abs and thick hair to be considered attractive. While we know this is an impossible standard for everyone to achieve, we still use this standard when evaluating the attractiveness of the people we see as well as what we see about ourselves in the mirror. Few people can live up to this unrealistic standard, so we hold attitudes that the people around us are all unattractive because none of them can live up to the unrealistic standard of attractiveness set by the media. Media influence has been found to be stronger on people's attitudes at a more general level—like opinions about society—than on a more specific level—like opinion about one's friends, one's own experiences, and oneself (Chock, 2011).

COMPARE & CONTRAST
ATTITUDE EFFECTS AND BELIEF EFFECTS

Compare: Attitude effects and belief effects are *the same* in the following ways:

- Both can occur in individuals as a result of media exposure.

- Both can occur immediately (during a media exposure or shortly after) or over a long period of continual exposure to media messages.

Contrast: Attitude effects and belief effects are *different* in the following ways:

- Attitude effects are evaluative judgments where individuals compare some element in a media message to their standard and decide whether the element meets the standard, falls short of the standard, or exceeds the standard.

- Belief effects are the acceptance that something is real or true.

Emotional-Type Effect

The media exert an **emotional-type effect** by making us feel things. They can trigger strong emotions such as fear, rage, and lust. They can also evoke weaker emotions such as sadness, peevishness, and boredom. Emotional reactions are related to physiological changes. In fact, some psychological theoreticians posit that emotions are nothing more than physiological arousal that we label (Zillmann, 1991). If a character on a YouTube video triggers a very high level of arousal, we might label this feeling love or we might label it hate; it depends on whether we are positive or negative about the character.

We have all experienced emotional changes while exposing ourselves to media messages. Horror movies trigger extreme fear, bloggers can make us feel outrage, magazine pictures can make us feel lust, and calm music can help us feel more peaceful.

iStock/FrancescoCorticchia

Have you ever become angry watching a sports game or sad at an ASPCA commercial? Then you've experienced an emotional-type effect.

The media also exert long-term emotional effects. One long-term emotional effect is desensitization. Over years of watching violence in the media, which rarely show victims suffering and instead focus on the perpetrators of the violence and how attractive they are, we gradually come to lose the ability to feel sympathy for victims both in media portrayals and in real life. We might regard the homeless as people who are victims of their own bad judgment and don't deserve much sympathy from us.

Physiological-Type Effect

Media can influence our automatic bodily systems, which are **physiological-type effects**. These are usually beyond our conscious control, such as the contraction of the pupil of the eye when we look at a bright light. We cannot control the degree to which the pupil contracts, but we can look away from bright lights and thus prevent the iris from contracting.

With the media, there are many physiological effects that usually serve to arouse us. A suspenseful mystery serves to elevate our blood pressure and heart rate. A horror film triggers rapid breathing and sweaty palms. Hearing a patriotic song might raise goose bumps on our skin. Viewing erotic pictures can lead to vaginal lubrication, penile tumescence, and increased heart rate (Malamuth & Check, 1980). A farce might make us laugh so hard that we are unable to stop, even when laughing becomes painful. Or listening to music can calm and relax us by reducing our heartbeat and bringing our rate of breathing down to a regular, slow rate.

Over time, our physiological responses to particular media messages can change. For example, when we see our first horror movie, our heart rate might go through the roof. But if we keep watching horror movies, we might find that it takes more and more gore to trigger any increase in heart rate. Gradually over many exposures to horror films, our physiological responses wear down.

Behavioral-Type Effect

Media can trigger actions. This is the **behavioral-type effect**. For example, after seeing an ad for a product, we might get on a website and order the product. Or we read about some disturbing event on a news site on the Internet and call a friend to talk about it.

There are also long-term effects to our behavior. For example, think about when you first got access to a computer to surf the Internet. Initially, you might have visited a lot of sites for a few minutes each. But over time, you developed a pattern of going to a few favorite sites and spending more and more time on particular sites. Perhaps you have reached the point where you spend almost all your waking hours playing certain games or connecting with friends on a social networking site. Perhaps your Internet behavioral habit is displacing other activities, such as exercising, hanging out with friends in real life, or going to class. Perhaps this behavioral habit has moved into an addiction. Many people continue interacting with friends on social networks for the purpose of getting emotional support even though research repeatedly shows that emotional support is far more satisfying offline than online (Trepte, Dienlin, & Reinecke, 2015).

Macro-Type Effect

The six types of effects presented above are all effects on individuals. The media also exert their influence on larger units such as organizations, institutions, and society; this influence results in **macro-type effects**. Some institutions, such as politics, have fundamentally changed due to the direct influence of the media, especially television and now the Internet. Other institutions—such as the family, society, and religion— have changed because of many different social pressures, and the media have served to heighten these pressures.

To illustrate this point, let's consider the institution of the family. In the span of a few generations, the makeup of the American family has changed radically. The number of traditional two-parent families has shrunk, eclipsed by childless couples, single parents, and people living alone. During the 40-year period starting in the early 1970s to 2009, the percentage of American households made up of married couples with children dropped from 45% to under 21%. Marriage also dropped from 75% of all adults in 1972 being married to 48% (U.S. Census Bureau, 2013).

One argument for the cause in the decline of the traditional family is that the rates of divorce are very high in the United States, and they have been climbing since television first penetrated our culture. In 1960, 16% of first marriages ended in divorce; 50 years later, that figure had increased to 50% (U.S. Census Bureau, 2013). Critics claim that the rise of the divorce rate and the portrayals of broken families on television are not a mere coincidence; they claim that the television portrayals have socialized people to believe that divorce and having children out of wedlock are acceptable. Critics point out that television too frequently portrays divorce, single-parent households, and alternative lifestyles. These portrayals, presented over many different kinds of shows and over many years, tend to be internalized by viewers as being indicators of what is normal. Over time, people become dissatisfied with their own marriages and seek adventure with other partners. Also, many popular television series have been portraying married life in a negative manner, thus giving young people the idea that marriage is an unattractive lifestyle.

The media have the potential to bring the family together to share a common experience. Families can build a bonding ritual around shared media behaviors and use those exposures as a chance to talk and bond. For example, in the 1970s, many households had only one television, and viewing was a common family activity (Medrich, Roizen, Rubin, & Buckley, 1982). However, few families now use television or other media in this way. Family members rarely share viewing time. Instead, family members are likely to watch very different shows at different times on different platforms, like laptops, smartphones, and iPods. In addition, the content different family members expose themselves to is fragmenting, so family members rarely share the same media experiences.

Also, parents have reduced the time they spend with their children—40% less time from the 1950s to the 1990s (Pipher, 1996) and that time is even less today. Pipher argues, "Rapidly our technology is creating a new kind of human being, one who is plugged into machines instead of relationships, one who lives in a virtual reality rather than a family" (p. 92). "When people communicate by e-mail and fax, the nature of human interaction changes" (p. 88). The conveniences of technology serve to cut us off from others. We depend less and less on others (at least face-to-face). People are likely to be regarded as things or services, rather than as human beings. Pipher said that 72% of Americans don't know their neighbors, and the number of people who say they have never spent time with the people next door has doubled in the past 20 years.

Even if we accept the argument that television has influenced the trend toward the breakdown of the traditional family, we must realize that there are also other influences, such as economic ones. For example, it takes more money to support a family. The median household income is now about $59,000 (Luhby, 2017), so both adults are likely to work, and this makes it harder for them to have children and raise

iStock/Fertnig

Family members tend to use television or other media at different times and on different platforms.

them at home. The percentage of women in the labor force has been steadily climbing. Now there are almost 75 million adult women in the U.S. labor force, with 70% of women with children under 18 working and 40% of women with children under 18 being the sole support of the household (DeWolf, 2017).

Another reason that family structure and family interaction have changed is that careers have become more important to many people than their families. Wage earners work longer hours, and this takes them away from the home for a higher proportion of their waking hours. There are strong stressors of time, money, and lifestyle, which make people regard the home as a place to recover from the workplace, not a place where they have high energy. For more than a generation, Americans have felt that family has not been of paramount importance in most people's lives (Pipher, 1996). The irony is that perhaps people are working longer hours so they can afford more of the things advertised on television and thereby achieve a happier life as promised by advertisers, but by spending less time with our loved ones, we are steadily becoming less happy.

Clearly, family structures and interaction patterns have been changing over the past 4 decades. There are many reasons for this. Media influence is a key element, but not the only one, in this change. The additional elements of economic demands, the rise in the importance of careers, and changes in lifestyle preferences have all contributed to the probability of change in the institution of family.

FOUR-DIMENSIONAL ANALYSIS

This section presents an extended example of analyzing a media effect using the four dimensions of timing, valence, intentionality, and type. For this example, let's consider the effect of Internet addiction, which has been a growing concern as critics of media influence now understand how successful media companies are at conditioning their audiences for repeated exposures. Many media companies are now becoming targets of criticism for their role in addicting people, particularly children, to their technological devices (Salon, 2018).

To begin this analysis, we first need to consider what is meant by *addiction*. Yes, media companies are very successful in conditioning audience members for repeat exposures to their messages and products. But is this addiction? The answer is no. Although the conditioning procedure used by media companies can lead to audience members becoming addicted, addiction is not just conditioning for habitual behavior. Addiction requires that the conditioning reach a point where people are no longer able to stop performing their addicted behaviors (Alter, 2017). In his book *Irresistible: The*

Rise of Addictive Technology and the Business of Keeping Us Hooked, Adam Alter (2017) explains that in the medical and psychology professions, the idea of addiction used to be limited to chemical dependency in which the human body becomes so dependent on the continual intake of chemicals (such as nicotine, alcohol, heroin, cocaine, oxytocin, etc.) that some people reach a point where they cannot stop themselves from consuming those chemicals. The consumption of these chemicals often leads to addiction because these chemicals stimulate the release of dopamine in the brain, which makes the person feel pleasure even to the point of euphoria. Over time as people consume these chemicals in order to experience pleasure, they find that they have to consume these chemicals in greater amounts and frequencies in order to trigger the same level of pleasure. Eventually they reach a point where the consumption of these chemicals becomes more important than everything else in life, so they sacrifice other things (such as family, friends, job performance, hobbies, etc.) that used to be important to them. As their quality of life deteriorates, so does their ability to control their consumption of these chemicals.

Recently, health professionals have recognized that addiction need not be triggered only by chemicals; it can also be triggered by learned behavioral patterns. Certain behaviors can trigger bodily responses that are identical to the bodily responses triggered by chemicals, even though those behaviors do not involve the person taking chemicals. Thus behaviors such as Internet gambling, shopping, viewing pornography, and engaging in social networking activities have also been found to trigger the release of dopamine. Over time, some people find this release so essential to their everyday lives that they cannot stop the behaviors they use to achieve this release and they exhibit all the signs of addiction. This connection between behaviors and dopamine production was first discovered by James Olds in 1954 in a series of experiments where Olds hooked up rats to a device that stimulated the rats' lateral hypothalamus, which is the pleasure center that releases a neurotransmitter called dopamine in the brains of organisms (Alter, 2017). In these experiments, rats had electrodes implanted in their brains then were put in a cage with a lever. Quickly the rates learned that when they pulled the lever, they would feel pleasure because the movement of the lever stimulated their brain's pleasure center by triggering the release of dopamine. Olds found that his rats would continue to pull the triggering lever over and over until they were completely exhausted; some rats even died from this exhaustion!

Alter (2017) explains that many Internet companies have become very successful at marketing their dopamine-delivery vehicles by the way they condition audiences for habitual use of their products. Thus Internet platforms are designed to provide people with a continual stream of immediate pleasure, in the form of making a winning bet, outbidding the competition on eBay, experiencing an erotic image, or increasing the number of one's Facebook friends. Platform designers build into their experiences all kinds of features to keep their audiences coming back for more and more by knowing how to construct their Internet platforms in a way to stimulate dopamine in the brains of their users.

Now let's use the four dimensions to analyze this media effect that is known as Internet addiction. By using the language provided by these four dimensions to think about this effect, you will be able to dig below the surface and understand the effect at a much deeper level.

As for timing, Internet addiction is clearly a long-term effect. You cannot become addicted by one exposure. In order for addiction to occur, people need to be conditioned over a long period of time so that they get caught in a pattern of habitual behaviors that they can no longer control.

As for valence, the effect is a very positive one—for the media businesses. When media businesses have conditioned audience members so completely that those people are addicted to their service, they can depend on this audience for a great deal of exposure for a long period of time. They can sell advertisers access to this audience and thus guarantee a steady income of advertising revenue. However, the effect is a negative one to those audience members. While the pleasure those audience members receive in the short term can be regarded as positive (who does not want more pleasure?), it becomes negative when people pass into addiction and can no longer control their exposures. When people become addicted to an Internet platform, they significantly decrease their attention to non-Internet activities. That is, face-to-face interactions with loved ones, friends, and other people trigger less pleasure. The challenges in their jobs and academic courses become less important, so they cut corners in those areas to shift time to their Internet activities. They care less about eating healthy (or at all), exercising, and sleeping than they care about achieving their next success on the Internet platform.

As for intentionality, people are intentional in seeking out pleasure from their use of the media; however, it is not likely that anyone is seeking addiction. Therefore the use of Internet platforms for the delivery of pleasure is, of course, intentional up to the point of addiction. Becoming more media literate will alert people to the path they get on when they increase their use of Internet platforms and help them monitor their usage so they can continue to enjoy the effects they intend to get while avoiding going too far in their behavioral conditioning and preventing themselves from entering into the unintentional extreme of addiction.

As for analyzing Internet addiction by type, things get more complicated because addiction suggests a variety of effects by type. Let's start with physiology. The experiencing of pleasure through the triggering of dopamine in the brain is a physiological response to engaging with an Internet site. Over time, people build a tolerance for lower levels of dopamine and require more intense triggering (or more frequent triggering) in order to achieve the level of pleasure they want to experience. This puts them on a path to addiction. The feeling of pleasure is an emotional effect that requires a physiological component, so emotions are linked with this type of physiological triggering. The addiction can be easily observed by watching people's behaviors. When people pass into the realm of addiction, their lives are dominated by behaviors that serve to feed their addiction. And what serves to maintain this increasing pattern of behavior is a set of beliefs that the increased exposures will deliver the expected pleasure and that stopping such behaviors will be truly devastating. So Internet addiction can be regarded as a physiological, emotional, behavioral, and belief effect. Trying to treat addiction as only one of these effects is likely to be unsuccessful because the addiction is a combination of all four.

As I hope you have seen in this extended example, using these four dimensions to analyze a media effect helps you develop a greater understanding of that effect. Some parts of this (and any) analysis are simpler than others. In this example, it was easy to see that

Internet addiction is a long-term effect that can vary by valence and intention depending on whether you conduct the analysis from the point of view of a media business or an individual audience member. Finally, the analysis by type shows you how complex addiction is and perhaps why it is such a challenge to overcome an addiction once it really takes hold of a person.

BECOMING MORE MEDIA LITERATE

Now that you have seen how the four-dimensional approach to media effects can broaden your perspective, let's see how good you are at internalizing this information. First, see how many different effects you can identify in the people around you (Exercise 13.1). Remember to consider long-term effects as well as immediate effects, positive effects as well as negative effects, and unintentional effects as well as intentional ones. Also, see if you can identify different types of effects.

Regarding Exercise 13.1 as a warm up, let's move on to a more rigorous challenge. Exercises 13.2 and 13.3 ask you to be more systematic and complete; that is, see if you can identify examples of both immediate and long-term effects across all six types. If you are not able to do this in one sitting, then keep these exercises in mind as you go through a typical week. See if you can spot different effects as they occur and thereby fill in some of the gaps in your charts. Also, you may find that some examples of effects have elements that would fit into several types. For example, you might learn something (cognitive effect) that leads directly to you doing something (behavior effect). Also, an immediate effect may suggest a longer-term effect. For example, you feel really good (emotional immediate effect) after a session of playing an electronic game, then later you notice that you have returned to the game again and play even longer (behavioral conditioning over the longer term).

Finally, take a look at Exercise 13.4 but do not feel you need to answer all those questions now. Keep these questions in the back of your mind. When you have a few minutes now and then in your everyday life, reflect on things like your expectations for romance, college, and career. Where did these expectations come from? Are they realistic? To what degree are you meeting these expectations? To what degree do your behavioral patterns conform to your beliefs about yourself and others? These are very important questions. Don't pressure yourself to answer these questions now; instead, let the answers come to you as flashes of insight as you encounter the problems and joys in your everyday life.

SUMMARY

A key step in increasing your media literacy is to expand your perspective about what is a media effect. Don't get trapped into thinking of the media only as kind of a candy store (see Box 13.1). Don't think that the media only affect others, such as young children who don't know any better or the criminal types who claim they copy what they see in the media.

BOX 13.1
CANDY AS AN ANALOGY FOR MEDIA EFFECTS

Many people think of media effects as if they were candy. As we walk down the street, there are people passing out all kinds of candy for free. They want us to taste their sweets, then come into the store and buy something. We are tempted. When we take a piece, it tastes good and makes us want another piece. Often we sneak another piece or two, thinking it can't hurt. But then a few minutes later, we experience a sugar rush followed by a crash of energy. Also, there is this lingering sweet taste in our mouths that becomes unpleasant as time goes by. We envision the sugar eating holes in our teeth. If we have kids with us, we find they are rambunctious and whine for more candy. And now we have to act like the bad guy and tell them no; it will spoil their dinner.

A lot of people think of the media as a candy store. Their messages are tempting, and we let ourselves sample and often like the experience. But afterward, we feel guilty. We feel we should have been doing something more substantial or productive with our time. We feel that those messages are now eating holes in our brains as we can't get a jingle, a song, or stupid joke out of our minds. If we have kids with us, we fear that they are soon going to imitate the bad language, bad attitudes, or bad behavior they have seen in the messages.

Yes, the media do offer lots of "candy" messages. If we indulge ourselves with a steady diet of candy over the years, we will clog up our arteries with fat and experience all sorts of negative health effects. But the media offer many other kinds of messages. If we can resist the initial temptation of candy and instead find the more nutritious messages in other parts of the media cafeteria, we can consume a more balanced and full range of vitamins and minerals. To live a more healthy life, we need to know what to consume and we need to exercise some self-discipline.

Because we are submerged in a media-saturated environment, effects are constantly happening to us as they shape our knowledge patterns, beliefs, attitudes, emotions, and behaviors. They even trigger physiological reactions, such as our heart rate, blood pressure, and other bodily functions. And we don't even need to experience a change in order to see that the media have had an effect on us because a prevalent effect is reinforcement—that is, solidifying our existing beliefs, attitudes, and behavioral patterns.

In our everyday lives, the immediate and long-term processes work together. The immediate process gives us a new fact that either extends our learning or adds weight to our already existing structure. In the long term, we look for patterns across these facts and infer conclusions about how the world operates. These generalized conclusions then become part of our knowledge structures. If we are not aware that we are making **generalizations**, then we cannot control that process and ensure that those generalizations are reasonable and accurate. Thus, faulty principles will get into our knowledge structures and lead us to make more defective conclusions and guide our search for facts in a faulty manner.

Being media literate requires that we understand the full range of media effects. We need to recognize when those effects are having a negative influence on us so we can protect ourselves. And we need to recognize when the effects are having a positive influence on us so we can appreciate and enhance their power.

Now that you have a broader appreciation for media effects, take a look at the list of effects in Appendix B (https://study.sagepub.com/potter9e). This list is not exhaustive. Instead, the list provides illustrations of all kinds of effects. Look for these media effects in your own lives, and let this selection of effects sensitize you to look for many other media effects.

Further Reading

Alter, A. (2017). *Irresistible: The rise of addictive technology and the business of keeping us hooked.* New York, NY: Penguin Press. (354 pages, including endnotes and index)

The author, an NYU business school professor, shows how behavioral addiction follows the same patterns and has the same causes as chemical addiction. He focuses his arguments on behavioral addiction to the Internet, especially shopping, social contacts, porn, and gambling. The first part of the book (three chapters) deals with the biology of addiction and how we have increased our understanding of behavioral addictions over the past few decades. Part 2 (six chapters) deals with how Internet designers engineer addiction. In Part 3 (three chapters), the author provides some suggestions for helping people avoid addiction and reducing it once it starts.

Bryant, J., & Oliver, M. B. (Eds.). (2009). *Media effects: Advances in theory and research* (3rd ed.). New York, NY: Routledge. (640 pages, including index)

This classic academic book presents a set of 27 chapters written by experts on a wide range of mass media effects. Each chapter provides an in-depth review of the research literature on a different effects theory (e.g., agenda setting, cultivation, social cognitive theory, etc.), type of effect (e.g., social perception, eating disorders, attitude change, etc.), or influence of type of content (e.g., sex, violence, educational television, etc.).

John, C. A. (2012). *The information diet: A case for conscious consumption.* Sebastopol, CA: O'Reilly Media, Inc. (150 pages; no index or reference list)

The author is a political consultant who became bothered by all the bad information available from the media, so he wrote this book to show people why they need to consume better information and how to do that. He uses food nutrition and the importance of dieting to avoid becoming obese as a metaphor to show why consumption of junk information can lead to problems of false understanding of our world.

Johnson, S. (2006). *Everything bad is good for you.* New York, NY: Riverhead Books. (250 pages, including end notes)

Steven Johnson, who is not an academic but a bestselling author, argues that the popular opinion that the media are harmful to us is wrong. Instead he says that exposure to media, especially television and video games, produces more net good than harm. He says that media messages are getting more complex, not simpler, over time. This makes exposure more challenging and hence more rewarding. The story lines of TV shows are much more complex and involved now than they were several decades ago. And today's video games are far more challenging than early video games. He says culture is getting more intellectually demanding, not less.

(Continued)

(Continued)

Nabi, R. L., & Oliver, M. B. (Eds.) (2009). *Media processes and effects*. Los Angeles, CA: SAGE. (643 pages with index)

This edited volume includes 37 chapters that focus on a wide variety of media effects topics. It is organized into six sections: conceptual and methodological issues; society, politics, and culture; message selection and processing; persuasion and learning; content and audiences; and medium issues.

Potter, W. J. (2012). *Media effects*. Thousand Oaks, CA: SAGE. (377 pages with index)

In this media effects book, I more fully develop the ideas that I am introducing in this chapter and the next in *Media Literacy*. I also present many more examples of media effects than I am able to present in the two effects chapters in this book.

Storr, W. (2014). *The unpersuadables: Adventures with the enemies of science*. New York, NY: The Overlook Press. (355 pages, including index and endnotes)

The author is a journalist who has interviewed people who hold beliefs at odds with scientific evidence (creationists, Holocaust deniers, etc.) to find out why they hold their beliefs. He concludes that all of human reasoning and knowledge is based on stories that we tell ourselves and that it is too psychologically troubling to change our stories, so we deny all those versions of the truth that do not conform to what we believe.

EXERCISE 13.1
THINKING ABOUT MEDIA EFFECTS

1. Pick some child with whom you have spent a fair amount of time. Can you think of any effects that child exhibited that could be regarded as a media effect? (List them below.)

   _____

   _____

   _____

2. Pick some adult with whom you have spent a fair amount of time—perhaps a parent or a neighbor. Can you think of any effects that adult exhibited that could be regarded as a media effect? (List them below.)

   _____

   _____

   _____

3. Pick a friend about your own age. Can you think of any effects that friend exhibited that could be regarded as a media effect? (List them below.)

   _____

   _____

   _____

4. Now think about yourself. Can you think of any effects that you exhibited that could be regarded as a media effect? (List them below.)

   _____

   _____

   _____

EXERCISE 13.2
RECOGNIZING IMMEDIATE EFFECTS

Think about the differences among cognitive, belief, attitude, emotion, behavior, and physiology effects. Then think about what has happened to you in your life after particular media exposures.

On a blank sheet of paper, divide the page into six rows and label them *cognitive, belief, attitudinal, emotional, behavioral,* and *physiological.*

For each row, see if you can list at least two effects that have happened to you immediately after being exposed to the media. Name the immediate effect, and then describe a specific example of how the media have affected you or someone you know. Use the list below to guide your thinking.

a. Cognitive: Media can immediately plant ideas and information.

b. Belief: Media can illustrate beliefs that we accept.

c. Attitude: Media can influence our evaluative judgments.

d. Emotion: Media can trigger an immediate emotional reaction, such as fear, attraction, sadness, and laughter.

e. Behavior: Media can trigger behavior.

f. Physiology: Media can arouse or calm you.

EXERCISE 13.3
RECOGNIZING LONG-TERM EFFECTS

Think about how the media may have exercised a subtle effect on you over the long term.

On a blank sheet of paper, divide the page into six rows and label them *cognitive, belief, attitude, emotion, behavior,* and *physiology.*

For each row, see if you can list two long-term effects. Next to each effect, describe specifically how long-term exposure to media has led to that effect on you. Use the list below to guide your thinking.

Long-term effects: Slow accumulation of information, attitudes, and images leads to beliefs about the real world.

a. Cognitive: Oftentimes, people will not expose themselves to the media with the purpose of learning anything. Rather, they will be interested in seeking escape or entertainment. This is especially true with television, radio, and film. However, acquisition of information and attitude change does take place. This type of learning is called *incidental learning.*

b. Belief: Erosion or reinforcement of values that are used as standards in evaluations.

c. Attitude: Erosion or building up of existing attitudes.

d. Emotion: People can build up a tolerance against emotional reactions over time and thus become desensitized.

e. Behavior: New behaviors can be learned in the short term but not performed until much later.

f. Physiology: Increased tolerance for certain content; physiological dependency on a medium or certain content.

EXERCISE 13.4
WHAT HAVE YOU INTERNALIZED FROM THE MEDIA CULTURE?

1. When you are driving and listening to your car radio, do you switch the channel, looking for something else, even when you are satisfied with the song you are currently hearing—thinking maybe a better song is on another station now? Do you flip through the channels on the television set looking for something better?

2. In romantic relationships, which is more important to you: commitment or perfection? When you are in a romantic relationship, are you happy when you make a lasting, strong commitment to the other person? Or do you worry that this person may not be the absolute best one for you and perhaps there is someone a little better out there?

3. In college, do you value learning or efficiency more? Do you make a commitment to each course, attend every session, and try to get all you can from them? Do you take a wide range of courses (some you know nothing about) to expand your experience? Or do you look for ways to spend your time better during class, such as going on a job interview, finishing a term paper for another course, or catching up on sleep? Do you look for courses on the basis of which ones require the least amount of work for the highest grades?

4. In your career, which will be more important to you: loyalty or success? Will you find a job and build your entire career there to pay back your employer for your first big opportunity? Or will you take the first job as a stepping stone to something better and leave as soon as you have learned all you can in that job?

5. When you have a major problem, are you upset when you cannot solve it in a short period of time?

© Jamaway/Alamy

14

HOW DOES THE MEDIA EFFECTS PROCESS WORK?

Key Idea: We need to be proactive—rather than reactive—in understanding how the media affect us. We also need to realize that there are many factors interacting in the effects process. When we understand these two ideas, we can achieve greater control over the process of effects.

The media effects process is complex. It is important to keep in mind how media influences us and how we can control that influence.

Two boys watch the movie The Deer Hunter, *a film in which American prisoners during the Vietnam War are forced by their captors to play the game of Russian roulette. Russian roulette is a game where one chamber in a revolver contains a bullet while the other chambers are empty. Each player in the game takes a turn pointing the gun at his head and pulling the trigger. If he is lucky and the chamber is empty, the gun does not fire and the player is saved. If he is unlucky, the chamber contains the bullet, which is then fired into his brain, killing him instantly.*

Several days after watching this movie, the boys are playing in their parents' bedroom and find a revolver under the bed. They decide to play Russian roulette. Eventually, the gun fires, killing one of the boys.

The tragic incident described above actually happened and when it was well covered by the press, it stimulated debate about who was to blame. There was a great deal of public criticism directed toward movies and television programs that were blamed for causing children to behave in violent ways. What this illustrates is that the public typically takes a reactive perspective; that is, when something happens that generates concern, the public likes to react to the event and debate where blame should be placed. While this reactive perspective is better than no perspective, a proactive perspective would be even better. For example, the public is concerned about risks—in this case, risks of harmful actions triggered by media portrayals—and educates people so that the probability of a tragedy occurring is greatly reduced.

When it comes to media effects, the media literacy perspective is much more oriented toward proactively dealing with potential risks through education rather than waiting until negative effects occur and then assessing blame when it is too late to take steps to prevent the problem from getting to a bad point. Learning how to be proactive will give you greater control over the process leading up to a negative effect. Also, it will allow you to position yourself better to achieve positive effects while you are avoiding negative ones.

To help you develop a more proactive perspective on mass media effects, this chapter will emphasize four ideas. First, it will show that media effects are constantly occurring. Second, it will illuminate the nature of factors that shape those effects. Third, it will help you develop a broader perspective on blame. And fourth, it will show you that you can control the effects process in your own life.

MEDIA EFFECTS ARE CONSTANTLY OCCURRING

A lot of people think about media effects categorically—that is, either an effect occurs or it does not. The problem with this type of thinking is that it is reactive. If an effect occurs and it is negative, then all we can do is feel bad about it and try to assess blame. Or if an effect occurs and it is positive, then all we can do is be thankful that it occurred and hope it occurs again. This perspective does not give you much control over the effects, because it is reactive. In contrast, media literacy helps you to develop a more proactive perspective, so that you can exercise some control over the probability of different media effects occurring. The more you understand about how the media exert their influence, the better you can help yourself avoid the negative effects and also increase the occurrence of positive effects. So in this section, I will show you the big picture about how the media exert their influence on all of us.

Manifested Effects and Process Effects

There are media effects that we can easily observe; these are the **manifested effects**. But there are also other things going on in our minds and bodies due to media influence. The media are constantly in a process of influencing how we think, feel, and act, whether we manifest these things or not. Let's call these other effects **process effects**, because we are always in a process of being influenced by mass media messages. If we limit our attention to only the manifested effects, we will greatly underestimate the degree of influence the media exert on us. Just because we do not see an outward manifestation of these things does not mean that the media are without influence. We also need to consider process effects.

To illustrate this distinction between manifested and process effects, let's return to the example at the beginning of this chapter. While the boys watched *The Deer Hunter*, they were being influenced by the messages presented in the movie. They felt excitement over the danger of the characters playing Russian roulette. Their attitudes were shaped that this game was a cool thing to play. There may have been no outward manifestation of these changes in emotions and attitudes, but this does not mean that the boys were not influenced by the media message. It was not until the boys discovered a revolver and started playing Russian roulette that was there a manifestation. If a parent had realized there were process effects occurring and did something to reduce those process effects, the boys could have been prevented from proceeding to such a horrible manifested effect.

The public and media critics are fixated on manifested effects. However, if we are to regard media influence from a media literacy perspective, we need to think more in terms of process effects. The more we understand about process effects, the more we can control media influence. Let's examine this in more detail by moving on to consider two kinds of process effects: baseline and fluctuation.

Baseline Effects and Fluctuation Effects

To illustrate the important difference between **baseline effects** and **fluctuation effects**, look at Figure 14.1. The horizontal lines represent time, and the vertical lines represent the degree of risk of experiencing an effect. Our **baseline** is our typical degree of risk that continues over time (see Figure 14.1a). Every once in a while something will happen to temporarily change that risk level (Figure 14.1b). Notice how there is a sudden spike from the normal baseline; this is a fluctuation effect. The fluctuation is usually temporary; after a brief period of time, the risk level returns to the base level.

FIGURE 14.1 ■ Baseline and Fluctuation Effects

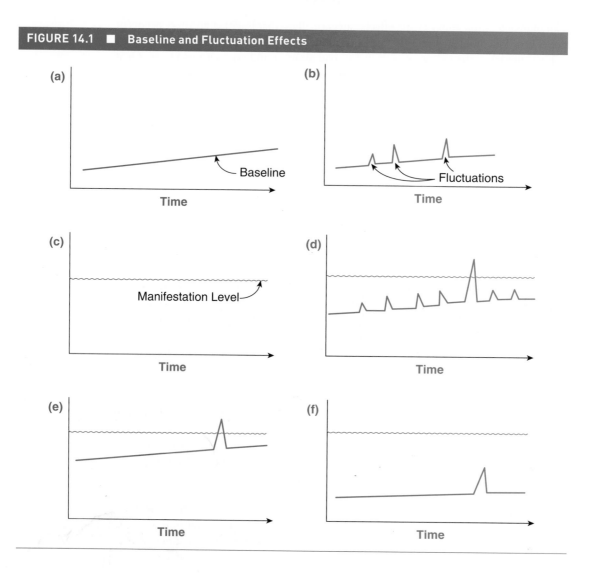

Now, let's add in the idea of a manifestation level. Think of the manifestation level as kind of a water level. Imagine yourself watching the surface of a lake, when suddenly a fish breaks through the surface and then dives back underwater. Until you see that fish break through the surface, you are not sure if there are any fish in the lake. Just because you do not see them, does not mean there are not fish—as well as turtles, eels, plankton, and even a Loch Ness monster—swimming around underwater. Observing what happens occasionally above water level does not tell you much about all the processes that we cannot see under the water. The same is true with media effects. There could be many effects (baseline effects and fluctuation effects) occurring under the manifestation level, and rarely will a fluctuation effect be strong enough to break through the manifestation level (see Figure 14.1d).

When we talk about media effects, we typically mean only fluctuation effects that break through the manifestation level—that is, those changes in behavior or knowledge that we can observe (see Figure 14.1d). For example, we notice that we are going to the kitchen to get that bag of potato chips to eat after watching a television commercial for that product. Or we watch a news program covering a campaign and notice that our attitude toward one of the candidates has changed. These are examples of effects we can observe; they have clearly manifested themselves. But if we limit ourselves to considering only fluctuations that have broken above the manifestation level, we lose the opportunity to learn about a great deal of effects activity that takes place underneath the manifestation level—these are the process effects.

When considering process effects, it is important to think in terms of baselines. As I said above, the baseline is the typical level of risk for an effect. It is fairly stable over time, but it can gradually increase or gradually decrease. Baselines are shaped by long-term conditioning. Some people are conditioned in a way that their baseline is very close to the manifestation level (see Figure 14.1e), so it does not take much in a media exposure to result in an effect being manifested. In contrast, other people have been conditioned in a way that their baseline is very far away from the manifestation level, so it is unlikely that any one media exposure will result in an observable effect (see Figure 14.1f).

COMPARE & CONTRAST
BASELINE EFFECTS AND FLUCTUATION EFFECTS

Compare: Baseline effects and fluctuation effects are *the same* in the following ways:

- Both refer to patterns of effects from media exposures.

- Both can be explained by combinations of factors of influence.

Contrast: Baseline effects and fluctuation effects are *different* in the following ways:

- Baseline effects express longer-term influence patterns that serve as an indicator of how close a person typically is to a manifestation level for an effect being observed.

- Fluctuation effects are typically immediate effects expressed as a temporary deviation off a baseline.

FACTORS INFLUENCING MEDIA EFFECTS

Every day, our baseline is being shaped by factors from the media and factors in our own lives. Some of those factors increase the likelihood of a particular effect being manifested, while other factors decrease that likelihood (see arrows in Figure 14.2). If there are more factors that increase the likelihood of manifestation, then the baseline will gradually ascend; if the factors that decrease the likelihood are more powerful, then the baseline will gradually descend. Notice that in Figure 14.2 there are more upward arrows than downward arrows; this indicates that there are more influences that serve to increase likelihood of manifestation compared to the influences that push the likelihood lower; as a result, the baseline gradually increases over time.

Many factors interact in the media effects process. In the following sections, I point out many of the more influential types of factors that are responsible for gradually changing a person's baseline and for triggering fluctuations off that baseline.

Baseline Factors

What are the general factors that are most influential on a person's baseline? I discuss seven of them in this section. Each of these seven types of factors exerts a subtle but continuing influence on a person, and this serves to make a person's baseline relatively fixed and enduring.

Developmental Maturities

We mature cognitively, emotionally, and morally as we age. Recall from Chapter 5 that when we are very young, our minds, emotions, and moral reasoning are beginning to develop and thus have a lower ceiling of capacity than when these are more fully developed. As we mature in these areas, we are able to process more information and to apply more sophisticated skills well. This gives us the capacity to move our baselines closer to the manifestation level for the effects we want to experience and away from the manifestation level for effects we want to avoid.

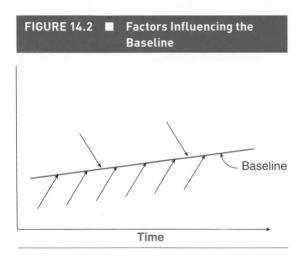

FIGURE 14.2 ■ Factors Influencing the Baseline

Baseline

Time

As children mature, they expand their cognitive abilities. That is, they are less influenced by a central, salient feature of a message and can process many more elements in a message, which allows them to understand context more fully; they are not limited to concrete thinking but get better at making inferences accurately; they are more sophisticated in making distinctions between fantasy and reality; and perhaps most important, they can think about thinking itself—that is, engage in meta-thinking—which helps them monitor their media exposures and the potential effects of those exposures on them (Wilson & Drogos, 2009). Thus as children age, they are more capable of staying in a self-reflexive exposure state where they can process media messages and learn from them. This makes it possible for them to exert greater control over the shape of their baselines as well as over fluctuations from those baselines.

As for emotional reactions, people at lower levels of maturity are limited in their capacity to control their emotions and behavior. Smith and Wilson (2002) found that fear reactions from news are affected by age. Older children are more likely to comprehend news stories, and this leads them to be more frightened by the happenings reported. Also, emotional reactions to violent action/adventure films are influenced by humor, but there is a gender difference. For example, research has found that females find that wisecracking heroes add to their emotional distress, whereas male viewers find that wisecracking heroes reduce their distress a bit (King, 2000).

Recall from Chapter 5 that we must be careful not to fall into the trap of believing that everyone of the same age has reached the same level of development cognitively, emotionally, and morally. Yes, children are highly susceptible to certain influences. But there is reason to believe that adolescents and adults can also be susceptible to these same influences.

Cognitive Abilities

The developmental maturities suggest potentialities; that is, at a given age, there are limits to what people can understand and how they go about reasoning. But developmental potentialities are not the same as actual abilities; that is, not everyone who has the same potential exhibits the same level of cognitive abilities.

There are four cognitive abilities—field dependency, type of intelligence, type of thinking, and conceptual differentiation—that are most relevant to media literacy (refer back to Chapter 5). Each of these has an influence on establishing a person's baseline for media effects. For example, people who are more field independent, higher on both fluid and crystalline intelligence, and more likely to differentiate information conceptually into categories will be more likely to control their baseline levels.

© ZUMA Press, Inc./Alamy

Knowledge Structures

People with the largest amount of knowledge learn most from media. When people have a great deal of knowledge on a particular topic, they have a strong, well-developed knowledge structure. They are usually motivated to acquire more information on various topics and thus seek out media that will provide them with this information. When they see a new message on the topic, they are able to integrate that new information quickly and efficiently into their existing knowledge structure.

With many topics, we have no choice but to rely primarily on media information. This is what makes the media so powerful as a socializing influence—we cannot check out the media information by comparing it to information from other sources, such as real-life experiences. For example, almost no one knows what it feels like to be a professional

Is it real? Viewers without actual experience of a Beverly Hills housewife may find it hard to judge the accuracy of media portrayals on the reality series *The Real Housewives of Beverly Hills*.

athlete. Sports interview shows and websites can give us some insights about what the life of a professional athlete might be like, but very few people have an opportunity to check those insights out for themselves. This is true for almost all content of news; viewers have no real-world experience about being a political leader, a celebrity coming out of rehab, or a crime scene investigator. The same is true for so-called reality programming; viewers have no real-world experience about being a Beverly Hills housewife, being 16 and pregnant, or singing their way to becoming an American idol. And this is certainly true for fictional programming; viewers have no real-world experience about being a vampire, a superhero, or even a surgeon, lawyer, or police officer. Because viewers do not have an opportunity to check out these things in their real lives, it is impossible for them to make valid judgments about how accurate these media portrayals are. When people are asked if TV entertainment is credible and a reasonable representation of the way people live, most people say yes. As you increase your amount of viewing, your perceptions of the reality of TV entertainment programs increase. That is, you are more likely to believe the real world is like the TV world. This is especially true among children and those who have the least amount of variety of real-world experiences.

Sociological Factors

The degree of **socialization** is related to the amount of influence the media will have. People who have been consistently socialized with particular values for a long period of time will have a relatively weighty baseline; that is, the baseline will be very resistant to change. It is unlikely that the media will be able to exert a strong enough influence to cause a fluctuation, especially one big enough to break through the manifestation level. For example, if a person is a senior citizen and has been exposed consistently to anti-aggression values all her life from parents, friends, educational institutions, church, and so on, she has a baseline far away from a behavioral fluctuation of aggression. She could watch an entire evening of highly aggressive media messages and not move anywhere near the level of manifesting aggressive behavior herself. If, on the other hand, another person has been taught by his father to fight back, has been taught that only the strong survive, and has been shown by his friends that the only way to get respect is to fight, he has a baseline fairly close to a manifestation level for aggression. It would take very little media influence to push this individual above that manifestation level.

We learn norms by observing other people in real life and through the media. The media present many characters who communicate a great deal of social information to viewers. These messages are especially influential on the socialization of children because young people have less experience in real life to counterbalance the media portrayals. In addition, many adults have very limited real-world information to counterbalance media portrayals, so they too are susceptible to media influence. For example, people who have never served in government, never become active in a political party, and never attended a political rally depend on the media to provide them with all their information about how the political system works and the qualities of the candidates running for office. These people with highly limited political experience have no way to check the media portrayals against the real world, so they must accept the stories the media present as accurate.

We are all influenced by institutions, parents, friends, and other social forces. For example, with children, parental involvement in media exposure serves to influence learning. Children increase their understanding and recall of both central and incidental program content when adults provide comments to guide their children's attention and understanding during viewing. The more a person identifies with a peer group and the more cohesive the group, the more the person will be influenced by the group and the less effect the media will have by themselves.

Lifestyle

People who have active lifestyles where they interact with many people and institutions are generally less affected by the media. In contrast, people who have fewer real-life experiences because of lack of money, education, or vitality are more likely to have much higher exposure to media that is not counterbalanced by other experiences. This is why the poor, individuals with low socioeconomic status, ethnic minorities, and the elderly are particularly susceptible to the influence of the media, especially television, because they expose themselves to a great deal of TV due to their sociological and psychological isolation. TV becomes their window on the world and their primary source of information.

Personal Locus

Recall from Chapter 2 that the personal locus is the combination of an individual's goals and drives for media exposures. This may be the most important factor so far because it reflects the five factors above and, more important, activates the power of those five factors. Furthermore, it determines the seventh factor, which is a person's media exposure habits. When a personal locus is strong, the person has the drive energy to make the most of his or her maturities, skills, knowledge structures, sociological factors, and lifestyle.

People who have a strong personal locus have more awareness of the effects process, so they have constructed their baselines to conform to their personal goals. This means that there are particular effects they want to achieve with the help of the media; for these effects, they have constructed a baseline fairly close to the manifestation level so that a single exposure to the proper media message can achieve the effect. People with a strong personal locus are also aware that there are some effects that they do not want to manifest themselves, so they construct baselines for those effects far from the manifestation level. To illustrate, let's say Jane and Phyllis both have a strong need to make friends. Jane is acutely aware of this need and uses the media to satisfy her need for friendship. She joins Facebook and actively searches out friends. She texts her new friends to find out more about their interests and consciously gravitates to those people with whom she shares the most interests. Over time, Jane has used the media to grow her circle of friends, and with her continual interactions, she builds more meaningful friendships both on Facebook and in the real world. In contrast, Phyllis feels lonely so she gravitates to television series where she can identify with certain kinds of characters. Over time, she gets pulled more into the world of those fictional characters and she feels as though she is part of their lives. However, since these media experiences are not interactive, Phyllis is only observing others and not building her friendship skills; thus, when she meets a person in real life, it is very difficult for her to interact in a friendly manner, and friendships are not manifested.

Media Exposure Habits

Each of us has a set of media exposure habits that focuses our attention on certain media and certain types of messages presented by those media. For example, some people like to surf the Internet and go to all kinds of sites indiscriminately. In this case, they are exposed to a very wide range of messages and no single type of message is likely to have much effect on their baseline. In contrast, other people might spend all their time playing violent video games and watching action/adventure movies. These people are likely to have a baseline very close to the manifestation level for aggressive behavior.

Fluctuation Factors

While understanding where your baselines are in the processes of influence, it is also important to monitor the factors that will move you off your baseline and create a fluctuation effect. In this section, I present six types of factors about the media as well as three types of factors about you that are important in assessing whether fluctuations will occur or not.

Content of the Messages

It matters what you expose yourself to in a particular exposure session. Let's say you have a habitual exposure pattern of horror and action/adventure shows, and your baseline is very high for an aggressive effect. If you watch another hour of video, will that be enough to push you above the manifestation level? It depends on what content you watch. If you watch a comedy in which the characters help each other and the themes are prosocial, then you are likely to move away from the manifestation level. But if you watch a highly violent program, then you will be more likely to move toward the manifestation level.

Context of Portrayals

The meaning of the messages arises from the way they are portrayed, especially social lessons. When the characters in a story are portrayed as being highly attractive, when their actions are portrayed as being justified, and when they are rewarded for those actions, then audiences will likely identify with those attractive characters, experience the action from their point of view, and learn from this vicarious experience. Audiences are likely to accept the meaning of the experience that was portrayed by those characters.

This is why the portrayal of violence in the media is so dangerous. The "good guys" are as likely as the "bad guys" to commit acts of violence. The good guys' violent acts are almost always portrayed as being justified, and they are rarely punished. The meaning of violence, then, is that if you are a good guy, violence is an essential and successful means of resolving conflict. Because each viewer regards himself or herself as a good guy, viewers learn that it is okay for them to use violence.

Cognitive Complexity of Content

When the message makes few cognitive demands on viewers, people can process its meaning easier (Lang, Potter, & Bolls, 1999). The more demands the narrative makes on the working memory, the less well facts will be comprehended and remembered (Fisch, 2000). For example, children remember news better from TV than from print, regardless of their reading proficiency. This is because TV news can provide information in several channels at once (pictures, words, and sound), and when the information is semantically redundant—that is, it complements and reinforces each other—learning is achieved better (Gunter, Furnham, & Griffiths, 2000). Children's comprehension of educational content from media messages is dependent on the degree to which the information is central to the narrative. Facts that are tangential to the main flow of a message are learned less well than facts that are central to the message. Also, people remember information better when emotional cues are also used (Bucy & Newhagen, 1999).

Motivations

When we have a conscious need for a particular kind of information, we will actively seek out this type of information in the media, and the chance of us learning from this experience is high. When we are passive, learning can still occur, but it is not as likely. Also, people who have a higher education and higher intelligence are more motivated to seek out information from the media. These people select the information that has the greatest utility to them.

States

A state is a temporary drive or emotional reaction that occurs in response to some stimuli. Oftentimes, something will happen in our lives that will cause us to feel angry or frustrated. This state can interact with media content and lead to certain effects. For example, someone who is frustrated and then views violence will be much more likely to behave aggressively than if only one of these conditions is present.

The media frequently alter our psychological states. Perhaps the most important of these states is arousal. When we are aroused, our attention is more concentrated, and the experience is more vivid for us. We will remember the portrayals more and will be more likely to act while aroused (Comstock, Chaffee, Katzman, McCombs, & Roberts, 1978; Zillmann, 1991).

Certain production techniques tend to arouse viewers. These techniques include fast cuts, quick motion within a frame, loud music, and sound effects. Also, certain narrative conventions (such as suspense, fear, life-threatening violence, and erotica) can lead to arousal.

Although most states are regarded as physiological or emotional ones, there are cognitive states also, and these are especially important with media literacy. If you find yourself confronting information about a topic where you have no context or background information, you will likely find yourself in a state of ignorance. This cognitive state of ignorance is usually associated with emotional states of frustration or despair. But the cognitive part of this state is keyed to a lack of informational context. Like all states, cognitive states are short lived because people will typically either avoid messages that trigger this state or search out more information on the topic, thus reducing the negative feeling about ignorance.

The *Fast and the Furious* franchise uses production techniques like explosions, car stunts, and life-threatening violence at the hands of actor Dwayne Johnson to arouse viewers.

Attaspix/Alamy

Degree of Identification

Identification with particular characters is also a key factor in the effects process because we typically pay more attention to those characters with whom we identify. We can form strong attachments to certain characters, depending on what those characters do and say

(Hoffner & Cantor, 1991). The stronger the attachment, the stronger the probability of an effect (Bandura, 1986, 1994) that will show up as a fluctuation.

We become involved in media-depicted events through a psychological relationship with characters in a two-step process. First, we make a judgment about how much we are attracted to the character. Attraction is linked to how much we feel that the character is like us or how much we would like to be like that character. Second, we engage in an "as if" experience in which we imagine ourselves in the role of the character. We frequently take these two steps while following stories in the media and this increases the degree to which stories can affect us.

PROCESS OF INFLUENCE

In the previous section, I laid out many individual factors that have been found to influence the baseline as well as trigger fluctuations off that baseline. While each of those factors was presented individually, you should understand that rarely does a factor act alone so that it is solely responsible for a fluctuation or a baseline. Instead, factors work together in a complex process such that combinations of factors must be present at certain times in order for changes to occur.

I presented those factors one at a time above so that you could get a sense for what the individual factors were. Also, media effects researchers typically test one factor at a time with experiments that attempt to hold all other factors constant while the researchers test whether or not a particular factor is associated with a particular media effect. Over time, as media researchers move on to more multivariate methods of data analyses, they have been testing combinations of factors and typically find things like **contingent influences**, **interactive influences**, and **asymmetric influences**. A contingent effect is one that shows up under certain conditions but not others. For example, age (Smith & Wilson, 2002) and gender (King, 2000) are typically found to suggest contingent effects, where particular effects may occur with younger children but not older children and some effects occur with males but not with females. Interactive effects are those where an effect does not occur unless several factors are present to interact. For example, if factor X is present by itself, there will be no effect. If factor Y is present by itself, there will be no effect. However, if both factors X and Y are present at the same time, their influence will interact and the effect will occur. Fire is an example of an interactive effect—requiring the presence of fuel, oxygen, and heat to be present at the same time in order for fire to occur; if any one of these three factors is missing, there will be no fire even though the other two factors might occur in abundance.

Asymmetric influences are when one factor influences another but not the other way around. For example, in autumn, the leaves on trees turn colors when the temperatures drop. The temperature drop influences the color of the leaves, but the color of the leaves does not influence the temperature. In the media effects literature, there are many examples of asymmetric influences. One recent example is from a study by Wright and Randall (2014), who found that support for same-sex marriage was not found to predict pornography consumption, but pornography consumption was found to predict support for same-sex marriage.

Because the media effects research literature is very large, with estimates of it being composed of more than 5,000 studies (Potter & Riddle, 2007), it offers many valuable insights into the complexity of the media effects process. However, the literature is difficult to read because the findings across studies often contradict one another. For example, recent research that examines the use of social networking sites presents findings that the use of social networking sites for political information narrows a person's learning because of selective exposure (Garrett & Stroud, 2014; Xu & Feng, 2014), while other researchers find that the use of these sites opens up users' minds and leads them to consider a wider range of points of view (Lee et al., 2014). Even within a single study there are often conflicting results. For example, Lewis, Tamborini, and Weber (2014) reported that cognitive conflict in a media story sometimes increased enjoyment and sometimes decreased enjoyment. It is frustrating to see equivocal results like this in the literature when we are looking for the clarity of simple findings. However, we must realize that the media effects process of influence is not a simple one. It is complex and involves many different factors in interaction. To understand this process, we need to analyze research findings to several layers of depth. When Lewis et al. did this in their study, they noticed that there were two different processes that people used to make sense of cognitive conflict in narratives. One process, which characterizes experiences of appreciation, is deliberative and slow and results from cognitive conflict. A second process, which characterizes experiences of enjoyment, is automatic and fast and occurs when cognitive conflict is inconsequential. Lewis et al. found that although both appraisal processes result from the same underlying framework of intuitive preferences, only the first process results from cognitive conflict.

THINKING ABOUT BLAME

Let's return once again to the Russian roulette situation from the beginning of this chapter and readdress the question: Should the media be blamed for the death of the boy who shot himself? This question is continually asked whenever we hear about a killing that is modeled after a portrayal in a movie, television show, or a video game. A death resulting from someone imitating something he or she saw in the media typically triggers public discourse that is usually very polarized, where different groups will blame other groups. For example, parents will blame the media. The media will blame the gun industry, lack of regulations on gun ownership, and the parents for leaving a loaded revolver where the boys could play with it. The gun industry will blame the parents and the boys by saying that guns do not kill people, people kill people. The arguments about who deserves all the blame are non-productive. The reality is that many factors contributed to the eventual death of the boy, so blame needs to be apportioned across all these factors

We need to understand that in our complex society, seldom does a single element cause an effect. There are always many influences, and those multiple influences work in combination. This is not hard for us to understand when it comes to knowing what causes a fire, for example. A fire requires fuel, oxygen, and heat. All three must be present to have a fire. With media effects, there are many factors about the media portrayal, factors in the life of the people involved, and factors about the real-world situation that all contribute to a probability that an effect will break through the manifestation level. No one of these factors is responsible by itself.

Who is to blame? It depends on how you ask the question. If the question is, "Should the gun manufacturers be held solely responsible for crimes committed using their guns?"

the answer is no, of course not, because there are other influences involved. If the question instead is, "Are the gun manufacturers blameless?" the answer again is no because their guns have been essential ingredients in many violent crimes. The key here is to recognize multiple influences and *not allow* any one of the influences to be absolved simply because it was not the *only* influence.

BECOMING MORE MEDIA LITERATE

The effects process is a complex one. That is why it requires that people increase their level of media literacy in order to appreciate the process of influence. People who are at low levels of literacy will believe the media exert no influence or that media influence only leads to effects in other people. This is faulty thinking.

The power to control media effects on oneself begins with an understanding about the wide variety of effects and how media influence works in combination with other influences. We need to think beyond those fluctuations that break through the manifestation level and also consider process effects. We also need to understand that baselines are even more important than fluctuations. This helps us take a proactive approach to media effects. When we understand where baselines are in relation to manifestation levels, we can help shape our baselines to bring them closer to the manifestation level for those effects we want to experience in our lives—effects such as high levels of learning, use of informed opinions, and the practice of behaviors that make us most happy and productive. At the same time, we need to shape our baselines for negative effects so that they move further and further away from the manifestation levels.

Let's see how well you are able to apply what you have learned in this chapter by undertaking Exercise 14.1. Consider each of the six short scenarios and see how well you can use the information you learned in this chapter to speculate about where the baseline is likely to be in each case. Then think about what factors must have occurred to create a fluctuation off that baseline.

Now let's make the exercise more real to you by identifying a media effect that you have experienced that you did not like (see Exercise 14.2). Think of yourself as a psychotherapist who will analyze your personality, habits, and environment to construct a profile of all the factors that likely led to that effect. At this point, don't worry about whether the scholarly research supports your profile; instead, just use your native intelligence and what you have learned in this chapter to make a reasonable argument for a set of factors.

SUMMARY

Media effects are constantly occurring in a complex process. Perhaps it would be useful to think of this in a metaphorical way (see Box 14.1) to make these ideas more accessible. We are all familiar with the idea that there is always weather and that its effect on us is constantly changing.

BOX 14.1
THE WEATHER AS AN ANALOGY FOR MEDIA EFFECTS

Media effects are like the weather in many ways. Weather is always there, but it can take many forms. Sometimes it makes you shiver, sometimes it makes you wet, and sometimes it gives you a painful sunburn—but it is all weather. Weather is very difficult to predict with any precision because the factors that explain the weather are large in number, and their interaction is very complex. Supercomputers are used to try to handle all those factors in highly complex models. They help increase the predictive accuracy on the broad level; that is, they can tell us how much rainfall and how many sunny days a particular locale will have this year. But they cannot tell us with accuracy who will get wet on which days. Although the weather bureau cannot control the weather, we as individuals can control the weather's effect on us. We can carry an umbrella, use sunscreen, or close ourselves off from elements we don't like. And we can run out to embrace a beautiful day.

Like the weather, the media are pervasive and always around us. Also, like the weather, media influences are difficult to predict because the factors that explain such effects are large in number, and their interaction is very complex. We use powerful computers to examine large sets of variables in trying to make such predictions, and we have learned much about media effects. We know that certain types of messages will lead to certain kinds of opinions and behaviors in general, but we cannot predict with precision whose opinion or behavior will be changed. And as individuals, we do not have much power to control the media, but we have a great deal of power (if we will use it) to control the media's effects on us. To know how to use this power, we must be sufficiently literate about media effects.

There is an important difference between the weather and the influence of the media on us. With the weather, we all recognize its different forms and know when they are happening. It is fairly easy to tell the difference between rain, fog, and snow because there is much tangible evidence whenever these occur. But with media influence, the effects are often difficult to perceive until someone points them out. Then they become easier to spot. We need to train ourselves to be able to spot manifestations of media effects—positive as well as negative. And we need to be sensitive to the fact that there are also process effects in addition to manifested effects.

With media influence, it is important to keep in mind three ideas. First, media effects are constantly occurring because we are constantly being influenced directly and indirectly by media messages. Second, the media work with other factors in our lives in exerting their influence. And third, you can control the effects process in your own life—if you understand how the process works.

By now you should have a basic knowledge structure about the wide variety of media effects and how the effects process works. This will give you a much better perspective on controlling the process and thereby achieving the effects you want. However, this chapter cannot give you much detail about all the different factors that change the probabilities of all the media effects that could occur. While I have alerted you to the different types of factors that have been found to influence many effects, you need to elaborate on the basic knowledge structure presented in this chapter by taking additional media effects courses and doing some additional reading of the relatively large literatures of media effects research studies.

Further Reading

Strasburger, V. C., & Wilson, B. J. (2002). *Children, adolescents, & the media.* Thousand Oaks, CA: SAGE. (539 pages, including appendices, references, and indexes)

This is a very readable book with lots of cartoons, pictures, and graphics. The content deals with how both children and adolescents are influenced by the media, particularly the content of advertising, violence, sexuality, drug use, music, and portrayals of food. It also has special chapters on the media of electronic games and the Internet. The authors take a public health perspective in showing the risks of different kinds of media content on individuals and society. The book concludes with chapters on recommendations to help individuals protect themselves as well as recommendations to others, such as programmers, advertisers, policymakers, educators, parents, and researchers.

Keeping Up to Date

Journal of Advertising (https://www.tandfonline.com/loi/ujoa20)

Journal of Advertising Research (http://www.journalofadvertisingresearch.com/)

Journal of Broadcasting & Electronic Media (https://www.tandfonline.com/loi/hbem20)

Journal of Communication (https://academic.oup.com/joc)

Journal of Communication Research (http://journals.sagepub.com/home/crx)

Journalism & Mass Communication Quarterly (http://journals.sagepub.com/home/jmq)

Media Psychology (https://www.tandfonline.com/loi/hmep20)

There are perhaps several hundred scholarly journals that publish research examining how media messages affect individuals and institutions. The seven journals listed above are the ones that account for most of that type of research published each year.

EXERCISE 14.1

DIAGNOSING RISK IN SIX SCENARIOS

Each of the six following scenarios features a person interacting with some media message(s). For each scenario, think about the following five things:

    a. Pick an effect that the person is at risk of fluctuating.

    b. Think about where the person's baseline is for that effect. What factors went into positioning that baseline where it is?

    c. What factors about a media exposure are likely to push the person toward the manifestation level?

d. What factors about the person's exposure experience or the person himself or herself are likely to push the person toward the manifestation level?

e. What could this person do to avoid being pushed toward the manifestation level?

Scenario 1: Bobby

Bobby is a 5-year-old who loves to watch action/adventure cartoons on Saturday morning television. His mother is happy that the television serves as a babysitter for Bobby, freeing time up for her to work in another part of the house.

Scenario 2: Jennifer

Jennifer reads every fashion magazine there is. She is obsessed with losing weight and wearing the right designer clothes.

Scenario 3: Cool Dude

Cool Dude is a sophomore in college. For the past 4 years, he has downloaded every track of heavy metal and rap music he can find. He stays up partying all night every night and sees himself as the center of social life at the school because of his dress, his talk, and his style.

Scenario 4: Alison

Four-year-old Alison has just watched Bambi's mother die in the movie. She is so grief stricken that she cannot take her nap.

Scenario 5: Percy

Percy is a teenager who has seen every horror film made. But now the thrill is gone. Recently, he has lost the ability to be scared while at the movies. Still, he continues to go to every new horror film—hoping that there will be some awesome special effect or super gruesome scene that can excite him.

Scenario 6: Harriet

Harriet was a nerd in middle school but now she has friends all over the world since her parents allowed her to set up a Facebook account. While she has developed a great deal more self-confidence, she is always tired because she spends more than 12 hours a day keeping up with her friends on Facebook.

EXERCISE 14.2

PROFILE THE PROCESS OF EFFECTS ON YOU

1. Think of a media effect that altered your behavior. (Perhaps you watched a violent movie and started behaving aggressively immediately afterward. Or perhaps you saw an ad for a product and immediately went to the store to buy it.)

   a. Look at the list of seven baseline factors presented in this chapter and write a profile of your baseline for that behavioral effect.

   b. Now write a profile using the six fluctuation factors presented in this chapter to identify a media message that would result in a large fluctuation spike through the manifestation level.

2. Think about a cognitive effect (refer to the previous chapter and Appendix B for choices). Construct a baseline for yourself on

(Continued)

(Continued)

that effect. How close is your baseline to a manifestation level?

- If the cognitive effect you selected is a positive one, what can you do to move your baseline closer to the manifestation level?

- If the cognitive effect you selected is a negative one, what can you do to move your baseline further away from the manifestation level?

3. Think about a negative attitude you have experienced. Construct a baseline for yourself on that effect.

- What can you do to move your baseline further away from the manifestation level?

- Profile the kind of media messages you should avoid in order to prevent a fluctuation off your baseline breaking through the manifestation level.

4. Think about a positive emotional effect. Construct a baseline for yourself on that effect.

- What can you do to move your baseline closer to the manifestation level?

- Profile the kind of media messages you should seek out in order to ensure that a fluctuation off your baseline would break through the manifestation level.

5. Think about other positive and negative effects using the four dimensions presented in the previous chapter. Then do the following for each of those effects:

- Profile your baseline.

- Profile media messages that would create larger fluctuations.

- Profile media messages that would lead to smaller fluctuations.

THE SPRINGBOARD

Chapter 15. Helping Yourself and Others to Increase Media Literacy

iStock/Wenjie Dong

15

HELPING YOURSELF AND OTHERS TO INCREASE MEDIA LITERACY

Key Idea: You have the power to develop media literacy strategies to influence society and other individuals, but first you need to increase your own level of media literacy.

The more active and aware you are when you engage with media, the more you will get out of your experiences with media.

Congratulations for having worked on building a full range of media literacy knowledge structures throughout the previous chapters. By now you should have a fairly good awareness about what it means to be media literate and have a good base of knowledge about the media industries, their audiences, their messages, and their effects on you and society.

You should now be asking yourself: How can I preserve the skills and knowledge structures I already have? How can I improve? And how can I help others improve? In this final chapter, I will help you fashion good answers to their questions. Think about what I say in this chapter as a platform—a jumping-off point for you to take greater control of the trajectory of your thinking as you glide through the rich atmosphere of media messages throughout the course of your life. First, I will help you understand how to develop your own personal strategy for continuing to increase your media literacy. Then I will make some suggestions about how you can help others increase their media literacy.

HELPING YOURSELF

The first thing you need to do is to develop a personal strategy for increasing your media literacy. The purpose of developing a personal media literacy strategy is to increase your control over the process of influence that is currently dominated by the media themselves. Here are 10 guidelines to help you develop your personal strategy.

Ten Guidelines

1. Strengthen Your Personal Locus

Remember that your personal locus is a combination of an awareness of your goals along with the drive energy to search out information and experiences to attain those goals. Begin by analyzing your personal goals by asking two questions. The first question is: How clear are my goals? If your goals are fuzzy, then you are likely to wander around looking for a better life and never find it. Clarity is required to give you direction. The second question is: To what extent are these goals really *my* goals? If the goals you seek to achieve have been programmed by someone else—like the media—then the achievement of such goals is not likely to make *you* happy or satisfied.

Once you *clearly* understand what *your* goals are, you need to ask yourself: Do I have enough drive energy to achieve my goals? A plan has little value unless you have the energy to enact it. With media literacy, you do not need a massive amount of energy because you are not going to change everything in a day or two. Instead, you need only a small amount of energy each day; the key to improvement is to keep at it. Each day pay a bit more attention to how you use the media and continually evaluate whether your media exposures are really achieving your goals. Evaluate those messages using your own standards, in place of the standards forced onto you by advertisers. When you continually engage in this process, you will find that you gradually increase your awareness of your own goals and standards, and you will find that there are many alternative ways of achieving your goals—some of which are more successful than the habits you have been relying on in the past.

We all have expectations about the appropriate amount of mental effort that is necessary to read a book, listen to a lecture on an iPod, play a video game, or watch a television program. Each medium requires a different amount of mental effort; each medium also requires a different kind of cognitive engagement. When a message meets our expectation, we typically continue our exposure but do so in an automatic state. However, when a message requires more effort than we expect, we might stop our exposure to that message and look for another message that requires less mental effort. This is a natural reaction, but sometimes it is helpful to stay with challenging messages and try to work through those challenges. The greater the mental effort expended, the higher the comprehension, learning, and eventual recall. Also, when you are willing to expend more mental energy when other people are not, you are getting more value from those messages and developing a stronger perspective that sets you apart from other people.

2. Develop an Accurate Awareness of Your Exposure Patterns

Periodically (maybe once a year), keep a diary of media usage for a week. By repeating this exercise, you can monitor your changing interests in media, vehicles, and messages. As you monitor changes, ask yourself the following types of questions:

- Am I broadening my exposure to different media, or am I staying primarily with only one or two?

- Am I broadening my exposure to different vehicles? For example, let's say you spend a great deal of time trying to increase your list of friends on Facebook. Ask yourself whether increasing your quantity of friends is really all you want to do. Perhaps increasing the quality of friendships becomes more important to you, so you seek out other Internet platforms where you can develop stronger friendships based on shared interests. Look for blogs and interest groups with people who share the same hobbies, concerns about social issues, or political attitudes as you do. You will have more in common with these kinds of people and this will offer a greater opportunity to build more meaningful relationships.

Explore a wider range of websites, new musical artists, new kinds of television shows, and different magazines. You don't have to like all these exposures; in fact, you are likely to hate many of them. But by trying new vehicles you are giving yourself opportunities to find even better messages than those delivered through your habitual exposures. And you are likely to discover new messages that you might like even better than the messages you usually get in your habitual patterns of exposure. If you do not occasionally explore the range of media messages, you will likely default to a narrower and narrower focus over time.

Think about the degree to which your current patterns of media exposure are meeting your personal goals. Make it a practice to ask yourself: Am I planning my media exposures to serve my own purposes, or am I just exposing myself to whatever comes along? If you are engaging in habitual exposure patterns with no personal goals, then you are clearly a tool of the mass media.

3. Acquire a Broad Base of Useful Knowledge

The key to knowledge is that it is useful; acquiring knowledge that is not useful does not help you. This means we must be continually aware of our needs for knowledge, then focus on satisfying those needs.

Try Exercise 15.1 and make an assessment now about your knowledge structures concerning the media. What have you learned from reading through the other 14 instructional chapters of this book? And what supporting experiences have you acquired throughout your life to this point that would contribute to your knowledge base about the media? If your assessment reveals gaps, do not let those deficiencies lead you to believe you have failed in some way. Instead, use this diagnosis as a way of showing you where you can direct your efforts to make the most difference in increasing your knowledge base.

iStock/alvarez

What are your personal goals for increasing media literacy?

There is always a gap between the knowledge we already have and the knowledge we need in order to understand the world better. Only you can close that knowledge gap for yourself. The means for closing the knowledge gap on a topic is under your control because the knowledge gap is influenced more by your interest in a topic than by our general level of education (Chew & Palmer, 1994). If we have high interest in a topic, we will search out information from many different media and many different sources. But when we have low interest in a topic, we allow the media to determine for us how much information we get.

4. Examine Your Mental Codes

As you engage in your habits of media exposures, periodically ask yourself why your habits are the way they are. To what extent have you programmed your habits to serve your needs? And to what extent have the mass media programmed your habits to meet their needs? By considering answers to these questions, you can reprogram your code to satisfy your own needs better. After this reprogramming, you can return to your routine exposures in a state of automaticity, but from that point onward your code will automatically be running in a way to deliver more on your goals rather than the media's goals.

Periodically work through your mental code to determine whether or not the beliefs that you currently hold are making you unhappy because they are not realistic and not reflective of who you really are. Examine your beliefs about the purpose of life, the meaning of friendship, the meaning of family, the nature of success, the role of a career in your life, what it means to be attractive, and the value of romance and love.

5. Examine Your Opinions

Ask yourself the following: Are my opinions well reasoned? Opinions are easy to create, but if they are not supported by facts and logic they can get you into trouble. Also, if you do not act in accordance with your opinions, then they are useless. Often people will hold critical opinions about things but then do nothing but complain. One example of this is that people like to criticize television in general as well as particular shows but then they keep exposing themselves to the shows that bother them. The Roper Organization, under the sponsorship of NBC in the early 1980s, had respondents in a national survey express their reactions to 17 particular TV shows—16 of which had been the targets of complaints about sex and violence from religious organizations. Only 13% of respondents said there was too much violence on the *Dukes of Hazard*, and 10% said there was too much sex on *Dallas*—these were the most negatively rated shows! But when asked about television in general, 50% of the respondents said that there was too much sex and violence on TV (The Roper Organization, 1981). Although this study was conducted before you were born, are the findings still valid for you? Do you incorporate the opinions you hear other people express about particular things then generalize to all things without doing some of your own checking of facts about your opinions?

6. Change Behaviors

To what extent do your behaviors match your beliefs? For example, if you think society is too materialistic, do you avoid buying material goods as much as possible? If you do keep your consumption of material goods at a minimum, then there is a match between your behaviors and your beliefs. But there are people who continually complain about waste in our materialistic society, then go out and buy lots of new things they don't need. In a recent survey, 82% of Americans agreed that most of us buy and consume far more than we need. And 67% agreed that Americans cause many of the world's environmental problems because we consume more resources and produce more waste than anyone else in the world. Yet we in the United States continue to consume nearly 30% of the planet's resources and services each year, although we account for less than 5% of the world's population. We can choose from more than 40,000 supermarket items, including 200 kinds of cereal. Do we really need all these material products?

Another example of a disconnect between beliefs and behavior is with pollution and cleaning up the environment. The media have put the issue of pollution on the public agenda as the prominence and length of these stories have increased dramatically from the 1970s to the 1990s (Ader, 1995). During that same period, air pollution went down about a third, but solid waste went up about 25%. While the amount of solid waste that is recycled continues to climb so too does the total amount of solid waste each year, even with drop offs in waste among some categories of trash such as paper due to digitization (Environmental Protection Agency, n.d.). When we put all these bits of information together, we see a pattern that Americans like to pressure governments to solve the problem of increased trash and pollution but are less likely to change their own habits to consume less and recycle more.

Changing your behavior to correspond with your beliefs demonstrates commitment to a moral responsibility of following through on your beliefs rather than simply blaming someone else and doing nothing, which has become a popular strategy for many of society's problems. The first step in behavioral change is a realistic assessment of the match between your beliefs and existing behaviors.

You could boycott advertisers, cancel subscriptions, and write letters when you see something you don't like in the media. This action, of course, will have almost no effect on the media themselves, unless large numbers of other people feel as you and do the same things. However, that is not a reason to stop yourself from doing these things. By taking action, you give yourself a sense of gaining control over the media, and this new sense of power will make a difference in your personal life.

7. Think About the Reality-Fantasy Continuum

Continually ask yourself about the degree to which something is real or fantasy; this is a continuum. Some messages will be easy to spot as fantasy, such as *Looney Toons*. But other messages may not be so obvious. Some have a realistic setting and some present realistic situations but are still fantasy, such as *Grey's Anatomy* or *Two and a Half Men*. Others may have a fantasy setting but deal with situations in a realistic manner, such as *Star Trek*. Distinguishing reality from fantasy in the media is often a difficult task that requires you to think about the many different characteristics of a message. So you must think analytically and break a message down into its component parts, then assess which parts are realistic. Do not try to categorize messages as simply being either real or fantasy; media messages always have elements of both.

Being aware of the fantasy-reality continuum is especially important now, when there are so many so-called "reality" programs on television. Although all of these programs have reality elements, they also contain many fantasy elements. And some of these reality shows may have a mix of elements that make them less real than some fictional programs. The distinction between shows labeled reality and those labeled fiction is not a sharp, clear line. Be careful of accepting the simple labels for messages. The important thing is to know when you are being exposed to fantasy so that you can process those messages differently. If you aren't sufficiently analytical, many messages with embedded fantasy might appear realistic.

Do not go on a quest to avoid fantasy merely because fantasy elements are dangerous to use in real-world expectations. There is a place for fantasy in the enjoyment of the media. Fantasy messages can be very entertaining because of their imaginative or humorous appeal. They can stimulate our thinking creatively. However, we must realize that fantasy is a tool to stimulate our imagination; it is not a model to imitate.

8. Become More Skilled at Designing Messages

Many media now not only offer you the chance to create your own messages, they require it. The best example of this is when you create a Facebook account, you must design your own page and you are expected to update it continually. How does your Facebook page compare to those of your friends? How well designed is it aesthetically? Do you have photos and graphics with your text? Would people want to visit your page just to see how well designed it is?

How well designed is your Facebook page from a personal information point of view? What have you decided to reveal about yourself? How will the information on your page affect your friends? Your parents? Future employers?

9. Do Not Take Privacy for Granted

In past generations, an individual's use of the media was a relatively private thing. However, today your media exposures are tracked in minute detail, and that information is sold to advertisers or to anyone else interested in your media use habits. When you post a message on your own web page, publish a blog post, or send a tweet, you initially have some control over who will see your message. But you soon lose that control when the web page server, web browser, blog owner, or Internet service provider can make copies of your messages, repackage them, and sell them to other users of the Internet. Once your message is sent in digital form, it can be endlessly copied, stored, and distributed to anyone. Therefore, before you digitize a message and put it out on the Internet, think about all of the potential audiences who could read that message—marketers, potential employers, friends, future spouse, children, parents, government officials, and on and on. What impression are you likely to create among all those audiences?

10. Take Personal Responsibility

This may be the hardest to do. We as Americans are fond of placing blame on others, because it allows us to feel that the problem lies elsewhere and therefore it is someone else's problem to fix. For example, let's consider the problem of overeating. The Centers for Disease Control and Prevention (2017) reports that the percentage of Americans who are obese increases dramatically with age with 9.4% children aged 2–5 years old being obese; 17.4% of children 6–11; 20.6% of adolescents 12–19; and 37.9% of adults 20 and older. This would seem to be a personal problem, but most people continue to eat too much and exercise too little. They wait for a government to impose some solution. By 2006, 16 states had imposed restrictions on junk food sales in public schools, and it appears that those restrictions were working to reduce weight gain. In a study of 6,300 public school children in 40 states, researchers found that children gained less weight from fifth through eighth grades if they lived in states with strong, consistent laws versus no laws governing snacks available in schools (Tanner, 2012). That is good news, but we need to ask whether people are so weak willed that they need the government to ban something before they will cut down their consumption of something harmful. Many people *are* that weak. Are you one of them?

Illustrations of Milestones

To help increase your awareness of differences in media literacy development, let's look at some examples of how people can react to different types of media content. Those reactions are best understood when compared to positions on the learning ladders of cognitive, emotional, moral, and aesthetic appreciation.

The learning ladders remind us that we can improve our degree of media literacy in four areas: cognitions, emotions, morality, and aesthetics. Progress up each of these ladders is accomplished by mastering the key skills of analysis, evaluation, grouping, induction, deduction, synthesis, and abstracting.

Cognitive Ladder

The first step on the cognitive ladder is awareness, which is the ability to perceive information elements in media messages. This requires the use of analysis. The next step is understanding. This is the ability to perceive the relevant components in any messages and then group them to see how those elements are related to each other. The next step is evaluation, which requires a good deal of contextual information to have templates with which to compare current messages. To do this well, a person needs a great deal of context in the form of elaborate knowledge structures. At the highest step, people are able to appreciate a message by comparing it to their understanding of the constraints and resources of the people who produced the message. The more elaborated a person's knowledge structure is about the media industries, the more the person will be able to appreciate the valuable elements in those messages and discount the other elements.

NetPhotos/Alamy Stock Photo

Emotional Ladder

At low levels of emotional development, people's emotions control them. They get aroused and angry without being able to control those reactions. They experience fear so strong they cannot shake it. Or they cry at a movie and cannot stop even though they are very embarrassed. Or they are unable to feel any emotions even though they long to do so.

At higher levels of emotional development, people can use the media to shape and control their emotions. For example, we have known for some time that stressed women

Once you post a blog or message on a webpage, it can be tracked and sold to anyone interested in your media use habits.

istock/porcorex

Chart your progress on learning ladders toward higher degrees of media literacy.

watch more game and variety shows as well as more television in total, whereas stressed men watch more action and violent programming (Anderson, Collins, Schmitt, & Jacobvitz, 1996). Depressed people especially use social media to escape unpleasant feelings and real-world stimuli, and their use of social media has been found to increase those feelings of depression (Shensa et al., 2017).

If people are aware of what they are doing, then the use of media to manage moods is a sign of high levels of media literacy; that is, people are consciously using the media as a tool to satisfy a particular need. If, in contrast, people are depressed and don't know what to do, they may watch television by default until they are tired enough to fall asleep. This is not an example of people controlling their exposure, so this is evidence of a low level of media literacy.

Moral Ladder

This requires the development of opinions about the ethical nature of media messages. Typically, we infer themes from shows by comparing elements in the portrayals against our personal values.

At the lowest level on this ladder, you construct your moral judgment of a message based purely on intuition or because someone else makes the judgment for you and you simply accept it. You see the elements in the show as an undifferentiated mass or blur. You make quick intuitive reactions about whether the show feels right or not, according to your values. If there is a fit, you are happy; if there is no fit, you have a negative reaction. You really can't articulate your reaction very well because it is primarily emotional. For example, if a respected friend tells you that *American Idol* is a morally reprehensible program that belittles people and crushes their dreams, you may simply accept this opinion without watching the show. If you accidentally find yourself exposed to it, you immediately have a negative reaction and turn it off.

At the middle levels of this ladder, you make a distinction among characters on their values and find yourself identifying with those characters who have the same values as you do. If those characters are portrayed positively (rewarded, successful, attractive, etc.), then you are happy.

At the higher levels, you think past individual characters to focus your meaning making at the overall narrative level. You separate characters from their actions so that you might not like a particular character, but still you like his or her actions in terms of fitting in with (or reinforcing) your values. You do not tie your viewing into one character's point of view but try to empathize with many characters so you can vicariously experience the various consequences of actions through the course of the narrative. During a narrative, you are able to assume different moral perspectives and more fully appreciate the action from all participants' points of view.

Aesthetic Appreciation Ladder

This development is oriented toward the cultivation of an enhanced enjoyment, understanding, and appreciation of media content. At lower levels on this aesthetic ladder, people have a very simple categorical opinion that the show is either good or bad. Not much reasoning goes into the intuitive decision, so viewers are not able to explain why they like something.

At the middle levels, people are able to distinguish acting from writing and directing. Viewers have the ability to perceive that one of these might be good while another is bad. Also, people are able to compare an artist's performance within this message with past performances and infer a trend in the work.

At higher levels, there is an awareness of media content as a "text" that provides insight into our contemporary culture and ourselves. An awareness of artistry and visual manipulation is also needed. This is an awareness about the processes by which meaning is created through the visual media. What is expected of sophisticated viewers is some degree of self-consciousness about their role as interpreters. This includes the ability to detect artifice (in staged behavior and editing) and to spot authorial presence (style of the producer/director).

Learning about visual conventions is not a prerequisite for interpreting visual messages. However, learning these conventions can help heighten our appreciation of artistry; it also provides viewers with the ability to see through the manipulative uses and ideological implications of visual images. This helps enhance critical viewing.

Can you make a quick assessment of your position on each of these four ladders? If you can, then your awareness is fairly high. But if you are unclear how to position yourself, then think about these ladders as you watch television or read a newspaper. As you reflect on your media exposures as they are happening, you will develop more insights about the levels at which you normally operate. Remember, you will move your positions on the ladders depending on the type of message and your mood. If you are simply looking for fantasy to help you relax, you are likely operating at lower levels. But you may be capable of operating at higher levels at other times. As you are exposed to media messages over a long period of time, develop a sense of where your "home position" is—that is, at what level you usually operate.

Now let's use these learning ladders as templates to examine some examples. This analysis will highlight the important differences across levels of media literacy.

Examples of Levels of Literacy

There are many different reasons why people expose themselves to different kinds of content, and there are many different benefits people can get out of any particular message. Because of this, it is not possible to analyze a message and assume that all those who are exposed will extract the same meaning or have the same experience from it. To illustrate these ideas, let's consider two examples: reality series on television and Facebook pages.

Reality series as a genre can appeal to viewers of all levels of media literacy. At a low level of literacy, people feel that the characters are real and that the situations actually happened as presented. They cannot explain why they like the characters or the show. Because they don't analyze it, they just let it be.

At a bit higher level of development, people will watch reality series because they feel a personal identity with the characters and enjoy their parasocial interactions with those

The reality series *Keeping Up With the Kardashians* can appeal to viewers of all levels of media literacy. At a low level, people might watch for the dramatic, flamboyant characters. At a higher level, the show can promote conversations about important topics like family values.

characters in their world, which is more exciting than their own barren existence. This leads to a strong emotional reaction. Other people will watch reality shows because they want to learn how attractive characters dress and act; this leads to some cognitive processing and evaluation of how characters look and act.

At a higher level, some people view reality series in groups so they can discuss the action as it unfolds. Or they will call their friends later and use the action as an important topic of conversation. These people use the viewing to maintain a community of friends that they would not have without the reality series. This requires a considerable amount of cognitive processing and emotional attachment.

At a higher level still, the viewing takes on an in-depth analysis of the aesthetic and moral elements displayed there. Viewers marvel at the editing that focuses their attention on the most exciting parts of the participants' lives and overdramatizes their mundane problems by blowing them up into huge moral dilemmas.

Now let's consider an example about creating a Facebook page. At a low level of media literacy, creating a Facebook page entails uploading snapshots a person thinks are cool. The person adds elements and sends messages to maximize the list of friends. Then the person spends a lot of time monitoring the growing list of friends and sending them all short, superficial messages to maintain contact.

At a higher level, users try to improve the artistic quality of their images and sounds so as to impress visitors to their page. They take pride in the increases in hits and friends that are attracted by their updates.

At the highest levels of media literacy, users are very strategic in using Facebook as a tool to create and maintain a personal image to satisfy specific goals, such as reinforcing a few key friendships, attracting a specific kind of romantic partner, or showing off web skills to a prospective employer. They are very conscious of what they reveal about themselves and make sure those revelations contribute substantially to constructing a positive image over the long term.

Remember that it is not the type of messages you watch or create that make you media literate. Instead, literacy is keyed to what you think and how you feel while you are engaging with the media. The more active and aware you are during those engagements, the more you will get out of the media and the more those experiences will help you achieve your personal goals.

HELPING OTHERS

In the previous section, the focus was on helping yourself increase your own level of media literacy. This section shifts the focus to helping others increase their levels.

First we examine how you can help others—especially children—interpersonally, then we look at more ambitious tasks of helping others by working with larger aggregates such as public education and society.

Interpersonal Techniques

Interpersonal techniques are the relatively informal things people use in their everyday lives to help others with their media literacy. Researchers have studied the techniques people use, mainly in family settings, and have found that techniques vary in their effectiveness (for review of this literature, see Nathanson, 2001a, 2001b, 2002). There seem to be three keys to helping others become more media literate. The first key is to be positive and constructive. If you want to be successful in helping others, you must show them that you have their best interests in mind and that you are not forcing your help on them for some ulterior motive, like exercising power over them.

We can help others achieve greater media literacy.

A second key is to be balanced. You should exhibit an attitude about the media that balances criticism with appreciation. There are some people who drive around town with a bumper sticker that says "Kill Your TV." It is hard to take those people seriously because they do not seem to realize the enormous positive influence that television has exercised on our culture. Trying to make people more media literate by only criticizing the media is like trying to make people healthy by only forcing bad-tasting medicine on them. Media exposures can be fun, so help people have more fun and increase the ways they can appreciate media messages. Then help people be more analytical about media messages so they can identify the elements that warrant criticism. When parents have only a negative, critical attitude about the media, rules become restrictive and are regarded as arbitrary by children. Many children fail to understand why certain kinds of content are bad for them when that content is fun and fulfills their immediate needs. These children are likely to subvert their parents' restrictions by continuing with exposures they find enjoyable.

A third key is to involve people's cognitive processes and help them get better at thinking for themselves. For example, if you want children to learn that certain content is harmful to them, you need to avoid simply telling them that. Instead, you need to help them analyze the content and see for themselves the silliness, the manipulation, or the harm.

Helping others become more media literate will become especially important to you when you become a parent and want to protect your children from negative risks of exposure. Realize that you cannot do everything, so pick your battles. Rather than try to deal with all forms of media content, I suggest you focus on two: food advertising and Internet use.

One type of message is the advertisement for food. There is a great deal of advertising of unhealthy foods to children in the United States (Page & Brewster, 2007) and other countries (Roberts & Pettigrew, 2007); advertisers use very sophisticated appeals that exaggerate health claims and imply that the advertised foods have the ability to enhance popularity, performance, and mood. These ads can have a detrimental influence on children who are not media literate enough to analyze their claims and find many of them to be silly or false. Studies have found that along with genetics and reduced rates of physical activity, the flood of advertising for high-calorie, low-nutrition foods leads to unhealthy eating and weight gain. In 2005, after criticism of the U.S. food industry for advertising's role in childhood obesity, national advertisers announced new policies to reduce children's exposure to ads for unhealthy foods. However, a content analysis that was conducted on television food advertisements aired just before and 1 year after these announcements found very few changes in food advertising seen by children (Warren, Wicks, & Wicks, 2007). And it is not likely that this type of advertising will become more responsible or will be reduced, especially because there is such a huge market for these foods. So the cycle will continue with more unhealthy foods being advertised, leading to more consumption of unhealthy foods, which leads food companies to produce more of this type of product to satisfy the growing market. The best hope you have to break this unhealthy cycle is to teach your children to take responsibility for their own actions and not to blame others, such as the government for lack of regulation, the food providers for providing what the market demands, or advertisers. When you blame others, the best that you can hope for is that those other people will change their practices. When you take responsibility for your own actions, you can move toward a healthier lifestyle immediately. When we realize that the percentage of overweight and obese children in the United States has more than tripled over the past 30 years (Warren et al., 2007), we can see that we need more children to view themselves less as victims of outside forces and more as people in control of their own lives.

A second type of special concern for parents should be with Internet messages. The Internet provides easy access for children to encounter all kinds of messages that are potentially harmful to them; I will focus your attention on three types in particular. One type of harmful message is that which contains material such as sexual matter and hate speech. Children's cognitive, emotional, and moral reasoning abilities are not developed well enough for them to process these messages in a way that protects them from harm. A second type of potentially harmful message includes communications from strangers who are trying to develop inappropriate relationships. The third type of message from which your children needs protection is from advertisers and others who solicit private information from your child.

Therefore, parents need to be careful in monitoring what sites their children visit. Parents need to tell their children never to give out any identifying information, such as an address, phone number, school name, and so forth, and never allow a child to arrange a face-to-face meeting with someone online. Parents who find information that may be illegal (such as child pornography or hate speech) should report it to authorities. Parents should build skepticism in their children because people on the Internet may not be who they claim to be; people can make up a persona in terms of gender, age, background, and so on. Parents should set time rules of access; too much contact can lead to addiction. And finally, surfing the Internet can be a fun activity for all family members to do together.

Parents, however, must be careful in how they guide their children. Findings from research suggest that children and adolescents often resist parental interference with their Internet experiences. In a national sample of 456 parents of children 10–16 years of age, Byrne and Lee (2011) found that children preferred that their parents empower them to protect themselves rather than restricting their use. But other research shows that younger children appreciate parental involvement. In an experiment, parents who created a Facebook page and "friended" their children were found to decrease conflict in their relationship. Even when the parent and child had a more conflicted relationship prior to the parent joining Facebook, the parent's presence on Facebook also enhanced the child's closeness with the parent (Kanter, Afifi, & Robbins, 2012).

Interventions

In contrast to the interpersonal techniques, which are typically informal things used in a person's everyday life, interventions are formal, carefully designed sessions that are intended to achieve particular media literacy goals. Media literacy interventions are designed by researchers and educators who select a target group, identify a particular risk that group may be experiencing from exposure to media messages, then deliver some sort of a treatment that includes media materials, mini-lectures, discussions of issues, and practicing some skill. Those treatments are typically designed to give members of the target group some information, insight, motivation or skill that will help them overcome some negative media effect or to inoculate them against experiencing a negative effect in the future (Potter & Byrne, 2009).

The design of a good media literacy intervention is a most challenging task, given the wide range of media effects (all of which can be either positive or negative for the individual) and the hundreds of factors about individuals and media messages that have been found to contribute to those effects (see Chapters 13 and 14). Over the years, media literacy scholars have tested various interventions and published their results in scholarly journals. Jeong, Cho, and Hwang (2012) conducted a meta-analysis of over 50 of those interventions and found that in general, media literacy interventions had positive effects on outcomes including media knowledge, criticism, perceived realism, influence, behavioral beliefs, attitudes, self-efficacy, and behavior. They also reported that interventions with more sessions were more effective, but those with more components were less effective. This means that designers of interventions need to simplify their treatments by focusing on one type of message or factor then repeat their treatment several times.

When interventions are designed with the right key influence, they can be successful. For example, Slater and Rouner (2002) focused on the influence of role modeling in entertainment programming. They found that when people do not have role models in shows, they are less involved in those shows and this makes them more susceptible to the influence of such messages. Thus, if these people were highly involved and were likely to argue against the messages, their low involvement would defuse the counter-arguments. Therefore a key to designing a successful intervention is to get people involved in the show by identifying with positive role models.

Rozendaal and colleagues (2011) argue that interventions to help children become less susceptible to advertising effects often do not work well because they are focused on simply providing conceptual knowledge of advertising. They point out that because much advertising is affect targeted and that children primarily process advertising under conditions of low elaboration, knowledge about advertising is not an adequate defense. They recommend that interventions aimed at increasing the advertising literacy among children need to focus on the actual use of conceptual advertising knowledge and attitudinal advertising literacy, which includes low-effort, attitudinal mechanisms that can function as a defense under conditions of low elaboration.

There are examples in the research literature where educators have designed interventions to increase the media literacy of the study's participants (usually children) and when they analyze their results, they find that the level of media literacy has declined rather than improved. This is known as a **boomerang effect**. An example of this effect was found by Byrne (2009), who performed an experiment of children in the fourth and fifth grades in an attempt to test how well her intervention could help children avoid behaving aggressively after being exposed to violence in the media. She had two interventions and a control group. One intervention consisted of an instructional lesson about not behaving aggressively. A second intervention was the same as the first but it also included a cognitive activity. Children who experienced only the instructional lesson actually increased their willingness to use aggressive behavior and this effect lasted over time—thus this treatment boomeranged. But the treatment with the lesson and the cognitive activity resulted in a reduction of willingness to use aggression, so it was successful. The lesson here is that people who are sincerely motivated to help others increase their media literacy may end up doing more harm than good.

Public Education

Perhaps you are interested in trying to increase the level of media literacy in large groups of people. The institution of education is a good place to start thinking about addressing this task.

Current Situation

Critics have observed that the United States has long lagged behind many other countries in developing media literacy courses and curricula in public schools (Brown, 1991, 1998, 2001; Considine, 1997; Davies, 1997; Kubey, 1997; Piette & Giroux, 1997; Sizer, 1995). They point to a long list of countries that are far ahead of the United States with media literacy curricula. These countries include Australia, Canada, United Kingdom, South Africa, Scandinavia, Russia, and Israel, as well as many other countries in Europe, South America, and Asia (Brown, 1991; Piette & Giroux, 1997). For example, Australia has had mandated media education from kindergarten to 12th grade since the mid-1990s. This curriculum stresses aesthetics and semiotics, with a liberal humanist approach to the popular arts (Brown, 1998).

In the United Kingdom and some Latin American counties, empowerment of media consumers is paramount, often focusing on industry control through corporate and governmental hegemony. Media education there stresses "representational" and oppositional ideologies, power, and politics and ways to participate in mainstream media or construct alternative media outlets (Brown, 1998, p. 45). This gap is getting smaller as many states have been enacting guidelines for media literacy (Zubrzycki, 2017).

Critics point out that the relative lack of attention to media education in the United States is a serious problem because the United States is the most media-saturated country

iStock/CEFutcher

Incorporating media literacy into schools and curricula in the United States presents many challenges and opportunities.

in the world. More time and money are spent on media consumption in this country than any other country in the world, yet our educational system virtually ignores media education (Sizer, 1995). This is not to say that there are no media literacy efforts in America's schools; however, their existence is rare and largely unsupported by the institution of education. For example, Brown (2001) characterizes the teaching of media literacy in this country as "isolated teachers introduc[ing] mass media topics into their classrooms, usually within the context of traditional content such as English or history social studies" (p. 683). He continues, "Schedules already crowded with curricular mandates had no time for yet another addition, so whatever media study could be introduced was typically integrated into already existing courses" (p. 683).

A few states have experimented with media literacy initiatives. Two decades ago, Kubey (1998) reported that there had been "significant statewide initiatives" in New Mexico and North Carolina, with "noteworthy developments" in Wisconsin and Minnesota. And Hobbs (1998) reported that media literacy concepts were included in the curriculum frameworks in more than 15 states. This is growing as "ongoing efforts are in place in many U.S. school districts. Interest in media education is even growing among mainstream education organizations and health professionals, including the National Association of Secondary School Principals and the American Academy of Pediatrics" (Hobbs, 1998, p. 24). Initiatives are growing, but we need to monitor whether this talk about the importance of media literacy and its inclusion in mission statements translates into meaningful implementation.

Barriers

Why is there so little sustained effort at developing and implementing media literacy curricula in the United States, while there are many good efforts in other countries? There appear to be many obstacles for further development of media literacy (for a more complete treatment, see Brown, 2001; Considine, 1997; Davies, 1997; Kubey, 1997).

Arguably, the most critical obstacle is the lack of centralized decision making concerning education in the United States. Brown (1998) points out that curriculum decisions are spread out over 15,000 school districts, each with its own school board and administrators. Kubey (1990) elaborates on this argument by pointing out that the United States is a huge country with a highly diversified population and no central governmental policy on media literacy to pull things together. Also, only approximately 4% of educational expenditures in the United States come from the federal government (Kubey, 1998). Thus, in this country, the power for curriculum decisions lies at the state and especially local levels. Each of these decision-making bodies has its mix of personalities, needs, and political agendas.

Not paying attention to the special circumstances in each school's culture has been credited in large part for the failure of media literacy efforts that were tried in the 1970s (Anderson, 1983). Hobbs (1998) extended this point by saying, "Media literacy initiatives have been most successful in school communities where teachers, parents and students have a shared, common vision about their love-hate relationship with media culture" (p. 23). Brown (1998) said, "If media literacy studies are to survive and grow, administrators in school systems and at individual schools must endorse and support them. They should not be left wholly dependent on the initiative and energy of isolated teachers" (p. 52). Brown called for a more holistic and continuing approach.

To succeed, a curricular program of media literacy must be developed through collaboration among teachers, administrators, specialists, and parents, who together must build it into the systematic education process. Media study should not be a mere appendage of a random elective course, nor should media technology be used merely as a tool or aid to teach other subjects. That means developing studies geared to the participants' successive levels of cognitive development based on educational and behavioral research findings. It also means continuing and integrating studies into successive grade levels through the school years. (p. 52)

But all this comes with a high cost. Other curricula must be replaced with the media literacy one. Teachers need significant training, and this will require reduced teaching loads. Parents will need to become much more involved. It also requires a sustained commitment that includes substantial training of media literacy teachers. Hobbs (1998) explained,

The most successful efforts to include media literacy in schools have taken 2 or more years of staff development to build a clearly defined understanding of the concept as it relates to classroom practice among a substantial number of teachers and school leaders within a school district. (pp. 23–24)

Then once trained, the teachers need to be supported continually by the institution rather than left on their own. Hobbs (1998) explains that a study of teacher performance in Great Britain yielded depressing results. Among the teachers who completed training in media literacy education, about 40% ended up doing nothing, 25% did something moderately well, 10% did something creatively exceptional, and the remaining 25% did something embarrassing, dangerous, or just a waste of time.

Unless resources are provided, there are significant barriers to implementation. For example, one study reported that although most high school teachers believe the study of media is important, 40% did not teach it at all because of constraints on time and curriculum space (cited in Brown, 2001). The same pattern was found in Maryland with language arts teachers; once again, the teachers regarded media literacy as important to teach, but the lack of training, materials, and time prevented many from teaching it (Koziol, 1989). Brown (2001) observed that few teachers receive training to deal with the challenge of teaching media literacy either in their college degree programs or in workshops for teacher certification. Most teachers, however, do feel that they are qualified to teach media literacy, even though only about one third had any training.

Curriculum designers often look to media literacy scholars for guidance. However, there is the lack of agreement among scholars about what media literacy is and what its goals should be (see Chapter 2). Two of the more persistent definitional issues when it comes to curriculum design are tone and texts. Regarding tone, Brown (1991) complained that "many media workshops and curricula are protectionist and defensive. They seek to inoculate consumers against blandishments of images and messages of media entertainment, news, and advertising" (p. 45). As for texts, Hobbs (1998) observed that although media texts have always been essential in education, rarely are those texts "considered beyond their function as conveyers of information" (p. 25). They need to be the objects of inquiry (Kress, 1992). Students need to analyze the people and corporations who produce and disseminate those texts and understand their motives. Also, the texts themselves need to be analyzed for what they leave out, how they are structured, and their basis for claims from both an aesthetic and moral perspective.

This diversity of opinion gets magnified as we move out to consumer activists, teachers, and school administrators. There is also a wide variety of opinion concerning the composition of a media literacy curriculum, what should be taught, how it should be taught, and how the effect of the teaching should be assessed. The good thing about this diversity is that it provides a wide range of ideas for instruction and a variety of curriculum models to the many different school systems in the United States. If most of the school systems were entrepreneurial and willing to search out the techniques that would fit the special culture in their district, then this variety would pay big dividends. But most school districts are very conservative about change. The teachers and administrators already feel they are asked to cover too many topics, so they cannot add another one without a great deal of debate.

The diversity of ideas among scholars appears more as an academic debate than as a convincing argument to shift resources. For scholars to present a convincing argument, they must present a perspective that integrates the best thinking into a clear set of principles that can guide their decision making in three key issues: curriculum design, teaching, and assessment.

What Can You Do?

When you become a parent, you can insist that your school district provide some sort of media education. You might have to begin small by volunteering in your child's classroom. Develop some mini-instructional units based on your own knowledge about media literacy. Typically, children will really like these sessions, because such sessions involve them in something they use every day. If your mini-units work well, students will talk about them, and other students will create a demand for similar instruction. By beginning small, you can grow a demand locally in your child's school.

Societal Techniques

With societal techniques, the focus is on exerting pressure on a particular part of the industry, the government, or some institution to increase public awareness about a problem or to bring about some particular change. To do this successfully, you will first need a strategy supported by a great deal of commitment. Your strategy will require many years of effort to effect a change. Also, it requires money. Often, people will start a PAC (political action committee) or a consulting firm that will then apply for grants to support its work.

Contacts are also extremely important. By linking up with other powerful people and groups, you could become part of something that could potentially have enough power to get the attention of the large media companies. Look at the list of citizen action groups in Appendix C (https://study.sagepub.com/potter9e). Contact those that are of most interest to you and ask them to send you information.

Changing media industry practices or content is very difficult. Remember that the industries have grown and developed in response to demands from the public. If an industry or a vehicle does not respond well to the demand, it loses money. Successful

CEOs have confidence that their decisions will result in greater profits. So don't expect change when you ask them to ignore their experience and to change their practices when they might risk losing millions of dollars by making those changes you suggest. This is why the public concern about television violence has resulted in so little change over the past 50 years. In explaining this non-action, Stuart Fishoff (1988), a psychologist who writes for television and movies, said,

> Let's suppose the results, the conclusions were incontrovertible—TV and film modeling of aggression and other anti-social values has significant effects on the viewing audience. Would it really make any difference to the gate keepers of media fare in Hollywood and New York? I submit the answer is not on your life! (p. 3)

He cites an important principle in psychology for his conclusion:

> The more far-reaching and costly the consequences of accepting a message, the more facts needed before an audience will be persuaded as to the accuracy of the message—and the more energy will be expended in denigrating both the message and the messenger in order to maintain existing belief. (p. 3)

Therefore, the media industries have been very slow in acknowledging the value of any of the research on negative media effects, whereas they use the research on positive effects to show that they are acting responsibly. This attitude has outraged many media critics and stimulated many average citizens to want to do something to remedy the problem.

Another example of a societal technique is the concern over protecting very young children from the effects of television advertising. In the early 1970s, some consumer groups were formed to protect children from what was being seen as abuses by broadcasters. Prominent among these groups was Action for Children's Television, which found examples of children's programs that contained as many as 16 minutes of ads per hour—far above the industry's self-imposed limit of 9.5 minutes. And the products advertised were largely non-nutritious snacks and deceptively presented toys. Many products were being pitched by characters from the programs, thus making the distinction between the show and the ad indecipherable, especially for young children.

This pressure influenced the Federal Trade Commission (FTC) to hold hearings throughout the 1970s. The FTC considered banning certain types of ads. But in the end, the FTC concluded that although there was evidence that television advertising created risks for children, no practical effective remedies were open to federal policymaking. The primary problems were determining who is a child; that is, at what age is a person no longer a child? Also, there was the fear that regulating advertising on children's television might cause broadcasters to stop programming for children.

Another example of a societal strategy took place in the fall of 1995, when some well-known political figures began a campaign to clean up talk shows on television. Headed by former Education Secretary William Bennett, Senator Joseph Lieberman (D-Conn.), and Senator Sam Nunn (D-Ga.), the campaign did not seek regulation of television content. Instead, it sought to influence public opinion and to shame certain television producers by characterizing the content of daytime talk shows as "lethal." These critics acknowledged that some of the 20 nationally syndicated talk shows dealt with serious issues of domestic abuse, drug abuse, and racism in a constructive way that enlightens viewers. But they pointed out that some shows had a circus atmosphere that included shouting matches, fistfights, foul language, and audience members yelling out unqualified advice. As an example of sleaze, they cited examples from the *Sally Jesse Raphael* show, which featured girls who were sexually active at the age of 10, and Jerry Springer, who hosted a show about a 17-year-old who had four children with her 71-year-old husband, whom she called "Dad" (Hancock, 1995).

There are many other examples of people and groups who have tried to influence public awareness of problems with media content and to bring about change in the media industries. These efforts have been more successful in raising public consciousness about these problems than they have been in bringing about changes in programming. This leaves us with the following question: Should we continue to try? The answer, of course, is yes.

Let's see how imaginative you are. Try Exercise 15.2. Be idealistic and dream about how you could make a huge difference. Of course, when we try to enact change in the real world, we need to scale back our expectations. Societal change of this type moves at glacial speed—it takes decades to see change. But remember that a glacier is exerting constant pressure, and change is happening constantly—but we can't see it happening because it is happening very slowly. The same is true with societal campaigns. But if we are committed and are able to exert constant pressure, we will eventually be able to effect changes.

SUMMARY

Media literacy is a perspective. To achieve this perspective, you need to increase your awareness and control. The exercises in this chapter are designed to help you make an assessment (and continue this practice over time) of your awareness about your own knowledge structures, about how your mind works, and about your ability to apply knowledge of the key elements in the effects process.

Media literacy is most clearly diagnosed when we compare people's patterns of thoughts and feelings to the positions on the learning ladders. Keep these ladders in mind during your exposures.

Once you develop your own strategy for increasing media literacy, you may want to help others do the same. Think about all the day-to-day informal things you can do to help the people around you understand the media better. If you get more involved in this task, then think about developing formal interventions and doing things to influence public education as well as society.

This book is now ending. What kind of an effect have you let it have on you? Did you read it critically by analyzing the information and arguments? Did you compare and contrast the points made here with your existing knowledge structures? Did you evaluate my arguments and positions, agreeing with some and disagreeing with others? Did you synthesize the information you found most useful into your own perspective on media literacy and your own set of techniques to achieve that perspective? If you answered yes to these questions, then you have reacted well cognitively to the book. The key to a high-quality cognitive reaction is not whether you agree with me and accept all this information. Instead, the key is that your mind was continually active as you read the book.

Did you have some strong emotional reactions while reading the book? For example, did you get upset with some of the information or arguments? Do you feel challenged and motivated to become more media literate? If you answered yes to these questions, then you have reacted well emotionally to the book. The key to a high-quality emotional reaction is not whether you have positive feelings about me or about the book. Instead, the key is that you were able to let your emotions become engaged by hating parts of the book and loving others.

Did you take moral positions throughout the book? For example, did you develop a sense of what is right with our culture (and what is wrong) because of the media? Did you make a strong commitment to yourself to do certain things to help yourself and others? If you answered yes to these questions, then you have reacted well morally to the book. The key to a high-quality moral reaction is not whether you agree with my positions. Instead, the key is that you are able to perceive a sense of right and wrong about certain conditions and to take a stand for yourself.

Finally, were you aware of aesthetic reactions to the book? Were there times when you appreciated the way I structured a chapter or the way I illuminated an important point? Did you find certain examples useful and creative? Did you feel that certain sections could have been written better? If you were able to answer these questions, then you were sensitive to the aesthetic features of the book. I, of course, hope that your aesthetic reactions were favorable. But whether favorable or not, the more aesthetic reactions you had and the more aesthetic awareness you exercised, the better for your media literacy development.

Most important, I hope you can see that you have achieved a significant degree of media literacy. You have many useful knowledge structures and many useful skills. As you continue developing these knowledge structures and skills, remember to be aware of what you are doing and stay in control of your progress. And make it fun!

Keeping Up to Date

There is a good deal of information about media literacy that is made available by various groups on their websites. While some of this information is offered for sale in the form of books, reports, CDs, and DVDs for a nominal price, a lot of this material is available for free. I recommend the following websites for media literacy organizations:

Center for Media Literacy	http://www.medialit.org
Center on Media and Child Health	http://cmch.tv/
Children Now	http://www.childrennow.org
Media Literacy Now	https://medialiteracynow.org/
National Association for Media Literacy Education	http://namle.net/

EXERCISE 15.1
AWARENESS OF YOUR KNOWLEDGE STRUCTURES

Below is a list of chapters in this book. Each one presents a knowledge structure on its topic.

1. For each chapter in the book, try to recall the structure of the content.

   a. Can you remember the key idea of that chapter? Can you remember major ideas or sections of the chapter?

   b. Then go back to the first page of that chapter and check your recall. If you remembered the key idea, give yourself 1 point, and give yourself another point for your recall of *each* major idea (the major points in the outline). Thus, your score should be somewhere between 0 and 5 for that chapter.

   c. Enter your score in the left column, which is labeled "Book."

   d. Do the same procedure for each of the chapters listed below.

Book	Ad Exp	PART I: INTRODUCTION
_____	_____	Chapter 1 Why Increase Media Literacy?
_____	_____	Chapter 2 Media Literacy Approach
		PART II: AUDIENCES
_____	_____	Chapter 3 Audience: Individual Perspective
_____	_____	Chapter 4 Audience: Industry Perspective
_____	_____	Chapter 5 Children as a Special Audience

		PART III: INDUSTRY
_____	_____	Chapter 6 Development of the Mass Media Industries
_____	_____	Chapter 7 Economic Perspective
		PART IV: CONTENT
_____	_____	Chapter 8 Media Content and Reality
_____	_____	Chapter 9 News
_____	_____	Chapter 10 Entertainment
_____	_____	Chapter 11 Advertising
_____	_____	Chapter 12 Interactive Media
		PART V: EFFECTS
_____	_____	Chapter 13 Broadening Our Perspective on Media Effects
_____	_____	Chapter 14 How Does the Media Effects Process Work?

2. Next, think about the additional reading you undertook after studying each chapter.

   a. For each book or article you read from the "Further Reading" list or from the reference list, give yourself 2 points.

   b. For each additional book you have read relevant to the topic since studying the chapter, give yourself 1 point.

   c. For each significant experience you have had concerning that topic since studying the chapter, give yourself 1 point. (A significant experience is an extended conversation you had with someone on

(Continued)

(Continued)

the topic of the chapter, consciously trying to apply the principles in that chapter, etc.)

d. Record your point totals for each chapter in the column labeled "Ad Exp" for Additional Experiences.

3. Look at the pattern of numbers across the chapters. What does this tell you about the state of your current knowledge structures?

a. Look down the "Book" column. If you have mostly 4s and 5s, you have a very strong set of knowledge structures. If you have mostly 3s, you have a good beginning set of knowledge structures. If you have some zeros, you need to go back and reorient yourself to the structure of information in those chapters.

Remember that having strong knowledge structures does not necessarily mean you have a great deal of knowledge on that topic, but it does mean that you are aware of the main ideas, and this will help you acquire additional knowledge much more efficiently.

b. Look down the "Ad Exp" column. If you have 3s or above, you are showing a strong commitment to extending your knowledge and elaborating your knowledge structures. Look where you have zeros and ask yourself why you were not willing or able to extend your knowledge.

c. Look at the total pattern of numbers. Were you stronger on certain chapters than others? It is understandable that you may have more interest in particular topics than others. But remember that balance is important. Be proud of your accomplishments—now build on them to overcome your weaknesses.

EXERCISE 15.2

FANTASIZING ABOUT YOUR SOCIETAL STRATEGY

Let's say that next year, you win $10 million in the lottery. After you pay your taxes, pay off all of your current debts, and splurge on all sorts of luxuries, you still have $3 million left over. So you decide to do something more worthwhile with your money and your life—you decide to set up a citizen action group that will help people become more media literate and change some of the things in society. Think about techniques as you address the following issues.

1. Goals: What would the goals be for your organization?

   a. List some interpersonal goals you would want to achieve.

   b. List some societal goals you would like to achieve.

2. Targets

   a. To reach those goals set above, which groups would you target for change (see Appendix C at https://study.sagepub .com/potter9e)? List those targets.

   b. For each target, what specifically would you want them to change?

3. Techniques: How would you stimulate that change?

   a. What things would you do to get the people in your targets to understand your point of view?

   b. What things would you do to get the people in your targets to change their behaviors?

   c. Barriers: What do you think would be the key barriers that might prevent you from achieving your goals?

CONFRONTING THE ISSUES

Now that you have read through the 15 instructional chapters, you are ready to apply what you have learned in a broad, systematic way. This section of the book presents you with six controversies about the mass media. See how well you can work through each of these controversies using your strengthening skills of analysis, evaluation, grouping, induction, deduction, synthesis, and abstraction. As context for understanding these controversies, use your four core media literacy knowledge structures—about the media industries, audiences, content, and effects. These six issues chapters give you a chance to continue elaborating your knowledge structures and to continue increasing the strength of your skills.

These six issues were selected because each attracts a high degree of public concern and criticism. Each has generated debate over various ways to deal with the problem that underlies the issue.

- Issue 1 presents the controversy about the ownership of media businesses. Critics argue that the industry has become too concentrated with too few companies owning too many media businesses. Are their arguments valid? What is at the root of this controversy?

- Issue 2 examines various answers to the question: Is there too much money being spent on sports?

- Issue 3 deals with the problem of what has been called "fake news." In how many different ways can news be regarded as fake?

- Issue 4 analyzes how we criticize advertising and whether those criticisms are valid and useful.

- Issue 5 tackles the persistent controversy over whether there is too much violence in the media and whether this type of content is harming individuals and society.

- Issue 6 examines the growing concern about privacy and how the new media environment is making it much more difficult for you to protect your privacy. What you don't know can hurt you.

While each of these six issues has generated considerable debate, rarely have these debates moved beyond a rather superficial level. To date, people who address these issues tend to have polarized positions, so these debates have generated more heat than light. As you read through these issues chapters, try to keep an open mind and understand what people on different sides of the controversy are arguing. Try to view the controversy from as many perspectives as possible. Do not be satisfied with surface arguments. Be rigorous in evaluating the evidence and arguments from all sides of the debate. Dig deep to uncover more layers underlying the controversy. Discuss the issue with your classmates and friends.

Each of these six chapters begins with a delineation of the issue to clarify its controversial nature and to outline what is being argued. However, I do not present arguments to lead you to think a certain way. Instead, I give you the raw material to think for yourself. So engage with the issues. If an argument does not sound convincing to you, analyze it to identify the problem. Challenge evidence that is presented. Keep digging through the controversy on your own. Through this process you will be developing your own well-informed opinions.

Five Generations of Kindle

ISSUE
1

OWNERSHIP OF MASS MEDIA BUSINESSES

Issue: The increasing concentration of media businesses ownership is an undesirable trend leading to harmful effects for the economy and society.

Jeff Bezos, CEO and founder of Amazon, announced he would purchase *The Washington Post* news organization for $250 million in cash in August 2013.

One of the most prevalent criticisms of the mass media concerns their ownership. Critics contend that there has been a trend toward concentration of ownership and that this concentration has been harming the economy and society.

This chapter presents an analysis of this issue by first delineating the main arguments of critics and defenders of this trend. Then we examine ownership patterns to determine the extent of the concentration. Next we examine the evidence of harm to see if it supports the claims of the critics. Finally, I present some guidelines and exercises to help you develop your own informed opinion on this complex issue.

DELINEATING THE ISSUE

This issue is driven by critics who are upset that fewer and fewer companies are owning more and more mass media businesses. On the other side of this issue are the large media companies that continue buying additional media businesses each year. Let's examine the arguments on both sides of this issue.

Arguments Against Concentration of Ownership of Media Companies

Critics who argue against the increasing concentration of ownership of media companies claim that this trend is harming the economy and society. They argue that when fewer owners control more of the mass media, competition is reduced and this harms the economy because these large companies increase the barriers to entry in their markets so that it becomes more difficult for new companies to break into those markets. As competition erodes, the incentives to keep quality high and prices low weaken. Thus consumers are harmed economically.

Critics also argue that concentration of ownership harms society in general. When fewer and fewer companies control the flow of information in a democracy, the population is exposed to fewer voices and this limits the range of information available to them to make informed decisions about important issues. Critics also fear that when the media are controlled by a few powerful businesspeople, there is a danger that the population will be subjected to the propaganda favored by the few people who control the flow of information.

Arguments for Concentration of Ownership of Media Companies

Defenders of the trend toward concentration take the position that the overall economy is strengthened when individual companies become stronger. Stronger companies have deeper pockets so they can develop better products to meet the needs of many more people. This stimulates more spending as more people buy those products. And in order to produce more products, these companies consume more raw materials and hire more workers.

Defenders argue that media companies are driven much more by economic goals rather than political ones, so they continually try to produce messages that appeal to the needs of consumers rather than try to fulfill their own political views.

EVIDENCE OF CONCENTRATION

In this section we examine the evidence for concentration of media ownership. First we look at the trend in concentration of ownership of media businesses both in the United States and internationally. Then we examine the reasons for such a trend.

Trend Toward Concentration

There is a good deal of evidence for patterns of concentration in all American industries, including the mass media. This trend is clearly illustrated by the research of Ben Bagdikian, who began conducting an analysis of media ownership patterns in 1983 in the United States. He reported that although there were about 25,000 media businesses, the top 50 of those businesses accounted for more than half of the revenues and audiences in their media markets. He warned that the decisions about most media content at the time were in the hands of 50 CEOs. Less than a decade later, Bagdikian (1992) reported that the number of companies that accounted for more than half of the media revenues and audiences had shrunk to 23, with 11 companies controlling most of the daily newspaper circulation, two companies controlling most of magazine revenues, five firms controlling more than half of all book sales, five media conglomerates sharing 95% of the recordings market, eight Hollywood studios accounting for 89% of U.S. feature film rentals, and the three television networks earning more than two thirds of the total U.S. television revenues (Bagdikian, 1992). By

Andres Burton/Getty Images

Of the big 5 media conglomerates, Warner and CBS control over 50% of the recordings market.

TIMELINE ISSUE 1.1
Media Mega-Mergers and Acquisitions

1985

1986: Capital Cities Communications, Inc. purchases American Broadcasting Company for $3.5 billion to create Capital Cities/ABC, Inc.

1986: General Electric Co. buys RCA Corp., parent company of National Broadcasting Co. and the NBC television network, for $6.4 billion. At the time, the deal was the largest non-oil acquisition in U.S. history. In the same year, Capital Cities bought ABC.

1989: Sony Corp. buys film and television producer Columbia Pictures Entertainment, Inc. for $3.4 billion.

1990: Warner Communications, Inc. and Time, Inc. complete a $14.1 billion merger, creating the world's biggest media conglomerate at the time.

1990

1991: Matsushita Electric Industrial Co. of Japan buys MCA, Inc. for $6.9 billion.

1993: The New York Times Co. buys Affiliated Publications, Inc., parent company of *The Boston Globe*, for $1.1 billion, the biggest takeover in U.S. newspaper history.

1994: Viacom, Inc. buys Paramount Communications, Inc. for $10 billion after winning a bidding war against QVC, Inc. to buy the movie, publishing, and sports company.

1994: Viacom, Inc. buys video rental chain Blockbuster Entertainment Corp. for $8 billion.

1995: Walt Disney Co. acquires Capital Cities/ABC, Inc. for $19 billion, making it the largest media company at the time.

1995: Westinghouse Electric Corp. buys CBS, Inc. for $5.4 billion, giving the new company 15 TV stations and 39 radio stations that, combined, provided it direct access to one third of the nation's households.

1996: Time Warner and Turner Broadcasting System complete a $7.6 billion merger. This becomes the world's biggest media company, with annual revenues of more than $20 billion.

1995

1996: Penguin Group, the international publisher, buys Putnam Berkley Group, a U.S. subsidiary of MCA (owned by Seagram Co.) for $336 million. Penguin is strong with backlist books (Arthur Miller, Gabriel García Márquez, Toni Morrison, E.L. Doctorow, Joyce Carol Oates), and Putnam has a strong front list (Stephen King, Terry McMillan, Tom Clancy, Patricia Cornwell).

1997: A merger of two radio companies creates Chancellor Media Corp., which took control over 103 radio stations that generate more than $700 million annually in revenue. The top-ranked radio group is Infinity Broadcasting ($1.1 billion in revenue annually), which is owned by Westinghouse Electric Corp.

1998: Compaq Computer Corp. buys Digital Equipment Corp. for $9.6 billion. This made Compaq one of the three largest computer companies in the world in terms of sales. This was the biggest buyout in the history of the computer industry to that point.

1999: Viacom announces a merger with CBS Television Network for $38 billion, making it the biggest deal between any two media companies. The merger combines film, television, radio, Internet sites, book publishing, and many other businesses.

1999: Clear Channel Communications, Inc. agrees to buy AMFM, Inc. for $16.6 billion in stock, creating the nation's largest radio company.

2000

2000: America Online, Inc. agrees to buy Time Warner, Inc. in a $164 billion merger agreement, the largest ever combination in the media industry.

2000: Time Warner, Inc. (record labels of Atlantic, Elektra, and Warner Brothers) and Britain's EMI Group (record labels of Virgin, Priority, and Capitol) agreed to merge their music businesses, thus creating the world's biggest music company, with combined annual revenues of $8 billion. The new firm would represent 2,500 musicians.

2005

2005: Paramount Pictures agrees to buy independent film studio DreamWorks SKG Inc. for $1.6 billion. The agreement does not include DreamWorks Animation SKG Inc.

2006: Walt Disney announces that it will buy Pixar, the successful animation studio majority owned by Apple's Steve Jobs, for $7.4 billion.

2006: Vivendi's Universal Music agrees to acquire BMG Music Publishing in a $2 billion deal. The acquisition makes Universal's music publishing holdings the largest in the world.

2006: Google, the Internet's leading search engine, announces that it is buying popular online video site YouTube for $1.65 billion.

2007: Google buys DoubleClick, Inc. for $3.1 billion, thus creating the largest repository of details about people's behavior online.

2007: NBCUniversal pays $925 million to buy cable network Oxygen, which was started by Oprah Winfrey and others in 1998.

2009: Walt Disney acquires Marvel Comics for $4 billion.

2010

2011: Comcast buys controlling interest (51%) in NBCUniversal for $30 billion.

2011: AT&T bids $39 billion to buy T-Mobile from Germany's Deutsche Telekom, thus adding 34 million customers to its existing base of 96 million and making it even larger than Verizon Wireless.

2011: Microsoft buys Skype (developed software that allows users to make voice and video calls over the Internet) for $8.5 billion.

2011: The Federal Communications Commission approves Comcast's takeover of a majority share of NBCUniversal from General Electric.

2013: A. C. Nielsen (the standard for TV ratings) acquires Arbitron (the standard for radio ratings).

2014: AT&T buys Direct TV for $67 billion.

2015

2016: Charter buys Time Warner Cable and Bright House for $65.5 to create the nation's second largest cable operator.

2018: The $85 billion merger between AT&T and Time Warner is approved. Time Warner is now WarnerMedia.

2020

Sources: Compiled from AP Online (2000), BtoBonline (2013), Chmielewski and Fritz (2009), Common Cause (n.d.), Fabrikant (1995), Greimel (2000), Hayes (2017), Hofmeister (1997a, 1997b), Holstein (1999), Lorimer (1994), Lyall (1996), McDonald (2000), and Menn (2007).

2004, when Bagdikian published the seventh update of his analysis, he claimed that the number of companies that generated most of the mass media revenue in the United States had shrunk to five.

During the 1980s, there were 2,308 mergers and acquisitions involving media companies for a total of $214 billion (Ozanich & Wirth, 1993). This merger activity increased during the 1990s, and has continued ever since (see Timeline Issue 1.1). This trend toward consolidation of resources in the media industries has given the CEOs of these newer, larger companies a greater concentration of power as they manage their increasing resources.

Media companies keep getting bought, merged, and reorganized, which makes it challenging to keep track of all this activity. For example, Westinghouse Electric Corporation began as a manufacturer of railroad air brakes in Pittsburgh in 1886. After about a century as a manufacturer of durable goods, it decided to expand its business and started buying other companies. In 1995, Westinghouse Electric Corporation bought one of the major television networks (CBS) for $5.4 billion, then spent another $9 billion buying cable channels and radio stations over the next 2 years. In 1997, it moved its headquarters to New York City and took the name CBS ("CBS Headquarters," 1997). Then CBS was acquired by Viacom, which was an established media conglomerate that had been founded by Sumner Redstone in 1971. In 2006, Redstone decided to separate CBS from Viacom. CBS Corporation was given Viacom's "slow-growth businesses"—namely, CBS, CBS Radio, Simon & Schuster, CBS Outdoor, Showtime, CBS Records, CBS Television Studios, and most television production assets. The new Viacom kept the high-growth businesses (MTV Networks and BET Networks, in particular) so it could generate sufficient revenue to allow for future acquisitions and expansion. In order to control both companies, Redstone created a company called National Amusements, which was an umbrella for both Viacom and CBS along with many other companies as they were acquired over the next decade. Many of the companies under the National Amusements umbrella are wholly owned by that company but others are partially owned or operate under close partnership agreements, so this structure is complex; however, what is clear is that Sumner Redstone is the CEO of National Amusements and he exercises considerable control over all the companies under his umbrella conglomerate (see Table Issue 1.1).

Merger activity shows no signs of slowing down; to the contrary, it appears to be increasing. The number of mergers among media-related companies more than doubled from 2011 to 2012, with over 1,350 mergers with a total value of almost $75 billion. However, 90% of these mergers were considered relatively small—that is, less than $50 million (BtoBonline, 2013). While relatively small mergers continue each year, there have also been some mega-mergers among media companies. In 2016, AT&T made a bid to acquire Time Warner, and the $85 billion merger was approved in June 2018. In the same month, the Department of Justice approved Disney's $52.4 billion merger with 21st Century Fox (Johnson, 2018).

Even newer media companies are becoming more powerful through mergers and acquisitions. For example, Facebook, which was founded in February 2004, began buying tech companies in 2005 and by the summer of 2018 had already spent over $23.1 billion in buying a total of 66 companies (Toth, 2018). The most notable of these acquisitions were the facial recognition platform Face.com ($100 million), the video advertising platform LiveRail ($500 million), the photo sharing app Instagram ($1 billion), the

TABLE ISSUE 1.1 ■ Most Powerful Media Companies Operating in the United States

Comcast ($84.5 billion annual revenue)

Founded in 1963; home office in Philadelphia, Pennsylvania; 139,000 employees

- Cable—largest broadcasting and cable company in the world; serves 23.6 million cable customers, and has 18 million digital cable subscribers; SportsNet, E! Networks, and the Golf Channel
- New Media—high-speed Internet access; serves 15.9 million high-speed Internet customers and 7.6 million voice customers. Comcast recently entered into a partnership with Verizon in which each company will market and sell the other's services.
- Sports—Philadelphia 76ers (basketball) and Philadelphia Flyers (hockey)
- NBC Universal—Comcast owns controlling interest at 51%; GE owns the other 49%
  - Television—NBC television network and 24 broadcast stations in major markets
  - Cable—40 cable TV stations, including MSNBC, CNBC, Bravo, USA Network, and SyFy
  - Film—Universal Studios
  - Internet—Hulu, Fandango, and others
  - Telemundo—16 Spanish-speaking broadcast stations in major markets
  - Other—Universal Theme Parks and Resorts
- Bought Time Warner in 2015 for $45 billion.
  - Broadcast Television—CW Network and Kids' WB!
  - Cable—Time Warner Cable (11 million subscribers); pay cable channels (HBO and Cinemax); nine local news cable channels; Turner Broadcasting System (CNN, Headline News, TBS, TNT, Turner Classic Movies, and The Cartoon Network)
  - Film—TV production and film production (Warner Brothers Pictures, New Line Cinema, Fine Line Features, New Line International, New Line Television, Castle Rock Entertainment, and Telepictures Productions); library of more than 6,000 films, 25,000 TV programs, and thousands of animated shows (such as Looney Tunes and Hanna-Barbera); Warner Brothers International Cinemas (123 screens in the United States and 650 screens in other countries)
  - Recordings—Warner Brothers Music Group, Atlantic, Elektra, and numerous smaller labels
  - Magazines—largest publisher of magazines in the United States, with over 140 magazines reaching more than 300 million people worldwide, including *Time, Life, People, Fortune, Money, Mad Magazine, Sports Illustrated, Entertainment Weekly, In Style, Sunset, Parenting, Southern Living,* and *Teen People*
  - Newspapers—seven dailies
  - Books—Little, Brown; Book of the Month Club; DC Comics (Superman, Batman, *Mad Magazine*, and 60 other titles)
  - Sports—Atlanta Braves (baseball), Atlanta Hawks (basketball), and Atlanta Thrashers (hockey)
  - Other—Warner Brothers Studio Stores (more than 150 worldwide); MovieFone

Sony ($70.2 billion annual revenue)

Founded in 1946; home office in Tokyo, Japan; 128,400 employees including nonmedia people

- Television—Columbia TriStar Television, HBO, and Cinemax
- Film—Sony Pictures Entertainment, Columbia TriStar Motion Picture Group, Columbia TriStar Home Video, and Columbia TriStar Television Group (*Spider-Man, Men in Black*)
- Recordings—owns more than 50 recording labels, including Sony Music Entertainment, CBS Records, Columbia Records, Epic, Legacy, TriStar Music, and RCA Records
- New Media—Sony PlayStation video games
- Other—Sony Electronics and Sony Ericsson Mobile Communications

(Continued)

TABLE ISSUE 1.1   ■   (Continued)

The Walt Disney Company ($55.3 billion annual revenue)

Founded in 1923 by Walt Disney; home office in Burbank, California; 180,000 employees

- Film—Walt Disney Studios, Touchstone Films, Miramax Films, Hollywood Pictures, Buena Vista Filmed Entertainment, Walt Disney Feature Animation, Buena Vista International, Pixar, and a partnership with Dreamworks
- Broadcast Television—10 TV stations; ABC Television Network
- Cable—ESPN, Fox Family, Toon Disney, and Disney Channel; also has holdings in Lifetime, A&E, History Channel, and Biography
- Radio—277 radio stations; ABC Radio Network
- Magazines—*Discover, Los Angeles Magazine*
- Books—Hachette Books (formerly Hyperion), ESPN Books, and Disney Publishing Worldwide
- Recordings—Walt Disney Records, Buena Vista Records, Hollywood Records, Mammoth Records, Lyric Street Records, and Wonderland Music Company
- Sports—Anaheim Angels (baseball) and Mighty Ducks of Anaheim (hockey)
- Other—11 theme parks; Marvel Comics (5,000 characters, including Spider-Man, X-Men, Iron Man, Hulk, and Fantastic Four); consumer products; The Disney Store; cruise line; petroleum and natural gas production interests

National Amusements ($26.9 billion)

Sumner Redstone founded Viacom in 1971, then after much merger activity spun off CBS Corporation into its own company in 2006; now Viacom and CBS Corporation, along with many other companies, are controlled by Redstone under the umbrella of National Amusements; home office in New York City; 925,920 employees

- Broadcast Television—CBS and UPN television networks; Paramount Television Studio (*JAG, Entertainment Tonight*), Spelling Television, and King World Productions (*Jeopardy, Wheel of Fortune*); Viacom Stations Group (39 TV stations)
- Cable—controls over 160 cable networks all over the world, including Comedy Central, Nickelodeon, MTV, VH1, TV Land, TNN (now Spike TV), CMT (Country Music Television), Showtime, and BET (Black Entertainment Television)
- Radio—Entercom and Infinity Broadcasting chain of 183 radio stations; CBS radio network; Westwood One; Metro Networks
- Books—Simon & Schuster, Scribner, Pocket Books, Anne Schwartz Books, Archway Paperbacks, Lisa Drew Books, Fireside, Free Press, MTV Books, Nickelodeon Books, Pocket Books, Star Trek Books, and Washington Square Press
- Film Production—Paramount Pictures (including a library of more than 2,500 titles), Nickelodeon Movies, MTV Films, Nickelodeon Studios, United International Pictures (33%), Spelling Films, Republic Entertainment, Worldvisions Enterprises
- Film Theaters—Paramount Theaters, Famous Players Theaters (1,700 screens in 13 countries), United Cinemas International
- Recordings—Famous Music (copyright holders of more than 100,000 songs)
- New Media—MTV Networks On Line, MarketWatch.com, CBS.com, CBSSportsLine.com, CBSMarketWatch.com, and Country.com
- Other—five amusement parks; TDI Worldwide and Outdoor Systems, which sell ad space on 210,000 billboards nationwide; *Star Trek* franchise

News Corporation ($8.1 billion annual revenue)

Founded in 1979; home office in New York City; 64,000 employees

- Broadcast Television—Fox Network; 27 stations in the United States plus many broadcast stations around the world
- Film—20th Century Fox, Fox 2000, Fox Studios, Fox Searchlight, and Fox Animation Studios Studio
- Radio—Fox Sports Radio Network
- Cable—FX Network, Fox Sports Net, Fox News Channel, Golf Channel, and National Geographic
- Magazines—several dozen magazines, mostly published in Australia
- Newspapers—175 newspapers internationally, including the *Wall Street Journal* and *New York Post*
- Books—HarperCollins, William Morris Books, Avon Books, and Regan Books
- Internet—owns AmericanIdol.com, AskMen, Fox.com, and other sites
- New Media—DirectTV, Sky Network TV

Sports—part owner of the Colorado Rockies (baseball) and the Staples Center

---

Sources: Compiled from Albarran (2002); Baker, Falk, and Manners (2000); Bettig and Hall (2003); CBS Corporation (n.d.); Chmielewski & Fritz (2009); Comcast. (n.d.); Croteau and Hoynes (2001); Flanigan (2003); Free Press (2012); NBCUniversal (n.d.); News Corporation (n.d.); Polman (2003); Sony Corporation (n.d.); The Walt Disney Company (n.d.); Time Warner (n.d.); Verrier and James (2003); Viacom (n.d.); and Yahoo Finance (2018).

virtual reality startup Oculus Rift ($2 billion), and the mobile instant messaging service WhatsApp ($19 billion).

Factors Driving the Trend

There are two salient factors that can be seen as responsible for the trend toward more concentration of ownership of media businesses. They are the factors of efficiencies and deregulation.

Efficiencies

Larger companies are able to operate more efficiently than smaller companies because of economies of scope and scale (recall these ideas from Chapter 7). They achieve these efficiencies through three types of mergers and acquisitions. First, there is the **horizontal merger**. This is when one media company buys another media company of the same type. An example is a newspaper chain buying another newspaper. This pattern was very popular during the 1980s, when newspapers were being gobbled up by chains at the rate of 50 to 60 per year. Thus newspaper chains share in the costs of covering national and international news over many newspapers. Also, when they buy materials (such as paper and ink) in very large quantities they can demand a lower wholesale price.

Second, there is the **vertical merger**. This is when one media company buys suppliers and/or distributors to create integration in the production and distribution of messages. An example is a book publisher buying a paper supply company (to help with production) and some bookstores (to help with distribution). Another example is Viacom, which owned television stations in Philadelphia, Boston, Dallas, Detroit, Pittsburgh, and

Miami. It added significant vertical integration through its ownership of Paramount Pictures, thus allowing Viacom to control the production and distribution of television programs to the television networks (CBS or UPN) and through the Blockbuster stores that it also owned at the time. In addition, it could promote those shows' soundtracks on MTV and VH1 and do book tie-ins through Simon & Schuster—all of which were also owned by Viacom.

Third, there is the **conglomerate merger**. This is when a media company buys a combination of other media companies and/or companies in a nonmedia business. An example is a film studio that buys a newspaper, several radio stations, a talent agency, and a string of restaurants. Conglomerates can better survive hard times when one sector of the economy is bad because they own businesses in other sectors that are likely to be doing well at that time. Therefore conglomerates can spread their resources around among all their businesses to help those businesses that happen to be struggling at any given time.

Federal Communication Chairman Tom Wheeler delivers opening remarks at the start of the Open Internet roundtable discussion, September 2014.

Regulation and Deregulation

In the early 1900s, the federal government became concerned over the degree of concentration in particular American industries. The government began monitoring the degree of concentration in American industries and forced very large companies (such as Standard Oil, American Tobacco, and AT&T) to split up when they had become too large and were becoming monopolies.

Within the mass media industries, the federal government instituted policies to try to encourage diversity of ownership and prevent monopolies. For example, when the radio industry was forming in the 1920s, the federal government became involved in controlling who was awarded a radio broadcasting license. Radio was different from all the other media industries at the time because radio required the use of the electromagnetic spectrum to send out (broadcast) its wireless signal. While an unlimited number of newspapers, magazines, and film theaters could exist in a given location, the same was not possible for radio. If you want to broadcast a radio or television signal, you must send your signal out on a frequency. If you and I wanted to use the same frequency to broadcast our different signals, then our signals would interfere with each other, and radio listeners would receive a garbled signal. Because there were only a limited number of frequencies made available for radio broadcasting on something called the **electromagnetic spectrum**, someone had to decide who got to use which frequencies. The federal government decided that it was the one to make the assignment of radio broadcasting frequencies, reasoning that the electromagnetic spectrum belonged to all Americans much like a national park or any other resource that should be shared by all citizens.

In the early days of radio broadcasting, the federal government decided to require individuals to apply for a broadcast frequency with the **Federal Communications Commission (FCC)**. The FCC was immediately flooded with applications for AM radio frequencies. But the AM band on the electromagnetic spectrum allowed for only about 117 broadcast frequencies. The FCC could have chosen 117 applicants and awarded each of them their own frequency. This would have led to 117 AM radio stations, with each using their frequency to broadcast their signal to the entire country. But that is not what the FCC did. Instead, the FCC divided the country into many local market areas and awarded some frequencies to each market. Also, each radio station was limited in the amount of power it could use to broadcast its signal so that the signals would not go beyond their local markets. This allowed the FCC to assign the same frequency to many different markets without having to worry about signals interfering with one another. The FCC chose this alternative because it wanted to spread the limited resource of broadcast frequencies around to as many different people as possible.

By keeping ownership of radio licenses at the local level, the FCC believed it was setting up a system whereby the stations would be operated in the best interests of their local communities. Private businesses were allowed to broadcast on these frequencies, provided they operate "in the public interest, convenience, and necessity." The federal government was able to regulate radio because of spectrum scarcity.

When television came along in the 1940s, the FCC used the same procedure of allocating broadcasting licenses to TV local stations in the 215 local markets across the United States. Now we have more than 6,800 broadcast television stations and 13,000 radio stations.

When the government felt that a media industry was too concentrated, it took steps to force those companies to sell off some of their vertically integrated businesses. For example, in the 1940s, the government felt the film industry was too concentrated, with a small number of film studios controlling film production, distribution, and exhibition. Under this pressure, the film studios sold off their theaters, which removed them from the exhibition sector, thus allowing theaters to compete for films. Another example is AT&T, which made electronic components, produced telecommunication equipment, and sold phone service, so the federal government in the 1970s began taking steps to break up the company to allow for more competition (Samuelson, 2006).

Then in the 1980s, the federal government began deregulating all industries, including the media industries. Up until the 1980s, the FCC had been preventing broadcasting monopolies from developing by limiting the number of stations any one company could own to seven AM, seven FM, and seven TV stations in total, with no two being in the same market. In the 1980s, the rules were relaxed to 12 AM, 12 FM, and 12 TV stations. Then the Telecommunications Act of 1996 further relaxed the limits to a significant extent in the guise of opening up competition. Also, the ban was lifted prohibiting a company from owning a TV and radio station in the same market. This deregulation triggered many mergers among media companies. During the 1990s, there was more than a total of $300 billion worth of major media deals in which companies bought multiple television and radio stations (Croteau & Hoynes, 2001). Since that time, the FCC has periodically held public hearings and continued to move in the direction of allowing more concentration of ownership. Now a single company can own as many television stations as it wants as long at the coverage of that set of stations does not exceed 39.5% of viewers; it can also own more than one television station in a TV market. As for radio, a company can own as many stations as it wants, including three to eight stations within a single radio market depending on the size of that market. Now one company (Clear Channel) owns more than 200 radio stations in the United States without violating the current "restrictions" on ownership.

Over time, broadcasters have chipped away at these regulations. Broadcasters have argued successfully that they were being unfairly limited in their rights to own multiple businesses. They pointed out that there were no ownership limits for magazines, book publishers, newspapers, and Internet sites; also, the previous limits on film studios had been relaxed. Consumer groups, who argued against relaxing the ownership rules, could present no convincing evidence that multiple ownership of broadcasting businesses caused harm to the public. In contrast, broadcasters showed that when businesses are consolidated, they are more efficient and that this efficiency benefits consumers.

Cable operators have also been fighting to have limits relaxed so that they can expand. In 2009, the FCC had limited cable systems from servicing more than 30% of the U.S. population. Comcast, the nation's largest cable company at the time with almost 25% of the nation's cable homes as subscribers, sued the FCC to raise their limit and won in a federal court of appeals, which reasoned that the restriction must be lifted to reflect the changing realities of the dynamic video marketplace where consumers have lots of alternatives to cable and therefore cable should not be regarded as a monopoly (Flint, 2009).

In recent decades, the trend to consolidation has grown stronger than the government's impulse to regulate. For example, in 1996, Congress passed the Telecommunications Act and largely removed the last remaining limitations to consolidation. In that year alone, there was $25 billion in merger activity in the broadcasting industry and another $23 billion in the cable industry (Jensen, 1997). Since 1996, the FCC has been less concerned with preventing monopolies within the United States and more concerned with allowing American companies to grow significantly stronger to compete and dominate in the world market (Albarran & Chan-Olmsted, 1998). Former FCC Chairman William Kennard said that he was merely recognizing the realities of globalization and new technologies.

One feature of the 1996 deregulation eliminated the longstanding restriction of allowing one company to own two television stations in the same market. It had long been believed that broadcast television stations were far too precious a local resource to allow one company to own more than one in a given television market. Almost all local markets had very few broadcast stations (typically three to five broadcast television stations), so it was important to have as many owners as possible to ensure a diversity of voices within that small number of stations in a market. However, over time, as greater numbers of people subscribed to cable television services, regulators came to believe that people in all local communities had access to many different voices, and therefore the limits on broadcast station ownership were no longer important.

All industries in the United States have been moving toward greater concentration. The key indicator that is used to measure this degree of concentration is the percentage of revenue in the industry that is generated by only the top four firms (CR4). Across all industries in the United States, the top four firms averaged 23% of revenue in 1997 and this increased 32% by 2012. Among all industries in the United States, the media industry has the highest degree of concentration. In 1997, the top four firms in the media industry generated 45% of the industry's total revenue and that increased to 53% by 2012. When we get inside the media industry, we can see that the most concentrated part is recordings—the top four firms in 2001 generated 98% of all revenue from recordings (see Table Issue 1.2). Even in the book industry, which is fairly unconcentrated relative to the other media industries, the top eight companies account for half of all book revenue. Furthermore, the figures in Table Issue 1.2, which reveal a high degree of concentration, are likely to underestimate the degree of concentration in the media industries because they do not take into consideration cross-ownership patterns; that is, they do not account for a firm owning and controlling revenue in several mass media industries at once. To see how much cross-ownership there is, look at what the top media conglomerates each control (see Table Issue 1.1).

EVIDENCE FOR HARM

The criticism about concentration of media ownership requires the critics to present evidence of harm. While there is ample evidence for the trend toward concentration, there is less evidence that this concentration results in harm. Let's examine those arguments for harm in four areas: increased barriers to entry, reduced level of competition, reduced number of public voices, and changes in content.

TABLE ISSUE 1.2 ■ Indicators of Concentration in Segments of the Mass Media		
CR4	**CR8**	**Mass Medium**
98	99	Recording industry
78	99	Motion pictures
77	91	Magazine
77	88	Radio
53	80	Cable and satellite television
48	69	Daily newspapers
30	50	Books
N/A	N/A	Broadcast television stations
N/A	N/A	Internet

CR4 = concentration ratio of the top four firms: percent of total revenues of the major four players in the industry; CR8 = concentration ratio of the top eight firms: percent of total revenues of the major eight players in the industry; N/A, not applicable.

Source: Compiled from Albarran (2002).

Increased Barriers to Entry

Has the trend toward concentration increased the barriers to entry so that an individual can no longer create a media business? The answer to this question depends on the media business. The barriers to entry into the radio and television broadcasting businesses have always been very high. But the barriers to entry into the newspaper, magazine, book publishing, recording, and Internet businesses have been low, and there is no evidence that concentration of ownership has increased the barriers to enter these markets.

It is also important to remember that during the last 3 decades when the trend toward concentration of ownership of media businesses has been so strong, there has also been the rise of the Internet, which has enabled all kinds of people to create their own newspapers and magazines in the form of blogs. It is now far easier to produce videos and attract an audience for them on platforms such as YouTube. Aspiring recording artists and book authors have much more opportunity to make their messages available without having to get signed to a recording studio or book publisher. And the companies that make the platforms to share all kinds of media messages are all relatively new and have become very prosperous (e.g., Amazon, Apple, Google, Facebook, YouTube, etc.). Meanwhile the traditional media companies find that their newspaper, magazine, radio, and broadcast TV businesses are struggling to adapt to the new media environment due to competition from new companies that offer better messages at lower—and sometimes free—cost to consumers.

Reduced Level of Competition

Although there is a clear trend toward concentration of ownership, this by itself has not eliminated competition. The big conglomerates still compete against one another and now they have to compete against many new Internet companies.

There is little evidence of vertical integration among companies providing computer services and hardware. "The computer industry is hugely splintered. Some firms sell components (Intel, AMD); some, software (Microsoft, SAP); some, services (IBM, EDS); some, hardware (Dell, Apple). There's overlap, but not much" (Samuelson, 2006, p. 45). Also, the Internet is dominated by newer companies such as Google, Facebook, and eBay, not the older established companies. While these newer Internet companies have already been engaged in a good deal of merger activity, they have not been buying traditional media companies.

Reduced Number of Public Voices

Critics argue that as concentration increases, the individual's access to the media is reduced. Access in this sense means the ability to get your particular point of view heard through someone else's media property. This is still relatively easy to do at the local level, such as with newspapers and small-circulation magazines. Most still print letters to the editors, and most buy articles from people with little journalistic experience. Also, most markets have call-in radio programs where you can get your voice heard. In contrast, national media properties, such as *Time* magazine or a TV or cable network, require a great deal of skill and good connections to get your voice heard because the competition to use those channels is so strong.

Many critics argue that the media industries lose diversity of voices when the industries become more concentrated. Fewer voices should mean fewer opinions getting aired. However, Einstein (2004) points out that "in study after study, scholars have determined that there is no proven causality between media ownership and programming content" (p. vii). Einstein argues that the reduction in the number of program choices is not due to consolidation but to television's reliance on advertising as its primary source of revenue. Because of this reliance, there are severe limits on content, which include time limits for program length, the "lowest common denominator" mentality, and an avoidance of controversy. In an analysis of the TV industry over the past 4 decades, Einstein reveals that as the industry became more concentrated, programming became more diverse. She said that diversity was at its peak in the late 1960s and then declined when the FCC imposed regulations about sharing programs through syndication. Then, when those syndication rules were relaxed and broadcasters could keep the programs they produced to themselves, diversity increased sharply.

Social media platforms allow users to express their opinions. Singer Katy Perry has over 109 million followers on Twitter.

MICHAEL CAMPANELLA/Redferns/Getty Images

The claim that the number of voices heard in the media has been narrowing due to the trend in concentration of ownership of the mass media businesses appears completely wrong when we consider the Internet. Platforms like Twitter have given absolutely everyone a voice. Anyone can now express any opinion at any time. Celebrities like Katy Perry have 109.5 million followers on Twitter (Statista, 2018j). Compare this to the highest-rated TV show, which has 18.6 million viewers, and *USA Today*, which is the largest circulation newspaper with 2.3 million readers.

Changes in Content

Critics argue that as competition among media companies decreases, the content of messages changes in a negative way. They claim that as companies grow larger, their content decreases in quality and that the messages are more likely to harm the public.

Has the quality of the media products declined? There is no evidence that it has. For example, research has not found that when a radio station is bought by a conglomerate the content degrades. Lacy and Riffe (1994) looked at the news content of radio stations and compared group ownership effects. They found that group ownership had no impact on the financial commitment or the local and staff emphasis of news coverage. Also, a study done on newspaper content could find no change in content after a newspaper was bought by a chain (e.g., see Picard, Winter, McCombs, & Lacy, 1988). No evidence of change was found with the stories, the range of opinions on the editorial page, or the proportion of the newspaper displaying news. Crider (2012) conducted a content analysis of news stories on radio station websites to determine the amount of local news, which was covered by journalists at the local stations, and syndicated content, which was imported from other news agencies. While it was found that local programming was less prevalent on smaller-market stations, there was no relationship between large corporate ownership and diminished local programming.

Has the trend toward concentration of ownership led to an increase in harmful content? This has not yet been tested directly but there is indirect evidence that concentration of ownership in the radio industry is associated with an increase in negative speech and obscenity. One research study found that as big broadcasters buy more radio stations, shock-jock programming often replaces local content. From 2000 to 2003, the nation's four largest radio companies racked up 96% of the fines handed out by the FCC, although their stations accounted for only about half the country's listening audience (Hofmeister, 2005).

YOUR OWN INFORMED OPINION

This is an issue about which you likely have some sort of an opinion. But to construct an informed opinion, you need to build it up from a deeper analysis of the situation. In this section, I lay out some steps for constructing an informed opinion on this topic. We begin by expanding your perspective on ownership then use this perspective to gather more evidence and re-examine previous evidence for harm. Next, we confront the idea that your opinion may be based on fundamental values.

Expanding Perspective

As you have seen above, the criticism of media ownership links ownership with control but this linkage is faulty as you will see in this analysis of ownership. If the big media conglomerates were each owned by one individual, then ownership and control would be the same thing. But this is not the case. While the media conglomerates own many media businesses, the media conglomerates themselves have a diversity of ownership; that is, none of these conglomerates is owned by one person or even a small number of powerful people. All of these large conglomerates are owned by millions of people—these are the shareholders of these publically traded companies. For example, the ownership of Disney is spread out over 1.5 billion shares of stock that are openly traded on the New York Stock Exchange. Only 35% of these shares are owned by individuals; the other 65% of shares are owned by institutions such retirement funds, governments, insurance companies, and mutual funds, which are themselves owned by millions of people. There are 2,663 of these institutions that own shares of Disney and none of these institutions owns as much as 7% of the company. As for individuals, Robert Iger, president of Disney, owns about 1.2 million shares, which is 00.08% of the company; thus if he were to increase his number of shares by 12 times, he still would not own as much as 1% of the company (Maverick, 2018).

While ownership gives you some control over a company, the ownership stake of each individual and each entity is so small that it is foolhardy to equate ownership with control. No single person or entity owns very much of any of these large media conglomerates. Stockholders get to vote for members of the company's board of directors, who in turn get to appoint the people who manage the company and make the business decisions. The power for controlling a company is much more concentrated in the managers than in the individual shareholders. But even among a company's top managers, their power is dispersed across their large staffs of advisers, analysts, as well as their subordinate managers who make the day-to-day decisions required to run the individual media businesses and departments. Thus the power to control the company is spread out over hundreds of individuals who are much less concerned with limiting voices or a range of media messages than they are with generating revenue. Managers have an economic responsibility to increase the wealth of the millions of owners of the company, and this requires them to increase profits so this money can be passed along to the owners either in the form of dividends on their shares of stock or by reinvesting in the company so that the value of the shares increases. Who benefits from the increasing profits? The answer is that millions of shareholders do, as well as millions of other people who depend on retirement benefits, insurance benefits, and services from governments.

Re-examining Evidence

Now that you have this expanded perspective on media ownership and who benefits from conglomeration, let's re-examine the evidence of harm. Applying Media Literacy Skills Issue 1.1 directs you to look again at the evidence for harm laid out previously in this chapter. But now think of harm not in terms of a general population but in terms of a very large part of the population that owns these companies.

Next, look carefully at your local market. Work through Applying Your Media Literacy Skills 1.2 to make a judgment about the degree of concentration in your local market. First gather information by seeing what you can find on the websites of the companies who operate media businesses in your local area. The website should provide you with enough information to get started but you will likely have to develop a search strategy to move beyond these websites to get good answers to all the questions in the exercise. After you have gathered this information, look for patterns across the media business.

Thinking About Underlying Values

When we dig deep into this issue of concentration of ownership of media businesses and get down to the bedrock, we can see that the debate rests on people's fundamental values, especially the values of localism and efficiency. Localism is the belief that society is better when power is spread out among as many people as possible and when governments preserve the differences across individuals and protect forums of information so that all voices can be heard. In contrast, efficiency is the belief that the economy works better when all resources are used most effectively and thus requires the elimination of waste from unnecessary duplication.

Both of these values are very American. They can be seen clashing in the way the founding fathers of this country wrote the Constitution. They can also be seen clashing in the way the government has viewed mass media businesses. And they can be seen clashing in our everyday lives. At times, we as consumers favor localism when we want a marketplace with as many voices as possible so we have lots of choices about how to satisfy our various needs for information and entertainment. But at other times, we favor concentration when we want a marketplace with easily available standard products for as low a price as possible.

Localism

Localism is a populist value. It is exhibited by the belief that control of important institutions should be spread out as much as possible so that many people share the power. Thus a considerable amount of power should exist at the local level, which is closest to individuals. It is based on the ideal that each person is a rational being, so each person should have an equal say in the political and economic arenas. This maximizes the freedom of each person. It also empowers all people by keeping them involved in as many important decisions as possible.

Localism is a part of the American tradition. The founding fathers of the United States followed this value when creating a democratic form of government rather than a more efficient totalitarian one (such as a monarchy) at the national level. They believed that the individual is more important than are institutions or governments. When government is necessary, it should be decentralized so as to be closer to the people's needs and more accountable to them, so they dispersed power by restricting the federal government from some areas and left decisions in these areas up to state and local governments. Thus, political power was structured so that it was spread out over many layers. America now has 18,000 municipalities and 17,000 townships. Within these, there are 500,000 local governmental units directly elected by local residents, and 170,000 of them have the power to impose taxes. Over time, the American public has retained its value for dispersion of power and has continued to support the overlapping, multilayered structure of government, even if it often seems inefficient.

Efficiency

Straining against this value of localism is a very strong trend toward concentration, consolidation, and centralization. Although almost every media company begins as a small, local operation, they take on the characteristics of big business as they grow. Big businesses are complex organizations that market many different products and services but do so under a strong centralized system to achieve a more efficient operation. Big businesses grow by claiming a larger share of the markets in which they compete. They accomplish this by acquiring control of more resources, and this often leads to buying—or at least investing in—other companies.

iStock/OJO_Images

As media conglomerates grow, fewer people exercise more control over more of the media.

General industry-wide trends show that fewer and fewer people control more and more of the media. And this trend will probably continue as the cost of buying and operating a media voice keeps going up and as entry into the industry becomes more difficult. Today, a person needs a great deal of money and expertise to attempt to buy a business in one of the established media industries. Because of this, only companies that already own media businesses are successful in acquiring new businesses. Entrepreneurs can still start a media business in the magazine, book publishing, and Internet industries, but those businesses begin as very small enterprises. Either those small companies go out of business quickly, or they grow successful and are usually bought by one of the big media **conglomerates**.

As media companies grow larger and more centralized, there is a danger that they will narrow the range of voices that will get heard. For example, if you send a letter to the editor of a newspaper with a circulation of 1,000, there is a good chance that your letter will get published. But if you send that same letter to a newspaper with a circulation of 1 million, your chance of being published is much smaller. Thus, the larger and more powerful the media company is, the less access you have for making a contribution to its messages or influencing the way it makes decisions. However, if your purpose is simply to get your voice heard, then you can contribute a comment to a blog or tweet it immediately. Although your posting may not be read by more than a handful of people, you have the power to keep posting in many different places; no media conglomerate is preventing you from creating your own audiences.

It is important for you to realize that there are two sides to this issue; that is, both sides have advantages and disadvantages. When you understand the arguments on each side of an issue, you are in a better position to create your own opinion in an informed manner.

Informing Your Opinion

By now you should have a better informed opinion about the ownership of the mass media businesses. However, this is an issue that is likely to keep changing as traditional media struggle to compete with newer media and as governments (both in the United States and around the world) struggle to figure out what the actual economic and social harms of concentration of ownership among conglomerates are and balance them against the benefits then decide whether to regulate or deregulate those conglomerates. This is a complex issue and one that is in constant change.

As you move into the future, try to keep an open mind and continually view the controversy from multiple points of view. Do not accept arguments on face value but demand credible evidence to support those arguments. Keep informing your opinion.

Further Reading

Bagdikian, B. H. (2004). *The new media monopoly*. Boston, MA: Beacon. (299 pages with endnotes and index)

Since 1983, Bagdikian has been conducting an economic analysis of the media industries to track the degree of concentration. With each new edition, the number of powerful companies shrinks as their media (as well as nonmedia) holdings dramatically grow. This book is a must-read for anyone concerned about how much power is being concentrated in the hands of a few CEOs of media holding companies.

Bettig, R. V., & Hall, J. L. (2003). *Big media, big money: Cultural texts and political economies*. Lanham, MD: Rowman & Littlefield. (181 pages with bibliography and references)

In this book, two professors at Penn State University argue that the media have been unfettered in their drive for greater profits and control over constructing meaning in our culture. They present a great deal of detail in support of this thesis in their six chapters. The authors demonstrate that the result of this media consolidation is that a few very powerful

(Continued)

(Continued)

companies are becoming even more invasive in our lives and are successfully supplanting family, friends, religion, and education as the controlling source of constructing meaning.

Downing, J. D. H. (2011). Media ownership, concentration, and control: The evolution of debate. In J. Wasko, G. Murdock, & H. Sousa (Eds.), *The handbook of political economy of communications* (pp. 140–168). Malden, MA: Wiley-Blackwell.

The author of this book chapter is an academic who does a good job of laying out the main arguments advanced over the years for the concern over growing concentration of ownership of the mass media. His tone is purely descriptive; that is, he avoids taking sides or making his own arguments about this controversy.

Einstein, M. (2004). *Media diversity: Economics, ownership, and the FCC.* Mahwah, NJ: Lawrence Erlbaum. (249 pages, including references, appendices, and indexes)

The author examines the issue of whether the consolidation in the media industries has led to a lessening of diversity. This book offers strong historical and economic perspectives on the issue. The author concludes that despite a clear consolidation of ownership of media properties and the narrowing in the number of people making decisions about media content, there is even more diversity in messages now than there was 4 decades ago.

Maney, K. (1995). *Megamedia shakeout: The inside story of the leaders and the losers in the exploding communications industry.* New York, NY: John Wiley. (358 pages, including index)

This is a well-written description of the major players in the technologies landscape in the mid-1990s. There are lots of anecdotes and stories about what has been happening in the telephone, cable, computer, wireless, and entertainment industries. The book is full of facts and personal descriptions of the personalities involved. However, things are happening so fast in these industries with new rollouts and buyouts that the book is likely out of date.

McChesney, R. W., Newman, R., & Scott, B. (Eds.) (2005). *The future of media: Resistance and reform in the 21st century.* New York, NY: Seven Stories Press. (376 pages with index)

This edited volume of 19 chapters plus an introduction was written by scholars who have been very concerned about the conglomeration of American media and the role of the FCC in not only allowing it to occur but in actually encouraging it. The authors document the increasing level of concentration in ownership of media properties by fewer and fewer companies and argue that this trend is harmful for consumers and citizens.

Keeping Up to Date

Columbia Journalism Review (http://www.cjr.org/resources/)

   This website allows you to check all the media holdings of many major conglomerates.

Vault.com (http://www.vault.com/wps/portal/usa)

This is a website that provides lots of useful information about various industries; particularly relevant to media literacy are the industries of publishing, newspapers, Internet and new media, music, broadcast and cable, advertising, and public relations.

APPLYING MEDIA LITERACY SKILLS ISSUE 1.1
CONFRONTING THE ISSUE OF CONCENTRATION OF MEDIA OWNERSHIP

1. Analysis: Digging deeper into the issue

   a. Can you think of additional reasons (beyond what was presented in this chapter) that add to the criticism for why the trend toward greater concentration of ownership is harmful? Can you find evidence to support these additional reasons?

   b. Can you think of additional reasons (beyond what was presented in this chapter) for why the trend toward greater concentration of ownership is something positive? Can you find evidence to support these additional reasons?

   c. Can you think of a bedrock value beyond localism or concentration that could be used as a perspective from which to view this issue?

2. Evaluation: Making judgments about the validity of the arguments

   a. Given the arguments presented in this chapter, which have the most valid evidence to support them?

   b. Which of the arguments have faulty support? For these, can you find strong evidence? Or should these arguments be rejected altogether?

3. Induction: Looking for patterns in the evidence

   a. Look for patterns (of support or faulty reasoning) across arguments.

   b. When you see a pattern, think about how you would continue to test it. What kinds of evidence would you need to see in order to increase your belief that those patterns really existed and were continuing into the future?

4. Synthesis: Constructing your informed opinion

   a. Which arguments of the defenders of the trend toward media ownership concentration are most valid and compelling?

   b. Which arguments of critics do you find the most valid and compelling?

   c. Can you think of a way to incorporate the arguments you identified in a and b into a single, well-integrated position that recognizes the value of both sides?

5. Abstracting: Expressing your position succinctly

In 200 words or less, can you express your informed opinion clearly and support it with compelling arguments?

APPLYING MEDIA LITERACY SKILLS ISSUE 1.2
ASSESSING THE CONCENTRATION OF MEDIA OWNERSHIP IN YOUR LOCAL MARKET

1. How many movie screens are there in your market?

   a. How many theaters control those screens?

   b. Are the theaters owned by chains? If so, how many chains control the total set of screens?

(Continued)

(Continued)

2. How many radio stations are there in your market?

    a. How many are group owned?

    b. How many of the stations are owned by companies that also own other media businesses in your market?

3. How many broadcast television stations are there in your market?

    a. How many are group owned?

    b. How many of the stations are owned by companies that also own other media businesses in your market?

4. Is your local newspaper owned by a chain? If so, does it own other media businesses in your market?

5. Are there any magazines published in your market and distributed only in your market? If so, does the controlling company also own other media businesses?

6. What is the name of the company that provides your market with cable TV service? Is that cable company a multiple system operator?

7. In total, how many different media outlets (voices) are there in your market? How many individuals or companies control these voices?

8. If you wanted to express yourself through the media in your market, how hard do you think it would be to gain access to one of these outlets?

    a. For example, assume that you wanted to criticize some new governmental regulation or tax policy in your local area. Which outlet would be most likely to give you space or time to speak out?

    b. Which outlet(s) do you think would be the hardest or impossible?

9. Given your answers to the questions above, how concentrated do you think your market is? Do you think it is more or less concentrated than the national market for mass media?

10. What are the harms to the local economy and society due to the degree of local concentration of media?

11. Given your answers to all the questions above, do you think the outlets in your local market are in the control of too few individuals?

TIMOTHY A. CLARY/AFP/Getty Images

SPORTS

Issue: The money cycle drives sports. Some people think the money cycle is destroying sports, while other people think that it is improving sports.

Sports are more than fun and games; they are also a big business in the United States, generating around $485 billion annually.

Sports have changed dramatically over the past 4 decades. The reason is money—big money. Globally, $1.3 trillion is spent annually on sports of all kinds (Plunkett Research, 2017) and this amount continues to increase each year—driven by the money cycle. This money cycle is especially influential in the United States, where sports revenue has climbed to $519 annually; this means that the United States, with less than 5% of the world's population, accounts for almost 40% of all the sports revenue generated globally.

DELINEATING THE ISSUE

The controversy concerning sports in the media is whether big money has ruined sports or whether it has made sports better. Like with the previous issue, the controversy in sports can be traced to people's values. Some people hold an egalitarian value where they cherish the similarities across all individuals and believe that everyone should be treated equally; they get upset when a few elites are treated massively better than the average person. In contrast, other people believe that there are enormous differences across individuals and that those who have an extreme degree of talent in some area should be rewarded massively. People with lesser talent need to appreciate the differences and admire those who perform at the top.

There is no ultimately correct position on this issue because there is no philosophical standard we can use to determine the worth of a person's talent or life. Instead, we let the economic marketplace tell us the value of talent. However, while markets are typically driven by the forces of supply and demand, there are times when irrational forces also drive markets, causing them to become inflated to a point where an irrational bubble of inflation bursts, thus setting off a market correction. The stock market has experienced many such bubbles and corrections, as has the economy in general. So at any given time, the market may be undervaluing or overvaluing particular resources.

With the issue of money in sports, your personal values are important. You must decide for yourself whether the money is now too much (i.e., the salaries of athletes are too high, the profits of team owners and leagues are too high, and the cost to the average fan is beyond affordability), or whether the money has made the games and the athletes better than ever. The key to being media literate is to get the facts and understand the arguments on both sides of this controversy. Then you can decide in an informed way which side makes more sense to you personally. In this chapter I will present some key facts to help you construct your informed opinion. First, I will show you how the money cycle is accelerating and how that acceleration is changing traditional sports. Then I will present two examples to illustrate the influence of the money cycle on the ancient sports of the Olympics as well as the creation of the newer sport of video gaming. The chapter concludes with some guidelines about how you can use this information to strengthen your skills of media literature and design a stronger knowledge structure on this topic.

THE MONEY CYCLE

The amount of time and money Americans spend playing, watching, and talking about sports increases each year. The key to making sense of these increases as well as the nature of sports today is to understand the **money cycle**. The mass media have been an integral part of making the money cycle possible. The media provide the means for advertisers to inject mammoth amounts of money into the cycle. Also, the media provide so much continual exposure for professional as well as college sporting events that millions of people have made sports an essential ritual in their lives. And the media have transformed hundreds of athletes into celebrities who can themselves command huge payments—for endorsing the products of commercial advertisers in addition to playing their games.

This money cycle has the following five components:

1. *Athletic talent* demands higher salaries plus bonuses each year. Because athletic talent is in short supply, talented athletes will find a team willing to pay a high salary and bonuses.

2. *Owners of teams* are willing to bid high for athletic talent so that they can field a competitive team that will attract fans to their games as well as fans to telecasts of their games. Because owners of other teams feel the same pressure to improve their teams, all owners continually drive up the salaries they pay to attract the best players and coaches.

3. *Television networks* compete against one another to attract fans, so they drive up the fees they pay for the right to telecast the games. Network programmers know that when they own the rights to telecast sports, their network generates higher revenues and the network gets stronger; in contrast, a network gets weaker when it lets a competing network outbid it for the telecasting rights.

4. *Advertisers* of certain products find sports fans an especially desirable audience. They pay sports telecasting networks a premium to get their persuasive messages to those audiences. They also use sports magazines, sports websites, and the sports sections of newspapers to reach their audiences.

5. *We, the public,* receive a lot of satisfaction in following our favorite sports teams, so we follow the games on television, tolerate the commercial interruptions, and buy the advertised products. Also, we find certain sporting events to be highly entertaining (*Monday Night Football*, the Super Bowl, playoff games), so we watch them even when we do not have a favorite team in the contests.

istock/manley009

The Staples Center is home to the Los Angeles Lakers and Los Angeles Clippers NBA teams, the Los Angeles Sparks WNBA team, and the Los Angeles Kings NHL team. Privately financed for $375 million, it is part of a larger retail, residential, and entertainment complex called L.A. Live.

When the five segments of the cycle cooperate and work well together, the cycle attracts more money into the cycle. The public watches more games and buys more advertised products, especially those products endorsed by athletes. With higher viewership for sports shows, television networks charge advertisers more for access to the viewers. The television networks make more money and can afford to pay the sporting leagues higher fees for the rights to televise the games. The leagues and owners make more money and can afford to pay more to attract the best players and thereby play more games, which attracts more fans.

The cycle keeps going around and around, each time at a higher level of salaries for players, which requires more income for owners and leagues, which demand bigger contracts from television networks, which must charge more for commercial time to advertisers, who want larger audiences, who want more exciting games, which requires better players, who want more money . . . and the cycle continues.

Let's take a closer look at each of these segments of the money cycle and make a distinction between the more *active* agents and the more *responding* agents in the cycle. The more active agents—the owners and players—have the most power in negotiating for money. The remaining agents—television networks, advertisers, and the public—are still essential to the money cycle, but their actions are largely in response to another agent; rarely do they initiate change.

Players

Salaries for players in all professional sports have been escalating in the past half century after the rise of television. To illustrate this trend, let's begin by turning the clock back to 1959, when Ted Williams, a future Hall of Fame player for the Boston Red Sox baseball team, was offered a contract for $125,000. Williams returned his contract unsigned to management; he was rejecting their offer. His reason for rejecting the contract was that it was for *too much money*. Williams argued that he was not worth that much money because he was coming off a year in which he hit "only" .259, which was a bad year for Williams, although it would be a better-than-average year for almost everyone who ever played professional baseball. Williams asked for a pay cut of 25%, which was the maximum pay cut possible.

Since the days of Ted Williams, salaries for Major League Baseball (MLB) players have been increasing rapidly. For example, in 2018, the MLB player with the highest salary was Mike Trout, who was paid $33.25 million to play centerfield for the Anaheim Angels (Badenhausen, 2018). This works out to a payment of about $205,247 for each of 162 games in the season. Thus Trout was paid more to play six innings than Ted Williams was paid to play an entire season. In 2018, there were 41 baseball players who were each paid at least $20 million (Badenhausen, 2018).

As for the National Basketball Association (NBA), Michael Jordan was earning $4 million during the 1995–1996 season, when he led the Chicago Bulls to their fourth championship in professional basketball in 6 years. He was named the most valuable player of the year, and many basketball fans still regard Jordan as the best basketball player of all time. A year later, he was a free agent and signed a new contract for $18 million, making him the highest-paid player in the league—temporarily (Rhodes & Reibstein, 1996). Now there are 38 players being paid more than $20 million per year in the NBA (Badenhausen, 2018).

Salaries for players in the National Football League (NFL) have also escalated dramatically. For example, the median earnings of the 2,000 NFL players in the 1999 season were $430,000; a decade later, it had increased to $770,000, and by 2018, it had increased to $860,000 (Woodruff, 2018).

Athletes can also command large fees for endorsing products. Companies are willing to pay huge fees to athletes who endorse their products because such endorsements work to increase sales. For example, Nike paid LeBron James $93 million for a 7-year endorsement deal ($13.3 a year), and Adidas paid Derrick Rose $185 million for 13 years ($14.2 million per year) (Saporito, 2012). While top professional athletes earn very large salaries from playing their sports, many earn much more money by endorsing commercial products (see Table Issue 2.1).

Until several decades ago, the owners and leagues were much more in control of players' contracts and salaries. Whitson (1998) explains that sport was commercialized early in the 20th century in the United States, where sports developed

> labor markets of athletic talent, in which wealthy teams offered "traveling players" financial inducements to come and play for them. It was this, of course, that created the phenomenon of the professional athlete, even though labor market mobility (and hence salaries) would quickly be contained by the emergence of cartels in all the major sports. (p. 60)

These cartels controlled player salaries and player movement, but this arrangement broke down as a result of labor challenges in the 1970s, and now there is a great deal of player movement and escalation of salaries.

To help control the rise of salaries and to try to create parity among teams, several professional sports have established salary caps for teams in their leagues. However, many owners have routinely ignored the caps for years. For example, in the 1995 NFL season, the salary cap was $37.1 million per NFL team, and 26 of the 30 teams in the league went over that maximum, with the Dallas Cowboys spending $62.2 million ("NFL Teams," 1996). By the 2018 season, the salary cap had been increased so high (to $177.2 million) that only three teams were exceeding the cap (Lewis, 2018, March 5). Not only are the salary caps much higher, teams have gotten more creative in the way they write player contracts so that they appear to be staying within the salary cap rules and therefore avoid paying fines for exceeding those caps.

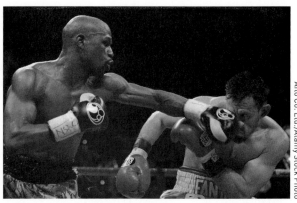

Boxer Floyd Mayweather, Jr. is currently the highest-paid athlete, having an annual income of $300 million.

Aflo Co. Ltd./Alamy Stock Photo

TABLE ISSUE 2.1   ■   Top-Earning Athletes in 2018

		2018 Income (in Millions of Dollars)		
Name	Sport	From Sport	From Endorsements	Total
Floyd Mayweather	Boxing	275.0	10.0	285.0
Lionel Messi	Soccer	84.0	27.0	111.0
Cristiano Ronaldo	Soccer	61.0	47.0	108.0
Conor McGregor	Mixed martial arts	85.0	14.0	99.0
Neymar	Soccer	73.0	17.0	90.0
LeBron James	Basketball	33.5	52.0	85.5
Roger Federer	Tennis	12.2	65.0	77.
Stephen Curry	Basketball	34.9	42.0	76.9
Matt Ryan	Football	62.3	5.0	67.3
Matthew Stafford	Football	57.5	2.0	59.5
Kevin Durant	Basketball	25.3	32.0	57.3
Lewis Hamilton	Racing	42.0	9.0	51.0
Russell Westbrook	Basketball	28.6	19.0	47.6
James Harden	Basketball	28.4	18.0	46.4
Canelo Alvarez	Boxing	42.0	2.5	44.5
Tiger Woods	Golf	1.3	42.0	43.3
Drew Brees	Football	29.9	13.0	42.9
Sebastian Vettel	Auto racing	42.0	0.3	42.3
Derek Carr	Football	40.1	2.0	42.1
Rafael Nadal	Tennis	14.4	27.0	41.4
Alex Smith	Football	40.4	1.0	41.4

Source: *Forbes* (2018b).

Why do owners continue to escalate salaries? The answer is that a star player at any price is a great investment. Not only can star players help their teams to win, but, more important, they also bring fans out to the stadiums and, even more important, attract television viewers for their games. This greatly increases the value of the franchise. For example, the Chicago Bulls franchise was valued at $17.5 million in 1985—Jordan's rookie year. In 1996, after the Bulls won their fourth NBA title, the franchise was valued at $178 million. The owner had a huge yearly income from broadcast rights, merchandising, and ticket sales. The Bulls play at the United Center, where there are 216 suites each selling for $175,000. In 1996, all games were sold out, and there was a waiting list of more than 17,000 fans for season tickets (Rhodes & Reibstein, 1996). Now the average NBA team is valued at $1.65 billion with even the least expensive teams being valued over $1 billion (Badenhausen, 2018).

Owners and Leagues

The major professional sports leagues are all very profitable, although there are times when they claim to be losing money. For example, in the summer of 2011 when the NBA players' contract had expired and league was negotiating a new deal with the players' union, the NBA claimed that during the previous season 22 of its 30 teams were unprofitable and the league lost about $300 million. The NBA made this claim despite a record $4.3 billion in revenue from television contracts and record attendance at the games (Pugmire, 2011). Further, the NBA argued that although it generated huge revenue, its expenses were too high (especially players' salaries) and it was asking players to take a pay cut.

However, when we look at the big picture, it appears that all the major sports leagues in the United States are doing well (see Table Issue 2.2). While the majority of income for all teams and leagues is from television broadcast rights, the owners of teams have been aggressive in developing additional revenue streams such as luxury skyboxes at stadiums and apparel merchandising. Also, the owners frequently raise the prices of tickets, concessions, parking, apparel, and other souvenirs.

College sports have become huge businesses of mass entertainment. Colleges own their teams and make a huge profit on marquee sports such as football and men's basketball. These sports are subsidized by students, who are regarded as amateur athletes

TABLE ISSUE 2.2 ■ The Big Four American Professional Sports Leagues				
	NFL	MLB	NBA	NHL
Number of teams in league	32	30	30	30
Games per season	16	162	82	82
Attendance per game	67,405	30,023	17,830	17,446
Average value per team (billions)	$1.97	$1.3	$1.65	$0.51
Annual revenue per league (billions)	$13.0	$9.5	$4.8	$3.7
Average salary per player (millions)	$2.7	$4.47	$7.15	$3.11

Source: Statista (2018i).

and therefore cannot be paid to play, although many are given scholarships. Even private colleges with high tuition can field a football team for about $2 million and a basketball team for less than half that; compare those figures to the annual payrolls of professional teams. Colleges share in TV money and also have revenue for tickets, parking, and concessions. While colleges do not play as many games per season as do pro teams, they have another source of revenue that pro teams do not have—donors who as athletic program boosters get to write off their donations as tax deductions. Colleges are looking for even more sources of revenue. College football is now selling naming rights to particular regular season games.

The salaries colleges pay to their football coaches keep increasing, especially recently. In 2006, the average salary of a Division I football coach was $950,000; by the fall of 2014, the average had doubled to $1.95 million (Brady, Berkowitz, & Schnaars, 2014). By 2018, the average salary being paid to football coaches across the five biggest football conferences was $3.6 million (Boyd, 2018).

College sports generate huge revenues at major universities. The 231 Division I schools generated a total of $9.15 billion from sports in 2016. Most of this revenue is generated by a small number of schools—with the top 24 earning more than $100 million a year, while almost half (44%) of those college programs each earned less than $20 million a year (Gaines, 2016). But their expenses are very high because universities support a wide range of sports programs (such as golf, tennis, track, volleyball, cross country, etc.) that generate almost no income, yet have considerable expenses. The American Council on Education explains that out of 1,000 college sports, "10 programs will have a net income of $9 million, and the remaining 990 will lose $1 million" (Suggs, 2018).

Television Networks

The biggest increase in sports revenue is from television. Without a television contract, no sports league could survive. The American Football League got started in the early 1960s with a TV deal of $1.7 million. Although this does not seem like much money today, it made the difference in whether the league survived in the early 1960s. In 1965, CBS paid $14.1 million to broadcast NFL games. By the mid-1990s, the NFL was charging $500 million per year for broadcasting rights, and this sum was so large that it had to be shared by five networks: ABC, NBC, ESPN, Fox, and TNT. In 2014, the NFL signed a contract that would generate an average of $4.9 billion per year for the league from 2014 to 2021 (Ozanian, 2016). The TV networks are willing to spend these large sums of money because the NFL generates strong TV ratings. In the fall of 2012, 31 of the 32 top-rated TV shows in the United States were NFL games (Eichelberger, 2013) and even though ratings of NFL games started falling in 2017, the games still generate higher ratings than most other television programs (Deitsch, 2018).

Steve Debenport/E+/Getty Images

Networks pay for a game's broadcasting rights and maximize return on the investment by using announcers and color commentators to fill airtime before, during, and after the game, when more advertising can be sold.

The television networks know they cannot depend on teams winning to keep increasing their viewership. With the four major professional sports (football, basketball, baseball, and hockey), each contest has only two teams, which means the number of losers is always the same as the number of winners. There is no way to increase the number of wins relative to the number of losses. Therefore, winning competition is not enough to market sports successfully. The television networks have had to develop other means to increase the size of the sports audience. The way they have done this is to shift the focus from sports to an entertainment formula. This means that the announcers must be good storytellers. The announcers must fill in the history of the teams and tell compelling stories like "there is a tradition of bad blood between the teams" or some other subplot to keep people watching the games, especially when the score is lopsided. Announcers must tell human interest stories about the struggles of individual players both on and off the field. And they must turn certain players into larger-than-life heroes, who can take over a game at any instant with their courage or superhuman abilities.

Certain players have been pushed into the spotlight each season, and those who performed well there became legends—players such as Babe Ruth, Wayne Gretsky, Magic Johnson, and Michael Jordan. Even non–sports fans knew who these people were, and those reputations attracted a lot of new fans to the games.

With television networks and advertisers putting so much money into these sports, they demand that the leagues make their sports even more exciting and more amenable to advertising. The leagues have complied. For example, the telecast of a football game is more than 3 hours long, although the game itself takes 60 minutes, and there is less than 10 minutes of action on the field during those 60 minutes that the clock is running. So the announcers must provide lots of anecdotes, statistics, and color commentary. The director must provide lots of replays, slow motions, shots of the crowd and cheerleaders, and so on.

Over the years, the professional sports leagues have changed the rules of their games to make them more exciting for fans. For example, the NBA created the 3-point basket, which added another dimension to the game and made it more exciting. Basketball now has a shot clock that requires players to shoot the ball at least every 24 seconds. The NFL changed the extra-point rule so that teams could go for 2 extra points, thus helping the team behind to catch up faster and make the game more interesting. Rules were changed to provide more protection for the most valuable offensive player—the quarterback—who needed more time to engage in the game's most exciting play, which is the long pass.

To accommodate advertisers, the NFL instituted the 2-minute warning in the mid-1960s to guarantee a break for commercial messages at a time when viewership is usually high. Also, the NFL and the NBA have frequent television time-outs. Uniforms are more colorful. All of these changes to the games were instituted to increase viewer interest and thereby provide advertisers with the largest possible audiences.

Advertisers

Advertisers pay huge fees to television networks to get their messages to their target audiences. During the first Super Bowl in 1967, the time to broadcast a 30-second ad cost advertisers $42,000; by 1995, the cost had increased to over $1 million. By 2018, the cost of showing one 30-second ad in the Super Bowl had increased to $5 million (Zarett, 2018).

Advertisers have also turned stadiums into advertising vehicles, with the naming of the stadiums and by putting ads on scoreboards, walls, ticket stubs, concession stand product packaging, and so on. Some basketball courts have ads painted on them; hockey arenas have ads on the ice and around the rink's walls. Some football teams have ads on their jerseys (e.g., the Nike Swoosh). In car racing, the drivers' uniforms as well as the cars are covered with ads.

In the spring of 2004, Major League Baseball even tried putting ads on the bases, but criticism flared up and the league has backed off, for now. One critic said that this "undermines the character of America's pastime at every level." This criticism makes one wonder whether the critic has seen a baseball game in the past 2 decades, with all the advertising that is already at the stadium. It is interesting to consider what another critic said as a way of thinking about what might be coming in the future: "How low will base-ball sink? Next year, will they replace the bats with long Coke bottles, and the bases with big hamburger buns?" (Penner, 2004, pp. D1, D8).

Businesses are happy to contribute large sums of money to sports—as long as those businesses get high visibility for themselves in return. For example, Frito-Lay gave $15 million to the Fiesta Bowl and in return received 3 years of sponsorship rights to that college football game. This means that the name of the game was changed to the Tostitos Fiesta Bowl, and this name had to appear on all the signage and be mentioned by all announcers referring to the game.

Public

The public has always been interested in sports. But for the money cycle to grow, the number of fans has to grow each year. Also, the commitment of those fans needs to grow each year so that those fans spend even more time watching the games, going to the stadiums, buying the team merchandise, and supporting all the advertisers. And most important, the general public in each locale must identify and support its local teams. All of these things have happened and continue to happen.

The media offer the public a great variety of sporting events, and people expose them-selves to these messages. In 1998, researchers estimated that there were more than 8,000 sporting events televised that year (Kinkema & Harris, 1998). That sounds like a huge number until you realize that this is an average of 22 events per day, and today this num-ber is likely to be much larger. With long tail marketing, there are many niche audiences for a much greater variety of sporting events. With interactive technologies, we have instant access to all kinds of sporting events beyond what the traditional media offer.

Not only does the money cycle depend on continued support from fans, but it requires support from non-fans also. This is most clearly seen in the building of new sports sta-diums across the country. The major sports leagues have been successful in getting local municipalities to finance a large part of these stadiums through public financing and taxes. In the 5-year period from the summer of 1998 to the summer of 2003, 12 new NFL foot-ball stadiums were opened—many in cities with existing football stadiums. Each of these new stadiums had between 82 (Seattle) and 208 (Washington, D.C.) premium skyboxes that the owners of the NFL teams could rent out to wealthy clients and businesses. But the sweetest part of most of these deals was that the NFL got the cities to pay for most of the construction costs. Only one owner (Daniel Snyder, owner of the Washington Redskins) paid for at least half of the construction costs; with three of the stadiums (Raymond James

Stadium in Tampa, Florida; Reliant Stadium in Houston, Texas; and the Coliseum in Nashville, Tennessee), the NFL saw to it that the cities paid the entire cost of the stadiums. Therefore, if you use an airport, rent a car, or pay for a hotel room in a city with an NFL team (or an MLB or NBA team), you are likely paying a tax that helps that city finance its stadiums (Metropolitan Sports Facilities Commission, n.d.).

Most cities feel that it is important to have major sports teams. Cities with such teams are willing to spend a great deal of public money to keep them, and those cities without

Sports fans are an integral part of the money cycle.

such a team are willing to spend a great deal of public money to attract such a team away from another city and to even build a news sports stadium. The costs of building professional sports stadiums are going up dramatically, and it is costing taxpayers a lot of money to have a team. For example, let's look at what happened in Houston, Texas. The city built the Astrodome at a cost of $35 million and opened it in 1965. Ten years later it opened the Compaq Center, which cost $27 million, as the home for the Houston Rockets of the NBA. Thus Houston had invested a total of $62 million to build venues for its big three professional sports teams. Then, in 2000, Houston opened Minute Maid Park, which cost $250 million to build and was designed for baseball only. Then 2 years later, Houston opened the brand-new Reliant Stadium for football only, at a cost of $449 million. This was replaced by the Toyota Center in 2003, which was built at a cost of $175 million (Reinken, 2003). By 2009, the cost of building a new NFL stadium surpassed $1 billion. The Dallas Cowboys' AT&T Stadium in Arlington, Texas, cost $1.3 billion to construct; the Minnesota Vikings' U.S. Bank Stadium cost $1.1 billion; San Francisco's Levi's Stadium cost $1.3 billion; and New York's MetLife Stadium cost $1.6 billion (Notte, 2017).

OLYMPICS

The ancient Olympics were a venue for amateur athletes to compete every 4 years. Of course, at the time, there were no professional sports. The ancient Olympics continued for more than 1,200 years, died out, and then were revived in 1896 as the "modern" Olympics. For a long time, the modern Olympics preserved its focus on amateur athletes and banned any professional athlete of any kind from participating.

Cities competed to host the Olympic games every 4 years. By 1932, the cost of hosting the games had increased to a point where cities could not make back all the money they spent, so it was a sacrifice to host the games. Still, many cities competed because it was prestigious to be the host city. It also provided a great public relations opportunity to show off the host city to the world.

Eventually, with the rise of television, networks were willing to pay the International Olympic Committee (IOC) fees for the rights to broadcast the games, and this helped host cities defray the costs of building all the venues and the cost of running the Olympics (see Table Issue 2.3). In 1964, NBC paid $1.5 million to the IOC for the rights to broadcast the Tokyo Summer Olympics. By 1980, the cost had skyrocketed to $85 million when NBC acquired rights to the Moscow Summer Olympics, despite the fact that the Soviets wanted $210 million plus $50 million in production equipment to be left behind. The broadcast was never made, though, due to the boycott of the 1980 games by the American government. ABC paid $225 million for the Los Angeles summer games in 1984 and $91 million for the winter games in Sarajevo. Despite losing money on the winter games, ABC came back with an even higher bid of $309 million for the 1988 winter games in Calgary. NBC got the 1988 summer games in Seoul, Korea, for $300 million. NBC paid $456 million for the 1996 Atlanta games, and CBS bid $375 million to broadcast the 1998 winter games in Nagano, Japan. NBC broke its record by bidding $705 million for exclusive U.S. rights to broadcast the 2000 summer games in Sydney, Australia, and another $545 million for the 2002 winter games in Salt Lake City. The total NBC package is worth about $1.3 billion—none of the other U.S. networks entered a bid (Nelson, 1995). NBC secured the rights to four Olympic games (the 2014 Winter games in Sochi, Russia; the 2016 summer games in Rio de Janeiro, Brazil; the 2018 winter games in PyeongChang, South Korea; and the 2020 summer games in Tokyo) for $4.38 billion. The network has a history of losing money on these broadcasts. In broadcasting the 2010 winter games, NBC lost $233 million (Flint, 2011).

TABLE ISSUE 2.3 ■ Television Broadcast Contracts for Summer Olympic Games		
Year	Host City	Fee (in Millions, $)
1960	Rome	0.6
1964	Tokyo	1.6
1968	Mexico City	4.5
1972	Munich	12.5
1976	Montreal	25.0
1980	Moscow	95.5
1984	Los Angeles	225.0
1988	Seoul	305.0
1992	Barcelona	401.0
1996	Atlanta	456.0
2000	Sydney	705.0
2004	Athens	793.0
2008	Beijing	894.0
2012	London	1,181.0
2016	Rio de Janeiro	963.0

Where does this money go? It is paid to the IOC, which also sells rights to broadcast the games to media in other countries. When ABC paid $309 million for the 1988 winter games, the European Broadcast Union (EBU, which represents 32 countries and a population of several hundred million) paid $5.7 million, and the Soviet Union (along with it Eastern European allies), North Korea, and Cuba paid a combined total of $1.2 million. Thus, it is clear that the United States (or rather, advertisers on U.S. television) really supports the games—without U.S. support, the Olympics would be very different.

PCN Photography/Alamy Stock Photo

Millions of viewers worldwide tuned in to watch Usain Bolt break world records in the 2016 Olympic games.

The IOC also sells to advertisers the rights to sponsor the games or show their products during the games. Real (1998) explains that American TV has increasingly borne the cost of hosting the Olympic games. In 1960, American TV money contributed about 0.3% of the cost of the games; in 1980, American money supported 6% of the cost; and in 1984, it contributed 50%. Now American TV totally supports the cost and allows the host city to make a big profit.

The Olympics have become a major venue for advertising. The modern Olympics have always accepted advertising. In 1896, there were ads for Kodak. Coke began its association with the games in 1928. But as the games got more expensive, planners needed more advertising revenue. The 1976 games in Montreal experienced a $1 billion deficit.

In 1984, when the Olympics were held in Los Angeles, the games not only covered their enormous costs but also made a huge profit of $215 million (Manning, 1987). They did this by selling corporate sponsorships of various events and locales. VISA alone spent $25 million on the rights and on promotions, and 146 corporations were official sponsors of various events. By the 1996 games in Atlanta, the IOC had signed up 180 companies and brands that used the Olympics for promotions (Grimm, 1996). The top 10 of these official sponsors (such as Coke and IBM) paid a total of $2.1 billion (Jensen & Ross, 1996). This more than offset the total cost of $1.7 billion for holding the 1996 Atlanta games (Boswell, 1996). Now, almost all athletes have corporate logos on their clothing. Sponsorships are sold for each event and for the games in general. Companies use the event as an opportunity for global marketing.

Ever since the Los Angeles games in 1984, the Olympics have been highly commercial and highly profitable for the host city. Now, competition among cities to host the event is very strong.

The Olympics are less profitable for the television network that outbids its competitors and is awarded the rights to broadcast the games. This huge expense for the broadcast rights is only the beginning. Production is another big expense. In the 1984 Los Angeles Summer Olympics, the United States sent 500 athletes to compete; ABC sent 3,500 people (1,400 engineers, 1,800 support personnel, and 300 network production and management people). To produce 188 hours of coverage, they used 205 cameras, 660 miles of camera cables, 4 helicopters, 3 houseboats, 26 mobile units, 35 office trailers, and 404 hardwired commentary positions. There were microphones on basketball backboards, underwater in the diving pool, in boxing ring posts, and on equestrian saddles. The cost of covering the games was $100 million. This is why the television networks must sell a great deal of advertising.

Ratings for the Olympic games have been dropping over the last 4 decades, from an average rating of over 20 down to an average rating of about 10 for the London Olympics in 2012 (Sandomir, 2012). Given the ratings drop and costs accelerating upward, television networks typically lose money televising the Olympic games; however, they continue to bid up the price for future telecasting rights. They reason that the Olympic telecasts attract large audiences that they can target their promotions for new entertainment shows. Thus, if those promotions can generate larger audiences for the shows premiering after the Olympics, the networks will more than earn enough to cancel out the loss of telecasting the Olympics and generate a larger overall yearly profit for the network.

Because of the highly commercial nature of the Olympic games, the IOC was unable to maintain the prohibition against professional athletes. Now the Olympics are very different than they were even 25 years ago. They are a showcase for the best athletes— professional as well as amateur—in the world. But even more important, they are a showcase for international companies that want to develop markets worldwide for their products and services.

VIDEO GAMING

Video gaming has become very popular among the general population over the past 3 decades. Now more than two thirds of all households play videogames, and 45% of all gamers are women. Gamers play an average of 6 hours globally and that figure is even higher (6.4 hours) in the United States. And almost one third (32.1%) of gamers said they would quit their job if they could support themselves as a professional video game player (Milligan, 2018). Video gaming has grown so popular that it is now a collegiate varsity sport and there are professional leagues.

Some colleges are making video gaming a varsity sport like soccer or basketball. Top players receive athletic scholarships worth up to $19,000 per year. These teams parallel other competitive college teams with money. Players wear team jerseys with logos of sponsors displayed, schools sell naming rights of their gaming rooms, and players practice up to 5 hours per day. The Collegiate Starleague now has 450 schools and 10,000 players, including well-known universities such as Harvard, Stanford, and Georgia Tech. They compete in the North American College Championship (NACC), where the championship team wins $30,000 in scholarship money (Gregory, 2015).

There are also professional leagues of video gamers, and these contests are regularly televised on major cable channels such as ESPN. TV money is flowing into the sport. According to SuperData Research, 93 million people will watch an e-sports event in 2015. When the League of Legends held its pro World Championship in October 2013, it drew a viewership of 32 million, which is more than Game 7 of that year's NBA Finals, which attracted 26.3 million (Gregory, 2015).

YOUR OWN INFORMED OPINION

Now that I have presented you with many facts about sports and the money cycle, you need to incorporate this information into the construction of your own informed opinion. First, you need to think about the big picture. Then you need to extend your knowledge about sports in general as well as about your own costs and benefits. Finally, think through the issue in a broader way to keep a broad perspective on this issue.

The Big Picture

This chapter has presented many figures illustrating how the money cycle has increased expenditures on sports over the years, and now more than $485 billion is spent on sports annually in the United States. Most of those figures have focused on the high-profile spectator sports, especially from the big four of American professional sports—football, baseball, basketball, and hockey. But if you look at Table Issue 2.2, you will see that the revenues of those four powerful sports leagues total $32 billion, which is a huge sum of money but only about 6.4% of the total revenue generated by sports in the United States each year. What generates the other 93.6%? Other spectator sports generate an additional $40 billion. This includes racing (especially horses and cars), golf, tennis, volleyball, and all other sports. Also, this figure includes all sports spectatorship at levels below professional, such as college and high school. So when we add up all of the money we pay to watch sports, this accounts for about 11.8% of all money spent on sports each year in the United States. The other 88.2% is money we spend on participating in sports, such as buying sporting goods, joining recreational centers and leagues, paying fees to play golf, and so on (Plunkett Research, Ltd., 2018).

While the sports industry in the United States employs about 1.3 million people, less than 1% of them are professional athletes; another 1% are umpires, referees, and officials; about 15% are coaches and scouts; and the rest work at gaming centers and sporting goods stores (Plunkett Research, Ltd., 2017).

The big picture then is that sports are extremely important to Americans—not just as fans but also as participants. Almost $9 out of every $10 we spend on sports is for participation. And our participation is stimulated by the performances we watch as fans of high-profile athletes in the media.

When you take a big-picture view on sports, you need to think beyond the mega-salaries paid to star athletes and think about how those athletes might be inspiring you to participate in sports yourself or to simply exercise. And as you expand your thinking, consider how those high-profile sporting contests may be teaching you lessons about preparing for challenges, setting goals, working hard, and excelling in the many various contests we face in our everyday lives. Professional athletes and their games do have much value to offer our economy and our society. You need to take that into consideration as you develop your own informed opinion on this issue about sports and whether they are worth it given the amount of resources being pulled into the accelerating money cycle.

Extend Your Knowledge

In this chapter, I have presented you with a great deal of detail about the sports money cycle but there is still much more you could learn. Try Applying Media Literacy Skills 2.1

to dig deeper into this issue. Then as you move forward in your life, keep thinking about how you keep up to date on this fast-changing cycle. Also, think about whether there should be limits on the growth of sports and if so, what should those limits be. If you think there should be no limits on the growth, then ask yourself three questions. First, are you willing to pay more for tickets, concessions, parking, and clothing with the logos of your favorite teams? Second, are you willing to pay more in taxes to municipalities so they can build stadiums and give tax incentives to sports teams so they will not move to another city? And third, are you willing to tolerate more commercial breaks that interrupt your viewing of sporting contests on television?

Cost-Benefit Analysis

Up to this point, we have focused on general trends in sports. You have seen that sports have become more exciting and entertaining to the general viewer over the past several decades. The public is showing increased interest in sporting events and personalities of all kinds. But the price for this continues to climb.

Now it is time to analyze your experience with sports in depth by going through Applying Media Literacy Skills 2.2 to conduct a cost-benefit analysis. Some of the costs to you are obvious. As a fan, you support your teams by buying tickets, parking, refreshments, and souvenirs at the games. But some costs are hidden. If you do not go to the stadium, you can still support your teams by watching them on television and buying products advertised on those telecasts. And even if you do not go to the games or watch the local teams on television, you are still supporting those teams financially through local taxes and paying the interest on revenue bonds your city council has sold to build the luxurious new stadiums that will keep owners from moving their teams elsewhere.

Clearly you are supporting the sports money cycle; you cannot avoid providing some support. So the big question for you now is: What am I getting back as benefits for all these costs? This part of the cost-benefit analysis is more difficult to conduct because the benefits cannot be neatly quantified like costs are (money and time). However, it is important that you really think about the satisfactions you derive from sports—from participating as well as watching.

Think About Implications

Think about the implications of the money cycle on sports in a broader way and moving into the future (Applying Media Literacy Skills Issue 2.3). How far have the changes in professional sports filtered down to college sports, high school sports, and recreational sports? Do the changes in professional sports negatively influence the expectations of those who play little league baseball; that is, is the pressure to win too high? Does it take the fun away from watching intramural sports or a community league game? What will the future be like if the sports money cycle continues? What are the dangers and benefits of this? Can you think of solutions to problems caused by the sports money cycle?

These Applying Media Literacy Skills exercises are rather involved. You may not want to do them all right now. That's okay. But keep them in mind and keep working on improving your opinion regarding the money cycle and sports. Take more control over the costs you give up and be more demanding of benefits. The more you think about these things, the more you will be using your informed opinion to use your resources more wisely and thereby increasing the value of the media to you personally.

Further Reading

Gaul, G. M. (2015). *Billion dollar ball: A journey through the big-money culture of college football*. New York, NY: Viking. (249 pages, including index)

This book is written by an investigative journalist and shows how college sports, especially football, have changed dramatically in the past few decades. Gaul addresses such questions as: Why do colleges pay coaches so much money? How do colleges make enormous incomes from their football programs? How have the lesser known college sports and women's sports been affected by the dominance of football in major colleges?

Raney, A. A. (2009). The effects of viewing televised sports. In R. L. Nabi & M. B. Oliver (Eds.), *Media processes and effects* (pp. 439–453). Los Angeles, CA: SAGE.

This chapter presents a relatively current review of the empirical literature on the effects of exposure to sports in the media.

Raney, A. A., & Bryant, J. (Eds.). (2006). *Handbook of sports and media*. Mahwah, NJ: Erlbaum.

This edited volume contains many chapters written by experts on sports in the media. It is organized into four sections of the development of sports media, the coverage and business of sports media, sports media audiences, and critical perspectives on sports media.

Wenner, L. A. (Ed.). (1998). *MediaSport*. New York, NY: Routledge. (336 pages with index)

This edited book contains 17 chapters in four parts: playing field, institutions, texts, and audiences. Although this book is now dated, with most of its research coming from the early to mid-1990s, it still presents valuable insights into how sports have developed primarily in the United States to become such a powerful economic and social force.

Keeping Up to Date

ESPN (http://espn.go.com)

This television cable network devoted to sports has a website that presents a great deal of current information about players, teams, and contests.

Plunkett Research (https://www.plunkettresearch.com/industries/sports-recreation-leisure-market-research/)

This company conducts and reports research on a wide variety of topics and its website is a valuable resource for information on sports statistics, such as players' salaries, value of different sports franchises, attendance at games, and so on.

USAToday Salaries Databases (https://www.usatoday.com/sports/)

This website presents a lot of detail about the salaries of professional athletes and teams in America's major sports.

APPLYING MEDIA LITERACY SKILLS 2.1
EXTENDING KNOWLEDGE

In this chapter, I have presented you with some facts to illustrate the money cycle with sports. Use this information as a jumping-off point and see what research you can do to update and expand on the points in this chapter by considering the following questions.

1. *Extend your knowledge.* Pick one of the main points in this chapter, and do your own research to expand your knowledge and update the information. Some topics are the following:

   - Product endorsements by professional athletes

   - Cost of sports stadiums and how they are financed

   - Comparison of player salaries across sports

   - Advertising expenditures by sport

   - Demographic profiles of fans in different sports

   - How the games have changed to make them more attractive to viewers

   - Who the owners of the sports teams are, and how they made enough money to be able to buy a sports franchise

2. *Analyze advertising content.* Watch several broadcasts of a particular sport but instead of paying most attention to the game, pay attention to the advertisements. Keep track of all ads. Then answer the following questions:

   - Which companies advertise the most on particular sports?

   - Which product categories are most often advertised by sports?

   - Given your answers to the above two questions, who do you think the target audiences are for those big advertisers?

   - What kinds of appeals are used in those ads; that is, what are the advertisers telling you about their products and why you should use them?

3. *Project trends.* Pick one sport and see if you can find salary information for what the average salary was and what the highest-paid players made in each decade.

   - Project that information into the future for 1, 2, and 3 decades. How much will the average player be making when you are 30, 40, and 50?

   - Break those salary figures down by game; that is, what will the average player and the highest-paid player make per game in the future?

   - What do you think your salary will be when you are 30, 40, and 50? How long will it take a pro player to earn what you make in a year?

4. *Get a historical perspective on these issues.* Talk to your father (or mother) and grandfather (or grandmother) about sports behaviors 40–50 years ago. Ask them the following questions:

   - Did they used to attend sporting events in person?

   - Did they follow sports through the media? Is so, which sports and which media?

   - Are they aware of any changes in their favorite sports over the past few decades? If so what is their reaction to those changes?

   - What is their reaction to the salaries paid to athletes today?

   - What is their reaction to the amount of advertising at the games and during media coverage?

APPLYING MEDIA LITERACY SKILLS 2.2
PERSONAL INVENTORY

This exercise is designed to guide you through a cost-benefit analysis of sports. Some of the questions in this cost-benefit analysis will require you to do some research on the Internet.

Begin by thinking about how many sports you follow. The big four are football, basketball, hockey, and baseball. But also think about golf, tennis, track, horse racing, car racing, volleyball, and so on. Think beyond professional sports and also include sports at the college and high school levels. Also, think about city leagues, YMCA leagues, children's leagues, and so forth.

Step 1: Estimate your direct costs.

Think about how much time and money you spend following sports and estimate your answers to the following questions.

1. For each sport, estimate how much time you spend going to games.
   - What is the cost of tickets?
   - What is the cost of transportation to the games?
   - What is the cost of parking at the games?
   - How much do you spend on food and drink at the games?
   - How much do you spend on souvenirs—programs, pennants, and so forth?
2. How much do you spend on items with team logos?
   - Clothing (hats, shirts, jackets, etc.)
   - Items for your car (flags, license plates, bumper stickers, etc.)
   - Items for your desk (cups, pens, calendars, etc.)
   - Sports gifts for others

3. How much money do you spend watching games on television?
   - Cost for special cable or pay TV sports services
   - Cost of parties for friends who watch the games with you
   - Cost of food and drink at sports bars while watching games
4. How much time do you spend in all the above activities?
5. How much time do you spend doing the following?
   - Talking about sports teams, players, and scores of games
   - Reminiscing about past good times
   - Complaining about bad games, plays, and players
   - Projecting into the future of your team, players' careers, or games

Step 2: Estimate your indirect costs.

1. How much money do you spend buying products advertised on sporting events?

   (To answer this completely, you need to analyze all the products advertising on all sports programs you watch and then find out what percentage of the purchase price of each of those products was spent on advertising of sports. To estimate your answer, think of the major sponsors of the teams you follow and add up all the money you spend each year on those products.)

2. How much money has your city spent to support the local sports teams?

   Think of the cost of building the stadiums, parking lots, and access roads to the professional, college, and high school sports. Try to estimate how much of your taxes go into supporting all these sports.

(Continued)

(Continued)

Step 3: Estimate your direct benefits.

1. How much satisfaction did you derive last season from the performance of the sports teams you followed? If you are a rabid fan and your teams all won championships, your satisfaction level should be extremely high. But think about the satisfaction you obtained from experiencing individual games and the performances of individual players.

2. How much satisfaction did you derive from displaying your teams' logos on your clothing, car, desk, and so on? Is it important to you that other people know which teams you support? If so, why? Do you identify so closely with a team that you, as a fan, feel partially responsible when they lose and that you have earned a celebration when they win?

Step 4: Estimate your indirect benefits.

1. How important are your teams to their home cities?

   • What economic benefits do the cities get by having those teams?

• What public relations benefits do the home cities get from supporting their teams?

• Do the teams need to win for the city to achieve these benefits?

2. Considering what the cities experience as benefits, how much of that passes down to individuals such as yourself?

Step 5: Compare costs to benefits.

Now that you have thought about the questions raised in the above four areas, make a comparison of the costs to the benefits. Do you feel that the benefits you derive (of all kinds) are more than enough to pay you back for all the time and money you put into your fan-ship?

• If yes, what is your most valuable benefit? Why do you value that so highly?

• If no, how can you bring this cost-benefit comparison more in line with the value you expect? Is there some way to reduce your costs while still getting the same benefits? Is there some way to increase the benefits without increasing your costs?

APPLYING MEDIA LITERACY SKILLS 2.3
THINKING ABOUT IMPLICATIONS

1. *Broaden your perspective.*

   • Think of the ramifications on lesser known sports venues.

      ○ Smaller colleges

      ○ High schools

      ○ Recreational leagues

   • Think of the ramifications on things beyond sports, such as the following:

   ○ Local taxes

   ○ Traffic patterns and congestion

   ○ Teaching your kids to play sports

   ○ Taking your family to sporting events

   ○ The cost of advertised products

   ○ The overall economy

   ○ Our sports as perceived by the rest of the world

2. *Imagine the future.*

- Think about where the money cycle is likely to take sports 5 years from now.
  - What will be the salaries of top players?
  - How many ads will be in TV shows of sports and at stadiums?
  - What will tickets cost?
- Think about what the benefits of being a sports fan will be 5 years from now.
  - Do you think the money cycle will be able to grow the benefits as much as they grow the costs?

3. *Analyze pros and cons.*

- Begin by making two lists: the pros and cons of the money cycle growing sports.
- Examine each pro that you have listed. Is there a con embedded in that pro? If so, remove the con element and add it to your con list.
- Examine each con that you have listed. Is there a pro embedded in that con? If so, remove the pro element and add it to your pro list.
- When you finish, you should have two pure lists—one list of only cons and one of only pros.
- Which list is longer? Does the longer list mean that your opinion is on this side?

4. *Recommend improvements.*

- What, if anything, should the following types of people do to improve the situation?
  - Elected leaders
  - Television networks
  - Future athletes
  - Advertisers
- Consider the potential outcomes if these individuals follow your recommendations, and answer the following:
  - What benefits will result to the sports money cycle?
  - What risks are there for making the situation worse?

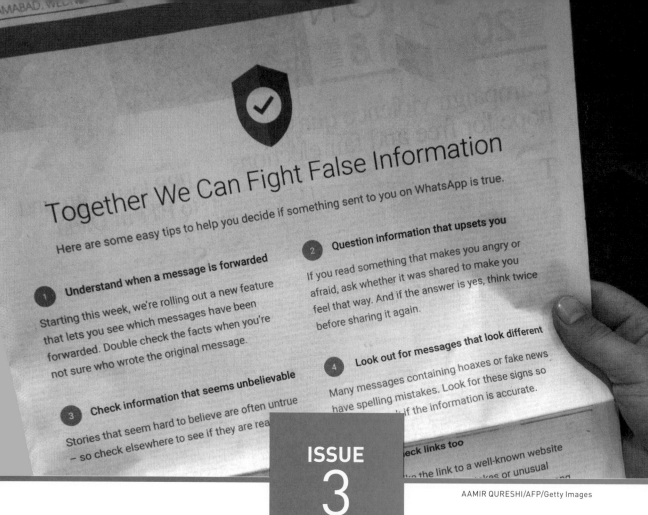

Together We Can Fight False Information

Here are some easy tips to help you decide if something sent to you on WhatsApp is true.

1 Understand when a message is forwarded

Starting this week, we're rolling out a new feature that lets you see which messages have been forwarded. Double check the facts when you're not sure who wrote the original message.

2 Question information that upsets you

If you read something that makes you angry or afraid, ask whether it was shared to make you feel that way. And if the answer is yes, think twice before sharing it again.

3 Check information that seems unbelievable

Stories that seem hard to believe are often untrue – so check elsewhere to see if they are rea...

4 Look out for messages that look different

Many messages containing hoaxes or fake news have spelling mistakes. Look for these signs so ... if the information is accurate.

...eck links too

...e the link to a well-known website ...kes or unusual

ISSUE

3

FAKE NEWS

*Issue: Criticizing media organizations for providing "fake news"
has arisen as a popular issue to debate. However, individuals on
both sides of this debate have a great deal of trouble identifying what is fake news, so
the arguments and suggested solutions fail to achieve enough depth
to illuminate the nature of the problem.*

The issue of "fake news" has come to the forefront of political discussion and public awareness in the past 2 years.

There has been growing criticism of news organizations for presenting "fake news." This is an important criticism because it is a serious indictment of the credibility of the institution of journalism, which we need to trust. If we cannot trust journalism in general to provide the population with accurate information about what the most important people and significant events are in our lives every day, then we cannot believe that the population is adequately informed to make good decisions about who our leaders should be, which problems are the most important, and how to solve those problems.

The term *fake news*, although only recently made popular, has already been used to criticize a variety of problems that vary by their contexts. Some varieties of fake news must be considered within a political context, others from purely financial motivations, and some have elements of both (see Tandoc, Lim, & Ling, 2018). Definitions of fake news range from narrow conceptualizations of "completely false information that was created for financial gain" (Silverman, 2016) to quite broad definitions that include any "news stories that have no factual basis but are presented as news" (Allcott & Gentzkow, 2017).

This chapter begins with an analysis of how this term has been used in order to answer the question: What is fake news? Then we turn our attention to the question: What can we, as news consumers, do to recognize fake news so that we can avoid its influence?

WHAT IS FAKE NEWS?

The phrase "fake news" implies there is something faulty with a news report or with a news organization that allows "fake" stories to be presented as news. The key to understanding this criticism is to identify what people mean when they say there is something fake about the news. In this section we will examine this criticism by applying five analytical dimensions in order to understand what people may be complaining about when they use the term "fake news." We begin with an analysis of the term by delineating it by (1) news criteria, (2) type of sender, (3) intention of sender, (4) accuracy, and (5) context.

Before we get started on this analysis, I need to clarify my use of some key terms. In this analysis, the word **fact** is used to designate something that (a) is a characteristic about a person, event, place, or time; (b) is presented as being true; and (c) can be verified. A **news story** (or "story" for short) is a sequence of facts presented to inform an audience. I use the term **newsworkers** to refer to all kinds of people who collect information and present it as news. Thus this is a general term that includes people who work individually (bloggers, tweeters, etc.) and people who work in news organizations (reporters, editors, opinion columnists, managers, production people, advertisers, etc.).

Delineation by News Criteria

One way we can analyze news to identify what people mean by "fake" is to consider the news criteria that journalists are trained to use. These criteria include the characteristics of **timeliness**, **significance**, **proximity**, **prominence**, **unusualness**, and **human interest** (Mediacollege.com, n.d.). Journalists are trained to believe that when something meets these criteria, it should be considered as newsworthy. When news organizations

The Los Angeles Times. Retrieved August 24, 2018 from http://www.latimes.com/latest/

Latest Headlines

RAMS 2:35 PM
Two years later, Sam Shields' concussion fog has lifted. His focus now is to corner a spot on the Rams' roster
By Helene Elliott

The nausea came over him in waves every day. He was dizzy, uncomfortable in bright light, and he couldn't bear being outside for very long. As much as cornerback Sam Shields missed football, simply watching a game on TV was too much for his concussion-muddled brain to process. "Mentally, at times...

BUSINESS 2:35 PM
IRS moves to block California and other states from helping residents avoid new tax-deduction limit
By Jim Puzzanghera

The Trump administration has delivered another blow to California. The Internal Revenue Service and Treasury Department on Thursday moved to block efforts by lawmakers in California and other Democratic-controlled states to help their residents avoid a new limit on state and local tax deductions....

ESSENTIAL POLITICS 2:20 PM
Actor Jeff Bridges says he was 'kinda shocked' after reading Times article on his property tax break
By Liam Dillon

Timeliness is one criterion that makes for a reputable news source. The *Los Angeles Times* website has a page showcasing its most current stories with time stamps indicating when each article was uploaded.

present stories that meet these criteria for newsworthiness, audiences are likely to consider those stories as "real" news. Conversely, when stories fail to meet any of these criteria, there is reason to consider them as fake news. Let's take a closer look at each of these six criteria to determine how solid they are as standards for deciding what is real news.

Timeliness

The word *news* means exactly that—a story about something that is *new*. Thus using this criterion, we should regard a story about something that is happening today as news; if this same thing happened last week, it can no longer be regarded as news.

This criterion, however, begins to break down when we consider stories across different types of media. For example, if we see a story about an event that occurred 5 days ago, we are likely to consider the story news if it appears in a weekly news magazine as we pull it out of our U.S. postal service mailbox. But if we read the same 5-day-old story on a website, we are likely to wonder why the website is presenting this story as "news."

Also, many events may continue for days or weeks. If a story about such an event is continually updated by showing developments as they unfold, then each of those stories is likely to be considered timely. However, such a judgment requires us to consider more than mere timeliness and also consider whether each additional story presents a sufficient amount of new material in order for us to conclude that each story is really news.

Significance

This criterion refers to how much impact the story is likely to have on the audience. Thus a crash of a private airplane where one person is killed holds less significance as news compared to a crash of a commercial airliner that kills hundreds of passengers. And if a story reports on the crash of an airplane that was operated by the same airline we will be using later today, it will have far more significance for us than if the story reports a crash of an airplane from an airline we have never flown.

Stories on events that convey a sense of resonance with an audience are more significant to those audience members than stories about events that have no relationship to their own experiences. However, the range of all possible things that might resonate with audiences is so broad and varied that it is not possible to draw a clear dividing line between events that are newsworthy because of significance and those that are clearly not. But journalists must continually draw that line in deciding what to cover. Thus a person who criticizes coverage of an event that she regards as having minor significance to her is on weak ground if she calls it fake news because she does not find the story significant enough.

Proximity

The criterion of proximity refers to how close events happen to an audience. Events are more newsworthy to the people in a town when those events occurred in their town rather than somewhere far away. However, proximity need not be limited to a geographical context; it can also be applied to a cultural context. For example, people in the United States might regard an event that occurred in England as far more newsworthy in proximity than if that same event occurred in Iceland, although Iceland is much closer to the United States than is England. But England is much closer to the United States culturally than is Iceland when we consider language and history.

Prominence

Famous people get more coverage just because they are famous. If you break your arm, it won't make the news; but if the Queen of England breaks her arm, it's big news. Thus the criterion of prominence refers to how well known a person or event is to the intended audience.

Unusualness

Events that are not typical are usually considered more newsworthy than events that occur every day. Thus, the cliché saying applies: If a dog bites a man, that is not newsworthy; but if a man bites a dog, that is news.

Human Interest

Human interest stories are a bit of a special case. They often disregard the main rules of newsworthiness; for example, they don't lose their timeliness as quickly, they need not affect a large number of people, and it may not matter where in the world the story takes place. Human interest stories appeal to the emotions. They aim to evoke responses such as amusement or sadness. Television news programs often place a humorous or quirky story at the end of the show to leave audiences with a feel-good reaction. Newspapers often have a dedicated area for offbeat or interesting items.

As you can see from the above analysis, each of these six criteria is relevant to determining how newsworthy something is, but none of them allow for a simple judgment. One reason for the difficulties in applying these criteria is that none of the six are categorical. That is, none offers a clear threshold to allow people to make simple classifications of being newsworthy versus not being newsworthy. Instead, each of the six offers a continuum of possibilities, so journalists must continually make judgments about whether something has enough characteristics of a criterion to be considered newsworthy. A second reason for the difficulty in applying these criteria is that they all interact with one another to force us to consider trade-offs. For example, something of moderate significance is typically news if it has occurred close to the audience but not if it occurred halfway around the world. In another example, a freaky happening (e.g., man bites dog) is high on the unusual criterion but negligible on the significance criterion. Given the degree of judgment required to use these criteria to decide what is newsworthy, it is not surprising that there is likely to be a wide range of opinion about whether any given story is newsworthy and therefore not fake news.

Delineation by Type of Sender

Another way that critics have identified news as being fake has been to focus on who is presenting a story as news. People who use this idea as the basis for their criticism make a distinction between legitimate professionals who present real news and others who present fake news. How do we distinguish between legitimate journalists and nonlegitimate journalists? Two ways have typically been used: one way is to look at the channels used to distribute the news, and the second is to use a standard of professionalism.

By Channel

For a long time, journalists were regarded as "reporters and editors working for newspapers, the broadcast media or wire services" (Donsbach, 2010, p. 43). With the rise of the digital media and the proliferation of websites and blogs that provide news stories, critics made an easy distinction by channel. They regarded the traditional news sites as mainstream and therefore legitimate, while the online sites were upstarts with no credibility and therefore not legitimate (McCaffrey, 2010). This is an easy distinction to make by channel, but when we start to analyze it, we can see that it loses its value. If we regard legitimate news and those stories produced by the mainstream news media, how do we define "mainstream"? Of course, we mean the television networks of ABC, CBS, and NBC, but do we also include Fox? Do we include non-broadcast TV networks like CNN? What about weekly newspapers? What about newspapers that have shifted from print to the Internet? You can see that this is a difficult distinction to make with adequate consistency.

Another problem with using channels to distinguish between legitimate and nonlegitimate news story providers is that many online news providers have been around long enough now to have established a solid reputation on par with the traditional mainstream news providers. Some news organizations are purely online sites with no print or broadcast outlets (e.g., Google News, Yahoo News, *The Huffington Post*, *Slate*, and Breitbart), and each has a staff of highly experienced journalists. Many of these online-only news sites have generated higher levels of trust for providing accurate news stories than many of the traditional news sites of newspapers and broadcast media (Engel, 2017).

While the mainstream media historically have earned a high level of trust for providing legitimate news, there are many examples where this trust has not been warranted. A high-profile example of this took place in 2004, when CBS news ran a report on *60 Minutes* that President George Bush Jr. had used his family connections to receive favorable treatment in the Air National Guard when he was a young man and eligible for the draft during the Vietnam War. Bloggers questioned the authenticity of the memos that CBS had used as the basis for its story. The bloggers were correct that the source memos were faulty, and CBS had to retract the story. Furthermore, Dan Rather, who was the news anchor at CBS, resigned in disgrace.

Another example of mainstream news media presenting nonlegitimate news occurred in 2015, when Brian Williams, anchor of *NBC Nightly News*, reported a story on air about him being in a helicopter covering the war in Iraq when the helicopter was shot down. When the story was found to be false, the credibility of the *Nightly News* program was damaged as viewers severely criticized the news anchor for knowingly lying on the air. NBC suspended him for 6 months without pay as a way of punishing him. At about the same time, Jon Stewart announced his retirement after anchoring the *Daily Show* since 1999 (Poniewozik, 2012). His viewers were sad to lose such an important news resource. Even though the public reactions were very different, both men shared many similarities. Both had loyal followings from people who wanted daily information on current events. Both were long-time anchors for evening news shows on major networks. But Williams worked for the news division of NBC where his show attracted 2 million viewers nightly, while

Brad Barket/Stringer/Getty Images Entertainment/Getty Images

Jon Stewart (right) hosted the satirical news program, *The Daily Show*, for 16 years before retiring in 2015. Comedian Trevor Noah (left) now hosts the show, which mixes comedy with political news.

Stewart worked for Comedy Central where his show attracted 3 million viewers nightly. But perhaps the most important difference was that while both men reported on current events, viewers could tell when Stewart was making something up and they appreciated his exhaustive research that was presented as satire to make fun of many current events rather than simply present them as facts.

The distinction by channel no longer works well. While the public may trust mainstream traditional news organizations generally more than newer online news organizations, there are many exceptions (Engel, 2017). That is, mainstream news organizations have made many high-profile mistakes, while some online news organizations have built solid reputations for providing good news coverage.

By Professionalism

A second way critics try to draw a line between legitimate and nonlegitimate newsworkers is to distinguish them by professionalism. However, there is a persistent question about whether journalism is a profession or not. Ornebring (2010) points out that professionalism in general is traceable to three qualities: knowledge, organization, and autonomy. He says that knowledge is composed of a cognitive base and particular skills. Organization refers to

> how a profession may require membership of professional associations that legitimately represent the profession as how practitioners must be able to earn a living from engaging full-time in their profession, and how formal codes of ethics organize the profession. (p. 569)

Autonomy refers to how professionals are able to do their jobs with a great deal of individual discretion, and external influence over the work process itself should be nonexistent or minimal. Thus applying these criteria of knowledge, organization, and autonomy, we can see that physicians are members of a profession. They are required to obtain a certain level of knowledge and skill that is tested before they are certified. While physicians are not required to join a professional association such as the American Medical Association (AMA), the AMA does control the education and certification of physicians. And physicians themselves decide what knowledge and skills are required for certification. Other professions (lawyers, accountants, building contractors, electricians, psychologists, public school teachers, masseuses, etc.) all have a governing organization that decides what knowledge and skills people must have in order to be certified as being a member of that profession and earn a license to practice that profession.

While many journalists typically regard their work as a profession, it is questionable about whether this characterization is accurate. Using Ornebring's three qualities as criteria, it appears that journalism does not qualify as a profession.

Knowledge Criterion. As for knowledge, there is no agreed-upon set of facts that journalists must share, nor is it possible to think of what such a set of facts might be given the wide variety of stories that journalists cover daily. A reporter working on crime stories would need a different set of knowledge than reporters covering government, sports, entertainment, religion, and so on. It is difficult to conceive of a test that would assess whether any kind of a journalist possessed enough knowledge to be considered a professional journalist. Thus, no such test exists.

Organization Criterion. Journalists do have professional organizations, such as the American Society of Newspaper Editors (ASNE) and the Society of Professional Journalists (SPJ). SPJ was founded in 1909 and now has nearly 300 chapters and 9,000 members of the media in the United States. Both of these professional societies have a code of ethics for their members. For example, the SPJ (Society of Professional Journalists, 2018) code of ethics states that professional journalists "believe that public enlightenment is the forerunner of justice and the foundation of democracy. Ethical journalism strives to ensure the free exchange of information that is accurate, fair and thorough." An ethical journalist acts with integrity, as defined by four principles: (1) seek truth and report it, (2) minimize harm, (3) act independently, and (4) be accountable and transparent.

Notice two things about this definition. First, it outlines what an "ethical journalist" does by saying that it "encourages" journalists to behave ethically. But it does not *require* such behavior. Therefore this definition suggests that people who are not ethical can still be regarded as a journalist. Also, notice that the four criteria are very open ended; that is, the definition does not specify the meaning of its key terms such as *truth, harm, act independently,* and *transparent.* Nor does the definition specify who journalists are accountable to—that is, who their constituents are. Should journalists be accountable to their news organizations, society at large, or some constituent within the general public, such as readers who desire a particular point of view in their news coverage? These are all important constituents but each has different expectations for journalists. To illustrate, if journalists are to be held accountable to society in general, then their stories need to provide all kinds of audiences with information in order to foster an open and civil exchange of views, even views they find repugnant. In contrast, if the primary constituent of a news organization is a particular group of people such as a niche audience along the political spectrum, then those audiences expect journalists to provide them information that supports their existing beliefs while discounting all other types of information. And if journalists' primary constituent is the news organization for which they work, then their focus needs to be on attracting a niche audience and conditioning those people for repeated exposures (recall this point from Chapter 4).

Oftentimes these constituents have different purposes for news so a journalist often cannot satisfy one constituent without alienating—or even angering—other constituents. For example, Benjamin Franklin's grandson, Benjamin Franklin Bache, inherited his grandfather's newspaper in 1790. Over the next decade, he railed against President John Adams's administration and sold lots of newspapers. In so doing, he angered Adams's party (the Federalists) to such an extent that his news stories were credited as a major influence in destroying the Federalist political party. Although the term "fake news" was not used in the 18th century, it is likely that people who favored the Federalist party regarded Bache's stories as fake and Bache as not a qualified journalist but instead as a political hack. Until the late 19th century, newspapers were typically niche oriented and each appealed to people of a particular political orientation. It was not until the rise of the penny press in the 1880s that newspapers tried to appear "objective" in their news coverage so as to expand their potential readership. That is, by trying to avoid offending readers of any political orientation, newspapers began attracting widespread readership.

However, in the 21st century, easy access to the Internet has enabled tens of thousands of people to create websites to present their political points of view to like-minded niche audiences, and many of these bloggers consider themselves to be legitimate journalists.

In 1922, the ASNE adopted a statement of principles that contained six articles of responsibility, freedom of the press, independence, truth and accuracy, impartiality, and fair play. The document was revised and renamed the "Statement of Principles" in 1975. Kaplan (2010) writes,

> This professional code of studied impartiality and rigorous factuality has been celebrated as American journalism's proudest, if most difficult to sustain, achievement. Considered a crucial tool for democracy, objectivity supposedly secures a space for neutral, factual information and public deliberation outside the corruption, rancor, and partisan spin that normally characterizes public discourse. (p. 25)

However, there is no licensing process for journalists to make sure they conform to the requirements of their profession like there is for other professions such as doctors, lawyers, accountants, and so on. Nor is there a professional organization that monitors their work and applies sanctions to those who violate the canon of ethics.

Autonomy Criterion. Journalists have always sought to be independent from outside pressures in a quest to report the news accurately. But this autonomy has focused on political influence—that is, protecting their independence from governmental interference with rights to obtain information and to report freely and openly. Journalists have been less vigilant about protecting their autonomy from economic influences. This led Ornebring (2010) to argue that journalism is currently undergoing a reverse professionalization; it is "becoming less of a coherent and autonomous occupation" and this is "thought to have negative effects on the status of journalism in society, the quality of journalism available to audiences, and, perhaps most importantly, the role of journalism as an institution of democracy" (p. 569).

As you can see from the analysis of type of sender, there is no professional organization that certifies who is a journalist and who is not. While there are professional societies that encourage journalists to adhere to particular guidelines, those societies have no power to require compliance. Therefore we cannot rely on an authority to tell us who we should trust as presenting real news and who we should regard as presenting fake news.

Delineation by Intention of Sender

The intention of the sender of a news story can be used as a criterion for determining what is fake news. If the purpose of news stories is to inform the public, then when senders deviate from this purpose and instead have a persuasive intent, these deviations can be regarded as fake news.

Sometimes such deviations are relatively easy to spot, such as advertorials, which are paid advertisements made to look like news stories. Oftentimes, advertisers who do not want audiences to discount their persuasive messages will make them look like news stories. Sometimes these advertorials are relatively easy to identify when the senders identify themselves as a sponsor (a commercial company, political party, or candidate running for office), although such designation may be only in the small print or a small company logo. But many times these sponsored stories do not identify who paid for the story placement, and this practice misleads audiences into thinking that a story is news when in actuality it is an advertisement.

Native advertising is a type of covert marketing practice where an ad mimics—or appears "native" to—the platform on which it appears. As a form of fake news, it "appropriates the look and feel of real news" (Tandoc et al., 2017, p. 11). Native advertising has evolved from the print advertorials of the analog era and has proliferated in the new digital media space (Carlson, 2015; Einstein, 2016; Sonderman & Tran, 2013). Many legacy and digital-only news media not only host native advertising but create this type of content on behalf of advertisers. However, this trend has not been good for informed citizenship. A growing body of academic research reveals that when native ads appear on news websites, less than 25% of adults are able to identify that what they are viewing is an advertisement rather than editorial content (Amazeen & Muddiman, 2018; Amazeen & Wojdynski, 2018). Similar results have been found for college-age, high-school, and middle-school digital natives (McGrew et al., 2017). Yet despite the difficulties audiences have in distinguishing between native and other covert content, publishers typically have not been helpful in alerting their audiences to the different types (Einstein, 2016).

Audiences who read an advertisement that looks like a news story but then realize that it is an ad feel misled and are likely to label that news story as being fake news. The facts presented in the story may all be accurate and the story may exhibit the characteristics of timeliness, significance, proximity, prominence, unusualness, and human interest. But if audiences realize that the story was paid for by a company trying to sell its product, then people will not regard it as legitimate news and will label it as fake news. In this case, the fakeness stems not from the story itself but from the intention of the sender.

It is much harder to spot the persuasive intent of senders of news stories when the sender has a point of view that heavily filters information and presents information that advocates their point of view while discounting or ignoring the existence of other points of view. We expect these types of messages to be labeled as editorials or opinion pieces; when they are labeled as such, audiences are alerted to treat them as essays that advocate for a point of view held by the sender of the message and not as a balanced presentation of facts. However, when audiences do not see something clearly labeled as persuasion, then they default to the assumption that the information is intended to inform them and this can be misleading.

This line between the two types of intentions has been blurring over time. And some editorial writers who have strong opinions on an issue allow their opinions to shape how they cover stories when they are performing reporter duties.

Delineation by Accuracy

A fourth possible way for people to arrive at a judgment that something is fake news is to use factual accuracy as a criterion. At first glance, factual accuracy seems to be a killer criterion capable of sharply delineating fake from real, but this is not the case when we analyze the idea of accuracy. Let's begin with the simplest designation of factual accuracy.

How Does This Bull Market End?

Probably the same way it began.

GILLIAN B. WHITE AUG 22, 2018

A Woman's Paycheck Is Influenced by Her Hometown—Even If She Doesn't Live There Anymore

In a new study, economists find women from places where sexist attitudes prevail end up earning less later in life.

VAUHINI VARA AUG 20, 2018

SPONSOR CONTENT

How Tech Brings Matcha from the Farm to Your Cup

The United States is currently in the throes of "Matcha Madness." Techology has become the key to take this rapidly popular drink into the mainstream.

AT&T BUSINESS

Teaching Kids to Code During the Summer—for $1,000 a Week

Are private summer camps exacerbating tech's diversity problem?

LINDSAY GELLMAN AUG 18, 2018

Native advertisements can look like regular articles. *The Atlantic* mixes sponsored content into their website's Business section.

Factual Accuracy

The building blocks of news stories are facts—that is, the *who, what, when, where,* and *why* of something. It is understandable that people would judge a story as real news when they believe that journalists present accurate facts, and they judge a story as fake when they believe that journalists present inaccurate facts either through sloppiness or through bias. This distinction sounds simple enough, but let's analyze it.

In order to make a judgment about whether a fact is accurate or not, we need a truth standard. Many facts have a clear truth standard that exists in our memories or that we can easily look up. For example, we can verify that Donald J. Trump was sworn in as president of the United States in January 2017. We may or may not like it, but this is a fact that can be verified as accurate. He is the 45th president of the United States. Or is he? Did you know that 44 people have been sworn in as president but because

Grover Cleveland served two non-consecutive terms in office, Cleveland is counted as the nation's 22nd and 24th presidents? Is it accurate to call Trump the 44th or 45th president? A case could be made for either. If we are counting the number of individuals who have served as president, then Trump is the 44th. But if we are counting the number of changes in leadership, then Trump is the 45th.

Often a fact may have more than one truth standard. For example, the U.S. Bureau of Labor Statistics (2018) reported in May 2018 that the unemployment rate had dipped to 3.8%, with 161,539,000 people currently working. However, in May 2018, the U.S. population was 327,988,000 people. So if we subtract the number of employed people from the number of people in the total population, we get a figure of 166,449,000 unemployed people, which is 50.8% of the U.S. population. Which figure is the accurate indicator of unemployment rate—3.8% or 50.8%? The answer is that both figures are accurate; understanding how both figures can be accurate requires us to understand how the figures are computed. That is, both figures are accurate computations but the numbers in the computations are different because of the differences in definitions of "unemployment." In everyday life, we define "unemployed" as simply not working, but the Bureau of Labor Statistics defines it very differently (see Box Issue 3.1).

BOX ISSUE 3.1

WHAT IS THE UNEMPLOYMENT RATE IN THE UNITED STATES?

Fact: In May 2018, the unemployment rate was 50.8%.

Rationale

- The U.S. population was 327,988,000 people.

- 161,539,000 people were working; 166,449,000 were not working.

- Therefore, 50.8% were unemployed.

Fact: In May 2018, the unemployment rate was 3.8%.

Rationale

- The U.S. Department of Labor recognized that 161,539,000 people were working in the United States as of May 2018.

- However, the U.S. Department of Labor does not use the total population figure to compute the unemployment rate; instead it uses a figure called the "labor force" to compute the percentage of people unemployed.

- The labor force begins with the total U.S. population then reduces that number by excluding the following people:
  - All people who are not at least 16 years old
  - All people serving in the military
  - All people who are institutionalized (prison, hospitals, etc.)
  - All people who cannot work due to some kind of handicap
  - All people who are retired
  - All people who do not want to work for some reason

Source: Bureau of Labor Statistics (2018).

People who want to argue that the unemployment rate is low will select the 3.8% figure, while people who want to argue that the unemployment rate is too high or misleading will select a higher figure. If we read several news stories on unemployment and notice that the figures differ across reports, we are likely to regard many of those reports as fake news by assuming that many of the figures are inaccurate. Our natural tendency is to pick one figure and regard that one as a fact while labeling all others as inaccurate. But when we do that, the fault lies with us in our misunderstanding rather than in the inaccuracy of any of the figures.

There are many examples of reported figures that appear to have a simple factual basis but that have multiple truth standards. For example, when I check my weather apps for the local temperature in my town of Santa Barbara, they each give me a different reading—sometimes a difference of as much as 20 degrees. How is this possible? Santa Barbara is a city with several very different microclimates. So the Santa Barbara temperature may be 60 degrees down by the beach, 70 degrees in the middle of the downtown area, and 80 degrees up on the hiking trails in the mountains. Each figure is an accurate reading of the temperature within some part of the city of Santa Barbara. I cannot rely on any one; instead when I am looking at the weather conditions to decide how to dress, I need to know what the weather is where I am going. It would be unfair for me to criticize my apps for providing me with "fake" readings of temperature because each app provides accurate information—but accurate for only one particular locale even though they all present their figure as the current temperature in Santa Barbara.

Thus making a judgment about whether a news story is fake or not is not as simple as comparing reported figures to one's belief about what those figures should be. It is much more complex because many facts have multiple truth standards. And even when a fact has only one truth standard, it can be reported inaccurately because all people involved in the news story and the reporting believed it to be accurate even though it was not. There are times where journalists interview "expert" sources who do not know the accurate figures for something but they answer the journalists' questions with their guesses, which are often inaccurate. When journalists have enough time, they check the accuracy of what experts tell them; but oftentimes, journalists do not check the accuracy because they trust the expert source. The inaccurate fact then gets reported as being true. Is this fake news? The journalist would say she was being accurate because she reported exactly what the expert source said. The source might say he was being accurate because he genuinely believed the fact to be correct.

Story Accuracy

Let's say that a journalist presents 20 facts in a news story and all the facts are accurate except for one. In this case, should we regard the story as accurate? Answering this question requires a judgment about the value of the entire story. This judgment is typically not as simple as deciding that the story is 95% accurate (19 facts out of 20 are accurate) so we should trust the story. Perhaps the one fact that is faulty is so important that it destroys the credibility of the entire story.

Delineation by Context

The word "story" in the phrase "news story" refers to the idea that newsworkers produce messages that present multiple facts arranged in a sequence that is intended to inform audiences about some event, person, or issue. This arrangement can be a simple listing of those facts. For example, a newsworker might list the bare facts of who, what, when, and where (see Box Issue 3.2). There may be nothing inaccurate about this story, but the story is so abbreviated that it does not offer audiences a context to help them understand the significance of the event being covered in the story. When editors think the story is about an important event, they ask reporters to gather more information and create a better treatment of the story. This process typically means giving audiences more context so they can appreciate the significance of the event.

BOX ISSUE 3.2
CONTEXT IN NEWS STORIES

Simple Listing of Facts

John J. Smith was arrested last night in his office at City Hall.

Negative Context for Smith

Mayor John J. Smith was arrested for the third time on charges of embezzlement, taken to the city jail where he spent the night locked up, then released on $100,000 bail early this morning.

Smith was charged with diverting more than $1 million of taxpayer funds away from city-approved projects and into areas that the indictment said benefited him personally.

"Smith continues to misappropriate public funds," said Horace T. Resnick, a city council member. "We on the city council have approved funding for some very worthy projects but the mayor continually refuses to transfer funds to these projects. This is an egregious abuse of power and he needs to be held accountable."

If Smith is convicted of the felony of embezzlement, he will immediately be removed from office.

Positive Context for Smith

Political opponents of John J. Smith put out an arrest warrant for the mayor last night. This is the third time this year that his opponents have tried to have him removed from office on charges of embezzling funds that were approved by the city council last year to build the Resnick Athletic Complex.

"Our city already has many athletic facilities," said Mayor Smith. "I cannot justify spending the money on something we do not need when we could spend it instead on something we desperately need, like sidewalks in neighborhoods around elementary schools. Children's safety is more important than the pet projects of a few council members."

When reporters are assigned to write a story about an event or a person that has a high degree of significance, they must gather more facts. Doing so requires journalists to make more filtering judgments about which facts to gather and how to arrange that greater number of facts in a sequence that conveys the significance. As newsworkers expand on the details, they are confronted by many decisions about which details to include and which to leave out. Also, they must decide the order in which they present the details, knowing that those details presented earlier in the story are more likely to be read than those details presented later. Also, we know from psychological research that the information presented first in a story is likely to frame audiences' expectations and thereby set them off on a particular path of interpreting the meaning of the presented elements. Box Issue 3.2 illustrates how the expansion of a story with more details provides a richer context for audiences to understand the meaning of an event—in this case, the arrest of a mayor. Notice that one way of telling the story presents Smith in a negative context, while another way of telling the same story presents Smith in a positive context.

Typically there are several different ways this significance can be conveyed, so when journalists construct their story to match the expectations of audiences, those audiences are more likely to regard the story as real news. But when journalists violate those expectations, audiences are more likely to regard the story as fake news.

Context gives readers more information to interpret the meaning of a story. But when newsworkers add context to their stories, they reveal their own personal biases. In the example of Mayor Smith, you can see that one journalist appears to have a negative perspective on Smith, while another journalist has a positive perspective. Recall from Chapter 9 that audiences expect newsworkers to present a balanced treatment of the people and events in their stories. But balance is difficult to achieve. Reporters could present an equal number of positive facts and negative facts, but this alone cannot guarantee balance because some facts may be more significant and carry more weight in the way audiences interpret meaning. So while balance is a worthy goal for reporters to try to achieve in every one of their stories, the judgment of whether balance was in fact achieved rests with audience members.

The key concern here is bias. When reporters research and write stories, they must make many decisions that are unavoidable. Some reporters approach this task like a scientist by keeping an open mind. As human beings, they may have opinions about an issue; but when they cover that issue as a scientist, they are willing to consider all points of view and present each one clearly and accurately. With this perspective, journalists see themselves as providers of full sets of information and then allow audiences to make up their own minds. Their goal is to contribute to a society in which differences of opinion exist but it is better to have informed opinions rather than uninformed opinions. In contrast, other journalists approach the task of reporting like a lawyer or debater. They use their own opinion (or the opinion of their editors) as a guiding point of view in collecting information and reporting that information. That is, they try to collect as much information as possible to support their own point of view; when they encounter information that is counter to their point of view, they either (a) refute it, (b) discount it, or (c) ignore it altogether because their purpose is to win the argument.

Stories that are written from an advocacy perspective stimulate much stronger emotional reactions in audiences. If audiences share the same opinion as the journalist, they feel good because there is more confirmation that their opinion is a good one. This is reinforcing and makes it more likely that those audiences will continue to seek out stories from that news provider. In contrast, if the audiences do not share the same opinion as the journalist, they feel bad. To handle these bad feelings they discount the story as being faulty; that is, it must be fake news.

Journalists are expected to be objective. However, recall from Chapter 9 that true objectivity is impossible to achieve. Instead journalists are more realistic and try to achieve neutrality, balance, completeness, and context in their news stories. Journalists who consistently demonstrate these characteristics in their news stories are regarded as providing real news. However, these characteristics are interpretations by the audience, that is, they must infer whether a story exhibits these characteristics from the way the story is presented. Not all audience members will make the same interpretations.

An Irony

News organizations are much more sensitive to violations of facts than to violations of bias. An example of this is the case of Jayson Blair, a 27-year-old reporter who was on the fast track at the *New York Times*. In order to enhance his career, he tried to write stories that would be so interesting that they would be selected for publication in the most prominent places in the newspaper. However, in order to write such stories, he liberally embellished the facts, even going so far as to make up whole stories. When *Times* editors finally began checking his stories, they found many fabrications and quickly fired Blair. But the damage to the credibility of the *Times* was done, and the editors felt compelled to publish a 14,000-word apologia on its front page (Wolff, 2003). Blair explained that he conducted extensive interviews for his stories and did a significant amount of research so his stories had a strong factual basis. However, when he wrote up his stories, Blair made changes to the names of people and places to protect the anonymity of the people he wrote about. He also rearranged facts and inferred information in order to fill in gaps so he could tell a more compelling story—a story that would be read and remembered so that his readers could more vividly understand the issues he was writing about, such as poverty and drug addiction. Thus the "truth" he was trying to communicate was more about big-picture patterns than the specifics of who did what to whom at an exact time and place (Wolff, 2003).

Context can illuminate the meaning of events and help audiences better understand the nature of those events, but context can also mislead audiences. Even a newspaper as respected as the *New York Times*, with its rigorous fact-checking apparatus, can still present stories that mislead audiences (Kurtz, 2018). Therefore it is important to be continually vigilant not only to the accuracy of facts in news stories but also to how the context of those stories can change meanings.

Conclusion

By now you should understand that there are many different things that could trigger an audience judgment that a news story is faulty and should be labeled as fake news. Perhaps the story is judged to be too old or lack enough significance to warrant coverage. Or perhaps audiences regard the sender as not being a journalist or being more interested in persuading rather than informing. Or perhaps audiences identify faulty facts or a misleading context. All of these perceptions can trigger a criticism of fake news. Given all these different bases for criticism, how can we deal with this issue in a media-literate manner?

MEDIA-LITERATE TREATMENT OF FAKE NEWS

Dealing with fake news is not easy. It requires constant vigilance, checking, and discounting. To make this task as easy as possible, I suggest a continuous four-step procedure as follows.

Be Skeptical

First, stay alert to the possibility that any news story can be fake in some way. This is an easy first step because it requires little effort. You simply rely on your emotional reactions to signal that something might not be right about the story. The challenge here is that you set a proper level of sensitivity to your **news radar**. If your radar is not sensitive enough, many false or misleading stories are not detected; if your radar is too sensitive, you are too compulsive and you waste time being concerned about perfectly good news stories. Achieving a proper level of sensitivity will develop from experience with particular news organizations and journalists. When a story raises a red flag for you, then move on to the next step.

Be Analytical

When you feel uncomfortable about a story, the next step is to analyze it to figure out what is bothering you. There are five analytical dimensions to use in trying to identify what might be wrong with the story (see Applying Media Literacy Skills Issues 3.1 and 3.2). Keep certain questions foremost in your mind as you are exposed to news stories. When you have difficulty answering these questions to your satisfaction or if the story makes you feel uncomfortable emotionally, red flag it. Once you've tagged a story as raising concerns for you, you need to check the facts as well as the way the facts are presented.

Evaluate Facts

The next step is to confirm that your feelings that something is wrong with the story are legitimate. The simplest of these tasks is to check the accuracy of a fact. Did the journalist identify all the sources of information? Did the journalist reserve anonymity for sources who may face danger, retribution, or other harm and have information that cannot be obtained elsewhere? When sources were identified, did the journalist explain why audience members should regard the source as credible? If the journalist presented two facts that seemed to oppose one another, did the journalist try to resolve the difference and explain how? Did the journalist label illustrations and re-enactments?

Evaluate the News Story

Does the journalist simply list facts or does the journalist try to provide context? When journalists provide context, do they take special care not to misrepresent or oversimplify in promoting, previewing, or summarizing a story? Are all instances of advocacy and commentary labeled?

More difficult is confirming the intention of the journalist; that is, was the journalist trying to be neutral and present the event as clearly and neutrally as possible? Or does the way the story is told lead you to be concerned that the journalist was trying to persuade you to a particular point of view?

If you have confirmed that a story is faulty in some way to regard it as fake news, then you need to discount it. Also, you need to think about whether this story is a "one off" for this journalist or whether he or she should never be trusted. This will require you to analyze other stories written by the journalist. And you will need to determine if the problem is bigger than any one newsworker and is systemic to the entire news organization.

YOUR OWN INFORMED OPINION

On this issue of fake news, it is important that you walk a fine line in order to construct an informed opinion. You need to be critical of news but not overly critical.

Be careful not to believe everything you hear in news stories. There are many stories that present inaccurate facts, and even the stories that contain only accurate facts can mislead you with an exploitive context because of the newsworkers' bias or a persuasive—rather than informative—intent. When you have well-developed knowledge structures in many different areas, it is easier to spot facts that may be inaccurate. And when you have a strong personal locus with a good awareness of your own needs for news information and a strong drive to satisfy those needs, you will be better able to perceive when news stories are trying to mislead you and to counter those subtle manipulations.

At the same time, be careful not to criticize everything you hear in news stories as being fake news. There are many news providers that genuinely try to check all facts and present news stories that are fair and balanced. Of course, there may be times when it looks like an inaccurate fact is reported; when you perceive this to be the case, check that fact's accuracy for yourself if possible instead of labeling the news organization as being sloppy or manipulative. This is not to say that there are no news organizations that operate as fronts for people with strong political or economic motives to try to persuade you rather than to inform you and let you make up your own mind. The key to dealing with this issue in a media-literate manner is to be skeptical and analytical so you can tell the difference between the news organizations you can trust and those you should not.

Further Reading

Kurtz, H. (2018). *Media madness: Donald Trump, the press, and the war over the truth.* Washington, DC: Regnery Publishing. (288 pages, including index)

This is a journalist's analysis of the press coverage of Trump's first year in office. Kurtz argues that the press's coverage of Trump was largely negative because of a bias among journalists to avoid normalizing his presidency. Rather than provide balanced coverage of his actions and words, the press amplified the negatives and downplayed the positives, which led Trump to criticize the press for continually presenting false news and in turn angered journalists and created a destructive cycle.

Levitin, D. J. (2016). *A field guide to lies: Critical thinking in the information age.* New York, NY: Dutton. (292 pages, including glossary and index)

Levitin, an academic and bestselling author, shows how facts presented in the media can be misleading or outright lies. The book is organized in three sections. The first section presents six chapters that show many ways that numbers can be used to mislead audiences. The second section (four chapters) shows how words can be used to distort meaning. The third section presents five chapters about how people can be misled by "facts" if they have insufficient background knowledge about science, logic, and statistics.

(Continued)

(Continued)

Nichol, T. (2017). *The death of expertise: The campaign against established knowledge and why it matters.* New York, NY: Oxford University Press. (252 pages, including index and endnotes)

This is an extended essay about how the culture has changed so that people no longer recognize expertise or care about it. With the rise of the Internet, information is so readily available on any topic that people can quickly access what look like facts. But because anyone can post anything on the Internet, most of that information is faulty because it is unchecked and unedited. And because people cannot tell the difference between good and bad information, the bad information carries as much weight as the good in shaping public opinion.

Keeping Up to Date

Mediacollege.com (http://www.mediacollege.com/journalism/news/newsworthy.html)

This webpage includes articles and examples illustrating what makes a story newsworthy.

APPLYING MEDIA LITERACY SKILLS ISSUE 3.1
BE ANALYTICAL

News Criteria Analytical Dimension

1. Is there something missing in the story that makes you feel it is not news?

   Is it significant enough?

   Is it timely enough?

2. Why is this story being presented as news when it does not meet enough "newsworthiness" criteria?

Type of Sender Analytical Dimension

1. If you feel the presenter of the story (reporter, editor, news organization) lacks a professional perspective worthy of being regarded as a journalist, what is missing?

2. Is your expectation for what journalists should do realistic?

Intention of Sender Analytical Dimension

1. Do you feel that this story lacks sufficient informative value?

   If so, what is missing?

2. Do you feel that this story has a persuasive intent?

   If so, what elements in the story make you feel that way?

Accuracy Analytical Dimension

1. Do you feel that the story presents inaccurate facts?

   If so, which facts do you believe are inaccurate and why?

2. Do you feel that the story is inaccurate because it lacks the presentation of key information?

If so, what critical information is missing?

Context Analytical Dimension

1. Do you feel the context is missing to help you interpret the meaning of events?

If so, what is missing?

2. Do you feel that the context presented by the journalist has systematically distorted the meaning of the event being covered?

If so, how?

3. Do you feel that the journalist has let his or her bias influence the story?

If so, do you think the bias is from lack of skill in presenting an adequate story?

Or do you feel that journalist has purposely presented a point of view in order to manipulate audiences?

APPLYING MEDIA LITERACY SKILLS ISSUE 3.2
THE ISSUE OF FAKE NEWS

1. Analyze an Unfamiliar Print Source of News

Select a newspaper, magazine, or online news source that you have never accessed before.

a. Analysis for Newsworthiness

Do you think the story contains enough newsworthy elements to warrant its presentation as news?

If so, which news criteria were most influential in your decision?

If not, what is missing? That is, what did this story need to exhibit more of in order for you to consider it newsworthy?

b. Analysis by Type of Sender

What can you find out about the person who wrote the story? Is this person a professional journalist? What is his or her education and experience?

What can you find out about the news organization? What is the news organization's reputation in the journalistic community and among audiences?

Who owns the news organization? Is it owned by a large conglomerate or is it independent?

c. Analysis by Intention of Sender

Do you sense that the story is more informative or persuasive?

What elements in the story led you to this conclusion?

d. Analysis by Accuracy

Do you judge any of the facts in the story as appearing to be inaccurate?

If so, why do you think they may be inaccurate? What are the sources of those facts?

If not, why do you feel all the facts are accurate?

Do you judge the overall story to be accurate?

(Continued)

(Continued)

   e. Analysis of Context

     Do you think the story is a simple listing of facts or is it a construction with context?

     If the former, do you think the story would have been better with context?

     If the latter, do you think the context was fair or manipulative?

2. Analyze an Unfamiliar Audiovisual Source of News

   Select a news story from television, radio, or the Internet. If you choose a website, find a story that has audio, video, and photos. Do the same five-step analysis as above. Pay special attention to the audio and visual elements.

3. Analyze a News Story From a Source of News Familiar to You

   Select a news story from a source of news that is familiar to you. Do the same five-step analysis as above. Pay special attention to your past experience with this source of news.

- In what ways does your past experience make this analysis easier?

- In what ways does your past experience potentially hinder you from conducting the analysis with a fresh perspective?

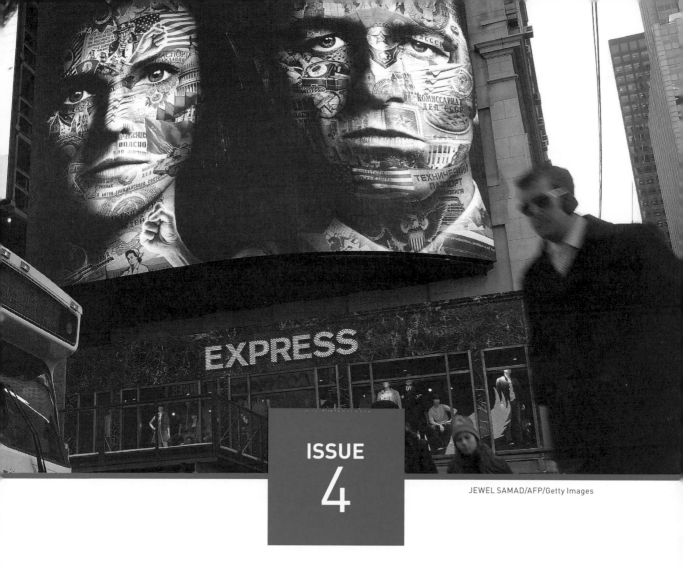

ADVERTISING

Issue: We live in a culture saturated with advertising messages.
Some popular criticisms of advertising form the public discourse, but the issues that
should concern us more lie at a deeper level.

A digital billboard of the TV show *The Americans* in Times Square. Whether you live in the big city or a small town, you are exposed to thousands of advertising messages every day.

Advertising is pervasive throughout our culture, as you saw in Chapter 11. We cannot avoid being continually exposed to ads of all kinds every day, everywhere. This leads us to criticize advertising for various reasons. In this chapter, we will analyze this criticism as we confront the issue about whether this criticism is warranted or not.

DELINEATING THE ISSUE

Some people regard advertisers as unscrupulous manipulators who will do or say anything to get you to give them your money. They think advertising has changed the culture for the worse by making us too materialistic—creating a throwaway society of products, ideas, and people.

Other people regard advertisers as American heroes who are responsible for keeping the economy fired up by creatively encouraging more and more consumption, which has produced the richest society ever—one with the highest standard of living and the most variety of everything imaginable. They see advertising as a glamorous profession for creative people—a fast track to a rewarding career.

Most people, however, do not criticize advertising, ignoring it as so much a part of the environment to be taken for granted. Every once in a while a particular ad might capture their attention by offending them and trigger a criticism.

Despite the fact that most of us have a positive or at least neutral attitude about advertising, we all have our pet peeves and find ourselves criticizing advertising from time to time. These criticisms typically stay on the surface; that is, we rarely dig down below the surface to try to find out what is really bothering us. However, when we expend the effort to analyze these surface criticisms, we will often find deeper insights that will direct our thinking into new areas or make us realize that our surface criticism was misdirected.

This condition raises the issue of whether advertising should be criticized more and, if so, what those criticisms should be. We begin this analysis by making a distinction among three kinds of criticisms. One kind of criticism is based on inaccurate ideas of advertising, so these criticisms are faulty. A second type of criticism is based on personal values. And a third type of criticism illuminates a difference between social responsibility and economic responsibility. We will examine each of these three kinds of criticism then I'll present some guidelines to help you work through these different kinds in constructing your own informed opinion of advertising.

FAULTY CRITICISMS

Three of the popular criticisms of advertising—advertising is deceptive, companies manipulate us using subliminal advertising, and advertising perpetuates stereotypes—are faulty. Let's examine why.

Advertising Is Deceptive

There is a federal law to ensure "truth in advertising," which is enforced by the Federal Trade Commission (FTC). The FTC was created in 1914 to protect America's consumers.

> Federal law says that ads must be truthful, not misleading, and, when appropriate, backed by scientific evidence. The Federal Trade Commission enforces these truth-in-advertising laws, and it applies the same standards no matter where an ad appears—in newspapers and magazines, online, in the mail, or on billboards or buses. (Federal Trade Commission, n.d.)

This sounds like a fairly clear statement of purpose, and it is. But determining whether advertising is truthful or misleading is often a very difficult task.

In everyday language, we think of deception as lying. Do ads lie? The answer is no in the sense that lying is making a claim that can be proven as false. Advertisers know that if they present a factual claim that they cannot support with evidence, their competitors will spot it and report them to the FTC. The FTC will investigate and punish those advertisers with fines or require them to pay for a corrective advertising campaign where they have to admit they lied. Therefore advertisers are careful to avoid outright lying; that is, they avoid making claims that can be tested and found to be false.

Advertisers, however, know they can stretch the truth or make the public believe exaggerated claims about their products without actually lying by using something called **puffery**. Puffery is a promotional statement that presents subjective claims that cannot be tested for truth although they convey the impression that they are truthful in saying that their product is superior or valuable (see Table Issue 4.1). Advertisers puff up their products with exaggerations that are expressions of opinion rather than claims of some objective quality or characteristic of the product. Thus puffery attempts to trick us into believing there is more to the product than there really is by creating the illusion that ads are making strong claims when, in fact, the claims are weak or even nonexistent (see Table Issue 4.2). From a legal point of view, these puffery claims are not deceptive, because they cannot be proven to be false. However, from a consumer point of view, puffery claims are misleading by design.

Another form of deception that is not illegal and not technically lying is the practice of advertisers hiring people to post positive reviews of their products online. While

TABLE ISSUE 4.1 ■ Puffery Techniques		
Technique	**Explanation**	**Examples**
Partial truth	An ad can present a kernel of truth but puff it up to make to sound bigger than it actually is, thus misleading the public.	Many brands that are labeled as a fruit juice drink contain only 10% fruit juice. Ads for many cereals show a brand as "part of this complete breakfast," which features several nutritious foods such as fruit, bread, and milk. This statement is literally truthful, but almost none of the nutrition in the claim comes from the cereal that is being advertised.
Pseudo-survey	A claim is made that is supported by a survey without providing enough detail to tell if the survey was any good.	"Four out of five dentists surveyed said they recommend X." Who are these five? Maybe they were paid to recommend it.
Pseudo-claims	An ad makes a clear claim for its product but does not give us enough detail to enable us to test it.	"This toothpaste fights cavities." But we are not told how. Is it a chemical in the toothpaste, the movement of the brush on the teeth, or the habit of brushing?
Comparison with an unidentified other	There is an implied comparison that makes the product sound superior, but it really is a meaningless claim.	"X has better cleaning action." Better than what? Better than another brand? Better than not cleaning?
Comparison of the product to its earlier form	A claim is made that the current version of the product is better than a previous version without explaining why.	"X is new and improved!" Again, on the surface, this seems like a good thing—until we start thinking about it. What was wrong with the old version? And what is wrong with this current version that will end up being new and improved again next year?
Irrelevant comparisons	A claim is made that the product is better than unspecified other products.	"X is the best-selling product of its kind." What kind? Maybe *kind* is defined so narrowly that there is only one brand of its kind. Also, maybe it is the best seller because it is the cheapest or because it wears out so fast.
Juxtaposition	No claim is made but a claim is implied from the visual, which leads viewers to associate the product with something positive.	A smiling person holds a product so that viewers associate happiness with the product.

70% of consumers say they trust the reviews from online review sites (such as Yelp, TripAdvisor, and Angie's List), up to 30% of those reviewers were found to be fake. That is, almost one third of product "reviews" were not reviews written by actual consumers of the products they were writing about; instead the glowing product recommendations were written by people hired by the advertisers. Some of these reviews are written by the owners of the businesses being reviewed, along with their friends, family members, and employees who post their reviews under false identities. A survey of Amazon's top 1,000 reviewers found that 85% had received free products from the companies they were reviewing (Grant, 2013). In addition, the buying of fake reviews by merchants hoping to boost sales of their products online continues to be a widespread problem not only on Amazon but also on Google and Facebook (Sterling, 2018).

TABLE ISSUE 4.2 ■ Examples of Puffery in Advertising	
Company	**Slogan**
Seattle's Best Coffee	Serving the best
Gillette Razors	The best a man can get
Folgers Coffee	The best part of wakin' up
Papa John's Pizza	Better ingredients. Better pizza
L'eggs Pantyhose	Nothing beats a great pair of L'eggs
U.S. Army	Be all you can be
Ford Trucks	Built Ford tough
Kellogg's Frosted Flakes	They're great!
Coors Light Beer	Cold as the Rockies

Companies Manipulate Us Through Subliminal Advertising

Is there such a thing as subliminal advertising? That is, are there subliminal messages that have a powerful effect on us? To answer this question, we first need to be clear about what "subliminal" means. The popularized version of subliminal persuasion suggests that the designer of a message is trying to deceive the audience by adding something to a message that is not consciously perceivable by the audience—but the person's unconscious mind still perceives that "extra message." For example, in the 1950s, James Vicary inserted messages of "Eat Popcorn" and "Drink Coke" into a theatrical film and claimed that the theater audience bought much more popcorn and Coke, even though no one reported seeing the ads because they were projected too quickly. Later, it was found that Vicary's results were a hoax. But this story has entered our folklore, and many people believe that unscrupulous advertisers are exposing us to subliminal messages all the time.

The idea of subliminal advertising having an effect on us is also a hoax. The word *subliminal* means below our threshold to perceive. For example, the human eye cannot see an image if it is shown for less than about one sixteenth of a second—that is below our line of ability to perceive an image. This is why we perceive movies as a smooth flow of moving images when, in actuality, what is being projected on the screen is a series of still shots. If those shots are projected at about 12 per second, we see

Meißner/ullstein bild via Getty Images

Think about the unconscious effect of this Lacoste advertisement. What does this image say about the brand of clothing without saying it in writing?

flicker in between shots, but we still perceive motion. Once those individual images are projected as fast as 16 per second, the flicker disappears; that is, it happens too fast to register an impression on us. The flicker between the individual images is still there, but we can no longer perceive it. Hollywood films are projected at 24 or more frames per second. At this speed, there is no chance for any individual frame to register a unique impression on us. So even if an advertiser placed an ad in one frame every second, each of those exposures would be too brief to cross the line of our ability to perceive them. If our sense organs cannot perceive an image, then it can have no effect on us. I'll further clarify this point with an audio example. You can train a dog to come to you when you blow a dog whistle, which emits a very high-pitched sound that the dog can hear but you cannot. The pitch of the sound is outside of the hearing range of humans; that is, the sound does not cross the line into our perceptual ability to hear it. Can you train a person to come to you every time you blow a dog whistle? No, because people cannot hear the whistle so they cannot know when you are blowing it, and therefore they cannot respond to a stimulus that they cannot perceive. Thus, because subliminal stimuli are outside a human's ability to perceive them, they can have no effect on humans.

When people use the term *subliminal advertising effects*, what they really mean is "unconscious effects of advertising." This unconscious influence is a powerful effect. In fact, advertisers depend on it; that is why they spend hundreds of millions of dollars on ad campaigns to embed their ads in highly cluttered environments—like in commercial pods on TV and radio, on the pages of newspapers and magazines, and on websites. Advertisers typically do not want their audiences to pay a high amount of attention to their ads and consciously process their claims. Instead, they want their images and jingles to flow into your mind unconsciously where they are not evaluated or their claims discounted. Then gradually over time, the ads alter our standards, our perception of needs, and our expectations for life. Advertising does this by showing us that we can change our attractiveness, body image, smell, whiteness of smile, relationships, self-image, and degree of happiness by using certain products. Advertisers can alter our perceptions of what is real. For example, until about the 1970s, advertisers used White actors almost exclusively, thus making audiences believe that minorities did not exist or, if they did, that they were unimportant. Then in the 1970s, African Americans began appearing on TV and eventually grew to about 10% of the actors in ads and in television shows; however, the portrayals of other ethnic minorities were almost nonexistent (Mastro & Stern, 2003). A recent analysis of advertising found that 19% of people featured in advertising are from minority groups. This study went beyond merely looking at the ethnicity of characters and also looked at other characteristics. The study found that 0.06% of people portrayed in advertising were disabled or from the LGBT community and just 0.29% were single parents. These figures indicate a serious underrepresentation of these groups, given that disabled people represent 17.9% of the population, the LGBT community comprises 1.7%, and single parents constitute 25% (Rogers, 2016).

Because ads do more than attempt to sell products, they also shape our perceptions of the importance of various types of people in our world and it is important to be concerned when patterns across media messages serve to distort our perceptions (Coltrane & Messineo, 2000). Although each ad is trying to get you to buy a particular product, at a deeper level, all ads are teaching you lessons about who are the in groups and out groups, who you should be in order to be happy, and how you need to look and act in order to be successful, happy, or even normal. To illustrate, let's consider how toothpaste is advertised. On the surface, toothpaste advertising appears to be simply an appeal to get you to use a particular brand of toothpaste. But it comes with several layers of deeper meanings embedded in the message. At a deeper level, the ad is a message about the importance of health. At an even deeper level, it conveys a message about consumerism— that is, the ad tells you that you need to buy something to clean your teeth; you cannot simply use water to brush your teeth. Also at a deeper level is implied permission to eat foods that might contribute to decay because as long as you use the product to brush your teeth, you need not feel guilty about eating things that promote tooth decay. You can see that a "simple" ad for a toothpaste carries with it several layers of meaning, some of which may be consciously processed (the surface claims made in the particular ad) and some of which are unconsciously processed (how to solve problems, the nature of health, etc.).

Advertising Perpetuates Stereotypes

Almost all advertisers must use stereotypes. A 30-second television commercial cannot develop a character in all the rich detail needed to make us feel that the character is more than a two-dimensional stereotype. Because advertisers tell their stories very quickly, they must simplify everything, including the characters.

When we analyze this criticism, we can see that the problem has less to do with stereotyping than with whether portrayals are negative or positive. If an entire class of people (such as all women or all African Americans) is portrayed with negative characteristics, then it is reasonable to argue that this is bad. If all young blonde women are portrayed as dumb, this is a negative stereotype and is offensive to many people. However, if an entire class of people is portrayed as being attractive, smart, and successful, it is not likely that people would be offended by this, although this too is a stereotype. Therefore the criticism that advertising uses stereotypes is largely a complaint about portraying groups in a negative way.

CRITICISMS BASED ON PERSONAL VALUES

There are three popular criticisms of advertising that are based on personal values. Thus these criticisms tell us more about the tolerance levels of the people complaining about the advertising than they tell us about the advertising per se.

Advertising Is Excessive

As you saw earlier in this chapter, our culture is saturated with advertising. Whether this is excessive requires an evaluative judgment. This means you must have a standard for what is an acceptable amount. If you have a high standard for excessiveness, then you will likely conclude that the amount of advertising has not yet reached that level, and therefore advertising is not excessive. So this criticism tells us more about people's standards than about how much advertising exists.

In public opinion polls, when people are asked, "Do you think there is too much advertising on television?" about 70% of people say yes. But if they are asked, "Do you think that your being shown all this advertising is a fair price for you to pay to be able to see 'free' television?" again 70% will say yes. But television is hardly free; it just seems free because you are not charged for each show you watch. Most of us pay an access fee to cable or satellite companies monthly. An even more hidden cost of television is our indirect support through buying advertised products. For example, when you buy soap or toothpaste, about 35% of the cost goes to advertising.

Let's examine this criticism more closely. Think about the situation with **junk mail**, which is unwanted mail that comes to you every day from two sources. One source is electronic, where the unwanted e-mail is called **spam**. It is estimated that each day there are 14.5 billion spam e-mails sent globally (Bauer, 2018), with many spammers sending out hundreds of millions of e-mails each day. E-mail providers have been working hard to improve their filters to screen out spam and prevent the flood of these unwanted messages from jamming their service. These filters have been successful in reducing the proportion of all e-mails that are spam from over 70% in 2014 down to under 50% in 2018 (Statista, 2018h).

The other source of junk mail is physical, in which direct marketers each day send out millions of pieces of paper with printed coupons and advertising appeals. In 2008, the average household was receiving 848 pieces of physical junk mail each year. This junk mail was estimated to weigh 40 pounds per person, and 40% of this junk mail ends up unopened in landfills each year. From an environmental point of view, this form of advertising does seem excessive.

You must decide for yourself whether you think advertising is excessive or not. When you are making this decision, consider what your standard is for an acceptable amount of advertising. How did you set this standard? And if you do decide that the amount of junk mail is excessive, then think about what should be done to deal with this excess. Should junk mail be outlawed? If so, what do you say to the junk mail industry that claims that the advertising it sends out generates $646 billion in sales each year (Caplan, 2008)? Marketers who use junk mail must send out large numbers of messages because their response rates are low; physical junk mail has a response rate of 4.4%, while spam has a response rate of only a 0.12% (Pulcinella, 2017). If we were to cut back this form of advertising drastically, wouldn't sales also drop drastically? If sales drop, companies who advertise their products would make less money, so they would pay less in taxes to support social services and have to lay off employees, which would increase unemployment and hurt the overall economy. When you call for limitations on any form of advertising, think about how those limitations could end up harming parts of the economy.

Advertising Manipulates Us Into Buying Things We Don't Need

The key to analyzing this criticism lies in addressing the question: How do we define a need? If we limit ourselves to the minimum needs for survival, then we must conclude that advertisers ask us to buy many, many things that are well beyond our need for basic survival.

When we analyze the idea of "need," we can see that we have many different kinds of needs in addition to basic survival. Psychologist Abraham Maslow pointed out that humans have a **hierarchy of needs**; that is, our needs are arranged by levels such that when our needs at a lower level are met, we move to needs at a higher level, so that we are always striving to satisfy some kind of need. Humans' most basic level of needs are those required for survival (food, water, shelter). The next level comprises the safety needs (freedom from attack from predators and disease). Next is the social level of needs (friendship, family, and belonging to groups). Then there is the self-esteem level of needs (achievement, confidence, respect from others). The highest level of need is **self-actualization** (fulfilling oneself through creativity and morality). For example, when our survival and safety needs are met, the drive to satisfy our needs shifts up to the social level in the hierarchy and we become focused on friendship or family problems. For these social needs, we need many different outfits of clothes to help us maximize our comfort in a variety of social situations. We need a certain type of car. We need to live in a certain kind of home. We need certain kinds of foods and beverages to go along with our lifestyles. We use all these products to define ourselves in social situations. Are these products luxuries or necessities? Each person must define what is a necessity for himself or herself.

Advertising Makes Us Too Materialistic

Some critics claim that advertising makes us too materialistic. However, when we analyze this criticism, we are faced with the question: How much is *too* much? Some people believe we should conserve natural resources and live at a lower level of consumption. Other people believe that we should always strive for more of everything; if it looks like we might run short of resources, we will be able to figure out a way to solve the problem. With less than 8% of the world's population, the United States consumes nearly 30% of the planet's resources. Americans can choose from more than 40,000 supermarket items, including 200 kinds of cereal. Do we really need all these material products?

Americans say they are dissatisfied with materialism despite all the abundance. In surveys, more than 80% of Americans typically agree that most of us buy and consume far more than we need. And about two thirds agree that Americans cause many of the world's environmental problems because we consume more resources and produce more waste than anyone else in the world (Debate.org, 2018; Koenenn, 1997). Yet we continue to consume at a greater rate each year. Clark (2000) reports that private materialism (individuals buying material goods for their own consumption) has been rising since 1960. Furthermore, private spending by Americans is reportedly approximately 50% to 90% higher than private spending by Europeans and a significant number of Americans spend more on material goods each year than they earn. Thus, the public is schizophrenic about consumption. We believe we are too materialistic but keep buying more products.

CRITICISMS ABOUT RESPONSIBILITY

The final four criticisms focus on responsibility. Each one shows that there is a conflict between economic responsibility and social responsibility. The people who run companies have an economic responsibility to the owners of their companies; it is their job to increase the wealth of those owners. However, the public is typically more concerned that companies be socially responsible. This does not necessarily mean that the public expects companies to contribute actively to social well-being (like being philanthropic), but it does mean that the public expects companies to avoid actively harming society.

We need to realize that with advertisers, the economic responsibility is more primary than the social responsibility. The first and overriding purpose of advertising is to increase sales and market share of advertisers' clients. If advertisers can satisfy this economic responsibility and also be socially responsible, they will do both. Advertisers are not trying to harm society, and they work hard to avoid offending consumers. However, there are times when they must make a choice when they cannot be both economically and socially responsible. When advertisers are faced with such a choice, they almost always choose economic responsibility. This can trigger some significant criticism. Let's examine four of these criticisms.

Advertising Potentially Harmful Products

There are some products that are potentially harmful to individuals and society, especially for some groups of people and especially when they are not used properly. Many of these products are legally available, and the marketers of these products are motivated to find new users as well as push existing users to buy more of the product. For example, manu-

© ZUMA Press, Inc. / Alamy

Repeated exposure to advertisements for potentially harmful products, like beer and liquor on TV, billboards, and at sports events, could encourage people to consume more.

facturers of alcoholic beverages, of course, know that it is legal to sell their beverages to adults but certainly not to adolescents and children. They also know that television is a powerful advertising medium but that there are always some adolescents and children in the TV audience for all shows. While beer companies have always used television for advertising, manufacturers of liquor avoided using television in an effort to be socially responsible. But during the fall of 1996, Joseph E. Seagram & Sons began airing spots for two whisky brands on independent TV stations around the country. The company was motivated by the desire to increase sales and felt it was bad business to continue avoiding the use of the powerful advertising medium of television. In defense of his company's move, Tod Rodriguez, general sales manager, said, "There are a lot worse things than alcohol ads on TV" (Gellene, 1996, p. D2). Many people found this incident very upsetting and the Seagram Company's reasoning very self-serving.

Anheuser-Busch, the number-one brewer in the United States, found that its beer sales were flat in 1998. At that time, the company's primary target audience was young men. To increase sales, Anheuser-Busch decided to also target a secondary audience: women. Anheuser-Busch felt that women were an underutilized group because women were accounting for only 17% of the company's sales. So Anheuser-Busch decided to break its self-imposed barrier of not targeting women and began advertising in daytime TV where there was a high proportion of women in the television audience. A consultant to the company said, "It should be done. For the beer people not to be selling full-bore ahead on one gender is absurd" (Arndorfer, 1998, p. 8).

Until the 1980s, pharmaceutical companies marketed their drugs only to physicians. Then in the 1980s, they began marketing to the general population. Pharmaceutical companies thought that they could increase sales of prescription drugs, especially anti-depressants, if they went directly to people and bypassed physicians. They reasoned that people with symptoms for certain diseases would pressure their doctors to prescribe the advertised medications. Of course, this introduced the risk that many healthy people would imagine they had the symptoms depicted in the drug ads and they too would pressure their doctors for prescriptions. This marketing strategy worked, because sales of antidepressants increased 400% from 1988 to 2008 and less than one third of people taking antidepressants had seen any kind of mental health professional in the past year (Wehrwein, 2011). This means that many people see an ad, think they are depressed, go to their family general practitioner, and get a prescription without seeing an expert in mental health. And the use of antidepressants continued to grow until by 2017, when more than one in every eight people age 12 and older in the United States was buying them (Sifferlin, 2017).

Liquor, beer, and pharmaceutical products are all legal, and each can be used in responsible and even positive ways by individuals. However, the aggressive expansion of persuasive messages in the mass media to encourage people to use more of these products is likely to risk greater harm to society.

Invading Protected Groups

Psychologists, parents, and social critics are concerned about protecting children from a barrage of advertising, especially of inappropriate products. Recall from Chapter 5 that young children have not developed to a point where they can understand certain elements about ads and therefore cannot protect themselves. Also, children have had less experience with products than have adults; therefore children are not as sophisticated in making decisions about how to spend their money. However, from an advertiser's point of view, children are regarded as an important and highly desirable target market and many advertisers are spending more money each year to convince children to consume their products. For example, tobacco companies have been targeting young people (ages 14–24) for decades as a prime market. In 1991, the Joe Camel campaign was launched to appeal to teens by focusing a lot of ads around high schools and colleges. In 5 years, the sale of Camels to teens went from $6 million to $476 million (Holland, 1998). Teenagers are three times as likely as adults to respond to cigarette ads; 79% smoke brands depicted as fun, sexy, and popular ("Study Links Teen Smoking," 1996).

Invading Privacy

In pursuit of their economic goals, advertisers continually invade your privacy by monitoring your economic transactions (as well as many other activities) and by invading your day-to-day lives with messages designed to alter your behavior. Advertisers collect information on every product you buy, they monitor your online shopping behavior, and they monitor your interests on blogs and social networking sites (see Issue 6 for a detailed treatment of this topic).

Retailing companies are becoming more sophisticated at assembling more detailed pictures of their customers by using **big data**, which refers to the huge amount of information companies have been gathering about everyone. Big data research firms are constantly expanding their databases that contain information on everyone's product purchases, media usage, and financial transactions. Retailers buy these data from the huge marketing research firms and use those data to target their consumers and send them advertising messages (Marr, 2017).

Advertisers are continually looking for ways to use this information to get you to buy more of their products. For example, online retailers know that 98% of visitors to online shopping sites leave without making a purchase. So they collect data on each of these people and send them messages to lure them back to what they visited. This is called **retargeting**. Advertisers want to know what you are thinking as you walk down the street so they can send an ad to your smartphone as you pass a store that has something you want. Companies like Loopt and Foursquare broadcast customers' locations from their cell phones to advertisers, so those advertisers can send special messages and discount offers to customers when they get close to one of their stores. Mobile advertising revenue was projected to increase to $25.8 billion by 2017, up from $2.3 billion in 2009 (Mobile Commerce, 2014). The goal is to make your smartphone as smart as you but quicker—to predict what you want before you know it (Pariser, 2011). If you trust that your phone is smarter than you are, then this is a good thing because it frees you from having to expend the mental energy required when you think for yourself.

The big companies that collect all these data do so without your explicit knowledge or permission. Whenever we download an app or have any dealings with a company online that requires us to set up a user account, we are asked to agree to a long list of things that are presented in many screens of jargon-laced language that few people understand. If you click on the "agree" button that is required to set up your account, you are giving up many of your rights to privacy and allow the firm to collect information about you and your transactions then sell it to other vendors.

Altering Needs

Perhaps the most powerful effect of advertising is that it alters our beliefs about needs in several ways. One way is that it has shifted our belief in needs from **public goods** to **private goods**. Public goods are those that are owned by society and are open for sharing for free or a modest fee (e.g., parks, beaches, city streets, bridges, public transportation systems, etc.). Private goods are those that you buy, own, and control (e.g. your clothing, car, furniture, phone, etc.). Harvard economist and social critic John Kenneth Galbraith (Arens, 1999) argued that advertising is fundamentally a negative force on society because it serves to shift a society's resources from benefitting the public to benefitting only individuals, and this leads to a great deal of waste. When we sell large cars and SUVs to individuals who rarely travel with many passengers, there is a waste of fuel, and we need to build more and more expensive highways and parking lots. But if that money were put into public transportation, the resources would be used much more efficiently, and everyone in the public would benefit more. Advertising is what drives private demand. If it weren't for advertising, consumers would buy much less, and some of the resources that currently go into satisfying private demand could be reallocated for the common good, such as public education, public parks, and public transportation.

In contrast to Galbraith, historian David Potter (Arens, 1999) regards advertising as a positive force on society. He sees advertising as a social institution comparable to the school and the church in its power to convey information and to teach values. An important value in America is the transforming of natural resources into abundance. Advertising supports this value and reinforces our inherent need to consume and enjoy it. Potter, however, does express some concern that advertising has no overriding responsibility to society. Other institutions (such as the family, education, religion, etc.) are altruistic; they try to improve the individual and society. Advertising is very different. Advertising is selfish; its only responsibility is to serve the marketing objectives of the company that pays for it.

Advertising has also conditioned us to believe that we have more and more needs. It does this by subtly and gradually shaping our standards about success, romance, and beauty and then leads us to believe that we are not living up to those standards. This triggers a false need to consume more in order to meet those standards. One example of this is with women's clothing. In 1930, the average American woman owned nine outfits. Now the average American woman buys more than 60 pieces of clothing each year (Wolverson, 2012).

Advertising conditions us to believe certain things about our standards for success and beauty. Does owning a designer purse make you successful? Designer purse companies say yes.

YOUR OWN INFORMED OPINION

It is important that you develop opinions about a cultural phenomenon as pervasive and as important as advertising. And it is essential that your opinions be informed by accurate facts rather than faulty information, by your own personal values that you use as evaluative standards, and by the differences between social responsibility and economic responsibility. You have begun this task by reading through the material presented above in this chapter. Now you need to continue this development of more informed opinions by using your media literacy skills (see Applying Media Literacy Skills Issue 4.1).

With entertainment and news-type messages, we are typically more active in searching for exposures and processing the information in those messages compared to advertising messages. In contrast, we encounter almost all advertising messages in a state of automaticity, where we are unaware of how much exposure we are experiencing. As we surf the Internet, listen to the radio, and flip through magazines, we are searching for entertainment and news messages and not paying much attention to all the ads embedded there. This is especially the case when we are multitasking.

To protect ourselves from all this unplanned advertising exposure, we remain in a state of automatic processing so we don't have to pay attention to all of the ads. However, exposure to the ads continues even though we are not paying attention to them, and this makes our exposure unconscious, which is what most advertisers want. When we are multitasking and not paying attention to ads, persuasive messages have a greater effect on us because we are much less likely to analyze the ad claims and counter-argue (Jeong & Hwang, 2012). During unconscious exposure, advertisers can plant their messages into our subconscious, where they gradually shape our definitions for attractiveness, sex appeal, relationships, cleanliness, health, success, hunger, body shape, problems, and happiness. For example, we might have the radio on in the car as we concentrate on driving, and when ads come on, we do not pay much attention. Then later, we find ourselves humming a jingle, a word phrase occurs to us, or we pass by a store and "remember" that there is a sale going on there. These flashes of sounds, words, and ideas emerge from our subconscious, where they had been put by ads that we did not pay attention to. Over time, all those images, sounds, and ideas build patterns in our subconscious and profoundly shape the way we think about ourselves and the world.

Further Reading

Jones, J. P. (2004). *Fables, fashions, and facts about advertising: A study of 28 enduring myths.* Thousand Oaks, CA: SAGE. (305 pages, including glossary and index)

The author is a college professor with 25 years' experience working in a major advertising agency. In this book, Jones confronts more than two-dozen beliefs that the public holds about advertising and shows how each of these is faulty.

Kirkpatrick, J. (2007). *In defense of advertising: Arguments from reason, ethical egoism, and laissez-faire capitalism.* Westport, CT: Greenwood Publishing. (200 pages with index)

Written by a professor of international business and marketing, this book analyzes much of the economic and philosophical bases used to criticize advertising and then argues that these criticisms are based on a faulty view of the world. The author concludes that advertising is good because it supports the rational self-interest of consumers.

APPLYING MEDIA LITERACY SKILLS ISSUE 4.1
CONFRONTING THE ISSUE OF MEDIA ADVERTISING

1. Analysis: Take a more in-depth look at how ads use puffery.

   a. Sample: I suggest you study a sample of somewhere between 20 and 50 ads. You need to look at enough ads so that you can see patterns, but you don't want to set up a task that is super burdensome. Go to your favorite magazine, website, and/or videos to access ads.

   b. Focus on product claims to answer the following questions:

   How many ads provide testable claims and how many rely on puffery?

   What techniques of puffery do you see most often?

   Are certain kinds of products more likely to use puffery?

2. Evaluation: Make informed judgments.

   a. Make a judgment about whether advertising is excessive.

   Think about your personal belief about how much advertising is appropriate for our culture. Where did you get this belief?

   b. Make a judgment about whether advertising has manipulated you to buy products you don't need.

   Think about what your needs really are. Has advertising changed your needs to make you consume more?

   c. Make a judgment about whether advertising has made you too materialistic.

   Think about your personal belief about how much materialism is appropriate. Where did you get this belief?

3. Compare/contrast: Look for differences and similarities across your advertising opinions.

   a. Which opinions are the most critical of advertising?

   b. Which opinions about advertising are the most important to you?

   c. Which opinions have you changed (or are likely to change) after reading this chapter and working through this exercise?

4. Synthesis: Construct your overall informed opinion about advertising.

   a. What things about advertising do you value most? List them.

   Why do you like these the most?

   b. What things about advertising do you dislike the most? List them.

   Do you dislike these things because they are likely to affect you or society?

   Do you dislike these things because they have already created harm or because you fear they will cause some harm in the future?

   c. Compare your two lists and make a judgment about whether you feel that advertising is more positive or more negative on balance.

   d. Can you think of a way to deal with your everyday exposure to advertising so that you reduce the risks of negative effects while at the same time increasing the probability of positive effects?

5. Abstracting: Express your opinion succinctly.

   a. Can you express your overall informed opinion about advertising in 50 words or less?

   b. Will the way you express your opinion stimulate other people to think like you?

ISSUE

5

MEDIA VIOLENCE

*Issue: The public has been complaining about violence in the
mass media as long as we have had mass media, but the media continue to present a
great deal of violence in their stories.*

There is no shortage of violence in the post-apocalyptic world of the film *Mad Max: Fury Road*. Will you be able to make an informed opinion about this film? Or will you allow emotional rhetoric to influence you?

People seem to have been complaining about violence in the media ever since storytellers have used the media. Criticism increases and decreases in cycles, and currently we are in a quiet part of the cycle after a lot of criticism during the 1990s (see Timeline Issue 5.1). But this topic could heat up quickly again at any time. When it does heat up, will you be ready with an informed opinion, or will you be swept away with all the emotional rhetoric?

DELINEATING THE ISSUE

The issue of media violence is typically expressed by the criticism that there is too much violence in the media. When we frame the issue in this way, we can analyze it like we did with the previous issues of media ownership, sports, and fake news. Such an analysis begins with the recognition that the criticism is an evaluative judgment that requires a person to compare the thing they are judging (in this case, media violence) to some standard that is typically a value that expresses the person's tolerance level for violence. Therefore people who have a low value for violence in stories will arrive at a judgment that there is too much media violence; conversely, people who have a relatively high value for violence (e.g., stories with aggressive characters make them feel powerful and aroused) will arrive at a judgment that there is not too much violence in the media.

With the issue of media violence, however, we should not be satisfied by tracing the controversy to differing values. There is more to it. We need to dig deeper into the other side of the evaluative equation, which is composed of the elements being evaluated—the portrayals that people perceive as violent. When we analyze public perceptions, we find that there are three faulty ones. In this chapter, we will examine those three faulty perceptions of the public. Then we will examine two faulty beliefs that are held by producers of media messages. The chapter concludes with a set of guidelines to help you move past this faulty thinking and thereby increase your media literacy.

THE PUBLIC'S FAULTY PERCEPTIONS

The public makes three kinds of faulty perceptions about media violence. These faulty perceptions are (1) equating violence with graphicness, (2) ignoring context, and (3) having a blind spot when it comes to harm from exposure to media violence.

TIMELINE ISSUE 5.1
Public Opinion About the Amount of Violence in the Media

1970

1975: A Gallup poll shows that two thirds of Americans find the present level of violent programming unacceptable (Cooper, 1996).

1985

1993: A poll shows that 70% of Americans feel that entertainment TV has too much violence, and 57% think that TV news gives too much attention to stories about violent crime (Galloway, 1993).

1994: A *Parents* magazine poll finds that an overwhelming majority of Americans—87% of those questioned—say that the media "contains too much violence" (Diamant, 1994).

1995: A *Time*/CNN survey finds that 52% of adult Americans say they are very concerned about the amount of violence depicted in movies, television shows, and popular music; another 25% say they are fairly concerned; only 9% say they are not concerned at all (Lacayo, 1995).

1997: A nationwide poll by the *Los Angeles Times* finds that two thirds of people think that television programming has gotten worse over the past decade, with 90% believing that television now has more violence and sex than it did 10 years ago (Lowry, 1997).

2000

1997: A *USA Weekend* write-in poll generates 21,600 responses, with 92% of those respondents saying they regard television content more offensive than ever, especially with violence, sexual content, and vulgarity.

1999: A Gallup poll finds that 75% of the public say they think there is a relationship between violence on television and the crime rate in the United States.

2013: An ICM poll finds that 73% of the public say they believe that on-screen violence (in the form of films, television, and computer games) encourages violence in society.

2015

Equating Violence With Graphicness

When the public criticizes the media for presenting too much violence in their stories, they are not really complaining about the amount of violence per se; instead they are complaining about graphic portrayals that offend them. People do not have a counter running automatically in their minds during their media exposures, so at any given time they cannot tell how many acts of violence they have witnessed in media portrayals. Instead, people continue tolerating acts of violence until one of those acts is presented in such a graphic way that it offends them. Because people do not like to be offended, they wish that they had not been exposed to that offensive portrayal. Thus the memory of an offensive act or two is what motivates their criticism, not an accumulation of acts reaching a certain number that surpasses people's value for tolerance.

This raises a question about all the violent portrayals that are not offensive. Are they okay to show? The answer to this question depends on whether you are a media scholar or not. Media scholars who carefully analyze media content for violent acts begin with a clear definition for violence. When they see an act that matches their definition, they count it. Therefore their content analyses of violence are sensitive to their definitions. Take a look at Table Issue 5.1 and try to answer those eight questions. If you answered no to all (or almost all) of them, you share the same conception of media violence as the general public. However, if you were a media scholar, you would likely have answered yes to all (or almost all) of them. Media scholars would answer yes to all these conditions because they know from research that people can be affected in a negative way when continually exposed to these conditions. In contrast, the public would answer no to all these conditions because they are not likely to be offended by portrayals in those conditions.

TABLE ISSUE 5.1 ■ Key Elements in Definitions of Violence
1. Does the act have to be directed toward a person? Gang members swing baseball bats at a car and totally destroy it. Is this violence?
2. Does the act have to be committed by a person? A mudslide levels a town and kills 20 people. Do acts of nature count? Remember that nature does not write the scripts or produce the programming.
3. Does the act have to be intentional? A bank robber drives a fast car in a getaway chase. As he speeds around a corner, he hits a pedestrian (or destroys a mailbox). Do accidents count?
4. Does the act result in harm? Tom shoots a gun at Jerry, but the bullet misses. Is this violence? Or what if Tom and Jerry are cartoon characters and Tom drops an anvil on Jerry, who is momentarily flattened like a pancake. A second later, Jerry pops back to his original shape and appears fine.
5. What about violence we don't see? If a bad guy fires a gun at a character off-screen and we hear a scream and a body fall, is this violence even though we do not see it?
6. Does the act have to be physical (such as assaults), or can it be verbal (such as insults)? What if Tom viciously insults Jerry, who is shown through the rest of the program experiencing deep psychological and emotional pain as a result? What if Tom embarrasses Jerry, who then runs from the room, trips, and breaks his arm?
7. What about fantasy? If 100 fighting men "morph" into a giant creature the size of a 10-story building, which then stomps out their enemies, does this count as violence?
8. What about humorous portrayals? When the Three Stooges hit each other with hammers, is this violence?

The public's conception of media violence is limited to physical violence that is depicted in a serious (non-humorous) manner and that results in severe physical harm to the victims that is presented graphically. Audiences' judgments about the degree of violence in a TV program or movie are related much less to the number of violent acts than to the degree of graphicness (Potter et al., 2002). For example, people might not think an action/adventure movie with wall-to-wall car chases and gunfire is more violent than a drama in which one character is unexpectedly shot and we see the bullet tearing through flesh and bone. A single highly graphic scene in a movie is much more likely to trigger the perception that the movie is violent compared to a movie with a constant stream of car chases, gunfights, and explosions where the victims were never shown in a graphic manner.

The public's conception of violence is keyed to whether the depiction is offensive or not. If the depiction dwells on graphic elements like blood and gore, then the depiction is likely to offend viewers and trigger complains. Thus, producers avoid offending audience members by sanitizing the violence. Producers know that if they remove the graphicness of violence by rarely showing harm to victims, audiences are much less likely to be offended. Research studies have repeatedly shown that audiences tolerate this **sanitized violence** but when the portrayal is unusually graphic, it interrupts viewers' flow of enjoyment and they experience strong negative emotions (British Broadcasting Corporation, 1972; Diener & De Four, 1978; Diener & Woody, 1981).

Another key element in the public's definition of violence is that humor is a camouflage. It appears that when humor blankets violence, the public does not see the violence. This is taken for granted by all kinds of people. An anecdote will illustrate this. A few years ago, I was meeting with the staff of the Viacom Standards and Practices Department in New York City. These seven women are charged with previewing the content to be aired on Viacom's cable channels of MTV, VH1, and Nickelodeon. I was watching a music video while the seven women in the room explained how they screened music videos to determine if those videos met their standards or, if in their judgment, there were things in the portrayals that would offend viewers. For an hour, the women showed parts of music videos and explained how they asked the various music groups to remove or tone down certain images that they felt were demeaning to women. Finally, when I was given a chance to ask a question, I said, "What about violence in the music videos?" Several women were eager to answer that they were sensitive to that issue and that the videos did not have any direct scenes of violence, although violence was implied in certain lyrics. Then I asked about violence on Nickelodeon. There was a rather long pause as the women looked at me as if I were a third grader who had just claimed that two plus two equals seven. One of the women looked very puzzled and said, "But there is no violence on Nickelodeon." I returned the puzzled look and replied, "What about your Saturday morning shows such as *Bugs Bunny* and *Ninja Turtles*?" Her puzzled look turned into a

© AF archive / Alamy

Would you consider the cartoon *Teenage Mutant Ninja Turtles* to be violent? Does the fact that the characters are cartoons make it acceptable for violent acts to be displayed to children?

big smile as she said, "But those are not violent. Those are cartoons!" Were these women naive? No, they had a highly sophisticated understanding of violence—as defined by the general viewing public. These women knew that the public was not concerned by the actions—even the most brutal—portrayed in cartoons.

What is the reason for humor camouflaging the violence? It appears that humor tends to remove the threat of violence in viewers' minds. For viewers to consider something violent, they need to feel a degree of personal threat. This insight can be found in the work of Barrie Gunter (1985) in the United Kingdom. He reported that viewers' ratings of the seriousness of violent acts were higher as the fictional settings were closer to every-day reality in terms of time and location. In contrast, Gunter found that violent acts "depicted in clearly fantastic settings such as cartoons or science-fiction were perceived as essentially non-violent, non-frightening and non-disturbing" (p. 245). Other researchers also report that people were much more concerned with acts that had a higher probability of occurrence, meaning the likelihood of the act happening to them in everyday life (Forgas, Brown, & Menyhart, 1980).

The public is also not concerned about acts of aggression and violence that result in non-physical harm, such as verbal aggression where characters inflict emotional, psychological, and social harm to their victims. Studies have shown the occurrence of verbal violence is far more prevalent—up to three times more frequent—than physical forms of violence (Greenberg et al., 1980; Martins & Wilson, 2012; Potter & Vaughan, 1997). For example, Martins and Wilson (2012) conducted a content analysis of the portrayal of social aggression in the 50 most popular television programs among 2- to 11-year-old children. Results revealed that 92% of the programs in the sample contained some social aggression. On average, there were 14 different incidents of social aggression per hour in these shows, or one every 4 minutes.

In summary, viewers who watch an average amount of television are likely to see one act of violence per week that is highly graphic in its depiction of serious physical harm. And this is the basis for their criticism that there is too much violence in the media. However, the average person is likely to view over 100 acts of physical violence per week—almost all of it sanitized or camouflaged with humor. Add to that another 200 to 300 acts of non-physical aggression in the form of hate speech, harsh insults, put-downs, and the like. Yes, indeed, there is a great deal of violence throughout the television landscape—far more than the average person perceives.

Ignoring Context

A second faulty belief held by the public is that the problem is keyed to the *amount* of violence instead of the *context* of the portrayals. Thus this criticism makes the argument that the harm to individuals and society would be reduced if the amount of violence presented in the media were reduced. The underlying assumption here is that harm is keyed to frequency of the portrayals. This belief is faulty because frequency is secondary to the more primary factor of context. It is the way violence is portrayed in the media that signals to audiences what the meaning of violence is, and that meaning is very influential in bringing about effects.

To illustrate this point, consider the following two scenarios. In the first scenario, there are two brothers who are selfish, petty, and physically ugly. Although they are weak, they each have a gun, which they use to extort money from hardworking "mom and pop" store owners in the neighborhood by pistol whipping them. At night they mug people and beat them up for fun. The victims of their violence are shown suffering all kinds of harm—fear, financial hardships, and physical pain. Eventually, the brothers are arrested and put in jail, where they are beat up by larger, stronger criminals. Their punishment is shown in detail as they work their way through the criminal justice system and are sentenced to long prison terms.

In the second scenario, the two brothers are young studs who are witty and highly intelligent. They spend their days hacking into private databases to find medical doctors who overcharge for their services and insurance investigators who cheat people out of their rightful benefits. At night they capture their targets and take them to their secret laboratory, where they torture them with high-tech devices and cutting-edge pharmaceuticals to get them to confess to their criminal behavior. While it is obvious that the targets are being tortured, the audience never sees any blood or gore. Afterward it is implied that the brothers kill their targets and carefully dispose of their bodies. However, they are eventually arrested and brought to trial, but the police are not able to find much evidence of their crimes so a jury finds them not guilty.

The first scenario is closer to what happens in real life. The audience is not likely to identify with the brothers, they are likely to be disgusted by the violence, and they are likely to have a good deal of sympathy for the victims. Audiences who watch this program are not likely to want to imitate the actions of the brothers or to commit violence themselves. Furthermore audiences are likely to believe that other people who watch these portrayals will also be less likely to want to commit violence. In contrast, the second scenario follows more closely the typical patterns of violent portrayals found in the media; that is, the perpetrators are glamorized and the violence is sanitized. People who watch these kinds of portrayals are more likely to believe that violence is often a good way to solve problems. If most media portrayals follow the first scenario, then it would be a good thing to increase the number of violent portrayals, because viewers would learn more about how violence occurs in the real world and how harmful violence is. However, if most media portrayals follow the pattern in the second scenario, then it would be a bad thing to increase the number of violent portrayals, because viewers would learn that violence is a good way of solving problems, that it is justified, and that only bad people experience harm.

The context in the way the violence is portrayed increases the probability of all

Peter Iovino/CBS via Getty Images

Is *Dexter*, a show about a forensic scientist who leads a secret life as a serial killer, too violent for TV?

sorts of negative effects. The sanitization of the violence leads viewers to become desensitized to the suffering of victims. The glamorization of violence leads viewers to become attracted to the violence and over time have their socialized inhibitions to performing violent acts eroded. The trivialization of violence with humor leads viewers to believe the risk to them of being punished is slight. If violence were presented in the context of a morality play instead of the way it currently is across the television landscape, then the repetitive exposure to media violence would be a positive thing for society because it would teach people that violence is not acceptable, that perpetrators are punished in all sorts of ways, that it is rarely if ever justified, and that it causes serious long-term harm to victims and their loved ones.

Blind Spot on Harm

If you ask the typical person, "Does violence in the media have any effect?" most people will say yes, recalling a horrible instance when someone copied a violent criminal act that was in a movie or in the news. However, if you were to ask those same people if violence in the media has had an effect on them, most would say no. Thus, most people believe that other people are at risk but think they are free from risk. This difference in perception between oneself and others has been labeled the **third-person effect**.

The reason for this third-person effect with media violence is because few people believe they behave aggressively after watching violence, but they have ample evidence that others are influenced to behave aggressively. There are frequent examples of copycat crimes and of kids going on shooting sprees at school in imitation of movie and video game violence. Also, many adults notice their children imitating violent television characters they see on action/adventure shows or on *World Wrestling Entertainment* shows. We all remember children (or even ourselves as children) racing around the house, chasing siblings and pets while imitating sounds and movements from violent portrayals. But we recognize we do not behave that way now, so there is no effect on us. But let's examine this more closely by considering verbal forms of violence in addition to physical forms. If you watch portrayals of daring criminals robbing a high-security bank and blowing up the cars and helicopters that chase them, you are not likely to imitate this form of violent behavior. But if you watch portrayals of characters insulting, verbally abusing, and embarrassing other characters in highly witty attractive ways, the probability of you trying to imitate such behave is rather high. When we consider verbal violence in addition to physical violence, we can see that even a presumably rarely occurring effect such as imitation is likely to be occurring with greatly more frequency than we had originally thought. What makes this opinion possible is a narrow conception of what effects are possible from exposure to media violence. Compared to physical aggression, social aggression is more imitable, so we should expect portrayals of social aggression to lead to more negative effects than portrayals of physical aggression. And these effects are not just imitations of behavior; they can be negative emotional effects. For example, Mares, Braun, and Hernandez (2012) conducted an experiment on middle school children by showing them programs popular with tweens (8 to 14 years old) where there were depictions of serious social conflicts. They found that habitual exposure was associated with expectations of encountering specific crowds in middle school (person schemata), with expectations of less friendliness and more bullying (behavioral scripts), and with greater anxiety about attending their future school. Similarly, those who saw high-conflict episodes anticipated more hostility and less friendliness in their future school and felt more anxious and less positive about going there than those who saw low-conflict episodes (effects that were partly mediated by perceptions of character hostility).

We, of course, need to be concerned with the imitation of violence as an important media effect, but there are many other effects that are also important (see Table Issue 5.2). Some of these effects are easier to spot than others and some are likely to result in a higher degree of harm than others, but all are important. All of these effects can happen to you and the people around you. Each of these has been well documented by research. Notice that some are immediate effects (meaning that they occur during exposure to the media violence), such as **imitation**, **disinhibition**, and **attraction**. Others are long-term effects (which take many exposures over a long period of time to build up to a manifestation),

TABLE ISSUE 5.2 ■ Immediate and Long-Term Effects of Exposure to Media Violence		
Effect	**Immediate Effect**	**Long-Term Effect**
Behavioral Effect	• Imitation/copying behavior: Exposure to media violence can trigger aggressive behaviors that mimic (or follow closely) the media portrayals. • Triggering novel behavior: Exposure to media violence can energize people to enact behaviors that are different from those depicted in the portrayal. • Disinhibition: Exposure to media violence can reduce viewers' normal inhibitions that prevent them from behaving in a violent manner. • Attraction: Many people are attracted to violence; this attraction is not necessarily to the violence per se but to the arousing nature of the portrayal.	• Training behavior: Violent video games can train players to kill; repeated playing establishes and reinforces behavioral patterns over time.
Physiological Effect	• Fight-or-flight: Exposure to violence can temporarily arouse people physiologically by increasing their blood pressure and heart rate.	• Physiological habituation: Repeated exposure to violent stimuli serves to erode the strength of automatic physiological responses to threats. • Narcoticization: Not only does habitual viewing of violence over time dull our reactions, but some people also continue to crave the strong "arousal jag" they used to get from violent exposures. But to experience the same degree of arousal, they search out more graphic and stronger forms of violence. Thus, violence acts like a drug in the sense that people grow a stronger dependence on it over time while the drug loses its strength.

Effect	Immediate Effect	Long-Term Effect
Emotional Effect	• Temporary fear: Exposure to violence can trigger intense fright reactions.	• Desensitization: Some portrayals are presented so often that we can no longer treat them with wonder or awe. Our tolerance has been increased so that those things that used to horrify or even upset us no longer do.
Attitudinal Effect	• Immediate creation/change of attitudes: A person's attitude can be created or changed with as little as a single exposure.	• Long-term reinforcement of attitudes: Because the media provide so many messages of violence and because those messages are usually presented with the same cluster of contextual factors, viewers' existing attitudes about violence are reinforced over time. This makes the attitudes stronger and therefore harder to change as time goes by.
Cognitive Effect	• Learning specific acts and lessons: Exposure to media violence can teach people how to use violence, even though they never act on that knowledge.	• Learning social norms: Repeated exposure to stories using violence as a successful way to solve problems leads people to believe that violence is an acceptable social tool. • Cultivation of unrealistic beliefs: Repeated exposure to stories using violence leads people to believe that the world is a violent place and that their chance of being victimized by violence is very high.
Effects on Society	Changing institutions: When violence permeates the media year after year in all kinds of programming, it puts pressure on institutions to change.	

Effects on Society (continued):

- Criminal justice system: When the public believes crime is one of the most important social problems, candidates for elective office run on a platform of getting tough on crime. Municipalities hire more police officers, arrests for certain crimes escalate, people are asked to give up certain rights, courts are under pressure to give stiffer sentences to criminals, the prison population increases, and states must build more prisons so they raise taxes.

- Educational system: Because of some high-profile shootings in public schools, many schools now have metal detectors at their doors; there are searches of lockers and restrictions on who can walk into a school building.

- Religion: When people are more fearful of society, they are likely to seek comfort in religions that offer strict moralities and hope for a better world.

- Family: Fear of victimization makes parents less trusting of their children. Couples who learn aggressive norms from violent portrayals may be less willing to deal with their problems by looking for peaceful solutions and instead are more willing to argue, feel more justified in those confrontations, and thus want to dominate the other in their resolutions.

such as **narcoticization**, **desensitization**, and **cultivation** of unrealistic beliefs. Notice also that although there are behavioral effects, there are also effects that are more physiological, attitudinal, emotional, and cognitive. When we take into consideration the full range of effects, it becomes easy to understand that there are likely many effects happening to everyone because of the widespread use of violence in media messages.

Perhaps the most prevalent effect of constant exposure to violence is an effect that is so subtle that most people overlook it. This is the effect of a cultivated belief that the world is violent and a related fear of being victimized. Of course, real-world violence and crime do exist, but they do not exist to the levels that the general public has been conditioned to believe. The crime rate in the United States increased from 1960 to 1990 then began falling. The FBI statistics show that in 1993 the number of property crimes per 1,000 people was 47.4 and this dropped to 24.5 by 2016, and the number of violent crimes per 1,000 people dropped from 7.5 in 1993 to 3.9 in 2016 (Gramlich, 2018a). While the crime rate was falling throughout the 1990s, a poll taken in 1996 found that only 7% of Americans believed that violent crime had declined in the previous 5-year period (Whitman & Loftus, 1996). Also, from March 1992 to August 1994, public perceptions of crime as the most important problem in the United States jumped from 5% to 52% (Lowry, Nio, & Leitner, 2003). And this disparity between the downward trend in crime and upward trend in concern about crime continues to grow. In a poll of likely voters in the 2016 election, 57% said that crime has gotten worse since 2008 (Gramlich, 2016).

Where do people get the idea that crime is a problem when they don't experience any in real life? From the media. The media constantly present stories about crime. There are cable TV shows that present one high-profile crime after another. Also, the media, through the news, present a constant stream of crime news that reinforces this impression that there is a great deal of terrible crime. Researchers have found a link between exposure to local television news, which is saturated with coverage of crime, and fear of crime (Romer, Jamieson, & Aday, 2003).

Given all these limitations on their perceptions of media violence (equating violence with graphicness, ignoring context, and the blind spot on harm), the public is routinely perceiving much less violence in the media presentations than there really are. So when the public complains that there is too much violence in the media, they are greatly underperceiving the amount. When we take a broader conception of violence (one that shows how exposure to media violence can lead to a wide range of negative effects), we can understand that the public's narrow conception of violence is truly faulty.

© Moviestore collection Ltd/Alamy

Social aggression is more imitable than physical aggression. The movie *Mean Girls* presents this aggression as witty and entertaining.

PRODUCERS' FAULTY BELIEFS

Producers of media messages also exhibit faulty beliefs, which also contribute to the problem. One of these is that violence is a necessary part of storytelling if they want to reach a large audience. A second faulty belief is that their violent stories should be held blameless when someone commits horrible acts of violence in real life and blames media exposure. Let's examine each of these faulty beliefs.

Violence Is Necessary to Storytelling

Violence is widespread throughout storytelling. Children's stories depend on violence ("Little Red Riding Hood," "Three Little Pigs," "Hansel and Gretel," and on and on). Much of our most revered literary writers present violence (e.g., all of Shakespeare's histories and tragedies present multiple acts of violence). Violence plunges characters into life-and-death situations and thereby heightens conflict and action, which are necessary storytelling features. However, there are other ways to attract audiences, heighten conflict, and arouse audience interest. Violence is a tool of storytelling, but not the only tool.

While there are certain audiences that like stories with violence, there are other audiences that do not. Research has repeatedly demonstrated that many people think that violence reduces their enjoyment of stories. For example, Weaver, Jensen, Martins, Hurley, and Wilson (2011) said, "It is widely assumed that children like violence in cartoons, but this assumption has not been supported in existing studies that show nonviolent programs are liked just as much or more than violent programs" (p. 49). They conducted an experiment to test this claim and found that violence had no relationship to whether children liked cartoons; they found that boys liked action in their cartoons and that violence could heighten the action. For girls, violence did not increase their enjoyment of either the action or the cartoons. In a meta-analysis of this literature, Weaver (2011) stated that violence has been found to decrease enjoyment of television programs among most people. However, there is a subset of the population that likes violence and searches it out, although most people do not like violence and try to avoid it.

Selective exposure is an important explanation. Some people seek out violent messages, and for them such messages satisfy a need and are enjoyable. But for most people, violence is not sought out. For example, violent video games have been found to attract people who have a high need for violence. These games then satisfy that need, and over time playing these games serves to reinforce those needs and make players more aggressive both in their game playing as well as in their real lives (von Salish, Vogelgesang, Kristen, & Oppl, 2011).

It is interesting to see what kinds of video stories people produce when they have an opportunity, which is what YouTube allows. A content analysis of the top-rated and most viewed videos on YouTube showed that the percentage of videos with violence was far less than on commercial mainstream television (Weaver, Zelenkauskaite, & Samson, 2012). The content analyses consistently showed that about 60% of television programs across the commercial mainstream contained some violence, while only 13% of videos on YouTube contained violence (Weaver et al., 2012).

Blame Others, Not Producers

When a high-profile act of violence—like a teenager taking guns to school or a movie theater and opening fire—occurs and the news media place it squarely on the public's agenda, many people blame the media. Media producers and programmers try to shift blame to the parents, gun sellers, or someone else. The belief that violent occurrences in society should be attributable to one and only one source is faulty. High-profile violent events are the result of many different kinds of influences over time. No one factor is sufficient, so the search for one place to assess blame is faulty. Blame should be shared.

YOUR OWN INFORMED OPINION

Now that you have seen some faulty public perceptions and some faulty producer beliefs exposed, it is time to work this understanding into your own opinion about media violence. Let's begin with examining the implications of this faulty thinking, so that you know what to avoid. Then you need to move beyond the faulty thinking.

Implications for Individuals

The way the public conceptualizes media violence is faulty. It is important that individuals broaden their perspective in order to realize that the context of portrayals is more primary than the frequency of those portrayals. When the context sanitizes the violence, it doesn't eliminate it; instead, by sanitizing violence, producers are merely masking its presence so that audiences will not be offended. But we *should be* offended by violent actions. We should see the suffering it creates in victims. We also need to avoid ignoring violence that is camouflaged by humor and violence that is more social and verbal in nature. In short, we need to broaden our conception of violence to match our broadened conception of effects.

The way the public defines violence creates an irony. The kind of violence that upsets people the most is precisely the type of violence that they need to be exposed to more. In contrast, it is the violence that most people do *not* complain about—or even perceive—that is doing them the most harm. When people are shown violence, they *should* be offended and they *should* complain. Such a reaction is the appropriate one to violent actions; it shows that people are sensitive to the violence. When they do not complain, this is a clear indication that they have been desensitized to the violence. There is a great deal of violence portrayed in the media, and the overwhelming majority of it is *not* met with complaints; thus, most people are desensitized to almost all of the violence they continually witness on TV.

If a show presents a highly graphic act of serious violence, people will be offended and complain that this type of portrayal is too violent and has no place in media messages. Their intention is to pressure the programmers to eliminate this type of content. The implication is that if the graphicness were reduced or if it were shown in a humorous context, the action would not be offensive to viewers.

When television programmers hear complaints about too much violence, the inclination of many creative types is not to reduce the amount of violent acts; instead, their typical response is to sanitize those acts. This means making the violence less graphic by showing less harm to the victims or to mask the harm with humor. **Sanitized violence** leads viewers to believe that violent acts are not such a big deal. So the less harm shown to the victims in television stories, the less chance that audiences will be offended; but at the same time, this sanitized violence is desensitizing viewers, so people are losing sympathy for victims in real life. So if producers eliminated all the acts of violence that people complain most about, they would likely be causing more harm to society.

Another irony is that while people are complaining about too much violence in the media, they are missing 99% of that violence because it has been sanitized, camouflaged, and limited to only physical violence. Thus they are focusing on violence that is less imitable and less likely to cause harm. The complaints are too narrow and focused on the wrong problem.

Implications for Producers

Producers of media messages are in the business of creating audiences so they can rent those audiences out to advertisers as well as sell access to their messages. They realize that there is a market for violent messages. But many of these messages create harm to individuals and society. While many of these harms cannot be attributable solely to media portrayals of violence, those messages are a contributing agent. We need to take an ecological approach and realize that societies are complex organisms that are sensitive to a wide range of factors.

We also need to take an economic approach and treat media organizations like businesses that consume resources and transform those resources into products that sometimes include harmful by-products (see Hamilton, 1998). For example, if the media were a manufacturing plant that were dumping harmful pollutants into the public water system or air, the Environmental Protection Agency would identify this as an economic problem and pressure the manufacturer to reduce the pollutants to pay a fine for the cleanup. If a steady stream of violent messages is attracting a particular audience that is predisposed to violent behavior in real life, then the companies providing this stream of messages that satisfy and reinforce that behavior should have an economic obligation to allocate some of their resources gained through the sale of these messages to the cleanup of the by-products of those messages.

Moving Beyond Faulty Thinking

In order for your opinion about media violence to be "informed," you need to move beyond faulty thinking. You can start this process by working to broaden your perspective on what kinds of portrayals constitute violence in the media. Try to write out a definition of violence in one sentence. When you finish, check your definition against the eight questions in Table Issue 5.1. Have you broadened your definition beyond that used by the general public? Is your definition as broad as that of media scholars?

Next, let's see how well you can apply your definition by conducting an analysis of media content (see Applying Media Literacy Skills Issue 5.1).

Now that you are sensitive to patterns of violence in media content, let's shift your attention to the effects possible from exposure to that content. Look at the six scenarios in Applying Skills of Media Literacy Issue 5.2. You will need to use the various descriptions of media effects as general principles and then compare them to the scenarios in a process of deduction. When a scenario fits the definition of a particular effect, then you can conclude that the scenario is an example of that effect. Make those deductions now then come back to the next section to see how your conclusions compare to mine.

Let's see what you concluded in Applying Media Literacy Skills Issue 5.2. I will present my conclusions but want you to realize that even if your conclusions differ from mine, this does not necessarily mean your conclusions are wrong. Perhaps a scenario triggered you to think of something you experienced in your life and thus you elaborated the scenario with many additional details. If those extra details support your conclusion, then feel confident in your conclusion.

Here are my conclusions. For the first scenario, I see a fairly standard imitation effect. In this situation, it is harmless, unless you get really carried away! But what is happening is that the viewing is getting you involved in the mayhem. Your heart rate and blood pressure increase. You are moving into a fight-or-flight mode. When you see your partner in a similar condition, you agree that wrestling would be a fun thing to do.

The second scenario presents a temporary fear reaction. The movie has planted strong images in your mind and a strong feeling of fear in your heart. Although your bedroom and surroundings are familiar, on this particular night, there is "something else in the room." That something else is not really a monster in the flesh but an apparition in your mind. This apparition can make your palms sweat and your heart pound—not very conducive to sleep!

The third scenario is likely a reinforcement of attitude effect. Most of the images the movie presented are probably not new to you. Although you likely have never seen a gang war in an inner city, you have these images through previous media exposures. And you have already held the attitude that inner cities and African American teenage males are highly dangerous. These are both stereotypes, of course. And the stronger the stereotypes, the less likely you will seek out real-world information to see if your attitude is distorted.

The fourth scenario is an attraction effect. You have a history of arousing and pleasurable experiences with past action/adventure films, especially those starring Steven Seagal.

The fifth scenario is a cognitive effect of generalizing patterns. Your recollection of several stories about local murders has led you to see a pattern. You can't recall many murders 5 years ago or when you were a child, so you see a trend to the pattern—there is an increase in the murder rate in your town. What may be happening is that the actual murder rate in your town is down (the murder rate in the United States as a whole has been declining the past decade), but the local news is getting better at presenting gruesome images that stay in your mind longer.

The sixth and final scenario is likely a desensitization effect. From watching so many acts of violence in the media, a simple fall seems like nothing. Also, because the victims of the serious acts of violence in the media rarely show any pain or harm, you think, "How can a silly slip hurt a young boy?"

The key to seeing value in your interpretations lies less in how often you agreed with me and more in how well you were able to apply the skill of deduction. In this case, you needed to have a set of good general principles in the form of clear definitions for a wide range of possible media effects. Then you needed to analyze the detail in the scenarios to find matches with the definitions. Finally you needed to reason logically using the particulars and general principles to arrive at your conclusions.

Keep working on your skill of deduction as you continue to confront this issue—as well as other issues. To be in a good position to do this, keep checking your general principles for their validity. Then when you encounter particulars (usually media message themselves or elements within them), conduct an analysis to make sure you really see what is there. Try to be logical—rather than intuitive—when reasoning to your conclusions.

Further Reading

Bushman, B. J., Huesmann, L. R., & Whitaker, J. L. (2009). Violent media effects. In R. L. Nabi & M. B. Oliver (Eds.), *Media processes and effects* (pp. 361–376). Los Angeles, CA: SAGE.

This chapter presents a relatively current review of the empirical literature on the effects of exposure to violence in the media. The authors focus on studies that take a strong psychological perspective and use the methods of experiment and survey.

Cantor, J. (2009). Fright reactions to mass media. In J. Bryant & M. B. Oliver (Eds.), *Media effects: Advances in theory and research* (3rd ed., pp. 287–303). New York, NY: Routledge.

This chapter reviews the literature on how violence and related media content have been found to trigger fear reactions in audiences, especially children.

Jordan, R. H., Jr. (2017). *Murder in the news.* Amherst, NY: Prometheus Books. (253 pages, including end notes and index)

This book presents the inside-the-industry story about why murder is so prominently covered in the news. The author is a journalist with 4 decades of experience as a TV reporter and anchor in Chicago, which has often been called the murder capital of the country. This is an easy-to-read reporting of an important issue in journalism, and the author uses lots of anecdotes to illustrate the reasons why murder is covered so often compared to other crimes and other more important events.

National Television Violence Study. (1996). *Scientific report.* Thousand Oaks, CA: SAGE. (568 pages with index)

The National Cable Television Association funded this $3.3 million project to examine the prevalence and context of violence on American television, the effects of warnings and advisories placed before violent programs, and the effect of public service announcements advocating the avoidance of violence. Some of the chapters are very technical and contain many statistics, but the overall report is one of the most comprehensive analyses of the issue of violence on television to date.

Potter, W. J. (1999). *On media violence.* Thousand Oaks, CA: SAGE. (304 pages with index)

In this book, I provide an in-depth analysis of the scholarly literature that deals with the effects of exposure to violence in the media.

Potter, W. J. (2003). *The 11 myths of media violence.* Thousand Oaks, CA: SAGE. (259 pages with index)

This book begins with a chapter illuminating the current state of public debate over media violence and ends with a chapter reflecting on the prognosis for change. In between are 11 chapters, each dealing with a faulty belief about media violence. Taken together, these myths lock people (the general public, people in the media industries, media regulators, and media researchers) into a maze of unproductive thinking. These myths include the following faulty beliefs: There is too much violence on television, the media are only responding to market desires, and reducing the amount of violence in the media will solve the problem.

Sparks, G. G., Sparks, C. W., & Sparks, E. A. (2009). Media violence. In J. Bryant & M. B. Oliver (Eds.), *Media effects: Advances in theory and research* (3rd ed., pp. 269–286). New York, NY: Routledge.

This chapter presents a brief history of the media violence controversy then moves on to review the research and theoretical work that tries to explain the phenomenon of violence in the media and how it affects audiences.

APPLYING MEDIA LITERACY SKILLS ISSUE 5.1
ANALYZE MEDIA CONTENT FOR VIOLENCE

1. Watch a television show that has a reputation for presenting a lot of violence. Use your definition and see how many actions fit your definition. Count them.

   How many acts would you have counted using a definition that was based on a "no" answer to all eight questions in Table Issue 5.1?

   How many acts would you have counted using a definition that was based on a "yes" answer to all eight questions in Table Issue 5.1?

2. Watch another program with violence; this time, pay attention to how the violence is portrayed.

   How much of the violence is committed by bad characters and how much by the "good guys"?

   How many of the violent acts are punished in the scene—that is, where the perpetrator is stopped in his or her actions or sanctioned in some way?

   How many of the violent acts show realistic harm to the victims?

   How many of the violent acts are portrayed as being justified?

   What does this pattern of context tell you about whether committing violence is good or bad? That is, what are the producers of this program teaching you about whether using violence is good or bad?

3. Watch a situation comedy and count the number of acts of verbal violence—that is, verbal put-downs, slurs, insults, and comments designed to embarrass another character.

   What kinds of characters commit the most verbal violence? Are they the main characters? Are they attractive?

   What happens to characters who commit acts of verbal violence? Are they punished or rewarded (by laughter) or neither?

   Are the victims of the verbal violence shown as being harmed? If so, what kind of harm, and how long does the harm last?

   What does this pattern of verbal violence and its context tell you about whether committing verbal violence is good or bad?

APPLYING MEDIA LITERACY SKILLS ISSUE 5.2
CAN YOU IDENTIFY THE NEGATIVE EFFECTS?

1. Do you or your children feel like wrestling after watching several hours of cartoons or *World Wrestling Entertainment* shows?

2. After watching a horror movie late at night by yourself, do you have a difficult time relaxing and falling asleep? Or do you lie awake in bed thinking that you should get up and check the locks once again or perhaps leave a light on in the hall?

3. You have seen a violent movie that took place in an inner-city ghetto. African American teenagers were dealing drugs and killing rivals with guns. You shake your head and think, "Inner cities are such war zones. I'm glad I don't have to travel through one of them!"

4. You're thumbing through the newspaper and notice that a new Steven Seagal action/adventure film has just been released. You feel excitement and can't wait until you get to see it.

5. You are watching the evening news and you hear about two brutal murders that took place last night in your town. You think back and remember previous newscasts about murders in your town over the past year. You conclude that the murder rate is sharply increasing.

6. You see a teenage boy slip on a puddle in a supermarket and fall down. You think, "Silly boy. It's his own fault for not looking where he was going. Besides, he's not really hurt." You walk away and do not give it another thought.

PRIVACY

Issue: The changes in media technologies have made it easier for marketers, governments, and criminals to invade your privacy.

Protecting your privacy, especially online, is important.

The issue of privacy has grown significantly over the past 2 decades as newer information technologies have changed the way information is generated, stored, and shared. When information was stored on paper, the files that recorded that information could be locked away and kept private. The information about us was scattered across all the people and businesses with whom we interacted. We expected each of those people and businesses to respect our privacy and trusted that they did not share our private interactions with third parties unless we gave them permission. Thus we controlled who we gave which bits of information to and who could share what bits of information. But all that has suddenly changed.

Information in almost all our exchanges (with banks, stores, governmental agencies, and even friends) is now recorded into electronic files that can be easily replicated and widely distributed to various **third parties**. Many of these third parties are information marketing businesses that pull information from many different sources to create databases that contain a huge amount of information about the details of our financial transactions, our friendships, our health, our whereabouts, and the thoughts we express. One of these companies is Acxiom Corporation, which operates more than 23,000 computer servers that are constantly collecting, collating, and analyzing more than 50 trillion unique data transactions every year. Acxiom has extensive data on 96% of American households and has amassed consumer profiles on 700 million consumers worldwide; each of these profiles contains at least 1,500 specific bits of information per individual, such as race, gender, phone number, type of car driven, education level, number of children, the square footage of the home, portfolio size, recent purchases, age, height, weight, marital status, politics, health issues, occupation, pet ownership and breed, and even whether a person is right or left handed (Goodman, 2015). Acxiom generates more than $1 billion a year selling this information (Acxiom, 2018).

Few of us are aware of how much information has been collected about us and how easily it is made available to marketers, governments, and anyone else who wants to buy even the most intimate details of our lives without our knowledge. Thus privacy has become one of the most important issues of media literacy. On one side of this issue are all the businesses, governments, and organizations who crave unlimited information about everyone so they can maximize their strategies to shape the attitudes and behaviors of others. On the other side of this issue is us, the public. Because we have been relatively unaware of how much privacy we have lost, we have been slow to engage with this issue. Therefore the purpose of this chapter is to show you what has been occurring over the past few decades to reduce your privacy so you can understand why this issue is so important.

DELINEATING THE ISSUE

Privacy is the secluding of personal information by individuals about themselves. In everyday language, privacy is characterized by a set of four ideas. The first idea is that individuals do not want to share all information about themselves with everyone; there are some things about themselves that they want to keep to themselves. Second, privacy is a variable condition; that is, a person might want to share some bits of information with some people but not with others. For example, we want our friends to have our phone numbers and e-mail addresses, but we want to keep this contact information away from telemarketers and other advertisers who might target us with a flood of unwanted messages. We want our physician to have a complete history of our medical conditions but we do not want to share this information with the public, and maybe not even with our friends or parents.

Third, individuals own their personal information and should be able to control it; if another person or an organization takes control of an individual's personal information without his or her permission, this is an invasion of the individual's privacy. Fourth, when we share some private information with another person and set boundaries on sharing that information, we expect that person to respect our boundaries. For example, when we give information about ourselves to our close friends, we expect them to follow a fundamental principle of fairness that they not share that information with a third party unless they first ask our permission or, at least, that they tell us that they have passed that information along to a third party. Many of us expect the same treatment when we interact with businesses; that is, when we buy something from an Internet retailer, we expect the retailer to respect our privacy and not share information about this transaction with other businesses.

All four of these ideas are routinely being violated by mass media businesses as well as other organizations and individuals. Three factors make this widespread violation possible. First, the technological advances of digitizing information along with the high-speed transmission capabilities made possible by computers and the Internet have allowed all kinds of people to gather information easily, store it, transform it, use it, and sell it to others. Second, regulations and laws to protect privacy favor businesses who want to acquire your information over consumers who want to protect their privacy. Third, the level of public awareness about this issue is very low; that is, few people understand the extent to which they have lost their privacy.

The issue of privacy is essentially the competition between threats and protections. At the present time, the threats are many and the protections are few, so the threats are far ahead in this competition.

One major source of these threats is criminals. These are the individuals, rogue gangs, and all kinds of organizations that hack into "secure" databases, steal information and even entire identities of people, and disseminate viruses that infect databases by disabling their use. The other major source of threats to our privacy is an assortment of non-criminals who coerce us into giving up our privacy, then with our "permission" collect massive amounts of previously private information on us and use it for their own marketing purposes and/or sell it to third parties. There are many organizations that continually invade our privacy in non-criminal ways, such as financial institutions, vendors (both Internet and brick and mortar), and governmental bodies that tax us or grant us licenses.

In this chapter, I will show you a wide range of threats to your privacy that are happening every day, then show you some ways you can try protecting your privacy in the digital age. We cannot rely much on governments to pass laws and regulations to protect our privacy, because governments have been very slow to act compared to the speed at which our privacy is being reduced to almost nothing. These threats to our privacy are so new and evolve so fast that regulators are just beginning to experiment with various restrictions and laws to try to protect us without violating the rights of legitimate businesses. In the meantime, you need to understand what these threats are so you can take steps now to protect your privacy while regulators are figuring out what to do.

CRIMINAL THREATS TO YOUR PRIVACY

iStock/peterhowell

Your activity on the Internet can be tracked, sold, and used in many ways, some legally and some illegally.

There has been a dramatic rise in cybercrime. The number of complaints of cybercrime reported annually to the Federal Bureau of Investigation's (FBI) **Internet Crime Complaint Center** (IC3) increased from 16,840 in 2000 to more than 300,000 in 2017 (FBI, 2018). While many of these cybercrimes are committed by individuals or small groups of **hackers**, some are committed by groups working for foreign governments. Over 20% of cyberattacks in 2017 came from China, 11% from the United States, and 6% from the Russian Federation (Sobers, 2018).

The cost of cybercrime has been growing dramatically. In 2001, cybercrime caused $17.8 billion in damage and this increased to over $600 billion by 2017, driven mainly by increases in attacks of **malware**, especially **ransomware** (McAfee, 2018). A *Forbes* article reveals how estimates of the cost of cybercrime typically underestimate the real cost, because they are limited to the direct costs to companies for restoring their databases once they are attacked by criminals as well as the costs they are forced to spend to buy protection services to prevent future attacks. Those cybercrime estimates ignore the follow-up costs such as how much money and time individual people must spend to recover from a company's data breach as well as the hacked company's loss of reputation, which can decrease the company's attractiveness to investors as well as suppress the company's future sales due to the loss of customers. When all of these expenses are considered, the total cost of cybercrime is more like $6 trillion per year (Eubanks, 2017). When we break this enormous cost down and realize this computes to $790 per person in the entire world, we can see that cybercrime is a huge problem!

In this section, we examine the threats to your privacy when people and organizations who have no rights to access your information use illegal means to invade your privacy. The three major types of threats from cybercriminals are stealing your private information, hijacking computers, and destroying information.

Stealing Private Information

We all have information that we want to keep private, but if it is stored on a computer, a mobile device, or on the **cloud**, criminals can steal it. In this section, we will examine first how cybercriminals can steal your private information both directly and indirectly. Then we will examine what those criminals do with this stolen information.

Direct Theft

Some cybercriminals steal private information directly from individuals by interacting with their victims on their own computers. The two most prevalent techniques used are **phishing** and **spyware**. When cybercriminals use the phishing technique, they typically pose as a reputable company in order to send messages to potential victims. Phishing is typically carried out by e-mail or instant messaging, and it often directs users to enter details at a fake website whose look and feel are almost identical to the legitimate one that it is pretending to be. For example, you might get an e-mail from someone who says she is a security officer at your bank and she wants to help you increase the security on your accounts at no charge to you. She urges you to click on the link provided. When you click on the link, a screen comes up that looks just like the sign-on screen for your bank, but it is really a website constructed by the phisher. You are asked to sign into your account and then to provide additional information (e.g., name, address, phone number, and social security number) to confirm that it is really you. After you provide this information, she says you have passed the security check and she is satisfied it is really you. Then she asks you to list your bank account numbers so she can increase the security on them. When you provide this information, you are not increasing your security; instead you are destroying your security by giving all this private information to a phisher.

Another commonly used phishing scam is for thieves to set up an electronic auction site where people bid on items (Lee & Light, 2003). The people who "win" this fake auction are told to send their name and address so the merchandise can be mailed. The recipients are told to wait until the merchandise arrives and check it out before paying for it, so the recipients are conned into believing they are dealing with a reputable company. But the merchandise never arrives and the thieves get away with the victim's name and address.

Cybercriminals can also access your private information by getting you to download spyware onto your computer or mobile device. Spyware is a small program that is typically downloaded automatically onto your computer when you open an e-mail attachment. Once the spyware program is on your hard drive, it begins collecting information about you without your knowledge, by recording keystrokes, sites visited, and even personal information such as credit card numbers, e-mail addresses, passwords, and so on.

Indirect Theft

Cybercriminals can steal enormous amounts of your private information without ever accessing your computer or even contacting you in any way. They hack into huge databases and steal your information—along with the information of millions of other individuals. Because private information about you exists in hundreds, and perhaps thousands, of different databases, cybercriminals have many sources. Every time you have engaged in any kind of a financial transaction (with a bank, insurance company, governmental agency, retailer, wholesaler, etc.) or social interaction (e-mails, uploads, downloads, postings, etc.) online, that institution stores that information in a data file and likely augments that information on you by buying additional data about you from other vendors. Most, but not all, of these companies try to protect their databases by using software that creates a **firewall**. However, it has been estimated that 41% of companies that have more than 1,000 sensitive files, including credit card numbers and health records, do not have firewalls to protect their databases (Sobers, 2018).

Hackers regard these firewalls as challenges and many hackers have been able to break through, or breach, many different kinds of firewalls. The Privacy Rights Clearinghouse (2018) reports that since 2005 when they began monitoring hacking activity, there have been 8,209 separate data breaches made public, and this totals more than 10.6 billion records hacked. The number of breaches has been growing each year and is expected to continue. In 2017, there were 130 large-scale, targeted breaches in the United States and that number was expected to grow by as much as 27% per year (Sobers, 2018). See Timeline Issue 6.1 for a few high-profile examples.

The cost to a company that has been hacked is staggering. In 2017, cybercrime costs accelerated, with organizations spending nearly 23% more than in 2016. In companies with over 50,000 compromised records, the average cost of a data breach is $6.3 million. When larger companies are hacked, the costs are much larger. For example, Equifax had to spend $4 billion to recover from its database being hacked in July 2017 (Sobers, 2018).

While hackers exhibit many purposes for their criminal activity, those purposes can be simply classified into two groups: economic purposes and political purposes.

Economic Purpose

Hackers motivated by an economic purpose hope to convert the information they steal into money. They can do this by either selling the information to other criminals or by using the information themselves to steal the identity of the people in the database they have hacked.

There is a robust market for stolen information on the dark web. There is now so much information available for sale that the prices for some data are remarkably low. For

TIMELINE ISSUE 6.1
Some Recent Security Breaches of Consumer Information

2000

2004: An employee at AOL steals 92 million e-mail addresses and sells them to a spammer for $28,000. It costs the company $400,000. The employee is found guilty in court, sentenced to 15 months in prison, and slapped with a fine.

2005: An employee of Bank of America loses computer tapes containing 1.2 million records consisting of personal information for credit cards used by federal employees.

2005: Hackers get into the database of CardSystems Solutions, Inc. and gain access to 40 million Discover, Visa, MasterCard, and American Express numbers.

2006: UCLA admits that hackers had gained access to personal information on about 800,000 of the university's current and former students, faculty, and staff members.

2006: A Department of Veterans Affairs data analyst takes home a database containing more than 26 million personal records on his laptop, which is stolen—exposing all the information necessary to swipe the identity of virtually every person released from military service since 1975.

2005

2007: Hackers access 94 million records of TJ Maxx.

2008: Hackers access 130 million records of Heartland.
2009: Hackers access 76 million records of the U.S. military.

2009: In May, hackers break into a Virginia state website used by pharmacists to track prescription drug abuse. They delete records on more than 8 million patients and replace the site's homepage with a ransom note demanding $10 million for the return of the records.

2011: Hackers access the names, addresses, passwords, and credit card details of 77 million accounts in a Sony network used to run their online gaming systems.

2010

2013: Twitter announces that hackers gained access to information (user names, e-mail addresses, and encrypted passwords) on 250,000 of its users.

2013: Target is hacked and credit card information is stolen from 110 million customers. Target has to pay out $10 million to customers.

2013: In June, Myspace has 360 million accounts hacked and usernames, e-mail addresses, and passwords are all stolen.

2013: In August, Yahoo says that 1 billion accounts had been breached, making it the largest hack on record. Hackers stole everything from dates of birth and e-mail addresses to encrypted security questions and answers and hashed passwords.

2014 : eBay has 145 million accounts breached.

2015

2015: In July, Hackers breach Ashley Madison, a dating website catering to married people, and steal information on 32 million users. Hackers then post data online about users' names, addresses, passwords, phone numbers, as well as their search histories.

2016: Uber has data stolen on 57 million riders and drivers.

2016: In May, LinkedIn has information from 117 million accounts stolen then publicly sold.

2017: In July, Equifax, the credit reporting bureau that collects extensive data on individual's purchases and payment histories to determine credit scores, has 143 million of its records hacked.

2018: In April, Facebook has 87 million accounts breached.

2018 : In June, Ticketfly has 27 million accounts hacked.

2020

Sources: "AOL Is Sued" (2006), D'Innocenzio and Collins (2013), Loobrok (2017), "Online Reputations in the Dirt" (2011), Privacy Rights Clearinghouse (2018), Rodriguez and Pierson (2011), and Sobers (2018).

example, the credit reporting bureau Experian says that people can now buy a social security number on the dark web for as little as $1, medical records for as little as $1, credit or debit cards for $5, bank information for $15, a valid driver's license for $20, diplomas for $100, and U.S. passports for $1,000 (Stack, 2018).

When criminals have a few bits of information about you (your name, birth date, and social security number), they can steal your identity. **Identity theft** is the using of key pieces of private personal information about an individual to assume that person's identity by applying for all kinds of economic resources (credit cards, loans, housing, licenses, etc.) and consuming those resources without the criminal paying for them. When the bills become due, the vendors contact the real person and expect payment. The real person, of course, did not make any of these purchases or benefit from any of these consumed resources but is still expected to pay back the vendors because those transactions were made in the victim's name. Victims of identity theft have only three options: (a) pay all the charges, (b) refuse to pay the charges and have their credit rating destroyed, or (c) try to convince vendors that they did not make any of the purchases, which is extremely difficult because it requires victims to prove the transactions were fraudulent although the vendors have evidence that the purchases were made in the victims' names.

According to complaints filed with the Federal Trade Commission (FTC), the most common form of identity theft is credit card fraud (133,015 complaints in 2017), followed by employment or tax-related fraud (82,051), phone or utilities fraud (55,045), and bank fraud (50,517). The total of all losses due to identity theft in 2017 alone was $905 million, which was a 21.6% increase over 2016 (Tatham, 2018).

Approximately 85% of victims of identity theft found out about the crime due to an adverse situation, such as being denied credit or employment, notification by police or collection agencies, or the receipt of credit cards they never ordered. Only 15% found out through a positive action taken by a business group that verified a submitted application or a reported change of address.

Although victims are finding out about the crime more quickly, it is taking far longer than ever—up to a decade—for them to recover fully from the identity theft. Victims struggle with credit scores that are unfairly low, and this forces them to pay increased interest on loans, higher credit card fees, and higher insurance premiums. Victims must battle with collection agencies and credit agencies that refuse to clear their records despite substantiating evidence of the crime. The emotional impact on victims is likened to that felt by victims of more violent crimes, such as repeated battering, violent assault, and even rape. Some victims feel dirty, defiled, ashamed, embarrassed, and undeserving of assistance. Others report that the effects of identity theft resulted in strained or dissolved relationships with a significant other or spouse or loss of family member support.

Political Purpose

Not all hackers have an economic purpose; some have a political purpose. That is, they breach a company's firewall to access private information to exert power over that company. These crimes are referred to as **hacktivism**.

One form of hacktivism is when political activists break into an organization's "secure" databases for the purpose of publically embarrassing that organization. For decades, the Chinese government has been sponsoring an ongoing campaign of stealing sensitive

Phishing and spyware are two popular ways for cyber thieves to steal your information.

iStock/ RapidEye

information from all kinds of businesses and governments then using that information to embarrass those organizations (D'Innocenzio & Collins, 2013, p. B4). These Chinese hackers broke through Google's firewall and accessed the Gmail account information of senior U.S. government officials, Chinese political activists, officials from Asian countries, journalists, and military personnel. Another example is when agents for the North Korean government hacked into Sony after the film company released a satirical movie (*The Interview*) about their leader, Kim Jong-un. The hackers extracted about 100 terabytes of information, then uploaded unreleased movies to a file sharing website and threatened to make public internal memos and e-mails that could embarrass many people at Sony (Altman & Frizell, 2015).

Private individuals also turn to hacktivism to embarrass their own governments or businesses when they believe those organizations are conducting nefarious activities in secret. A popular site where hacktivists publish stolen data is WikiLeaks, which is an international not-for-profit organization founded by Julian Assange in 2006. For example, in 2016, someone hacked into the protected files of the Democratic National Committee then published on WikiLeaks 44,053 e-mails and 17,761 attachments from the top strategists in the presidential campaign of Hillary Clinton. When this information was made public, it embarrassed the Clinton campaign to such an extent that it has been blamed as the reason Clinton lost the election. Hacktivists have also used WikiLeaks to publish embarrassing information hacked from the private files of various organizations of the U.S. government, including the Army (e.g., a manual for dealing with prisoners at Guantanamo Bay), the State Department, the Central Intelligence Agency, and Immigration and Customs Enforcement. Hackers have also used WikiLeaks to publish stolen information about scandals around the world that governments have tried to keep secret (Lohrmann, 2017).

Hijacking

A second major criminal threat to your privacy is the **hijacking** of your computer, which occurs when hackers take over the control of your computer. One form of hijacking is with the use of ransomware where hackers freeze your computer so you cannot use it. The frozen screen explains that hackers now completely control your computer and will not unfreeze it until you pay a ransom. Typically hackers will avoid doing this to individual computers and instead target the servers in large companies where they can demand much more money as a ransom to unfreeze all the computers throughout the organization's computer network.

The use of ransomware is growing at an alarming rate. Ransomware damage costs exceeded $5 billion in 2017, which was 15 times the cost from the previous year. It was estimated that the cost of ransomware will increase to $11.5 billion by 2019, when a business will fall victim to a ransomware attack every 14 seconds. The health care industry has the highest number of ransomware attacks and this is expected to quadruple by 2020

(Sobers, 2018). By 2017, hackers were breaching a major healthcare database every day (SecureLink, 2018).

Another form of hijacking is when criminals hack into your computer and link it up with other hijacked computers to create a **botnet**. A botnet is a network of infected computers (bots) that is remotely controlled by hackers who put these computers into round-the-clock service sending spam, phishing for credit card numbers, spying on Internet traffic, or logging users' keystrokes. Some of these botnets have been found to send out 30 billion spam e-mails per day. Almost all of this is done without the knowledge of the individuals who own the computers in the botnet (Sarno, 2011).

Another form of hijacking, which is done by advertisers, is to take over your homepage with a browser or to implant a search engine on your computer's hard drive. This appears innocent enough, but this browser or search engine is designed to direct you only to certain advertised websites. One is SearchCoolWeb, which provides a page of all kinds of interesting topics that you can click on to play games or go shopping. Although this page looks like a service helping you in your Internet surfing, your browser has actually been hijacked and your Internet browsing is being controlled by the hijacker who directs you to certain websites while preventing you from accessing other websites.

Destroying Information

A third type of criminal activity is the use of viruses to destroy information stored electronically. A **computer virus** is a small string of code (typically 2 to 4 kilobytes) that insizes itself into a normal software program, often affixing itself to file extensions that end in .COM or .EXE. The string of viral code hides itself among the normal code and is latent until it is activated, at which time it begins to destroy your stored information either by erasing lines of existing data, by reformatting large sections of your memory, or by erasing file addresses on your directory, thus making it impossible for your computer to find those existing files.

Computer viruses are highly contagious. Each time an infected computer interacts with another computer, the virus gets passed along. Because most viruses remain hidden, most users have no idea they are passing around the virus until it is too late.

Sony Pictures cancelled the release of the satirical comedy *The Interview*, about a plot to assassinate North Korean leader Kim Jong-un, in December 2014, after hackers launched a cyberattack on the company.

The number of viruses has grown dramatically in less than 3 decades. In 1986, the National Computer Security Association estimated that there were only four known computer viruses. By 2000, it was estimated that there were over 50,000 identified viruses. In 2011, Symantec Corporation, which markets Norton Utilities computer software, estimated that there were over 1 million viruses (DaBoss, 2013). Then a short 4 years later, it was estimated that there were 1 million computer viruses being introduced worldwide each day (Harrison & Pagliery, 2015). One of the most serious recent viruses, called Wannacry, infected over 400,000 computers in at least 150 countries in 2017 before it was recognized and programmers could write code to protect computers from this particular virus. Wannacry cost the users and companies of the infected computers a combined $4 billion to recover from this single virus. Users who installed updated software to protect them from the Wannacry became immune to further attacks of that virus; however, there were 5.4 billion attacks of that virus within its first few months of use (Sobers, 2018).

NON-CRIMINAL THREATS TO YOUR PRIVACY

In contrast to the threats outlined above, the practices that I present in this section are legal. Commercial entities, such as legitimate businesses and research firms, frequently access information about you that you may prefer to keep private, or assume is being kept private. The motivation behind these types of threats is financial gain for the organizations that use these data. That is, some commercial entities use this information themselves for their marketing—to direct you toward certain products and services and entice you to buy them. Other organizations gather this information so they can sell it to other organizations.

The threats to our privacy presented in this section are all legal because—whether you realize it or not—you have given your permission to allow companies to gather private data and use it in any way they want, even selling it. Whenever we apply for a credit card, a checking account, a store discount card, phone service, or membership to websites, we are asked to read a very long document; buried in all that small type and legalese are clauses that grant the provider of the service we are seeking the right to collect all kinds of information about us as we use their service. Furthermore, additional clauses grant the provider of the service the right to share any or all of that information with "third-party providers," which means any organization that is not directly involved in the transactions between you and the company that is asking you initially for the information. When most of us are faced with reading such a document, we quickly scan through it until we get to the end where we click on the "accept" button with relief that the application process is finally over and we can now access the service. Then as we use the service, we are largely unaware of the degree to which the service provider is monitoring our activities, recording information, using the information to control our use of the service, then selling that information to other organizations.

Collecting and Selling Information

Every time you use your computer, your activities are being monitored. **Internet Service Providers (ISPs)** collect information on which websites you visit and for how long. Search companies such as Google and Yahoo have been collecting data on all your searches for years (Levy, 2006), and these companies are encouraging you to make even more of your personal data available to them as they update their customer agreements.

Facebook is a prime example of an Internet service that has grown very sophisticated in monitoring you. Facebook makes a copy of everything all users post through its service; this includes photos, text, audio, video, links, personal information, and even every e-mail. In addition, Facebook also monitors every opinion expressed. Facebook founder

Mark Zuckerberg explained that Facebook not only owns the right to use this material but that it retains the right in perpetuity, even after users quit the site (Sarno, 2009a). In 2011, Facebook added a facial recognition feature, which was presented to users as an added bonus of using the site—that is, users could pass a cursor over a photo of a picture of a person they do not recognize, and the person's name pops up. This, of course, is also a major benefit to Facebook itself because this feature makes it possible for Facebook to keep better track of who your friends are and what you say to each of them. With innovations like facial recognition, Facebook has become the repository of identity for much of the Internet ("Trolling for Your Soul," 2011).

Facebook has been very successful in collecting everything it can about you then selling marketers access to it. Facebook's annual revenue in 2007 was $153 million and this increased to $40.7 billion in 2017 (Statista, 2018k). How did it generate that income when it doesn't sell anything to users? The answer is that it sells its users' information and attention to all kinds of marketers. When Facebook prepared to go public in 2004, it had to disclose its financial records as a requirement to issue publically traded stock. In those initial financial documents, Facebook estimated that each of its users was worth $80.95 to the company. Over time as Facebook monitored how much information it was collecting from users and how much they were selling that information for, Facebook revealed that each profile page was worth $1,800 and that your friendships were worth $0.62 each (Goodman, 2015, p. 55). So while Facebook does not ask you for a monetary payment to set up an account, it does require that you grant them permission to collect all your information (all your thoughts, expressed needs, friendships, pictures, and lifestyle indicators) and use it all in any way it wants. And when he has been questioned about privacy, Facebook's CEO Mark Zuckerberg said that "privacy is no longer the social norm" (Goodman, 2015, p. 71).

In April 2018, Zuckerberg was called to testify on privacy and data mining in front of the U.S. Senate Committees on Commerce and the Judiciary. During the 5-hour session, when Zuckerberg was asked about what Facebook does with users' information, he said, "Yes, we store data . . . some of that content with people's permission" (Watson, 2018), although he continually emphasized that Facebook was concerned about protecting the privacy of its users. He repeatedly denied that Facebook sells user information to advertisers but said that Facebook uses that information to help advertisers place their ads in Facebook in a highly targeted manner. So while Facebook may not sell the information itself directly to advertisers, it is clearly selling access to that information.

Zuckerberg does appear to be very concerned about this issue when it comes to his own privacy. In 2013, he bought the four homes surrounding his house in Palo Alto, California, for $30 million then tore them down to create a privacy barrier around his home. Also, he has taped over camera lenses on his computers to prevent them from recording his sessions (Oremus, 2018). During his congressional testimony, when Senator Dick Durbin asked Zuckerberg if he would be comfortable sharing the name of the hotel he stayed in last night, Zuckerberg replied, "No. I would probably not choose to do that publicly, here." He said, "I think everyone should have control over how their information is used" (Watson, 2018).

Because Congress is now very concerned with privacy, Zuckerberg is being forced to walk a very fine line with very strong pressures on either side. On one side is the pressure to make the public and potential regulators believe he is being responsible about protecting the privacy of Facebook users, and the pressure from the other side is to preserve his business model that makes it essential to use as much private user data as possible to continue generating billions of dollars of ad revenue. While Zuckerberg is now choosing his words very carefully, other Internet moguls are more frank. In December 2009, CNBC's Maria Bartiromo asked Google CEO Eric Schmidt about privacy concerns resulting from Google's increasing tracking of consumers. Schmidt replied, "If you have something that you don't want anyone to know about, maybe you shouldn't be doing it in the first place" (Goodman, 2015, p. 77).

With the rise in popularity of **social networking sites (SNSs)**, a new industry of monitoring has grown. Called **sentiment analysis**, companies now sift through millions of postings across SNSs to monitor the rise and fall of popularity for various topics, needs, products, and services (Kennedy, 2012).

ISPs and SNSs are second parties—that is, you are interacting with them directly. An industry of third-party companies has grown dramatically as new companies acquire information from numerous second parties and collate that information into even larger databases. For example, BlueCava is compiling a database of the usage of every computer, smartphone, and online-enabled gadget in the entire world and linking those data to information about their users. In this massive task, it uses programs such as Phorm, which mines the activity of ISPs using a method called deep packet inspection to analyze the traffic that flows through their servers and builds a comprehensive profile of each customer's activity on each ISP (Pariser, 2011).

Another tool that data miners use is called a **cookie**, which is tiny computer file that is planted on your hard drive when you access many websites. Cookies are what make monitoring of your Internet activities possible. Most people only have a fuzzy idea about what a cookie is or they have no idea at all.

Netscape created cookies as an innovative browser feature in 1994. It told users that cookies would make their experiences with Internet sites easier, especially those sites that offered "shopping cart" services such as Amazon. The idea was to allow consumers to click from page to page, choosing items to buy, while a virtual clerk kept track of the items by listing them in a small file that Netscape called a cookie. The cookie also contained the user's name, address, and credit card information. Cookies stayed on the computer hard drive so that when the user went shopping again, his or her information was automatically accessed, making it more convenient for the user not to have to re-enter all the payment and mailing information. Because the purchasing information was also stored, this made it easy for the Internet vendor to access the information and direct consumers to certain items. Vendors could also upload this information, making it easy for them to construct a profile of your browsing history and interests.

When Netscape first developed cookies, it did not tell consumers how they worked. As the use of cookies grew in frequency, there were few complaints from consumers. But eventually, some consumers figured out that there was this clandestine activity taking place on their hard drives. When some news articles reported on the cookie technology in January 1996, a firestorm of criticism erupted as people began realizing how their privacy was being invaded without their knowledge. Officials at Netscape were surprised by the criticism and dismissed it. For example, Alex Edelstein, Netscape's product manager for Navigator 2.0, declared that cookie technology was an insignificant issue and would "blow over" (Pew Internet & American Life Project, 2000). But it didn't blow over. In subsequent public opinion polls, many people who understood what cookies were continued to criticize their use. In a 2000 poll, more than half (54%) of Internet users said they believed that websites' tracking of users is harmful because it invaded their privacy. Just 27% said tracking is helpful because it allows the sites to provide information tailored to specific consumers, but another 27% said they would never provide personal information (Pew Internet & American Life Project, 2000).

Under pressure, Netscape added a tool to allow users to disable cookies for the next version of its web-browsing software, but users had to find out on their own what this tool was and the tool was not very easy to use. Netscape continued with an **opt-out default**, in which it continued to use cookies unless a user specifically opted out. Therefore, users would continue to have cookies implanted on their machines unless they took affirmative steps to reject cookies, which meant that users who did not know what cookies were or that they had the option to opt out still had no control over cookies. With Netscape, a user had to dig two menu screens down in the browser to find the place to opt out of cookies.

Microsoft built in cookie controls in its more recent versions of Internet Explorer. Internet users are now alerted when a site tries to place a third-party cookie—that is, one that could help track their activities all across the web. But even with these new tools provided by Internet browsers, only about 10% of people were found to set their browsers to block cookies, because many people still do not know what cookies are or how to prevent them (Pew Internet & American Life Project, 2000).

Cookies are now used by other companies in addition to ISPs and online stores. There are now "third-party advertising networks," which use cookie files to track a user's activities all across the web and trigger advertisements according to each user's apparent interests and needs. One of these third-party advertising networks is DoubleClick, which sprang up to oversee banner ads on websites. You can check your Internet browser to see what cookies have been automatically downloaded to your computer (see Table Issue 6.1). It is likely that there are many cookies stored on your computer. Look at the list. Some of the names of the cookies are clear enough to tell you who is responsible for putting that cookie on your computer, but some of the names are very cryptic and tell you nothing about who is responsible.

Some shocking uses of cookies have come to light. These examples show how powerful cookies are in monitoring activity on one's computer. For example, Pharmatrak, Inc., a Boston technology firm, acknowledged tracking consumers' activities on health-related sites without informing the public (Pew Internet & American Life Project, 2000). Some agencies of the federal government have also been found to engage in monitoring private individuals by using cookies. The federal Office of National Drug Control Policy (the so-called "drug czar's office") was found to use cookies to track web surfers' drug-related information requests. The FBI developed "Carnivore," a device that silently intercepts all traffic to and from a suspect's e-mail account without the person's knowledge or permission. It is similar to a wiretap without a court order.

The use of media technologies to monitor your activities is not limited to your use of computers; it extends to phones and other mobile devices. Every time you make a phone call, an entry is made in a database that indicates the number you called and how long you were connected. With mobile phones, records are kept about where you called from. With GPS technology, people can find where you are even when you are not making a

TABLE ISSUE 6.1   ■   **How to Check Your Computer for Cookies**

If you have never checked your computer for cookies, make sure you do this exercise as soon as possible. Instructions are provided below for the most popular web browsers.

Google Chrome

1.   When Chrome is open, the word "Chrome" appears on the upper left corner. Click on "Chrome."

2.   On the drop-down menu, click "Preferences."

3.   A settings screen will appear. Scroll to the bottom of this screen and click on "Advanced," which will present you with more options. The first set of options is labeled "Privacy and Security." For each of these options, there is a switch on the right that allows you to turn that option on or off.

Microsoft Explorer

1.   Look at the top right of your browser's page and click on the "Tools" tab. This will give you a drop-down menu.

2.   At the bottom of the drop-down menu is "Internet Options." Click on "Internet Options."

3.   You will see a box with seven tabs across the top. Click on the "Privacy" tab.

4.   On the left of the box, you will see a settings bar. If you move the bar up, it will increase your security; if you move the bar down, it will decrease your security. As you move the bar, you can see a description on the right that indicates how you are changing the settings on cookies.

Safari

1.   When Safari is open, the word "Safari" appears on the upper left corner. Click on "Safari."

2.   On the drop-down menu, click "Preferences."

3.   A box will appear in the middle of your screen. Across the top of that box are icons. Click on the "Privacy" icon and you will be shown your options for allowing (or preventing) cookies and tracking.

Mozilla Firefox

1.   When Firefox is open, the word "Firefox" appears on the upper left corner. Click on "Firefox."

2.   On the drop-down menu, click "Preferences."

3.   A new screen will appear with several options listed on the left side. Click on "Privacy & Security" to update your options.

phone call, and advertisers can use this information immediately. For example, Placecast uses GPS tracking data on people's smartphones to track potential consumers and send them enticing offers when they get close to a particular store.

The digitization of information, along with the popularity of mobile devices and other wireless connections, has made it possible for organizations to monitor virtually all of your activities. Every time you use a credit card or check to pay for something or scan a store card for discounts, those purchases are recorded. In 2010, Americans used debit and credit cards for $3.7 trillion in purchases. Now there are smartphone apps that let you buy merchandise on your way to a store, such that you just walk in and pick up your purchase and have your bank account automatically debited for the purchase price. This is a big move toward paperless transactions ("Money? There's an App for That," 2011). Unlike cash, purchases made with cards and phones leave electronic evidence that can be collated with other databases so that a full picture of all your purchases is assembled and sold to marketers who want to know your buying habits.

Many companies provide services in which they monitor where you are every minute of every day. If you have a mobile device, it is likely to have a GPS tracker that tells your service provider where you are at all times. Phone companies like Verizon and AT&T already have these data about where you travel each day and all the calls you make and to whom. They sell these data to city planners, commercial interests, and others. Other companies (such as Facebook, Twitter, and Google+) all have "check in" features that broadcast your location to people in your network. Facebook created Facebook Offers, where companies track users they think are potential customers and send them coupons and announcements for special deals on their products. Facebook users can then click on the offers, which lets people in their network know what products they are buying (Tucker, 2014). Marketers love this because they know consumers exert a strong influence on one another.

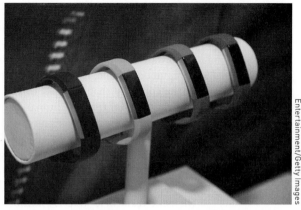

Devices like the Fitbit claim to provide health benefits by tracking and monitoring your daily activity.

There are also companies that sell tracking devices so you can monitor the activities of people around you. For example, Navizon sells a device that can be plugged into a wall outlet and monitors every phone using Wi-Fi within a given area (Tucker, 2014, p. 17). Also, apps like Sonar could identify the VIPs in the room; Banjo will tell you the names of nearby Twitter, Facebook, and Instagram users.

Companies also sell us devices to help us monitor our own activities but then collect those data and sell them to marketers. For example, Apple, Nike, and FitBit sell smartwatches that track users' movements, sleep, and heart rate, among other things. Jawbone previously sold a device that that recorded users' sleeping (130 million hours), walking (more than 1.6 trillion steps), and eating (180 million items of food) patterns and sold this information to marketers (Walsh, 2014).

Companies continue to develop new technologies to gather even more information on consumers. Many manufacturers are now embedding sensors into their products to allow them to monitor the use of their products. With cars, insurance companies can now monitor the driving styles of their customers and offer them rates based on their competence (or recklessness) rather than their age and sex ("Building With Big Data," 2011). Google has taken street-level photographs of every house and business in every neighborhood on Earth, and satellites take pictures of your house in enough detail to show what is in your backyard. Cameras are everywhere to record your movements in public when you drive, when you are in stores or public buildings, or even when you are walking down the street.

While many of these technological innovations offer considerable benefits to us, they also seriously invade our privacy. Many of these invasions occur without our knowledge. For example, in November 2011, news broke that a company called Carrier IQ had installed software on 150 million phones. The software accesses users' texts, all histories, web usage, and location histories without users' knowing consent. In February 2012, it was revealed that the apps people had downloaded from Facebook, Yelp, Foursquare, Instagram, and others were uploading contact information from iPhones and iPads (Calabresi, 2012).

Beware when a company offers you a "free" app. Once you install that app on your computer or phone, it begins collecting all kinds of information about you then sends it to the company that "gave" it to you. Businesses regard the digital mobile network as a global system for tracking human beings and collecting information about them. So does the law enforcement community, which also has easy access to your phone conversations if you use mobile devices. While landline phone information is protected as being private and law enforcement agencies need a warrant to tap into your landline phone calls, this is not the case with cell phones. A 1986 law has a loophole that allows warrantless searches of stored communications. In 2011, there were 3,000 legal wire taps of landline phones; the same year, there were 1.3 million taps on cell phone tracking data from federal, state, and local law enforcement. The U.S. Marshals Service reports that the average time it takes to find a fugitive has dropped from 42 days to 2 days (Calabresi, 2012).

With the Internet and cell phones, employers are now more easily able to monitor the activities of their employees. For example, Dow Chemical Company monitors its employees and fired 50 employees after a search of their e-mail revealed pornography or violent images. A survey found that more than 75% of employers say they monitor how their employees use their work computers (checking websites and using e-mail) and also monitor their office phone calls (Levy, 2006).

The extent of monitoring individuals' activities has gotten so large that it has triggered the attention of the FTC, which has started pressuring the tech industry to do more to protect consumer privacy. Concerns over consumer privacy are even greater since the growth in the "Internet of Things," which refers to products (like home appliances, cars, etc.) that now come with sensors that report consumer usage back to the manufacturers (Bailey, 2015).

Not only do commercial businesses collect massive amounts of information on all of us, so too do law enforcement agencies. These agencies claim that they are only monitoring criminal activity when they use their cameras and devices to surveil e-mails and cell phone activity. However, because they do not know ahead of time which crimes will be committed, when, and by whom, they end up monitoring everyone all the time. And when their own monitoring devices don't provide them with enough information, they pressure commercial companies to provide them with the additional data. For example, in 2013, AT&T received 300,000 requests from law enforcement agencies for information relating to both criminal and civil cases. While most of these (248,000) followed the law by including subpoenas, many did not. In 2009, Sprint disclosed that it has even created a law enforcement portal that gives police the ability to ping without a warrant any one of Sprint's mobile phones in order to geo-locate users in real time—a feature that was used more than 8 million times in that 1 year (Goodman, 2015).

Few people realize how much governmental agencies have been invading our privacy by continually monitoring our activities in all kinds of ways. This is why the WikiLeaks story was so shocking to the public. In March 2017, WikiLeaks published nearly 9,000 pages of documents detailing CIA hacking tools that they have been using as cyberweapons that allow them to invade privacy such as hacking into smartphones, smart TVs, Wi-Fi routers, and computers—anything that is connected to the Internet. Using a program they call "Weeping Angel," the CIA had been secretly recording conversations through the microphones built into these devices. The CIA was also found to be accessing private information on supposedly secure apps before those apps could encrypt the data ("Surveillance," 2017).

A lot of your information that you might think is private is easily accessible by anyone and much of it is free (e.g., check out 123people.com, PeekYou.com, and Snitch.name). Anyone can get access to satellite pictures of any neighborhood at Zillow.com. You can even find out who owns each property, when they bought it, and how much they paid for it on BlockShopper.com (Sarno, 2009b).

Most of the information that is collected about you is assembled into databases by companies who sell it rather than give it away. Some companies that collect information from their customers promise not to sell it but then are later forced to do so. For example, in 2000, Toysmart.com filed for bankruptcy, and the FTC forced the company to sell off customer data to the highest bidder. The firm had promised site users that it would not divulge information gleaned from tracking users' activities on the site, but a court-appointed overseer believed the customer list was a valuable asset that could be sold to help pay off the firm's creditors. In this case, the court ruled that it was more important for a bankrupt company to partially pay back some of its creditors than it was to protect the privacy of its customers.

Controlling

The reason marketers, government agencies, and other organizations collect and buy so much information about us is so they can exercise control over what we think and how we act. And they know that the better that information is (our deepest values, fears, and motivations), the more power they can exercise in the shaping of our attitudes and behaviors. For example, when we shop at a virtual store, we think we are browsing through all their products. In reality, those sites are controlling our shopping by using the information they have about us to guide us to certain products and away from others. These sites claim that this guidance is a benefit to us—that is, it makes for a more efficient shopping experience when we are shown only products that are likely to interest us. But much of this guidance is influenced by advertisers who pay the sites to direct our attention to their products.

The most sophisticated "guidance" algorithms have been developed by Google. When we do a search on Google, we think we are being shown the most relevant information on the topic expressed in our keywords but in reality we are being directed to a small list of sites that have largely been determined by paid placement. **Paid placement** is a method developed by Google as part of its search algorithm where companies can improve their placement when Google presents the results of a search. The more a company pays to Google, the more likely that company will appear at the top of the search list of results.

Our Internet searches are also controlled by our past history, which presents another problem. When our present and future searches for information and products are controlled by our history, then we continue to be exposed to the same things, and this tends to narrow our Internet experiences over time. For example, retailers like Amazon collect information about all your purchases as well as previous shopping activity on its site and they use that information to guide your current shopping activity. These retailers tell you that they are doing this for your benefit so that your shopping experience can be more efficient as they guide you to those products that they believe are likely to interest you most based on your browsing history. However, this serves to limit your choices.

It's not just retailers who exercise considerable control over you; search engines do the same thing. For example, Google, in addition to using keywords and advertiser placement in their search algorithms, also uses a person's search history. In his fascinating book *The Filter Bubble: What the Internet Is Hiding From You*, Eli Pariser (2011) says that if you do a Google search and ask your friend to do a Google search for the same term at the same time, the results of the two searches will be different because Google adjusts its search algorithm across individuals based on the individual's "personal interests" as determined by their browsing and purchasing histories. Google claims this is an innovation designed to tailor searches to individuals and thus make searches more useful to each user. However, Pariser points out that the effect of this tailoring of searches tends to narrow our exposure to a range of information rather than opening us up to find genuinely new information on the Internet.

Spamming

The using of the media to invade your privacy with unsolicited and unwanted messages that are designed to get you to buy a product or service is called **spamming**. It is especially focused on e-mail accounts but also applies to text messages sent to your phone and all kinds of attention-getting devices (pop-ups, banners, etc.) that clutter webpages as we surf the Internet.

Spamming can be considered an invasion of our privacy because we have not given spammers our e-mail addresses or invited them to correspond with us. So when we get an unwanted message from a spammer, we feel somewhat violated as we wonder how they got our e-mail address and why they think we would possibly be interested in any of the products they want us to buy. And spam can be regarded as a major irritant if it dominates our e-mails or slows down our e-mail servers.

Each year the amount of spam increases. In 2004, it was estimated that 15 billion pieces of spam were sent every day, and this number accounted for over 60% of all e-mail messages ("Can Spam," 2004). By 2011, Pingdom estimated that 300 billion e-mails were being sent each day and that 89.1% of them were spam. Fortunately for us, most e-mail providers have good spam filters that are continually updated, so most of this spam is filtered out and we do not have to see it. That means the average e-mail account receives about 100 spam messages every day. However, the danger with spam filters is that someone else is deciding what is spam; therefore, you may end up filtering out some messages that you might want to read.

Spammers operate on a hit rate of 25 sales per 1 million e-mails. Therefore they are motivated to increase the number of messages they send. When spammers send out 30 million e-mails a day, they are achieving an exposure rate about equal to major advertisers who spend several million dollars a week to use the traditional media to expose their targeted consumers to their ad messages.

The key to becoming a successful marketer through spamming is to have access to millions of valid e-mail addresses. Where do spammers get such access? One way is to buy lists; spammers can buy 100 million e-mail addresses for as little as $2,000. A second way is to hack into a large company's database and steal the addresses. Or they might hack into a company's private e-mail directory and steal those e-mail addresses. Sometimes they rely on both methods. For example, in the summer of 2004, AOL, after fighting a daily battle with spammers who were clogging their service with unwanted e-mails, found out that one of its employees had sold AOL's list of 92 million e-mail addresses to a spammer for $100,000. The spammer used the addresses to promote his online gambling business, then sold those addresses to other spammers for tens of thousands of dollars himself (Gaither, 2004b).

ISPs are especially wary of spammers because a sudden surge of hundreds of thousands of messages can slow their systems down, and a flood of a million messages can crash their systems. Slow service and crashed systems anger customers, and customers of an ISP that has frequent slowdowns and crashes will switch to another ISP that is faster and more reliable. Therefore, ISPs have been forced to hire large staffs of technical people to identify spammers and write programs quickly to filter out as much spam as possible.

Spammers fight back. For example, in the spring of 2013, Spamhaus, an anti-spam watchdog group, was almost destroyed by a massive **denial-of-service attack** where spammers jammed Spamhaus with so much information it shut the service down (Satter, 2013). Another example of spammer retaliation was a 2003 attack on Monkeys.com, which was publishing blacklists of spammers. After a year and a half, spammers had had enough of Monkeys.com and they continually inundated the website with a mass spam e-mail assault for 10 days until the website had to close down. The owner of Monkeys .com said, "I underestimated both the enemy's level of sophistication, and also the enemy's level of brute malevolence" (Gaither, 2004a, p. C1).

One example of a huge spammer group calls itself the Alabama Spammers. This group dialed into EarthLink's high-powered servers and established several dozen connections simultaneously. EarthLink's spam abuse team spotted the attack within minutes, but it usually takes an hour to identify the accounts and manually terminate all the connections; meanwhile, the Alabama Spammers were able to send out thousands of messages. EarthLink filed civil lawsuits against 100 companies, accusing them of hijacking EarthLink customer accounts to send spam under the RICO Act (Racketeer Influenced and Corrupt Organizations Act), which has been used to attack Mafia operations (Gaither, 2004a). The suit contended that in 2003, spam cost U.S. businesses $10 billion. One of the companies named in the suit is OptInRealBig.com (now Media Breakaway) and its owner, Scott Richter. This company uses contests and promotions to gather information on Internet users, then sells those addresses to other spammers. Richter's past promotions include selling a diet pill named Inferno, a copy of Jennifer Lopez's engagement ring, Iraq's most-wanted playing cards, and an herbal supplement for "penile fitness." He sends out several hundred million e-mails each day, making his company one of the largest spammers. Richter does not like the term *spammer* and says, "We're a powerhouse in the e-mail marketing world. I stand up for what I do" (Jerome & Bane, 2004, pp. 125–126).

Spammers are not limited to e-mail; they have invaded Amazon with a proliferation of messages in the form of e-books. Users of Amazon's Kindle get on Amazon to buy e-books and download them to their Kindle. But the offerings for books are being clogged with spam in the form of Private Label Rights (PLR) content, which typically sells for about 99 cents each. Why are these PLR e-books regarded as spam? The answer is that most of these books are written by people who simply take an already published book that is selling well and make a few minor changes to target it better to a different demographic, and they do this multiple times in order to achieve a high volume of sales. Aspiring spammers can even buy a DVD called *Autopilot Kindle Cash*, which promises to teach them how to publish 10 to 20 new Kindle books a day without writing a word. These books are then listed on Amazon along with more legitimate books and the list of offerings gets enormously clogged with these bogus e-books. How bad is the problem? In 2002, there were 215,000 traditional books published in the United States; people could buy a paper copy from a traditional publisher or bookstore. In the same year, there were 33,000 non-traditional books published (these are typically self-published by individual authors without the use of a book publisher). So, the number of non-traditional books published in 2002 was only 15% of the number of traditional books published in that 1 year. By 2010, the number of traditional books had grown to 316,000, while the number of non-traditional books grew to 2.8 million or 886% the size of traditional book publishing ("Spam Clogging Amazon's Kindle," 2011).

Another form of spamming is with the use of **adware**, which is advertising-supported software. When you access some commercial sites, the site will send a small program to your computer. This adware is embedded in your hard drive where it automatically downloads advertisements to your computer and continually displays those ads as pop-ups, banners, in-text links, autoplay video commercials, and other commercial content on the browsers. Additionally, this ad-supported application can initiate redirects to various websites and collect browsing-related information without users' permission.

The war between spammers and Internet companies has continued to escalate. The Internet companies have technicians set up spam traps—called honey pots—to collect spam e-mail and analyze it to figure out what spammers are doing; then they devise anti-spam software to screen it out. In response, spammers buy the anti-spam software to figure out how to get around it. Each week, the sophistication of each side increases as they learn about the creative techniques developed by the other side.

PUBLIC OPINION AND REGULATIONS

Public opinion is strongly in favor of personal privacy. However, it is difficult for regulators to establish laws that draw a clear line distinguishing what is private and what is public. Although there are a few laws in existence, it is exceedingly difficult to prosecute and punish offenders.

Public Opinion

Privacy has become a much more important issue to the American public in the past few decades. A Lou Harris poll found that the percentage of Americans concerned about their privacy rights grew from 34% in 1970 to 90% in 1998 (Identify Theft Resource Center, 2002). Public opinion polls over the last 2 decades have consistently shown that the public exhibits a growing concern about how companies and the government are chipping away at their privacy, especially with the use of the Internet. Nine out of 10 people do not like the idea of opting out, which places the burden on people to know when their privacy is being invaded and take action to find a way to prevent these intrusions; instead, the public prefers the default to be opt in, which requires companies to ask for express permission to gather data on individuals and to sell that data (Electronic Privacy Information Center, 2013). Furthermore, in public opinion polls, over half and sometimes as high as two thirds of the population believes that the tracking of their web activities should be illegal and there should be federal legislation to outlaw it. People feel that the current self-regulatory environment is insufficient to protect their privacy. A 2014 survey found that 91% of Americans "agree" or "strongly agree" that people have lost control over how personal information is collected and used by all kinds of entities. Some 80% of social media users said they were concerned about advertisers and businesses accessing the data they share on social media platforms, and 64% said the government should do more to regulate advertisers. A 2017 survey found that less than 10% of respondents believed that the social media platforms they used were protecting their information. And while 74% said that it is very important to them to control who gets to use private information about them, only 9% said they feel they had enough control over their data use. This explains why two thirds of Americans believe that current laws are not good enough to protect their privacy, and 64% think that there should be more regulations of advertisers (Rainie, 2018).

There is evidence that people are growing more aware of the threats to their privacy and doing something about it. A survey by the Pew Research Center found that 54% of mobile users decided not to install an app after learning about the amount of information it would collect, and 30% of mobile users uninstalled an app after discovering that it was collecting personal information that they did not want to share. Also, younger cellphone users were twice as likely as older users to report that a company or a person had accessed their phone in a way that felt like privacy invasion (Electronic Privacy Information Center, 2012).

Regulations

While these threats to privacy continue to grow and become more serious, regulators and law enforcement agencies have been very slow to respond adequately. One problem that explains this slow response is limited jurisdictions. All law enforcement agencies have a constrained geographical location in which to operate, but Internet activities take place in cyberspace. For example, the United States might pass a federal law making spam illegal, but spammers who live outside the geographical boundaries of the United States can still send millions of messages to people whose computers are located within the United States. Therefore, it is not clear whether these spammers have broken a law and, if so, who is in charge of enforcement and what rights the enforcers have to go into other countries to bring the spammers to justice in the United States.

There are areas where governments have begun to address some of these threats with additional laws. For example, the FTC instituted some regulations that it called the CAN-SPAM Act (Controlling the Assault of Non-Solicited Pornography and Marketing Act) in 2003, then tightened its regulations in 2008. This act essentially requires senders of e-mail messages to more clearly identify themselves and to allow receivers of the messages to opt out of receiving any future messages from the senders. In the fall of 2004, California passed a law against spyware—the placing of software on a personal computer to collect information about the computer's owner (Lawrence, 2004). Other states are following suit. However, at this point, the problem of increasing threats to individuals' privacy is growing faster than is government regulation to protect individuals.

The federal government has been slow to pass new regulations and laws to control these threats, because the agencies that are charged with enforcing the existing regulations and laws are having so much trouble with this enforcement. It is expensive to track down violators, and when those lawbreakers are identified, they simply move out of the country and thus avoid punishment. For example, the first financial penalties to a spammer were handed down in California in October 2003, when PW Marketing and its owners, Paul Willis and Claudia Griffin, were fined $2 million for sending unsolicited or misleading e-mails. The spammers fled the country to avoid the judgment (Healey, 2003). On January 1, 2004, a new law took effect outlawing many of the tricks spammers use. In response, many spammers simply moved their operations outside the United States so they could continue with their same business practices and avoid prosecution. The virtual geography of the Internet does not lend itself to the traditional ways of thinking about laws and enforcement.

Industry groups are working hard right now to protect their business practices that give them access to all kinds of information about you. If they get their way, they will continue to have the right to plant cookies on your hard drive; monitor your shopping and all other activities; gather unlimited amounts of information about you; send advertising to you through all kinds of media, especially computers and mobile devices; and sell information they collect about you to other advertisers. When these businesses offer you options to restrict their use of your information, they place the burden on you to tell them no (opt out), rather than accept the burden themselves to ask for your consent (opt in).

Over the past few decades, the U.S. Congress has held hearings about Internet privacy and various legislators have introduced bills but no significant legislation has passed. However, the European Union instituted a set of major regulations called the General Data Protection Regulation (GDPR) in the spring of 2018 (https://gdpr-info.eu/). The GDPR was immediately called the world's toughest rule to protect people's online data because it not only gives people much more control over their personal information, but it also restricts how businesses obtain and handle the information. As for empowering people, the GDPR gives people the right to request their online data, ask for deletions from those databases, and ask that the trail of information left when browsing social media be reduced. Businesses must also more clearly detail how someone's personal information is being handled, and the GDPR has created more limitations on how advertisers are allowed to use personal information. Companies face fines if they do not comply, with tech giants risking penalties greater than $1 billion. Privacy groups preparing class action–style complaints under the new law may put even more legal pressure on companies.

The European Union says its 28 member countries are also setting the bar for stricter enforcement of anti-trust laws against tech behemoths and are paving the way for tougher tax policies on companies. The new privacy rules are part of a "strong European tradition" of policing industries to protect the environment and public health, even if it does "constrain business," said Margrethe Vestager, Europe's top anti-trust official (Satariano, 2018).

The GDPR has forced major tech companies all over the world to revise their policies to comply so they can continue to do business in Europe. This breakthrough set of regulations has stimulated Brazil, Japan, and South Korea to follow Europe's lead, with some having already passed similar data protection laws. European officials are encouraging copycats by tying data protection to some trade deals and arguing that a unified global approach is the only way to crimp Silicon Valley's previously unchecked power (Satariano, 2018).

Europe's proactive stance is a sharp divergence from that of the United States, which has taken little action over the years in regulating the tech industry. Most recently, the Trump administration has sought to cut taxes and roll back regulation. However, many American tech companies do a significant amount of business in Europe, so they know they need to respond to these new regulations. To meet the GDPR's requirements, Facebook and Google have deployed large teams to overhaul how they give users access to their own privacy settings and to redesign certain products that may have sucked up too much user data. Facebook said it had roughly 1,000 people working on the initiative globally, including engineers, product managers, and lawyers. Also, the Silicon Valley companies are quickly adding lobbyists to influence other European regulations before they spread. Google and Microsoft are already among the five biggest spenders on lobbying in the European Union, with budgets of about 4.5 million euros (or $5.3 million) each (Satariano, 2018).

YOUR OWN INFORMED OPINION

Living in this information-rich world has many advantages. These extensive information resources help businesses to monitor our developing needs as well as to construct the products and experiences that can satisfy those needs. These databases help organizations spot problems early (about health, crime, transportation, weather, resource shortages, etc.) and help them monitor their strategies designed to reduce problems. The rapid sharing of information among these databases makes it highly efficient to complete purchases, to get medical diagnoses, to travel, to connect with friends, and to find the experiences and information we want when we want them.

However, there are also many disadvantages of living in this information-rich world—the most serious of which is the virtual elimination of personal privacy. Once we complete a transaction of any kind that has an electronic component, we forever lose control over the information that is created by that transaction. That information is duplicated many times as it is added to countless databases that are continually expanding your electronic profile. The information you think is being "protected" behind firewalls is frequently accessed illegally by hackers and even legally by marketers as well as people working in a variety of governmental agencies.

With this issue of privacy, the essential first step is that you become informed about the risks to your privacy. If you remain ignorant about these risks, you will continue to lose much of your privacy and possibly even your identity. Then once you know about the risks to your privacy, you need to do something to protect yourself, at least from the most serious threats. In this section, I will help you by providing a series of three suggestions. First, you need to make an information assessment. Second you need to make a threat assessment. And third, you need to create a privacy strategy.

Information Assessment

An information assessment begins with you identifying what information is currently available on you. Then you need to organize that information by levels of privacy you want to maintain.

Take an Inventory About What Information Is Publically Available About You

Search websites where you have accounts or that you frequently visit (see Applying Media Literacy Skills Issue 6.1). Focus on sites in the following areas: finances, shopping, health care, education, government, and social.

Go to one of the following websites: PeekYou.com, www.intelius.com, and Snitch .name. Type in your name and see what information others can easily get about you.

Map Your Information by Privacy Levels

To keep this task relatively simple, think of just three levels—purely personal, limited sharing, and public. Research has shown that we vary what we disclose to friends, family, acquaintances, and so on (Vitak, 2012).

Stay vigilant to protect your privacy.

Now create a map by drawing three concentric circles. The resulting picture will have a small circle in the middle that is surrounded by an intermediate band (like a donut) and an outer band (like a big donut). Inside the smallest circle in the middle, write down those deep, dark secrets that you absolutely want to keep private. This is your central deep vault of secrets.

Next, divide the intermediate band into neighborhoods, with one neighborhood for each type of person in your life. For example, you may have a neighborhood for close friends, work colleagues, parents, siblings, medical professionals, counselors, and so on. For each neighborhood, think about what kinds of information you would be willing to share with the people in that neighborhood.

Finally, label the outer band "the public." Write things in this public band that you want everyone to know about you.

After you have finished your desired privacy map, start checking it against reality. Look at your postings on SNSs, the words and pictures you post, your contributions to blogs, and your e-mail history. Are you consistently sharing the right information with the right people? If not, what changes do you need to make to protect your privacy configurations?

If you have been careful about sharing the right kinds of information with each kind of person, ask yourself how much you trust those people to avoid passing along information you wanted them to have with other people whom you did not want to have that information about you.

The purpose of this step is to stimulate you to think about what privacy means to you. Is your conception of privacy too complicated? Is it realistic? How much can you trust the people around you to understand and respect your expectations for privacy?

Threat Assessment

The next step is to examine how much you can trust your Internet services to respect your privacy (see Applying Media Literacy Skills Issue 6.2). Start with the sites you visit most and look carefully at their privacy statements. All sites are required to provide you with such a statement, especially those that require you to sign an agreement to be granted access to them. Can you understand what those privacy statements are saying or are they written in a way to confuse you?

What is the privacy default on those sites? Is the default an opt-out policy rather than an **opt-in policy**? With opt in, the default is privacy, and consumers have to do something to grant advertisers permission to send them a message or to record information in a cookie; that is, advertisers cannot send e-mail to consumers or record information in cookies on consumers' computers unless they first ask those consumers and are explicitly granted permission. In contrast, with an opt-out policy, the default is that businesses have the right to send any information and to create cookies until consumers tell them to stop.

Businesses overwhelmingly prefer the opt-out option because they can do whatever they want until a person tells them to stop, and few people tell businesses to stop because most people are not aware of how those businesses are invading their privacy. When this is explained to people, 86% of Internet users say they prefer opt-in privacy policies.

Most regulations, however, are being crafted to favor businesses. For example, the policy negotiated by the Clinton administration, the FTC, and a consortium of web advertisers gave websites the right to track Internet users unless the users take steps to opt out of being monitored. These privacy standards were regarded as being so favorable for online advertisers that shares in DoubleClick rose 13% in 1 day (Pew Internet & American Life Project, 2000).

To protect their privacy, a relatively small number of savvy users are devising their own opt-in policies and deciding that some websites are not worthy of getting their personal information. Also, 24% of Internet users said that they have provided a fake name or personal information to avoid giving a website real information, 9% of Internet users have used encryption to scramble their e-mail, and 5% of Internet users have used "anonymizing" software that hides their computer identity from websites they visit. But most people do not know how to protect themselves, and 56% of Internet users did not know what cookies were, much less know how to avoid them. Only 10% of Internet users have set their browsers to reject cookies (Pew Internet & American Life Project, 2000).

Think about what you do to create threats. Think about what you post on websites that can be accessed by people you do not know. Things you post today can be copied to other sites, where they can be copied to still other sites, and so on; even if you erase an image you posted, that image may be out there on the web in hundreds of different places. Even more dangerous, those images (as well as your words, your voice, etc.) can be distorted from the original message you posted so that what is widely disseminated is a distortion that could embarrass you.

Now broaden your scope. Think about all the threats—legal as well as illegal—that I outlined previously in this chapter. Then think about the threats to the neighborhoods on your privacy map.

Privacy Strategy

We cannot depend on other people to have our best interests at heart and protect us. Furthermore, it is unlikely that regulators will ever catch up with the technology that keeps developing new ways to invade our privacy. The responsibility rests with each of us to protect our own privacy. If we do not do the work to protect ourselves, we will likely have very little privacy left.

Start with the threats you have identified up to this point (see Applying Media Literacy Skills Issue 6.3). Now make a list of the things you can do to reduce—and even eliminate, if possible—those threats.

Remove Private Information

When you find something you don't like shared, contact the website to ask to have it changed or taken down. Find the phone number or an e-mail address of the person who has the authority to take down the information. Most websites have a "Contact Us" link. If you don't know who runs the site, go to Google and type "whois www.name-of-site .com" (include the quotes). If it is the site's policy not to remove content, ask whether your name can be removed from the post or whether content can be blocked from appearing in search engines.

Even if you are able to remove information about yourself on all the websites you have identified, there is still likely to be information about you in existing databases and that information will be sold to other companies that will use it in the future. To eliminate this type of threat, go to primary data brokers (such as Intelius) and search for yourself on these sites and ask to be removed. Primary data brokers collect information from public records. Also, go to secondary data brokers (like Spokeo) and search for yourself on these sites and ask to be removed. Secondary data brokers aggregate information from primary brokers and add data collected from social networks and other online sources. Also, go to a site like Abine, which is a privacy company that maintains a list of 25 major data vendors and provides instructions about how to opt out of each of them.

Be vigilant. Search for yourself on people-finder sites every few months to make sure data collectors have not added you back again. For more instructions, go to a site like Account Killer, which shows you how to delete your profiles on the big networks.

When you join a new site like Gmail, provide as little personal information as possible. When an account will not let you leave fields blank, fill in the fields with fake information. If you must provide an e-mail address, create a new e-mail account in order to complete the registration and then when you get the e-mail confirmation, cancel the e-mail account. Check your account settings and make sure your profile is private and can't be found in search engines. You might want to use a pseudonym but remember that there are companies like PeekYou that collect information about all of your pseudonyms, so this technique may not work.

Correct Inaccuracies

There are places where you want there to be information available about you—accurate information. When you find inaccurate information, contact the website to get those inaccuracies corrected.

Remember that what you have posted yourself is your responsibility. For example, if you posted a compromising picture of yourself in full party mode on your Facebook page last year and now you think it is "inaccurate" because that is really not you now, you can remove those images but Facebook will retain a copy and there may also be many other copies that visitors to your site have made over the last year.

Continually Monitor Threats

Be skeptical about requests for information about you. Do you know who is asking for this information? If so, do you trust that person or organization? On social networks, be very careful about accepting requests from strangers. Those requests may come from advertisers, spammers, or even predators. Never give out information you want kept private unless you know who is asking for it and what their privacy policy is.

It is especially important to monitor your financial transactions to make sure the purchases that are charged to you are purchases you have made. Keep up to date on looking at all charges on all your credit and debit cards and deductions to your checking account. Also, monitor your credit history to see if unauthorized individuals or companies are accessing your information. Now all 50 states give residents three free credit checks each year from the three major credit reporting bureaus. Go to AnnualCreditReport.com to check on your credit. See who has been accessing your credit information. Do you recognize those people and businesses, such as your bank, places where you have applied for employment, and the like? If not, then there may be attempts to steal your identity.

Download Software to Protect Your Computer From Threats to Your Privacy

While major ISPs, such as Google's Gmail, Microsoft's Hotmail, and your own university that provides you with an e-mail account, have large staffs who work every day to identify threats and filter them out, it is still a good idea to download software to protect your own computer. There are several companies (such as Norton and McAffee) that sell software that you download onto your computer's hard drive and creates a firewall to screen out all kinds of threats, especially spam, spyware, and adware. Or you could go online and find software that you can download for free. This is called freeware and there are many services available for download, but these are usually targeted to one threat such as spyware only or adware only. If you decide to try freeware, make sure you go to a reputable site that includes product reviews, so that you know you are downloading something that will help you. If you do not check out the software first, you may end up downloading a program that appears to offer protection but is really an adware or spyware program rather than a program that protects you.

Set Up Your Internet Browsers to Disallow Cookies as the Default

Allow cookies only from sites you trust, such as your online bank, which will require cookies for you to log onto your account and access your money.

Cookies themselves are not inherently bad or necessarily invasive to one's privacy. But they open the door for widespread abuse. In the most comprehensive and extreme cases, a web company could build a profile of an Internet user that combines information about her purchases, her taste in music, the investment information she seeks, the health issues that concern her most, and the kind of news stories that seize her interest. When you allow cookies to exist in your hard drive, a hacker could get into your computer and by reading the information in your cookies infer a great deal about your interests, finances, health, personality, and lifestyle.

In conclusion, following the guidelines I have provided will require a good deal of work. Think of it as making an investment in your peace of mind. The investment is relatively small compared to the effort you will need to expend dealing with the negative consequences later.

Further Reading

Calvert, C. (2004). *Voyeur nation: Media, privacy, and peering in modern culture*. New York, NY: Basic Books. (274 pages)

This book clearly shows how our culture has become obsessed with voyeurism, which has been made possible by technological advances in surveillance along with a governmental Big Brother mentality. However, the legal system has not kept pace with this phenomenon, so our privacy is being severely limited. The author is a professor at Pennsylvania State University and an expert in media law, privacy, and their interrelation.

Goodman, M. (2015). *Future crimes: Everything is connected, everyone is vulnerable, and what we can do about it*. New York, NY: Doubleday. (392 pages plus endnotes and index)

Written by an expert in law enforcement, this book presents a lot of startling facts about how privacy in America has largely dwindled to almost nothing because of the availability of technologies that we have come to depend on and take for granted. After presenting an overwhelming case for how our privacy is being invaded in 16 chapters, the author presents a short four-page appendix of a few suggestions about what we can do to protect what little privacy we have left.

Jones, M. L. (2016). *Ctrl+Z: The right to be forgotten*. New York: New York University Press. (267 pages, including endnotes, bibliography and index)

Written by an academic, this book is an examination of the legal issues in the United States and other countries concerning the public's right to privacy. It focuses on the European idea of people's right to be forgotten and shows how this idea is needed to be enacted in legislation in countries around the world to give people more options about how they can protect themselves from invasion from digital media.

MacKinnon, R. (2012). *Consent of the networked: The worldwide struggle for Internet freedom*. New York, NY: Basic Books. (294 pages, including endnotes and index)

While this book is primarily focused on showing how countries around the world, including the United States, use laws and policing to prevent people from openly sharing information, it also tells many stories about how those governments as well as businesses use the Internet to invade people's privacy without their knowledge or consent. In her last chapter, MacKinnon presents a detailed plan for how people need to stop taking their rights for granted and instead work to build what she calls a "netizen-centric" Internet.

O'Neil, C. (2016). *Weapons of math destruction*. New York, NY: Crown. (259 pages, including endnotes and index)

The author is a mathematician who has worked at hedge funds and start-up companies developing predictive models using data mined from the Internet. In this book, she argues convincingly that these models are harming all kinds of people and institutions because of the way they value certain things and ignore other factors. She presents many examples from education, business, voting, and health care to illustrate that when big corporations use big data to drive greater profits, many individuals are discriminated against without their knowledge or consent. Also these models tend to limit opportunities for certain kinds of people and lead them down a path toward greater risks to their health, financial well-being, and success in work.

Pariser, E. (2011). *The filter bubble: What the Internet is hiding from you.* New York, NY: Penguin Press. (294 pages)

The author is an Internet activist who criticizes how certain web services (particularly Google, Netflix, Amazon, Facebook, and Pandora) are recording your browsing information and using it for commercial marketing purposes.

Solove, D. J., Rotenberg, M., & Schwartz, P. M. (2010). *Privacy, information and technology* (2nd ed.). New York, NY: Aspen Publishers. (320 pages with index)

Written by three law school professors, this book takes a strong legalistic approach to the problem of protecting people's privacy when they access media messages.

Tucker, P. (2014). *The naked future: What happens in a world that anticipates your every move?* New York, NY: Current. (268 pages, including endnotes and index)

The thesis of this book is that big data—companies collecting information about everything you do—will lead to a better future for everyone despite the almost total elimination of personal privacy. The author argues that the use of big data will improve research on health, crime prevention, education, and personal relationships.

Keeping Up to Date

Electronic Frontier Foundation (https://www.eff.org/)

> This is a non-profit organization that bills itself as the "first line of defense" when the public's freedoms in the networked world come under attack. Founded in 1990, it champions the public interest by defending free speech, privacy, and consumer rights. Get on the official website and click on the "Privacy" tab to get updated information on litigation and news stories, resources, and research papers.

Electronic Privacy Information Center (http://epic.org/)

> Established in 1994 in Washington, D.C., EPIC is a public interest research center with the mission of focusing public attention on emerging civil liberties issues and protecting privacy, the First Amendment, and constitutional values.

National Cybersecurity Center (http://cybercenter.org)

> Created by the U. S. Department of Homeland Security in 2008, the NCC monitors and shares information about cyber security among the federal government's communication networks, particularly the National Security Administration, the Federal Bureau of Investigation, and the Department of Defense.

APPLYING MEDIA LITERACY SKILLS ISSUE 6.1
INFORMATION ASSESSMENT

1. Analysis: Search websites to inventory the information that is available about you.

   a. Financial

   What information do financial institutions (banks, credit unions, investment companies) provide about you on their websites?

   b. Shopping

   Do you have store cards that enable you to get discounts at checkout?

   Have you set up accounts on merchants' websites (Amazon, Macy's, etc.)?

   c. Health care

   What information does your health insurance carrier provide?

   Do you have a website account with your physician, clinic, hospital, and so on?

   Do you have a website account with a veterinarian for your pet?

   d. Educational institutions

   What records do your high school and college make available online?

   Do you have a student loan account?

   e. Government

   What information do local, state, and federal governments provide?

   - Agencies that levy and collect taxes (Internal Revenue Service, Social Security Administration, etc.)

   - Licensing agencies (driver's license, car registration, certifications, etc.)
   - Property registrations (ownership of buildings and land, liens, zoning variations, etc.)
   - Policing agencies (arrest records, criminal registries, etc.)
   - Voting lists

   f. Social

   What information about yourself have you shared on e-mail?

   What information about yourself have you posted on SNSs?

   Are you a member of social organizations that require membership and have a website? If so, what information have those organizations gathered about you?

   Do you have a personal blog or website?

2. Grouping: Once you have listed the information available about you, organize it into groups to create your desired privacy map.

   a. Purely personal: What information do want to keep most private? This is the information you don't want to share with anyone unless it's your best best friend.

   b. Limited sharing: This is information you are willing to share on a limited basis.

   c. Public information: This is information that you are willing to share with everyone.

APPLYING MEDIA LITERACY SKILLS ISSUE 6.2
THREAT ASSESSMENT

1. Evaluation: Use your desired privacy map as your standards and compare the information available on you to those standards.

Some of that information may meet a standard.

- ○ Some information you think should be public is now available to everyone.
- ○ Some information that you feel should be available to only one type of individual or company is on a website that requires a password and can only be accessed by people whom you think are okay.

Some of that information may fall short of your standard.

- ○ You have put information on a public website that you feel should be limited to only certain kinds of individuals.
- ○ A website you trusted to limit the available of information about you has violated that trust.

2. Analysis

Get onto those websites that have information about you that you think is especially important to protect (financial records, health history, etc.).

Find their privacy statements and analyze all that legalese to see if you can understand your rights.

What does the site promise to protect?

With whom will the site share what kinds of information?

What is their justification for this?

How well do you feel your information on each site is protected from access by criminals who may try to steal your personal information, assume your identity, or change some of your information?

APPLYING MEDIA LITERACY SKILLS ISSUE 6.3
DEVELOPING A PRIVACY STRATEGY

Synthesis: Now that you have analyzed your world to identify what information is available about you and have evaluated the appropriate levels of privacy for different kinds of information, you are ready to synthesize all that information in the formulation of a strategy that will help you immediately reduce threats then over the long term continue to keep those threats to a minimum.

You must create your own plan given your particular needs; however, I will guide you in that task by providing five suggestions:

1. Remove private information from places where it is currently available.

2. Correct any inaccuracies in information that you want to continue being made available.

3. Continually monitor threats.

   Monitor updates to companies' privacy policies.

   Check with credit monitoring bureaus to see that your credit score has not changed.

   Check public sites to monitor what information is available on you.

   Google your name.

   Check PeekYou.com, www.intelius.com, and Snitch.name.

(Continued)

(Continued)

4. Download software to protect your computer from threats to your privacy.

Anti-virus software

Anti-spam software

Ad blockers

Spyware checkers

5. Set up your Internet browsers to disallow cookies as the default.

When companies require cookies in order for you to access their services (such as banks), make sure you know and trust the company before allowing cookies.

GLOSSARY

Above-the-line employees: people who are hired for their specific creative talents to make media messages (actors, directors, writers, composers, etc.)

Abstracting: the skill of creating a brief, clear, and accurate description capturing the essence of a message in a smaller number of words (or images, sounds, etc.) than the message itself

Activation: an immediate behavioral effect where a media message triggers behavior suggested (but not actually depicted) in that message

Active mediation: a media literacy technique that parents use with children that focuses on parents talking to their children during media exposures in order to help their children understand media messages better and to help them avoid negative effects

Adaptation stage: the fifth and last phase in the life cycle pattern of the development of a mass medium where the medium redefines itself in the media marketplace and provides different messages or services not provided by the other media

Adware: advertiser-supported software that is a form of spamming; when you access a commercial site, that site sends a program to your computer that automatically plays ads and downloads more ads to your computer

Analog coding: the recording, storage, and retrieval of information that relies on the physical properties of a medium; thus a sound is recorded, stored, and retrieved in a different manner than is a photographic image

Analysis: the skill of breaking down a message into meaningful elements

App: a computer-based application program that can be downloaded off the Internet to a person's computer or mobile device

Asymmetric influences: when one factor influences another but not the other way around

Attention: exposure to a media message that takes place in the attentional state; conscious awareness of the media message

Attentional exposure state: the experience of being aware of a media message and actively processing its information while being exposed to the message

Attitude: an evaluative judgment made by comparing something with a person's standard

Attitudinal-type effect: a type of media-influenced effect that is manifested as the acquisition of a new attitude or the triggering, alteration, or reinforcement of existing attitudes

Attraction: an immediate behavioral effect where a media message attracts our exposure so we access a website, turn on the television, buy a book, and so on

Audience conditioning: a strategy used by media organizations to make their existing audience members want to continually expose themselves to their subsequent messages

Automatic exposure state: the experience of being exposed to a media message without being aware of the message

Automatic routines: sequences of behaviors or thoughts that we learn from experience then apply again and again with little effort; think of these as computer programs that run in the back of our minds without us consciously paying attention to them

Automaticity: an exposure state where we put our minds on "automatic pilot" and filter out almost all message options

Baseline: a way of thinking about a person's typical probability of manifesting an effect

Baseline effect: a form of process effect that alters a person's baseline by moving it up gradually to the manifestation level, moving it down away from the manifestation level, or reinforcing its position thus making it more difficult to move in the future

Behavioral-type effect: a type of media-influenced effect that is manifested as the triggering of actions in a person or over time of altering as well as reinforcing patterns of action

Belief: faith in the existence or truth of something

Belief-type effect: a type of media-influenced effect that is manifested as the acquiring of a belief or the long-term alteration as well as reinforcing of an existing belief

Below-the-line employees: people who work in the media industries and exhibit skills that are not especially unique; that is, the skills required to do their jobs are widespread in the population

Big data: huge databases created and expanded by research firms that continually collect information from everyone whenever they go online, carry a GPS-equipped smartphone, communicate with friends through social media or chat applications, and shop; the key characteristics of these huge databases are that they are high volume, high velocity, and high variety

Blog: short for web log; Internet sites set up by individuals, businesses, and news organizations that are designed to attract the attention of as many visitors as possible with text, audio, and video

Boomerang effect: when researchers find that the interventions they have designed to improve media literacy have had the opposite effect; that is, the interventions actually resulted in decreasing media literacy or in increasing the negative effects they were designed to reduce

Bootlegging: a form of media message piracy that refers to the unauthorized recording of a live delivery of a message then the subsequent distribution of that recording

Bot network activity: a technique used by spammers and hackers to hijack your computer so it can use your IP (Internet Protocol) address and not their own so their activities cannot be traced back to them

Botnet: a network of infected computers (bots) that is remotely controlled by hackers

Brick-and-mortar stores: retail stores that people can physically (compared to virtually) visit in order to browse, touch the products (such as books, recordings, and DVDs), talk to live salespeople, buy the products, and leave the store with the physical product

Buying funnel: a way of thinking about interacting with potential customers who are on the Internet to get them to visit your website then moving them step by step from interest to awareness of your product to a positive attitude, to product purchase, to reinforcement, and to advocacy

Campaign strategy: The planning document that companies or advertising agencies develop to sell a product or service

Characterizational feature: refers to ads that focus on how users feel when using the product being advertised, that is, the psychological consequences of the consumption

Cloud: a network of computers used to store information from individuals and organizations

Cognitive development: the maturation of the human mind throughout childhood and throughout life; as the mind matures, it increases in its abilities for perception and reasoning

Cognitive-type effect: a type of media-influenced effect that is manifested as the acquisition of information (factual or social) as well as the triggering, alteration, or reinforcement of a mental process

Competencies: the ability to accomplish a task successfully, such as matching the meaning of a media message element; in contrast to skills, competencies are categorical (that is, either you can perform the task successfully or you cannot)

Complex interdependence: the relationship among the five players in the economic game as they negotiate exchanges of resources

Computer virus: a small computer program that is downloaded into a person's computer and attaches itself to existing computer programs then begins infecting those programs by erasing or rearranging data

Conceptual differentiation: the ability to classify objects into a large number of mutually exclusive categories

Conglomerate merger: one company buys other companies that can be in the same industry (same type of business or a company's suppliers and distributors) as well as in other industries

Conglomerates: very large companies that own and operate many businesses across different industries

Content analysis: a social scientific research method that focuses on certain characteristics of media messages (such as the demographics of characters or the portrayals of violence) and counts how frequently those characteristics occur

Contingent influences: some factors of influence contribute to a media effect only under certain conditions or only with certain types of people

Continuous partial attention: a long-term cognitive effect where the media reinforce a pattern of continually fading in and out of attention for media messages as we conduct multiple activities at the same time so that we lose the ability to devote full attention to any one thing

Contrast effect: an immediate attitudinal effect where people judge things in their real life as unfavorable (such as the attractiveness of their romantic partner) because their standards have been set unrealistically high by media messages

Convergence: the moving together over time of things that were separated into a common group; this is a powerful force on the mass media that has three manifestations: technological, business, and psychological

Cookies: tiny computer files that are planted on your hard drive when you access websites; these files store information about your browsing history and preferences and are activated next time you access the website that created the cookie

Copy platform: Advertisers' planning document to guide the design of each individual ad in an advertising campaign

Copyleft: the removing of restrictions so that the media messages are free and all users have the right to distribute copies and modified versions of a work; based on the values of openness and common ownership

Copyright: the legal establishment of ownership of a media message; based on the idea that the creative products of artists should be protected so that these artists can make a living and therefore be willing to create more products

Counterfeiting: a form of media message piracy that refers to the duplication of a copyrighted message along with its packaging and selling it as the real product

Co-viewing: a media literacy technique that parents use with children that focuses on watching television with their children; it is believed that this has a positive effect because when parents co-view, their children do not watch undesirable programming or exhibit undesirable behaviors

Creative commons: the sharing of resources for the common good such that everyone is allowed open access to the work of others and given the freedom to change that work and build on it for the common good

Cross-media promotion: advertising your media message in another medium so as to attract people in that medium to try exposing themselves to your message

Cross-vehicle promotion: advertising your media message in another vehicle so as to attract people in that medium to try exposing themselves to your message

Crystalline intelligence: the ability to memorize facts as well as the facility to absorb the images, definitions, opinions, and agendas of others

Cultivation: a long-term belief effect where after exposure to many media messages we come to believe the real world is like the world depicted in the media

Decline stage: the fourth phase in the life cycle pattern of the development of a mass medium where the medium loses audience members and revenue due to competition from a newer medium that provides better messages or the same messages in a better way

Deduction: the skill of using general principles to explain particulars

Default strategy: when audience members do not think about their media exposures and do not make active decisions as they negotiate their resources of time and money; instead, they continue with their automatic habits that follow a goal of maintaining a minimal level of uninterrupted satisfaction

Demographic segmentation: identifying a niche audience by their enduring characteristics, such as gender, ethnicity, and so on

Denial-of-service attack: when hackers flood a website or e-mail service provider with so much information that the site crashes; typically done by spammers who retaliate against anti-spamming sites who are filtering out the messages of spammers

Denoted meanings: standard meanings for symbols that are shared by all people; these are the dictionary-type meanings we memorize for words and symbols when we are in elementary school

Desensitization: a long-term emotional effect where the continual exposure to a certain kind of media message erodes the intensity of our emotional reaction; for example, repeated exposures to acts of aggression lead us to reduce our sympathy for victims of aggression

Developing news events: newsworthy occurrences that change over the course of days or weeks; journalists continue to file updated stories, realizing that each story is only partial and may contain inaccurate information

Digital coding: the recording, storage, and retrieval of information that uses a sequence of symbols or bytes (usually numbers) that are not dependent on the physical characteristics of any one medium

Digital Rights Management (DRM): the media industries' use of technological devices to control audiences' use of copyrighted materials, especially limiting users' exposure time or number of viewings

Direct support of media: consumers make payments directly to media companies in exchange for access to their messages

Disinhibition: a long-term behavioral effect where exposure to violent messages over time reduces the socialized inhibitions that prevent us from behaving in a violent or aggressive manner

Displacement: a long-term behavioral effect where the media gradually change how we spend our time by shifting our behaviors into media usage and away from other activities

Economies of scale: the high costs of making the first copy of a media message are spread out over many copies; as additional copies are produced, the high cost of making the initial copy is averaged over a greater number of copies and the cost per copy is reduced

Economies of scope: the high costs of making a media message spread out over different messages; when an original message is translated into similar messages and distributed through different media

Efficiency value: the belief that power in the government and the economy should be concentrated in the hands of a few people or businesses so that decisions can be made more quickly and enacted more smoothly

Electromagnetic spectrum: a range of frequencies that are used for broadcasting messages without wires; in the United States, the Federal Communications Commission is in charge of assigning frequencies to individuals and businesses for transmission of radio, television, and cell phone signals

Electronic games: platforms offering competitive experiences using electronic devices (video, computer, smartphone, etc.)

Emotional development: the maturation of one's abilities to recognize and understand the emotions in oneself and in others as well as the ability to control one's own emotional reactions

Emotional intelligence: the ability to understand and control one's emotions

Emotional-type effect: a type of media-influenced effect that is manifested as the triggering of an emotional reaction or the altering of emotional patterns over time

Evaluation: the skill of judging the value of an element; the judgment is made by comparing a message element to a standard

Exposure: the condition of being in proximity (place and time) to a message, having the message occur within our perceptual abilities, and leave some impression (however slight) in our minds; thus there are three hurdles for exposure: physical, perceptual, and psychological

Exposure states: four qualitatively distinct psychological states people can be in when experiencing a media message; these four states are automatic, attentional, transported, and self-reflexive

Extensive learning: an immediate cognitive effect of acquiring information that serves to create new links among existing knowledge structures or stimulates the creation of a new knowledge structure

Fact: a bit of information that (a) is a characteristic (about a person, event, place, or time), (b) is presented as being true, and (c) can be verified, which is in contrast with the terms *belief* and *opinion* that refer to personal interpretations that cannot be verified using a truth standard; while beliefs and opinions can be based on facts (or not), they are not themselves facts

Factual information: discrete bits of information that can be confirmed by objective sources; examples include names (of people, places, characters, etc.), dates, titles, and definitions

Fair use: allows for the quoting of portions of a copyrighted work for purposes of news reporting, criticism, and teaching

Family hour: the hour early in prime time (8 p.m. to 9 p.m.) that television programmers regard as a time when children are watching in large numbers, so they purportedly present less offensive programming in terms of portrayals of violence, sexual activity, and bad language

Federal Communications Commission (FCC): an agency established by the U.S. Congress in the 1920s to regulate the new broadcasting industry and later the developing telecommunication industry; focuses primarily on establishing national standards for developing information technologies as well as regulating ownership of broadcasting and telecommunication businesses

Field independency: a natural ability to distinguish between the signal and the noise in any message; the noise is the chaos of symbols and images, whereas the signal is the information that emerges from the chaos

Fight-or-flight: an immediate physiological effect where a media message depicts a threat to a character in a story and this triggers an automatic bodily response in audience members that prepares them to stand and fight off the threat or to flee from it to safety

Filtering: the information-processing task where we continually make decisions about filtering out media messages (ignore them) or filter them in (pay attention to them)

Firewall: a software program that is part of a computer network that blocks unauthorized access into the network while permitting members of the network to send out communications

Flow: when playing video games, the experience of being so focused on playing the game and achieving one's goals that the player loses track of time and place

Fluctuation effect: a form of process effect where there is a temporary deviation off a person's baseline

Fluid intelligence: the ability to be creative, make leaps of insight, and perceive things in a fresh and novel manner

Follow-on users: users of a copyleft message who take an original message, add something to it, then pass it on to other users who can also add something to it

Frame: a set of experiences we use to interpret media messages; frames are composed of our beliefs, preferences, emotions, and so on

Functional feature: refers to ads that focus on the advantages about how the advertised product can be used

Game engines: the basic programming needed to support an electronic game; users work off this basic programming to customize a game by designing various characters, settings, and rules of their own choosing

General entertainment story formula: the generic structure of all entertainment-type stories; the story begins with a conflict or a problem, the conflict is heightened throughout the story as the main characters try to solve the problem, and the story is resolved in a climactic scene

Generalization: a long-term cognitive effect that involves a process of observing a few occurrences of something in media messages, perceiving a pattern that ties together those occurrences, and then inferring that the pattern reflects something more general than those specific occurrences

Genre: refers to kinds of message and suggests that there are categories within which media messages can be organized; the most general genres of media messages are entertainment, news/information, and persuasive messages (such as commercial messages and public service announcements)

Geodemographic segmentation: identifying a niche audience by a combination of where they live and their demographic characteristics

Geographic segmentation: identifying a niche audience by where its members live and shop

Grouping: the skill of determining which elements are alike in some way; determining how a group of elements are different from other groups of elements

Hackers: people who use computer programming to break through firewalls designed to protect databases; their motive is to steal information, cause havoc with that information, or simply overcome the challenge of defeating security systems

Hacktivism: the using of hackers' techniques to break into organizations' secure databases for the purposes of either damaging those databases or using the information to publically embarrass the organization

HDTV: high-definition television; video that has substantially higher (five times) resolution than standard television

Hierarchy of needs: an organization of human needs as conceptualized by psychologist Abraham Maslow, in which human needs are arranged by five levels: survival, safety, social, self-esteem, and self-actualization; when the needs at a lower level are met, we focus on the needs at a higher level

Hijacking: when hackers use your computer without your permission and often without your knowledge

History stealing: a form of commercial mining where an Internet vendor records your activity on its site as it is allowed to do but then it also allows other vendors to record this information

Horizontal merger: one company buys another company of the same type so as to increase the number of outlets for the same products/services

Human interest: a news selection criterion that refers to the degree to which something would appeal to emotions of audiences; events that are likely to trigger emotions of admiration, appreciation, amusement, fear, and anger are more likely to be considered newsworthy

Hyper-localism: the specialization of news vehicles in response to the fragmenting audience

Hypermnesia: a long-term cognitive effect that is the opposite of forgetting information over time; instead, people seem to be able to recall more information over time without additional exposures to that information because their minds organize previously exposed information in ways that make it easier to recall

Identity theft: thieves use technology and media to access your personal information, then use that information to get credit cards and other forms of your identity sent to them

Imitation: an immediate behavioral effect where a media message triggers behavior that emulates the behavior depicted in the media message

Inbound marketing: a much newer method that uses the Internet primarily, in which advertisers design a website for their product then wait for people to declare their interest in the product by visiting the website; once these "inbound" potential consumers get on their website, advertisers take them through a step-by-step procedure to get them to buy the product (this procedure is called the sales funnel)

Indirect support of media: consumers pay extra for advertised goods and services and this extra amount flows from the advertisers to the media companies

Induction: the skill of inferring a pattern across a small set of elements, then generalizing the pattern to all elements in the set

Information-processing tasks: a sequence of tasks of filtering media messages, then matching meaning and meaning construction

Innovation stage: the first phase in the life cycle pattern of development of a mass medium; it is characterized by technological and marketing innovations

Inoculation: an immediate attitudinal effect where designers of persuasive messages expose audiences to a preview of a message counter to their position so as to immunize those audience members against being influenced by the counter message later

Intensive learning: an immediate cognitive effect of acquiring information that adds additional examples to a person's existing knowledge structure and thus elaborates it

Intentionality of effects: refers to the motives of both the senders of media messages as well as the audiences of those messages

Interactive influence: some factors of influence contribute to a media effect only when particular other factors of influence are present

Interactive media: media platforms allow, and typically require, their audiences to create the content, either by themselves, in interaction with other audience members, or in interaction with employees of mass media organizations; audience members are not paid for creating any of this content (to the contrary, audience members not only create the content for free but they often pay the interactive mass media companies for access to the content either through subscription fees, as with many games, or by agreeing to be exposed to advertising)

Internet addiction: a long-term behavioral effect where people become addicted to accessing the Internet and lose control over their behavior

Internet Crime Complaint Center: abbreviated as IC3, this is a division of the U.S. Federal Bureau of Investigation (FBI) that investigates complaints from citizens who have been victimized by a criminal using the Internet; examples of these crimes are typically identity theft, hacking into secure databases, and the planting of malware on computers

Internet Service Providers (ISPs): media companies that offer users a way to connect to the Internet through wires or Wi-Fi

Junk mail: unwanted mail that is sent to you either virtually through e-mail (called spam) or physically through the postal service (called direct mail marketing)

Knock-off series: a new television series where producers try to copy the formula of a successful television series from other producers

Knowledge structures: sets of organized information stored in a person's memory

Lateral thinking: a problem-solving method (in contrast to vertical thinking) that uses intuition and creative insights more than logic

Learned helplessness: a long-term behavioral effect where the media, especially television and Internet, have conditioned our behaviors to such a degree that we are helpless to change our behavior

Learning agendas: a long-term cognitive effect where we infer a pattern across many media messages that tells us what is important (that is, what should be on our agenda of things to pay attention to)

Life cycle pattern: a sequence of five stages of development typically followed by all mass media; the five stages are innovation, penetration, peak, decline, and adaptation

Localism value: the belief that power in the government and the economy should be spread out over as many people as possible so that everyone has a voice as well as an influence on every decision

Long tail marketing: a strategy of identifying smaller niche audiences that have been ignored by other media companies; the "long tail" refers to the extreme ends on the bell curve and ignores the fat middle where the majority is represented

Lowest common denominator: a programming principle where a media company (especially television) tries to attract the largest audience possible by creating messages that will not offend anyone and thus appeal to a wide range of people

Macro-type effect: a type of media-influenced effect that is manifested as the gradual altering or reinforcing of processes in aggregates of individuals such as organizations, institutions, and society

Magic window: a perspective that regards media messages as a window on the world that presents the actual occurrences from the real world in an undistorted manner

Malware: any software intentionally designed to cause damage to a computer, server, or computer network; as an umbrella-like term, malware includes computer viruses, worms, Trojan horses, ransomware, spyware, adware, and scareware, among others

Manifested effect: a media-influenced effect that can be observed and can be easily attributed to media influence

Marketing concept: a practice among marketers that begins with research to identify audience needs, then creates the types of messages that can satisfy those particular needs

Marketing convergence: using the advantages of technological convergence across channels of media to attract niche audiences for a particular message with as many platforms as possible

Marketing innovation: an essential characteristic of the innovation stage in the development of a mass medium where marketers attract new users to their medium and convince them that the new medium is a superior way for those users to access media messages

Marketing perspective: a belief among managers of media companies that it is their job to identify existing needs in various niche audiences then develop media messages to satisfy those needs

Mass audience: the outdated conceptualization of the media audience as being a very large mass with no social organization or interaction among audience members, who are heterogeneous, anonymous, and interchangeable

Mass communication: the outdated conceptualization that media send messages to a mass audience in a one-way flow with no feedback

Maturation: the natural development of one's natural abilities physically, cognitively, emotionally, and morally as one ages

Meaning construction: the information-processing task where we engage in a process of creating our own meaning for a media message; this process is usually engaged when we have no denoted meaning already residing in our memory or when the denoted meaning does not satisfy our current needs

Meaning matching: the information-processing task where we engage in a process of recognizing elements (referents) in a media message then automatically access our memory to find the meanings we have memorized for those elements

Media literacy: a set of perspectives that we actively use to expose ourselves to the mass media to interpret the meaning of the messages we encounter; media literacy is multidimensional, consisting of cognitive, emotional, aesthetic, and moral dimensions; and media literacy is a continuum, not a category

Mental codes: rules for decision making that we have learned through exposure to media messages; these codes are stored in our memory and are automatically activated when we engage in information-processing tasks of filtering and meaning matching

Messages: the instruments that deliver information to us from the media

Metered paywall: a device used by websites where visitors are allowed to access a certain number of pages, then their access is denied until they pay the subscription fee to give them further access

Middle-ware market: the making available of programming packages, guidelines, and game engines to people who want to design electronic games but lack the programming skill to create them from scratch

MMORPGs: massively multiplayer online role-playing games; Internet-based platforms that attract thousands of game players from all over the world who want to create a persona in a fantasy world and compete for virtual rewards in those worlds

Money cycle: the continual and accelerating flow of money in sports from the public to advertisers, to television networks, to leagues and owners, then to players

Monopolistic competition: the economic condition within most media industries where there are a few powerful companies that control the majority of resources and compete aggressively among themselves

Moral development: the maturation of one's ability to reason about the ethical value of the motives and consequences of the decisions of others and oneself

Narcoticization: a long-term behavioral effect where the media act like a powerful drug by giving us excitement during early exposures that conditions us for repeat exposures that deliver less excitement, thus driving us to want more to achieve the same excitement as our initial exposure

Native advertising: a type of false news because the message appears as a news story when it is really a covert marketing practice; the message, which is an ad, mimics the conventions of a news platform by appearing to be "native" to that platform and the ad appropriates the look and feel of real news

Negative mediation: a media literacy technique used by parents when viewing television with their children; parents point out the harmful things in messages, such as when characters behave in antisocial ways, in order to help their children learn to avoid performing those negative behaviors in their own lives

Net loser: people and organizations who complete economic exchanges with resources of less value compared to the resources they gave up in the exchange

Net winner: people and organizations who complete economic exchanges with resources of greater value compared to the resources they gave up in the exchange

News-framing influences: the factors that shape how journalists do their jobs and construct the news; the major news-framing influences are commercialism, the marketing perspective, organizational structures, ownership, use of sources, branding, values, hyper-localism, and story formula

News perspective: a view of what is news that is developed on the job by journalists as they learn to work within all the news constraints and story formulas

News radar: your default sensitivity that spots potentially bad news stories; the ability to spot things in news stories that trigger you to analyze the facts and the way the story is told

News story: a sequence of facts presented to inform an audience

Newsworkers: the people who collect information and present it as news; thus, this is a general term that includes people who work as individuals (bloggers, tweeters, etc.) and people who work in news organizations (reporters, editors, opinion columnists, managers, production people, advertisers, etc.)

Next-step reality: the idea that media messages must be based on real-world elements (recognizable characters, situations, etc.) so that audiences can relate to what happens in those messages but then the messages must also take a step away from pure reality by adding fantasy elements in order to capture and hold the audience's attention

Niche audience: a relatively small audience that is defined by a shared interest or need

Nonimpulsiveness: the willingness to avoid rushing into decisions for the sake of efficiency and instead analyzing messages carefully to insure greater accuracy

Open source software: computer software that is free to anyone who wants to use it and/or alter it

Opt-in policy: the default is privacy; providers of services are not allowed to gather information on their users and to sell that information until users grant permission to do so

Opt-out default: the default is no privacy; providers of services are allowed to gather information on their users and to sell that information until users tell them to stop; it is the users' responsibility to inform the site when they do not want to be subjected to these practices

Outbound marketing: the traditional method advertisers use to engage their targeted consumers by designing ads to attract their attention then placing those ads in traditional media outlets (television, radio, newspapers, and magazines) where advertisers know there are high concentrations of their targeted consumers in the audience

Paid placement: advertisers pay a fee to web browsers and online retailers so that when visitors to their sites do a search, the results of those searches are influenced in part by how much advertisers have paid to have their products moved up to the top of those search results listings

Payola: an illegal practice where record companies pay radio disk jockeys to play their records on the air

Paywall: a device used by websites where visitors are allowed to access some content while most of the content is walled off from them until they pay the subscription fee for access

Peak stage: the third phase in the life cycle pattern of development of a mass medium where the medium commands the most attention from the public and generates the most revenue compared to other media

Penetration stage: the second phase in the life cycle pattern of development of a mass medium where it continues to attract larger numbers of audience members of all kinds

Perceptual exposure: the media message falls within a human's bandwidth of visual and/or auditory perception

Personal locus: a person's plan for building knowledge structures about the media along with the psychic energy needed to execute the plan

Phishing: a technique used to acquire sensitive information from unaware users by seemingly trustworthy message senders; victims receive an e-mail message that typically directs them to a fake website whose look and feel are almost identical to the legitimate one (like a bank or insurance company) and the victim is asked to sign in and divulge private information

Physical exposure: the message and the person occupy the same physical space for some period of time

Physical feature: refers to ads that focus on something about the product itself, such as its ingredients or other physical properties of the product

Physiological-type effect: a type of media-influenced effect that is manifested as the triggering of an automatic bodily function, such as increasing blood pressure or heart rate

Piracy: the unauthorized use of copyrighted material; with media messages, it typically takes three forms: bootlegging, counterfeiting, and sharing copyrighted messages without paying for access

Positive mediation: a media literacy technique used by parents when viewing television with their children; parents point out the good things in those television messages to help their children learn positive lessons about life

Prime time: a television viewing term that refers to the hours of the day when the audience is largest for television, so networks and stations present their strongest programming then and charge their highest advertising rates; those hours are 8 p.m. to 11 p.m. every day except Sunday when prime time begins at 7 p.m.; in the central time zone, prime time begins and ends 1 hour earlier than in the other time zones

Privacy: the secluding of personal information by individuals about themselves

Private goods: things that individuals buy, own, and control

Process effect: a media-influenced effect that is continually occurring without being easily observed

Professional responsibility perspective: a belief among journalists that it is their responsibility to inform the public about the most important and significant events of the day so that people can use the information to make better decisions as citizens of that society

Profit: the positive difference between a company's revenue and expenses; often used mistakenly as a synonym for *revenue*

Prominence: a news selection criterion that refers to how well known people and events are to an audience

Proximity: a news selection criterion that refers to how close events happen to an audience either geographically or culturally

Psychological convergence: the breaking down of barriers between audiences and mass media organizations as well as the barriers separating audience members from one another due to geography or other social constraints

Psychographic segmentation: identifying a niche audience by their psychological and lifestyle characteristics

Psychological exposure: a media message creates a trace element in a person's mind

Public domain: the idea that a media message is available for anyone to use; the message is not protected by a copyright that requires the public ask for permission and/or pay for the use of the message

Public goods: things that are owned by society and are open for sharing for free or at a modest fee

Puffery: a technique used by advertisers to use words in a way that it appears they are making claims for the superiority of their products when, in fact, they are not making any product claims that can be tested

Quality audience strategy: attempting to attract a particular kind of audience; *quality* refers to kind of audience, not to an elite audience

Quantity audience strategy: attempting to attract as large an audience as possible

Ransomware: a type of malware that prevents or limits users from accessing their system, either by locking the system's screen or by locking users' files unless a ransom is paid

Restrictive mediation: a media literacy technique that parents use with children that focuses on setting and enforcing rules about media exposure, particularly with television and other screens

Retargeting: online retailers collect data about the products a person searches for when he or she visits the site; the retailer then later sends that person messages about those products to lure the individual back to the site and stimulate a purchase

Revenue streams: sources of income for a business

ROA: return on assets; the comparison of a business's annual profit compared to the size of its asset base expressed as a percentage

ROR: return on revenue; the comparison of a business's annual profit compared to its annual revenues expressed as a percentage

Sanitized violence: media portrayals typically clean up the way violence is portrayed so as not to offend viewers with graphicness and the suffering of victims

Search engine: a service provided usually free to Internet users that allows them to type in a key term and the service provides them with a list of Internet sites relevant to that term

Self-actualization: the highest level of need in Maslow's hierarchy of human needs; the needs at this level focus on fulfilling oneself through creativity and morality

Self-reflexive exposure state: the experience of being exposed to a media message with a high degree of awareness of the media message as well as a high awareness of standing apart from the message while analyzing it

Sentiment analysis: the process of computationally identifying and categorizing opinions expressed in a piece of text, especially in order to determine whether the writer's attitude toward a particular topic, product, and so forth is positive, negative, or neutral

SEO (Search Engine Optimization): the process of improving the position and visibility of a website on search engines (Google, Yahoo!, Bing, etc.)

Significance: a news selection criterion that refers to how much impact the story is likely to have on the audience; coverage of events that convey a sense of resonance with an audience is more significant to those audience members than stories about events that have no relationship to their own experiences

Simplified extended conflict: a news story formula that tells journalists to look for some angle of conflict that appears very simple, then structure their stories to emphasize the simple conflict between two people or two points of view

Skills: tools we use to build strong knowledge structures; the seven fundamental skills necessary with media literacy are analysis, evaluation, grouping, induction, deduction, abstraction, and synthesis

Sleeper effect: long-term attitudinal effect where a person creates a negative attitude about a particular message during an exposure to a message because of a dislike for the source, but then over time the attitude changes to a positive one because the person forgets about the source while remembering the message

Social class segmentation: identifying a niche audience by the level of their social class, such as lower class, middle class, and upper class

Social cocooning: long-term behavioral effect where people form technological bubbles around themselves to separate them from their real-world surroundings

Social information: a type of information that is characterized by rules and patterns about how individuals behave around other people; this information, which cannot be verified by authorities in the same way factual information can be, is typically inferred as individuals observing how people behave in social interactions and the consequences of those behaviors

Social networking: a behavior exhibited by humans as they make contact with other humans by forming groups both formal and informal

Social networking sites (SNSs): platforms for individuals and businesses to create an identity on the Internet and provide information to friends and the public about themselves (e.g., Facebook, LinkedIn, etc.)

Socialization: long-term effect where we use media messages to form our beliefs about how society works in the real world

Spam: unsolicited and unwanted e-mail messages sent to you and hundreds of millions of others daily by marketers

Spam filters: software used by Internet service providers that screens out messages that have been identified as coming from spammers so that you never see these messages

Spamming: using the media, especially e-mail, to invade your privacy with unsolicited and unwanted messages

Spin-off series: a new television series that is a direct extension of a successful television series by the same producers

Spyware: a small program that is inadvertently downloaded by computer users when they access certain websites; the program installs itself on a person's computer then it collects information about users without their knowledge

Story formulas: the guidelines that producers of media messages use to attract audiences, hold their attention throughout the message, and condition them for repeat exposures; audiences use these guidelines to follow messages and make sense of them

Subliminal advertising: there is a belief among conspiracy theorists that advertisers use subliminal techniques to manipulate audiences of their advertising unfairly, but this is a false belief because *subliminal* means that the message elements are outside the ability of humans to perceive them

Synthesis: the skill of assembling information elements into a new structure to reveal new relationships among the elements

Talent: an economic resource of above-the-line media employees that refers to their ability to attract and condition audiences for repeat exposures

Technological convergence: the breaking down of barriers that separated the different media channels of communication (such as print media, broadcast TV, film, computers, etc.) primarily due to the digitization of information so that a message could move seamlessly across all media channels of communication

Technological innovation: a characteristic of the innovation stage in the development of a mass medium where inventors develop a new form of transmitting information

Telescoping: the way electronic game players keep the big picture of the overall game in mind while focusing on the immediate objectives that face them at any one point in the game

Third parties: people and organizations outside of our direct interactions where we are the first party and the other (a friend, a bank, a store, etc.) is the second party in the interaction; when the second party shares or sells information from an exchange to a third party without our permission, it is a violation of our privacy

Third-person effect: the widespread belief in the public that exposure to media can harm other people (the third person) but not themselves personally

Timeliness: a news selection criterion that refers to how recently an event has occurred; the more recent the event, the more likely it meets this criterion of newsworthiness

Timing of effects: focuses on when a media-influenced effect is manifested; it has two values of immediate (where the manifestation occurs during the media exposure or shortly after) and long term (where the manifestation does not occur until the person has experienced many exposures to media messages)

Tolerance for ambiguity: the willingness to follow situations into unfamiliar territory that go beyond our preconceptions and take us out of our comfort zone

Transported exposure state: the experience of being exposed to a media message and being swept away by it into a different place and time such that you lose sense of your current physical surroundings and current point in time

Trolling: the posting of willfully inflammatory, off-topic, or simply stupid remarks on the blogs of others

Type of effect: refers to the form of the manifestation of the effect in individuals (cognitive, attitudinal, emotional, physiological, or behavioral) and in larger aggregates (macro-type effect)

Unavoidable constraints: factors that put limitations on the way news is presented; the major constraints are deadlines, geographic focus, and resource limitations

Unusualness: a news selection criterion that refers to how untypical events are; occurrences that are rare are considered more newsworthy

Valence of effects: refers to whether an effect is positive or negative

Vehicle: the means by which a media company sends its messages to audiences; for example, with television, the vehicles are the programs

Vertical merger: one company buys suppliers and/or distributors to create integration in the production and distribution of products/services

Vertical thinking: a problem-solving method (in contrast to lateral thinking) that is based on a standard step-by-step logical progression

Viral spiral: an upward spiral of innovation on the Internet made possible by the Internet's open networking structure that gives all people free access to ideas, so that the creators of those ideas can easily disseminate them widely and allow others to build on those ideas and extend them in creative ways

Web 1.0: designation for older Internet companies (such as Yahoo, AOL, and Netscape) that provided services that were proprietary, that is, their source code was kept secret so competitors could not use it

Web 2.0: designation for a perspective about the Internet that fosters a social dynamic where people have the freedom to share their work through all sorts of open websites; users are free to access all these sites, use whatever they want, create their own messages, and make their messages available to anyone

REFERENCES

Abelman, R. (1999). Preaching to the choir: Profiling TV advisory ratings users. *Journal of Broadcasting & Electronic Media*, *43*, 529–550.

Acxiom. (2018). Financial summary. Retrieved from https://investors.acxiom.com/financial-information/default.aspx

Ader, D. R. (1995). A longitudinal study of agenda setting for the issue of environmental pollution. *Journalism & Mass Communication Quarterly*, *72*, 300–311.

Albarran, A. B. (2002). *Media economics: Understanding markets, industries and concepts* (2nd ed.). Ames: Iowa State Press.

Albarran, A. B., & Chan-Olmsted, S. M. (1998). The United States of America. In A. B. Albarran & S. M. Chan-Olmsted (Eds.), *Global media economics: Commercialization, concentration and integration of world media markets* (pp. 19–32). Ames: Iowa State University Press.

Allcott, H., & Gentzkow, M. (2017). Social media and fake news in the 2016 election. *Journal of Economic Perspectives*, *31*(2), 211–236.

Alter, A. (2017). *Irresistible: The rise of addictive technology and the business of keeping us hooked*. New York, NY: Penguin Press.

Altheide, D. L. (1976). *Creating reality: How TV news distorts events*. Beverly Hills, CA: SAGE.

Altman, A., & Frizell, S. (2015, January 5). Hollywood hacked: Why no company is immune. *Time Magazine*, p. 26.

Amazeen, M. A., & Muddiman, A. R. (2018). Saving media or trading on trust? *Digital Journalism*, *6*, 176–195.

Amazeen, M. A., & Wojdynski, B. W. (2018, February 7). The effects of disclosure format on native advertising recognition and audience perceptions of legacy and online news publishers. *Journalism*. doi:10.1177/1464884918754829

American Obesity Association. (2004, June 24). *AOA factsheets*. Retrieved from http://obesity.org

Anderson, C. (2006). *The long tail: Why the future of business is selling less of more*. New York, NY: Hyperion.

Anderson, D. R., Collins, P. A., Schmitt, K. L., & Jacobvitz, R. S. (1996). Stressful life events and television viewing. *Communication Research*, *23*, 243–260.

Anderson, J. A. (1983). Television literacy and the critical viewer. In J. Bryant & D. R. Anderson (Eds.), *Children's understanding of television: Research on attention and comprehension* (pp. 297–327). New York, NY: Academic Press.

Angwin, J. (2009). *Stealing MySpace: The battle to control the most popular website in America*. New York, NY: Random House.

AOL is sued over privacy breach. (2006, September 26). *Los Angeles Times*, p. C2.

AP Online. (2000, March 13). *Timeline of major media mergers. Financial Section*.

Arens, W. F. (1999). *Contemporary advertising* (7th ed.). Boston, MA: Irwin McGraw-Hill.

Arndorfer, J. B. (1998, December 21). A-B looking for women via daytime TV programs. *Advertising Age*, *69*(51), 8.

Aslam, S. (2018a, January 1). *Twitter by the numbers: Stats, demographics & fun facts*. Retrieved from https://www.omnicoreagency.com/twitter-statistics/

Aslam, S. (2018b, February 5). *YouTube by the numbers: Stats, demographics & fun facts*. Retrieved from https://www.omnicoreagency.com/youtube-statistics/

Austin, E. W. (1993). Exploring the effects of active parental mediation of television content. *Journal of Broadcasting & Electronic Media*, *37*, 147–158.

Austin, E. W., Bolls, P., Fujioka, Y., & Engelbertson, J. (1999). How and why parents take on the tube. *Journal of Broadcasting & Electronic Media*, *43*, 175–192.

Badenhausen, K. (2018a, February 7). NBA team values 2018: Every club now worth at least $1 billion. *Forbes*. Retrieved from https://www.forbes.com/sites/kurtbadenhausen/2018/02/07/nba-team-values-2018-every-club-now-worth-at-least-1-billion/#563cd4af7155

Badenhausen, K. (2018b, April 11). Major league baseball's highest paid players for 2018. *Forbes*. Retrieved from https://www.forbes.com/sites/kurtbadenhausen/2018/04/11/major-league-baseballs-highest-paid-players-for-2018/#bb4a4a65e3fb

Bagdikian, B. (1992). *The media monopoly* (4th ed.). Boston, MA: Beacon.

Bagdikian, B. (2004). *The new media monopoly* (7th ed.). Boston, MA: Beacon.

Bailey, B. (2015, January 7). FTC chief says gadget industry must prioritize privacy. *Santa Barbara News Press*, p. A1.

Baker, C. (2003, August). Cracking the box office genome. *Wired*, p. 52.

Baker, M. R., Falk, L., & Manners, J. (2000, January). The big media road map. *Brill's Content*. pp. 99–102.

Bandura, A. (1986). *Social foundations of thought and action: A social cognitive theory.* Englewood Cliffs, NJ: Prentice Hall.

Bandura, A. (1994). Social cognitive theory of mass communication. In J. Bryant & D. Zillmann (Eds.), *Media effects* (pp. 61–90). Hillsdale, NJ: Lawrence Erlbaum.

Barthel, M, (2018, June 13). Newspaper fact sheet. *Pew Research Center*. Retrieved from http://www.journalism.org/fact-sheet/newspapers/

Bash, A. (1997, June 10). Most parents don't use ratings to guide viewing. *USA Today*, p. 3D.

Battles, K., & Hilton-Morrow, W. (2002). Gay characters in conventional spaces: Will and Grace and the situation comedy genre. *Critical Studies in Media Communication*, *19*, 87–106.

Bauder, D. (2000, March 14). CBS to air two reality TV shows. *Tallahassee Democrat*, p. B1.

Bauer, E. (2018, February 1). 15 outrageous email spam statistics that still ring true in 2018. *Propeller*. Retrieved from https://www.propellercrm.com/blog/email-spam-statistics

Bauer, R. A., & Bauer, A. (1960). America, mass society and mass media. *Journal of Social Issues*, *10*, 3–66.

Baym, N. K., & Boyd, D. (2012). Socially mediated publicness: An introduction. *Journal of Broadcasting & Electronic Media*, *56*, 320–329.

Bazarova, N. N. (2012). Public intimacy: Disclosure interpretation and social judgments on Facebook. *Journal of Communication*, *62*, 815–832.

Beam, R. A. (2003). Content difference between daily newspapers with strong and weak market orientations. *Journalism & Mass Communication Quarterly*, *80*, 368–390.

Becker, L. B., Kosicki, G. M., & Jones, F. (1992). Racial differences in evaluation of the mass media. *Journalism Quarterly*, *69*, 124–134.

Bettig, R. V., & Hall, J. L. (2003). *Big media, big money: Cultural texts and political economies.* Lanham, MD: Rowman & Littlefield.

Bialik, K., & Matsa, K. E. (2017, October 4). Key trends in social and digital news media. *Pew Research Center*. Retrieved from http://www.pewresearch.org/fact-tank/2017/10/04/key-trends-in-social-and-digital-news-media/

Bielby, D. D., & Bielby, W. T. (2002). Hollywood dreams, harsh realities: Writing for film and television. *Context*, *1*, 21–27.

Blumer, H. (1946). Collective behavior. In A. M. Lee (Ed.), *Principles of sociology* (pp. 185–186). New York, NY: Barnes & Noble.

Boczkowski, P. J., & Mitchelstein, E. (2013). *The news gap.* Cambridge, MA: MIT Press.

Bollier, D. (2008). *Viral spiral: How the commoners built a digital republic of their own.* New York, NY: The New Press.

Boswell, T. (1996, July 20). Between the commercials, waiting for the real show. *Washington Post*, p. G9.

Boxman-Shabtai, L., & Shifman, L. (2014). Evasive targets: Deciphering polysemy in mediated humor. *Journal of Communication*, *64*, 977–998.

Boyd, J. (2018). *List of top FBS head coach salary for NCAA football in 2018*. Retrieved from https://www.boydsbets.com/highest-paid-college-football-coaches/

Brady, E., Berkowitz, S., & Schnaars, C. (2014, November 20). Higher demands, higher salaries. *USA Today*, pp. C1, C7–C9.

British Broadcasting Corporation. (1972). *Violence on television: Programme content and viewer perceptions*. London, England: Author.

Brooks, D. (2011). *The social animal: The hidden sources of love, character, and achievement*. New York, NY: Random House.

Brown, J. A. (1991). *Television "critical viewing skills" education: Major media literacy projects in the United States and selected countries*. Hillsdale, NJ: Lawrence Erlbaum.

Brown, J. A. (1998). Media literacy perspectives. *Journal of Communication, 48*, 44–57.

Brown, J. A. (2001). Media literacy and critical television viewing in education. In D. G. Singer & J. L. Singer (Eds.), *Handbook of children and the media* (pp. 681–697).Thousand Oaks, CA: SAGE.

Brown, J. D., El-Toukhy, S., & Ortiz, R. (2014). Growing up sexually in a digital world: The risks and benefits of youths' sexual media use. In A. B. Jordan & D. Romer (Eds.), *Media and the well-being of children and adolescents* (pp. 90–108). New York, NY: Oxford University Press.

Brownfield, P. (1999, July 21). As minorities' TV presence dims, gay roles proliferate. *Los Angeles Times*, p. A1.

Bruner, J. S., Goodnow, J., & Austin, G.A. (1956). *A study of thinking*. New York, NY: John Wiley.

BtoBonline (2013, January 2). Media M&A activity in 2012 doubled. *AdAge*. Retrieved from http://adage.com/article/btob/media-m-a-activity-2012-doubled/288333/

Bucy, E. P. (2004). The interactivity paradox: Closer to the news but confused. In E. P. Bucy & J. E. Newhaghen (Eds.), *Media access: Social and psychological dimensions of new technology use* (pp. 47–72). Mahwah, NJ: Lawrence Erlbaum.

Bucy, E. P., & Newhagen, J. E. (1999). The emotional appropriateness heuristic: Processing televised presidential reactions to the news. *Journal of Communication, 49*, 59–79.

Buerkel-Rothfuss, N. L. (1993). Background: What prior research shows. In B. S. Greenberg, J. D. Brown, & N. Buerkel-Rothfuss (Eds.), *Media, sex and the adolescent* (pp. 5–18). Cresskill, NJ: Hampton.

Building with big data (2011, May 28). *The Economist*, p. 74.

Bullas, J. (n.d.) 35 mind numbing YouTube facts, figures and statistics–Infographic. Retrieved from https://www.jeffbullas.com/35-mind-numbing-youtube-facts-figures-and-statistics-infographic/

Bureau of Labor Statistics (2015, December 17). Occupational outlook handbook summary. Retrieved from https://www.bls.gov/news.release/ooh.nr0.htm

Bureau of Labor Statistics. (2018, June 1). The employment situation—May 2018. Retrieved from https://www.bls.gov/news.release/archives/empsit_06012018.pdf

Byrne, S. (2009). Media literacy interventions: What makes them boom or boomerang? *Communication Education, 58*, 1–14.

Byrne, S., & Lee, T. (2011). Toward predicting youth resistance to Internet risk prevention strategies. *Journal of Broadcasting & Electronic Media, 55*, 90–113.

Calabresi, M. (2012, August 27). The phone knows all. *Time*, pp. 30–31.

Calvert, C. (2004). *Voyeur nation: Media, privacy, and peering in modern culture*. New York, NY: Basic Books.

"Can Spam" (2004, January 5). *Providence Journal*, p. A8.

Cantril, H. (1947). The invasion from Mars. In T. Newcomb & E. Hartley (Eds.), *Readings in social psychology* (pp. 619–628). New York, NY: Holt.

Caplan, J. (2008, December 15). De-cluttering your mailbox. *Time*, p. 58.

Carlson, M. (2015). When news sites go native: Redefining the advertising–editorial divide in response to native advertising." *Journalism, 16*, 849–865.

Cassata, M., & Skill, T. (1983). *Life on daytime television*. Norwood, NJ: Ablex.

Castronova, E. (2001, December). *Virtual worlds: A first-hand account of market and society on the cyberian frontier.* CESifo Working Paper Series No. 618. Munich, Germany: Center for Economic Studies & Ifo Institute for Economic Research.

Castronova, E. (2005). *Synthetic worlds.* Chicago, IL: University of Chicago Press.

CBS Corporation. (n.d.). Retrieved from http://en.wiki pedia.org/wiki/CBS_Corporation

CBS headquarters, name taken over by Westinghouse. (1997, December 2). *Santa Barbara News- Press,* p. A6.

CBSNews.com (2009, February 11). *V-chip still not taking flight.* Retrieved from http://www.cbsnews .com/8301-207_162-303136.html

Centers for Disease Control and Prevention. (2017, May 3). *National Center for Health Statistics: Obesity and overweight.* Retrieved from https://www.cdc.gov/nchs/ fastats/obesity-overweight.htm

Cheang, M. (2016, June 2). Why are there so many movie sequels? *Star 2.com.* Retrieved from https://www.star2 .com/entertainment/movies/movie-news/2016/06/02/ why-are-there-so-many-movie-sequels/

Chew, F., & Palmer, S. (1994). Interest, the knowledge gap, and television programming. *Journal of Broadcasting & Electronic Media, 38,* 271–287.

Chmielewski, D. C. (2011, May 31). Bringing order to YouTube's chaos. *Los Angeles Times,* B1, B3.

Chmielewski, D. C., & Fritz, B. (2009, September 1). Marvel makes for mightier mouse. *Los Angeles Times,* pp. A1, A7.

Cho, H., Shen, L., & Wilson, K. (2014). Perceived realism: Dimensions and roles in narrative persuasion. *Communication Research, 41,* 828–851.

Cho, S. (2007). TV news coverage of plastic surgery, 1972–2004. *Journalism and Mass Communication Quarterly, 84,* 75–89.

Chock, T. M. (2011). Is it seeing or believing? Exposure, perceived realism, and emerging adults' perceptions of their own and others' attitudes about relationships. *Media Psychology, 14,* 355–386.

Christianson, P. G., & Roberts, D. F. (1998). *It's not only rock & roll: Popular music in the lives of adolescents.* Cresskill, NJ: Hampton.

Clark, T. N. (2000, September). Is materialism rising in America? *Society, 37,* 47–48.

CNN Library. (2018, March 22). *Facebook fast facts.* Retrieved from https://www.cnn.com/2014/02/11/ world/facebook-fast-facts/index.html

Coltrane, S., & Messineo, M. (2000). The perpetuation of subtle prejudice: Race and gender imagery in 1990s television advertising. *Sex Roles: A Journal of Research, 42,* 363–389.

Columbia Broadcasting System. (1980). *Network prime time violence tabulations for 1978–1979 season.* New York, NY: Author.

Comcast. (n.d.). Retrieved from http://en.wikipedia .org/wiki/Comcast

Common Cause. (n.d.) Media mega mergers: A timeline. Retrieved from http://www.commoncause.org/ site/pp.asp?c=dkLNK1MQIwG&b=4923181

Comstock, G.A. (1989). *The evolution of American television.* Newbury Park, CA: SAGE.

Comstock, G. A., Chaffee, S., Katzman, N., McCombs, M., & Roberts, D. (1978). *Television and human behavior.* New York, NY: Columbia University Press.

Connell, S. L., Lauricella, A. R., & Wartella, E. (2015). Parental co-use of media technology with their young children in the USA. *Journal of Children and Media, 9,* 5–21.

Considine, D. M. (1997).Media literacy: A compelling component of school reform and restructuring. In R. Kubey (Ed.), *Media literacy in the information age* (pp. 243–262). New Brunswick, NJ: Transaction Publishers.

Cooper, C. A. (1996). *Violence on television: Congressional inquiry, public criticism and industry response.* New York, NY: University Press of America.

Coyne, S., & Whitehead, E. (2008). Indirect aggression in animated Disney films. *Journal of Communication, 58,* 382–395.

Crider, D. (2012). A public sphere in decline: The state of localism in talk radio. *Journal of Broadcasting & Electronic Media, 56,* 225–244.

Croteau, D., & Hoynes, W. (2001). *The business of media: Corporate media and the public interest.* Thousand Oaks, CA: Pine Forge Press.

Csikszentmihalyi, M. (1988). The flow experience and its significance for human psychology. In M. Csikszentmihalyi & I. S. Csikszentmihalyi (Eds.), *Optimal experience: Psychological studies of flow in consciousness* (pp. 15–35). New York, NY: Cambridge University Press.

DaBoss. (2013, February 2013). *Number of viruses.* Retrieved from https://www.cknow.com/cms/vtutor/number-of-viruses.html

D'Alessio, D., & Allen, M. (2000). Media bias in presidential elections: A meta-analysis. *Journal of Communication, 50,* 133–156.

Danny. (2018, April 26). 37 mind blowing YouTube facts, figures, and statistics – 2018. *MerchDope.* Retrieved from https://merchdope.com/youtube-stats/

Dating Sites Reviews. (2018, June 10). *Online dating statistics and facts.* Retrieved from https://www.datingsitesreviews.com/staticpages/index.php?page=Online-Dating-Industry-Facts-Statistics#ref-GODI-2018-15

Davenport, T. H., & Beck, J. C. (2001). *The attention economy: Understanding the new currency of business.* Boston, MA: Harvard Business School Press.

Davies, M. M. (1997). Making media literate: Educating future media workers at the undergraduate level. In R. Kubey (Ed.), *Media literacy in the information age* (pp. 263–284). New Brunswick, NJ: Transaction Publishers.

Davis, B. (1990). Media hoaxes. *Wilson Library Bulletin, 64,* 139–140.

Debate.org. (2018, June 25). *Is modern society too materialistic?* Retrieved from http://www.debate.org/opinions/is-modern-society-too-materialistic?ysort=3&nsort=5

Dehnart, A. (2018, February 14). *The most-popular reality TV shows of 2017.* Retrieved from https://www.realityblurred.com/realitytv/2018/02/most-popular-reality-tv-shows-2017-ratings/

Deitsch, R. (2018, January 3). Why the NFL's ratings saw a steep decline in 2017. *Sports Illustrated.* Retrieved from https://www.si.com/tech-media/2018/01/03/nfl-ratings-decline-espn-fox-nbc-network-tv

DeWolf, M. (2017, March 1). 12 stats about working women. *U.S. Department of Labor Blog.* Retrieved from https://blog.dol.gov/2017/03/01/12-stats-about-working-women

Diamant, A. (1994, October). Media violence. *Parents Magazine, 69,* 40.

Diefenbach, D. L., & West, M. D. (2007). Television and attitudes toward mental health issues: Cultivation analysis and the third-person effect. *Journal of Community Psychology, 35,* 181–195.

Diener, E., & De Four, D. (1978). Does television violence enhance programme popularity? *Journal of Personality and Social Psychology, 36,* 333–341.

Diener, E., & Woody, L. W. (1981). TV violence and viewer liking. *Communication Research, 8,* 281–306.

D'Innocenzio, A., & Collins, T. (2013, February 3). Hackers make their way into Twitter. *Santa Barbara News-Press,* pp. B1, B4.

Donsbach, W. (2010). Journalism as the new knowledge profession and consequences for journalism education. *Journalism, 15,* 661–677.

Dorr, A. (1981). Television and affective development and functioning: Maybe this decade. *Journal of Broadcasting, 25,* 335–345.

Dorr, A. (1986). *Television and children: A special medium for a special audience.* Beverly Hills, CA: SAGE.

Dorr, A., Kovaric, P., & Doubleday, C. (1989). Parent-child coviewing of television. *Journal of Broadcasting & Electronic Media, 33,* 35–51.

Dow, B. J. (2001). Ellen, television, and the politics of gay and lesbian visibility. *Critical Studies in Media Communication, 18,* 123–132.

Doyle, G. (2002). *Understanding media economics.* London, England: SAGE.

Drapes, M. R., & Lichtenberg, N. R. (2008). *Vault guide to the top media & entertainment employers.* New York, NY: Vault.com, Inc.

Dunn, A. (1999, July 8). Most of Web beyond scope of search sites. *Los Angeles Times,* Home Section, p. 1.

Dunn, J. (2017, June 9). TV is still media's biggest platform – but the internet is quickly gaining ground. *Business Insider.* Retrieved from http://www.businessinsider.com/tv-vs-internet-media-consumption-average-chart-2017-6

Eichelberger, C. (2013, January 30). NFL sees modes revenue growth as sponsors stay shaky on economy.

Bloomberg. Retrieved from http://www.bloomberg.com/news/2013-01-30/nfl-sees-modest-revenue-growth-as-sponsors-stay-shaky-on-economy.html

Einstein, M. (2004). *Media diversity: Economics, ownership, and the FCC*. Mahwah, NJ: Lawrence Erlbaum.

Einstein, M. (2016). *Black ops advertising: Native ads, content marketing, and the covert world of the digital sell*. New York, NY: O/R Books.

Electronic Privacy Information Center (2012, September 5). Pew survey finds most mobile users avoid apps due to privacy concerns. Retrieved from http://epic.org/privacy/survey/

Electronic Privacy Information Center (2013). Public opinion on privacy. Retrieved from http://epic.org/privacy/survey/

Eller, C. (1999, July 9). Literary manager built career by not following script. *Los Angeles Times*, pp. C1, C5.

eMarketer. (2014 April). Time spent per day with major media in the United States from 2009 to 2014 (in minutes). *Statista—The Statistics Portal*. Retrieved from https://www.statista.com

eMarketer. (2017a, May 1). *US adults now spend 12 hours 7 minutes a day consuming media: US adults will spend more than half the day with major media*. Retrieved from https://www.emarketer.com/Article/US-Adults-Now-Spend-12-Hours-7-Minutes-Day-Consuming-Media/1015775

eMarketer. (2017b, October 9). *eMarketer updates US time spent with media figures*. Retrieved from https://www.emarketer.com/Article/eMarketer-Updates-US-Time-Spent-with-Media-Figures/1016587

Engel, P. (2017, March 27). These are the most and least trusted news outlets in America. *Business Insider*. Retrieved from http://www.businessinsider.com/most-and-least-trusted-news-outlets-in-america-2017-3

Entertainment Software Association. (2017). 2017 essential facts about the computer and video game industry. Retrieved from http://www.theesa.com/article/2017-essential-facts-computer-video-game-industry/

Entertainment Software Association. (2018, January 18). *US video game industry revenue reaches $36 billion in 2017*. Retrieved from http://www.theesa.com/article/us-video-game-industry-revenue-reaches-36-billion-2017

Environmental Protection Agency. (n.d.). National overview: Facts and figures on materials, waste and recycling. Retrieved from https://www.epa.gov/facts-and-figures-about-materials-waste-and-recycling/national-overview-facts-and-figures-materials

Eron, L. D., Huesmann, L. R., Lefkowitz, M. M., & Walder, L. O. (1972). Does television violence cause aggression? *American Psychologist*, *27*, 253–263.

Eubanks, N. (2017, July 13). The true cost of cybercrime for business. *Forbes*. Retrieved from https://www.forbes.com/sites/theyec/2017/07/13/the-true-cost-of-cybercrime-for-businesses/#61ea9c344947

Fabrikant, A. S. (1995, August 1). Disney to buy ABC for $19-billion. *Santa Barbara News-Press*, pp. A1, A2.

Fabrikant, G. (2004, September 23). CBS fined $550,000 for Super Bowl. *Santa Barbara News Press*, p. B1.

Facebook. (n.d.). Retrieved from http://en.wikipedia.org/wiki/Facebook

FBI (2018, May 7). Latest internet crime report released. Retrieved from https://www.fbi.gov/news/stories/2017-internet-crime-report-released-050718

FCC finds no indecency in the airing of "Private Ryan." (2005, March 1). *Los Angeles Times*, p. E12.

Federal Communications Commission (FCC). (2003, June 2). *Media ownership policy reexamination*. Retrieved from http://www.fcc.gov/ownership

Federal Trade Commission (n.d.). Truth in advertising. Retrieved from https://www.ftc.gov/news-events/media-resources/truth-advertising

Ferguson, D. A. (1992). Channel repertoire in the presence of remote control devices, VCRs, and cable television. *Journal of Broadcasting & Electronic Media*, *36*, 83–91.

Fernandez-Collado, C., Greenberg, B., Korzenny, F., & Atkin, C. (1978). Sexual intimacy and drug use in TV series. *Journal of Communication*, *28*, 30–37.

Fico, F., & Soffin, S. (1995). Fairness and balance of selected newspaper coverage of controversial national, state, and local issues. *Journalism & Mass Communication Quarterly*, *72*, 621–633.

Fisch, S. M. (2000). A capacity model of children's comprehension of educational content on television. *Media Psychology, 2*, 63–91.

Fisher, D. A., Hill, D. L., Grube, J. W., Gruber, E. L. (2007). Gay, lesbian, and bisexual content on television: A quantitative analysis across two seasons. *Journal of Homosexuality, 52*, 167–188.

Fishman, J. M., & Marvin, C. (2003). Portrayals of violence and group difference in newspaper photographs: Nationalism and media. *Journal of Communication, 53*, 32–44.

Fishoff, S. (1988, August). *Psychological research and a black hole called Hollywood*. Paper presented at the annual meeting of the American Psychological Association, Atlanta, GA.

Flanigan, J. (2003, September 7). GE's broad vision may transform media. *Los Angeles Times*, pp. C1, C4.

Flint, J. (2009, August 29). Appeals court sides with Comcast in market-share battle with FCC. *Los Angeles Times*, p. B2.

Flint, J. (2010, November 9). PTC study shows almost 70% jump in bad language on broadcast TV. *Los Angeles Times Business Online*. Retrieved from http://latimesblogs.latimes.com/entertainmentnewsbuzz/2010/11/ptc-study-shows-almost-70-jump-in-bad-language-on-broadcast-tv.html

Flint, J. (2011, June 8). NBC secures the Olympics through 2020. *Los Angeles Times*, pp. D1, D16.

Foehr, U. G., Rideout, V., & Miller, C. (2000). Parents and the TV ratings system: A national study. In B. S. Greenberg, L. Rampoldi-Hnilo, & D. Mastro (Eds.), *The alphabet soup of television program ratings*. Cresskill, NJ: Hampton.

Forbes. (2018a, June 17). The world's highest paid celebrities. Retrieved from https://www.forbes.com/celebrities/list/#tab:overall

Forbes. (2018b, June 26). The world's highest-paid athletes. Retrieved from https://www.forbes.com/athletes/list/#tab:overall

Foreman, J. (2009, June 6). Drug labels, ads at center of battle. *Los Angeles Times*, pp. E1, E5.

Forgas, J. P., Brown, L. B., & Menyhart, J. (1980). Dimensions of aggression: The perception of aggressive episodes. *British Journal of Social and Clinical Psychology, 19*, 215–227.

Free Press. (2012). Who owns the media? Retrieved from http://www.freepress.net/ownership/chart

Friedman, T. (1995). Making sense of software: Computer games and interactive textuality. In S. G. Jones (Ed.) *CyberSociety: Computer-mediated communication and community* (pp. 73–89). Thousand Oaks, CA: SAGE.

Friedson, E. (1953). The relation of the social situation of contact to the media in mass communication. *Public Opinion Quarterly, 17*, 230–238.

Fritz, B. (2009, September 9). Friends in fantasy and reality. *Los Angeles Times*, pp. A1, A8.

Frosch, D. L. Krueger, P. M., Hornik, R. C., Cronholm, P. F., Barg, F. K. (2007). Creating demand for prescription drugs: A content analysis of television direct-to-consumer advertising. *Annals of Family Medicine, 5*, 6–13.

Gabrielli, J., Traore, A., Stoolmiller, M., Bergamini, E., & Sargent, J. D. (2016). Industry television ratings for violence, sex, and substance use. *Pediatrics, 138*, e20160487.

Gaines, C. (2016, October 14). The difference in how much money schools make off of college sports is jarring, and it is the biggest obstacle to paying athletes. *Business Insider*. Retrieved from http://www.businessinsider.com/ncaa-schools-college-sports-revenue-2016-10

Gaither, C. (2004a, May 23). Can spam be canned? *Los Angeles Times*, pp. C1, C4.

Gaither, C. (2004b, June 24). Insider arrested in spam scheme. *Los Angeles Times*, pp. C1, C9.

Galloway, S. (1993, July 27). U.S. rating system: Sex before violence. *Hollywood Reporter*.

Gans, H. J. (2003). *Democracy and the news*. New York, NY: Oxford University Press.

Gardiner, B. (2010, July). Sony's wins and losses. *Wired*, p. 18.

Gardner, R.W. (1968). *Personality development at preadolescence*. Seattle: University of Washington Press.

Garrett, R. K., & Stroud, N. J. (2014), Partisan paths to exposure diversity: Differences in pro- and counterattitudinal news consumption. *Journal of Communication, 64*, 680–701.

Geddes, B. (2014). *Advanced Google AdWorks* (3rd ed.). New York, NY: Wiley.

Gellene, D. (1996, September 24). Seagram plans more TV ads for whiskey. *Los Angeles Times*, p. D2.

Gerbner, G., Gross, L., Morgan, M., & Signorielli, N. (1980). The "mainstreaming" of America: Violence profile no. 11. *Journal of Communication*, *30*, 10–29.

Gibbs, Nancy. (2012, August 27). Your life is fully mobile. *Time*, pp. 32–39.

Giddings, S., & Kennedy, H. W. (2006). Digital games as new media. In J. Rutter & J. Bryce (Eds.), *Understanding digital games* (pp. 129–147). London, England: SAGE.

Gilligan, C. (1993). *In a different voice*. Cambridge, MA: Harvard University Press.

Glascock, J. (2001). Gender roles on prime-time network television: Demographics and behaviors. *Journal of Broadcasting & Electronic Media*, *45*, 656–669.

Gleick, J. (2011). *The information: A history, a theory, a flood*. New York, NY: Pantheon Books.

Goldberg, B. (2013). *Bias: A CBS insider exposes how the media distort the news*. Washington, DC: Regnery Publishing

Goldberg, L. (2018, May 12). Here are all the broadcast TV shows that were canceled this season (and why). *Hollywood Reporter*. Retrieved from https://www.hollywoodreporter.com/live-feed/broadcast-canceled-shows-2018-definitive-guide-1107043

Goldstein, D. (1999, September 25). Biggest-grossing movies gross in other ways. *Tallahassee Democrat*, p. B1.

Goleman, D. (1995). *Emotional intelligence*. New York, NY: Bantam.

Good news is no news. (2011, June 4). *The Economist*, p. 36.

Goodman, M. (2015). *Future crimes: Everything is connected, everyone is vulnerable, and what we can do about it*. New York, NY: Doubleday.

Gramlich, J. (2016, November 16). Voters' perceptions of crime continue to conflict with reality. *Pew Research Center*. Retrieved from http://www.pewresearch.org/fact-tank/2016/11/16/voters-perceptions-of-crime-continue-to-conflict-with-reality/

Gramlich, J. (2018a, January 30). 5 facts about crime in the U.S. *Pew Research Center*. Retrieved from http://www.pewresearch.org/fact-tank/2018/01/30/5-facts-about-crime-in-the-u-s/

Gramlich, J. (2018b, April 10). 5 facts about Americans and Facebook. *Pew Research Center*. Retrieved from http://www.pewresearch.org/fact-tank/2018/04/10/5-facts-about-americans-and-facebook/

Grant, K. B. (2013, March 3). Online reviewers won't tell you. *Wall Street Journal*, p. F3.

Greenberg, B. S., Edison, N., Korzenny, F., Fernandez-Collado, C., & Atkin, C. K. (1980). In B. S. Greenberg (Ed.), *Life on television: Content analysis of U.S. TV drama* (pp. 99–128). Norwood, NJ: Ablex.

Greenberg, B. S., Rampoldi-Hnilo, L., & Hofshire, L. (2000). Young people's responses to the age based ratings. In B. S. Greenberg, L. Rampoldi-Hnilo, & D. Mastro (Eds.), *The alphabet soup of television program ratings*. Cresskill, NJ: Hampton.

Greenberg, B. S., Stanley, C., Siemicki, M., Heeter, C., Soderman, A., & Linsangan, R. (1993). Sex content on soaps and prime-time television series most viewed by adolescents. In B. S. Greenberg, J. D. Brown, & N. Buerkel-Rothfuss (Eds.), *Media, sex and the adolescent* (pp. 29–44). Cresskill, NJ: Hampton.

Gregory. S. (2015, March 27). Meet America's first video game varsity athletes. *Time*. Retrieved from http://time.com

Greimel, H. (2000, February 5). Mannesmann agrees to buyout. *Tallahassee Democrat*, p. E1.

Grimm, M. (1996, June 10). Olympic grab bag. *Brandweek*, pp. 26–28, *30*, 32.

Gross, L. (2001). *Up from invisibility: Lesbians, gay men and the media in America*. New York, NY: Columbia University Press.

Gunter, B. (1985). *Dimensions of television violence*. Aldershot, England: Gower.

Gunter, B., Furnham, A., & Griffiths, S. (2000). Children's memory for news: A comparison of three presentation media. *Media Psychology*, *2*, 93–118.

Haberkorn, J. T. (2009). A poverty of information: Public health and the local television news

(Doctoral Dissertation, University of Delaware, 2009). *Dissertation Abstracts International: Section B: The Sciences and Engineering, 69*, 5346.

Hall, A. (2003). Reading realism: Audiences' evaluations of the reality of media texts. *Journal of Communication, 53*, 624–641.

Hamilton, J. T. (1998). *Channeling violence: The economic market for violent television programming*. Princeton, NJ: Princeton University Press.

Hampton, K. N., Livio, O., & Sessions Goulet, L. (2010). The social life of wireless urban spaces: Internet use, social networks, and the public realm. *Journal of Communication, 60*, 701–722.

Hancock, E. (1995, October 27). Culture cops take on sleazy TV talk shows. *Santa Barbara News-Press*, p. A1.

Harrington, C. L. (2003). Homosexuality on All My Children: Transforming the daytime landscape. *Journal of Broadcasting & Electronic Media, 47*, 216–235.

Harris, J. L. (2014). Demonstrating the harmful effects of food advertising on children and adolescents: Opportunities for research to inform policy. In A. B. Jordan & D. Romer (Eds.), *Media and the well-being of children and adolescents* (pp. 52–69). New York, NY: Oxford University Press.

Harrison, K. (2006). Scope of self: Toward a model of television's effects on self-complexity in adolescence. *Communication Theory, 16*, 251–279.

Harrison, V., & Pagliery, J. (2015, April 14). Nearly 1 million malware threats released every day. *CNN Tech*. Retrieved from http://money.cnn.com/2015/04/14/technology/security/cyber-attack-hacks-security/index.html

Hartman, T. (1999, March 22). Movie characters aren't reaping what they sow. *Tallahassee Democrat*, p. A1.

Haven, K. (2007). *Story proof: The science behind the startling power of story*. Westport, CT: Libraries Unlimited.

Havens, T., & Lotz, A. D. (2012). *Understanding media industries*. New York, NY: Oxford University Press.

Hawkins, R. P. (1977). The dimensional structure of children's perceptions of television reality. *Communication Research, 7*, 193–226.

Hayes, D. (2017, December 14). Disney-Fox deal: How it ranks among biggest all-time mergers.

Deadline Hollywood. Retrieved from https://deadline.com/2017/12/biggest-media-mergers-disney-fox-deal-list-1202226683/

Healey, J. (2003, October 25). Pair ordered to pay $2-million fine for spam. *Los Angeles Times*, pp. C1, C2.

Hetsroni, A. (2007). Three decades of sexual content on prime-time network programming: A longitudinal meta-analytic review. *Journal of Communication, 57*, 318–348.

Himes, S. M., & Thompson, J. K. (2007). Fat stigmatization in television shows and movies: A content analysis. *Obesity, 15*, 712–718

Himmelweit, H. (1966). Television and the child. In B. Berelson & M. Janowitz (Eds.), *Reader in public opinion and communication* (2nd ed., pp. 67–106). New York, NY: Free Press.

Himmelweit, H., Oppenheim, A., & Vince, P. (1958). *Television and the child*. Oxford, England: Oxford University Press.

Hobbs, R. (1998). The seven great debates in the media literacy movement. *Journal of Communication, 48*, 16–32.

Hoffner, C., & Cantor, J. (1991). Perceiving and responding to mass media characters. In J. Bryant & D. Zillmann (Eds.), *Responding to the screen* (pp. 63–101). Hillsdale, NJ: Lawrence Erlbaum.

Hofmeister, S. (1997a, February 19). $2.7-billion deal would create no. 2 radio group in U.S. *Los Angeles Times*, p. D1.

Hofmeister, S. (1997b, February 19). Seagram to buy USA Networks for $1.7-billion. *Los Angeles Times*, p. D1.

Hofmeister, S. (2005, September 8). Study ties indecency to consolidation of media. *Los Angeles Times*, pp. C1, C11.

Holcomb, J., Gottfried, J., & Mitchell, A. (2013, November 14). News use across social media platforms. *Pew Research Center*. Retrieved from http://www.journalism.org/2013/11/14/news-use-across-social-media-platforms/

Holland, J. (1998, January 15). Internal records show tobacco firm targeted teenagers. *Santa Barbara News-Press*, p. A2.

Hollenbeck, A., & Slaby, R. (1979). Infant visual and vocal responses to television. *Child Development, 50*, 41–45.

Holstein, W. J. (1999, September 20). MTV, meet 60 Minutes. *U.S. News & World Report*, pp. 44–46.

Huston, A., Wright, J. C., Rice, M. L., Kerkman, D., Seigle, J., & Bremer, M. (1983, June). *Family environment and television use by preschool children*. Paper presented at the Biennial Meeting of the Society for Research on Child Development, Detroit, MI. (ERIC Document Reproduction Service No. ED230293)

Identity Theft Resource Center. (2002). Facts and statistics. Retrieved from http://www.idtheftcenter.org/facts.shtml

IMDbPro. (2018, June 20). *Box office mojo*. Retrieved from http://www.boxofficemojo.com/alltime/world/

Internet Live Stats. (2018a, May 22). *Total number of websites*. Retrieved from http://www.internetlivestats.com/total-number-of-websites/

Internet Live Stats. (2018b, June 10). *Google search statistics*. Retrieved from http://www.internetlivestats.com/google-search-statistics/

Ito, M., Horst, H., Bittanti, M., Boyd, D., Stephenson, B. H., Lange, P. G., . . . Robinson, L. (2009). *Living and learning with new media: Summary of findings from the Digital Youth Project*. Cambridge, MA: MIT Press.

James, P. D. (2009). *Talking about detective fiction*. New York, NY: Alfred A. Knopf.

Jamieson, K. H., & Waldman, P. (2003). *The press effect: Politicians, journalists, and the stories that shape the political world*. New York, NY: Oxford University Press.

Jamison, L. (2018, June 10). The digital ruins of a forgotten future. *The Atlantic*. Retrieved from https://www.theatlantic.com/magazine/archive/2017/12/second-life-leslie-jamison/544149/

Jeffres, L. W. (1994). *Mass media processes* (2nd ed.). Prospect Heights, IL: Waveland.

Jenkins, H. (2006). *Convergence culture: Where old and new media collide*. New York, NY: New York University Press.

Jenkins, H., Ford, S., & Green, J. (2013). *Spreadable media: Creating value and meaning in a networked culture*. New York, NY: New York University Press.

Jensen, C. (1995). *Censored: The news that didn't make the news—and why*. New York, NY: Four Walls Eight Windows.

Jensen, C. (1997). *20 years of censored news*. New York, NY: Seven Stories Press.

Jensen, J., & Ross, C. (1996, July 15). Centennial Olympics open as $5 bil event of century. *Advertising Age, 67*(29), 1–2.

Jeong, S.-H., Cho, H., & Hwang, Y. (2012). Media literacy interventions: A meta-analytic review. *Journal of Communication, 62*, 454–472.

Jeong, S.-H., & Hwang, Y. (2012). Does multitasking increase or decrease persuasion? Effects of multitasking on comprehension and counterarguing. *Journal of Communication, 62*, 571–587.

Jerome, R., & Bane, V. (2004, May 3). Spam I am. *Money*, pp. 125–126.

Johnson, C. (2006a, Sept. 17). Cutting through advertising clutter. *CBS News*. Retrieved from https://www.cbsnews.com/news/cutting-through-advertising-clutter/

Johnson, S. (2006b). *Everything bad is good for you*. New York, NY: Riverhead Books.

Johnson, T. (2018, June 27). How the Disney-Fox deal got DDOJ's greenlight quicker than expected. *Variety*. Retrieved from https://variety.com/2018/politics/news/disney-fox-merger-justice-department-1202859900/

Jones, J. P. (2004). *Fables, fashions, and facts about advertising: A study of 28 enduring myths*. Thousand Oaks, CA: SAGE.

Jones, M. L. (2016). *Ctrl+Z: The right to be forgotten*. New York, NY: New York University Press.

Jordan, A. B. (2001). Public policy and private practice: Government regulations and parental control over children's television use in the home. In D. G. Singer & J. L. Singer (Eds.), *Handbook of children and the media* (pp. 651–662). Thousand Oaks, CA: SAGE.

Jordan, A. B., & Romer, D. (Eds.). (2014). *Media and the well-being of children and adolescents*. New York, NY: Oxford University Press.

Jordan, R. H., Jr. (2017). *Murder in the news*. Amherst, NY: Prometheus Books.

Kagan, J., Rosman, D., Day, D., Albert, J., & Phillips, W. (1964). Information processing in the child: Significance of analytic and reflective attitudes. *Psychological Monographs*, *78*, 1–37.

Kaiser Family Foundation. (1999). *Parents and the V-chip*. Menlo Park, CA: Author.

Kaiser Family Foundation. (2003). *Sex on TV 3*. Menlo Park, CA: Author.

Kaiser Family Foundation (2010). Daily media use among children and teens up dramatically from five years ago. Retrieved from https://www.kff.org/disparities-policy/press-release/daily-media-use-among-children-and-teens-up-dramatically-from-five-years-ago/

Kaniss, P. (1996, December 19). Bad news: How electronic media muddle the message. *Philadelphia Inquirer*, p. A35.

Kanter, M., Afifi, T., & Robbins, S. (2012). The impact of parents "friending" their young adult child on Facebook on perceptions of parental privacy invasions and parent–child relationship quality. *Journal of Communication*, *62*, 900–917.

Kantrowitz, B. (2006, October 30). Brush with perfection. *Newsweek*, p. 54.

Kaplan, M. A. (2010). *Friendship fictions: The rhetoric of citizenship in the liberal imaginary*. Tuscaloosa: University of Alabama Press.

Kaye, B. K., & Sapolsky, B. S. (2001). Offensive language in prime time television: Before and after content ratings. *Journal of Broadcasting & Electronic Media*, *45*, 303–319.

Kennedy, H. (2012). Perspectives on sentiment analysis. *Journal of Broadcasting & Electronic Media*, *56*, 435–450.

Kepplinger, H. M., Geiss, S., & Siebert, S. (2012). Framing scandals: Cognitive and emotional media effects. *Journal of Communication*, *62*, 659–681.

Kerr, A. (2006). *The business and culture of digital games: Gamework/gameplay*. London, England: SAGE.

King, C. M. (2000). Effects of humorous heroes and villains in violent action films. *Journal of Communication*, *50*, 5–25.

King, P. M. (1986). Formal reasoning in adults: A review and critique. In R. A. Milnes & K. S. Kitchenor (Eds.), *Adult cognitive development: Methods and models* (pp. 1–21). New York, NY: Praeger.

Kinkema, K. M., & Harris, J. C. (1998). MediaSport studies: Key research and emerging issues. In L. A. Wenner (Ed.), *MediaSport* (pp. 27–54). New York, NY: Routledge.

Knobloch-Westerwick, S., & Meng, J. (2009). Looking the other way: Selective exposure to attitude-consistent and counterattitudinal political information. *Communication Research*, *36*, 426–448.

Koenenn, C. (1997, May 14). Let's get simple. *Los Angeles Times*, p. E1.

Kohlberg, L. (1966). Moral education in the schools: A developmental view. *School Review*, *74*, 1–30.

Kohlberg, L. (1981). *The philosophy of moral development: Moral stages and the idea of justice*. New York, NY: Harper & Row.

Koziol, R. (1989, August). *English language arts teachers' views on mass media consumption education in Maryland high schools*. Paper presented at the annual conference of the Association of Education in Journalism and Mass Communication, Washington, DC.

Kress, G. (1992). Media literacy as cultural technology in the age of transcultural media. In C. Bazalgette, E. Bevort, & J. Savino (Eds.), *New directions: Media education worldwide* (pp. 190–202). London, England: British Film Institute.

Kubey, R. (1990). Television and family harmony among children, adolescents, and adults: Results from the experience of sampling method. In J. Bryant (Ed.), *Television and the American family* (pp. 73–88). Hillsdale, NJ: Lawrence Erlbaum.

Kubey, R. (1997). A rationale for media education. In R. Kubey (Ed.), *Media literacy in the information age* (pp. 15–68). New Brunswick, NJ: Transaction Publishers.

Kubey, R. (1998). Obstacles to the development of media education in the United States. *Journal of Communication*, *48*, 58–69.

Kunkel, D., Eyal, K., & Donnerstein, E. (2007). Sexual socialization messages on entertainment television: Comparing content trends 1997–2002. *Media Psychology*, *9*, 595–622.

Kunkel, D., & Wilcox, B. (2001). Children and media policy. In D. G. Singer & J. L. Singer (Eds.), *Handbook of children and the media* (pp. 589–620). Thousand Oaks, CA: SAGE.

Kurtz, H. (2018). *Media madness: Donald Trump, the press, and the war over the truth.* Washington, DC: Regnery Publishing.

Lacayo, R. (1995, June 12). Are music and movies killing America's soul? *Time*, pp. 24–30.

Lacy, S., & Riffe, D. (1994). The impact of competition and group ownership on radio news. *Journalism & Mass Communication Quarterly*, 71, 583–593.

Lang, A., Potter, R. F., & Bolls, P. D. (1999). Something for nothing: Is visual encoding automatic? *Media Psychology*, 1, 145–163.

Lang, B. & Lieberman, D. (2018, May 8). Do media chiefs deserve the lavish pay packages they rake in? *Variety*. Retrieved from https://variety.com/2018/biz/news/media-ceo-salaries-compensation-1202801551/

Law, C., & Labre, M. P. (2002). Cultural standards of attractiveness: A thirty-year look at changes in male images in magazines. *Journalism & Mass Communication Quarterly*, 79, 697–711.

Lawrence, F., & Wozniak, P. (1989). Children's television viewing with family members. *Psychological Reports*, 65, 395–400.

Lawrence, S. (2004, September 24). Governor signs bills on vaccine, "spyware". *Los Angeles Times*, p. A6.

Lee, J. K., Choi, J., Kim, C., & Kim, Y. (2014). Social media, network heterogeneity, and opinion polarization. *Journal of Communication*, 64, 702–722.

Lee, K., & Light, J. (2003). Law and regulation, part I: Individual interests. In L. Shyles (Ed.), *Deciphering cyberspace: Making the most of digital communication technology* (pp. 293–322). Thousand Oaks, CA: SAGE.

Lee, M., & Solomon, N. (1990). *Unreliable sources: A guide to detecting bias in news media.* New York, NY: Carol.

Leo, J. (1999, September 27). And now . . . smut-see TV. *U.S. News & World Report*, p. 15.

Levy, S. (2006, September 11). Will you let them store your dreams? *Newsweek*, p. 12.

Lewis, E. (2018, March 5). NFL salary cap for 2018 season set at $177.2 million. Retrieved from http://www.nfl.com/news/story/0ap3000000919680/article/nfl-salary-cap-for-2018-season-set-at-1772-million

Lewis, R. J., Tamborini, R., & Weber, R. (2014). Testing a dual-process model of media enjoyment and appreciation. *Journal of Communication*, 64, 397–416.

Lichter, L. S., & Lichter, S. R. (1983). *Prime time crime.* Washington, DC: The Media Institute.

Lih, A. (2009). *The Wikipedia revolution: How a bunch of nobodies created the world's greatest encyclopedia.* New York, NY: Hyperion.

Lim, S. S., Vadrevu, S., Chan, Y. H., & Basnyat, I. (2012). Facework on Facebook: The online publicness of juvenile delinquents and youths-at-risk. *Journal of Broadcasting & Electronic Media*, 56, 346–361.

Lindstrom, M. (2016). *Small data: The tiny clues that uncover huge trends.* New York, NY: St. Martin's Press.

Linthicum, K. (2009, June 5). Wikipedia limits Scientology access: The encyclopedia site shuts out computers from the church's Los Angeles headquarters. *Los Angeles Times*, p. B2.

Lippmann, W. (1922). *Public opinion.* New York, NY: Harcourt, Brace.

Livingstone, S. (2014). Risk and harm on the internet. In A. B. Jordan & D. Romer (Eds.), *Media and the well-being of children and adolescents* (pp. 129–146). New York, NY: Oxford University Press.

Lohrmann, D. (2017, February 22). *The dramatic rise of hacktivism.* Retrieved from https://techcrunch.com/2017/02/22/the-dramatic-rise-in-hacktivism/

Loobrok, R. (2017, May 26). *Hacking scandals: The biggest, baddest, and scariest.* Retrieved from https://www.orangewebsite.com/articles/biggest-hacking-scandals-of-all-times/

Lorimer, R. (1994). *Mass communications: A comparative introduction.* Manchester, England: Manchester University Press.

Lowry, B. (1997, September 21). TV on decline but few back U.S. regulation. *Los Angeles Times*, pp. A1, A40, A41.

Lowry, D. T., Nio, R. C. J., & Leitner, D. W. (2003). Setting the public fear agenda: A longitudinal analysis of network TV crime reporting, public perceptions of crime, and FBI crime statistics. *Journal of Communication*, *53*, 61–73.

Luhby, T. (2017, September 12). Middle class income tops $59,000. *CNN Money*. Retrieved from http://money.cnn.com/2017/09/12/news/economy/median-income-census/index.html

Lyall, S. (1996, November 27). Penguin's deal to buy Putnam will create major publishing force. *Santa Barbara News-Press*, p. A6.

MacKinnon, R. (2012). *Consent of the networked: The worldwide struggle for Internet freedom*. New York, NY: Basic Books.

Malamuth, N. M., & Check, J. V. P. (1980). Penile tumescence and perceptual responses to rape as a function of victim's perceived reactions. *Journal of Applied Social Psychology*, *10*, 528–547.

Malito, A. (2017, June 17). Grocery stores carry 40,000 more items than they did in the 1990s. *MarketWatch*. Retrieved from https://www.marketwatch.com/story/grocery-stores-carry-40000-more-items-than-they-did-in-the-1990s-2017-06-07

Maney, K. (1995). *Megamedia shakeout: The inside story of the leaders and the losers in the exploding communications industry*. New York, NY: John Wiley.

Manning, R. (1987, December 28). The selling of the Olympics. *Newsweek*, pp. 40–41.

Mares, M-L., Braun, M. T., & Hernandez, P. (2012). Pessimism and anxiety: Effects of tween sitcoms on expectations and feelings about peer relationships in school. *Media Psychology 15*, 121–147.

Market Mogul Team. (2018, April 3). *Amazon's annual revenue over the years*. Retrieved from https://themarketmogul.com/amazon-annual-revenue/

MarketWatch.com. (2018, June 10). *eBay, Inc.* Retrieved from https://www.marketwatch.com/investing/stock/ebay/financials

Marr, B. (2017, March 14). The complete beginner's guide to big data in 2017. *Forbes*. Retrieved from https://www.forbes.com/sites/bernardmarr/2017/03/14/the-complete-beginners-guide-to-big-data-in-2017/#4bb7fdc27365

Martins, N., & Wilson, B. J. (2012). Mean on the screen: Social aggression in programs popular with children. *Journal of Communication*, *62*, 991–1009.

Marwick, A., & Ellison, N. B. (2012). There isn't Wifi in heaven! Negotiating visibility on Facebook memorial pages. *Journal of Broadcasting & Electronic Media*, *56*, 378–400.

Mastro, D. E., & Greenberg, B. S. (2000). The portrayal of racial minorities on prime-time television. *Journal of Broadcasting & Electronic Media*, *44*, 690–703.

Mastro, D. E., & Stern, S. R. (2003). Representations of race in television commercials: A content analysis of prime-time advertising. *Journal of Broadcasting & Electronic Media*, *47*, 638–647.

Matsa, K. E. (2017a, June 16). Network news fact sheet. *Pew Research Center*. Retrieved from http://www.journalism.org/fact-sheet/network-news/

Matsa, K. E. (2017b, July 13). Local TV news fact sheet. *Pew Research Center*. Retrieved from http://www.journalism.org/fact-sheet/local-tv-news/

Maverick, J. B. (2018, June 12). The top 5 Disney individual shareholders. *Investopedia*. Retrieved from https://www.investopedia.com/articles/markets/102715/top-5-disney-shareholders.asp

McAfee. (2018, February). *Economic impact of cybercrime—No slowing down*. Retrieved from https://www.mcafee.com/us/resources/reports/restricted/economic-impact-cybercrime.pdf

McCaffrey, P. (Ed.). (2010). Editor's introduction. In P. McCaffrey (Ed.), *The news and its future* (pp. 3–5). New York, NY: H. W. Wilson.

McCombs, M., & Reynolds, A. (2009). How the news shapes our civic agenda. In J. Bryant & M. B. Oliver (Eds.), *Media effects: Advances in theory and research* (3rd ed., pp. 1–16). New York, NY: Taylor & Francis.

McCombs, M. E., & Shaw, D. (1972). The agenda setting function of the mass media. *Public Opinion Quarterly*, *36*, 176–187.

McDonald, M. (2000, March 27). L.A. is their kind of town. *U.S. News & World Report*, p. 45.

McGrew, S., Ortega, R., Breakstone, J., & Wineburg, S. (2017). The challenge that's bigger than fake news: Civic reasoning in a social media environment. *American Educator*, *41*, 4–39.

Meadowcroft, J., & Reeves, B. (1989). Influence of story schema development on children's attention to television. *Communication Research*, *16*, 353–374.

Mediacollege.com (n.d.). What makes a story newsworthy? Retrieved from https://www.mediacollege .com/journalism/news/newsworthy.html

Mediakix. (2017, September 14). *How the Internet became home to hundreds of millions of blogs in less than 25 years*. Retrieved from https://mediakix.com/2017/09/how-many-blogs-are-there-in-the-world/

Medich, R. (2002, October 18). Flashes. *Entertainment*, p. 16.

Medrich, E. A., Roizen, J. A., Rubin, V., & Buckley, S. (1982). *The serious business of growing up: A study of children's lives outside school*. Berkeley: University of California Press.

Menn, J. (2007, April 17). Google plan raises privacy issue. *Los Angeles Times*, p. C1.

Messaris, P. (1994). *Visual "literacy": Image, mind, and reality*. Boulder, CO: Westview.

Metallinos, N. (1996). *Television aesthetics: Perceptual, cognitive, and compositional bases*. Mahwah, NJ: Lawrence Erlbaum.

Metropolitan Sports Facilities Commission. (n.d.). Next generation of sports facilities. Retrieved from http://www.msfc.com/nextgen.cfm

Mifflin, L. (1997, February 22). Parents give TV ratings mixed reviews. *New York Times*, p. A6.

Milligan, M. (2018, March 28). Gaming gores mainstream for bother playing and watching. *Limelight*. Retrieved from https://www.limelight.com/blog/state-of-online-gaming-2018/

Mnookin, S. (2002, August 19). The tobacco sham. *Newsweek*, p. 33.

Mobile Commerce. (2014, December 14). *Boosted by mobile, global ad revenue to hit $545 billion in 2015*. Retrieved from http://mcommerce.name/mobile-advertising/boosted-by-mobile-global-ad-revenue-to-hit-545-billion-in-2015-study-2/

Mohr, P. J. (1979). Parental influence of children's viewing of evening television programs. *Journal of Broadcasting*, *23*, 213–228.

Money? There's an app for that. (2011, May 28). *The Economist*, p. 79.

Money Morning (2013, Dec. 20). What is the impact of Bitcoin on the U.S. dollar? Retrieved from http://moneymorning.com/2013/12/20/impact-bitcoin-u-s-dollar/

Moon, S. J., & Hadley, P. (2014). Routinizing a new technology in the newsroom: Twitter as a news source in mainstream media. *Journal of Broadcasting & Electronic Media*, *58*, 289–305.

Morrissey, B. (2013, March 21). *15 alarming stats about banner ads*. Retrieved from http://digiday.com/publishers/15-alarming-stats-about-banner-ads/

Nathanson, A. I. (2001a). Mediation of children's television viewing: Working toward conceptual clarity and common understanding. In W. B. Gudykunst (Ed.), *Communication yearbook 25* (pp. 115–151). Mahwah, NJ: Lawrence Erlbaum.

Nathanson, A. I. (2001b). Parent and child perspectives on the presence and meaning of parental television mediation. *Journal of Broadcasting & Electronic Media*, *45*, 201–220.

Nathanson, A. I. (2002). The unintended effects of parental mediation of television on adolescents. *Media Psychology*, *4*, 207–230.

Nathanson, A. I., Eveland, W. P., Park, H.-S., & Paul, B. (2002). Perceived media influence and efficacy as predictors of caregivers' protective behaviors. *Journal of Broadcasting & Electronic Media*, *46*, 385–410.

National Center for Education Statistics (2012). Program for International Student Assessment. Retrieved from http://nces.ed.gov/surveys/pisa/index.asp

National Television Violence Study (NTVS). (1996). *Scientific report*. Thousand Oaks, CA: SAGE.

NBCUniversal. (n.d.). Retrieved from http://en.wikipedia .org/wiki/NBC_Universal

NCTV says violence on TV up 16%. (1983, March 22). *Broadcasting Magazine*, p. 63.

Nead, N. (2018, June 18). *Media and entertainment industry overview*. Retrieved from https://investmentbank .com/media-and-entertainment-industry-overview/

Nelson, J. (1995, August 8). NBC gets Olympic TV rights in coup. *Santa Barbara News-Press*, p. A12.

Neuman, W. R. (1991). *The future of the mass audience.* New York, NY: Cambridge University Press.

Neuman, W. R. (Ed.). (2010). *Media, technology, and society: Theories of media evolution.* Ann Arbor: The University of Michigan Press.

News Corporation. (n.d.). Retrieved from http://en.wikipedia.org/wiki/News_Corporation

NFL teams dodge salary cap. (1996, January 2). *Santa Barbara News-Press*, p. B5.

Notte, J. (2017, August 15). 10 of the most expensive NFL stadiums your precious tax dollars paid for. *TheStreet.* Retrieved from https://www.thestreet.com/slideshow/14272534/1/these-are-the-10-most-expensive-nfl-stadiums-your-precious-tax-dollars-paid-for.html

NumberOf.net (2015). Number of users on Twitter. Retrieved from http://www.numberof.net/number-of-users-on-twitter/

Olivarez-Giles, N. (2011, June 14). Facebook's growth is slowing, study says. *Los Angeles Times*, p. B3.

Oliver, M. B. (1994). Portrayals of crime, race, and aggression in "reality based" police shows: A content analysis. *Journal of Broadcasting & Electronic Media, 38*, 179–192.

Online reputations in the dirt. (2011, April 30). *The Economist*, p. 65.

Opree, S. J., Buijzen, M., van Reijmersdal, E. A., & Valkenburg, P. M. (2014). Children's advertising exposure, advertised product desire, and materialism: A longitudinal study. *Communication Research, 41*, 717–735.

Oremus, W. (2018, April 5). How Mark Zuckerberg protects his own privacy online and what that tells us about how he treats ours. *Slate.* Retrieved from https://slate.com/technology/2018/04/how-mark-zuckerberg-protects-his-own-privacy-online.html

Ornebring, H. (2010). Technology and journalism-as-labour: Historical perspectives. *Journalism, 11*, 57–74.

Ozanian, M. (2016, January 13). The bottom line on Rams move to LA. *Forbes.* Retrieved from https://www.forbes.com/sites/mikeozanian/2016/01/13/the-bottom-line-on-rams-move-to-la/#e1b70dd26fdf

Ozanich, G. W., & Wirth, M. O. (1993). Media mergers and acquisitions: An overview. In A. Alexander, J. Owers, & R. Carveth (Eds.), *Media economics: Theory and practice* (pp. 115–133). Hillsdale, NJ: Lawrence Erlbaum.

Page, R., & Brewster, A. (2007). Frequency of promotional strategies and attention elements in children's food commercials during children's programming blocks on US broadcast networks. *Young Consumers, 8*, 184–196.

Parenti, M. (1986). *Inventing reality: The politics of the mass media.* New York, NY: St. Martin's.

Pariser, E. (2011). *The filter bubble: What the Internet is hiding from you.* New York, NY: Penguin Press.

Pashler, H. E. (1998). *The psychology of attention.* Cambridge, MA: MIT Press.

Passy, C. (2014, August 17). Reality TV won't tell you. *The Wall Street Journal Sunday*, F3.

Patterson, T. (1980). *The mass media election.* New York, NY: Praeger.

Penner, M. (2004, May 7). Baseball cancels plans for movie ad on bases. *Los Angeles Times*, pp. D1, D8.

Perrin, A., & Jiang, J. (2018, March 14). About a quarter of U.S. adults say they are "almost constantly" online. *Pew Research Center.* Retrieved from http://www.pewresearch.org/fact-tank/2018/03/14/about-a-quarter-of-americans-report-going-online-almost-constantly/

Pettegree, A. (2014). *The invention of news: How the world came to know about itself.* New Haven, CT: Yale University Press.

Petty, R. E., & Cacioppo, J. T. (1986). *Communication and persuasion: Central and peripheral routes to attitude change.* New York, NY: Springer-Verlag.

Pew Internet & American Life Project. (2000, August 20).*Trust and privacy online: Why Americans want to rewrite the rules.* Retrieved from http://www.pewinternet.org/2000/08/20/trust-and-privacy-online/

Pew Research Center. (2012, September 27). *In changing news landscape, even television is vulnerable: Trends in news consumption 1991-2012.* Retrieved from http://www.people-press.org/2012/09/27/in-changing-news-landscape-even-television-is-vulnerable/

Pew Research Center (2014, March 26). Key indicators in media & news. *Retrieved on* January 31, 2015 from http://www.journalism.org/2014/03/26/state-of-the-news-media-2014-key-indicators-in-media-and-news/

Piaget, J. J. (2012). *Language and thought of the child.* New York, NY: Routledge.

Picard, R. G., Winter, J. P., McCombs, M., & Lacy, S. (Eds.). (1988). *Press concentration and monopoly: New perspectives on newspaper ownership and operation.* Norwood, NJ: Ablex.

Piette, J., & Giroux, L. (1997).The theoretical foundations of media education programs. In R. Kubey (Ed.), *Media literacy in the information age: Current perspectives, information and behavior* (Vol. 6, pp. 89–134). New Brunswick, NJ: Transaction Publishers.

Pingdom. (2017, May 10). *Report: Social network demographics in 2017.* Retrieved from https://royal.pingdom.com/2017/05/10/social-media-in-2017/

Piotrowski, J. T. (2014). The relationship between narrative processing demands and young American children's comprehension of educational television. *Journal of Children and Media, 8*, 267–285.

Pipher, M. (1996). *The shelter of each other.* New York, NY: Putnam.

Plack, C. J. (2005). Auditory perception. In K. Lamberts & R. L. Goldstrone (Eds.), *Handbook of cognition* (pp. 71–104). London, England: SAGE.

Plunkett Research, Ltd. (2017). Sports industry statistic and market size overview, business and industry statistics. Retrieved from https://www.plunkettresearch.com/statistics/Industry-Statistics-Sports-Industry-Statistic-and-Market-Size-Overview/

Plunkett Research, Ltd. (2018, June 27). *Sports & recreation business statistics analysis, business and industry statistics.* Retrieved from https://www.plunkettresearch.com/statistics/sports-industry/

Polman, D. (2003, June 1). FCC vote may prove a windfall for media giants. *Santa Barbara News-Press*, pp. B1, B2.

Poniewozik, J. (2012, September 24). Check please: Fact-checking has been good newsin 2012, but it's only a start. *Time*, p. 68.

Potter, R. F. (2002). Give the people what they want: A content analysis of FM radio station home pages. *Journal of Broadcasting & Electronic Media, 46*, 369–385.

Potter, W. J. (1986). Perceived reality in the cultivation hypothesis. *Journal of Broadcasting & Electronic Media, 30*, 159–174.

Potter, W. J. (1987a). Does television viewing hinder academic achievement among adolescents? *Human Communication Research, 14*, 27–46.

Potter, W. J. (1999). *On media violence.* Thousand Oaks, CA: SAGE.

Potter, W. J. (2003). *The 11 myths of media violence.* Thousand Oaks, CA: SAGE.

Potter, W. J. (2018). *The skills of media literacy.* Santa Barbara, CA: Knowledge Assets.

Potter, W. J., & Byrne, S. (2009). Media literacy. In R. Nabi & M. B. Oliver (Eds.). *Handbook of media effects* (pp. 345–357). Thousand Oaks, CA: SAGE.

Potter, W. J., Pashupati, K., Pekurny, R. G., Hoffman, E., & Davis, K. (2002). Perceptions of television: A schema approach. *Media Psychology, 4*, 27–50.

Potter, W. J., & Riddle K. (2007). A content analysis of the media effects literature. *Journalism & Mass of Communication Quarterly, 84*, 90–104.

Potter, W. J., & Smith, S. (2000). The context of graphic portrayals of television violence. *Journal of Broadcasting & Electronic Media, 44*, 301.

Potter, W. J., & Vaughan, M. (1997). Aggression in television entertainment: Profiles and trends. *Communication Research Reports, 14*, 116–124.

Potter, W. J., & Ware, W. (1987). An analysis of the contexts of antisocial acts on prime-time television. *Communication Research, 14*, 664–686.

Pritchard, D. A. (1975). Leveling-sharpening revised. *Perceptual and Motor Skills, 40*, 111–117.

Privacy Rights Clearinghouse. (2018, July 1). *Data breaches.* Retrieved from https://www.privacyrights.org/data-breaches

Prot, S., Anderson, C. A., Gentile, D. A., Brown, S. C., & Swing, E. L. (2014). The positive and negative effects of video game play. In A. B. Jordan & D. Romer (Eds.),

Media and the well-being of children and adolescents (pp. 109–128). New York, NY: Oxford University Press.

Pugmire, L. (2011, July 1). Labor woes shut NBA down. *Los Angeles Times*, pp. C1, C8.

Pulaski, M. A. S. (1980). *Understanding Piaget: An introduction to children's cognitive development* (Rev. and exp. ed.). New York, NY: Harper & Row.

Pulcinella, S. (2017, August 30). Why direct mail marketing is far from dead. *Forbes*. Retrieved from https://www.forbes.com/sites/forbescommunicationscouncil/2017/08/30/why-direct-mail-marketing-is-far-from-dead/#5e3ea97b311d

Purcell, K., & Rainie, L. (2014, December 8). Americans feel better informed thanks to the internet. *Pew Research Center*. Retrieved from http://www.pewinternet.org/2014/12/08/better-informed/

Rainey, J. (2007, March 12). Media's focus narrowing, report warns. *Los Angeles Times*, p. A8.

Rainie, L. (2018, March 27). Americans' complicated feelings about social media in an era of privacy concerns. *Pew Research Center*. Retrieved from http://www.pewresearch.org/fact-tank/2018/03/27/americans-complicated-feelings-about-social-media-in-an-era-of-privacy-concerns/

Rainie, L., & Perrin, A. (2017, June 28). 10 facts about smartphones as the iPhone turns 10. *Fact-tank*. Retrieved from http://www.pewresearch.org/fact-tank/2017/06/28/10-facts-about-smartphones/

Rampoldi-Hnilo, L., & Greenberg, B. S. (2000). A poll of Latina and Caucasian mothers with 6–10 year old children. In B. S. Greenberg, L. Rampoldi-Hnilo, & D. Mastro (Eds.), *The alphabet soup of television program ratings*. Cresskill, NJ: Hampton.

Ranson. J. M. (2017, Oct. 30). How many copies does the average book sell? *Quora*. Retrieved 6/14/2018 from https://www.quora.com/How-many-copies-does-the-average-book-sell

Real, M. R. (1998). MediaSport: Technology and the commodification of postmodern sport. In L. A. Wenner (Ed.), *MediaSport* (pp. 14–26). New York, NY: Routledge.

Reingold, J., & Wahba, P. (2014, September 22). Where have all the shoppers gone? *Fortune*, pp. 81–84.

Reinken, T. (2003, August 19). Dome and other homes. *Los Angeles Times*, p. A10.

Revers, M. (2014). The twitterization of news making: Transparency and journalistic professionalism. *Journal of Communication*, *64*, 806–826.

Rhodes, S., & Reibstein, L. (1996, July 1). Let him walk! *Newsweek*, pp. 44–45.

Rideout, V. J., Foehr, U. G., Roberts, D. F., & Brodie, M. (1999). *Kids & media @ the new millennium*. Menlo Park, CA: Kaiser Foundation.

Rigby, S. (2014, June 4). Movie streaming and downloads to overtake box office in 2017. *Digital Spy*. Retrieved from http://www.digitalspy.com/movies/news/a575450/movie-streaming-and-downloads-to-overtake-box-office-in-2017/

Roberts, M., & Pettigrew, S. (2007). A thematic content analysis of children's food advertising. *International Journal of Advertising*, *26*, 357–367

Robertson, L. (2001, March). Ethically challenged. *American Journalism Review*, pp. 20–29.

Rocheleau, M. (2017, March 7). Chart: The percentage of women and men in each profession. *Boston Globe*. Retrieved from https://www.bostonglobe.com/metro/2017/03/06/chart-the-percentage-women-and-men-each-profession/GBX22YsWl0XaeHghwXfE4H/story.html

Rodriguez, S., & Pierson, D. (2011, June 2). China hackers accessed accounts, Google says. *Los Angeles Times*, pp. AA1, AA4.

Rogers, C. (2016, December 6). Just 19% of people in ads are from minority groups, new research finds. *Marketing Week*. Retrieved from https://www.marketingweek.com/2016/12/06/lloyds-diversity-report/

Romer, D., Jamieson, K. H., & Aday, S. (2003). Television news and the cultivation of fear of crime. *Journal of Communication*, *53*, 88–104.

The Roper Organization. (1981). *Sex, profanity and violence: An opinion survey about seventeen television programs*. New York, NY: Information Office.

Rozendaal, E., Lapierre, M. A., van Reijmersdal, E. A., & Buijzen, M. (2011). Reconsidering advertising literacy as a defense against advertising effects. *Media Psychology*, *14*, 333–354.

Rubenking, B., & Lang, A. (2014). Captivated and grossed out: An examination of processing core and sociomoral disgusts in entertainment media. *Journal of Communication, 64,* 543–565.

Rubin, A. M., Perse, E. M., & Taylor, D. S. (1988). A methodological examination of cultivation. *Communication Research, 15,* 107–133.

Salon, O. (2018, Feb. 5). Former Facebook and Google workers launch campaign to fight tech addiction. *The Guardian.* Retrieved from https://www.theguardian .com/technology/2018/feb/05/tech-addiction-former -facebook-google-employees-campaign

Samuelson, R. J. (2006, October 30). The next capitalism. *Newsweek,* p. 45.

Sandomir, R. (2012, August 13). NBC improves on Olympic ratings. *New York Times.* Retrieved from http:// www.nytimes.com/2012/08/14/sports/olympics/nbc -improves-on-olympic-ratings.html?_r=0

Sang, F., Schmitz, B., & Tasche, K. (1992). Individuation and television coviewing in the family: Development trends in the viewing behavior of adolescents. *Journal of Broadcasting & Electronic Media, 36,* 427–441.

Sapolsky, B. S., Molitor, F., & Luque, S. (2003). Sex and violence in slasher films: Re-examining the assumptions. *Journalism & Mass Communication Quarterly, 80,* 28–38.

Sapolsky, B. S., & Tabarlet, J. (1990). *Sex in prime time television: 1979 vs. 1989.* Unpublished manuscript, Department of Communication, Florida State University, Tallahassee.

Saporito, B. (2012, November 5). What's in a name? *Time,* pp. 54–55.

Sarno, D. (2009a, February 17). For Facebook, privacy issues remain a factor. *Los Angeles Times,* p. C3.

Sarno, D. (2009b, August 16). It's getting hard to hide in cyberspace. *Los Angeles Times,* pp. B1, B4.

Sarno, D. (2011, July 17). How to safeguard your PC from hackers. *Los Angeles Times,* pp. B1, B7.

Satariano, A. (2018, May 24). G.D.P.R., a new privacy law, makes Europe world's leading tech watchdog. *New York Times.* Retrieved from https://www.nytimes .com/2018/05/24/technology/europe-gdpr-privacy.html

Satter, R. (2013, March 28). Record-breaking cyberattack hits anti-spam group. *Santa Barbara News-Press,* pp. B1, B2.

Saxon, J. (2018, June 1). *Why your customers' attention is the scarcest resource* in 2017. Retrieved from https://www .ama.org/partners/content/Pages/why-customers -attention-scarcest-resources-2017.aspx

Sayre, S., & King, C. (2003). *Entertainment & society: Audiences, trends, and impacts.* Thousand Oaks, CA: SAGE.

Schmierbach, M., Xu, Q., Oeldorf-Hirsch, A., & Dardis, F. E. (2012). Electronic friend or virtual foe: Exploring the role of competitive and cooperative multiplayer video game modes in fostering enjoyment. *Media Psychology, 15,* 356–371.

Schrag, R. (1990). *Taming the wild tube: A family guide to television and video.* Chapel Hill: University of North Carolina Press.

Schramm, W., Lyle, J., & Parker, E. B. (1961). *Television in the lives of our children.* Stanford, CA: Stanford University Press.

Schudson, M. (2003). *The sociology of news.* New York, NY: Norton.

Schumpeter, J. (2011, April 16). Fail often, fail well. *The Economist, 399,* p. 74.

Schwartz, B. (2004). *The paradox of choice: Why more is less.* New York, NY: HarperCollins.

Schwartz, S. (1984, Winter). Send help before it's too late. *Parent's Choice,* p. 2.

Scott, D. M. (2013). *The new rules of marketing and PR* (4th ed.). Hoboken, NJ: Wiley.

Second Life (n.d.). What is second life? Retrieved from http://secondlife.com/whatis/?lang=en-US

SecureLink (2018, February 14). Healthcare data: The new prize for hackers. Retrieved from https:// www.securelink.com/blog/healthcare-data-new -prize-hackers/

SelectUSA. (2018, June 18). *Media and entertainment spotlight.* Retrieved from https://www.selectusa.gov/ media-entertainment-industry-united-states

Shafer, D. M. (2014). Investigating suspense as a predictor of enjoyment in sports video games. *Journal of Broadcasting & Electronic Media, 58,* 272–288.

Shambaugh, J., Nunn, R., Breitwieser, A., & Liu, P. (2018, June). The state of competition and dynamism: Facts about concentration, start-ups, and related policies. *The Hamilton Project*. Retrieved from http://www.hamiltonproject.org/papers/the_state_of_competition_and_dynamism_facts_about_concentration_start_

Shearer E., & Gottfried, J. (2017, September 7). News use across social media platforms 2017. *Pew Research Center*. Retrieved from http://www.journalism.org/2017/09/07/news-use-across-social-media-platforms-2017/

Shensa, A., Escobar-Viera, C. G., Sidani, J. E., Bowman, N. D., Marshal, M. P., & Primack, B. A. (2017). Problematic social media use and depressive symptoms among U.S. young adults: A nationally-representative study. *Social Science Medicine, 182*, 150–157.

Shiver, J., Jr. (2004, October 22). Viacom, Disney fined by FCC over TV ads. *Los Angeles Times*, p. C2.

Sifferlin, A. (2017, August 15). 13% of Americans take antidepressants. *Time*. Retrieved from http://time.com/4900248/antidepressants-depression-more-common/

Signorielli, N. (1990). Television's mean and dangerous world: A continuation of the cultural indicators perspective. In N. Signorielli & M. Morgan (Eds.), *Cultivation analysis: New directions in media effects research* (pp. 85–106).Newbury Park, CA: SAGE.

Signorielli, N., & Kahlenberg, S. (2001). Television's world of work in the nineties. *Journal of Broadcasting & Electronic Media, 45*, 4–22.

Silver, N. (2012). *The signal and the noise: Why so many predictions fail—but some don't*. New York, NY: Penguin.

Silverblatt, A., Smith, A., Miller, D., Smith, J., & Brown, N. (2014). *Media literacy: Keys to interpreting media messages* (4th ed.). Westport, CT: Praeger.

Silverman, C. (2016, December 6). This analysis shows how fake election news stories outperformed real news on Facebook. *Buzzfeed News*. https://www.buzzfeednews.com/article/craigsilverman/viral-fake-election-news-outperformed-real-news-on-facebook

Simon, H. (1956). Rational choice and the structure of the environment. *Psychological Review, 63*, 129–138.

Singer, D. G., & Singer, J. L. (Eds.). (2001). *Handbook of children and the media*. Thousand Oaks, CA: SAGE.

Sizer, T. R. (1995). Silences. *Daedelus, 124*, 77–83.

Slater, M. D., Long, M., Bettinghaus, E. P. (2008). News coverage of cancer in the United States: A national sample of newspapers, television, and magazines. *Journal of Health Communication, 13*, 523–537.

Slater, M. D., & Rouner, D. (2002). Entertainment-education and elaboration likelihood: Understanding the processing of narrative persuasion. *Communication Theory, 12*, 173–191.

Smiley, J. (2006, June 18). Selling between the lines. *Los Angeles Times*, p. M1.

Smith, S. L., & Wilson, B. J. (2002). Children's comprehension of and fear reactions to television news. *Media Psychology, 4*, 1–26.

Smythe, D.W. (1954). Reality as presented on television. *Public Opinion Quarterly, 18*, 143–156.

Sobers, R. (2018, May 18). 60 must-know cybersecurity statistics for 2018. *Varonis*. Retrieved from https://blog.varonis.com/cybersecurity-statistics/

Society of Professional Journalists. (2018). SPJ Code of Ethics. Retrieved from https://www.spj.org/ethics code.asp

Solove, D. J., Rotenberg, M., & Schwartz, P. M. (2010). *Privacy, information and technology* (2nd ed.). New York, NY: Aspen Publishers.

Sonderman, J., & Tran, M. (2013). Understanding the rise of sponsored content. *American Press Institute*. Retrieved from http://www.americanpress institute.org/publications/reports/white-papers/understanding-rise-sponsored-content/"\t"_blank

Sony Corporation. (n.d.). Retrieved from http://en.wiki pedia.org/wiki/Sony

Sowell, T. (2008). *Economic facts and fallacies*. New York, NY: Basic Books.

Spam clogging Amazon's kindle. (2011, June 17). *Los Angeles Times*, p. B4.

Stack, B. (2018, April 9). Here's how much your personal information is selling for on the dark web. *Experian*. Retrieved from https://www.experian.com/

blogs/ask-experian/heres-how-much-your-personal-information-is-selling-for-on-the-dark-web/

Statista (2018a, May 24). *Percentage of the U.S. population who have completed four years of college or more from 1940 to 2017, by gender.* Retrieved from https://www.statista.com/statistics/184272/educational-attainment-of-college-diploma-or-higher-by-gender

Statista (2018b, May 27). Number of establishments in the media industry in the United States from 2007 to 2016, by sector. Retrieved from https://www.statista.com/statistics/184708/establishments-in-the-us-media-industry-by-sector/

Statista (2018c, June 1). Media advertising spending in the United States from 2015 to 2021 (in billion U.S. *dollars).* Retrieved from https://www.statista.com/statistics/272314/advertising-spending-in-the-us/

Statista (2018d, June 8). Estimated number of World of Warcraft subscribers from 2015 to 2023 (in millions). Retrieved from https://www.statista.com/statistics/276601/number-of-world-of-warcraft-subscribers-by-quarter/

Statista (2018e, June 9). Percentage of U. S. population who currently use any social media from 2008 to 2017. Retrieved from https://www.statista.com/statistics/273476/percentage-of-us-population-with-a-social-network-profile/

Statista. (2018f, June 14). Percentage of U. S. adults who own a smartphone from 2011 to 2018. Retrieved from https://www.statista.com/statistics/219865/percentage-of-us-adults-who-own-a-smartphone/

Statista. (2018g, June 18). Distribution of advertising spending in the United States from 2010 to 2020, by media. Retrieved from https://www.statista.com/statistics/272316/advertising-spending-share-in-the-us-by-media/

Statista. (2018h, June 24). Global spam volume as percentage of total e-mail traffic from January 2014 to March 2018 by month. Retrieved from https://www.statista.com/statistics/420391/spam-email-traffic-share/

Statista. (2018i, June 26). Average annual player salary in the sorts industry by league in 2017/18 (in million U. S. dollars). Retrieved from https://www.statista.com/statistics/675120/average-sports-salaries-by-league/

Statista. (2018j, June 29). Twitter accounts with the most followers worldwide as of June 2018 (in millions). Retrieved from https://www.statista.com/statistics/273172/twitter-accounts-with-the-most-followers-worldwide/

Statista. (2018k, July 1). Facebook's annual revenue and net income from 2007 to 2017 (in million U.S. *dollars).* Retrieved from https://www.statista.com/statistics/277229/facebooks-annual-revenue-and-net-income/

Statista. (2018l). Number of magazines in the United States from 2002 to 2016. Retrieved from https://www.statista.com/statistics/238589/number-of-magazines-in-the-united-states/

Sterling, G. (2018, April 24). *Reports: Fake reviews are a growing problem on Amazon, Google.* Retrieved from https://searchengineland.com/reports-fake-reviews-are-a-growing-problem-on-amazon-google-296742

Sternberg, R. J., & Berg, C.A. (1987). What are theories of adult intellectual development theories of. In C. Schooler & K.W. Schaie (Eds.), *Cognitive functioning and social structure over the life course* (pp. 3–23). Norwood, NJ: Ablex.

Stewart, L. (2004, March 24). Study criticizes school over diversity, graduation rates. *Los Angeles Times*, p. D5.

Storr, W. (2014). *The unpersuadables: Adventures with the enemies of science.* New York, NY: Overlook Press.

Strasburger, V. C. (2014). Wassssup? Adolescents, drugs, and the media In A. B. Jordan & D. Romer (Eds.), *Media and the well-being of children and adolescents* (pp. 70–89). New York, NY: Oxford University Press.

Strasburger, V. C., & Wilson, B. J. (2002). *Children, adolescents, & the media.* Thousand Oaks, CA: SAGE.

Stroud, N. J., Muddiman, A., & Lee, J. K. (2014). Seeing media as group members: An evaluation of partisan bias perceptions. *Journal of Communication, 64,* 874–894.

Study links teen smoking to popular ads. (1996, April 14). *Santa Barbara News-Press*, p. A2.

Suggs, D. W., Jr. (2018, June 27). Myth: College sports are a cash cow. *American Council on Education.* Retrieved from http://www.acenet.edu/news-room/Pages/Myth-College-Sports-Are-a-Cash-Cow2.aspx

Sunstein, C. R. (2006). *Infotopia: How many minds produce knowledge*. New York, NY: Oxford University Press.

Surveillance: Is the CIA really spying on you? (2017, March 24). *The Week*, p. 18.

Sykes, J. (2006). A player-centred approach to digital game design. In J. Rutter & J. Bryce (Eds.). *Understanding digital games* (pp. 75–92). London, England: SAGE.

Tamborini, R., Grizzard, M., Bowman, N., Reinecke, L., Lewis, R. J., & Eden, A. (2011). Media enjoyment as need satisfaction: The contribution of hedonic and nonhedonic needs. *Journal of Communication*, *61*, 1025–1042.

Tandoc, E. C., Jr., Lim, Z. W., & Ling, R. (2018). Defining "fake news." *Digital Journalism*, *6*, 137–153.

Tanner, L. (2012, August 13). School junk food bans may really help curb obesity. *Today.com*. Retrieved from http://www.today.com/id/48646703/site/todayshow/ns/today-back_to_school/t/school-junk-food-bans-may-really-help-curb-obesity/#.UTJMCxl0yUY

Tatham, M. (2018, March 15). Identity theft statistics. *Experian*. Retrieved from https://www.experian.com/blogs/ask-experian/identity-theft-statistics/

Taylor, S. E., & Howell, R. J. (1973). The ability of three-, four-, and five-year-old children to distinguish fantasy from reality. *Journal of Genetic Psychology*, *122*, 315–318.

Taylor, T. (2012). *The instant economist*. New York, NY: Plume.

The basics of selling on eBay. (2007). *Student guide*. San Jose, CA: eBay.

The new tech bubble. (2011, May 14). *The Economist*, p. 13.

The Walt Disney Company. (n.d.). Retrieved from http://en.wikipedia.org/wiki/Disney

Thompson, C. (2009, September). The new literacy. *Wired*, p. 48.

Time Warner. (n.d.). Retrieved from http://en.wikipedia.org/wiki/AOL_Time_Warner

Toth, S. (2018, Jan. 4). 66 Facebook acquisitions—the complete list (2018)! *TechWyse*. Retrieved from https://www.techwyse.com/blog/infographics/facebook-acquisitions-the-complete-list-infographic/

Trepte, S., Dienlin, T., & Reinecke, L. (2015). Influence of social support received in online and offline contexts on satisfaction with social support and satisfaction with life: A longitudinal study, *Media Psychology*, *18*, 74–105.

Trolling for your soul. (2011, April 2). *The Economist*, p. 58.

Tucker, P. (2014). *The naked future: What happens in a world that anticipates your every move?* New York, NY: Current.

Turow, J. (1992). *Media systems in society*. New York, NY: Longman.

Turow, J. (2010). *Media today* (3rd ed.). New York, NY: Routledge.

Tversky, A., & Kahneman, D. (1973). Availability: A heuristic for judging frequency and probability. *Cognitive Psychology*, *4*, 207–232.

"Unkind unwind." (2011, March 19). *The Economist*, pp. 76–78.

U.S. Census Bureau (2009). *The 2009 Statistical Abstract: The national data book, Table 1089*. Washington DC: Department of Commerce.

U.S. Census Bureau. (2013). *Statistical abstract of the United States: 2012*. Washington, DC: Department of Commerce.

U.S. Census Bureau. (2017). *Statistical abstract of the United States: 2016*. Washington, DC: Department of Commerce.

Valkenburg, P. M., Krcmar, M., Peeters, A. L., & Marseille, N. M. (1999). "Instructive mediation," "restrictive mediation," and "social coviewing." *Journal of Broadcasting & Electronic Media*, *43*, 52–66.

Van Damme, E. (2010). Gender and sexual scripts in popular US teen series: A study on the gendered discourses in One Tree Hill and Gossip Girl. *Catalan Journal of Communication & Cultural Studies*, *2*, 77–92.

Van Der Heide, B., D'Angelo, J. D., & Schumaker, E. M. (2012). The effects of verbal versus photographic self-presentation on impression formation in Facebook. *Journal of Communication*, *62*, 98–116.

van der Voort, T. H. A. (1986). *Television violence: A child's-eye view*. Amsterdam, The Netherlands: North-Holland.

Verrier, R., & James, M. (2003, October 9). GE, Vivendi finalize NBC Universal deal. *Los Angeles Times*, pp. C1, C11.

Viacom. (n.d.). Retrieved from http://en.wikipedia.org/wiki/Viacom

Vitak, J. (2012). The impact of context collapse and privacy on social network site disclosures. *Journal of Broadcasting & Electronic Media, 56*, 451–470.

Vivienne, S. & Burgess, J. (2012). The digital storyteller's stage: Queer everyday activists negotiating privacy and publicness. *Journal of Broadcasting & Electronic Media, 56*, 362–377.

von Salisch, M., Vogelgesang, J., Kristen, A., & Oppl, C. (2011). Preference for violent electronic games and aggressive behavior among children: The beginning of the downward spiral? *Media Psychology, 14*, 233–258.

Walsh, B. (2014, November 24). Data mine. *Time Magazine*, pp. 35–38.

Walsh, D. (1994). *Selling out America's children*. Minneapolis, MN: Fairview.

Wang, Z., & Tchernev, J. M. (2012). The "myth" of media multitasking: Reciprocal dynamics of media multitasking, personal needs, and gratifications. *Journal of Communication, 62*, 493–513.

Ward, S. C. (2014). From e pluribus unum to caveat emptor: How neoliberal policies are capturing and dismantling the liberal university. *New Political Science, 36*, 459–473.

Warren, R., Wicks, J. L., & Wicks, R. H. (2007). Food and beverage advertising to children on U.S. television: Did national food advertisers respond? *Journalism and Mass Communication Quarterly, 84*, 795–810.

Wartella, E. (1981). The child as viewer. In M. E. Ploghoft & J. A. Anderson (Eds.). *Education for the television age* (pp. 28–17). Springfield, IL: Charles C Thomas.

Watson, C. (2018, April 11). The key moment's from Mark Zuckerberg's testimony to Congress. *The Guardian*. Retrieved from https://www.theguardian.com/technology/2018/apr/11/mark-zuckerbergs-testimony-to-congress-the-key-moments

Weaver, A. J. (2011). A meta-analytical review of selective exposure to and the enjoyment of media violence. *Journal of Broadcasting & Electronic Media, 55*, 232–250.

Weaver, A. J., Jensen, J. D., Martins, N., Hurley, R. J., & Wilson, B. J. (2011). Liking violence and action: An examination of gender differences in children's processing of animated content. *Media Psychology, 14*, 49–70.

Weaver, A. J., Zelenkauskaite, A., & Samson, L. (2012). The (non) violent world of YouTube: Content trends in web video. *Journal of Communication, 62*, 1065–1083.

Wehrwein, P. (2011, October 20). Astounding increase in antidepressant use by Americans. *Harvard Health Blog*. Retrieved from http://www.health.harvard.edu/blog/astounding-increase-in-antidepressant-use-by-americans-201110203624

Whitman, D., & Loftus, M. (1996, December 16). Things are getting better? Who knew? *U.S. News & World Report*, pp. *30*, 32.

Whitson, D. (1998). Circuits of promotion: Media, marketing and the globalization of sport. In L. A. Wenner (Ed.), *MediaSport* (pp. 57–72). New York, NY: Routledge.

Wikipedia: Statistics. (2018, June 10). Retrieved from https://en.wikipedia.org/wiki/Wikipedia:Statistics

Williams, T. M., Zabrack, M. L., & Joy, L. A. (1982). The portrayal of aggression on North American television. *Journal of Applied Social Psychology, 12*, 360–380.

Williams-Grut, O. (2017, December 20). The cryptocurrency market is now doing the same daily volume as the New York Stock Exchange. *Business Insider*. Retrieved from http://markets.businessinsider.com/currencies/news/daily-cryptocurrency-volumes-vs-stock-market-volumes-2017-12-1011680451

Wilson, B. J., & Drogos, K. L. (2009). Children and adolescents: Distinctive audiences of media content. In R. L. Nabi & M. B. Oliver (Eds.). *Media processes and effects* (pp. 469–485). Thousand Oaks, CA: SAGE.

Wilson, B. J., & Weiss, A. J. (1992). Developmental differences in children's reactions to a toy advertisement linked to a toy-based cartoon. *Journal of Broadcasting & Electronic Media, 36*, 371–394.

Wilson, T. D. (2002). *Strangers to ourselves: Discovering the adaptive unconscious*. Cambridge, MA: Belknap Press.

Witkin, H. A., & Goodenough, D. R. (1977). Field dependence and interpersonal behavior. *Psychological Bulletin, 84*, 661–689.

Wolff, M. (2003, May 26). Troubled times. *New York*, pp.18–21.

Wolverson, R. (2012, August 6). Need for speed: Glamorizing cheap fashion costs more than you think. *Time*, p. 18.

Women's Media Center (2017, March 22). Women's Media Center Report: Women journalists report less news than men; TV gender gap most stark. Retrieved from https://www.womensmediacenter.com/about/press/press-releases/womens-media-center-report-women-journalists-report-less-news-than-men-tv-g

Woodruff, J. (2018, July 1). How much money does an NFL player make a year? *Chron*. Retrieved from https://work.chron.com/much-money-nfl-player-make-year-2377.html

Wright, A. (2007). *Glut: Mastering information through the ages*. Washington, DC: Joseph Henry Press.

Wright, P. J., & Randall, A. K. (2014). Pornography consumption, education, and support for same-sex marriage among adult U.S. males. *Communication Research, 41*, 665–689.

Wulff, S. (1997). Media literacy. In W. G. Christ (Ed.). *Media education assessment handbook* (pp. 123–142). Mahwah, NJ: Lawrence Erlbaum.

Xu, W. W., & Feng, M. (2014). Talking to the broadcasters on Twitter: Networked gatekeeping in Twitter conversations with journalists. *Journal of Broadcasting & Electronic Media, 58*, 420–437.

Yahoo Finance. (2018, May 23). *How would mergers in media industry unfold for the markets*? Retrieved from https://finance.yahoo.com/news/mergers-media-industry-unfold-markets-142902731.html

Yee, N. (2002, October). *Ariadne—Understanding MMORPG addiction*. Retrieved from http://www.nickyee.com/hub/addiction/home.html

YouTube (2018). YouTube in numbers. Retrieved from https://www.youtube.com/intl/en-GB/yt/about/press/

Zarett. E. J. (2018, February 4). How much do Super Bowl commercials cost in 2018? *Sporting News*. Retrieved from http://www.sportingnews.com/nfl/news/super-bowl-2018-how-much-do-super-bowl-commercials-cost-nbc-coca-cola-hyundai/1qap05f9qd6hd1kn2i9lahwlk3

Zephoria Digital Marketing. (2018, May). *The top 20 valuable Facebook statistics*. Retrieved from https://zephoria.com/top-15-valuable-facebook-statistics/

Zhang, Y., Dixon, T.L. & Conrad, K. (2010). Female body image as a function of themes in rap music videos: A content analysis. *Sex Roles, 62*, 787–797.

Zillmann, D. (1991).Television viewing and physiological arousal. In J. Bryant & D. Zillmann (Eds.). *Responding to the screen: Reception and reaction processes* (pp. 103–133). Hillsdale, NJ: Lawrence Erlbaum.

Zubrzycki, J. (2017, July 28). More states take on media literacy in schools. *Education Week*. Retrieved from http://blogs.edweek.org/edweek/curriculum/2017/07/media_literacy_laws.html

INDEX